THE GOOD
FISHING
GUIDE

This is a Carlton Book

Text copyright © 2001 Thomas Harmsworth Publishing Company
Design copyright © 2001 Carlton Books Limited

This edition first published in 2001 by
Carlton Books Limited
20 Mortimer Street
London W1T 3JW

ISBN 1 84222 233 3

A CIP catalogue record for this book is available from the British Library

10 9 8 7 6 5 4 3 2

Printed and bound in Great Britain

THE GOOD
FISHING
GUIDE

CARLTON
BOOKS

Contents

Abbreviations

The following abbreviations are used throughout the book:

S, salmon;

T, trout;

MT, migratory trout,

NT, non-migratory trout;

C, char;

FF or **FW**, freshwater (ie coarse fish);

RD, River Division (or its equivalent);

s, season;

m, month (National Rivers Authority list only);

f, fortnight;

w, week;

d, day;

t, ticket;

ns, nearest railway station;

m means mile or miles, except when it is used in conjunction with t, ie, **mt**, when it means monthly ticket. Likewise, **st** means season ticket, **wt** weekly ticket, **dt** daily ticket, and so on.

Fishery Agents

ENGLAND

FPD Savills, 20 Grosvenor Hill, Berkeley Square, London W1X 0HQ (Tel: 020 7499 8644, Fax: 020 7495 3773, Internet: www.fpdsavills.co.uk.).

Hatton Fishing Tackle, 64 St Owen Street, Hereford (Tel: 01432 272317). Up-to-the-minute information on fishing on Wye and Lugg.

Knight Frank, 20 Hanover Square, London W1R 0AH (Tel: 020 7629 8171, Fax: 491 0854, Internet: www.knightfrank.com).

Sale & Partners, 18–20 Glendale Road, Wooler, Northumberland (Tel: 01668 281611, Fax: 01668 281113). Tweed salmon fishing *(see advt)*.

Strutt & Parker, 37 Davies Street, London W1Y 2SP (Tel: 020 7629 7282, Fax: 020 7499 1657).

WALES

Knight Frank, 14 Broad Street, Hereford HR4 9AL (Tel: 01432 273087, Fax: 275935, Internet: www.knightfrank.co.uk2).

Chester-Master Ltd, Dolgarreg, North Road, Builth Wells, Powys LD2 3DD. Salmon fishing on Wye, Usk and tributaries. By the day or week. (Tel: 01982 553248, Fax: 553154).

SCOTLAND

Bell-Ingram, Durn, Isla Rd, Perth PH2 7HF (Tel: 01738 621121, Fax: 630904). Deveron, Cassley, Dee, etc.

CKD Finlayson Hughes, Lynedoch House, Barossa Place, Perth PH1 5EP. (Tel: 01738 451600, Fax: 01738 451900). Agents for fishing on a wide range of estates throughout Scotland.

Knight Frank, 2 North Charlotte Street, Edinburgh EH2 4HR (Tel: 0131 225 8171, Fax: 4151, Internet: www.knightfrank.co.uk).

JH Leeming, Stichill House, Kelso, Roxburghshire TD5 7TB. (Tel: 01573 470280, Fax: 01573 470259, Internet: www.scotborders.co.uk.). 24-hour information service, Freephone 0800 387 675. River Tweed.

Strutt & Parker, 37 Davies Street, London W1Y 2SP (Tel: 020 7629 7282, Fax: 020 7499 1657, telex: 8955508 STRUTT G).

Thurso Fisheries Ltd, Thurso East, Thurso, Caithness KW14 8HP (Tel: 01847 8963134. Fax: 01847 896295). River Thurso.

Fishing Holiday Agents

Angling Club Lax-, PO Box 3363, 123 Reykjavik, Iceland, E-mail: arnibald@ismennt.is. Tours on 16 first-class salmon rivers, also sea trout, brown trout and char in rivers and lakes. Self-catering Accommodation and jeep transport.

Arthur Oglesby, 9 Oatlands Drive, Harrogate, N Yorks HG2 8JT. Tel/Fax: 01423 883565. Host to parties on such rivers as the Spey in Scotland, the Varzuga and Kitza in Russia, Orkla in Norway, Alagnak in Alaska and the Ranga in Iceland *(see advt)*.

Hermitage Holidays, Vinyl House, Almond Grove, Newhall, Derbys DE11 0RD, Tel: 44 12 83 21 09 19. Fully catered holidays in France, with 16-acre carp fishing lake.

Chris Hill, 8 Augusta Road, Newtown, Hobart, Tasmania, Australia 7008, E-mail: tastrout@southcom.com.au. 3- to 7-day packages, trout fly fishing in Western Lakes and others.

Mike Hopley, PO Box 4273, Soldotna, AK 99669, USA. rufishn@alaska.net. Guided Alaskan fishing, with accommodation, featuring Kenai River salmon, and saltwater halibut.

Paradise Bay Lodge, Chibuene, Vilanculos Mainland, Mozambique, c/o PO Box 1667, Nigel, Gauteng, Rep of South Africa, Tel/Fax: (27-11) 8143938, Internet: www.oribi.co.za/pab/default.

htm Big game fishing for sail and marlin, wahoo, barracuda, and other species, with accommodation.

QUEST Global Angling Adventures, 3595 Canton Highway, Suite C-11, Marietta, Georgia 30066. Peacock bass fishing excursions throughout Venezuela, Brazil and Peru, with 3 to 6 full days of fishing.

Roxton Bailey Robinson, Field Sports and Safaris, 25 High Street, Hungerford, Berkshire RG17 0NF. Tel: 44 (0) 1488 683222, Fax: 44 (0) 682777, Internet: www.roxtons.com.

Salmon fishing in Russia, Norway, Iceland, Alaska, Scotland. Saltwater and deep sea fishing in Bahamas, Cuba, Kenya, Mexico. Trout fishing in UK, USA, Argentina, and elsewhere.

Top End Sportfishing Safaris, PO Box 194, Howard Springs, NT 0835, Australia. Tel: 00 61 8 8983 1495, Fax: 00 61 8 8983 1456.

Viv's Barramundi & Sportfishing Safaris, PO Box 95, Howard Springs, NT 0835, Australia. Tel: 00 61 8 8983 2044, Fax 00 61 8 8983 2786, E-mail: helent@taunet.net.au

British Fish Farms

Anna Valley Trout Farm Ltd, Andover, Hants (Tel: 01264 710382).

Berkshire Trout Farm, Hungerford, Berkshire RG17 0UN (Tel: 01488 682520, Fax: 01488 685002). Brown and rainbow trout.

Bibury Trout Farm, Bibury, near Cirencester, Gloucestershire GL7 5NL. Rainbow and brown trout bred on Coln. (Tel: 0128574 0212/215, Fax: 01285 740392). Catch Your Own fishery on R Coln.

Clearwater Fish Farm, East Hendred, Wantage, Oxon OX12 8LN (Tel: 01235 833732, Fax: 01235 835586).

Exe Valley Fishery Ltd, Exbridge, Dulverton, Somerset, TA22 9AY (Tel: 01398 323328, Fax: 01398 324079). Rainbow trout available.

Kilnsey Park Trout Farm, Kilnsey, Skipton, North Yorkshire BD23 5PS (Tel: 01756 752150, Fax: 752224).

Loch Leven Fishery, Kinross Estates Office, Kinross KY13 7UF. Trout. (Tel: 01577 863407, Fax: 863180).

Ludworth Trout Farm, Marple Bridge, Cheshire SK6 5NS (Tel: 0161 449 9520).

Ruskin Mill Aquaculture Project, Harsley Mill, Harsley, Stroud, Gloucestershire GL6 0PL. Trout and carp (Tel: 01453 833379).

Trent Fish Culture Co Ltd, Mercaston, Ashbourne, Derbyshire DE6 3BL. Brown, rainbow and American brook trout. Ova, fry, yearlings and 2-year-olds 1.5lb to 2lb; larger fish on application. (Tel: 01335 360318).

Upper Mills Trout Farm, Glyn Ceiriog, Nr Llangollen LL20 7HB (Tel: 01691 718225, Fax: 01691 718188).

Watermill Trout Farms Ltd, Welton Springs, Louth, Lincs LN11 0QT. Brown and rainbow trout (Tel: 01507 602524, Fax: 01507 600592, Telex: 56528).

Westacre Trout Farm, King's Lynn, Norfolk. Brown and rainbow trout for immediate delivery (Tel: 01760 755240, Fax: 01760 755444).

Further information about **British Fish Farms** can be had from **British Trout Farmers' Restocking Association**, Secretary, T Whyatt, Allenbrook Trout Farm, Brockington, Wimbourne St Giles, Dorset BH21 5LT (Tel: 01725 517369, Fax: 517769).

Fishing Schools and Courses

Arthur Oglesby, 9 Oatlands Drive, Harrogate, N Yorks HG2 8JT (Tel/Fax: 01423 883565).

The Arundell Arms, Lifton, Devon PL16 0AA (Tel: 01566 784666, Fax: 01566 784494). A full range of residential courses from beginners to advanced. Private tuition also offered.

Game Angling Instructors Association, Little Saxby's Farm, Cowden, Kent TN8 7DX (Tel: 01342 850765, Fax: 01342 850926). The

Association has approximately 90 members both in the UK and abroad, qualified as Advanced Professional Game Angling Instructors, offering a range of tuition from simple casting lessons to full residential courses. Members can be contacted through the Secretary.

School of Casting, Salmon & Trout Fishing, Michael Waller and Margaret Cockburn, Station House, Clovenfords,

Galashiels, Selkirkshire TD1 3LU (Tel/Fax: 01896 850293). Brown trout, sea trout and salmon on River Tweed and other waters in area.

Seafield Lodge Hotel, Alasdair Buchanan, Grantown on Spey, Moray PH26 3JN (Tel: 01479 872152. Fax: 01479 872340). Access to seven miles of Association water.

These below are members of the **Register of Experienced Fly Fishing Instructors and Schools** (Reffis), sponsored by Farlow's of Pall Mall, 5 Pall Mall, London SW1Y 5NP (Tel: 020 7839 2423, Fax: 01285 6437, Internet: www.farlows.co.uk/farlows/). Most members of Reffis offer fishing, as well as instruction. For full list of members, contact Reffis Chairman, Richard Slockock, Lawrences Farm, Tolpuddle, Dorchester, Dorset DT2 7HF (01305 848460/849060 Fax).

Caithness & Sutherland Angling Services, Lesley Crawford, Askival, Caithness KW14 7RE (01847 81170). Tuition and guiding on many Caithness and Sutherland wild brown trout lochs, plus various renowned salmon and sea trout rivers.

Blackwater Fly Fishing Instruction and Guide Service, Doug Lock, Ghillie Cottage, Kilbarry Stud, Fermoy, Co. Cork, Ireland (Tel: 025 32720). Spey casting tuition and salmon fishing 'off the reel', on Munster Blackwater River. Approved farmhouse accommodation.

Clonanav Fly Fishing Centre, Andrew Ryan, Ballymacarbry, Clonmel, Co Waterford, Eire (Tel/Fax: 052 36141).

Colebrook Park Fly Fishing School, Patrick Trotter, Colebrook Estate, Brookeborough, Co. Fermanagh, Northern Ireland BT94 4DW (Tel 01365 531402).

Esk and Borders Instruction and Guide Service, T E King, Netherknock, Bentpath, nr Langholm, Dumfriesshire, Scotland DG13 0PB, (Tel: 01387 370288). Packages for salmon and night fishing for sea trout, for all anglers from beginner to expert.

Fishing Breaks Ltd, Simon Cooper, 23 Compton Terrace, London N1 2UN (Tel: 020 7359 8818, Fax: 4540). Stillwater and chalk-stream trout (R Test and others).

Half Stone Sporting Agency, Roddy Rae, 6 Hescane Park, Cheriton Bishop, Exeter EX6 6SP (Tel/Fax: 01647 24643). Brown trout, sea trout and salmon fishing, let by day, week, or season. Private beats on Exe, Taw or Mole.

David Henderson, 31 Craigie buckler Terrace, Aberdeen. Fishing for salmon, sea trout, browns and rainbows, on numerous beats with easy reach of Aberdeen. Tackle and transport provided.

Highland Angling Services, Robert Brighton, 12 Fyrish Crescent, Evanton, Ross-shire, Scotland IV16 9YS (Tel: 01349 830159). Highland loch fishing, with tackle and transport.

Ian Moutter, South Wing, Borthwick Hall, Heriot, Midlothian, Scotland EH38 5YE (Tel: 0131 557 8333, Fax: 0131 556 3707). Instruction on river and stillwater fisheries in the Scottish borders, specialising in salmon and sea trout.

John Pennington, 24 Upper Burnside Drive, Thurso, Caithness KW14 7XB (Tel: 01847 8946410). Fishing and guiding on Halladale River.

Rainbow Springs Angling Centre, Brian Wallis, Whitehill, Redberth, Pembroke. (Tel: 01646 684038, Mobile, 07880 950173). Fly fishing in and around the Pembrokeshire coast and National Park. Transport, permits, equipment arranged.

Simon J Ward, Guide and Instructor, 20 Primrose Way, Locks Heath, Southampton, Hampshire SO31 6WX (Tel: 01489 579295). Chalk streams in southern England.

Wessex Fly Fishing School, Southover, Tolpuddle, Dorchester, Dorset DT2 7HF (Tel: 01305 848460, Fax: 01305 849060). Lakes, pools, chalk-stream fishing for trout on Rivers Piddle and Frome.

Westlake Fly Fishing, Ian Hockley, 78 Grove Street, Wantage, Oxon OX12 7BG (Tel: 01235 227228).

West Wales School of Fly Fishing, Pat O'Reilly A.P.G.A.I., Ffoshelyg, Lancych, Boncath, Pembrokeshire SA37 0LJ (Tel/Fax: 01239 698678). Trout, sea trout and salmon on Rivers Teifi, Cych and Gwili, and private lakes. Beginners' and advanced courses. Personal tuition also offered.

Disabled Facilities

List of Wheelyboat Locations

The numbering below refers to positions on the map, and also signifies the HIN (hull identity number) of the individual boat. Gaps in the numbering may signify that there is more than one boat at a location, or that a boat's use has been suspended.

Ardleigh Reservoir, Colchester, Essex. Tel: 01206 230642. Trout and coarse fish.

Barton Broad, The Nancy Oldfield Trust, Neatishead, Wroxham. Tel: 01692 630572. Coarse fish and boating for pleasure; also accommodation available all year.

Bewl Water, Lamberhurst, Kent. Tel: 01892 890352. Trout.

Blagdon Lake, Blagdon, Avon. Tel: 01275 332339. Trout.

Bough Beech Reservoir, Sevenoaks, Kent. Tel: 01732 851544. Trout fishing and trips for the disabled.

Bridgend, Mid Glamorgan, Wales. Private disabled use.

Butterstone Loch, Dunkeld, Perthshire. Tel: 01350 724238. Trout.

Carsington Water, nr Ashbourne, Derbyshire. Tel: 01629 540478. Trout.

Clatworthy Reservoir, Taunton, Somerset. Tel: 01984 624658. Trout.

Coate Water, Swindon, Wiltshire. Tel: 01793 522837 or 490150. Trout and coarse fish.

Darwell Reservoir, near Robertsbridge, East Sussex. Tel: 01580 880407. Trout and pike.

Ellesmere, Shropshire. Tel: 01691 623461. Fishing and general boating for pleasure.

Elsham Country Park Lake, South Humberside. Tel: 01652 688698. Trout.

Esthwaite Water, Ambleside, Cumbria. Tel: 015394 36541. Trout.

Exeter Canal, Devon (c/o Orcombeleigh, Exmouth). Tel: 01395 272644. For use of MS Society guests at Orcombeleigh, Exmouth.

Eyebrook Reservoir Trout Fishery, Caldecott, Leicestershire. Tel: 01536 770256. Trout.

Farmire Fishery, nr Knaresborough, N. Yorkshire. Tel: 01423 866417. Trout.

Fingask Loch, Blairgowrie, Perthshire. Tel: 01250 875402. Trout.

Foremark Reservoir, Milton, Derbyshire. Tel: 01283 703202 or 01332 380770. Trout.

Friday Island, Poole Keynes, Cirencester, Gloucestershire. Tel: 01285 770226. For disabled visitors to Friday Island.

Fritton Lake and Country Park, Norfolk. Tel: 01493 488288. Coarse fish.

Gartmorn Country Park, Clackmannanshire, Scotland. Tel: 01259 214319. Trout.

Grafham Water, nr Huntingdon, Cambridgeshire. Tel: 01480 810531. Trout.

Hanningfield Reservoir, South Hanningfield, Essex. Tel: 01268 710101. Trout.

Harewood House Lake. Harewood Estate, Harewood, Leeds. Tel: 0113 2181006. Boating for pleasure, fishing being developed.

Hillend Reservoir, nr Caldercruix, Strathclyde. Tel: 01236 843611. Trout.

Kennet & Avon Canal, Hungerford, Berkshire. Tel: 01488 682567. Pleasure boating. Disabled private owner willing to help other disabled people.

Kielder Water, Falstone, Northumberland. Tel: 01434 250232. Trout fishing and The Calvert Trust waterborne pleasures for disabled children.

Lake of Menteith, Stirling, Scotland. Tel: 01877 385664. Trout.

Latimer Park Lakes, Chesham, Bucks. Tel: 01494 76633. Trout.

Leaplish Waterside Park, Kielder Water, Northumberland. Tel: 01434 250312. Trout and coarse fish.

Linlithgow Loch, West Lothian, Scotland. Tel: 0831 288921. Trout.

Llandegfedd Reservoir, Pontypool, Gwent, S. Wales. Tel: 01495 755122. Trout.

Llyn Alaw, Lantrissant, Holyhead, Anglesea, N. Wales. Tel: 01407 730762. Trout.

Llyn Brenig, Cerrigydrudion, N. Wales (7 miles SW of Denbigh). Tel: 01490 420463. Trout.

Llysyfran Maenclochog, Dyfed, S. Wales. Tel: 01437 532694. Trout.

Loch Achonachie Angling Club, Dingwall. Secretary: Mr George S Cameron. Tel: 01349 862455. Trout.

Loch Tay: Kenmore Hotel, Kenmore. Contact Mr Paul Fishlock. Tel: 01887 830765. Salmon and brown trout. Salmon fishing is free to disabled anglers.

Loch Venacher, Stirling, Scotland. Tel: 01786 841692. Mobile: 0373 958922. Trout.

Lochore Meadows Country Park, Fife, Scotland. Tel: 01592 414300. Trout and coarse fish.

Maes y Clawdd, nr Bala, Gwynedd, North Wales. Tel: 01678 530239. Trout.

Newmill Trout Fisheries, Cleghorn, Lanarkshire, Scotland. Tel: 01555 870730. Trout.

Ormesby Broad, The Eels Foot Inn. Tel: 01493 730342. Alternatively contact The Broads Authority. Tel: 01493 740539 or mobile: 0411 439180. Coarse fishing, bird watching, photography or simple boating trips for disabled persons.

Packington Trout Fisheries, Packington Park, Warwickshire. Tel: 01676 522754. Trout.

Parklake Fishery, Dungannon, Co. Tyrone. Tel: 01868 727327. Trout.

Peckham Copse, Chichester, West Sussex. Tel: 01243 788434. Trout.

Pitsford Water, nr Northampton. Tel: 01604 781350. Trout.

Portree, Isle of Skye. Tel: 0147 082304. Trout.

Powdermill Water, Sedlescombe, East Sussex. Tel: 01424 870498. Trout.

Ravensthorpe Reservoir, nr Northampton. Tel: 01604 770875. Trout.

Rib Valley Lake, Westmill Farm, Ware, Herts. Tel: 01920 484913. Trout. (Additional facilities under construction for season 2000).

Richmond Park, Surrey. Tel: 0181 948 3209. For disabled people at PHAB's Holly Lodge Project, Richmond Park.

River Yare, Beauchamp Arms, Buckenham Ferry, Norfolk. Tel: 01508 480247. Coarse fish especially pike.

Roadford Reservoir, Lifton, nr Oakhampton, Devon. Tel: 01409 211507. Trout.

Rooksbury Mill, Andover, Hampshire. Tel: 01264 352921. Trout.

Rutland Water, Normanton Lodge, Edith Weston, Leicestershire. Tel: 01780 686441. Trout.

St John's Loch, Caithness, Scotland. Tel: 01847 851270. Trout.

Stocks Reservoir. Slaidburn, Lancashire. Tel: 01200 446602. Trout.

Sutton Bingham Reservoir, nr Yeovil, Somerset. Tel: 01935 872389. Trout and coarse fish.

The Lough, Thurstonfield, Carlisle, Cumbria. Tel: 01228 576552. Trout.

The Serpentine, Hyde Park, London. Tel: 0171 262 1330. General boating for pleasure.

Tildarg Fishery, Ballyclare, N. Ireland. Tel: 01960 340604 or 322216. Trout.

Toft Newton Reservoir, nr Lincoln. Tel: 01673 878453. Mobile: 0850 606630. Trout.

Upton Warren Sailing Lake, nr Droitwich, Worcs. Tel: 01527 861426. Pleasure boating and angling.

Vicarage Spinney, Little Linford, Milton Keynes. Tel: 01908 612227. Trout.

Walton Hall Trout Fishery. Waterton Park, Walton, West Yorkshire. Tel: 01924 242990. Trout.

Weirwood Reservoir, nr East Grinstead, West Sussex. Tel: 01342 822731. Trout and coarse fish.

Wentwood Reservoir. Wentwood Fly Fishing Association. Caldicote, Monmouthshire, S Wales. Contact Mr D G P Jones, Hon Sec. Tel: 01291 425158. Trout.

Wimbleball Reservoir, Brompton Regis, Somerset. Tel: 01398 371372. Trout.

Fishing in England and Wales

Environment Agency Structure, Close Seasons, Licence Duties etc.

The Environment Agency was created in 1996 from the National Rivers Authority, which had come into existence with the privatisation of the Regional Water Authorities. The Agency works to improve fish stocks, by checking, rescuing and stocking; to improve water quality, habitat and river flows; to protect fisheries from poaching, and enforce fishing and water byelaws generally; and to help anglers through supply of information, restoration and promotion of fisheries, and protection of wildlife.

The Agency is also responsible for the issue of compulsory rod licences. In England and Wales anyone aged 12 years or older who fishes for salmon, trout, freshwater fish or eels must hold an Environment Agency rod licence. And in addition, permission to fish, if necessary, must be gained from the owners or tenants of the fishing rights. Failure to produce a valid Agency rod licence when fishing is a criminal offence. Rod licence income helps the Agency to perform its necessary duties.

Rod licences are available from post offices in England and Wales. Licences are also obtainable from some larger fisheries, Regional Environment Agency offices, or by post from Environment Agency National Rod Licence Administration Centre, PO Box 432, Richard Fairclough House, Knutsford Road, Warrington WA4 1HH. Concessionary rates are available for persons aged 12 to 16, aged 65 years and over, or in receipt of incapacity benefit or severe disability allowance. War pensioners in receipt of an unemployability supplement are also entitled to the concession. Full season and concessionary junior rod licences can be purchased by telephone 7 days a week from 8.00 a.m. to 8.00 p.m. on 0870 1662662. Licence charges for 1999/2000 are as follows:

Salmon and Migratory Trout – Full season £57.00 (concessionary rate £28.50), 8 consecutive days £16.50, Single day £5.50.

Non-migratory Trout and Coarse – Full season £16.00 (concessionary rate £8.00), 8 consecutive days £6.00, Single day £2.00.

Where local rules and regulations permit, up to 4 rods may be used at a time when fishing for coarse fish and eels. One rod licence will be required for a maximum of 2 rods and rods must be fished no more than 3 metres apart. A maximum of 2 rods can be used on stillwaters for salmon and trout but only one rod may be used when fishing for salmon, trout and migratory trout on rivers, streams, drains and canals.

Anglers are reminded that the expression 'immature' in relation to salmon means that the fish is less than 12in long; taking immature salmon is prohibited throughout England and Wales. In relation to other fish the expression 'immature' means that the fish is of a length less than that prescribed by byelaw. Unless otherwise stated, it may be assumed that the length is measured from the tip of the snout to the fork of the tail.

The word 'salmon' means all fish of the salmon species. The word 'trout' means all fish of the salmon species commonly known as trout. The expression 'migratory trout' means trout that migrate to and from the sea. The expression 'freshwater (ie coarse) fish' means any fish living in fresh water except salmon, trout, all kinds of fish which migrate to and from tidal water, eels and their fry.

National Salmon Byelaws: In April 1999 Ministers confirmed new Agency fisheries byelaws to protect stocks of early-run salmon. The byelaws are designed to increase the stock of early-run salmon by reducing the number killed by both anglers and nets. The national byelaws relating to rods are as follows: Any angler catching a salmon before 16 June must return it with minimum injury. Angling for salmon before 16 June can only be with artificial fly or artificial lure. N.B. More stringent existing local regulations will remain in force, such as fly only at certain times on several rivers including the Usk, Wye, Dee.

NOTE: In the following lists the **telephone numbers** are those at which to contact officers during office hours. For the reporting of pollution an emergency hotline exists on a 24-hour free service: 0800 807060. Environment Agency general enquiries may be made through Tel: 0645 333111.

Abbreviations: The following abbreviations are used throughout the book: S, salmon; T, trout; MT, migratory trout; NT, non-migratory trout; C, char; FF or FW, freshwater (ie coarse fish); s, season; m, month (Following list only); f, fortnight; w, week; d, day; t, ticket; ns, nearest railway station. In the lists of fishing stations the abbreviation m means mile or miles, except when it is used in conjunction with t, ie, mt, when it means monthly ticket. Likewise, st means season ticket, wt weekly ticket, dt daily ticket, and so on.

Environment Agency

For general enquiries, you should call your *local* Environment Agency office. The national general enquiry line (0645 333 111) should only be used if you are unsure who to contact at the local office.

There is a 24-hour emergency hot-line for reporting all **environmental incidents** relating to air, land and water: 0800 807060. There is also a River Level Line for five of the Regions, as follows: North East, 0930 107701; North West, 0930 107702; Midlands, 0930 107703; Welsh 0930 107704; South West, 0930 107705.

Regions of the Environment Agency

SOUTHERN REGION, Guildbourne House, Chatsworth Road, Worthing, Sussex BN11 1LD (Tel: 01903 832000, Fax: 01903 821832).
Regional Fisheries, Recreation, Conservation and Navigation Manager: Ian Johnson.
Rivers controlled: Darent, Cray, Medway, Stour, Eastern Rother, RM Canal, Adur, Arun, Ouse, Cuckmere, all rivers in Pevensey Levels, Test, Itchen, Hamble, Meon, Beaulieu, Lymington, Fletch, Keyhaven, Eastern Yar, Medina, and the tributaries of all these rivers.

Area offices.
Kent: Kent Fisheries Team Leader, Orchard House, Endeavour Park, London Road, West Malling, Kent ME19 5SH. (Tel: 01732 875587, Fax: 01732 875057).
Sussex: Sussex Fisheries Team Leader, Saxon House, Little High Street, Worthing BN11 1DH (Tel: 01903 215835, Fax 01903 215884).
Pollution reporting: emergency hotline: 0800 807060.

Hampshire/Isle of Wight: Hampshire/Isle of Wight Fisheries Team Leader, Colvedene Court, Wessex Way, Colden Common, Winchester, Hampshire SO21 1WP (Tel: 01962 713267, Fax: 01962 841573).
Pollution reporting, to above office numbers, or outside office hours: 24-hour emergencies – Freephone: 0800 807060.

SOUTH WEST REGION, Headquarters: Manley House, Kestrel Way, Exeter, Devon, EX2 7LQ (Tel: 01392 444000, Fax: 01392 444238).
Regional Headquarters: Fisheries, Recreation Conservation and Navigation Manager: E S Bray.
Regional General Manager: Katharine Bryan.

Cornwall Area:
Sir John Moore House, Victoria Square, Bodmin, Cornwall PL31 1EB (Tel: 01208 78301, Fax: 78321).
Fisheries, Ecology and Recreation Manager: M P Willans.
Rivers controlled: Camel, Fowey, Looe, Lynher, Plym, Tamar, Tavy, Yealm and tributaries, including Bude Canal.

Devon Area:
Exminster House, Miller Way, Exminster, Devon EX6 8AS (Tel: 01392 444000, Fax: 01392 442109).
Fisheries, Ecology and Recreation Manager: S R Douglas.
Rivers controlled: Avon, Axe, Dart, Erme, Exe, Lyn, Otter, Taw, Teign, Torridge and tributaries, including Exeter and Tiverton Canal.

North Wessex Area:
Rivers House, East Quay, Bridgwater, Somerset TA6 4YS (Tel: 01278 457333, Fax: 01278 452985).
Fisheries, Ecology and Recreation Manager: E R Merry.
Rivers controlled: Axe, Bristol Avon, Brue, Parrett and their tributaries, including Tone, Huntspill, King's Sedgemoor Drain and Bridgwater and Taunton Canal.

South Wessex Area:
Rivers House, Sunrise Business Park, Higher Shaftesbury Road, Blandford Forum, Dorset DT11 8ST (Tel: 01258 456080, Fax: 455998).
Fisheries, Ecology and Recreation Manager: G Lightfoot.
Rivers controlled: Hampshire Avon and Stour, Frome, Piddle, Brit and Char. (All rivers entering the sea between Lyme Regis and Christchurch).

Rod Seasons

Devon and Cornwall Areas
Salmon: Avon – 15 April to 30 November (E). Erme – 15 March to 31 October. Axe, Otter,

Sid – 15 March to 31 October. Camel – 1 April to 15 December. Dart – 1 February to 30 September. Exe – 14 February to 30 September. Fowey, Looe – 1 April to 15 December. Tamar, Tavy, Lynher – 1 March to 14 October. Plym – 1 April to 15 December. Yealm – 1 April to 15 December. Taw, Torridge – 1 March to 30 September. Lyn – 1 February to 31 October. Teign – 1 February to 30 September. Lim – 1 March to 30 September. **Migratory trout**: Avon – 15 April to 30 September. Erme – 15 March to 30 September. Axe, Otter, Sid – 15 April to 31 October. Camel, Gannel, Menalhyl, Valency – 1 April to 30 September. Dart – 15 March to 30 September. Exe – 15 March to 30 September. Fowey, Looe, Seaton, Tresillian – 1 April to 30 September. Tamar, Lynher, Plym, Tavy, Yealm – 3 March to 30 September. Taw, Torridge, Lyn – 15 March to 30 September. Teign, – 15 March to 30 September. Lim – 16 April to 31 October. **Brown trout**: Camel, Fowey – 1 April to 30 September. Other rivers and streams – 15 March to 30 September. All rivers in North and South Wessex Areas – 1 April to 15 October. All other waters – 15 March to 12 October. **Coarse fish and eels**: Rivers, streams, drains, Kennet and Avon Canal, Bridgewater and Taunton Canal – 16 June to 14 March. Enclosed waters, no close season.

North and South Wessex Areas
S, Frome and Piddle – 1 March to 31 August. Other rivers – 1 February to 31 August. MT, 15 April to 31 October, NT. Rivers 1 April to 15 October. Reservoirs, lakes and ponds 17 March to 15 October. Rainbow trout – still waters only – no closed season. FF all waters. 16 June to 14 March following year.

NORTH WEST REGION, Richard Fairclough House, Knutsford Road, Warrington WA4 1HG (Tel: 01925 653999, Fax: 01925 415961).
Principal Fisheries, Recreation, Conservation and Biology Manager: Dr M Diamond.
Pollution reporting: Tel: 01925 53999.

North Area
Area Fisheries, Ecology and Recreation Manager: N C Durie, Ghyll Mount, Gillan Way, Penrith 40 Business Park, Penrith, Cumbria, CA11 9BP (Tel: 01768 866666, Fax: 01768 865606).
Rivers controlled: Esk, Liddel, Lyne, Irthing, Petteril, Wampool, Caldew, Ellen, Derwent,

Eamont, Eden, Cocker, Ehen, Irt, Esk, Brathay, Duddon, Crake, Rothay, Leven, Kent, and their tributaries. Lakes Derwentwater, Thirlmere, Ullswater, Haweswater, Bassenthwaite, Windermere, Wastwater, Coniston Water, Esthwaite Water, Grasmere, Rydal Water.

Central Area
Area Fisheries, Ecology and Recreation Manager: Dr D Evans, Lutra House, Dodd Way, Walton Summit, Bamber Bridge, Preston, Lancashire PR5 8BX (Tel: 01772 339882, Fax: 01772 627730).
Rivers controlled: Ribble, Hodder, Lune, Wyre, Calder, Crossens, Yarrow, Douglas, Alt, Keer and their tributaries.

South Area
Area Fisheries, Ecology and Recreation Manager: A R Lee, Appleton House, 430 Birchwood Boulevard, Birchwood, Warrington, Cheshire WA3 7WD (Tel: 01925 840000, Fax: 01925 852260).
Rivers controlled: Roch, Irwell, Tame, Etherow, Mersey, Goyt, Bollin, Dean, Weaver, Dane, Gowey, and their tributaries.
Close seasons: Salmon, 1 November to 31 January, except R. Eden system – 15 October to 14 January. Migratory trout, 16 October to 30 April, except rivers Annas, Bleng, Esk, Mite, Irt, Calder, Ehen and all tributaries – 1 November to 30 April. Trout, 1 October to 14 March. Coarse fish, 15 March to 15 June (no close season for coarse fish in enclosed waters).

NORTH EAST REGION, Rivers House, 21 Park Square South, Leeds LS1 2QG (Tel: 0113 244 0191, Fax: 0113 246 1889).
Regional Fisheries Officer: Steve Chambers (Tel: 0113 231 2465, Fax 0113 231 2375).
Northumbria Area, Tyneside House, Skinnerburn Road, Newcastle Business Park, Newcastle upon Tyne NE4 7AR (Tel: 0191 203 4000, Fax: 0191 203 4004).
Rivers controlled: Aln, Coquet, Fant, Wansbeck, Blyth, Tyne, Wear, Tees, Derwent.
Close seasons: S – 1 November to 31 January. MT – 1 November to 2 April. NT – 1 October to 21 March, excluding Kielder Water, Broomlee Lough, Craglough Loch, Greenlee Lough, Derwent Reservoir, and East and West Hallington where the close season is 1 Nov to 30 Apr.

Dales Area
Coverdale House, Amy Johnson Way, Clifton Moor, Yorks YO3 4UZ, (Tel: 01904 692296, Fax: 01904 692297).

Rivers controlled (together with South Yorkshire Area): Tees, Swale, Ure, Esk, Derwent, Wharfe, Nidd, Ouse, Aire, Calder, Rother, Don, Dearne and Hull system.
Close seasons: for River Tees and tributaries northward as per Northumbria Area. For Staithes Beck, River Esk and tributaries of the Ouse and Humber, as per Southern Yorkshire Area.

Ridings Area
Phoenix House, Global Avenue, Leeds LS11 8PG (Tel: 0113 244 0191, Fax: 0113 213 4609).
Close seasons: S – 1 Nov to 5 April. MT – 1 Nov to 5 April. NT – 1 October to 24 March.

ANGLIAN REGION, Kingfisher House, Goldhay Way, Orton Goldhay, Peterborough PE2 5IZR (Tel: 01733 371811, Fax: 231 840).
Regional Fisheries, Ecology and Recreation Manager: John Adams.

Northern Area
Waterside House, Waterside North, Lincoln, LN2 5HA. (Tel: 01522 513100).
Fisheries, Ecology and Recreation Manager: Irven Forbes.

Central Area
Bromholme Lane, Brampton, Huntingdon PE18 8NE (Tel: 01480 414581).
Fisheries, Ecology and Recreation Manager: Debbie Jones.

Eastern Area
Cobham Road, Ipswich, Suffolk IP3 9JE (Tel: 01473 727712).
Fisheries, Ecology and Recreation Manager: Dr Charles Beardall.
Close Seasons: S and MT 29 September–last day of February. T 30 October–31 March. Rainbow T; no close season on enclosed waters, otherwise 30 October–31 March. FF 15 March–15 June on rivers, streams, drains, all waters in Broads area, and some SSSIs.
Emergencies: A 24-hour service is provided at Regional Headquarters, Tel: 01733 371811. Emergency hotline: 0800 807060.

MIDLANDS REGION, Sapphire East, 550 Streetsbrook Road, Solihull B91 1QT (Tel: 0121 711 2324, Fax: 0121 711 3990).
Fisheries, Ecology, and Recreation Manager, Midlands: Martin Stark
Area Fisheries, Recreation and Ecology Manager: A S Churchward, Lower Severn Area EA, Riversmeet House, Newtown Industrial Estate, Northway Lane, Tewkesbury, Glos GL20 8JG. (Tel: 01684 850951).
Rivers controlled: Severn, Warwickshire Avon, and all other tributary streams in the Severn south of Worcester and all other canals and pools. The Agency also owns or rents water on the Avon and Severn.
Area Fisheries, Recreation, Ecology and Navigation Manager: Dr J V Woolland, Upper Severn Area EA, Hafren House, Welshpool Road, Shelton, Shrewsbury SY3 8BB (Tel: 01743 272828).
Rivers controlled: Severn and tributaries north of Worcester, Teme, Vyrnwy, Tanet, Banwy, Tern, Roden, Mease, Perry and all other canals and pools.

Trent Area
Area Fisheries, Recreation and Ecology Manager: K Miller, Lower Trent Area EA. Trentside Offices, Scarrington Road, West Bridgford, Nottingham NG2 5FA (Tel: 0115 9455722).
Rivers controlled: Trent, east of Dove confluence, Soar, Derbyshire Derwent and their tributaries, all canals and pools.
Area Fisheries, Recreation and Ecology Manager: M J Cooper, Upper Trent Area EA, Sentinel House, Wellington Crescent, Fradley Park, Lichfield, Staffs WS13 8RR (Tel: 01543 444141).
Rivers controlled: Trent west of Dove confluence, Tame, Dove, Manifold, Churnet and their tributaries, all canals and pools.
Close seasons: Brown trout: 8 October to 17 March inclusive. Rainbow trout: 8 October to 17 March inclusive in all rivers, streams, drains and canals. In reservoirs, lakes and pools there is no national close season, although owners/ managers may wish to impose their own. Salmon: 8 October to 31 January inclusive. Catch and release method restrictions apply from 1 February to 15 June inclusive, when all salmon caught must be returned alive to water. Freshwater fish: 15 March to 15 June inclusive in all rivers, streams, drains, canals and on specified stillwater SSSIs. On stillwaters (excluding specified SSSIs) there is no national close season, although owners/managers may wish to impose their own. Eels: There is no national close season, but hook and bait restrictions apply in all rivers, streams, drains, and canals from 15 March to 15 June inclusive.
Pollution reports: Please report any pollution or dead fish to the following Freephone number: 0800 807060.

THAMES REGION, Kings Meadow House, Kings Meadow Road, Reading, RG1 8DQ (Tel: 0118 953 5000, Fax: 0118 950 0388).

Fisheries & Conservation Manager: David Willis (Tel: 0118 953 5502).

Area Fisheries and Ecology Manager (West): J Sutton, Lambourne House, Howbery Park, Wallingford, Oxon OX10 4BD (Tel: 01491 828353). River Thames (source to Hurley); Rivers Churn, Coln, Windrush, Evenlode, Cherwell, Ray, Cole, Ock, Thame, Wye, Oxford Canal; Kennet, Kennet and Avon Canal, Lambourne, Pang, Leach, Enborne.

Area Fisheries and Ecology Manager (North East): M Thomas, 2 Bishops Square, Business Park, St Albans West, Hatfield, Herts AN10 9EX (Tel: 01707 632 315). Rivers Lee, Stort, Rib, Ash (Herts), Mimram, Beane and tributaries, Roding, Rom, Beam, Ingrebourne and tributaries, Colne, Colnebrook, Ver, Misbourne, Gade Chess and tributaries. Grand Union Canal, Slough Arm, Paddington Arm. Brent, Crane and Duke of Northumberlands River.

Area Fisheries and Ecology Manager (South East): Dr A Butterworth, Swift House, Frimley Business Park, Camberley, Surrey, GU16 5SQ (Tel: 01276 454 425). Rivers Thames (Wargrave to Yantlet), Loddon, Blackwater, Wey, Mole, Wandle and 5 London tributaries. Canals: Basingstoke and parts of Grand Union and Regents.

River Pollution, Fish Mortality and Disease: Reports by members of the public: phone FREEFONE RIVER POLLUTION. This number covers the whole of the Thames Region catchment 24 hours a day, 7 days a week; or phone 0800 807060.

Seasons: Salmon and trout (excluding rainbow trout): 1 April to 30 September; enclosed waters: 1 April to 29 October. Rainbow trout: 1 April to 30 September (does not apply to enclosed waters). Freshwater fish: 16 June to 14 March.

Please report salmon or sea trout captures to Reading Office, Tel: 0118 953 5511.

ENVIRONMENT AGENCY, WALES, Rivers House/Plas-yr-Afon, St Mellons Business Park, Cardiff CF3 0LT (Tel: 02920 770088, Fax: 02920 798555).

Regional Fisheries, Conservation, Recreation, Navigation Manager: Dr Michael Evans.

AREAS OF THE AGENCY
Northern Area: Ffordd Penlan, Parc Menai, Bangor, Gwynedd LL5 2EF (Tel: 01248 670770).

Area Fisheries, Ecology and Recreation Officer: A J Winstone.

Enforcement Officer: Mark Chapman.

Rivers controlled: Dee (Welsh) Clwyd, Elwy, Alwen, Alyn, Ceiriog, Ceirw, Lliw, Tryweryn, Twrch, Bala Lake and their feeders. Also waters in an area bounded by watersheds of rivers (including their tributaries and all lakes) running into the sea between the eastern boundary of the Division's area at Old Gwyrch, Denbighshire, and the southern extremity at Upper Borth, Cardiganshire: Dulas, Conway, Lledr, Llugwy (with Lakes Elsi, Crafnant, Cowlyd, Eigiau, Conway, Melynllyn, Dulyn), Aber, Ogwen (with Lakes Anafon, Ogwen, Idwal, Ffynnon, Loer), all waters in Anglesey, Seiont, Gwyrfai, Llyfni (with Lakes Padarn, Cwellyn, Gader, Nantlle), Erch, Soch, Rhydhir, Afon Wen, Dwyfawr, Dwyfach (with Lake Cwmystradlyn), Glaslyn, Dwyryd, Prysor (with Lakes Dinas, Gwynant, Llagi Adar, Trawsfynydd, Gamallt, Morwynion, Cwmorthin), Glyn, Eisingrug (with Lakes Techwyn Isaf, Techwyn Uchaf, Artro, Mawddach, Eden, Wnion (with Lakes Cwm Bychan, Bodlyn, Gwernan, Gregennen), Dysynny, Dovey, Dulas, Twmyn (with Lake Tal-y-Llyn).

South West Area: Llys Afon, Hawthorne Rise, Haverfordwest, Pembs.

Area Fisheries, Ecology and Recreation Officer: P V Varallo.

Enforcement Officer: Steve Williams

Rivers controlled: Neath, Afan, Kenfig, Ogmore, Ewenny, Llynfi, Tawe, Afan, Kenfig, Gwendraeth Fawr, Gwendraeth Fach and Loughor. Towy, Teifi, Taf, Eastern and Western Cleddau, Gwaun, Nevern, Aeron, Clarach, Rheidol, Ystwyth, Wyre, and the tributaries of these rivers.

South East Area: Rivers House, St Mellons Business Park, Cardiff CF3 0LT (Tel: 02920 770088).

Area Fisheries, Ecology and Recreation Officer: J Gregory.

Enforcement Officer: Steve Barker.

Rivers controlled: Thaw, Ely, Taff, Rhymney, Usk and tributaries, including Cilienni, Honddu, Yscir, Bran, Cray, Senni, Tarrell, Cynrig, Crawnon, Rhiangoll, Gwyne-fawr, Grwynefechan, Olway, Afon Lwyd and Ebbw and tributary Sirhowy. Wye and all rivers and brooks of the Wye watershed including Monnow, Trothy, Lugg, Arrow, Ithon and Irfon.

24-hour pollution emergency freephone: 0800 807060.

Fishing Stations in England

Main catchments are given in alphabetical order, fishing stations listed in mouth to source order, first main river, then tributaries. Where national borders are crossed – e.g. Wye and Border Esk – allocation has been arbitrary. Some small streams have been grouped in counties rather than catchments.

Environment Agency rod licences are now required almost everywhere in England and Wales for all freshwater fishing. Details appear on pages 11–15. A list of fishing clubs appears at the end of each national section. 'Free fishing' means only that a riparian owner is reputed to allow fishing without making a charge. It does not imply a right and such information should be checked locally before an attempt to fish is made. All charges shown are exclusive of VAT unless otherwise stated. Reduced charges to juniors, the disabled, pensioners, and in some instances to ladies, are now quite commonplace. In many instances, they are specified. Where they are not, they may nevertheless be in force. If in doubt, ask when booking.

ADUR

(For close seasons, licences, etc, see Southern Region Environment Agency, p12).

Rises SW of Horsham and flows into the English Channel at Shoreham. Sea trout, trout, and very good coarse fishing, with match weights in excess of 70lb.

Shoreham (W Sussex). Bass, codling, flats, eels, mullet from harbour and shore. Church Farm, Coombes BN15 0RS, has 2 coarse lakes, with carp, chub, roach, etc. Dt £6, conc.

Upper Beeding (W Sussex). Chub, bream, perch, rudd, roach, dace, eels and pike. CAL-PAC fishes 3,000 yds of prolific tidal stretch. Dt £4, conc, from bailiff on bank. No night fishing. Open 15 Jun–15 Mar.

Bramber and **Steyning** (W Sussex). Bream, roach, chub, dace, pike and carp. Pulborough AS has 3m from Bramber Bridge upstream to Streatham Old Railway Bridge. On tidal water, low water best. Dt £4 (£2.50, conc). River also has run of sea trout. Dt from Hyde Square News, Hyde Square, Upper Beeding, or Prime Angling, 74 Brighton Rd, Worthing.

Henfield (W Sussex). Henfield & Dist AS has fishing rights on 7m of Mid and Upper Adur, from Streatham Bridge to Wineham, with sea trout, brown trout, very large pike, carp, perch, eels, and other coarse species, and coarse fish-

ing in lakes and ponds, with large carp. No dt, membership £40, conc for juv, OAP. Apply to Hon Sec. Worthing & Dist Piscatorial S has two stretches of Adur fishing in vicinity, with bream, carp, chub, pike, perch, gudgeon, roach, rudd, tench; Patching Pond, 4m west of Worthing; Laybrook Fishery, 2m from Ashington. Dt £5–£2.50 from Worthing and Littlehampton tackle shops. Society is affiliated with Sussex Anglers Consultative Association. Tackle shops: Ken Dunman, 2 Marine Place; Prime Angling, 74 Brighton Rd, both Worthing.

ALDE

(For licences, etc, see Anglian Region Environment Agency, p14)

A small Suffolk stream, rising near Saxmundham and flowing into the North Sea at Orford Haven, 6½ m NE of Felixstowe. Sea fish.

Aldeburgh (Suffolk). Bass, codling, flat-fish, etc, can be taken in estuary from jetty and boat; cod and whiting from beach; October and November best months. Hotels: Brudenell, White Lion, Wentworth, East Suffolk *(see also Suffolk, Sea Fishing Stations)*.

Snape (Suffolk). River tidal. Mullet, bass, eels below sluice. Fishing free. Other free fishing at Thorpness Mere, nr Leiston. Tackle shop: Saxmundham Angling Centre, Market Place, Saxmundham, Tel: 01728 603443: day tickets, details of local lake fishing for carp, tench, perch, bream, rudd and pike, and details of local fishing clubs. Hotels: White Hart, Bell.

ALN
(For close seasons, etc, see North East Region
Environment Agency, p13)

Short Northumberland river, flowing into
North Sea at Alnmouth. Trout and sea trout,
occasional salmon; usually a late run river.

Alnwick (Northumberland). Aln AA water
(owned by the Duke of Northumberland), 7–9
miles of trout, sea trout and salmon. Stocked
yearly with 500 brown trout, av 1¼lb. Portion
running through grounds at Lesbury House private. Visitors (excl Sundays) mt £40, wt £25, dt
£8, under 12 free, with adult, from Murraysport,
Narrowgate, Alnwick, and Leslie Jobson, Tower
Showrooms during business hours. Coquet and
Till within easy reach. Hotels: White Swan and
Hotspur, Alnwick; Schooner, Alnmouth.

ANCHOLME
(For close seasons, etc, see Anglian Region
Environment Agency, p14)

This river, in South Humberside and
Lincolnshire, with its tributaries drains about 240
square miles of country. Falls into the Humber
at **South Ferriby**, where there is a sluice and
tidal lock. The lower part is embanked for about
19 miles and is owned by Anglian Water. The
fishing rights are leased to Scunthorpe and
District Angling Association. Temporary membership day permits are obtainable from their
bailiffs on the bankside. The river is abundantly
stocked with coarse fish, especially roach and
bream, and recently perch. Winter shoals found
mainly at **Brigg**. Other choice sections at
Broughton, Snitterby, Horkstow areas.
Fishing accesses: South Ferriby Sluice, 4m from
Barton upon Humber; Saxby Bridge, 6m
from Barton upon Humber; Broughton,
Castlethorpe, **Cadney** and **Hibaldstow
Bridges** near Brigg through which town river
passes; Brandy Wharf, Snitterby, **Bishop
Bridge**, 6m from **Market Rasen**.
Improvement work recently completed at
Scabcroft, Broughton and Brigg. Disabled fishing
stands at Brigg and at Hibaldstow Bridge. At
Barton upon Humber are **Barton Broads**
mixed coarse fishery, 6½ acres, Malt Kiln Lane,
for tickets, see Goole; **Pasture House
Fishery**, 20 acres, and Hoe Hill Lake, on banks
of Humber, 9 acres with roach, rudd, carp,
bream, tench, chub. Dt £2.50 from Mrs K Smith,
Barton upon Humber, Tel: 01652 635119;
Winter Brothers Pond, East Halton, 21 acre
coarse lake, dt £1. Mr Winter, Marsh Lane, East

Halton, Tel: 01469 40238. Tackle shop: Boyalls,
High St, Barton upon Humber.

ARUN
(For close seasons, etc, see Southern Region
Environment Agency, p12).

Rises on NW border of Sussex, flows past
Horsham and enters English Channel at
Littlehampton. Noted coarse-fish river, largely
controlled by clubs. Some sea trout; May to
October.

Littlehampton (Sussex). See under Sea Fishing
Stations. HQ of Littlehampton and Dist AC is at
Arun View Hotel, right by river. Billingshurst AS
has R Arun fishing at Pallingham, and three lakes.

Arundel (W Sussex). River tidal and mainly
mud-bottomed. Roach and dace run large;
bream, perch, pike, chub and occasional sea
trout. Bass and mullet taken in fair numbers June,
July, August between Ford railway bridge and
Arundel, where fishing is free. Leger best method
when tide running; trotting down successful in
slack water. Victoria AC has 5m of bank north of
Arundel town, with roach, dace, bream to 6lb;
mullet and bass in summer months. Dt £2 from
Black Rabbit, Offham; George and Dragon,
Burpham; or Tropicana, 6 Pier Rd, Littlehampton.
Castle Trout Pond, Mill Rd, Arundel, open June
to Sept, Tel: 01903 8837427. Hotels: Norfolk
Arms, Swan, Howards.

Chalk Springs Fishery, Park Bottom,
Arundel, West Sussex BN18 0AA. Four lakes,
clear water, stocked with brown and rainbow
trout of 2–20lb. Dt £27.50. Part-day £17.50,
£16.50, £22.00. Refreshments, lodge on lakes,
tuition, tackle for hire and sale. Tel: 01903
883742.

Amberley (W Sussex). Chub, bream, roach,
dace, rudd, eel, perch, pike. Worthing Piscatorial
Society control stretch from Houghton Bridge
to Bury. Dt from Houghton Bridge Tea Rooms,
Amberley, and Worthing tackle shops. Rother
AC has two stretches on the Arun: ½m from
Greatham north, on west bank, and 1½m
from Stopham Bridge north, on west bank. The
Central Association of London and Provincial
Angling Clubs hold both banks downstream of
Houghton Bridge to South Stoke, tidal water.
Railway station 2 mins walk from fishery. Dt £5
from bailiff on bank, £4 conc in advance from
Swan Public House. No night fishing on CAL-
PAC water. This area to Stopham involved in
Sussex RD improvement scheme.

Pulborough (W Sussex). Pike, bream to 7lbs, roach to 2½lbs, chub, dace, perch, rudd, large carp. Central Association of London and Provincial ACs leases tidal stretch. at Swan Meadow. Station is 7 mins walk from fishery. Dt £4, conc, from bailiffs. No night fishing on CAL-PAC water. Pulborough and District AS has fishing on the tidal Arun from Pulborough to Greatham Bridge, approx 3m, 1m on **Rother**, 3m on **Adur**; also 11 lakes, incl **Duncans Lake**, Pulborough (good for young anglers) and 6 small lakes near **Ashington**, coarse fish. St £55, conc, from Sec. At **Wisborough Green** Crawley AS has water; dt. At **Horsham** is Newells Pond Carp fishery, 2 lakes of 4.2 acres each. St only, from Tim Cotton, Newells Pond House, Newells Lane, Lower Beeding RH13 6LN. Worthing PS has Laybrook Lakes, Pulborough, and Doctors Lake, Horsham. Dt from Houghton Bridge Tea Rooms, Amberley, and Worthing tackle shops. Whitevane Coarse Fishery, Mrs Teresa Yeates, Forest Grange, Off Forest/Pease Pottage Rd, Horsham (Tel: 01403 791163): 10 acre lake with large carp, roach, rudd, tench, perch, etc. Dt £7, 2 rods, night ticket £12, 24 hr £17, conc. Furnace Lakes, Slinfold (Tel: 01403 791163), 4m from Horsham: 6 acre lake with carp to 32lbs, large rudd, bream, etc, and 2½ acre lake, mirror and common carp, roach, skimmer bream, etc; dt £8 2 rods, £10 3 rods, 24 hr £17, conc. Hawkins Pond, 10 Bunting Close, Horsham RH13 5PA (Tel: 01293 610309): 11 acre lake, specimen fishery with carp to 32lb, pike to 28lb. Limited membership, but permits offered. At Pease Pottage, New Pond, Parish Lane. Mixed coarse, pike to 28lb. St only, £36, conc half price. Contact O Thayre, 10 Murray Court, Broadfield, Crawley.

Rudgwick (W Sussex). Roach, bream, chub, perch, pike, carp, large eels. Southern Anglers fish ½m non-tidal river at Bucks Green, u/s of road bridge. Tickets for members guests, £5–£4; also exchange tickets with four other clubs for several Sussex and Hampshire waters. Annual subscription £40, conc. Rudgwick AS fishes from Slinfold to Gibbons Mill. Hazelcopse, Knowle Lane, nr Rudgwick (Tel: 01403 822878): 2 lakes of 7 acres, with rainbow and brown trout, and salmon. Dt £22, 4 fish, catch and release after limit, barbless hooks. Tackle shops: Tropicana, Littlehampton; Prime Angling, 74 Brighton Rd, Worthing.

Tributaries of the Arun
WESTERN ROTHER:

Petworth (W Sussex). Pike, perch, roach, dace, chub, few trout and sea trout. Leconfield Estate operate a commercial fishery, and let trout rods on their section of the Rother. Contact Smiths Gore, Estate Office, Petworth. Hants and Sussex AA has 5½m in all, limited dt; also stretch downstream from Coultershaw Mill to Shopham Bridge, and 1m (N bank only) from Shopham Bridge. Then both banks for 1m from Fittleworth Bridge. St £21 + £10 joining fee, dt £2.50, from Sec. Contact Richard Etherington, South Dean, Tillington, Petworth GU28 0RE, Tel: 01798 343111, for 1½m stocked fly fishing on Rother for browns and rainbows, 3 miles from Petworth. **Burton Mill Pond** holds good pike, perch, roach, rudd, carp, tench. **Duncton Mill**, Dye House Lane, Duncton, Petworth GU28 0LF (Tel: 01798 342294). 8-acre trout farm and fishery, on chalk spring fed lakes; brown, brook, tiger and rainbow trout, average bags 3 fish, 7½lb total; all facilities, incl tuition and rod hire.

Selham (W Sussex). Pitshill Fly Fishing Waters: 1½m part double bank downstream from Lods Bridge; also ½m of tributary. R Etherington, South Dean, Tillington, Petworth, Tel: 01798 343111. Stocked with b and r trout.

Midhurst (W Sussex). Rother AC has six stretches of river and four lakes; coarse fish incl dace, roach, rudd, bream, tench, perch, carp, pike, eels. Tickets for Rother £3, Rotherfield Pond £5 conc, from Backshalls Garage, Dodsley Lane, Easebourne, Midhurst. Membership from Treasurer.

Chithurst (W Sussex). Petersfield & Dist AC is affiliated to the Hants and Sussex Anglers Alliance who have fishing on the Arun, **Rother**, and 11 stillwaters. Fishing is predominantly coarse with most species. Permits for Heath Lake, 22 acres (with carp to 27lb), Petersfield, from local tackle shop. Enquiries to Hon Sec. Tel: 01730 66793. Southern Anglers have water on Rother at Habins Bridge, **Rogate**, approx ½m d/s of pumping station, north bank only, with trout, grayling, chub and dace; also Stepstones Lakes, Dumpford, nr Rogate, 3 small lakes containing carp, tench, roach, rudd, and large eels. Dt on river, £4, from club Committee members, or Sec, Mr B Smith, Tel: 023 9247 2110. Tackle shop: Rods and Reels, 418 Havant Rd, Farlington.

AVON (BRISTOL)
(For close seasons, licences, etc, see South West Region Environment Agency, p12).

Coarse fishing now excellent in places. Large chub, barbel, pike, bream, roach. Trout in weir pools, including exceptional specimens occasionally, and in some tributaries. Much of Avon controlled by Bristol, Bath and Wiltshire Anglers, a merger of 11 clubs known as "the Amalgamation". Fishing includes many stretches of Bristol Avon, Somerset Frome, Bristol Frome, stretches on Brue, and coarse lakes. Membership costs £27 (concessions for ladies, juniors and pensioners), obtainable from tackle shops in the main Avon centres or Hon Sec. Dt waters.

Bristol. On Avon and Frome and in Somerset. Some free fishing on Environment Agency licence from Netham Weir u/s to Hanham, towpath only. Good sport with trout on **Blagdon Lake**, **Chew Valley** and **Barrow Reservoirs** (see Somerset streams, lakes and reservoirs). Among coarse fishing lakes in area are **Bowood** (2m W of Calne, dt at waterside); **Longleat** (see Warminster); **Bitterwell Lake** (N of Bristol) excellent bream, roach, rudd, a few common, mirror and crucian carp, perch. Tuck shop and tackle sold. Dt on bank, £3 per rod, £1.50 conc and after 4pm, from Mrs M Reid, The Chalet, Bitterwell Lake, Ram Hill, Coalpit Heath, Bristol BS17 2UF (Tel: 01454 778960). Tickenham Pond, **Tickenham**: trout fly fishing; contact M Rutland, 43 Blackthorne Gardens, Worle, Weston S M. **Henleaze Lake** (north of Bristol, dt June–Sep from R W Steel, 63 Hill View, Henleaze, Bristol). **Abbots Pool**, Abbots Leigh, is run by North Somerset Council, PO Box 146, Town Hall, Weston-super-Mare BS23 1LH (01934 888888). Tackle shops: Veals, 61 Old Market St BS2 0EJ (Tel: 0117 9260790); Fish and Field, 60 Broad St, Chipping Sodbury; Scotts, 42 Soundwell Road, Staple Hill; S Shipp, 7 Victoria St, Staple Hill; Avon Angling Centre, 348 Whitewell Road, St George; Bristol Angling Centre, 12 Doncaster Road, Southmead.

Keynsham (Avon). Chub, perch, eels, roach and dace. Free fishing on Environment Agency licence at R **Chew** confluence, end of recreation ground, left bank; also R Chew in Keynsham Park. Keynsham AA has water at Swineford, all coarse fish; stretch of R Chew from Keynsham Mill to Compton Dando; also Century Pond, carp roach, bream, tench. All waters members only. Special facilities for young anglers. St £11, dt £4 from Keynsham Pet Shop, High St, Keynsham, or Veals, Old Market, Bristol BS2 0EJ (Tel: 0117 9260790). Bathampton AA has stretch of R Chew at Keynsham; Bristol & West of England Federation has water here; BB&WAA has six stretches of river here and one at **Willsbridge**. Tackle shop: Keynsham Pets and Garden Centre, Bath Hill, High St.

Saltford (Avon). BB&WAA has stretch at Swineford. Bathampton AA has 2½m; most coarse fish, including carp and tench, few large trout. St £15, dt £2 from local tackle shops and Hon Sec.

Bath (Avon). Coarse fish; barbel present from here to Limpley Stoke; few large trout. Also good base for Rivers Chew and Frome, with reasonable trout fishing. Some free Avon fishing at Pulteney Weir d/s to Newbridge, along towpath; Bathampton Weir u/s to car park, most of footpath. Bath AA are part of BB&WAA, and has water at Kensington meadows and from Bathampton to city weirs. Good trout fishing in tributary streams, all preserved. **Kennet and Avon Canal** to Winsley Hill preserved by Bathampton AA. Assn also fishes on Newton Park, Hunstrete and Lydes Farm, also Box Brook nr Bathford on A4, fly only. Contact K Rippin, The Grove, Langridge, Bath. Tackle shop: I M Crudgington Ltd, 37 Broad Street BA1 5LT (Tel: 01225 464928) has information and tickets for Bath AA and Bathampton AA waters.

Batheaston (Avon). BB&WAA has two fields here.

Bathampton (Avon). All-round fishing. BB&WAA has water. Bathampton AA has water here, and at **Kelston**, **Newton St Loe**, **Newbridge**, **Saltford**, and on **Kennet and Avon Canal**, **Hunstrete**, **Newton Park** and Lydes Farm, and **Box Brook**. Members only, St £17.50, conc £4.50, from Hon Sec. and tackle shops in Bristol, Bath, Keynsham, and Chippenham.

Claverton (Avon). Bathampton AA has 2m; very good chub, and barbel.

Warleigh (Avon). Bathampton AA has 4 meadows here: (as Claverton above). BB&WAA has 5 meadows.

Limpley Stoke (Wilts). Good all-round fishing; large carp, with tench, chub, roach bream and trout; fly-fishing on **River Frome** at Freshford and **Midford Brook** at Midford; preserved by Avon and Tributaries AA. Bathampton AA holds **Kennet and Avon Canal** from Limpley Stoke to confluence with Avon at Bath (5½m): dt from Hon Sec, tackle shops.

Midford (Avon). **Midford Brook**; trout only; preserved and stocked by the Avon and Tributaries AA.

Freshford (Avon). BB&WAA has water on Avon here; dt issued. **Frome**: trout, coarse fish, stocked and preserved by Avon and Tributaries AA; from Avon up to Farleigh Hungerford. Limited dt for members' guests. Association also has part of Avon, Freshford to Avoncliffe, fly only water on **Midford, Wellow** and **Cam Brooks**.

Bradford-on-Avon (Wilts). Coarse fish, including pike, few trout. **Kennet and Avon Canal**; coarse fish.

Melksham (Wilts). Coarse fish, few trout. BB&WAA has Lacock stretch 1m from Melksham: excellent barbel. Baits from Gogoozler, Marina. Leech Pool Farm has coarse fishing at **Broughton Gifford**.

Lacock (Wilts). BB&WAA has water here. Dt on site for **Silverlands Lake**. Carp and tench.

Chippenham (Wilts). Chub, barbel, bream, perch, roach, carp, pike. Chippenham AA has water, details from B Duffield (Tel: 01249 655575); st £20, wt £10, dt £3.50 from Rob's Tackle, 22 Marshfield Road, who also have dt for **Sword Lake**, coarse, and **Sabre Lake**, coarse with carp. BB&WAA has about 1½m between here and **Lacock**. Calne AA has **River Marden**, st £17, dt £3, from T K Tackle. **Devizes AA waters: 15m of Kennet and Avon Canal**, 1m of Avon at Beanacre, Melksham, various coarse, dt £3.50, conc. Melksham AC has Avon from Beanacre to Whaddon, st £10, dt £2. These and others from Rob's Tackle (*above*) or T K Tackle, 123a London Rd, Calne. Mill Farm Trout Lakes, Worton, nr Devizes, Tel: 01380 813138, 2 dt lakes, 3½ acres. Bill Coleman. Ivy House Lakes, nr Swindon, all species, carp to 20lbs. Dt £3, conc. P and J Warner, Tel: 01666 510368. Tackle shop: House of Angling, 59/60 Commercial Rd, Swindon SN1 5NX.

Christian Malford (Wilts). Several fields controlled by BB&WAA here, and at **Sutton Benger**. Calne AA has 2 meadows on church side. Tickets from T K Tackle, 123A London Rd, Calne. Somerfords FA has water upstream from Seagry to Kingsmead Mill (part of it, from Dauntsey road bridge, is trout water) and 2m above Kingsmead Mill on left bank and 1m on right bank. Good chub and perch. Assn also has water on **Frome**. Dt for trout and coarse fishing issued. Golden Valley FC has water at Seagry.

Malmesbury (Wilts). Bristol, Bath and Wiltshire AA has fishing here, members only; trout and coarse fish; also Burton Hill Lake. Membership £25, conc. RD licences from Sports and Leisure, 36 High Street.

Lower Moor Fishery, Oaksey Malmesbury, Wiltshire SN16 9TW. Tel: 01666 860232. Forty acres of excellent trout fishing on two lakes: Mallard Lake (34 acres), any kind of fly fishing, stocked rainbow and brown; Cottage Lake (8 acres) confined to nymph and dry fly on floating line. Dt £20 or £12 (4 and 2 fish limits). Fine fly hatch, exceptional mayfly and damsel. Open end of Mar to New Year's Day.

Tributaries of the Avon (Bristol)

FROME (Bristol): Rises near Chipping Sodbury and joins Avon estuary near Bristol. Small tributaries upstream provide ideal conditions for trout. Fishing on **Mells River**, **Whatley** and **Nunney Brooks**. Coarse species are barbel, bream, carp, eel, perch, roach, tench, chub and grayling. BB&WAA has water at **Stapleton**.

Frampton Cotterell (Glos). Most of lower Frome controlled by Bristol, Bath and Wiltshire Anglers.

Yate (Glos). Frome Vale AC has water from Moorend Weir to viaduct. Dodington Park Lake, 6m; carp, perch; preserved. Tanhouse Farm, Yate Rocks, has coarse fishing lake.

CHEW: From Confluence to Compton Dando, coarse fish; thereafter, trout.

Keynsham (Avon). Keynsham AA has fishing (*see Avon*).

Malmesbury (Wilts). Free fishing on Environment Agency licence at Sherston Avon u/s of Cascade at Silk Mills; Tetbury Avon u/s Station Yard Weir, Fire Station, left bank. Club also has long stretch of **Woodbridge Brook**.

Chewton Keynsham (Avon). Water held by BB&WAA. Stretch in Keynsham Park free to licence holders.

Compton Dando (Avon). Mainly trout, grayling and dace. Keynsham AA also has water from Keynsham Mill to Compton Dando; all coarse fishing; see entry under *Avon*.

Pensford (Avon). Trout and coarse fish. Lakes: **Hunstrete Park Lakes**; 3 lakes with carp, tench, bream, roach, perch; Bathampton AA; members only.

Stanton Drew, Chew Magna, Chew Stoke (Avon). Trout dominant; some roach and dace. No spinning. Dt from local inns and Bristol tackle shops from June 15 to Sept 30 (Mon–Fri only). **Emborough Pond**; carp, tench, roach, perch; dt (limited) from bailiff. *(For Chew Reservoirs, see Somerset (lakes and streams)).*

BOYD BROOK: Trout in upper reaches, coarse fish, **Golden Valley FC has stretch above and below Bitton.**

CAM BROOK: Trout. Avon and Tributaries AA has water (members only). Cameley Trout Lakes are at Temple Cloud. St and dt, apply to J Harris, Tel: Temple Cloud 52790/52423.

BYE (BOX) BROOK: Trout, coarse fish. Bathampton AA has water at **Shockerwick** (Som) and **Box** (Wilts); members only, st £17.50, conc. By Brook Fly FC and Two Mills Flyfishers has water for members. Manor House Hotel, Castle Combe, has ½m of good trout fishing in grounds.

SEMINGTON BROOK: Trout, coarse fish. Lavington AC has Bulkington Brook. St £15 and st £3. Concessions for juniors. Members only. Tel: 01380 830425. For **Erlestoke Lake**, D Hampton, Longwater, Erlestoke, Devizes, Wilts SN10 5UE. Coarse fish, carp to 24lb. Members, limited dt. St £70, wt £30, dt £7. Juv £15, £3. Ban on nut baits and keepnets. Tackle shop: Steve's, 26 High St, Warminster.

FROME: Coarse fish, trout.

Frome (Som). Frome and Dist AA has 12 miles above and below town, and coarse fishing lake at Marston, 3m from Frome. Regular matches. Membership £10 pa, conc, dt £2, conc. Information from R Lee, Tel: 01373 461433. Two coarse lakes, just off A36 road between Bockington and Warminster: Brookers Wood, and Cuckoo's Rest. Dt £3.50 from tackle shops. BB&WAA has fishing at **Beckington**. Witham Friary Lake coarse fishing open all year, Witham Hall Farm, Witham Friary, nr Frome. Tel: 01373 836239. Tackle shops: Haines Tackle, 47 Vallis Way, Frome BA11 3BA (Tel: 01373 466406); Frome Angling

Centre, 11 Church St BA11 1PW (Tel: 01373 467143). Hotel: George, Market Place.

Wolverton (Avon). Trout, coarse fish.

MARDEN: Coarse fish, trout.

Calne (Wilts). Trout, barbel, chub, rudd, carp, golden orfe, tench, pike, perch, roach, dace, bream; fly fishing 1 Apr–15 Jun; 6m held by Calne AA: st £17, conc, dt £3. Assn also fish section of R Avon at Christian Malford, and Spye Park Lake. Disabled stages available, jun coaching and matches. **Bowood Lake**, large pike (to 26lb), perch, carp, tench, roach. Details from Bowood Estate, Calne, Wilts SN11 0LZ, Tel: 01249 812102, who issue st £99–88, jun conc. Waiting list. North end of lake private. *Note: access to lake only at Pillars Lodge entrance on Calne – Melksham road.* Tickets for Sabre Lake, nr Calne, and other local waters, from T K Tackle, 123a London Road.

AVON (Hampshire)
(For close seasons, licences, etc, see South West Region Environment Agency p12)

In years gone by the most famous mixed fishery in England. In its upper reaches, the Avon is a typical chalk stream, populated by free-rising trout and grayling.

Christchurch (Dorset). Avon and Stour. Excellent sea and coarse fishing in Christchurch Harbour, which is leased to Christchurch AC. Bass, mullet, flounders and (higher up) dace, roach, bream and eels. Other Club waters include several stretches of Dorset Stour from Christchurch Harbour to Wimborne, lakes and gravel pits with large carp and pike. Membership £80 per annum. Dt for these waters and the Royalty Fishery on the Avon (excluding Parlour and Bridge Pool) can be obtained from Mr G K Pepler, Davis Tackle Shop, 75 Bargates, Christchurch, Tel: 01202 485169. June 16 to Mar 14 inclusive. The Royalty Fishery price structure ranges between £30 per day for salmon, sea trout and coarse fishing, to double rod £75, and £8 single rod for coarse and sea trout fishing, with concessions. Davis will supply brochure on receipt of request and SAE. Top Weir Compound, Parlour and Bridge Pool (best sea trout pool) permits from Fishery Manager; advance bookings only, except 1 Nov–14 Mar, when coarse dt are obtainable for Parlour and Compound. No advance bookings on Main River. All salmon to be returned. Permits for fishings on Stour and in Christchurch Harbour also obtainable from Davis Tackle Shop (see also Stour (Dorset)) and Pro Fishing Tackle. For other salmon and sea trout fishing apply early in writing to the Royalty Fisheries Manager, Bournemouth and West Hants Water Plc, George Jessel House, Francis Avenue, Bournemouth BH11 8NB. Dt also from Head Bailiff, 2 Avon Buildings, Christchurch. Small coarse fisheries in vicinity: Gold Oak Farm, 7 lakes with carp and tench, Hare Lane, nr Cranborne, Tel: 01725 517275; Beeches Brook Fishery, Forest Rd, Burley, Tel: 01425 402373; Turf Croft Farm, Forest Rd, Burley, Tel: 01425 403743; **Hordle Lakes**, Golden Hill, Ashley Lane, **New Milton**, Tel: 01590 672300: coarse fishery on 7 lakes. Dt on site. Good sea fishing at Mudeford; boats. Tackle shops: Davis, 75 Bargates; Pro Fishing Tackle, 258 Barrack Rd. Both open 7.30 am, 7 days a week. Hotel: Belvedere, 59 Barrack Road.

Winkton (Dorset). Davis Fishing Tackle, 75 Bargates, Christchurch now sole agents for coarse fishing on this fishery. Season is June 16 to March 14; good roach, large chub and barbel, pike; also dace, perch. Dt £5. Salmon fishing is offered, March 15 to June 15 only. Details from Davis Tackle, Tel: 01202 485169. Hotel: Fishermans Haunt.

Ringwood (Hants). Ringwood & Dist AC has fishing on rivers as follows: **Avon**; Breamore, 1½m (barbel, chub), Fordingbridge (trout), Ibsley, 2m (S and specimen coarse fish), side streams at Ibsley, Ringwood, 2m (coarse fish), East Mills, 1½m (coarse fish), Fordingbridge Park, ¼m (coarse fish); **Stour**; 12 stretches totalling more than 12m (coarse fish); **Test**; over 2m at Broadlands Est. (members only); also 9 still waters totalling over 120 acres. Dt for much of the water from tackle shops. Dt £5 from Ringwood Tackle for ¾m both banks above Ringwood; 1¼m E. bank below and several coarse fishing lakes, dt £4. **Beeches Brook**, Forest Rd, Burley BH24 4DQ (Tel: 01425 402373) is dt coarse lake off A31 to Southampton. Dt £5, advance booking advisable. **High Town**, Ringwood: 23 acre pit containing most coarse species. Tickets from Ringwood and Christchurch tackle shops. Other dt waters: river at Lifelands Fishery; Martins Farm Carp Lake, W Ball, Woodlands, **Wimborne** BH21 8LY (Tel: 01202 822335); Hurst Pond. Tackle shops: Ringwood Tackle, 5 The Bridges, West Street, Ringwood BH24 1EA (Tel: 01425 475155); Hales Tackle; Davis, Christchurch. Hotels: Crown, Star Inn, Fish Inn, Nag's Head, White Hart.

Fordingbridge (Hants). Trout, grayling, perch, pike and roach. Park Recreation Ground has fishing, dt from Council grounds staff, Sept to Mar. Burgate Manor Farm Fishery let to Wimborne AC. Albany Hotel has short river frontage (licences obtainable). Few dt for Bickton Estate water from river bailiff, 2 New Cottages, **Bickton**; St (trout streams) £300, st (coarse) £35, st (salmon) £60, dt (trout streams) £12. No licence needed as block licence purchased. Tackle shop on premises. East Mills Manor, Shepherds Spring Restaurant has 1½m of river and lake. Dt water. Two excellent stillwater fisheries in the vicinity. **Damerham** and **Lapsley's Fishery** (ex Allens Farm). Hotel: Ashburn.

Breamore (Hants). Bat and Ball Hotel has 2m of salmon, trout and coarse fish on dt basis, from £2.50. Phone Breamore 252.

Salisbury (Wilts). Avon, Bourne, Ebble, Nadder and Wylye; trout, grayling, coarse fish; preserved. Salisbury and Dist AC has water on Avon at Charford, within city boundary, **Durnford**, **West Amesbury**, Ratfynn, Countess Farm, and Durrington; on Upper Avon; plus **R Wylye** at **Stapleford**; **R Bourne** at **Hurdcott** and **Gomeldon**; **R Ebble** at **Bishopstone** and **Knighton**; coarse fishing on R Stour at Wimborne; coarse fishing on six lakes and fly fishing for rainbows on one small lake. Dt for waters within city boundary from Reids Tackle or John Eadie (below). Club also issues permits for Charlton fishing, from Post Office, Downton Cross Roads. All details from Secretary. The Piscatorial Society has Avon fishing nr **Amesbury**, members only. Other local clubs: Tisbury AC has Wardour Castle Lake and Dinton Lake, and 3m of R Nadder, with bream, carp, roach, tench, etc; Downton AA has 2½m of Avon with specimen chub, roach, barbel, etc. Membership for both these at Reids Tackle (below). Langford Fisheries have 22 acre trout lakes at Duck St, **Steeple Langford**. Good dry fly fishing, catch and release, boats and permits on site. Fishing includes 1m of R Wylye. Tel: 01722 790770. London AA has **Britford Fishery**; excellent coarse fishing, good sport with trout, some salmon. Members only; no dt. **Avon Springs Fisheries**, Recreation Rd, Durrington SP4 8EZ (Tel: 01980 653557): 2 spring fed lakes beside R Avon, of 3 and 5 acres, stocked with brown and rainbow trout from 2lb to double figures. Best rainbow 1998, 16lb 4oz; best brown, 17lb, 1oz. Prices are as follows. Lakes: st from £798–£270. Full dt

£30, 4 fish limit; half-day £23, 3 fish; evening £16, 2 fish; juv £19–£15. River: dt £35, 2 fish limit. Accom, nr fishery: Parkhouse Motel (Tel: 01980 629256); Plum and Feather, Shrewton (Tel: 01980 62021). Waldens Coarse Fishery, Walden Estate, **West Grinstead** SP5 3RJ (Tel: 01722 710480) has coarse fishing on 5 lakes, total 7.5 acres. Tackle shops: John Eadie, 20 Catherine Street; Reids Tackle, Kingsway House, Wilton SP20 0AY. Hotels: County, White Hart; Red Lion; Grasmere; Old Mill, Harnham; Lamb, Hinton; Bell, South Newton.

Netheravon (Wilts). Trout, grayling; preserved. The 6m from **Enford** to **Bulford** is The Services Dry Fly FA (Salisbury Plain) water; strictly members only, no tickets.

AVON (Hampshire) tributaries

BOURNE: Enters near Salisbury. Trout, grayling, coarse fish. Fishing stations: **Porton** and **Salisbury** (Wilts).

EBBLE: Joins Avon below Salisbury; good trout fishing, but mostly private.

WYLYE: Trout, grayling.

Wilton (Wilts). 6 miles preserved by Wilton Fly Fishing Club, full-time keeper, club room, wild brown trout (stocked with fry and fingerlings), grayling. Closed membership of forty five, no dt. Wyle Fly FC has stretches at **Steeple Langford**, **Quidhampton**, and elsewhere. Members and their guests only.

Stapleford (Wilts). Salisbury AC has fishing here; members only. (See Salisbury.)

Warminster (Wilts). Hunters Moon Lodge, Henford Marsh BA12 9PA has fishing for guests and club members. Tel: 01985 219977 or 212481. **Longleat** Estate owns just over 2m of upper river. Excellent coarse fishing in three lakes in Longleat Park; Bottom and Middle, mixed fishing, Top Lake, specimen carp. Tickets are issued by Bailiff, Nick Robbins Swancombe Cottage, Crockerton, Warminster (Tel: 01985 844496, mobile: 05896 25999). Dt £5, 24 hr £10. The Sutton Veny Estate, Eastleigh Farm, Bishopstrow, Warminster BA12 7BE (Tel: 01985 212325), lets rods, part rods and quarter-rods on 4m of Wylye, chalk stream dry fly and upstream nymph only, brown trout. Autumn nymph fishing for grayling. B & B: Roger Dale, Mill Farm, Hill Deverill (Tel: 01985 840448).

NADDER: Tributary of Wylye. Trout, grayling, roach, dace, chub. Mostly preserved by landowners. Fishing stations: **Wilton**, **Tisbury**. Tisbury AC has 3m, guest tickets from Sec R Fogerty (Tel: 01722 716529). Exchanges with Warminster and Salisbury clubs. Club also has Old Wardour and Dinton Lakes; carp, roach, tench. St £25 plus £4 joining, conc. Tackle shop: Reid's Tackle, Wilton, nr Salisbury. Hotel: South Western; Tisbury AC HQ.

AXE
(For close seasons, licences, etc, see South West Region Environment Agency, p12)

Rises in Dorset and flows south to the English Channel at Axemouth. Trout, sea trout and salmon. Fishing difficult to come by, but one or two hotels can provide facilities.

Seaton (Devon). Trout, salmon. Some sea trout fishing from L Burrough, Lower Abbey Farm, Axminster, and from Ackermans. Axe estuary fishable (for bass, mullet, flounders, etc), on £2 dt from harbour filling station, Axemouth. Tackle and licences: F Ackerman & Co Ltd, Fore Street (see Sea Fishing Stations). Hotel: Pole Arms. Sea trout, rainbow and wild brown trout fishing at **Colyton**: dt £3 from Mrs E Pady, Higher Cownhayne Farm, Colyton EX13 6HD, (Tel: 01297 552267). Two farmhouse holiday apartments to let, on weekly or weekend basis.

Axminster (Devon). Axe, Yarty; trout and salmon. Trouting good especially in April and May. Taunton Fly Fishing Club has beats on the Axe at Chard, Tytherleigh, Musbury. At **Uplyme**, Amherst Lodge, Dorset DT7 3XH (Tel: 01297 442 773): day ticket fishery with four fly fishing lakes and three coarse lakes. Hotels: Cavalier, Bear Inn, Colyton.

Crewkerne (Som). Axe (3m off); trout. Parret (1m off); trout, roach, dace. Stoke-sub-Hamdon AA has trout fishing from Bow Mills to Creedy Bridge on **Parret**; members only. Fees, £6, £3. Wt also. Yeovil AA has trout and coarse fishing on **Yeo** and tributaries; dt £4 from tackle shops. Trout fishing in **Sutton Bingham Reservoir**, near Yeovil. Tackle shops: Yeovil Angling Centre, 27/29 Forest Hill; Stax Angling and Saddlers, Montacute, nr Yeovil (Tel: 01935 822645).

BLACKWATER (Essex)
(For close seasons, licences, etc, see Anglian Region Environment Agency, p14)

Rises in NW of county, flows by Braintree to Maldon and empties into North Sea through large estuary. Coarse fish include pike, chub, rudd and some carp.

Maldon (Essex). Maldon AS has river, canal and pond fishing in Maldon area; three stretches totalling 1½ of **R Blackwater**, **Chelmer Navigation Canal**, Longford. All coarse, carp over 45lb, tench, roach, rudd, bream, dace, gudgeon, perch, pike. Membership £45, conc. Dt for Chelmer and Blackwater canal sections only, from bailiff on bank or tackle shop. RMC Angling **Chigborough** gravel pits of 8½ acres at **Drapers Farm**. Coarse fish, tench, bream, crucian, etc. St £20, conc. £10. Dt £1.50, jun conc, from Essex Angling Centre (Tel: 01621 840414). RMC Angling run many other fisheries throughout southern England, and they may be contacted at The Square, Lightwater, Surrey GU18 5SS (Tel: 01276 453300). Tackle shop: Essex Angling Centre, 48 The Street, Heybridge, Maldon. Hotels: Swan, White Hart, King's Head.

Chigboro Fisheries, Maldon, Essex CM9 7RE (Tel: 01621 857368). Home Water: 16-acre lake with brown and rainbow trout of average weight 2lb 6oz, fly only. Lake record, 19¼lb. 4 boats. St from £145. Dt £23(full limit), or £14.50 (half limit). Slough House Water: four acres, stocked brown and rainbow, average 2½lb. Record 16/4lb. St £320, dt £32, 4 fish, combined water ticket, £27. No boats, rod and tuition. Coarse fishing: 4 lakes, 20 acres total, large carp and other species, incl catfish. St £100–£60, dt £9–£5.

Witham (Essex). Blackwater and **Brain**. Coarse fish. Kelvedon and Dist AA has 7½m from here to **Braintree**; members only. **Witham Lake**, 5½ acres; **Bovingdon Mere**, **Hatfield Peverel**; 4 acre lake coarse fishery, Colchester APS waters. Tackle shop: E & J Tackle, 16 Church St.

Kelvedon (Essex). Kelvedon and Dist AA has various stretches as well as water on Suffolk **Stour**, **Tiptree Reservoir**, between Colchester and Witham, **Seabrook Reservoir**, nr **Chelmsford**, Hunts Farm Reservoir, between Maldon and **Colchester**, all good carp waters, **Silver End Pits**, 6 acres each, and two 2 acre pits at **Layer Marney**. St £52, conc, from tackle shops in Chelmsford, Witham, Tiptree and Colchester. Maldon AS has water here and at **Feering** and **Braxted**; members only (see Witham, Coggeshall and Maldon). Tackle shop: E & J Tackle, 16 Church St, Witham.

Coggeshall (Essex). Coarse fish. Colchester APS fish Houchins Reservoirs, (see Colchester).

Braintree (Essex). Braintree and Bocking AS owns most of water on main river, both banks, from Shalford to Bradwell Village and on **Pant**. Well stocked with roach, perch, rudd, dace, and chub. St £17, Juv £6, OAP £2 from subscription Sec D Clack, (Tel: 01376 44201). For Gosfield and Sparrows Lakes see Essex (Streams and Lakes). Hotels: Horne, White Horse, Nag's Head.

CHELMER and CAN: Coarse fish.

Chelmsford (Essex). River stocked: roach, dace, bream, tench, carp, pike, perch. Public fishing in town parks. Dt £3 for towpath between Brown's Wharf and Ricketts Lock, and for **Heybridge Canal** from Beeleigh to Hall Bridge from bailiff on bank. Chelmsford AA has fishing as follows: 14m of Chelmer and Blackwater Canal, from Chelmsford to Maldon; Boreham Mere, Boreham; Blunts Mere, Cants Mere and Wick Mere, **Ulting**; Broads Mere and Tuftnell Mere, **Great Waltham**; Braxted Hall Estate fishing, of reservoir and 2 lakes, **Braxted**. All mixed fisheries, with carp, bream, tench, rudd, roach, barbel, chub; all members only, except canal, dt £3 conc, on bank. St £45, conc. Instruction is offered, and matches are organised. Contact Secretary Mrs I Lewis (Tel: 01245 264832). Newland Hall Fisheries, **Roxwell**, Chelmsford CM1 4LH (Tel: 01245 231463) have Brook, Moat, Park and Osiers Lakes, total of approx 10 acres. The fishing is for carp, roach, tench, etc, with match weights exceeding 100lb. Platforms for disabled. Dt, two rods, £7–£8, conc. RMC Angling gravel pit at **Boreham** offers good carp fishing. St £20, conc. £10. (For RMC Angling, see Chertsey.) Blasford Hill Fisheries, Little Waltham, nr Chelmsford (Tel: 01245 357689): lakes stocked with carp, tench, roach, and other species. Dt £5, conc, on bank or from Edwards Tackle, 16 Broomfield Rd (Tel: 01245 357689). Tackle shops: Edwards (above); Gibson's Sports, Moulsham St; Ronnie Crowe, 63 Maldon Rd, Gt Baddow, Chelmsford CM2 7DN (Tel: 01245 471246), who has permits for all local clubs. Boreham tackle shop: Bevans Carp and Tackle, Main Rd, Boreham, specialist in carp tackle. Hotels: County; White Hart, Witham.

BLYTH (Northumberland)
(For close seasons, licences, etc, see North East Region Environment Agency, p13)

Rises near Throckington and flows 20m to North Sea at Blyth. Trout and grayling with coarse fish (especially roach) in lower reaches. All stretches controlled by Bedlington and Blagdon AA, members only, no tickets.

BRUE
(For close seasons, licences, etc, see South West Region Environment Agency, p12)

Rises in Mendips and flows to Bristol Channel at Burnham. Coarse fish throughout. From West Lydford to Glastonbury, a number of weirs provide deep water in which coarse fish predominate. A good late season river, contains numbers of most coarse species.

Highbridge (Som). Roach, bream, etc. North Somerset AA fishes Rivers **Kenn**, **Axe**, **Apex Pit**, between Highbridge and Burnham, (match record 35lb 11oz), Newtown Pond, Highbridge (carp to 20lb), Walrow Ponds, North Drain. Weston-super-Mare AA has **River Axe** fishing, Old R Axe, South Drain. Bridgwater AA has **Huntspill River**, **Kings Sedgemoor Drain**, North and South Drains. Emerald Pool Fishery, off Puriton Rd, Highbridge (Tel: 01278 794707), purpose-made lake stocked with large carp, tench, perch, bream, etc. Dt and refreshments on site. Lands End Fisheries, Heath House, Wedmore BS28 4UQ (Tel: 07977 545882), two lakes with various carp species and others. Dt £5. Permits for these and local fishings, and club information from tackle shops P & J Thyer, 1A Church Street, Highbridge TA9 3AE (Tel: 01278 786934), or Richards Angling Centre, 12 Regents Street, Burnham on Sea. Highbridge AA is part of N. Somerset AA, and holds junior matches, and other events. Further information from Hon Sec. Huntspill River. BB&WAA has water on Brue and **Axe** at **Wedmore**, as well as Pawlett Ponds and other lakes. Hotels: Highbridge; The George (clubs accommodated). Lamb Guest House, 11 Church St, is recommended locally, for visiting anglers.

Bason Bridge (Som). Area around milk factory noted for carp; fish run up to 16lb or so. Also roach, chub, tench, perch and pike.

Mark (Som). Carp, pike, perch, roach, chub, tench. N Somerset AA has 2½m on river and 3 to 4m on North Drain; dt and wt from Hon Sec. Highbridge AA also has water on North Drain. Inn: Pack Horse.

Glastonbury (Som). Roach, bream, chub, etc, in lower stretches of River Brue. Glaston Manor AA has approx 12m of water from Lydford to **Westhay**. Membership and season tickets are obtainable from tackle shops: Street Angling Centre, 160 High Street, Street BA16 0NH (Tel: 01458 447830); Thatchers Tackle, 18 Queen St, Wells (Tel: 01749 67513).

BUDE RIVER AND CANAL
(For close seasons, licences, etc, see South West Region Environment Agency, p12)

Bude Canal has 1¼ miles of wider than average canal with good banks and full variety of coarse fish. Apply to Hon Sec, Bude AA.

Bude (Cornwall). Bass from beaches, breakwater and rocks; bass and mullet in estuary of Bude River. Details from Hon Sec Bude & Dist SAA. Bude Angling Association has fishing on a total of 6½m of banks of **Tamar** and **Claw** from near Bude to half way to Launceston. Wild brown trout and some dace in downstream beats. Membership £5, wt £5, dt £3. Membership enquiries (with 50p if map req.) to Hon Sec, Bude AA. **Tamar Lake** and **Crowdy** (trout reservoir) controlled by SW Water (see Cornwall lakes, etc). **Bude Canal** (roach, bream, eels, dace, perch, carp to 25lb and tench) 1m from town centre towards Marhamchurch leased by Bude Canal AA; wt £15, dt £3, £1.50 jun and OAP, on bank. Tackle shop: Bude Angling Supplies, 6 Queen St, Bude.

BURE
(see Norfolk and Suffolk Broads)

CAMEL
(For close seasons, licences etc, see South West Region Environment Agency, p12)

A spate river, rising on Bodmin Moor near Davidstow, flowing about 30m to enter the Atlantic between Pentire and Stepper Points. Salmon, sea trout and small brown trout. Grilse from June, with the main runs in October, November and December. Sea trout from June to Aug. Best brown trout fishing in tributary De Lank. Salmon fishing in upper reaches dependent on heavy rainfall. There is a voluntary restriction in operation covering the whole river. No fishing in April and Sept, and a limit of 2 salmon per day and 4 per week, and 4 sea trout per day; also no selling of fish and no maggots. Salmon season ends 15 Dec.

Wadebridge (Cornwall). Trout, sea trout, salmon; good mullet and flounder fishing in tidal reaches; estuary is now a bass nursery area, boat fishing for bass prohibited, shore fishing allowed. Approx 6m held by Wadebridge and Dist AA at Pencarrow, Grogley, Wenford, and **River Allen** above Sladesbridge, 5½m. Membership of Wadebridge & Dist, via a year long list, is £40. Dt on all waters except Grogley, £15, wt £45, conc, and sea-fishing boat bookings, from Marcus Watts, The Bait Bunker, 5 Polmorla Rd, Wadebridge PL27 7NB (Tel: 01208 816403). Hotels: Molesworth Arms, Bridge-on-Wool, Swan, Lanarth, and Country Club, St Kew. (For sea fishing see Padstow.)

Bodmin (Cornwall). A few miles from the Camel and Fowey, where Bodmin AA issues visitor permits (10 per day) on some 12 miles of the best water. Details from Hon Sec. Wt £40, dt £15 from May 1–Nov 30. No permits in Dec. St, wt and dt from Hon Sec. Concessions for jun and OAP. Free maps and licences from Hon Sec R Burrows, 26 Meadow Place, Bodmin, Tel: 01208 75513, on receipt of sae. Mr T Jackson, Butterwell, Nanstallon, Bodmin PL30 5LQ has 1½m salmon and sea trout fishing, occasional day permits with preference given to residents, fly only, June–Aug. Self-catering cottage and limited B & B. Tel: 01208 831515. Fenwick Trout Fishery, Old Coach Rd, Dunmere, Bodmin PL31 2RD (Tel: 01208 78296) features 2 acre lake stocked with rainbow trout, record 13lbs 3oz, and 570yds of salmon fishing on R Camel. Dt £18, 4 fish; £15 salmon river bank permit. Lakeview Park Holiday Village, **Lanivet**, has 3 coarse fishing lakes, 6 acres, stocked; specimen carp, bream, tench. Dt £4, conc. (Tel: 01208 831808). Temple Trout Fishery, Temple Rd, Temple PL30 4HW (Tel: 01208 821730); 2 gravel pits totalling 7 acres, stocked with brown and rainbow trout; fish from 1¾lb to 17lb; dt £20.50 or £12, good access for disabled. Innis Moore Trout Fishery, 7 acres. Contact tackle shop: Roger's, Stan Mays Store, Higher Bore St, Bodmin PL31 1DZ (Tel: 01208 78006) (closed Wednesday), who also issue tickets for Fowey (Lostwithiel AA waters) and Camel (Bodmin AA waters). Hotel: Penhallow Manor, Launceston PL15 7SJ.

CHESHIRE (Lakes/Reservoirs)

APPLETON RESERVOIR, nr **Warrington**. Trout fishery controlled by Warrington AA. Members only, membership is by annual subscription plus joining fee, with generous concessions. This is one of the larger fishing clubs of Great Britain, controlling approximately 60 fisheries on rivers, lakes, reservoirs, canals and pools. The club keeps a coarse fishing close season between 15 Mar–15 Jun. See club list, for address.

ARNFIELD RESERVOIR, Tintwistle, nr Manchester. NWW trout fishery. Contact S Cuthberth, Tel: 0831 518284, or C.A.R. manager Peter Sharples. (See Greater Manchester.)

BLACKSHAW MOOR LAKES, Leek. 4 acre coarse fishery; carp, tench, bream, roach. Prince Albert AS water, members only.

BOSLEY RESERVOIR. Fishing station: **Bosley**. Roach (good), bream, pike, perch, carp. Prince Albert AS water, members only.

BOTTOMS RESERVOIR. High Peak, Cheshire. £2 coarse dt on bank. Information from D Blackburn, Woodhead Rd, Tintwistle, Hyde, Cheshire SK14 7HS.

BOTTOMS RESERVOIR. Macclesfield, Cheshire. Prince Albert AC. 5 permits per day issued from Barlows, Bond St, Macclesfield.

CAPESTHORNE POOLS, Siddington. Large carp, tench, bream, roach, rudd and pike. Park, Top and Garden pools controlled by Stoke-on-Trent AS. No tickets. Stock pond has excellent carp and tench. Dt £6, ½ day £4 from K Whalley, East Lodge Capesthorne (Tel: 01625 861584).

DOVE MERE, SAND MERE, Allostock, Knutsford. Prince Albert AS waters, members only. Heavily stocked, including large carp. St £55; waiting list.

GREAT BUDWORTH MERE. nr **Northwich**, 50 acre lake holding good bream, pike, etc. Northwich AA; tickets from Hon Sec, st only, £20 plus £20 joining fee, conc. **Pickmere** and **Petty Pool** are assn waters nearby.

HORSECOPPICE RESERVOIR, Macclesfield. Trout fishing leased to Dystelegh Fly FC (see Bollinhurst). Members only, no permits.

LANGLEY BOTTOMS and **LAMALOAD RESERVOIRS**. Nr **Macclesfield**. Langley Bottoms now coarse fishing, Prince Albert AS, members only. Lamaload, Good fly fishing for trout. Prince Albert AS. Limited dt £8 from Barlows Tackle, 47 Bond St, Macclesfield. Further information, contact Peter Sharples, Conservation, Access and Recreation Manager, North West Water Ltd. (See Greater Manchester.)

LEADBEATERS RESERVOIR. Bollington and Royal Oak AC, T Woolley, 51 Palmerston St, Bollington SK10 5PW. Dt from Barlows, Bond St, Macclesfield.

LYMM DAM, Lymm, beside A56. 15 acre lake, good all year round fishing with big carp and pike. Lymm AC water, 50 pegs, bookable for matches. Contact Hon Sec for this and seven other dt waters. Membership £27 per annum.

OULTON MILL POOL. Fishing station: Tarporley. Well stocked with good carp, bream, tench and pike. Dt from Mill Office.

RIDGEGATE RESERVOIR, Macclesfield. Macclesfield Fly FC, dt £12, from D J Harrop, School House, Macclesfield Forest, Macclesfield SK11 0AR. More information from Peter Sharples, Conservation, Access and Recreation Manager, North West Water Ltd. (*See Greater Manchester.*)

ROMAN LAKES LEISURE PARK, Marple, nr Stockport SK6 7HB, Tel: 0161 427 2039. Roach, perch, bream, carp to 30lb, pike to 20lb. Dt £3.75, with concessions from Lakeside Cafe.

ROSSMERE LAKE. 6 acres. Fishing station: **Wilmslow**. Heavily stocked. 80 match pegs. Prince Albert AS, members only.

TEGGSNOSE RESERVOIR, Macclesfield. Trout, Macclesfield Waltonian AC. Dt from Barlows Tackle Shop, 47 Bond St, Macclesfield. Information, Peter Sharples, Conservation, Access and Recreation Manager, North West Water Ltd. (*See Greater Manchester.*)

THORNEYCROFT HALL LAKES, Gawsworth. Prince Albert AS water, members only. Carp, tench, roach, pike.

WALL POOL LODGE, Off Church Lane, Gawsworth, SK11 9RQ (Tel: 01260 223442); 3 lake complex with coarse fishing, open all year round, dawn to dusk. Dt on bank, £5 one or two rods, conc for OAP and juv. Matches and night fishing by arrangement. Barbless hooks.

COLNE (Essex)
(For close seasons, licences, etc, see Anglian Region Environment Agency, p14)

Rises in north of county and flows to North Sea via Colchester. Improving as coarse fishery.

Colchester (Essex). Colchester APS controls two short stretches, with roach, chub, perch, pike, bream, dace; no tickets. The society's other waters, with excellent catfish, carp and pike fishing, include **Layer Pit**; pike, perch, bream, roach, rudd, tench, carp; Houchins Reservoirs, Coggeshall, coarse, large catfish; five stretches on Suffolk **Stour**; Hatfield Peverell Lakes; Witham Lake; Olivers Lake at Witham; Preston Lake, 20 acre mixed coarse fishery, and Bovingdon Lakes, good carp. Members only on all waters except Oliver's Lake, dt from E & J Tackle (below). St £49, conc to jun, OAP, disabled. Colchester Piscatorial Society has water on Langham Ponds, Stour and Colne; members only. ½m of Colne fished by Kelvedon AA. Tackle shops: W E Wass, 24 Long Wyre Street; K D Radcliffe, 150 High St; Carp Unlimited, Unit 16, Peartree Business Centre, Colchester. Witham tackle shop: E & J Tackle, 16 Church St. Hotels: George, Red Lion.

Aldham (Essex). Colnes AS has water at Fordham and Aldham, 3 stretches of Stour near Bures, 3 reservoirs, 1 lake and 2 ponds, and Blackwater stretch. Most species. Improved access for disabled. Members only, £20, conc, from Sec P Emson, Emson & Son Tackle Shop, 88 High St, Earls Colne, Colchester CO6 2QX.

Halstead (Essex). Halstead and Hedingham AC waters are: stretch of R Colne; several miles of **R Pant**; Sparrows Pond, **Gosfield**, with coarse fishing incl carp, tench, bream etc; **Halstead Reservoir**, with carp, tench, rudd; **Stebbing Reservoir**, with carp, bream, perch; Gosfield Sandpits, with tench, bream, perch, etc. Membership £20, conc, from Bill's Tackle, Braintree (Tel: 01376 552767). No day permits.

COQUET
(For close seasons, licences, etc, see North East Region Environment Agency, p13)

Rises in Cheviots and enters North Sea near Warkworth. Salmon, sea trout and trout. Sport still very good. Facilities for visitors. Good run of spring salmon.

Warkworth (Northumberland). Trout, sea trout; salmon from Feb onwards to late summer and autumn. Duke of Northumberland leases large part of his water to Northumbrian Anglers Federation. St £55 salmon, £35 trout. Concessions for OAP. Applications to Head Bailiff, Thirston Mill, Felton, Morpeth NE65 9EH, Tel: 01670 787663, or tackle dealers for trout permits only. Additional permit for tidal section. Permits for 2m beat, situated 1m d/s from Weldon Bridge, Longframlington, £16 or £11, from Murraysport, Narrowgate, Alnwick.

Acklington (Northumberland). Trout, sea trout and salmon. Northumbrian AF water on Coquet and tributary, Thirston Burn.

Felton (Northumberland).Salmon, sea trout (spring and autumn), trout. Northumbrian AF; trout permits from Post Office (see *Warkworth*).

Weldon Bridge (Northumberland). Nearest station: Morpeth, 9½m. Trout (sea trout and salmon, late summer and autumn). Anglers Arms Hotel, Weldon Bridge, Morpeth NE65 8AL, has fishing, maximum 3 rods, on 1m north bank. Free for residents, otherwise £10 dt. Tel: 01665 570655/570271.

Rothbury (Northumberland). A late salmon run and excellent sea trout fishing in June and Oct. Brown trout, including fish to 3lb. Northumbrian AF has 4m of Coquet (see *Warkworth*). Thropton & Rothbury AC has 1½m on Coquet around Rothbury, 2–3m on tributaries. Main runs of salmon and sea trout, Sept and Oct. Non members welcome, dt £7, conc, from Thropton P O, and Morpeth tackle shop. **Fontburn Reservoir**, Ewesley, nr Rothbury, trout fishery of 87 acres stocked with rainbow and American brook trout, fly or worm permitted. Record rainbow, 20lb 14oz. Dt £11, £9 conc, 6 fish. Tel: 01669 621368. Hotel: Whitton Farm House.

Holystone (Northumberland). Salmon (late), trout; mostly private. Holystone Burn, trout; Grasslees Burn, trout. Inn: Salmon, where particulars may be had.

Harbottle (Northumberland). Good trout and some late salmon fishing on Coquet and Alwin. Upper Coquetdale AC has extensive parts of upper river; members only.

CORNWALL
(streams, lakes, etc)
(For close seasons, licences, etc, see South West Region Environment Agency p12)

ARGAL RESERVOIR, nr **Penryn**. SWW coarse fishery of 65 acres, with carp to 30lb, large perch, pike, bream, tench, eels. St £110, dt £4.50, conc; open all year, 24 hr day. Permit from self-service kiosk.

BOSCATHNOE RESERVOIR, Penzance; 4 acre, stocked SWW coarse fishery, with bream, roach, tench, crucian carp, gudgeon, eels. Permits £4.50, conc, st £110 or £70, with conc, from Newtown Angling Centre, Newtown, Germoe, Penzance (Tel: 01736 763721), or Headmoor Stores, Golval (Tel: 01736 65265); or H Symons, Ironmonger, Market Place, St Ives.

BUSSOW RESERVOIR, St Ives. SWW coarse fishery, with bream, roach, tench, carp, eels, rudd, perch, etc. Open all year, 24 hour day, permits £4.50 from Newtown Angling Centre, Newtown, Germoe, Penzance (Tel: 01736 763721); Atlantic Fishing Tackle, 36 Wendron St, Helston; or H Symons, Ironmonger, Market Place, St Ives TR26 1RZ (Tel: 01736 763721). Other coarse fisheries near St Ives: Nance lakes, with carp, roach, rudd, bream; Woonsmith, with carp, roach, tench, rudd, bream, etc, and trout; Sharkeys Pit, **Hayle**: carp, roach, rudd, gudgeon, eels; Permits from H Symons, Ironmonger, Market Place, St Ives TR26 1RZ (Tel: 01736 796200).

STITHIANS RESERVOIR, Redruth. 247 acres. SWW brown and rainbow trout fishery; fly, spinning, bait fishing zoned. Season Mar 15–Oct 12. Full st £90, dt £7, conc. Limited boats, bookable 24 hrs in advance. Permits from Londis Supply Store, Stithians (Tel: 01209 860301); Peninsula Watersports Centre, Stithians (Tel: 01209 860409).

PORTH RESERVOIR, Newquay. 40 acres, SWW fishery, bream, rudd, tench, roach, perch, eels, and carp. Open all year, 24 hour day, permits £4.50, conc, from self-service unit at car park.

CROWDY RESERVOIR, Camelford. 115 acre SWW trout fishery, stocked with brown trout fry, supplemented with rainbows. Fly, spinning and bait fishing zoned. Season Mar 15–Oct 12. Full st £110, dt £7.50, conc, from Spar Shop, Camelford PL32 9PA (Tel: 01840 212356).

SIBLYBACK LAKE, Liskeard. 140 acres. Fly only, premier SWW fishery, with stocked rainbow trout. Season Mar 24–Oct 31. Permits £14 from self-service kiosk, st £375, conc, Watersports Centre, Siblyback, Common Moor, Liskeard. Ranger (Tel: 01579 342366).

COLLIFORD LAKE, Liskeard. 900 acres. SWW fly fishery, with natural brown trout. Full st £110, dt £7.50, conc. No boats. Open 15

Mar–12 Oct. Permits from Jamaica Inn PL15 7TS (Tel: 01566 86177), off A30 at Bolventor.

CONSTANTINE BROOK. Fishing station; **Constantine**, ns Penryn WR, 6m. Trout. Constantine joins estuary of **Helford River**. Sea fishing off Helford Mouth (see Falmouth). Ashton, near **Helston, Wheal Grey Pool**; stocked coarse fishery with large carp.

DRIFT RESERVOIR. Near **Penzance** (3m); 65 acres in quiet valley. Wild brown and stocked rainbow trout (fly only). Limit, 3 rainbows per day, no limit on wild browns. St £120, wt £22 and dt £8, £6, conc, from warden on reservoir, by car park, or Mr Terry Shorland, Driftway, Drift Dam, Penzance (Tel: 01736 363869). 7m from Penzance, **Tin Dene Fishery**: 3 pools with carp to 25lb, roach, rudd, etc, trout; dt £3, conc. Mr J Laity, Bostrase, Millpool, Goldsithney TR20 9JG, Tel: 01736 763486. **St Buryan Lake** carp pool, Tel: St Buryan 220. Tindeen Fishery, John Laity, Bostrase, Millpool, Penzance (Tel: 01736 763486): quiet 2 acre pool with carp to 28lbs, tench, roach, rudd, etc.

GWITHIAN BROOK. Fishing station: **Camborne**. No longer recommended for trout fishing. Several coarse lakes in area, also very good beach and rock fishing. Camborne AA is sea fishing club. Tackle, baits and tickets from The County Angler, 39 Cross Street TR14 8ES. Hotels: Regal, Tyack's.

HAYLE. Fishing stations: **Relubbus, Hayle Causeway** and **Gwinear**. Trout and sea trout. Good beach fishing near Hayle, and estuary fishing very good, particularly for bass, mullet and flats; plenty of natural bait. Marazion AC has 3 coarse pools in St Erth, nr Hayle, tickets from The County Angler, see above. Tackle shop: Angoves Sports, 40 Fore St, Copperhouse, Hayle TR7 4DY (Tel: 01736 752238).

WEST LOOE RIVER. A small spate river running through Herodsfoot to the Looe estuary. Good runs of sea trout, which fish well in summer. Liskeard & District AC has water. Tickets from Looe Tropicals and Pets shop in East Looe. **East Looe River** also fishes well for sea trout, but local knowledge is required. 6m west of Looe on B3359, Shilla Mill Lakes and Lodges: 2 coarse lakes, one specimen carp lake. Fishing is for guests, no day permits. Contact Mr & Mrs J Pearce, Lanreath, Looe PL13 2PE (Tel: 01503 220886). Hotels: Punch Bowl, Lanreath; Kylmiarven, Looe.

Good sea fishing. Tackle and tickets from Looe Tropicals and Pets, Buller St, Tel: 01503 326535.

LYNHER. A noted salmon and sea trout river with a reputation for early fish. Rises on Bodmin Moor, as do Fowey and Camel, and runs to Tamar estuary via Saint Germans. Smaller than Fowey but more natural, there being no big reservoirs in catchment to modify spates. Good runs of sea trout (end Mar to end May), smaller sea trout and grilse from June, and good summer night fishing for sea trout. Season ends 14 Oct, end of season has good salmon fishing, given some rain.

Callington (Cornwall). Liskeard and District AC has several good beats on Lyner, also on **Fowey** and **Inny River** (tributary of Tamar), all providing salmon and sea trout. For sea trout only, club has beats on **Seaton** and **West Looe Rivers**. Membership from Trevor Sobey, Trevartha Farm, Liskeard. Dt and wt from Tremar Tropicals, Liskeard, Looe Tropicals and Pets shop in East Looe, or Watson's hairdressing in Pannier market, Callington. Siblyback and Colliford Lakes are near. Royal Albert Bridge AC has 2 acre coarse fishing lake at **St Germans**.

LUXULYAN RIVER. Fishing station: **Par**. Heavily polluted, but tributary **Redmoor River** has good head of trout. Sand-eels at Par Sands, mackerel from the bay, pollack by Gribben Head and near harbour, and bass between harbour and Shorthorne Beach. Boats for hire at Par and Polkerris. Hotels: Royal, Par; Carlyon Bay, St Austell.

MELANHYL. Newquay. Brown trout and occasional sea trout. Contact. Sec, St Mawgan AC or The Merrymoor Inn, Mawgan Porth for tickets.

OLD MILL RESERVOIR. Dartmouth. 4 acre SWW coarse fishery with carp, roach, rudd, bream, tench, eels. Open all year, 24 hour day. Season ticket only, on application to South West Water Peninsula Fisheries, Higher Coombepark, Lewdowne, Okehampton, Devon EX20 4QT, Tel: 01837 871565.

PETHERICK WATER. Fishing station: **Padstow**. Small trout. Estuary now a bass nursery area, prohibiting fishing for bass. Other species scarce.

RETALLACK WATERS. St Columb, TR9 6DE, Tel: 01637 880974. 20 acres of water, with separate coarse and specimen lakes; carp and pike to 25lb, roach, rudd, tench, eels. Dt £5, tackle and bait from The Tackle Cabin on site. Open 7 days a week. Meadowside Coarse Fishery, Winnards Perch, St Columb; 3 lakes with carp and mixed coarse fish. Dt £3.50, £4.50 2 rods, conc. Mrs Holmes, Tel: 01637 880544.

ST ALLEN RIVER, Truro. St Allen and **Kenwyn** Rivers at Truro; **Tresillian** River (3m from Truro on St Austell road); **Kennel** or **Perranarworthal** River (5m from Truro); a few sea trout run into **Lower Tresillian** River. Gwarnick Mill Fly Fishing Lake, St Allen, Truro TR4 9QU (Tel: 01872 540487); lake of 1½ acres fed by St Allen River, with rainbow trout av 2lb, and wild browns; dt £16 for 4 fish, £10 for 2 fish. At **Perranporth**, nr Redruth, Bolingey Coarse Fishing Lake, coarse fish. Dt £5. Contact John and Maddy, Tel: Truro 572388. Hotel: The Morgans, Perranporth (see also Sea Fishing Stations)

ST AUSTELL. Roche (St Austell) AC has club waters in area at St Dennis, Rosevean, St Blazey, Bugle and Glynn. Coarse fishing for perch, roach, rudd, carp, tench, eels and pike. Members only. Tackle and information from The Bait Bunker, Polmorla Rd, Wadebridge.

SEATON RIVER. Rises near Liskeard, runs through Hessenford to the sea across the beach at Seaton. It fishes well for sea trout from May onwards, with occasional browns. Liskeard and Dist AC has lower stretch, which is the only fishable part of river. Tickets from Looe Tropicals and Pets shop in Looe, or from Tremar Tropicals shop in Liskeard.

TAMAR LAKE (UPPER), Bude. 81 acres, SWW coarse fishery with carp, bream, tench, roach, rudd, eels. Dt £4.50, £3.50 conc, from self-service kiosk on site. Tamar Lake (Lower) now closed.

TIDDY. Fishing station: **St Germans**. Sea trout to Tideford, trout elsewhere.

VALENCY. Fishing station: **Boscastle**. Valency is 4m long; holds small trout and few sea trout. Hotels: Wellington, in Boscastle (Environment Agency licences); Eliot Arms, Tregadillet 15m. Sea fishing good for bass, mackerel, pollack, etc.

WHITEACRES COUNTRY PARK, White Cross, **Newquay** TR8 4LW. Four

stocked coarse fishing lakes in 28 acres. Carp to 25lb, tench 7lb, large bream and roach. Night fishing, matches and competitions. Tel: 01726 860220.

CUCKMERE
(For close seasons, licences, etc, see Southern Region Environment Agency, p12)

Formed by two tributaries, which join at Hellingly, and enters sea at Cuckmere Haven, west of Beachy Head. Mainly coarse fish, roach, bream, chub, carp, perch, dace and pike.

Alfriston (E Sussex). Fishing controlled by the Southdown AA, membership from The Polegate Angling Centre or any Eastbourne tackle shop. Dt £5 for several club fisheries. Below Alfriston Lock the river is salt and tidal, being open to mouth at Cuckmere Haven. In summer grey mullet are plentiful near Exceat Bridge (Eastbourne–Seaford road); also bass and occasionally sea trout. Cuckmere is tidal to ½m upstream from Alfriston. At **Berwick**, Langley AC has coarse fishing on Batbrooks Pond; club also fishes **Langney Haven**, **Hurst Haven**, **Kentland Fleet**. Tickets from Tony's Tackle, Eastbourne.

Hailsham (E Sussex). Cuckmere 2m. Southdown AA (formed 1997 from merger of Hailsham AA and Compleat Anglers FC) has extensive fishing on Cuckmere between Alfreston and Horsebridge (Hailsham); **Wallers Haven**; **Pevensey Haven**; **Abbotts Wood**, lake 3½ acres, and other waters. Membership £40, conc, dt £5 on some fisheries from Hon Sec or tackle shops: Hailsham Bait & Tackle, Battle Rd, Hailsham; Polegate Angling Centre; Tony's Tackle, both Eastbourne; Anglers Den, Pevensey Bay.

CUMBRIA (lakes)
(See English Lake District)

CUMBRIA (streams)
(For close seasons, licences, etc, see NW Region Environment Agency, p13, unless otherwise stated)

ANNAS. Fishing station: **Bootle**. Small trout; good sea trout and salmon; late. Millom AA has fishing, also water on **Esk**, **Lickle**, **Irt**, **Duddon**, **Devoke Water**, **Black Beck** and **Lazy**. St £70 + £10 entrance from Hon Sec Millom & Dist AA. Dt £15 from Duddon Sports. Environment Agency licences from Waberthwaite PO, Haverigg PO, Millom PO.

BLACK BECK. Fishing station: **Green Road**. This stream rises on Thwaites Fell, and in 7½m reaches Duddon Estuary. Millom AA has water, entrance, Race Grove, The Green, nr Millom. Tickets from secretary.

CALDER. Empties into Irish Sea some 150 yards from mouth of Ehen. Salmon, sea trout, a few brown trout. Sea trout run large; 10lb and more. Best June onwards: good salmon fishing, July–Oct.

EHEN. Outflow of Ennerdale Water. Flows into Irish Sea on west coast of Cumberland. Salmon, sea trout (June to Oct) and brown trout. Engremont Anglers' Assn has good salmon and sea trout fishing for 7m both banks, from **Engremont** to Sellafield; st £30, wt £30; May 1–Oct 31 apply Hon Sec or tackle shop. Hotels: Black Beck, Egremont and Sea Cote (St Bees). Good fishing in upper reaches held by Wath Brow and Ennerdale AA; st and wt. Tackle shop: W Holmes, 45 Main Street, Egremont, Tel: 01946 820368, has permits for Ehen, Ennerdale Lake and other local fishing.

ELLEN. Rises on Great Lingy Hill and flows into the Solway Firth at Maryport. Salmon and sea trout runs increasing; best late July onwards. Good brown trout fishing (Mar–June best).

Aspatria (Cumbria). Trout, sea trout, and salmon from July. Hotels: Grapes, Sun.

ESK. Rises near Scawfell and flows into Irish Sea near Ravenglass. Good runs of salmon, sea trout, July onwards.

Ravenglass (Cumbria). Salmon, sea trout. Rivers Mite and Irt here join Esk estuary (see also Irt). Millom AA has 620 yds south bank on Esk at Ravenglass, in three stretches. Membership, wt and dt from Sec. May and June are best for trout; June, July, Aug for sea trout; Sept, Oct for salmon.

Eskdale (Cumbria). Trout, sea trout, salmon; various private owners. Millom & Dist AA fishes Dalegarth Estate water, two beats at Gill Force and Beckfoot; good fly fishing, and worming; also stretch at Brantrake, with sea trout from June, salmon from July, Sept–Oct best months. Contact Hon Sec. Inexpensive fishing on **Wastwater** and **Burnmoor Tarn**. Good sea fishing for bass within five miles.

IRT. Outflow of Wastwater, joining Esk in tidal water. **Bleng** is main tributary. Runs of salmon and sea trout July onwards, some heavy fish taken. Gosforth Angler's Club has stretch, weekly permits obtainable.

Holmrook (Cumbria). Salmon, sea trout, brown trout. Short free stretch in village. Enquire at hotel. Lutwidge Arms Hotel is sole agent for supply of permits for 1½m of Sporting Tribune water, limit of 6 rods. Wt £50, dt £11. Tel: 0194672 4230. Millom AA holds two stretches, apprx 1,200 yds, Holme Bridge and Drigg Village; tickets from Holmrook Garage; Waberthwaithe and Haverigg P Os. Tackle shop: E W Mitchell & Son.

Netherwastdale (Cumbria). On **Wastwater Lake**; trout, permits (see English Lake District). Greendale Tarn and Low Tarn feed Wastwater. Sport is good in May and June.

MITE. Flows south for short course from slopes near Eskdale to join estuary of Irt and Esk at **Ravenglass**. A late river. Sea trout, good brown trout, occasional small salmon later on, but few opportunities for visitors.

POAKA BECK. Barrow AA, J R Jones, 69 Prince St, Dalton in Furness LA15 8ET. Dt from secretary.

WAMPOOL. Fishing stations: **Wigton** and **Curthwaite**. Wampool, under the name of Chalk Beck, rises on Broad Moor. Sea trout in lower reaches mostly free.

WAVER. Trout stream, flowing into the Solway Firth. Some water free, but most subject to agreement by farmers and landowners. Environment Agency licences may be obtained from Saundersons (Ironmongers), 11–13 King Street, **Wigton** CA7 9EB. Waver has run of sea trout and herling, particularly in its lower reaches.

Wigton (Cumbria). Springfalls (Tel: 01697 345012), Longthwaite, nr Wigton has stocked tarn with rainbow and brook trout.

CRUMMOCK BECK (tributary of Waver). Flows into Holm Dub, tributary of Waver. Free, but difficult to fish. (For licences, see Waver).

Leegate (Cumbria). Waver, 1m E.

WHICHAM BECK. Fishing Station: **Sile Croft**. After a course of 6m runs into Haverigg

Pool, which joins Duddon estuary at Haverigg (NWW).

DARENT

(For close seasons, licences, etc, see Southern Region Environment Agency, p12)

Rises by Westerham and enters Thames estuary at Dartford. Water retention has been improved by weirs. Modest trout fishing in upper reaches, coarse fishing downstream, roach, dace, chub.

Dartford (Kent). Dartford and Dist A & PS has lakes along river valley which hold coarse fish, (Brooklands, see Kent) plus stretches of Medway, Beult and L Tiesse, members only, Long waiting list. RMC Angling has 3 gravel pits at Sutton-at-Hone, with carp, tench and other species. St £40, conc. (See Chertsey.) Darenth Fishing Complex (Tel: 01322 290150): 2 syndicate lakes, Toplake, and Big Lake, which contain carp over 30lb; and 2 day/night ticket lakes, Tree, and Long Lake, with good head of small carp, and other coarse fish, incl occasional catfish to 35lb. Also stocked beginners' pond. For further details contact Tackle Box, Watling St, Dartford DA2 6EG (Tel: 01322 292400). Lamorbey AS fishes 3 acre lake at Lamorbey Park, **Sidcup**; 28 swims, tench, rudd, crucian carp; dt on part of water, £4, conc. Access for disabled. Tackle shops: Bob Morris, 1 Lincolnshire Terrace, Lane End; Angling Centre, 84 Lowfield St; Tackle Box (above). Sidcup tackle shop: Kent Particles, 10 Halfway St.

Shoreham (Kent). Trout, chub, roach, dace. Darent Valley Trout Fishers have good 2½m stretch of water between Shoreham and Eynsford; strictly members only (waiting list). Sepham Trout Fishery is nearby, at Sepham Farm, Filstone Lane, Shoreham TN14 5JT. Tel: 019592 2774.

Sevenoaks (Kent). River preserved. Holmesdale AS has the following waters, for members and guests only: **Chipstead Lakes**, with bream, roach, perch, rudd, carp, pike; **Longford Lakes**; similar variety of coarse species; Montreal Lakes nr **Riverhead**, Sevenoaks; mainly junior water. Joining fee £15, annual subscription £40 from Mrs Lancefield, 33 St Johns Rd, Sevenoaks; and from tackle shops: Angling Centre, 218 Main Rd, Biggin Hill; A & I Tackle, Sevenoaks Rd, Green Street Green; Manklows Kit & Tackle, 44 Seal Road, Sevenoaks. Manklows will supply useful general information about local fishing.

Tributary of the Darent

CRAY: Coarse fish.

Crayford (Kent). Thameside Works AS, (members of Rother Fisheries Association) has fishing for bream, roach, perch, rudd, pike, carp, tench; members only. They also have a lake at Northfleet and Shorne Country Park lakes. Coarse fish. Dt for Shorne only, £2.50, £1.50 jun. from bailiff. Membership from R Graham, 186 Waterdales, Northfleet DA11 8JW (Tel: 01474 351456). SAE, please. **Ruxley Pits**, **Orpington**, coarse fish; Orpington & Dist AA has 5 lakes, 40 acres in a nature reserve, all coarse fish, pike to 28lb, large tench. Dt for Mondays to Fridays, from tackle shop: A & I Fishing Tackle, 33 High St, Green St Green, Orpington BR6 6BG (Tel: 01689 862302). Other Assn waters: R Medway and Eden nr Tonbridge; R Teise at Yalding.

DART

(For close seasons, licences, etc, see, South West Region Environment Agency p12)

The East and the West Dart rise two miles apart on Dartmoor. East Dart runs to Postbridge and thence to Dartmeet, where it unites with West Dart which flows through Two Bridges. The West Dart above Dartmeet (with the exception of the right bank from Huccaby Bridge to Dartmeet), and the East Dart above Dartmeet (with the exception of the left bank from Wallabrook Junction to Dartmeet), belong to Duchy of Cornwall. The river has runs of salmon and peal (sea trout). Best months for salmon are May to Sept in the lower reaches and also higher up, depending on water. For peal May to Sept are favoured in the main river, and tidal water of Totnes Weir Pool in May and June. Wild brown trout are mainly small.

Dartmouth (Devon). In river, fishing for ray, bass, whiting, mackerel, garfish, mullet, and pouting. Coastline for dogfish, bull huss, bass, wrasse, whiting, dad, plaice, turbot, conger. Boats effective in river and sea. Skerrie banks and wrecks popular venues. Flatfish off sand. Club: Dartmouth & Dist AA, clubroom open at weekends. Salmon, peal and trout fishing in Dart on Dart AA water (see Totnes, Buckfastleigh) and a trout reservoir. Lake; Slapton Ley; pike, rudd, etc, 8m (see Devonshire, small streams and lakes). Also, **Old Mill**, SWW carp pool, dt. Tackle and frozen baits from Sport 'n' Fish, Fairfax Place. Hotel: Victoria, Victoria Rd.

Totnes (Devon). Salmon, peal, trout. Dart AA controls Dart from Staverton Weir to Austins Bridge, left bank only; Totnes Weir Salmon av 10lb; peal 2lb in May–June and about 1lb thereafter. 4lb and 5lb peal not rare. School peal run from late June to mid-Aug. Nearly all peal caught after dark in normal conditions; Aug usually best. Fly only for peal and trout. Newhouse Fishery, Moreleigh, Totnes TQ9 7JS, Tel: 01548 821426, has 4 acre trout lake open all year. Dt £16, 4 fish. Half day £10, 2 fish. New Barn Angling Centre, Totnes Rd, Paignton, has coarse and trout ponds. Tel Paignton 553602. Hotels: Seymour, Royal Seven Stars and Cott Inn (at Darlington). Sea Trout Inn TQ9 6PA (Tel: 01803 782274) is close to the river at Staverton, and sells tickets on behalf of Dart AA. Dt £10 brown trout, £15 sea trout, £20 salmon; £20 for Totnes Weirpool.

Buckfastleigh (Devon). Salmon, peal, trout. SWW Plc has fishery, ¼m Dart, Austins Bridge to Nursery Pool; salmon, sea trout. St £45, 16 rods. Tel: 01392 219666. Holne Chase Hotel, nr Ashburton TQ13 7NS (Tel: 01364 631471, Fax 631453), has about 1m right bank upstream from bridge, with 7 pools; fishing for hotel guests only, £25 per rod day; ghillies and tuition if required. Hotel can arrange fishing on the Moor with Duchy permit, and a further 7m through the Dart Anglers' Association. Permits also from Watercress Farm, Kerwells, Chudleigh, N Abbot TQ13 0DW. Fishing is near Ashburton.

Princetown (Devon). Permits for salmon and trout fishing on main river, **East** and **West Dart**, **Wallabrook**, **Swincombe** and **Cherrybrook** from most tackle shops in S Devon; also the Prince Hall Hotel, Two Bridges Hotel, both Princetown; Mabin's News, Fore St, Buckfastleigh; and Princetown Post Office. Salmon best May–Sept. Charges: S and MT, st £125, wt £70, dt £20; T, st £55, wt £15, dt £4. Prince Hall Hotel, nr Two Bridges, Dartmoor PL20 6SA (Tel: 01822 890403) has fine riverside location; hotel stocks flies and Duchy licences, and will advise on local fishing, tuition, ghillie service, etc.

Hexworthy (Devon); Salmon, sea trout (peal), brown trout. Forest Inn Hotel, Hexworthy PL20 6SD, Tel: 01364 631211, E-mail: forestinn@hotmail.com; dt, wt or st, at hotel, for Duchy of Cornwall water. Ghillie, instruction offered; Inn buys catch. Good centre for E and W Dart and Cherrybrook.

DEBEN
(For close seasons, licences, etc see Anglian Region Environment Agency, p14)

Short Suffolk river (about 30 miles long) rising near Debenham and flowing to North Sea near Felixstowe. Coarse fishing.

Woodbridge (Suffolk). Tidal. Roach, pike, tench, perch above town. Club: Woodbridge and Dist AC, who also has Loam Pond, Sutton, and Holton Pit; st £12, dt £2, from tackle shop or Saxmundham Angling Centre or Anglia Photographics, Halesworth. Framlingham & Dist AC (Tel: 01473 611116) has about ½m of Deben at Campsey Ashe, single bank, with roach, perch, pike and some bream; also Haywards Reservoirs at **Wickham Market**, Youngmans Reservoirs at Charsfield, and two other still water fisheries, at Parham and **Framlingham**. All waters coarse fishing, members only, except Haywards, dt £3 from Stuart Clay Traps, Melton; Markhams, Woodbridge Rd, Ipswich; or Saxmundham Angling Centre. Membership £25 p.a., conc. Hotels: Bull, Crown.

Wickham Market (Suffolk). Roach, perch, pike. Woodbridge AC has river and Wickham Market Reservoir.

DERWENT (Cumbria)
(For close seasons, licences, etc, see South West Region Environment Agency p12)

Rises on north side of Scafell and flows through Borrowdale, Derwentwater and Bassenthwaite Lakes to the Solway Firth at Workington. Salmon and trout practically throughout length. A late river. Best months for salmon, July to October. Trout fishing on some stretches excellent. River also holds pike and perch.

Cockermouth to **Workington** (Cumbria). Salmon, sea trout, brown trout. Trout and salmon fishing may occasionally be permitted on dt. Enquiries to Fishery Manager, Cockermouth Castle. Permit charges under review. Permits for **Cocker** also (limited). Waters through town can be fished on permit from Tourist Information Office, Town Hall, Market St, CA13 9NP (Tel: 01900 822634), by residents and visitors staying locally on weekly basis. Cockermouth AA, Ken Simpson (Tel: 01900 815523), has water on Cocker (members only) but issues dt for **Cogra Moss. Mockerkin Tarn** stocked with carp. Fishing within reach on Bassenthwaite, Loweswater, Crummock and Buttermere. Nr

Cockermouth are Gilcrux Springs Trout Farm, Gilcrux, (Tel: 01697 322488), with American brook, rainbow trout; also Ellerbeck Farm and Fishery, Brigham (Tel: 01900 825268), coarse fishing on day permit. Tackle shops: Graham's Guns and Tackle, 9–15 South William St, Workington (Tel: 01900 605093); Complete Angler, 4 King St, Whitehaven (Tel: 01946 695322); Field & Stream, 79 Main St Keswick (Tel: 017687 74396). Hotels: Trout, Globe, Cockermouth Pheasant, Bassenthwaite Lake, Sun, Bassenthwaite.

Bassenthwaite (Cumbria). Derwent, 1m N; trout, salmon; private. Lakes: Bassenthwaite; pike, perch, trout, occasional salmon (see English Lake District – Bassenthwaite). Hotels: Swan, Pheasant, Armathwaite Hall (Tel: 017687 76551).

Keswick (Cumbria). For rivers Derwent and Greta. Salmon, trout (average ¼lb), pike, perch, eels; mid-August onwards for salmon. Portinscale to ½ mile above Bassenthwaite Lake, Keswick AA water. Assn stocks Derwentwater and Rivers Derwent and Greta with 1,000 12in browns each year. Visitors salmon wt £75, dt £20. Trout permit includes Derwentwater, wt £25, dt £5 (reductions for juniors on all fishing) from Field and Stream, 79 Main Street, or Keswick PO (Tel: 017687 72269). Visitors st by application to Sec. Tickets issued for Derwent cover Greta also. For full details of water controlled by Keswick AA, write to secretary, enclosing sae, or contact local tackle shop or main post office. Hotels: Hazeldene, Queen's Royal Oak, Lake, George, County King's Arms. The Derwentwater Hotel. Permit charges subject to annual review.

Borrowdale (Cumbria). Trout, salmon; gin-clear as a rule and best fished after dark. Lakes: Derwentwater; trout, perch, pike; small charge for fishing. Watendlath Tarn 2m S; Blea Tarn, 4m S; trout. Hotels: Scafell; Borrowdale; Stakis Keswick Lodore CA12 5UX (Tel: 017687 77285), free trout permits for patrons, mid-week only.

Tributaries of the Derwent (Cumbria)

COCKER: Salmon, sea trout, trout. July to October best for migratory fish. Mostly private, but dt for Cockermouth AA water (and for **Loweswater, Buttermere** and **Crummock Water**).

Scalehill (Cumbria). Cockermouth. 7m Cocker: Salmon, sea trout, trout. Private. National Trust lakes. Hotel: Scale Hill.

Cogra Moss. 40 acre trout reservoir 8m S of Cockermouth. Browns and rainbows. Contact Cockermouth AA.

NEWLANDS BECK: not worth fishing.

GRETA: Trout (av ¼lb); salmon.

Threlkeld (Cumbria). Keswick AA has fishing here (tickets see Keswick). Best months for salmon Sept and Oct; mostly spinning and worm fishing. Glenderamackin Beck; trout; fishable throughout length, but very narrow and fish few and far between.

DEVON
(streams and lakes)
(For close seasons, licences, etc, see SW Region Environment Agency, p12)

AVON. Rises on Dartmoor and flows 22m SE, entering English Channel near Thurlestone via long, twisting estuary. Tide flows to Aveton Gifford. Trout (3 or 4lb), sea trout, salmon.

Thurlestone (Devon). Near mouth of Avon estuary. Capital bass fishing off Bantham Sands at mouth.

Aveton Gifford (Devon). Sea trout (end of May onwards), some salmon; good dry-fly trout water (3 to the lb). Banks heavily wooded; good wading. Mt, ft, wt, from post office at Loddiswell, and P O'Neil, 55 Church Street, Kingsbridge.

Loddiswell. Brown trout, salmon, sea trout; Avon FA has a total of 14½m. No day tickets. Capital bass and pollack in Kingsbridge estuary. Hotels: King's Arms; Buttville; Torcross (for Slapton Ley).

Brent (Devon). Salmon, trout, sea trout. Mrs J Theobald, Little Aish Riding Stables, South Brent, issues dt for stretch of Aish Woods. Red Brook, 2m N; trout. Black Brook, 2m S; trout. Hotel: Anchor.

AVON DAM (8m NE of Totnes). SWW, brown trout fishery, zoned worm, spinning and fly fishing free to Environment Agency licence holders. No boats. Season March 15–Oct 12. Reservoir is about 1½m beyond **Shipley Bridge**, car parking on site.

BELLBROOK VALLEY TROUT FISH-ERY, Oakford, Tiverton EX16 9EX, Tel/Fax: 01398 351292. Set in picturesque Devon valley. Three specimen lakes, min stock 3lb, and 3 normal fishing lakes; specimen fishing, dt £37, 4 fish, various other permits obtainable. Record 1995, 21lb 12oz. Tuition. Corporate party days. Accommodation at fishery farmhouse.

BLAKEWELL FISHERY, Muddiford, Blakewell Lane, nr Barnstaple EX31 4ET. Brown and rb. trout av. 2¼ lb. Various day permits from £20, 5 fish, to £12, 2 fish, from fishery. Tackle hire and tuition on site. This establishment also runs a commercial fish farm. Richard or John Nickell (Tel: 01271 344533).

BURRATOR RESERVOIR, Yelverton. 150 acres, South West Water. Zoned fly fishing and spinning for brown and rainbow trout. Open Mar 15–Sept 30. Dt £7.50, st £110 (concessions), from Yelverton Garage, Yelverton.

CRAFTHOLE, nr **Torpoint**. A popular little SWW fishery of 2 acres, dammed, stocked with carp and tench. Season permit, with limited day permits. Contact South West Water Peninsula Fisheries, Higher Coombepark, Lewdowne Okehampton Devon EX20 4QT (Tel: 01837 871565).

DARRACOTT, Torrington. 3 acre coarse fishery run by South West Water, with carp, tench, bream, roach, rudd, perch, eel. Open all year, 24 hour day. St £70, dt £4.50, conc, from N Laws, Summerfields Tackle, 3 Golflinks Rd, Westward Ho! (Tel: 01237 471291); or Whiskers Pet Centre, 9 The Square, Torrington (Tel: 01805 622859).

ERME. Rises on Dartmoor and flows 14m S to Bigbury Bay. Trout.

FERNWORTHY RESERVOIR, near **Chagford**, on Dartmoor. South West Water. 76 acres, natural brown trout fishing, largest 4lb 2oz. Open May 1–Oct 12. Dt £7.50, concessions. Self-service unit by Boathouse.

JENNETTS RESERVOIR, Bideford. 8 acres, South West Water coarse fishery, with carp principally, to 23lb, as well as tench, bream, roach, perch, eels. Open all year, 6.30am to 10.00pm. Permit, £4.50, £3.50, conc, from N Laws, Summerlands Tackle, 16–20 Nelson Rd, Westward Ho! (Tel: 01237 471291).

KENNICK RESERVOIR, Christow. A SWW Dartmoor fishery, with stocked rainbow trout. Boats on first-come first-serve basis, Allenard Wheelyboat for disabled. Permits from

self-service kiosk, £14 per day, full season £375, conc. Open 26 Mar–31 Oct.

MELBURY RESERVOIR, Bideford. 12 acre SWW reservoir, open all year, 6.30am to 10.30pm. Carp, bream, roach, perch, eels. Permits £4.50, £3.50, conc, from N Laws, Summerlands Tackle, 16–20 Nelson Rd, Westward Ho! (Tel: 01237 471291).

MELDON RESERVOIR (3m SE of Okehampton). 54 acres, natural brown and stocked rainbow trout. Spinning, bait and fly fishing, SWW fishery, free to Environment Agency licence-holders. Season Mar 15–Oct 12.

LYN, near **Lynmouth** (Devon). This beautiful river has good run of salmon, July onwards. Also sea trout and brown trout; latter small. Environment Agency **Watersmeet** and **Glenthorne** fisheries: Limits, 2 salmon, 6 sea trout, 8 trout. Restricted season and methods. Salmon and sea trout: wt £35, dt £13.50. Trout: st £27.50, wt £10, dt £3, from Brendon House Hotel, Brendon EX35 6PS (Tel: 01598 741206); Tourist Information Centre, Town Hall, Lynton; Lynmouth P O. Season March 1–Sept 30. Mrs Lester, Glebe House, Brendon, issues dt for 3m (both banks) of East Lyn. Other contacts for East Lyn fishing are Rising Sun Hotel, Harbourside, Lynmouth EX35 6EQ; Doone Valley Riding Stables, Brendon. Tackle shops: D & M Woolgrove, 13 The Parade, Minehead. *(See also Sea Fishing Stations).*

PLYM. Devon salmon and sea trout river which rises above Lee Moor and flows southwest to Plymouth, skirts the east of the town to enter the Sound on the south side.

Plymouth (Devon). Good runs of sea trout on Plym and Tavy. Salmon run late on Plym, Oct to 15 Dec. Plymouth and Dist Freshwater AA has R Plym from Plymbridge upstream for about 3m, and Tavy, north of Tavistock. Annual subscription £80, from Hon Sec D L Owen, Tel: 01752 705033. Dt for first mile from D K Sports, or from Snowbee (UK) Ltd, *(below)*. Length above Bickleigh Bridge, controlled by Tavy, Walkham and Plym FC. Club issues tickets (salmon, sea trout, brown trout) for its water, here and on Tavy, Meavy and Walkham. Salmon st £100, dt £15, brown trout st £40, mt £20, wt £15, dt £5, from DK Sports *(below)*; Tavistock Trout Fishery (Tel: 01822 615441); Yelverton Garage (Tel: 01822 853339). *(See Tamar – Tavy).* Sea fishing excellent. Tackle shops: D K

Sports, 88 Vauxhall St; Snowbee (UK) Ltd, Unit 2a, Parkway Ind. Estate, St Modwen Rd Plymouth PL6 8LH (Tel: 01752 672226), Osborne & Cragg, 37 Bretonside.

MEAVY. Tributary of the Plym, on which Burrator Reservoir blocks salmon migration. Joins main river at Shaugh Bridge. Fishing governed by overspill when Burrator is full. Fishing stations: **Shaugh** and **Clearbrook**.

OAREWATER, Brendon. Trout.

ROADFORD FISHERY, nr **Okehampton**. SWW fishery, with wild brown trout. More than 700 acres, catch and release policy, barbless hooks. Permits £13.50, conc, from Angling and Watersports Centre, Lower Goodacre. Open 24 Mar–12 Oct. Enquiries, Tel: 01409 211507.

SID, Sidmouth. Trout.

SLADE RESERVOIRS, Ilfracombe. South West Water fisheries. **Upper Slade** now closed to public owing to dangerous banks, **Lower Slade,** coarse fishing for pike, carp, tench, bream, roach, rudd, gudgeon and perch. St £70–£110, conc £35–£50; dt £4.50, conc £3.50, from Slade Post Office, 80 Slade Rd EX34 8LQ, or Variety Sports, 23 Broad St, Ilfracombe EX34 9EE (Tel: 01271 862039).

SLAPTON LEY, Dartmouth 7m. Pike, rudd, roach, eel and perch. Part of National Nature Reserve, boats only, bank fishing prohibited. For day tickets only, £7–£11, £10–£16, £13–£21, for one, two or three anglers, apply Field Centre, Slapton, Kingsbridge TQ7 2QP (Tel: Kingsbridge 580685). Life-jackets on site, compulsory for anglers under 18 years of age. Also in vicinity, Coombe Water Fishery, Coombe Lane, **Kingsbridge**, with carp, tench, rudd, eel; dt on site. Tackle shops: Sport and Fish, 16 Fairfax Place, Dartmouth; Anchor Sports Cabin, Bridge St, Kingsbridge TQ7 1SB (Tel: 01548 856891). Hotels: The Torcross and (in Slapton) the Tower Inn. Many guest houses.

SQUABMOOR RESERVOIR. E Budleigh. Bait fishing for coarse fish, with carp to 25lb, tench, bream, roach, rudd, eels. St £100–£65, conc, dt £3.50, conc, from Exeter Angling Centre, Smythen St, Exeter; Knowle Garage, Knowle, or Tackle Shop, 20 The Strand, Exmouth. **Hogsbrook Lake**, 2½ acres, at Woodbury Salterton is dt coarse fishery nearby.

Contact Woodbury Park, Woodbury Castle, Woodbury, Exeter EX5 1JJ.

STAFFORD MOOR FISHERY, Winkleigh EX19 8PP (Tel: 01805 804360). Two lakes of 14 acres and 8 acres; and 2 of 1½ acres; all regularly stocked with rainbow trout, average weight 1½lb. Tackle, over 300 patterns of flies on sale, tied at fishery by Ms Marilyn Nott. Single permit £5, 1 fish, extra fish £4.50.

TRENCHFORD RESERVOIR (8m NE of **Newton Abbot**). SWW pike fishery of 45 acres, pike to 30lb. Open all year. Dt £4.50, conc, from self-service kiosk.

VENFORD RESERVOIR, Ashburton. Brown and rainbow trout. Spinning and bubble-float fishing, free to licence-holders. Season: March 15–Oct 12. Contact SWW, for more details.

WISTLANDPOUND RESERVOIR, South Molton. SWW natural brown trout fishery. Fly only, open Mar 15 1–Oct 12. Dt £7.50, conc, from Post Office, Challacombe EX31 4TT; The Kingfisher, Barnstaple; Variety Sports, Ilfracombe.

YEALM. Rises on southern heights of Dartmoor and flows 12m south and west to English Channel, which it enters by a long estuary. Trout, sea trout, occasional late salmon. Fishing private. Estuary is now a bass nursery, bass fishing prohibited.

Newton Ferrers (Devon). On estuary. One of finest deep-sea fishing stations in south-west. Hotel: River Yealm, Tel: 01752 872419, has its own harbour frontage and jetty.

DORSET (streams)
(For close seasons licences, etc, see South West Region Environment Agency, p12)

BRIT and **ASKER**. Fishing station: **Bridport**. Trout. Rivers mostly private or over-grown, but Civil Service Sports Council has stretch of Brit for members only. 7/8 Buckingham Place, Bellfield Rd, High Wycombe HP13 5HW. Also **Radipole Lakes**; dt for latter: coarse fish. Tickets from Weymouth tackle shops. Dt for **Osmington Mills Lake** (carp and tench) on site only. Trout fishing at **Watermill Lake**, well stocked with rainbows. Mangerton Mill, Bridport, DT6 3SG (Tel: 01308 485224).

CHAR. Fishing station: **Charmouth**. Char is

some 7m long; trout, private. General sea fishing. Hotels: Queen's Arms, Hammons Mead.

CORFE. Rises 1m W of Corfe Castle and runs into Poole Harbour 5m down. Coarse fishing sometimes permitted by landowners. Dt can be obtained for Arfleet Lake at Corfe Castle.

DURHAM (reservoirs)

DERWENT. Edmundbyers. 1,000 acre trout water. Hotel: Lord Crewe Arms. *Reservoir also partly in Northumberland.*

SMIDDY SHAW, and **WASKERLEY**. Good trouting, preserved by North-West Durham AA (Tel: 07974 819153). Limited dt £9, Waskerley only, in the hut by the reservoir. Smiddy Shaw, members only. Season April 1–Sept 30. Nearest towns: **Wolsingham**, **Consett** and **Stanhope**. Hotel: Royal Derwent at Allensford.

EDEN
(For close season licences, etc, see North West Region Environment Agency, p13)

Rises south of Kirkby Stephen and empties into Solway Firth 5m NW of Carlisle. Salmon, sea trout, brown trout and grayling. Still some spring fish, but now more a back-end river. Sea trout in lower and middle reaches and tributaries from June onwards. Trouting best in middle and upper reaches, fish run to good average size for north. Chub in parts.

Carlisle (Cumbria). Salmon in spring and autumn, sea trout and herling in July and August, brown trout fair, some chub and dace. Carlisle AA has 7m on Eden, permits from Murrays, *below*, visitors salmon st £100, wt £50, dt £25; trout £17, wt £7, dt £2. **Thurstonfield Lough**, Thurstonfield CA5 6HB; 25 acres, dt £17, boat £5, 4 fish limit. ½ day and evening tickets, self-catering accom. (Tel: 01228 576552). Three lakes of 25 acres with trout and coarse fishing, and salmon and sea trout in adjacent rivers, at Oakbank Lakes Country Park, Longtown CA6 5NA. St £60 and dt £8, conc, tel: 01228 791108. Tackle shop: Murrays 16 Fisher St CA3 8RN (Tel: 01228 523816), permits and tuition. Hotels: Crown and Mitre, Central, Hilltop, many guesthouses.

Wetheral (Cumbria). Salmon and sea trout preserved for 3m, both banks from Warwick Bridge upstream, by the Yorkshire Fly-fishers' Club here and at Great Corby; Cairn Beck, 2m,

Irthing, 3m N. Scotby Beck, 2m W at Scotby. Hotel: Crown.

Armathwaite (Cumbria). Salmon, trout, grayling. Croglin Waters, 3m E.

Lazonby (Cumbria). Salmon, trout and grayling. 1m of fishing, M Rhodes, 1 Sunray Terrace, Lazonby CA10 1AB; permits from post office, Midland Hotel, and Joiners Arms. Mixed fishery at Crossfield Farm, Kirkoswald, Penrith. Record ide caught, 1993, 3lb 4½ oz. Special match tickets on offer. Trout limit 2 fish. Disabled facilities. Holiday accom. on site. Tel: 01768 896275.

Great Salkeld (Cumbria). Fetherston Arms Hotel, Kirkoswald, has 2½m (Lazonby 284). High Drove Inn has salmon and trout fishing; salmon 75p day, trout 50p.

Langwathby (Cumbria). Salmon, trout; preserved by Yorkshire FFC.

Culgaith (Cumbria). Trout; preserved by Yorkshire FFC from Culgaith to below Langwathby apart from vicinity of Watersmeet. Winderwath, left bank is Penrith AA water. Hotels: Black Swan, Culgaith, King's Arms, Temple Sowerby.

Temple Sowerby (Cumbria). Salmon, trout, grayling; preserved (with some miles of Eamont) by Yorkshire FFC; members only. Penrith AA (with 35m of fishing in all) has Powis House Water above Bolton Village; water upstream of Oustenstand Island. Wt and st issued at various prices for different stretches. (*See Penrith.*) King's Arms Hotel has trout fishing for guests on 1½m of Eden; licences and tickets at hotel; trout average 1lb.

Kirkby Thore (Cumbria). Salmon, trout and grayling. Penrith AA preserves 2m brown trout fishing on main river and Kirkby Thore Beck near Long Marton.

Appleby (Cumbria). Eden trout are very free risers, averaging about ¾lb with better fish to 3 and even 4lb. Appleby AA has 14m of R Eden, excellent fly fishing water, and offers dt £6 for stretch ¾m above Jubilee Bridge (fly section and bait section), or £15 for stretch between Bolton Bridge and Ouenstands Bridge (all fly fishing). Membership £70, non-resident, £35, resident, conc, from H Pigney and Son (*below*). Tufton Arms, Market Square CA16 6XA (Tel: 017683

51593), and Sandford Arms, Sandford CA16 6NR (Tel: 017683 51121) have tickets for guests on Appleby AA water; Tufton Arms has salmon and trout flies; good quality rods for sale; tuition and courses from John Pape; also late availability sporting agency. Tackle and permits from H Pigney & Son, Chapel St, Appleby CA16 6QR (Tel: 017683 51240).

Kirkby Stephen (Cumbria). Kirkby Stephen and Dist AA has about 15m on main river and becks, fly only. (See Belah and Scandal Tributaries). Visitors' st £70, joining fee £15, from Hon Sec. Dt £15 from Robinson, Market Street. Fly fishing ponds at Bessy Beck Trout, Tel: 015396 23303. For Eden Valley Trout Lake, Little Musgrave, a secluded fishery with brown and rainbow to 8lbs, contact Bearsett, Rowgate CA17 4SR (Tel: 017683 71489/51428). H Parr, 280 Park Rd, Blackpool, runs local fishing courses and holidays. Licences from Mounsey, Newsagent, 46 Market St. Tackle and tickets from H S Robinson, 2 Market St. Hotels: Kings Arms, Pennine, Black Bull, White Lion, Croglin Castle.

Tributaries of the Eden

PETTERIL joins Eden at Carlisle. Good trout fishing, but lower half mostly private.

Plumpton (Cumbria). Trout.

IRTHING: Rises on Grey Fell Common and joins Eden east of Carlisle. Salmon, trout, grayling and few sea trout.

Brampton (Cumbria). Irthing; 1m N; Gelt, 1m S; trout, grayling, chub. Brampton AS preserves; st (£16), wt (£12), dt (£4) and Environment Agency licence from Sports Haus, Front St. Trout average ½ to ¾lb, early months best. Tackle shops: Sporting Guns and Fishing Tackle, 2 Market Place; W Warwick, Front Street. Hotels: White Lion, Scotch Arms, Sand House, Howard Arms.

Gilsland (Cumbria). Haltwhistle & Dist AA fishes 14m, brown trout only. Visitors welcome, dt £20, wt £50, from Haltwhistle tackle shops (see Haltwhistle).

EAMONT flows from Ullswater Lake. Penrith AA has approx 6m of this water. Lake Ullswater good trout fishing; free, but Environment Agency licence required.

Penrith (Cumbria). Eamont, 1m S; trout. Upper portion (trout and salmon) preserved by Penrith AA (fly fishing only for visitors) from Pooley Bridge on both banks to below Stainton; also on **Eden, Lowther** and on becks. Visitors weekly ticket covering a variety of fishings, £20–£40, dt £6–£10, from Sykes Guns & Tackle (see below); the Punchbowl Hotel, Askham, Penrith, or J Banks, 23 Newton St, Penrith (Tel: 01768 866062). Trout fishing at **Blencarn Lake**, 15 acres, from Mr and Mrs J K Stamper, Blencarn Hall CA10 1TX (Tel: 0176 888284). Dt £16–£10, 4 and 2 fish, fly only; facilities, piers for disabled. Yorkshire Flyfishers preserve left bank of Eamont from Brougham Castle down to Barrack Bank and then on left bank only to below Udford; members only. Other water on Eamont private. Coarse fish at Whins Pond, **Edenhall**; Mrs Siddle, Tel: 862671. Sockbridge Mill Trout Farm, Tel: 01768 865338, off B5320, is suitable family venue, fishing dt £1.50 + £1.65 per lb caught. Hemmingways, Old Barn, Skelton, Penrith CA11 9SE (Tel: 017684 84439) runs boat fishing trips in Lakeland, with permits, tuition, etc, provided. Mainly pike, trout, salmon, char fishing.

Haweswater, 10m SE; currently, no permit is required (see Westmorland lakes). Crown & Mitre Hotel, Bampton Grange, has 3m of trout fishing on Lowther to residents. Other hotels: Crown, George, Gloucester Arms, Edenhall, near Langwathby. Tackle shop: Charles. R. Sykes, Guns & Tackle, 4 Great Dockray CA11 7BL (Tel: 01768 862418).

Pooley Bridge (Cumbria). Eamont; trout. Penrith AA water.

Patterdale (Cumbria). The becks Goldrill, Grizedale, Deepdale and Hartsop, free. Aira Force below NT property (3m), free. N Hawes and Riggindale Becks, permits N West Water. Blea Tarn and Smallwater, N West Water.

Ullswater. Trout numerous, average three to pound. Evening rise during May and June yields heavy baskets; six brace of trout in evening quite common. Day fishing also good; and heavier fish begin to move about middle of May. Numerous boats. Angle Tarn, permits. Greenside Reservoir, Red Tarn, Grizedale Tarn, free. Hotels: Ullswater, Patterdale; White Lion, Brotherswater; Glenridding (boats).

LOWTHER (tributary of Eamont): No fishing for salmon, spawning river only. Sport with trout remains good (av ¾lb). Crown and Mitre Hotel, **Bampton** (via Penrith), has more than

3m fishing for guests (trout and late salmon) including Haweswater Beck; a good centre, only 100 yds from river. Penrith AA holds substantial stretches of good fly water on river; other assn water on Eden and Eamont. Licences from hotel or post offices.

LYVENNET: Good trout stream; runs in a few miles below Temple Sowerby. Leave from farmers in some parts. 1m preserved for Yorkshire Flyfishers' Club.

BELAH: Flows from Pennine fells to join Eden 2m below Kirkby Stephen. Lower reaches, from Brough Sowerby, rented by Kirkby Stephen and Dist AA; members only.

SCANDAL BECK, Smardale (Cumbria) and **Crosby Garrett** (Cumbria): Kirkby Stephen & Dist AA has water. *(See Kirkby Stephen under Eden.)*

ENGLISH LAKE DISTRICT
(For close seasons, licences, etc, see North West Region Environment Agency, p13)

BASSENTHWAITE, 5m Cockermouth; 8m Keswick. Long famous for its pike, also perch and some brown trout. Over Water trout fishery is near Bassenthwaite village, *see below*. Hotels: Pheasant Inn; Swan; Armathwaite Hall CA12 4RE (Tel: 017687 76551).

BIGLAND WATERS, Bigland Hall Estate, **Backbarrow** LA12 8PB. 13 acre coarse fishery and 16 acre fly only trout lake (barbless hooks only), plus beginners lake. Trout dt £15, 4 fish, £10, 6 hours, 2 fish; coarse dt £4, conc. Contact the Fisheries Manager, Tel: 015395 31728.

BLEA TARN. About 2m above Watendlath Tarn; perch; some trout. National Trust. Permits from Mrs Myers, Blea Tarn Farmhouse.

BLELHAM TARN. Ns **Windermere**. Pike, perch, roach, eels, brown trout. Now controlled by WADAA, open all year. Assn also controls fishing bank nr boathouse and rocks at northern end of tarn. Livebaiting prohibited. Limited permits from Go Fishing, Bowness-on-Windermere.

BORRANS RESERVOIR South Lakeland. Managed by North Tyneside M.B.C., Educational Dept, High Borrans, Outdoor Pursuit Centre, Windermere.

BROTHERSWATER. Good trout and pike. National Trust, fishing free.

BUTTERMERE. National Trust lake. Char, trout, pike, perch. Permits (wt £10, dt £3) which also cover Crummock and Loweswater, from Mr & Mrs Parker, Dalegarth Guest House, Buttermere, Cockermouth CA13 9XA (Tel: 017687 70233). Rowing boats for hire.

CLEABARROW TARN, Windermere. WADAA fishery, 2 acres, 20 pegs. No close season. Well stocked, carp (17lb), tench (5lb), bream (7lb), roach, rudd, golden rudd, gudgeon. Fishery is weedy, strong tackle recommended. Dt £4.00, conc, from Tourist Information Centres, and local tackle shops. Night fishing is strictly prohibited.

CODALE TARN, 4m from **Grasmere**. Perch, some trout; free. Hotels: *(see Grasmere)*.

CONISTON. Trout, char, perch, pike. Free, licence needed. Boats from Coniston Boating Centre, Lake Rd, Coniston, Tel: 015394 41366. Tackle and licences from David Wilson, Tackle and Sports Shop, Tilberthwaite Ave, or Sun Hotel, both Coniston. Local club is Coniston and Torver DAA, which has fishing on Yew Tree Tarn, fly only, dt £6, conc. Hotels: Sun, Black Bull, Crown, Ship Inn.

CRUMMOCK WATER. National Trust lake. Pike, trout, char, perch; salmon and sea trout from Cocker sometimes caught by trolling. Fishes best June and July. Dt £1.50, (covering also Buttermere and Loweswater) from Mr & Mrs McKenzie, Wood House, Buttermere, CA13 GXA (Tel: 017687 70208). Rowing boats for hire, £5–£16. Best periods for Crummock, Buttermere and Loweswater are: trout, late May and early June (good mayfly hatch); char, July and August (special technique required: trolling 60 to 90 feet down). Accom at Wood House, also self-catering.

DERWENTWATER. Keswick. Trout, very good size, are best fished for from a boat in mayfly season. Stocked annually with 1,000 12in browns by Keswick AA. Good sized perch and pike, salmon present but rarely taken. Wt £25, dt £5 (which includes all KAA waters) from Field and Stream, Keswick, or Keswick P O. Boats may be hired from Nicoll End, and Keswick landings. Many hotels and guest houses.

DEVOKE WATER near **Ravenglass** (5m

E). Moorland tarn offering sport with fair-sized trout. Millom AA holds rights. Membership and dt obtainable from Sec; Haverigg PO; Bridge Garage, Holmerook; Waberthwaite PO.

DRUNKEN DUCK TARNS, Ambleside. Brown trout to 4½lb, rainbow to 6lb. Wt £60, dt £12 (reductions for ½ day and evenings), from Drunken Duck Hotel.

DUBBS TROUT FISHERY, Windermere. A quiet upland reservoir, controlled by WADAA, open 15th March–31st Dec inclusive. Stocked rainbow and brown trout to 10lb, fly only, 2 fish limit. Dt £10 from Ings Filling Station (A591), tourist information centres, local fishing tackle shops.

EASEDALE TARN, 3m from **Grasmere**. Good perch, few trout. Free fishing. Managed by National Trust, The Hollens, Grasmere, Cumbria LA22 9QZ, Tel: 015394 35599.

ENNERDALE, ns **Whitehaven**. Trout, char; controlled by Ennerdale Lake fisheries formed by Egremont Anglers, Wath Brow and Ennerdale Anglers; St £12 and wt £7 from Wath Brow Post Office, Cleator Moor, or W N Holmes, Main St, Egremont. Enquiries to D Crellin (Hon Sec.), (Tel: 01946 823 337).

ESTHWAITE WATER (nr **Hawkshead**, Lancashire). 280 acres stocked trout fishing. Rainbows to 16lb 3oz, browns to 7lb 4oz. spinning, worming or fly. Boats with o/b, also boat for disabled. Dt from Hawkshead Trout Farm, The Boathouse, Ridding Wood, Hawkshead LA22 0QF (Tel: 015394 36541); from Hawkshead Tourist Information., or from Hawkshead PO. Accommodation plentiful.

FISHER TARN, ns **Kendal**, 3m. Kendal's water supply. Trout. Fisher Tarn Anglers, A Moore, 65 Waterside, Kendal, Cumbria. Dt from Sec or D Bird, 1 Rydal Mount, Kendal, Cumbria.

GHYLL HEAD TROUT FISHERY, Windermere. 11 acre WADAA stocked fishery, fly only. Open 15th March–31st Dec. Rainbow and brown trout, 2 fish limit. Dt £10 from Beech Hill Hotel (A592 Bowness – Newby Bridge road), Tourist Information Centres, local tackle shops.

GRASMERE, ns **Windermere**. Summer fishing, pike over 20lb regularly caught, perch,

eels, roach, trout; WADAA water, open 16th June–14th March inclusive. Live-baiting with fish is strictly prohibited, dead baiting and lure fishing are the most productive methods. Find underwater drop-offs for the best sport. Boat fishing can be good, boats from boathouse at northern end of lake. Dt £4 (juv/OAP £2.00), wt £10.00 (juv/OAP £5.00). St £30.00 (juv/OAP £15.00). This permit also allows fishing on Rydal Water, River Rothay, River Brathay, High Arnside Tarn, Moss Eccles Tarn, School Knott Tarn & Hayswater. Permits from: Tourist Information Centres, local fishing tackle shops, Barney's News Box, Grasmere (6.00 am–5.30 pm)

GREAT RUNDALE TARN, ns **Long Marton**, 5m. Seamore Tarn and Little Rundale Tarn are in the vicinity. Small trout.

HARLOCK RESERVOIR, South Lakeland. Trout water managed by Barrow AA, Hon Sec J R Jones, 69 Prince St, Dalton in Furness, Cumbria LA15 8ET.

HAWESWATER, ns **Penrith** or **Shap**. A good head of wild brown trout, char, gwyniad and perch. Bank fishing, fly only, free to all holders of Environment Agency licence. No maggot or loose feeding.

HAYESWATER RESERVOIR, Patterdale. WADAA water, 34 acres, 9m north of Ambleside, open 15th March–30th Sept. Brown trout, fly only, stocked annually. Dt £4 (juv/OAP £2.00), wt £10.00 (juv/OAP £5.00), st £30.00 (juv/OAP £15.00). This permit also allows fishing on Grasmere, Rydal Water, High Arnside Tarn, Moss Eccles Tarn, School Knott Tarn & Rivers Rothay and Brathay. Permits from: Tourist Information Centres, local fishing tackle shops.

HIGH ARNSIDE TARN, Ambleside; SCHOOL KNOTT TARN, Windermere; MOSS ECCLES TARN, Hawkeshead. Three small fly fisheries stocked by WADAA, open 15 March–30 Sept. Dt £4, juv/OAP, £2, wt £10–£5, st £30–£15, from TICs, local tackle shops, Coniston Sports.

HIGH NEWTON TROUT FISHERY, High Newton. WADAA trout fishery, 10.8 acres, open 15th March–31st Dec, rainbow and brown trout. Dt £8.00. The reservoir is very well stocked with rainbow trout on a regular basis and, in addition, for the 1997 season the

Association has introduced a large stocking of bigger rainbow trout between 3–10lb which are all tagged and dye marked. These are sport fish and must be returned if captured before the 1st September. The tagged fish are in addition to normal stockings which will continue as usual. All anglers must use barbless hooks (squashed barbs) and the use of buoyant lures or boobys on sunken lines is prohibited. Permits from Newby Bridge service station; tackle shops or TICs.

HOLEHIRD TARN, Windermere, 3 acre WADAA water, open all year round. Carp (18lb), crucian carp (1lb), tench (5lb), roach (2lb), bream (6lb), rudd, chub (5lb), gudgeon. Dt £4.00 (juv £2.00). The number of anglers permitted at Holehird is limited to 10 at any one time, consequently a peaceful day is usually guaranteed. Four day permits are sold per day and only from Go Fishing, Gillys Landing, Glebe Road, Bowness-on-Windermere (Tel: 015394 47086). Permits may be obtained in advance of fishing from either of these shops or by sending a cheque made out to WADAA with s.a.e to Mr. C. J. Sodo, Ecclerigg Court, Ecclerigg, Windermere, Cumbria LA23 1LQ (Tel: 015394 45083). Fishing is permitted from one hour before sunrise to one hour after sunset. Overnight parking or night fishing is strictly prohibited.

KENTMERE FISHERY, nr Windermere, (Tel: 01768 88263, evenings only). Two lakes, of 20 and 4 acres with brown and rainbow trout, and 400 yds of Kent River, with sea trout and two salmon pools. Dt £18, 4 fish limit, half-day or evening £12. Permits from WOOFS Newsagents, Staverley.

KILLINGTON RESERVOIR, ns **Oxenholme,** 3m. Trout, pike, perch. Leased to Kent AA. St £11, wt £4.50, dt £2 from Kendal tackle shops or Keeper at reservoir. Concession st to jun. Parties should book in advance through Kent AA Sec.

KNOTT END TARN: Birkby, Ravenglass. Regular stocking of brown trout to 6lb. Dry fly and nymph (barbless hook) only. Fly casting instruction, also suitable for handicapped anglers. Day tickets, 8am–5pm, £12. Evenings: £12. Bookings to W Arnold, Tel: 01229 717255. Tackle and information from Esso Garage, Holmrook.

LONGLANDS LAKE. Cleator, West Cumbria. Wath Brow and Ennerdale Anglers,

stocked monthly. Day tickets from Farrens Family Store, Cleator, or Wath Brow GPO.

LOUGHRIGG TARN, nr **Ambleside.** Pike, perch, roach, rudd, dace, brown trout and eels; apply to M A Murphy, Tarn Foot Farm, Loughrigg, nr Ambleside (Tel: 015394 32596).

LOWESWATER. National Trust lake. Pike, perch, trout (av 1½-2lb but hard to catch; fly only up to June 16); no fishing from Oct 31–Mar 15. For dt £3, wt £10, apply to Mr and Mrs Leck, Water End Farm, Loweswater (Tel: 01946 861465).

MEADLEY RESERVOIR. Cleator Moor, West Cumbria. Brown trout and rainbow. Permits from E G & J Littlefair, Wath Brow Stores & PO, 121/2 Ennerdale Road, Wath Brow, Cleator Moor, Cumbria CA25 5LP.

MOCKERKIN, near Loweswater. Tarn stocked with carp by Haigh AA, Whitehaven.

OVER WATER, nr Bassenthwaite, and 7m north of Keswick. 30 acre brown trout fishery, fly fishing by boat, float tubing permitted. Stocked regularly. Good coarse fishing in winter, with roach, dace, perch, pike to 28lbs. Permits from Overwater Hall Hotel. Information from Stan Edmondson, Troutdale Cottage, Borrowdale, Keswick CA12 5UY (Tel: 01768 777293).

PENNINGTON RESERVOIR, South Lakeland. Trout fishing, Barrow AA. Dt from secretary. For further information contact Paul Phillips, Team Leader, NWW Ltd, Woodland Office, Thirlmere Keswick, Cumbria (Tel: 017687 72334).

RATHERHEATH TARN, Kendal. 5 acre WADAA coarse fishery, open all year. Carp (20lb), tench (5lb), roach (2lb), bream (7lb), rudd, crucian carp, perch, gudgeon. Dt £4 (juv £2) from: Plantation Bridge Filling Station, A591 (Open 7.00 am–9.00 pm), Tourist Information Centres, local tackle shops. A special platform for disabled anglers stands just inside the entrance gate 10 metres from the car park. Fishing is permitted from one hour before sunrise to one hour after sunset. Overnight parking or night fishing is strictly prohibited.

RYDAL WATER, Ambleside. WADAA water, open 16th June–14th March. Pike, perch, eels, trout. Rydal Water offers similar fishing to Grasmere and is a popular pike fishery producing fish to the mid-20lb mark. Parking is at White Moss Common or Rydal Village. Most pike are caught near underwater features around the islands and off the various points. Boat fishing is not permitted. The Association wants to conserve pike stocks in all fisheries so please use adequate tackle and has unhooking gear at hand. Dt £4 (juv/OAP £2.00), wt £10.00–£5, st £30.00–£15.00). NB. This permit also allows fishing on Grasmere, River Rothay, River Brathay, High Arneside Tarn, Moss Eccles Tarn, School Knott Tarn & Hayswater. Permits from: Tourist Information Centres, local tackle shops, Barney's News Box, Grasmere (7.00 am–6 pm)

SKELSMERGH, ns **Kendal**, 3m. Now privately owned, with large tench and perch regularly caught. Dt £5 on bank.

SPRINKLING TARN. Right up Stye Head Pass. Trout. Good on a favourable day until July.

STYE HEAD TARN. Same information as Sprinkling Tarn.

THIRLMERE. Perch, pike, trout. Free fishing to Environment Agency licence-holders. No maggots, live baits or loosefeeding. For further information contact Peter Guy, C.A.R. Manager, NWW Ltd, Pennine House, Stanley St, Preston PR1 4DR (Tel: 01772 822200), or Roy McGuffie, Woodland Manager, Northern Estates Office, The Old Sawmill, Thirlmere, Keswick, Cumbria CA12 4TQ (Tel: 017687 72334).

ULLSWATER, nr **Penrith**. Covers 2,200 acres. Permits £5 daily, from tackle shops. Pike, perch, brown trout. Rowing boats and powered boats on water. Hotel: Ullswater, Glenridding CA11 0PA (Tel: 017684 82444) has private fishing for guests only.

WATENDLATH TARN. Keswick 3m. Brown and rainbow trout fishery, fly only, stocked weekly; boats. Open March to Dec, dt half-day, evenings. Apply to Stan Edmondson, Watendlath Trout Fishery, Borrowdale, Keswick CA12 5UY (Tel: 017687 77293). Mr Edmondson also has day tickets for 1m fishing on **River Cocker**.

WINDERMERE, nr **Windermere**. Largest English lake, 10½m long and nearly 1m wide. Good pike and perch, also eels, char and trout (trout best March–June), and roach now caught in numbers. Fishing free, apart from Environment Agency licence. Big fish taken by trolling. Boats from Bowness Bay, Waterhead Bay and Fell Foot NT Park. Local association, Windermere, Ambleside & Dist AA, has special corporate membership arrangement with 60 hotels, which give residents 2 rods per day on WADAA fisheries. Assn waters include 4m of Windermere Lake shore at Graythwaite Estates, near south-west end of lake; also **Grasmere**, **Rydal Water**, Rivers **Rothay**, **Brathay**, 6 tarns, Ghyll head and Dubbs Trout Fisheries, High Newton Reservoir, Grange-over-Sands. Details are elsewhere in text. **Ratherheath** and **Cleabarrow** Tarns are now coarse fisheries, dt £4, from local tackle shops: Go Fishing, Robinson Place Bowness-on-Windermere LA23 3DQ; Carlsons Tackle Shop, 64/66 Kirkland, Kendal. Hotels: Lonsdale, Lake Rd; Cragwood Country House; Applegarth; Oakthorpe; Ambleside; Skelwith Bridge; Langdale Chase; Fisherbeck. All these offer free fishing on WADAA waters.

YEW TREE TARN, near **Coniston**. Rainbow and brown trout, fly only, no boats; apply Lake District National Park Information Centre, Ruskin Avenue, Coniston.

ESK (Border)

(Esk in England is under North West Region Environment Agency; close seasons, licences, etc, see p13. For statutory close season in Scotland, see Fishing in Scotland; no licence needed).

Rises in Dumfriesshire and flows into the Solway Firth but is classed as an English river. Upper reaches of Esk and main tributary, Liddle Water, good for brown trout but rivers are primarily sea trout and salmon waters from Langholm and Newcastleton to the mouth. Heavy run of sea trout and herling from July to September. Salmon in late autumn, September and October being best months. Chub and dace in lower reaches provide good sport in winter.

Canonbie (Dumfries and Galloway). Salmon, sea trout, herling, trout; The Buccleuch Estates Esk and Liddle Fisheries issue permits. Fly fishing; spinning and worming allowed only when river level exceeds markers provided. St £44 to £348, wt £9 to £117, dt £7 to £37. Up to 28 May ½ price. From G Graham, River-watcher, Hagg on Esk, Canonbie DG14 0XE. Six private beats are let on weekly basis to parties of 3 rods, directly by Buccleuch Estates Ltd, Ewesbank (Tel: 013873 80202). Liddle tickets from J D Ewart, Douglas Square, and Mrs B Elliott, Thistlesyke, both Newcastleton. Also contact Stevenson and Johnstone, Bank of Scotland Buildings, Langholm, Dumfriesshire DG13 0AD. No licence needed. Hotels: Cross Keys, Canonbie.

Langholm (Dumfries and Galloway). Salmon, sea trout, herling, brown trout. Certain stretches of Esk and its tributary the Liddle, are under the control of Esk and Liddle Fisheries (see above). Netherby Estate, Longtown, issues permits for salmon and sea trout fishing at **Netherby**, through Edwin Thompson & Co, Bute House, Rosehill, Carlisle CA1 2RW. Sunday fishing and night fishing allowed on Netherby waters; restrictions on spinning and worm fishing. Full particulars from secretary. Tackle shop: Patties of Dumfries. Hotels: Eskdale, Douglas or Cross Keys (Canonbie).

Westerkirk (Dumfries and Galloway). Salmon, sea trout, herling, trout.

Tributaries of the Border Esk

LIDDLE: Salmon, sea trout, herling, brown trout.

Newcastleton (Roxburgh). Salmon, sea trout, herling, brown trout. Esk and Liddle Fisheries have much water. Tickets for 5m stretch. (See Canonbie). Bailey Mill Farm Holidays and Trekking Centre, Bailey TD9 0TR (Tel: 016977 48617) offer fishing holidays on 7m of Liddle, with accommodation, also 12m of Esk nr **Longtown**. Oak Bank Fisheries, Longtown, have trout and carp fishing. Tickets from local tackle shops.

LYNE: Lyne rises on Bewcastle Fells and joins Esk ½m above Metal Bridge. Salmon, sea trout, herling, trout.

SARK: Trout stream about 10m long, forming for a short distance boundary between England and Scotland, and emptying into Solway at **Gretna**. For Sark fishing, contact Annan and Dist AC.

KIRTLE WATER: Stream which empties into the Solway at Kirtlefoot. Sea trout, herling, trout. Rigg and Kirtleside farm, Rigg.

Kirtlebridge (Dumfries and Galloway). Sea trout and trout; short free length. Winterhope Burn. Penoben Burn. Annan, 3m SW. Well-

stocked reservoir 3m off, **Middlebie Dam**, fishable by permit; trouting very good.

Kirkpatrick (Dumfries and Galloway). Trout.

ESK (Yorkshire)
(For close seasons, licences, etc, see North East Region Environment Agency, p13)

Rises on Westerdale Moor and runs into sea at Whitby. Salmon, sea trout, trout and grayling. Good runs of sea trout, river has twice held British record, 1994 was highest ever total. The River Esk Action Committee, representing riparian owners and anglers, is dedicated to the furtherance and improvement of this once great salmon river. In partnership with the National Park and Environment Agency, it is carrying out an annual programme of habitat improvement and restocking, using own hatchery. For further information, please contact Egdon Estate Office (Tel: 01947 895466/7).

Whitby (Yorks). Salmon, sea trout, trout, grayling, eels; largely preserved by the Esk FA from Whitby to beyond Glaisdale. Visitors' tickets from Mr Sims, Ruswarp Boat Landing, Whitby. No maggot fishing is allowed. Fishing from Iburndale Beck down to Ruswarp Dam. St, dt. Salmon, sea trout and brown trout. Tackle shop: Whitby Angling Supplies, 65/67 Haggersgate, Whitby. Hotels: Wheatsheaf; Horseshoe.

RUSWARP (Yorks): Salmon, sea trout, trout, grayling, eels; preserved for 2m by Esk Fishery Association. Tickets from Mr Sims, Ruswarp Boat Landing, Whitby.

Sleights (Yorks). Salmon, sea trout, trout, grayling, eels; preserved by Esk Fishery Association. Tickets from Boatyard, Ruswarp.

Goathland (Yorks). Murk Esk; trout. Goathland FC water.

Grosmont (Yorks). Trout, salmon; preserved by the Esk FA above to Glaisdale, and below to Whitby.

Egton Bridge (N Yorks). Salmon, sea trout; some water preserved by the Esk FA. Other water (1¼m both banks) owned by Egton Estate, Estate Office, Egton Bridge, nr Whitby YO21 1UY (Tel: 01947 895466/7). Tickets issued throughout season, 3 rods per day. Trout fishing in **Scaling Dam** (worm and fly). Hotels: Horse Shoe; Wheatsheaf Inn; Station.

Glaisdale (N Yorks). Salmon, sea trout, trout; preserved below by the Esk FA *(see Whitby)*. Hotel: Angler's Rest. Esk FA bailiff, D J Swales, Rosedene, Priory Park, Grosmont, Whitby YO22 5QQ (Tel: 01947 895488). Dt from Yorkshire Water.

Danby (N Yorks). Salmon, sea trout, brown trout, grayling, preserved by landowners and Danby AC. Danby AC has about 8m of water stocked each year with approx 800 11in brown trout; also water between Castleton and Leaholm; st (limited) £12, dt £3, (£6 Oct), conc. from Duke of Wellington (Danby); Post Offices, Castleton and Danby; F Farrow, 11 Dale End, Danby (Club bailiff). Restrictions on method according to date. Accommodation, licences, tickets, at Duke of Wellington. Tackle shops: Angling Supplies, 65 Haggersgate Whitby; Keiths Sports, 31 Milton St, Saltburn-by-Sea.

Tributaries of the Esk (Yorkshire)

MURK ESK: Salmon and trout. Tributaries are: Little Beck, Brocka Beck, Eller Beck, Little Eller Beck. Fishing station: **Grosmont**.

COMMONDALE BROOK: Commondale (Yorks). Trout: preserved by the owners.

ESSEX (streams, lakes and reservoirs)
(For close seasons, licences, etc. see Anglian Region Environment Agency, p14)

ARDLEIGH RESERVOIR, nr **Colchester**. Off the A137, stocked with rainbow trout (20,000 in season). Fly only reservoir season: Mar 15 to Oct 31. Any legal method in Oct and coarse season. Coarse fishing allowed June–Feb, but restricted to arms of reservoir before Oct 1; excellent pike fishing. Wick Lane Ponds open all year, coarse fishing. 15 rowing boats, outboards allowed. Tackle and flies sold on site, tuition obtainable when required. St £500–£360, dt £14, beginners £5, conc. Boats £9–£7.20. Enq to Fisheries & Estate Officer, Ardleigh Reservoir, nr Colchester, Essex CO7 7PT (Tel: 01206 230642), enclose SAE.

BERWICK PONDS, **Rainham**. Operated by Berwick Ponds, 105 Suttons Avenue, Hornchurch RM12 4LZ. Tench, roach, bream, pike, carp. Dt £4, £1.50 extra rods; OAP £1.50, jun £2.50 from bailiff on bank. Night fishing £5.50, 24 hours £7.

CONNAUGHT WATERS, **Chingford**. Roach, bream, carp; free.

EPPING FOREST PONDS. Fishing permitted in most ponds except where prohibited by notices, namely Alexandra Lake, Eagle Pond, Shoulder of Mutton Pond. Charges apply to the following: Ornamental Water, Perch Pond, Hollow Pond, Connaught Water, Highams Park Lake, Wake Valley Pond, pay bailiff on site. The remaining are free. Further information from Forest Information Centre, Tel: 020 8508 0028, or Superintendent of Epping Forest, The Warren, Loughton, Essex IG10 4RW.

FISHERS GREEN, **Waltham Abbey**. Pike, tench, bream, roach, barbel, chub, perch, eels. An RMC Angling restricted permit fishery of 68 and 65 acre gravel pits, 3,900m of R Lea, 3,160 of Lea Relief Channel. St £42, no dt. Concessions for jun, OAP, dis. *(For RMC Angling, see Chertsey.)*

GOSFIELD LAKE, **Halstead** (Essex). 45 acres; well-stocked with carp, perch, roach, tench, pike. Inquire C W Turp, Gosfield Lake Ltd, Church Road, Gosfield. Dt (7.30am–7.30pm) £4, concessions to jun, obtainable from the shop.

GREEN OAKS FISHERIES, Potash Rd, **Billericay**. 2½ acre lake stocked weekly, open 8am till dusk all year round. Instruction, refreshments and flies for sale on site.

HANNINGFIELD RESERVOIR. Near **Chelmsford**. Excellent brown and rainbow trout fishery, average weight 2lb, good numbers of fish to 24lb 10oz. Regular stocking. Bank and boat fishing, incl boats for disabled. Season: End Mar–Oct 31. Full St: £435; Mon–Fri: £370; named week-day: £265; Sat and Sun £340, weekend one named day £290. Dt, 6 fish, £15. Motor boats £18 per day, rowing boats £10.50. Part day and evening boats also for hire. All prices include VAT. Car parks and fishing lodge. Total catch around 50,000, average weight 2lb, Enquiries to Fisheries Manager, Fishing Lodge, Giffords Lane, South Hanningford CM3 8HX (Tel: 01268 710101) shop, (Tel: 01245 212031) office. Internet: www.eswater.co.uk.

HATFIELD FOREST LAKE. Near Hatfield Broad Oak and Bishop's Stortford. National Trust property.

HOOKS MARSH. 40 acre RMC Angling gravel pit nr **Waltham Abbey**. Bream, tench, roach, perch and pike. Dt £3, conc, from Hall's Tackle, 44 Highbridge St, Waltham Abbey EN9 1BS, or on bank. Hall's also sell tickets for two coarse fisheries with carp, at **Clavershambury**.

LAYER PITS. 6m S of **Colchester**; controlled by Colchester APS; coarse fish; members only.

NAZEING MEADS, Meadgate Lane, Nazeing, Essex. Four gravel pits totalling 125 acres. Carp are main species, with large bream, roach, tench, eels and pike. Enquiries to Lee Valley Regional Park Authority Information Centre, Abbey Gardens, Waltham Abbey, Essex EN9 1XQ (Tel: 01992 702 200/Fax 230).

STAMBRIDGE FISHERIES, Stambridge Road, **Great Stambridge**, Essex SS4 2AR (01702 258274). Three lakes, of 16, 20 and 40 swims each, and carp to 10lbs or 20lbs, depending on water. Mirror, common, leather and wild, also crucian carp; roach, rudd, golden rudd, bronze and silver bream, and other species. No pike or zander. Dt from £3.50 on bank, night fishing by pre-booking; bait and tackle on site, all facilities.

STANFORD-LE-HOPE. Two RMC Angling gravel pits, 13 acres. Large carp, crucian, perch, pike, roach, tench. St £24, concessions to jun, OAP, dis. No dt. (For RMC Angling, see Chertsey.)

MARDYKE: Fishing stations: **Purfleet** and **Ockendon**. Rises by East Horndon and flows 12m to Thames at Purfleet. There are some club lengths. Moor Hall & Belhus AS has 2 members only coarse fisheries at South Ockendon, st on application to Sec.

PANT. **Bocking**. Upper part of R Blackwater (see Blackwater in main list).

ONGAR. Coarse fish; good chub, roach, dace and perch.

PASSINGFORD BRIDGE. Roach, chub, pike, bream, carp, tench. Barkingside and Dist AS has 1½m downstream; bailiff on water. Dt from bailiffs on bank for ¾m upstream of bridge. Woodford AS has 1½m north of bridge; Elm Park AS has water; dt from bailiff. **Romford**.

SOUTH WEALD LAKES. Weald, Thorndon, South Belhus Woods and Danbury

Country Parks all have fishing run by Essex County Council. Usual freshwater fish, esp. carp. St £60 (Weald and Thorndon only), dt £3.20, £1.60 jun, OAP; on lakeside or from Weald Office, Weald Country Park, South Weald, Brentwood, Essex CM14 5QS Tel: 01277 216297.

WANSTEAD & WOODFORD LAKES AND PONDS. **Eagle Pond**, **Snaresbrook** (roach, perch, carp); **Knighton Wood Pond**, **Woodford**; **Hollow Pond**, **Whipps Cross**; all free.

OTHER TICKET WATERS. Priory Lakes, Priory Park, **Southend**; Eastwood Pit, **Rayleigh**; Essex Carp Fishery (crucian carp, bream) at Mollands Lane, **South Ockendon**; Old Hall Lake, **Herongate**; Moor Hall Farm Fishery, **Aveley**; Raphael Park Lake, **Romford**; Danbury Park Lakes, near **Chelmsford**; Harwood Hall at Corbets Tey, and Parklands Lake, both near **Upminster**; Warren Pond, **Chingford**; carp, bream. Tickets mostly from bailiffs on site. Essex tackle shops: Essex Angling & Sport, 5 Broadway Parade, Elm Park; Avenue Angling, 22A Woodford Avenue, Ilford; Angling Centre, 226 Hornchurch Rd, Hornchurch.

For Walthamstow reservoirs, see under London.

EXE

(For close seasons, licences, etc, see South West Region Environment Agency p12)

Rises in Somerset on Exmoor and runs south through Devon to Exmouth. Salmon and trout, with grayling and coarse fish in lower reaches. At several points on upper reaches trout fishing (moorland) and salmon fishing may be had by hotel guests.

Exeter (Devon). Bream, carp, dace, gudgeon, pike, perch, roach, rudd, tench and eels. **Exeter Ship** and **Tiverton Grand Western** Canals contain bream, carp, pike, perch, rudd, roach, tench, eels and dace. Better part of Exeter canal from Broadwater (lime Kilns) to Turf (where canal enters Exe estuary). Hotels on canal banks: Double Locks, Turf. Exeter & Dist AA (amalgamation of local clubs) has coarse fishing rights on R Exe, on **Culm** and **Creedy**, from City Basin to Turf Basin on Exeter Ship Canal, and on ponds at Kingsteignton, Sampford Peveril, Feneck. St, visitors wt, dt. For fishing on Tiverton Canal contact Tiverton AC (Tel: 01884 242275) or tackle shops. At Exwick right bank visitors may fish for ½m, and from Exwick Mills d/s 400 yds below Exwick Rd Bridge. Environment Agency has 3m of salmon fishing on lower Exe in Cowley and Countess Wear areas. Dt £4, st £60, fly or spinning, from Feb 14 to Sept 30, from tackle shops in Exeter, Taunton, Tiverton. Apply Exeter AC, Smythen Street. Dt £3, wt £10 for Exeter & Dist AA waters from tackle shops. South View Farm Fishery, Shillingford St George, Exeter EX2 9UP (Tel: 01392 832278): 6 acres of coarse fishing on 3 lakes, with various species of carp to 20lb, tench, rudd and other coarse; £5 dt on bank, facilities on site. 2m W of city, **Haldon Ponds** trout fishery, stocked with rainbows to 10lb, b to 7lb. Wt £35, dt £6, evening £3. Rods limited. Boats. Phone Exeter 32967. One permit a day for salmon fishing (weekdays only) from Exeter Angling Centre, Smythen Street (Tel: 01392 436404/435591); Brailey's Field Sports Centre, Market St.

Brampford Speke (Devon). Salmon, trout, dace, roach, chub; preserved. Pynes Water, from here down to Cowley Weir (2½m) fished by local syndicate. Exeter & Dist AA water towards Stoke Canon (see Culm).

Silverton (Devon). Trout, chub, roach, dace, pike, perch; preserved. Exeter & Dist AA has coarse fishing on Culm here (see Exeter and Culm).

Bickleigh (Devon). Trout, salmon. Fisherman's Cot Hotel has a short stretch adjoining hotel for salmon and/or trout. Mainly for residents, but a few £12 dt on offer.

Tiverton (Devon). Exe, Lowman and Little Dart; trout, salmon. **Tiverton Canal**; bream, pike, perch, roach, tench. Tiverton & Dist AC has river, canal and lake fishing in vicinity. Canal dt from tackle shops, other waters, members only. Exe preserved for 2m both above and below town (trout and grayling) by Tiverton FFC, fly only. St £12 for residents only. River walk in Tiverton, ½m, free trout fishing to juv. Hotels: Bark House at Oakford Bridge; Fisherman's Cot, Bickleigh (beat on Exe). Tackle shop: Exe Valley Angling.

Dulverton (Som). Salmon, trout, grayling. Usually good run of salmon (May onwards and autumn) to Dulverton and beyond, depending on water conditions. Trout fishing good on Exe and **Barle** (four to lb). For 540m single bank, contact Lance Nicholson (see below). Grayling less plentiful. Guests at Carnarvon Arms (see advt) may fish on 5m of Exe and Barle; individual

beats, ghillie service, and instruction on site. Wt £100–£130 (S). Dt (S) £12–£25. Trout dt £7–£12. A few day tickets sometimes for non-residents. Some free fishing for guests at Lion Hotel, Bank Square, Dulverton TA22 9BU (Tel: 01398 323444). Royal Oak, Winsford TA24 7JE (Tel: 01643 851455) has a mile of river, free fishing for guests. **Exe Valley Fishery**, Exebridge, Dulverton TA22 9AY (Tel: 01398 323328, Fax: 324079). One large and two small lakes stocked with rainbows averaging 2lb+. Dt £5.50 (£3.80 per kilo caught extra) on site throughout year, 5 fish limit; evening £3.30, 3 fish limit. At **Broford**, 5m double bank of Little Exe, with wild brown trout, fly only. Dt £10, from tackle shop: Lance Nicholson, High St TA22 9HB (Tel: 01398 323409). Accom. at Anchor Inn, Exebridge, Dulverton.

Tributaries of the Exe

CREEDY: Trout, coarse fish.

Cowley Bridge (Exeter). Coarse fish. Exeter and Dist AA has rights, left bank only (see Exeter).

Crediton (Devon). Trout. Yeo 3m; trout. Crediton FFC has over 5m, mainly double bank, on Rivers Creedy, Culvery and Yeo, also 1½m on R Taw. Five day visitor tickets £25, from Hon Treasurer Howard Thresher, 30 Tuckers Meadow, Crediton EX17 3NX. Oldborough Fishing Retreat, Aboveway Rd, Morchard Bishop EX17 6SQ: 2 acre lake with good sized mirror and common carp, perch, roach, bream, etc. Book in advance Dt £4.

CULM: Trout, coarse fish, few grayling.

Stoke Canon, **Rewe** and **Silverton** (Devon). Dace, chub, roach, perch and occasional grayling. Exeter and Dist AA has water.

Hemyock (Devon). Trout, small and few. Lower water preserved and stocked by Hemyock-Culmstock syndicate.

Clayhidon (Devon). Upper Culm FA preserves about 4m in this district (see Hemyock). No Sunday fishing. Hotel: Half Moon.

Killerton (Devon). National Trust controls coarse fishing on Killerton Estate; tickets from tackle shops for Exeter AA water.

BARLE: Runs through beautifully wooded valley and holds salmon (av 7–10lb) and trout (av 8–10in).

Tarr Steps (Som). Salmon, trout. Tarr Steps Hotel, Hawkridge TA22 9PY, has 6m of salmon and brown trout fishing, fly only. Non-residents welcome, dt salmon from £20, trout from £10. Tel: 01643 851293, Fax: 01643 851218.

Simonsbath (Som). Exmoor Forest Hotel has rights on approx 1m of Barle, commencing 1½m below Simonsbath Bridge, free to hotel guests. St £50 to dt £3.50, for non-residents. E.A. licences at hotel. Spinning for salmon allowed. Convenient for **Wimbleball Reservoir**.

FAL
(For close seasons, licences, etc, see South West Region Environment Agency, p12)

Rises near Roche and flows about 23 miles, due south, past Grampound and Tregony to the English Channel at Falmouth.

Falmouth (Cornwall). Trout fishing in Argal Reservoir, coarse fishing in College Reservoir: large pike and carp. Trout in some of the small streams flowing into creeks around Falmouth. 2 acres coarse fishing at Tory Farm, Ponsanooth (Tel: 01209 861272), speciality, carp. Dt on site. Tackle shop: The Tackle Box, Falmouth.

Tregony (Cornwall). Trout, 2m off runs Polglaze Brook, 4m long; trout.

FOWEY
(For close seasons, licences, etc, see South West Region Environment Agency p12)

Rises on Bodmin Moor, runs down a steep valley at Golitha and enters sea by estuary at Fowey. Cornwall's foremost sea trout river. Run of big sea trout in April and May followed by peal until mid-June. Night fishing for sea trout excellent in July, Aug and early Sept. Grilse run from July, salmon fishing is good with autumn rain in Sept. There is also a good late run, until mid Dec.

Fowey (Cornwall). Capital sea fishing (see *Sea Fishing section*). Boat hire for estuary fishing from Fowey Diving Services, 21 Station Rd, Fowey PL23 1DF (Tel: 01726 833920). Tackle shops: Leisure Time, 10 The Esplanade; Fowey Marine Services, 23/27 Station Rd. Hotels: Fowey; Ship; Fowey Hall; Marina; Fowey Marine Guest House (Tel: 01726 833920).

Lostwithiel (Cornwall). Sea trout, salmon,

brown trout. Fishing for rod and line below Lostwithiel Bridge free. Lostwithiel FC has approx 2m double bank fishing, with disabled platforms on two pools; season tickets £55, conc, may be purchased from Treasurer, F Cox, Cott Rd, Lostwithiel; day tickets £10, conc, from Lostwithiel Angling Centre, Queen St; Roger's Tackle Shop, Higher Bore St, Bodmin PL31 1DZ (Tel: 01208 78006). National Trust has water at Lanhydrock.

Respryn Bridge (Cornwall). Most water above the bridge is in the hands of Lanhydrock AA, NT Cornwall Regional Office, **Lanhydrock Park** PL30 4DE. St £45 (waiting list), wt £25, dt £10, juv st £22.50. Artificial bait only. Free fishing on section between Respryn Bridge and footbridge. Hotels: Royal Talbot, King's Arms, Earl of Chatham, Royal Oak, Globe, Trevone Guest House and Restormel Lodge.

Liskeard (Cornwall). Liskeard and Dist AC has several good beats on Fowey, also **Lynher**, and on minor rivers, West Looe, Seaton and Inny. Membership from T Sobey, Trevartha Farm, Liskeard; Looe Tropicals and Pets shop in Looe, or from Tremar Tropicals shop in Liskeard.

FROME AND PIDDLE
(Dorset)
(For close seasons, licences, etc, see South West Region Environment Agency, p12)

Frome rises above Hooke in West Dorset and flows into the English Channel at Poole Harbour near Wareham. Piddle rises in a mill pond 1 mile north of Piddletrenthide and enters Poole Harbour near mouth of Frome near Wareham. Both are chalk streams and closely preserved but sport may sometimes be had. Some very good sea trout have been caught in the Frome, which also receives a run of heavy salmon. Trout in both rivers plentiful and good. Bass run up to where the river enters Poole Harbour. Piddle carries very small stock of heavy salmon. River is in fine condition due to successful efforts of River Piddle Protection Association.

Wareham (Dorset). On Frome and Piddle; salmon, sea trout, trout, grayling, pike, roach and dace. Free coarse fishing on towpath side of R Frome, from Wareham South Bridge downstream. E.A. licence required. Salmon and trout preserved. Morden Estate Office, Charborough Park, Wareham, sometimes has rods for entire season (never for day or week) as follows: salmon, Frome and Piddle; trout, Piddle and

Bere Stream, and River Stour, coarse fishing. Environment Agency lets 14 rods for the season (on the basis of 2 per day) for fishery on Piddle; salmon, sea trout (details from Area Conservation Officer). South Drain nr Poole Harbour is Wareham & Dist AS water. Club has 22 local waters, membership £24, £5 jun. Hotels: Red Lion and Black Bear. Tackle shop and bait: G Elmes & Son, St John's Hill; Guns & Sports, 24 South Street.

Wool (Dorset). Frome: Salmon, sea trout. Spring salmon scarce, summer and autumn fish plentiful in Frome. Woolbridge Manor (100 yards from river) has 1¼m; fly and spinning. Salmon run large, fish over 20lb not rare. Summer run of grilse 6 to 10lb. Season 1 Mar to 31 Aug. St £200, dt £25, approx. For details write to Mr Bowerman, Morden Estate Office, Charbourgh Park, Wimborne, Dorset. Nr **Puddletown**, **Pallington Lakes**, **Tincleton**, one trout, one coarse, one carp and tench only. Daily stocking. Trout dt £19; 4 fish limit. Coarse fishing £4, conc. Records include salmon 19lb, r trout 11lb 12oz and carp 22½lb. Tel: 01305 848141. At **Tolpuddle**, and 7m from Dorchester, **Wessex Fly Fishing**, Lawrences Farm DT2 7HF (Tel: 01305 848460): 12 chalk streams, beats on Rivers Frome and Piddle, lakes and pools; tuition (Reffis member). Catch and release on rivers, 10 fish limit, barbless hooks. Lake dt £24, ½ day £20, evening £15; rivers, from £17 to £55, depending on season and beat. Tackle shop on site, also self-catering accom and B & B.

Dorchester (Dorset). Frome: brown trout and grayling; Dorchester FC has 6½m water in vicinity of Dorchester. U/s dry fly or nymph fishing. Limited dt £20, from J Aplin (see below). Rest of river preserved by landowners. Dt and licences from tackle shop. Dorchester and Dist AS issues coarse fishing dt for short stretch of **Stour**. At **Kingcombe**, Higher Kingcombe Farm. 8 ponds – coarse fishing; Paul Crocker Tel: 01300 320537, St £75, £3 full day, £2 evenings, £5 night. **Rawlsbury Waters**, 4 small trout lakes, Tel: 01258 817446. **Flowers Farm Lakes**, Hilfield, Dorchester, Dorset DT2 7BA Tel/Fax: 01300 341351; trout fishery of 5 lakes, brown and rainbow. Dt £18, £14, £10.50. Limit, full day limit 4 fish. Open all year. Tickets for Luckfield Lake Fishery, 1½ acres, Broadmayne, with carp, and for R Frome fishing, from Tackle shop: John Aplin, Specialist Angling Supplies, 1 Athelstan Road, Dorchester DT1 1NR (Te;: 01305 266500). Hotel: King's Arms.

GIPPING (Orwell)
(For close seasons, licences, etc, see Anglian Region Environment Agency, p14)

Rises between Stowmarket and Bury St Edmunds, and flows into the North Sea by an estuary near Ipswich. Coarse fish.

Ipswich (Suffolk). Most coarse fish. From Yarmouth Rd Bridge to Norwich Railway Bridge, 1m, dt on bank. 2m stretch from Railway Bridge to Sproughton Bridge, dt from tackle shops. Town section, st or dt on bank. Gipping APS controls 10m between Stowmarket and Ipswich, and issues dt for small section of river from Sproughton to Ipswich, from Ipswich tackle shops; members only on other fishings, which include several coarse lakes in vicinity. **Alton Water**, 350 acre coarse fish reservoir at Anglian Water Services Ltd, Holbrook Rd, Stutton, Ipswich IP9 2RY (Tel: 01473 589105), under control of AW, with bream to 7lb and pike to 25lb, plus roach and perch. St £25, dt £2.50, conc, on site or from local tackle shops. Tackle shops: Breakway Tackle, Bramford Rd; Viscount Tackle, Clapgate Lane; R Markham, Woodbridge Road East; Bosmere Tackle, 57 High Street, Needham Market.

Stowmarket (Suffolk). Permits to fish Green Meadow stretch from Bosmere Tackle, see below. Stowmarket and Dist AA has short stretch of **Rattle**; members only. Gipping Valley AC fishes river here, and at **Needham Market** and **Claydon**; also **Needham Lake**, 10 acres: most coarse fish stocked. Membership from Bosmere Tackle, 57 High St, Needham Market.

GLOUCESTERSHIRE (streams)

BIDEFORD BROOK. Fishing station: **Awre**. Rises in Abbot's Wood and flows 7m to Severn estuary; coarse fish; preserved. **Blackpool Brook** enters at Awre; Forest of Dean AC; members only.

CONE. fishing station: **Woolaston**. Cone rises by Hewelsfield, and is 5m long. Eels and flounders.

FROME. Rises near Cheltenham and flows into Severn estuary. Coarse fish; a few trout higher up. Fishing stations: **Stonehouse** (Glos), coarse fish, and **Stroud** (Glos), a few trout and coarse fish. Several brooks in vicinity. Pike and coarse fishing in Stroudwater Canal. Stroud AA controls 2m Thames at Lechlade and 1m at Newbridge. Stroud tackle shop: Batemans Sports, Kendrick Street, GL5 1AB (Tel: 01453 764320), issue st £10, £3.50 juv, for local club waters, including Frome at **Eastington** and **Whitminster**, canal from Stroud to Thrupp, tickets for gravel pits, a total of 21 different venues.

NAILSWORTH BROOK (tributary of Frome): Fishing stations: **Nailsworth** (Glos) and **Woodchester** (Glos). Brook reported polluted in parts. Lakes: Longfords Lake, pike, carp. Woodchester Park lakes: pike, perch, roach, tench, brown and rainbow trout; now preserved.

HOPE BROOK. Fishing station: **Westbury-on-Severn**, ns Grange Court, 1½m. Hope Brook rises 2m above Longhope, runs 5m to Westbury and Severn estuary (1m). Coarse fish, mostly preserved. Inn: Red Lion.

LITTLE AVON: Small Gloucestershire stream flowing into Severn estuary.

Berkeley (Glos). Coarse fish, trout, Waterley Brook. Fishing below Charfield preserved. Close by station rises Billow Brook, which runs thence 3m to estuary. Clubs have water on **Gloucester and Berkeley Canal**; 16m Sharpness to Gloucester.

LYD. Chub, roach, perch. Fishing station: **Lydney**. Lydney AA holds stretch from railway station to Tufts Junction. Club also has **Lydney Lake** (carp, roach and perch). **Lydney Canal** and a dam.

GREATER MANCHESTER RESERVOIRS

These are trout fisheries, unless otherwise stated. More information may be obtained from C.A.R. Manager Peter Sharples, North West Water Ltd, Woodhead Road, Tintwhistle, Hadfield via Hyde, Cheshire SK13 1HS, Tel: 01457 864187; C.A.R. Manager Phil Luff, NWW Ltd, Rivington Water Treatment Works, Horwich, Bolton BL6 7RN, Tel: 01204 696118.

BOLLINHURST RESERVOIR, Disley. Leased by Dystelegh Fly FC. Contact G Heywood, 10 Marlett Ave, Disley, Stockport. Members only, no permits.

BUCKLEY WOOD RESERVOIR, Rochdale. Rochdale Waltonian Anglers, (see *club list*).

CASTLESHAW (LOWER) RESERVOIR, Oldham. Oldham United Anglers, J K Lees, 10, Packwood Chase, Oldham (Tel: 0161 624 5176).

GORTON (LOWER) RESERVOIR. Coarse permits on bank, suitable for disabled anglers. Contact Manchester City Council (*below*).

GORTON (UPPER) RESERVOIR, 'Lawrence Scott Arm'. Coarse fishing permits on bank. Further details from Manchester City Council, Leisure Dept, Debdale Centre, Debdale Park, 1073 Hyde Road, Gorton, Manchester M18 7LJ (Tel: 0161 223 5182).

HOLLINGWORTH LAKE, Littleborough. Fishing for roach, perch, pike, tench, carp bream. Contact Chief Warden, Visitors' Centre, Hollingworth Lake Country Park, Rakewood Rd, Littleborough, Lancs OL15 0AQ (Tel: 01706 373421). Tickets from Visitors' Centre, or from ranger on bank.

JUMBLES RESERVOIR, Bradshaw Rd, **Bolton**. Free fishing to licence-holders. Contact C.A.R. Manager Phil Luff, NNW Ltd (see *Thirlmere*).

KITCLIFFE RESERVOIR, Rochdale. Oldham United Anglers, see *Castleshaw*.

LITTLE SEA RESERVOIR, Oldham. Oldham & Dist Amalgamated AA. B Boff, 369 Shaw Rd, Oldham.

LUDWORTH RESERVOIR, Stockport. Crossland's AC, Mr L Donaldson, 57 The Ridgeway, Romiley, Stockport SK6 3HA. Dt for members guests only, from Stockport Angling Centre, 145 Wellington Rd North, Stockport SK4 2PF.

OGDEN RESERVOIR, Rochdale. Oldham United Anglers, see *Castleshaw*.

RUMWORTH LODGE, Bolton. Royal Ashton AC, D T Dobson, 1 Parkway, Westhoughton. Dt water.

WALKERWOOD TROUT FISHERY, Brushes Road, **Stalybridge** SK15 3QP (Tel:

0421 619399). Fly only, all browns to be returned. Best brown 7lb, best rainbow 14lb 8oz. Dt £15, 4 fish, at car park. A range of season tickets on offer. Internet: www.walker-wood.free-online.co.uk

WATERGROVE RESERVOIR, Rochdale. Dt from warden on site at the sailboard club, or from Hollingworth Lake.

HAMPSHIRE (Streams, lakes and canal)
(For close seasons, licences, etc, see Southern Region Environment Agency, p12)

BASINGSTOKE CANAL. Fishing stations: **Greywell, North Warnborough, Odiham, Winchfield, Crookham, Fleet, Farnborough, Aldershot, Ash Vale.** Pike, carp, roach, good tench, perch; fishing from towpath only; dt for 17m of Hampshire section from Greywell Tunnel to Ash Lock from tackle shop Noels Tackle, 314 Fernhill Rd, Cove. Andover AC has fishing. Further enquiries about Basingstoke Canal to BCAA Sec, R Jenkins, 26 Tintern Close, Basingstoke RG24 9HE. Farnborough AS also has rights on **Whitewater** at **Heckfield, Loddon** at **Winnersh, Ash Vale Lake**, 5 acres, **Shawfields Lake**, 3 acres, mixed, and gravel pits. St £13 from Raison's, 2 Park Road, Farnborough for **Willow Park Fisheries**, Ash Vale, 3 lakes stocked with carp, tench and other coarse fish. Bait and refreshments on site. Dt on site £1 and £1.50, concession for jun. Four RMC Angling gravel pits at **Frimley**. Carp, crucian carp, bream, perch, tench, perch, rudd, eel and pike. Large specimens recorded. No night fishing, no dt. St £24, ½ price conc. (For RMC Angling, see Chertsey.) Tackle shops: Two Guys, 27 Burnby Close, Basingstoke; Raison's, 2 Park Road, Farnborough; Tackle Up, 151 Fleet Road, Fleet; The Creel, 36 Station Road, Aldershot.

BEAULIEU. The Beaulieu River is approx 14 miles long. Tickets for tidal stretch, Bailey's Hard to Needs Ore (bass, mullet), st £17, dt £2.50, from Harbour Master, Buckler's Hard (Tel: 01590 616200) or Resident Land Agent, John Montagu Building, Beaulieu (Tel: 01590 612345). Access from Bailey's Hard and Buckler's Hard. Coarse fishing on **Hatchett Pond** (Forestry Commission); bream, carp, tench and pike; tickets from Forestry Commission, Queen's House, Lyndhurst SO43 7NH (Tel: 02380 283141), campsite offices during camping season and local tackle shops (st £60, wt £9, dt

£5, VAT incl, jun conc, barbless hooks only). Children may fish free on Janesmoor Pond. Hotel: Montagu Arms. Accommodation at Newhouse Farm, Tel: 01590 612297.

DAMERHAM TROUT LAKES, The Lake House, Damerham Fisheries, **Fordingbridge**, SP6 3HW (Tel: 01725 518 446/Fax 471). Six lakes, and river for St holders. R and b trout. Open March to October. Season rods only, full, half, quarter, guest, prices on application. Lunch in 16th C. thatched cottage adjacent fishery.

FLEET POND. Fishing station: **Fleet**. Cove AS water. No tickets. Tackle shop: Fleet S C, 182 Fleet Road.

HAMBLE. Sea trout and trout. **Bishop's Waltham.** Fishing mostly private.

HOLBURY TROUT LAKES, Lockerley, Near **Romsey**, Hants SO51 0JR (Tel: 01794 341619). Fishery of 4 lakes, stocked with rainbow and blue trout (average caught 3lb, largest 13lb 9oz), and ⅔m of River Dun, both banks, stocked brown trout. Dry fly and nymph only on river, wet and dry fly on lakes. No catch and release. Various tickets, incl full dt for lakes and river £44, limit 6 fish; full season, lakes only, £650, limit 26 × 4 fish; half day £25, river only, 26 × half day £400. Full facilities on site, and tuition if required.

LYMINGTON RIVER. Fishing station: Lymington. Sea trout (2–11lb), brown trout (¾ to 1lb). Sea trout best June to Sept. Fishing improved by Brockenhurst Manor FFC; private. Mixed fishery at Sway Lakes, Barrows Lane, Sway Lymington, Tel: 01590 682010. Carp over 20lb. Dt on bank. Tackle and bait from Loni's Angling Centre, Gore Rd, New Milton.

MEON. Trout; sea trout in lower reaches. Fishing station: **East Meon**; Hants and Sussex Alliance has water; inquire Hon Sec. Portsmouth Services FFA has 5 miles on Meon and 2¼ miles on Itchen below Winchester. Membership is immediately obtainable for serving personnel, those retired may have to wait 2 years. Serving members £80, retired £160, guests £16 per day. Portsmouth and Dist AS (members of Hants & Sussex Alliance) holds some 20 waters around **Portsmouth** and across Hampshire and W Sussex, which include coarse fishing on Arun, Rother, Ember, and Wallington. Dt on some waters. Membership £58 per annum, plus £15 joining fee, conc

Enquiries to Hon Sec, or local tackle shops. Other fisheries in vicinity: at Staunton Country Park, Havant PO9 5HB (Tel: 023 9245 3405): a 3 acre lake with carp, bream roach, dt from Park Office 10.00–16.00. Meon Springs Fly Fishery, Whitewood Farm, East Meon, Petersfield GU32 1HW (Tel: 01730 823249): 2 small lakes between East and West Meon. Chiphall Lake Trout Fishery, 5 acres: Northfields Farm, Wickham. Wintershill Lake, Wintershill Farmhouse, Durley SO32 2AH (Tel: 01489 860200): trout fishing on 3½ acres. For full season, half season, and day rods contact Lake Bailiff, Tel: 023 8060 1421. Tackle shops: Rover's, 178B West St, Fareham; Alan's Marine, and Merrett's, both Portsmouth.

SANDLEHEATH. Six lakes and three chalk stream beats at **Rockbourne Trout Fishery**, Sandleheath, Fordingbridge, Hampshire SP6 1QG. Excellent fishing for rainbow trout in lakes and brown trout and grayling in streams, fly only, various period terms from dt £32, limit 5 fish, ½ day £28, 4 fish. Special winter tickets, also. Blocks of tickets at discount. Concessions for juv. Tuition, tackle hire, licensed cafeteria. Tel: 01725 518603.

WAGGONERS' WELLS, near **Haslemere**. Three lakes; National Trust waters, now managed by Greyshott AC. Coarse fishing; carp, roach, tench, gudgeon, a few trout. Dt from Greyshott Tackle, Crossway Road, Greyshott, Hindhead, or bailiff on bank. Hotel: Punchbowl Hotel, Hindhead.

WARBURN. Dace, trout, salmon; preserved; leave sometimes from landowners; joins sea at **Key Haven**.

HERTS AND GREATER LONDON
(Reservoirs and lakes)
(see also London Reservoirs)

ALDENHAM (Herts). **Aldenham Country Park Reservoir**. Managed by Herts CC. Coarse fishing, incl. tench, pike to 37lb, carp to 39lb, plus very good roach and bream. No night fishing. Dt £3 (jun, OAP £1.50), punt £6–£4. Dis free. From bailiff on site or from Park Manager, Park Office, Dagger Lane, Elstree, Herts WD6 3AT. Tel: 020 8953 1259; or 01831 837446, bailiff's mobile phone.

Shepperton (Middx); **Ashmere Fisheries**, Felix Lane, Shepperton TW17 8NN. Four lakes, total 20 acres, stocked with rainbow trout.

Boats. Annual membership only, £350–£585. Apply Mrs Jean Howman, Ashmere Fisheries, Felix Lane, Shepperton (Tel: 01932 225445, Fax: 253793).

STANSTEAD ABBOTS. RMC Angling coarse fisheries consisting of 5 gravel pits with carp over 40lb, mill stream and part of main river. Other species include roach, tench, dace, pike, barbel. Season tickets £30. Concessions to jun, OAP, dis. No dt. (For RMC Angling, see Chertsey.)

TRING (Herts). Four large reservoirs: **Marsworth**, **Startops End** and **Wilstone** (2m from Tring) main feeders for Grand Union Canal. Good fishing for specimen hunters. Bream over 10lb, former British record tench 12½lb, pike to 26lb, many large roach, specimen catfish. Sunday fishing now permitted. St £80 (including night fishing), conc, dt £4, conc £3, evening £3. Tickets obtainable on bank from bailiff, B C Double, Reservoir House, Watery Lane, Marsworth HP23 4LX (Tel: 01442 822379). The fourth reservoir is a private trout fishery. The Tring Anglers have extensive fishing on Wendover and Aylesbury Arms of Grand Union Canal; Oxford Canal north of Kiddlington; **R Thame** at Chearsley and Shabbington Island and Ickford; **R Ouzel** nr Newport Pagnell and Stoke Hammond; **R Ivel** at Shefford, plus lakes and ponds which include an excellent bream fishery. Club also fishes Oxford & Dist AA waters on Thames and elsewhere, Reading & Dist AA waters incl Kennet, and has a comprehensive sharing scheme with Barnet & Dist AC. St £32, dt £3 where applicable, conc half price. Tackle shop: Chiltern Tackle, Western Rd, Tring.

HULL
(For close seasons, licences, etc, see North East Region Environment Agency, p13)

Tidal river between Hempholme and Hull is free of any permit charge and is popularly fished by an increasing number of coarse anglers. Upstream of Beverley first-class sport may be had with roach, dace, pike, chub, bream, etc. West Beck is an excellent but preserved trout fishery of chalk-stream character.

Hull (North Humberside). River polluted. Drains giving good coarse fishing. Free fishing on E.A. licence from North Frodingham to Hull. Hull & Dist AA has water on **Derwent** at **Breighton**, **Wressle** and **Newton**; on the **Rye** at **Butterwick** and **Swinton**; and on the **Trent**

at **Carlton**. Also the **Brandsburton Ponds** (open all the year), Tilery Lake, the Broomfleet, Motorway, and other ponds, 9m of **Market Weighton Canal**, 17m from Hull, mixed coarse fishery, 1m of **R Foulness**, north bank. Membership is unrestricted. Stone Creek and Patrington Haven hold flounders. Good sea fishing. Burstwick Watersports have coarse fishing nr **Burstwick**; dt £2 or £1.50. Contact P Hall, Tel: 01482 26455. Rush Lyvars Lake, coarse fishery at **Hedon**, dt £1.20. Tel: 01482 898970. **Pickering Park Lake** owned by City Council, fine pike. Coarse dt £1.10. Tel: 01482 222693. At Aldbrough on Sea, Lambwath Lakes, 5 pond complex of 120 pegs, good match fishing for carp, tench, orfe and bream. D Heslop, 999 Sutton Rd, Hull HU8 0HU. Tackle shops: Fishing Basket, 470 Beverley Road; Everett's Fishing Tackle, 691 Holderness Rd; G W Hutchinson & Co, 27 Anlaby Rd; B B Fishing Tackle, 567 Holderness Rd.

Beverley (N Humberside). Tidal River Hull and drains give good coarse fishing; from Hull Bridge upstream through **Arram**, **Aike Wilfholme**, **Baswicke** and **Hempholme** to Frodingham Beck: North East Region Environment Agency, for enquiries; weedy June to Nov. **Beverley Beck**, canalised stream, 1m long, 60 pegs, good access for disabled. Stocked with most coarse species, but mainly roach to 2lb, bream 7lb, tench and chub. Dt £2.50, jun 50p, from Total Petrol Station, Waterside Rd, Beverley. Further information: Paul Caygill, Tel: 01964 542677. Dt £2 for 2 coarse ponds in Lakeminster Park, Tel: 01482 882655. **Leven Canal** (6m): coarse fish, Hull AA water except for 250 yds to right of bridge, Trailer and Marina Ltd, Tel: 01482 896879. Fine tench. Dt from Minster Tackle, 3 Flemingate, Everett's Fishing Tackle, Beverley, Leven Marina, and 11 The Meadows, Leven. Hotel: Beverley Arms.

Brandesburton (N Humberside). River Hull 3m W, excellent coarse fishing in gravel pits (see Hull).

Wansford (N Humberside). Free left bank below Lock Dow to Brigham. **Driffield Canal Fishery**, from Town Lock, Driffield along B1249 to Snake Holme Lock, ½m west of Wansford. Trout, both bait and fly. **West Beck** preserved by Golden Hill AS and West Beck PS; members only. Fishponds Farm and Fishery, Woldgate, Boynton, nr **Bridlington** YO16 4XE, has 3 coarse fishing ponds. Dt £3, 2 rods. Barbless hooks, no groundbait, no keepnets. Tel: 01262 605873.

Tributaries of the Hull

FOSTON BECK (or **KELK** or **FROD-INGHAM BECK**):

North Frodingham, Foston-on-the-Wolds and **Lowthorpe** (N Humberside). Rises in Yorkshire wolds; true chalk stream containing brown trout averaging well over the pound. Preserved.

DRIFFIELD BECK:

Driffield (N Humberside). Provides chalk stream fishing for trout and grayling of high order. Driffield AA. Kellythorpe Trout Lake now in private hands. For **Pickering Trout Lake**, Newbridge Rd, Pickering, N Yorks.

ISLE OF MAN

The geographical nature of the Isle of Man tends to dictate the type of river, fish and hence fishing one may encounter when angling in the Island. Being a relatively mountainous place, rivers and streams are small, swift flowing and very clear. There are very few coarse fish on the Isle of Man but nevertheless excellent sport can be had in the numerous trout streams where the art of approach to the river bank and the gentle and accurate cast of the true angler becomes vital.

There are very few preserved stretches of river in the Island and a well chosen word with the land owner is often all that is required to enable an angler to fish in peace. Approx one half mile of the River Douglas through the Nunnery Estate is exclusively reserved for the Manx Game FC. Small sections of the rivers Dhoo and Glass can only be fished under permit from the Douglas and District Angling Club. Applications for membership should be sent to Sue McCoubrey, 47 Hildesley Road, Douglas (Tel: 628460). Subscriptions are now £15, £6 junior.

Natural baits (worms, bread, cheese) and artificial baits are allowed on the Island's rivers, ponds and streams but anglers are reminded that only artificial baits are allowed when reservoir fishing (except Eairy Dam). Further details of all freshwater angling can be obtained from the Freshwater Fishery Inspector, Cornaa, Maughold.

Anglers must abide by the regulations wherever they fish. (1) Not to use or carry a gaff or tailer. (2) Not to use a line that exceeds 10lb breaking strain). (3) Not use more than one hook on a line unless (a) Pennel or Stewart tackles are being used for bait fishing; (b) a 'point with two droppers' is being used for fly fishing only; (c) a spinner is being used for spinning only. (4) Not use a spinner except (a) in a reservoir where the spinner does not exceed 10 grams in weight and does not exceed 65 millimetres in length, inclusive of hook and dressing; or (b) in a river where the spinner does not exceed 15 grams in weight and does not exceed 100 millimetres in length, inclusive of hook and dressing. (5) Not to use a hook larger than No 6 Redditch scale, unless the hook is comprised in an artificial fly. (6) Return to the water all fish foul hooked. (7) Return to the water unharmed any freshwater fish hooked which is less than 18 cm in length overall. (8) Chest waders prohibited. (9) Must have and use landing nets when fishing in reservoirs at all times, and when fishing for migratory species in rivers.

The river fishing season commences on 1 April, and finishes on the 30 September for trout and 31 October for salmon. The reservoir season begins on 10 March and continues until 31 October. A freshwater fishing licence is required to fish any river or pond, and a separate licence required to fish a reservoir.

Salmon fishing takes place mainly in the autumn as the Island does not enjoy a spring run. Salmon and sea trout are usually taken during or after spate conditions. There is a bag limit for the rivers of 6 trout or salmon, of which no more than 2 may be migratory fish in any one day. Fish are small and rarely if ever exceed 20lb – a more reasonable average would be 5–10lb.

There is a bag limit for the rivers of 6 trout or salmon, of which no more than 2 may be migratory fish in any one day; and a bag limit for the reservoirs of 4 fish in any one day. Anglers must not continue to fish after catching and killing the maximum number of fish.

The Department of Agriculture, Fisheries and Forestry pursues a continual stocking programme of rivers, ponds and reservoirs.

Fishing Licences
Freshwater fishing licences are obligatory by law, and cost as follows. Reservoirs: £85 for season, £28 for one week, £10 for one day. Other waters: £28 for season, £10 for one week, £5 for one day. Concessions for juniors.

They are obtained from: I.O.M. Department of Agriculture, Fisheries and Forestry, Mount Havelock, Douglas, Tel: 01624 685857; from Department of Tourism & Leisure, Information Bureau, Sea Terminal, Douglas, from local com-

missioners offices in Onchan and Laxey, and from most post offices.

No licence required for sea fishing, which from pier, rocks or boat is excellent, especially for pollack – locally called callig – mackerel, cod and codling, whiting and plaice. Chief bait for ground fish is mackerel, but lugworm, sand-eels and shellfish also found. Jigging with white and coloured feathers and artificial sand-eel for pollack, mackerel and cod is successful. Good centres for most species are Peel, Port Erin, Port St Mary and Ramsey. Department of Tourism & Leisure, Douglas, issues useful booklet on sea and river fishing.

At present there are 8 reservoirs open for trout fishing, mostly fly and spinning only: the West Baldwin Reservoir, near the centre of the Island. A main road goes along its shallow side, but much of it is hardly fished. Clypse and Kerrowdhoo Reservoirs lie, one beyond the other, about 1½ miles north of Onchan Village. A private road runs, off the road to Grange Farm, to the attendant's house where there is room to park cars. Ballure Reservoir is just south of Ramsey. Access is by a private road branching off the main road to Douglas, on the Douglas side of the MER crossing near the town boundary. Cringle Reservoir is just north of the road from Ronague to Foxdale and is on the south slopes of South Barrule. Cars can be parked on the reservoir land. Sulby Reservoir is close to the A14 Sulby–Snaefell road. Block Eairy Reservoir stands at 750 feet above sea level, just west of Sulby Valley. Fishing involves steep hill walk. Fly fishing and spinning. Eairy Dam is alongside the A24 Douglas to Foxdale road. It is not a water supply and restrictions on the use of live bait do not apply. Reservoirs are stocked on a weekly basis with browns and rainbows up to double figures. There is a limit of 4 fish. There are also several private stillwater fisheries, including Kennislough, Lower Ballaclucas Farm, Trolloby Lane, Marown (Tel: 01624 851887); ¾ acre lake, stocked with large rainbow trout. Principal rivers as follows:

COLBY RIVER. Trout. This stream is 4m long; preserved in lower reaches.

DOUGLAS RIVER. Salmon, sea trout, trout. Douglas formed by junction of Dhoo and Glass, half a mile above the town of **Douglas**. River Dhoo is private fishing to Braddan Bridge, above which, somewhat polluted by agriculture. Glass largely rented by Douglas AC. Manx Game FC has fishing on these rivers, residents only, no guest tickets.

GLEN MOOR BURN, 3m long. Trout; fishing free, but not very good. Fishing station: **Kirk Michael**.

LAXEY RIVER. Trout; free but poor. This stream is 5m long. 1m above junction with sea at Laxey, Glen River (trout), 3m long, joins on right bank. Fishing station: **Laxey**.

NEB. Trout; mostly free and good; salmon from Aug. Neb (sometimes called Peel River) rises above **Little London** and Blabae and runs 3m to **Glen Helen** (Hotel: Glen Helen). It then runs 4m to **St John's**. Here **Foxdale River**, 6m long, joins on left bank. Hence to **Peel** is 3m. 3m S is **Glen Maye River** 4m long; sea trout below waterfall, trout above. **Cornaa River** starts below North Barrule, and runs to sea at Port Cornaa. River has big pool ½m up from sea, and further pools from Ballalass Glen, upstream.

SANTON BURN. 6m long; trout; mostly preserved, but poor; salmon from Aug. Fishing station: **Santon**.

SILVER BURN. Trout, sea trout; free. This stream rises on the slopes of South Barrule, runs 5m to **Ballasalla**, where Awin Ruy, 4m long, joins on left bank. Silver Burn runs 3m to the sea at **Castletown**. Best sport downstream for about 1m to Castletown.

SULBY. Salmon (from Aug), sea trout; free; moderate in lower reaches only, upstream from Claddaghs, poor.

WYLLIN BURN. 4m long; trout; free; fishing poor. Near **Kirk Michael**.

(For further information about sea fishing on the Island, see under Sea Fishing Stations)

ISLE OF WIGHT
(For close seasons, licences, etc, see Southern Region Environment Agency, p12)

Freshwater fishing on the Island is better than is generally appreciated. The **Yar** from St Helens, Bembridge, to Alverstone holds fair numbers of roach, dace and rudd, with perch, carp and bream to 7lb in some stretches. Isle of Wight Freshwater AA has coarse fishing for dace, roach, carp, bream, perch, tench, pike and others at Yarbridge and Alverstone on Yar, dt on bank for Alverstone only; **Gunville Pond**, Newport, Merstone Fishery, 3 coarse lakes (both members only), **Somerton Reservoir**,

Cowes, dt from bailiff. IWFAA membership £25, conc £10. At Morton Farm, Brading, Tel 01983 406132, is coarse fishing on small lake and R Yar. Hale Manor Lakes are both 1 acre, carp and mixed coarse. Hale Manor, Arreton, Tel: 01983 865204. Ideal junior coarse ponds at Jolliffes Farm, Whitewell, Tel: 01983 730783. Gillees Pond, Stag Lane, Newport: carp, rudd, roach, bream. Dt £2 from Scotties, *below*. Tackle shops: The Sport and Model Shop, 9 Union Street, Ryde; N R Young, The Sports Shop, 74 Regent Street, Shanklin; W Bates & Son, 5 Springhill, Ventnor; The Sports & Model Shop, Ryde; David's Food Market, Lane End Court, Bembridge; 'Scotties', 11 Lugley St, Newport and 22 Fitzroy St, Sandown. Light sea fishing, for which freshwater tackle may be employed, at Whippingham (River Medina), Fishbourne (Wootton Creek) and in Bembridge Harbour; mullet, bass, flatfish, etc.

ITCHEN
(For close seasons licences, etc, see Southern Region Environment Agency, p12)

Rises some miles north-west of Petersfield and flows via Winchester into Southampton Water at Southampton. Famous Hampshire chalk stream. Trout fishing excellent, but strictly preserved for most part. Some salmon and sea trout lower down, but also preserved. Principal tributaries are **Arle** and **Candover Brook**; both strictly preserved.

Southampton (Hants). Itchen and Test estuaries. Pout, whiting and eels in Southampton Water; and whiting, bass, grey mullet from the piers and quays. Free coarse fishing from public footpath between Woodmill and Mansbridge. **Lower Itchen Fishery**, Gaters Mill, Mansbridge, west End, offers salmon, brown trout and night sea trout fishing on season basis, and some dt. Contact Embley Ridge, Gardeners Lane, Romsey, Hants, or Tel: 0585 175540. **Leominstead Trout Fishery**, Emery Down, **Lyndhurst** SO43 7GA has 8 acres of trout and coarse fishing, trout dt £25, 5 fish limit. Coarse dt £5, jun £2.50. Tel: 023 8028 2610. Mopley Farm Cadland Fishery, c/o The Ruffs, Blackfield SO45 1YX (Tel: 023 8089 1617); several coarse ponds with specialist carp fishing, mirror, common, ghost, to 26lb plus. Access for disabled; various permits, incl dt on bank, £5.50, conc, night permit £7.50. For Holbury Manor Pond, with tench, carp, pike, roach, contact Gang Warily Recreation and Community Centre, Newlands Rd, Fawley SO45 1GA, Tel: 023 8089 3603. Tackle shop: Bells Sports, 9 New Rd, Hythe, Southampton.

Eastleigh (Hants) Trout, salmon and grayling; preserved. Eastleigh & Dist AC has various game and coarse fishing, incl 3 stretches of river, Upper and Lower Itchen Navigation, and 12 lakes. Dt £4, conc, for one of these, Lakeside Park, Eastleigh, from tackle shops. Membership £47 pa, joining fee £6. Bishopstoke FC has water, which affords excellent sport. Water holds large trout. Salmon run right up to Brambridge. Some sea trout also come up; private. Junior st from Borough Council for Bishopstoke Riverside Rd stretch. Tackle shop: Eastleigh Angling Centre, 325 Market Street.

Bishopstoke (Hants), ns Eastleigh. Salmon, trout and grayling; preserved by Bishopstoke FC and other owners.

Winchester (Hants). Trout above city; trout and grayling below. Free fishing on NRA licence between the city weirs, and the left bank of the **Itchen Navigation**, between Blackbridge and St Catherine's Lock. Portsmouth Services FFA has 1¾ miles below town; terms of club membership are described under R Meon entry. The Rod Box, London Road, King's Worthy, Winchester SO23 7QN, Tel: 01962 883600, offers dry fly fishing on st and dt basis and other rods on celebrated private stretches of the **Test** and on the **Itchen**, **Arle Anton**, and **Whitewater**, and on lakes. Charges on request. Tackle shop: The Rod Box (*above*).

Itchen Abbas (Hants). Trout; preserved by riparian owners. **Avington Trout Fishery**, three lakes plus stretch of R Itchen, provide excellent trout fishing. Open all year, stocked daily. Limit 2 brace. St and dt. British rainbow record broken there several times. (Tel: 01962 779 312.) Tackle Shop: The Rod Box, Kingsworthy, Winchester. Many hotels.

Alresford (Hants). **Candover Brook**, **Alre**, **Itchen**; trout; preserved by riparian owners. Grange Lakes, Alresford Pond; coarse fish; preserved.

KENT (lakes and streams)

BEWL WATER: The Fishing Lodge, **Lamberhurst**, Tunbridge wells TN3 8JH, (Tel: 018922 890352); 770 acre SW fly-only trout fishery. St (full) £499, 6 fish daily. (Mon–Fri) £390. Dt £14. Evenings, £11, 4 fish. Concessions for beginners and jun, with reduced limits. Motor and pulling boats, £19.50 and £12; evenings: £13.40 and £8. Courses of instruction, wheely-

boat for disabled on water. Season: April 3–Oct 31. Bewl Bridge Flyfishers' Club offers various advantages to members. Enquiries to Peter Firth, The Goal, Lower St, Tilmanstone CT14 0JD (Tel: 01304 611301).

BROOKLANDS LAKES, 20 acres, almost in centre of Dartford. Dartford and Dist APS, variety of coarse fish, carp to 30lb, tench, bream, roach, pike; dt £4–£6, conc, from bailiffs on bank. Tackle shop: Dartford Angling Centre, Lowfield St, Dartford.

BOUGH BEECH RESERVOIR. Near **Tonbridge**. 226 acres, trout fishing on season ticket only, dt for pike and coarse. Trout fishing Apr–Jun, coarse Jul–Mar, pike in Oct. Tickets from Mr E Crow, Honeycroft Farm, Three Elm Lane, Golden Green, Tonbridge TN11 0BS, Tel: 01732 851544.

BURNHAM RESERVOIR (3m north of **Maidstone**). Coarse fishery of 12 acres; carp to 30lb, 100lb bags of bream, good roach and chub. No day tickets, but membership offered. £43 pa, joining fee £15, conc. Contact Medway Victory Angling and Medway Preservation Society, 33 Hackney Rd, Maidstone, Kent ME16 8LN.

CHIDDINGSTONE CASTLE LAKE Good coarse fishing, especially carp. No night fishing. Prepaid booking advisable at weekends. Dt £8 from Custodian. One onlooker only, per fisherman, £3.50, no children. Apply to the Administrator, Chiddingstone Castle, near **Edenbridge** TN8 7AD (Tel: 01892 870347).

LARKFIELD LAKES. Three pits of 47, 20, 27 acres. Carp, tench, pike, bream, eels, roach, perch. St £34. Concessions on all for jun, OAP, dis. No dt. Applications to RMC Angling (see *Chertsey*).

LONGFORD LAKE. **Sevenoaks**. Private water of Holmesdale AS, who also have junior water Montreal Park Lakes; fishing for members and guests only, membership from Hon Sec; from Manklow Tackle Shop, 44 Seal Rd, Sevenoaks; A & I Tackle, Green St Green, Orpington.

LULLINGSTONE LAKE, near **Eynsford**. Trout. Kingfisher APS; no tickets.

MID KENT FISHERIES, Chilham Water Mill, Ashford Rd, **Chilham** CT4 8EE (Tel:

01227 730668, Fax: 738894). Coarse fishing on 18 lakes, from 26 to 3 acres, well stocked with all species. Catches include British record carp 55lb 15oz, bream to 15lb, perch, rudd, tench, and pike to 36lb. Purpose built match fishing lake with 104 pegs. St £125, half price concessions for OAP, juv, dis. A £5 dt is offered on one lake, with same conc. Trout fishing on river, £35–£18 per day, pre-booking only.

MOTE PARK LAKE. **Maidstone** (see Medway). Coarse fishery of 26 acres; large carp, roach, tench, bream; no day tickets, but membership is open, contact Medway Victory Angling and Medway Preservation Society, 33 Hackney Rd, Maidstone, Kent ME16 8LN.

PETT POOLS. Fishing stations: **Winchelsea**, 2m; Rye, 4m. 25 acres, coarse fish; dt £4 (limited) from T G King, Market Stores, Pett Level, nr Hastings TN35 4EH.

ROMNEY MARSH. Much good fishing on marsh, especially in main drains to Rother; best in summer (large bream shoals); water on low side in winter. Clubs with water here are: Ashford and Dist APS; Cinque Ports AS; Clive Vale AC (who fish Jury's Gap Sewer; Clive Vale reservoirs (carp), Ecclesbourne Reservoir, Hastings), Hastings, Bexhill and Dist AA (members only); Rye and Dist AS; Tenterden and Dist APS; Linesmen AC (also waters on **Medway**, **Beult** and **Stour**; details: Hon Sec). Tackle shops; Romney Tackle, The Avenue, New Romney; Point Tackle Shop, Dungeness, and Hastings tackle shops: Steve's, White Rock; Angling Centre, The Bourne.

ROYAL MILITARY CANAL. Summer fishing only; level partially lowered in winter for drainage. Stations: **Hythe** and **Ashford**. Cinque Ports AS has 7m from Seabrook outfall to Giggers Green; carp, bream, roach, rudd, tench, eels, tench, perch, pike; most sections have dt from bailiff or tackle shops. West Hythe Ballast Pit is members only. Rother FA fishes 3m from Appledore Dam to Iden Lock. Dt £3 from bailiff on bank. Sperringbrook Sewer, nr Appledore, is CALPAC water, and may be fished from Mock Hill Farm to Arrow Head Bridge. Tackle shops: Ashford Angling Centre, 3B Stanhope Sq; Hythe Angling, Dymchurch Rd.

SCHOOL POOL. At Oare, 1½m N of **Faversham**. Controlled by Faversham AC; large pool containing carp (30lb plus), tench, bream, roach, rudd and pike. Dt £5 in advance

only, from Mr and Mrs Kennett, 14 Millfield, Faversham, Tel: 01795 534516. Faversham AC also has Bysington Lake and Oare Lakes, Faversham, mixed fisheries with carp, tench, roach, etc. Members only. Twin Lakes, Uplees Rd, nr Oare, Faversham: dt £6 for carp, tench, roach, perch fishing. Tackle shop: Ashford Tackle, St Marys Rd, Faversham.

LANCASHIRE AND CUMBRIA
(Westmorland) streams
(For close seasons, licences, etc. see North West Region Environment Agency, p13 unless otherwise stated)

BELA. Cumbrian trout stream, flowing from Lily Mere to estuary of Kent at Milnthorpe. Much of its course is through low-lying country with heavy water. Size of fish better than in some northern streams; many dry-fly reaches. Salmon and sea trout below Beetham Mills private. One of the earliest of northern streams; fishing starts March 3.

Milnthorpe (Cumbria). Trout. Preserved by Milnthorpe AA and confined to members and guests. Association also preserves St Sunday's Beck from Deepthwaite Bridge and Peasey Beck from Farleton Beck downwards and thence, from confluence of these streams, to Beetham Mills, which is as far as salmon run. Fishing below mills private. Sport very good in March, April, May and Aug. Licences and tackle from Kendal Sports, Stramongate, Kendal. Hotels at Milnthorpe: Cross Keys, Bull's Head, Coach and Horses; Wheatsheaf at Beetham.

Oxenholme (Cumbria). Bela, 2m E. Beehive Beck, 1m E. Old Hutton Beck, 3m SE. **Killington Reservoir**; large area of water, 3m E. Pike, perch and some big trout. Now privately fished. (See Kendal).

CONDOR. Fishing station: Galgate. Brown trout and sea trout.

DUDDON. Fishing station: **Broughton-in-Furness**. Sea trout, salmon. Millom & Dist AA has rights to 366 yds of north bank from Duddon Bridge downstream, and Hall Dunnerdale stretch. Assn also has water on **Esk**, **Lickle** (which joins Duddon on left bank, close to Broughton-in-Furness), **Annas**, **Irt**, **Lazy**, **Devoke Water** (salmon, sea trout, trout); **Black Beck**; also **Baystone Bank**, Copeland. Membership and day tickets for Assn waters from Sec; Bridge Garage, Holmrook; Waberthwaite PO; Haverigg PO, Millom.

Ulpha (Cumbria). Good sea trout and salmon, few brown trout. All river below down to Ulpha Bridge private. **Devoke Water** (large trout) may also be fished from here. Millom AA has rights, wt and dt, limit 6 fish. Applications for membership to Hon Sec. Below this point Duddon runs into estuary. Hotel: Old King's Head.

KENT: Fast-flowing salmon and trout stream running into Morecambe Bay. Fishing reported much improved following pollution and drainage schemes. Salmon, sea trout, trout.

Kendal (Cumbria). Salmon, sea trout, trout. A few spring salmon with main run and sea trout moving up about June; fairly plentiful Aug onwards. Fishing for the public at Lower Levens Farm: st £85, day permits £5 and B & B £10 per night from Mrs Parsons, Olde Peat Cotes, Sampool Lane, Levens, Near Kendal LA8 8EH, (Tel: 015395 60096.) South of the town to Basinghyll Bridge (both banks) held by Kent AA. Tickets and licences from Kendal Sports (see below). Kendal & Dist AC fishes pond at Old Hutton, and both river and pond fishing nr Grange-over-Sands. **Killington Reservoir** (ns Oxenholme), is property of British Waterways; pike, perch and trout. Fishing rights leased to Kent AA, st £30, dt £5. Tackle shops: Carlsons Fishing Tackle, 64 Kirkland, Kendal; Kendal Sports, 28–30, Stramondgate, who issue licences. Hotels: County, Globe.

Staveley (Cumbria). Trout, salmon and sea trout in Sept and Oct. Staveley and Dist AA has 4m of local Kent and Gowan fishing. Tickets from D & H Woof, 22 Main Street, Staveley. Hotels: Eagle and Child, Duke William, Railway.

MINT (tributary of Kent): Best fished from Kendal. Joins Kent about 1m above town; holds good head of small trout. Kent AA has lowest water *(see Kendal).*

SPRINT (tributary of Kent): Joins Kent at Burneside. Burneside AA (see Burnside) has about 1m of fishing from junction with Kent. Kent AA has ½m (L bank only). Salmon and sea trout from Aug; brown trout small; banks much wooded.

KEER: Rises 4m above Borwick, runs into Morecambe Bay 3m below **Carnforth**. Good sea trout and brown trout (no coarse fish). Carnforth AA has water; wt and dt on application to Hon Sec. Wych Elm Fly Fishery,

Milnthorpe Rd, Holme, Carnforth LA6 1PX (Tel: 01524 781449): 2 acre lake with rainbow, brook, brown trout; dt £20, 4 fish, £11 half day, 2 fish.

LEVEN: Drains Windermere, and is joined by River Crake (from Coniston Water) at Greenodd, near Ulverston, before flowing into Morecambe Bay. Salmon, sea trout, trout. Ulverston AA has members only fishing on R Crake.

Ulverston (Cumbria). Salmon, sea trout, trout. Ulverston AA has members only salmon and sea trout fishing on **R Crake**, **Knottallow Tarn**, brown trout, and coarse on **Ulverston Canal**, 1¼m long, specimen tench, carp, etc; restocked; dt from Canal Tavern Inn; Angling and Hiking Centre, Rawlinson St, Barrow-in-Furness, Coopers, White Hart Yard, Ulverston. Match permits from AA Sec. Lakes: **Knottallow Tarn** (brown trout fishing, on associate membership to visitors). Hotels: Armadale, Sun, Queen's, King's, Bay Horse, Lonsdale House.

Lake Side (Cumbria). Salmon, trout, pike, perch, trout. Some free fishing; other sections of the shore private; inquire locally.

TORVER BECK (tributary of Coniston lake), Torver (Cumbria). Lakes: Coniston, 1m E; pike, perch and trout, Goat's Water, 3m NE. Beacon Tarn, 5m S. Hotel: Church House Inn.

CRAKE (tributary of Leven):

Greenodd (Cumbria). Crake; salmon, sea trout, trout. From Sparks Bridge to Little Dicks Bridge, Ulveston AA, members only. Assn. offers £2.50 dt on bank for **Ulverston Canal** fishing: coarse fish. **Rusland Pool River**, tributary of Leven. Forestry Commission, Satterthwaite issues tickets. Tackle from Coopers of Ulveston, 1 White Hart Yard.

Coniston (Cumbria). Yewdale Beck, Torver Beck, 2½m S. Duddon, 8m west; salmon, sea trout. Millom & Dist AA has water at **Duddon Bridge** and **Hall Dunnerdale**. Membership and tickets, *see Devoke Water.* Coniston Lake: pike, perch, char, trout and eels. Char fishing very good from May to October. Lake free to holders of E.A. licence. For boats and tackle, *see Coniston, English Lake District.* River Crake flows from S end of Coniston Lake; salmon, sea trout. Esthwaite Lake, 4m east; stocked trout fishery *(see Hawkshead).*

GRIZEDALE BECK (tributary of Leven): **Hawkshead** (Cumbria). Forestry Commission, small brown trout, low population at present, let to Grizedale AC. Contact Mr Grant, via The Theatre in the Forest, Hawkshead LA22 0QJ.

RIVERS ROTHAY & BRATHAY, **Ambleside**. WADAA fisheries. Open, brown trout 15th March–30th Sept, migratory trout 15th March–14th Oct. These rivers are the main feeders to Windermere and offer small river fishing for brown trout, seatrout and the very occasional salmon. They are best fished when above normal level using worm or fly. Maggots, cheese and offal baits are prohibited. The Association does not control all the fishing on these rivers and anglers should ascertain where angling is permitted. The large pool near the head of Windermere contains pike and perch as well as trout. Autumn fishing is usually best when lake trout and sea trout take up residence in the river prior to spawning. At this time of year very large trout can be caught. Dt £4.00 (juv/OAP £2), wt £10–£5, st £30–£15, from Tourist Information Centre, local fishing tackle shops. NB. This permit also allows fishing on Grasmere, Rydal Water, High Arnside Tarn, Moss Eccles Tarn, School Knott Tarn & Hayswater.

TROUTBECK (trib of L Windermere)

Scandal Beck, Ambleside; trout, preserved.

WINSTER: Parallel with Windermere for 6m. Joins the sea by **Grange-over-Sands**. Sea trout, brown trout, eels. Kendal & Dist AC has R Winster fishing at **Meathop**, nr Grange-over-Sands, stocked with coarse fish. Other club waters nearby include Witherslack Hall Tarn, roach, perch, eels, pike. Membership open. Wigan & Dist AA has 2m of river at Grange, with brown trout, sea trout and eels, dt £2. Assn also fishes 18 stillwaters in vicinity of **Wigan**, **Chorley** and **Hindley**, and 2 canals, all coarse fishing with day tickets; also stretches of **Rivers Ribble Elston**, **Wyre** at **St Michaels**, **Douglas** at **Wigan**, coarse fishing, members only. Contact Membership Sec.

LANCASHIRE
(lakes and reservoirs)
(see North West Region Environment Agency, p13, unless otherwise stated)

ANGLEZARKE RESERVOIR, **Wigan**. Trout, Ribble & Wyre FA. Dt from bailiff, £1–£1.20. For further information contact P Luff, NNW Ltd (see Greater Manchester).

BARROW-IN-FURNESS RESERVOIRS. Barrow AA has trout fishing in 5 reservoirs. No tickets. Furness FA (Game section) issues day tickets for stocked waters. Coarse section fishes 5 waters, 3m from Barrow-in-Furness, Ormsgill Reservoir.

BARNSFOLD WATERS. 7m NE of **Preston**. Two trout lakes, 22 acres, fly only. St and dt £18 to £7. Boats £5 to £12. F J Casson, Barnsfold Waters, Barns Lane, Goosnargh, Preston PR3 2NJ. Tel: 01995 61583. Tackle shop on premises.

BLACKMOSS RESERVOIRS, **Pendle**. Brown trout dt from Barley Information Centre. For further information contact Blackmoss FA, S Ogden, 4 The Bullion, Barley, Burnley, Lancs (Tel: 01282 611743).

BUCKLEY WOOD RESERVOIR, **Rochdale**. Leased by NWW to Rochdale Walton AS. Inquire Hon Sec (see also Mersey and Rochdale).

BROWNHILL RESERVOIR. Between Colne and **Foulridge**. Feeder for Leeds and Liverpool Canal. Holds brown trout; preserved by Colne AA, tickets for members' guests only.

CANT CLOUGH RESERVOIR, **Burnley**. NNW Ltd (see Thirlmere).

CHURN CLOUGH RESERVOIR, **Pendle**. Possibly to be re-let. NNW Ltd (see Thirlmere).

CLOWBRIDGE RESERVOIR, **Rossendale**. Coarse dt on site at Rossendale Valley Water Park Shop. NNW Ltd.

COLDWELL (LOWER) RESERVOIR, **Pendle**. Nelson AA. Trout day ticket from Coldwell Inn Activity Centre. For further information, NNW Ltd.

DEAN CLOUGH RESERVOIR, **Hyndburn**. Brown and Rainbow trout, fly only, Lancashire FFA water, dt £10, 2 fish limit, from Hyndburn Angling Centre, 71 Abbey Street, Accrington (Tel: Acc. 397612). For further information contact NNW Ltd (see above). Lancashire FFA also has members' access at Stocks Reservoir.

DILWORTH (UPPER) RESERVOIR, **Ribble Valley**. Trout, Ribchester and Dist AA, D Harwood, Ribblesdale House, Blackburn

Road, Ribchester, Preston PR3 3ZQ. Dt from Happy Shopper, Higher Rd, Longridge. For further information contact C.A.R. Manager Peter Guy, NNW Ltd (see *Thirlmere*).

DINGLE RESERVOIR, Blackburn. Dingle Fly Fishing Club. Dt £10–£7 from Bungalow sited on reservoir, and the Black Dog Hotel, Belmont. For further information contact Phil Luff, NNW Ltd (see *Greater Manchester*).

EARNSDALE RESERVOIR, Darwen. Brown and rainbow trout. Darwen AA has rights on reservoir; good fly water, dt £8, 2 fish, from Anglers Den, Darwen. For further information contact Phil Luff, NNW Ltd.

ENTWHISTLE RESERVOIR, Blackburn. Entwhistle Flyfishers, I A Rigby, 10 Wayoh Croft, Edgeworth, Bolton BL7 0DF. Dt £14. For further information contact Phil Luff, NNW Ltd (see *Greater Manchester*).

GRIMSARGH RESERVOIR, Preston. Red Scar AA, N Watson, 14 Farrington Lane, Ribbleton, Preston. Dt from Mrs D Dewhurst, 14 Longridge Rd, Ribbleton PR2 6LX.

GRIZEDALE LEA RESERVOIR. 9m south of Lancaster. Rainbow trout, 1 Apr–30 Nov; Kirkham and Dist FFC water, fly only, limit 3. Membership £150 plus £150 joining fee. Dt (limited), from Hon Sec, or from A Helme, The Veterinary Surgery, 13–17 Freckleton St, Kirkham, Preston; or from K Curwen, 59 Broadwood Drive, Fulwood, Preston.

HAGGS RESERVOIRS. Hynburn Road, **Accrington**. Roach, carp, chub, tench, Accrington AC water, members only. Water has disabled platform. Club also fishes Martholme length of **R Calder**, at **St Harwood**, coarse fishing, members only.

HEAPY RESERVOIRS. Chorley. Reservoirs I, 2, 3 and 6, roach, carp, perch, bream, tench. Wigan and Dist AA water. Dt on all except no. 6. St £16, juv £2. Map books £1.25 + SAE from Membership Sec K Hogg, 95 Holme Terrace, Wigan WN1 2HF or from bailiffs.

HODDLESDEN, Blackburn. Trout, Darwen Loyal Anglers, T Berry, 5 Springvale, Garden Village, Darwen BB3 2HJ.

LANESHAW RESERVOIR, Pendle. Trout fishing dt from The Sweet Treat, 51

Keighley Rd. For further information contact NNW Ltd (see *above*).

MITCHELS HOUSE RESERVOIRS, Higher Baxenden. Accrington & Dist FC waters; stocked fortnightly with 14in rainbows. Dt £8, 2 fish limit. Membership is open.

OGDEN RESERVOIR, Rossendale. Haslingden and Dist Fly FC; Trout fishing dt £14.50, 3 fish limit; contact W Monk, 6 Ryde Close, Haslingden. For further information contact Phil Luff, NNW Ltd (see *above*).

PARSONAGE RESERVOIR, Hyndburn. Trout fishing, Bowland Game FA, B Hoggarth, I Moorfield Rd, Leyland, Preston PR5 3AR, dt from Roe Lee Tackle Box, 336 Whalley New Rd, Blackburn, Tel: 01254 676977.

PENNINGTON FLASH, Leigh. Good coarse fishing. Pennington Flash AA issues st £2.50 and dt 50p. Inquiries to G Unsworth, 142 Chestnut Drive S, Leigh, Lancs.

LOWER RIVINGTON RESERVOIR. Managed and stocked by First Organisation, St Thomas Centre, Ardwick Green, N Manchester M12 6F2. Permits. For further information contact Phil Luff, NNW Ltd (see *above*).

UPPER RODDLESWORTH RESERVOIR. 35 acres in West Pennine Moors, managed by Horwich and Dist Fly Fishers Club. Stocked with rainbows to 9lb, and wild brown population. Day ticket £9 from The Black Dog Inn, Belmont; Royal Arms Hotel, Tockholes; or Fisheries Officer (Tel: 01254 704113). For further information contact Ian Watson, Manor Barn, Lower Hill, Tockholes, Lancs BB3 0NF. NWW Ltd owned reservoir.

LOWER RODDLESWORTH and **RAKE BROOK RESERVOIRS, Chorley**. Coarse fisheries with pike to 30lb, managed by Withnell AC. Dt from Brinscall Post Office, School Lane, Brinscall. NNW Ltd. For further information contact Withnell AC sec, B Wren, I Belmont Close, Brinscall, Tel: 830935 01254.

SABDEN RESERVOIR. Whalley Rd, **Sabden**. Accrington and Dist FC trout water. Members only.

STOCKS RESERVOIR. Slaidburn. 320 acre trout fishery, stocked weekly with brown, and rainbow trout, also indigenous stock of wild browns. Fly only, there is a close season. Boat and bank fishing, 20 boats and tackle in site, outboard an optional extra, Wheelyboat for disabled. St, wt, dt. 3 and 2 fish limit. Tickets from Mr Ben Dobson, Stocks Fly Fishery, Catlow Rd, Slaidburn BB7 3AQ (Tel: 01200 446602). Telephone before coming.

SWINDEN RESERVOIR, Burnley, 10 minutes' drive from town centre. Trout fishing, Burnley Angling Society. Dt £10 from Roggerham Gate Inn, below reservoir, or from Higher Cockden Farm, ½m away. For further information contact NNW Ltd (see above).

WALVERDEN RESERVOIR, Pendle. Coarse fishing for perch, tench, pike, eels, carp, roach. Dt and st from bailiffs on site. Further information from Pendle Leisure Services, Outdoor Recreation, Guy Syke, Colne, Lancs BB8 0QD (Tel: 01282 661230).

WITHNELL RESERVOIRS. Withnell Fisheries Ltd, Oakmere Ave, Withnell, nr Chorley, manage 3 reservoirs fishable with season ticket, £55. Waiting list, which restricts fishing to local anglers. Contact T F Hampson, 279 Hulton Lane, Bolton BL3 4LF.

WORTHINGTON RESERVOIRS. Wigan. 3 reservoirs of 5, 7 and 3 acres, all coarse with roach, perch, carp, bream, barbel. Wigan & Dist AA water, dt £2. For Assn fishing, see River Winster. Enquiries to K Hogg, Membership Secretary, 95 Holme Terrace, Wigan WN1 2HF. Tackle shops: Angling Centre, 15 Orrel Rd, Orrel, Wigan: Lake View Tackle, 38 Lodge Rd, Orrel, Wigan; and many others in Chorley, Westhoughton, Blackburn, Leyland, and Preston.

LEE OR LEA

(For close seasons, licences, etc, see Thames Region Environment Agency, p15)

Walton's river; flows through Bedfordshire and Hertfordshire then along boundary between Essex and Middlesex to join Thames near Blackwall; 46m long. Urban development and canalisation have largely removed its charm, but still holds good quantities of barbel, and large bream, carp, pike, chub, perch. Very little free fishing, but permits are obtainable from bailiffs on most stretches.

Tottenham (London). Fishing controlled by Lee Anglers' Consortium, Peter Green, PO Box No 19426, London E4 8UZ (Tel: 01279

654434). St £20, dt 2.50. Good access points are at Lea Bridge Rd, Hackney Marshes, Carpenters Rd, Dace Rd. Dt from bailiffs. Picketts Lock and Stonebridge Lock are popular fisheries, used for matches, with good roach and bream. TW reservoirs close to Tottenham Hale (roach, perch, carp, bream, pike; or stocked with brown and rainbow trout) (see under London). D/s of Enfield Lock, **Ponders End** is a good venue with large shoals of bream and roach. Tackle shop: Don's, 239 Fore Street, Edmonton N18 2TZ (Tel: 020 8807 5396/5219).

Enfield Lock (Middx). Plenty of roach, perch, bream, tench and pike. Day tickets. Controlled by Lee AC (see Tottenham).

Waltham Abbey (Herts): **Lee Relief Channel** from Hooks Marsh to Highbridge St, Waltham Abbey: 1½m of bank, mixed coarse fishing, with chub, tench, bream, carp, pike, and occasional bags of roach. This fishery is run by Lee Valley Regional Park Authority, Information Centre, Abbey Gardens, Waltham Abbey, Essex EN9 1XQ (Tel: 01992 702 200, Fax: 230). Dt should be obtainable on bank, in 2000/2001 season. LVRPA permits cost £2.80, day, £5 two rods, conc. Tackle shop: P & B Hall, 44 Highbridge Rd.

Cheshunt (Herts). Good chub, roach, bream fishing, controlled by Lee AC. (See Tottenham). Red Spinner AS has Cheshunt South Reservoir; carp. Members only. Annual subscription £250, plus £125 joining fee. Kings Arms and Cheshunt AS run Brookfield Lake, with carp, tench, bream, perch; dt £3 per rod, £5, 2 rods, from Simpsons below. Other society waters include local rivers, lakes and gravel pits. Matches, outings, newsletter organised, new members welcome. **North Met Pit**, gravel pit of 58 acres, various coarse species incl large carp, pike, tench; LVRPA water, st only; also **Bowyers Water**, 35 acre gravel pit, with carp and pike, st only, contact LVRPA (see Waltham Abbey). Tackle shop: Simpsons, Nunsbury Drive, Turnford EN10 6AQ, Tel: 01992 468799.

Wormley (Herts). **King's Weir Fishery**, Mrs B Newton, Slipe Lane, Wormley EN10 6EX (Tel: 01992 468394): (½m R Lee, both banks, and 1/2m of bank at Langridge Lake). Large carp (30lb), chub, dace, perch, bream, barbel, and pike. Dt £9 for 9 swims on Wier Pool; Back Stream, members only, £45 st, plus £4 key. Swims for disabled. **Slipe Lane Pits**, 4 gravel pits of 25 acres with large tench, bream, carp, pike, catfish. Dt on bank. Run by LVRPA (see *Waltham Abbey*).

Broxbourne (Herts). **Redlands Carthagena Fishery**, consisting of weir pool, 2 lakes (one with carp to 32lb); ¾m of Old R Lee, 1m of Lee Navigation, bream, tench, carp, chub, roach, rudd. St only, £40–£75, juv, OAP £25, from P Brill, Carthagena Lock. Tel: 01992 463656. Towpath from Nazeing New Rd to Dobbs Lock, £2.50–£1.50, from bailiff on bank. **Old Mill and Meadows Fishery**, Mill Lane, Weirpool, Lee Navigation, with roach, chub, pike, perch, run by LVRPA (see *Waltham Abbey*). Day tickets from bailiff on bank.

Hoddesdon (Herts), ns Rye House or Broxbourne. On Lee, Stort and New River Lee: Dobbs' Weir Fishery, Essex Rd; roach, pike, chub, carp, barbel. Dt from bailiffs. Admirals Walk Lake, 25 acre gravel pit at Conker lane, pike, tench, bream, roach, carp; both fisheries run by LVRPA (see *Waltham Abbey*). For coarse fishing at Crown Fishery, Dobbs Weir Rd, with carp to 35lb, catfish to 40lb, tench to 11lb, dt £4–£6, membership £25, contact Tackle Shop, 315 Amwell St, Hoddesdon EN11 8TP (Tel: 01992 462044).

Rye House (Herts). Roach, chub, dace, bream, pike, perch, tench. Rye House Bridge to October Hole is London AA water; West Ham AC controls east bank and Lee AC, west bank, at Fieldes Weir. Dt from bailiff.

St Margaret's (Herts). Old River Lee. River fishing from towing-path. Lee AC (see *Tottenham*).

Ware (Herts). River Lee Navigation, controlled by Lee AC, Tel: 020 8524 0869. Ware AC have members only carp ponds. Membership £14, concessions. Rib Valley Fishing Lake, Westmill Farm, Ware (Tel: 01920 484913) 13 acres, rainbow trout from 2lb. Dt £26, 4 fish, to £16, 2 fish.

Hertford (Herts). For **Lee**, **Mimram**, **Beane**, **Rib** and **New River**. Lee Anglers' Consortium (see *Tottenham*) controls the Lee angling from Hertford to Stort Confluence at Feildes Weir. Very good coarse fishing. Access points at Folly Bridge, Mill Rd, Marshgate Drive. London AA has stretch from Town Mill gate to junction with Lee Navigation (¾m); members only. For Hertford AC contact C Bite, Tel: 01992 467585. for Ware AC contact D

Bridgeman, Tel: 01920 461054; both clubs have local fishing. Tackle shop: Pro-Angling, Ware Rd, Hertford. Hotels: Salisbury Arms, Dimsdale Arms, White Hart, Station.

Hatfield (Herts). Hatfield and Dist AS has rights on river from Mill Green to Essendon (about 2½m); including 7-acre Broadwater (large carp and bream). Members only.

Luton (Beds). Tring Reservoirs (10m); Grand Union Canal (10m); Great Ouse (20m). Clubs: Milton Keynes AC leases **Milton Keynes Lakes** from AW; Leighton Buzzard AC (Tel: 01582 28114), Ampthill & Dist AC (Tel: 01525 715457). Tackle shop: Dixons, 95 Tavistock St, Bedford.

Tributaries of the Lee

STORT: Preserved from source to Bishops Stortford.

Roydon (Essex). Roach, dace, perch, pike, chub, bream, carp, rudd, gudgeon, eels, bleak, pope. Globe AS fishes Stort and backwaters here, with the species listed. Members only, £35 fee, conc. Water between road bridge and railway bridge is Two Bridges AS fishing; Hon Sec B Bird, 8 Ducketts Mead, Roydon. Global Enterprises Ltd, Roydon Mill Park, Roydon, Essex (Tel: 01279 792777) has 2m free fishing for guests camping or caravanning. This includes well stocked weir pool; 40 acre water-ski lake with carp to 30lb, pike to 25lb, and bream to 10lbs. Dt £5 per rod, or £15 for 2 rods, 24 hrs. Lychnobite AS leases Temple Farm Fishery, (about 2m of fishing) with Dt from bailiff on water. Two RMC Angling gravel pits of 16 acres plus 160 mtrs R Stort at **Ryemeads**, offering large pike, chub, dace, tench, bream and roach. No day tickets. St £22, concessions for jun, OAP, dis. *(For RMC Angling, see Chertsey.)*

Harlow (Essex). Coarse fishing at Netteswell Pond, Oakwood South Pond and on south bank of Stort Navigation between Burnt Mill Lock and Harlow Lock, all managed under agreement between Harlow Council and Stort Valley AC. Species are carp, roach, rudd, bream, tench, perch, pike, etc. More details from either club Secretary (Tel: 01279 437888); or bailiff (Tel: 01279 864874). Enquiries to Parks and Landscapes Services, Mead park Depot, River Way, Harlow CM20 2SE (Tel: 01279 446407). Boxmoor and Dist AS has stretch of Sort Navigation. *See Boxmoor.* London AA has water at **Spellbrook** and **Thorley**. Enquiries to Hon

Sec. Tackle shop: Harlow Angling Centre, 5 Long House, Bush Fair.

Sawbridgeworth (Herts). Good head of all coarse fish with many large roach; fishes best Sept onwards. Sawbridgeworth AS has from confluence at Spellbrook to confluence of Little Hallingbury Brook, left hand bank; pike fishing (after Oct 1). Visiting parties welcome; apply Hon Sec for reservation. Mixed lake fishery ½m from Sawbridgeworth Station, on Little Hallingbury Rd. Members only, £3 per rod.

Bishop's Stortford (Herts). Navigational stretch opened by British Waterways. Bishop's Stortford and Dist AS has coarse fishing to Spellbrook Lock (tickets), a length at Harlow, Cam at Clayhithe, lakes, 10 acre gravel pit. Tackle shop: Anglers Corner, 40A Hockerill St. Hotels: Foxley, George.

ASH: Fishing stations: **Widford** (Herts) and **Hadham** (Essex); a few trout, pike, etc; preserved.

RIB: Trout, coarse fish. For Rib Valley Fishing Lake, see *Ware*.

BEANE: This once-excellent trout stream has been largely ruined by abstraction. Some stretches still hold good fish, however. No public fishing except at Hartham Common, Herts.

MIMRAM: Trout, preserved.

LINCOLNSHIRE
(small streams)
(For close seasons, licences, etc, see Anglian Region Environment Agency, p14)

GREAT EAU or **WITHERN**. Rises above Aby and flows some 12m to sea at Saltfleet; coarse fish; much free water; fishes best in autumn.

Saltfleet (Lincs), ns Saltfleet, 3m. Grayfleet, South Eau, and Mar Dyke; coarse fish; some free water. At Saltfleetby St Peters is pond on which fishing is permitted by dt, purchased from shop near pond; no Sunday fishing. Sea trout in Haven in Sept; also flounders.

Louth (Lincs). Great Eau private above bridge on main Louth-**Mablethorpe** road, including Calceby Brook, Aby and South Ormesby Park; free below to licence holders as far as Gayton lugs, thence ½m private to members of Mablethorpe, Sutton-on-Sea

Dist AC (also another ¾m stretch). Louth Crown & Woolpack AC has small coarse pond at Charles St, good tench, membership £10. **Theddlethorpe** (Mablethorpe Dist AC), and free below Cloves Bridge. Altogether 10m free fishing to licence-holders; coarse fish, including good roach, bream, perch, pike, rainbow trout (few and mostly small) and grayling. **Lud** generally free below Louth to Alvingham. Coarse fishing in ponds at **Louth**, **North** and **South Somercotes**, **Fulstow**, **Saltfleetby**, **Legbourne**, **West Ashby**, **Hogsthorpe**, **Chapel St Leonards**, **Skegness**, **Wainfleet**, **Authorpe**, **Addlethorpe**, **Alford**, **Farlesthorpe**, **Spilsby**, all on dt from local tackle shops. Sutton Brick Pits, Alfred Rd, **Sutton-on-Sea**; dt at adjacent houses. Hatton Lake, trout, Tel: Wragby 858682. **Louth Canal** from **Alvingham** to sea outlet at **Tetney** controlled by Witham and Dist JAF; coarse fish. Tackle shops: Castaline, 18/20 Upgate, Louth (Tel: 01507 602149); Belas, 54–56 High Street, Mablethorpe. Hotels: Kings Head, Lincolnshire Poacher, both Louth.

STEEPING. Rises 5m above **Spilsby** (1m off on left bank), runs thence to **Wainfleet** and joins the sea 4m below near **Skegness**; coarse fish; Croft AC has stretch at Haven House; tickets. Witham and Dist JAF controls 20m from Wainfleet upstream, and **Wainfleet Relief Channel**. £2.50 temporary members ticket from Storr's Shop, Market Place, Wainfleet. Spilsby AA has **Ereby Canal**; good bream, tench, perch, etc; members only; confined to 13m radius; st and dt from Hon Sec or Higgs Bros Tackle Shop, Spilsby, who also issue licences.

LINCOLNSHIRE
(small lakes and ponds)

Ashby Park Fisheries, Horncastle LN9 5PP, Tel: 01507 527966. 6 lakes, mixed coarse fishing with carp to 21lb 9oz, bream to 9¾lb, and most other species, incl eels to 5¾lb. Dt £4 and bait on site.

Baston Fen Fishery, Baston, Bourne. Mixed coarse and specimen lakes with some very large bream. Mrs Wyman, Tel: 01778 560607.

Belleau Bridge Lake, Belleau Bridge Farm, **Alford**. 6 acre coarse fishery, dt from Mr Harrop, Tel: 01507 480225.

Brickyard Fishery, South Rd, **South Somercoates**, Louth LN11 7PY, Tel: 01507 358331. 4 acre coarse fishing water, dt £4 on site.

Charles Street Pond, Louth. 1 acre lake with crucian carp and tench. St only, from local tackle shops, open all year.

Fish Pond Farm, Usselby, **Market Rasen**, LU8 3YU, Tel: 01673 828219. 2 lakes, mixed coarse fishing, dt on site, £3, B & B & meals.

Goltho Lake, Goltho Wragby LN3 5JD, Tel: 01673 858358/858907. Lincoln, 10m. 2 acre mixed coarse fishery, dt £2 on site.

Grange Farm Leisure, **Mablethorpe**. 4 coarse lakes, 1 trout and 1 carp lake. Dt only, sold on site. Also tackle and bait shop, and cafe. Tel: 01507 472814.

Grimsthorpe Lake, Grimsthorpe and Drummond Castle Trust, Tel: 01778 591205. 36 acres, mixed coarse fishing.

Hartsholme Country Park Lake, Skellingthorpe Rd, LN6 0EY, Tel: 01522 686264; 27 acre lake, mixed coarse fishery, permits on site, st £16.50, dt £2.50.

Hatton Trout Lake, Hatton, nr Wragby, Tel: 01673 858682. Dt on site, £7.50–£5.

Haverholme Park Lakes, nr Sleaford; contact D J Inger, 13 Goodson Close, Boston. Carp average 2–3lbs, roach, bream, perch. Dt £3.50 on bank.

Lake Helen, near Sutterton. Mixed coarse fishery of 2.75 acres; contact H Greeves, Tel: 01205 460681, or Anglian Region EA.

Herons Mead Fishing Lake, Marsh Lane, Orby, Skegness, Lincs PE24 (Tel: 01754 873357); coarse fishery, carp to 20lb, roach, rudd, perch, etc; dt £3.50, on bank. Facilities, refreshments on site.

Hill View Lakes, Skegness Rd, **Hogsthorpe**, Chapel St Leonards, Tel: 01754 872979. Three lakes, two mixed coarse, one carp. Barbless hooks only.

Hollands Park, Wedland Lane, **Thorpe St Peter**, Tel: 01754 880576. Coarse fishing lake, dt £250 on site.

Lakeside Leisure Ltd, **Chapel St Leonards** PE24 5TU, Tel: 01754 872631. Three mixed coarse lakes, one with 10 species, the others 20 and 24 species respectively, dt on site, £3.20, £4.50 double.

Mill Road Fishing Lakes, Skegness. Two small lakes with common and mirror carp, roach, bream, tench. Information from P Cumberworth, Mill Road, Addlethorpe, Skegness (Tel: 01754 767586).

North Kelsey Park, North Kelsey LN7 6QH, Tel: 01831 132819. Large lake, mixed coarse fishery, dt on site.

North Thoresby Fisheries, Fen Lane, North Thoresby. 3 lakes, 2 fishable on dt. 1 acre trout, 4½ acre coarse, mostly carp. Contact J Casswell, Tel: 01472 812518.

Oham Lake, **Alford**. 2 acre coarse fishery, with tackle shop and other facilities on site. Contact C Beckenham, Maltby le Marsh, Alford (Tel: 01507 450623).

Olsten Fishery, Mill Lane, **Legbourne**, Louth LN11 8LT, Tel: 01507 607432; coarse fishing in lake, trout in chalk stream. Trout dt £12–£5, coarse £3.50, on site.

Pelican Pond, **Barton-on-Humber**, Tel: 01652 33600. 80 acre coarse fishery with large stocks of roach, tench, pike, eels, bream. St only, on bank. Contact North Lincs Sailing Club, Pasture Rd.

Redlands Pits, Lolham Level Crossing, West Deeping. Three lakes with tench and rudd fishing. Deeping St James AC, Tel: 01778 346355.

Rossways Water, 189 London Rd, **Wyberton** PE21 7HG, Tel: 01205 361643. Two lakes mixed coarse fishing, carp to 30lb, large bream and tench. Dt £3, subject to availability. Barbless hooks only. Caravans to let on site.

Skegness Water Leisure Park, Walls Lane, Ingoldmells. 7 acre lake with tench, perch, bream, golden orfe, and carp. Dt from manager's office, Tel: 01754 76019.

Starmers Pit, Tritton Rd, **Lincoln**, Tel: 01522 534174. Lincoln AA water; 7 acre lake, mixed coarse fishery with large pike, eels, carp, bream and tench. Dt on site.

Sycamore Lakes, Skegness Rd, **Burgh-le-Marsh** PE24 5LN, Tel: 01754 811411. 5 acre mixed coarse fishery of four lakes, with carp to 32lb, tench, rudd, roach, perch, orfe; Woodland Lake stocked with smaller fish, ideal for matches; dt £3.50, conc, at lakeside. Tackle and bait shop, lakeside cafe, holiday cottages to let on site.

Tattershall Leisure Park, Sleaford Rd, Tel: 01526 343315. 7 lakes, mixed coarse fishing, dt on site, £2.

Thorpe Le Vale Fishery, **Louth**. 5 acre trout fishery, brown and rainbow. Fly only. Dt from G Wildsmith, Thorpe le Vale, Ludford, Louth, Tel: 01472 398978. Season, Mar–Dec.

Toft Newton Trout Fishery, Toft-next-Newton, **Market Rasen** LN8 3NE (Tel: 01673 878453 or 08050 606630). 40 acre reservoir, bank and boat fly only fishing, stocked twice weekly, rainbow and brown trout. Season varies, usually 1 Mar–15 Dec. Dt £15, 6 fish, £7, 2 fish. Boat £9, £4.50 ½ day, disabled boat and facilities. Tackle hire and tuition on site.

Vickers Pond, Main Road, Saltfleetby, **Louth**. 1.5 acre lake with tench, bream, carp and grass carp. Dt on site. No groundbait, and carp not to be kept in nets.

Warren Pond, Warren Rd, **North Somercotes**. Small pond with carp, rudd, perch and bream. Mr Lowis, Tel: 01507 358350.

White House Fishery, Crossroads, **Baston Fen**, nr Market Deeping, Tel: 01778 342 155. Two lakes with rainbow, brown and brook trout. Tickets £6.50, 2 fish. Coarse lake, carp to 15lbs: tickets £5–£3.

Willow Lakes, Grantham. 5 lakes, 1 carp, 4 mixed coarse, dt on site. Contact Mr Chilton, Newark Rd, Foston, Grantham, Tel: 01400 282190.

Woodlands Fishery, Ashby Rd, **Spilsby**, Tel: 01709 754252. Three coarse lakes with mixed species, best carp 15lb 1oz, tench over 5lb, roach 2lb, best mixed bag 1997 31lb. dt £3.50, £5 two rods, conc. Tackle and refreshments on site.

LONDON
(Thames Water Reservoirs)

Most of the waters referred to below are in the area termed Greater London. All are easily accessible from Central London. A number are rented by angling clubs and reserved for members, but at others fishing is offered to the general public at modest charges on season or day ticket basis.

It seems appropriate to mention here two important angling bodies: first, the **London Anglers' Association**, which has water on many miles on rivers, streams and lakes (125 fisheries in all). The Association now has about 5,000 full members through 160 affiliated clubs. It has offices at Izaak Walton House, 2A Hervey Park Road, Walthamstow, London E17 6LJ (Tel: 020 8520 7477). For a brochure and application form please send a stamped addressed envelope to the above address. Annual membership (associate) £21.50. Jun, OAP, regd disabled £8.50.

The Central Association of London and Provincial Angling Clubs (CALPAC) has about 120 affiliated clubs and fisheries on rivers, canals and lakes in the South of England. Day tickets issued for many fisheries. Full details from Hon Sec.

Among tackle shops in Central London are: Hardy Bros, of 61 Pall Mall; C Farlo0w & Co Ltd, 5b Pall Mall Tackle dealers in the suburbs are too numerous to list. Tackle shops in Metropolitan area listed under individual centres.

Thames Water Reservoirs where fishing rights are let to clubs include the following:

Cheshunt (South) to Red Spinner AS, members only, no day tickets.

Cheshunt (North) to Kings Arms A.C.

Reservoirs open to the public for game fishing (stocked with rainbow or brown trout).

Walthamstow Nos 4 & 5 are stocked with brown and rainbow trout. Bank fishing, fly only on **5**.

East Warwick, fly only, let to syndicate.

Reservoirs open to the public for coarse fishing.

West Warwick Reservoir, **Walthamstow Nos 1, 2 & 3**, **High** and **Low Maynard**, **Coppermill Stream**. Dt on all except West Warwick and Lockwood, st only. Best catches to date include carp 34lb, pike 29lb, bream 13lb, perch 4lb 10oz, plus large roach, barbel, chub and dace.

LUNE

(For close seasons, licences, etc, see North West Region Environment Agency, p13)

Rises on Ravenstonedale Common (Westmorland) and flows through beautiful valley into Irish Sea near Lancaster. Excellent sport with salmon, sea trout and brown Lower reaches also well-stocked with coarse fish. August to October best for salmon and sea trout.

Lancaster (Lancs). Salmon, sea trout, trout, coarse fish. Environment Agency has Halton and Skerton Fisheries. Salmon, Jun 16 to Oct 31, sea trout, May 1 to Oct 15, brown trout Mar 15 to Sept 30. Coarse fishing June 16 to Mar 14, all weekdays only. Salmon, catch and release only, on E.A. waters. Permits for Upper and Lower Beats, Halton, also Skerton; £6 salmon, £4 trout, from 1 M Robinson, Newsagents, 6 Sycamore Rd, Brookhouse, Nr Lancaster (Tel: 01524 770544). Evening permits for sea trout on both beats at Halton, £7.50, from Anne Curwen, Greenup Cottage, Hornby Rd, Caton, LA2 9JB (Tel: 01524 770078). Mrs Curwen also sells permits for Lancaster and Dist AA, Caton fishing. Lansil Sports and Social Club has 1½m both banks just above tidal stretch, with additional coarse fishing for usual species plus specimen bream (12lb+). Salmon st £55 + £25 joining fee, other fishing, £25, conc. Littledale Fishery, nr Caton, mixed coarse; tickets from Morecambe Angling Centre, Thornton Rd, only (Tel: 01524 832332). Lonsdale AC fishes **Lancaster Canal**, northern stretch, tench, pike, mixed fishery; 2 lakes, and Upper Swantley mixed fishery. Open membership and dt, from tackle shops: Charlton and Bagnall, 3/5 Damside St (Tel: 01524 63043); Stephen J Fawcett, Gunsmiths & Fishing Tackle, 7 Great John Street (Tel: 01524 32033), who supply licences and specialist information on Lune, Greta, Wyre and Wenning; Gerry's of Morecambe, 5–7 Parliament St, Morecambe; Morecambe Angling Centre (above).

Halton (Lancs). Lune; salmon, sea trout, trout, coarse fish. Permits for Halton top and bottom beats, and other stretches, from 1 M Robinson, Newsagents, 6 Sycamore Rd, Brookhouse, Nr Lancaster (Tel: 01524 770544). Permits for Environment Agency water from Mrs Curwen, Greenup Cottage, Hornby Rd, Caton LA2 9JB.

Caton (Lancs). Lancaster and Dist AA has fishing over 6 bank miles divided into three sections. Dt is sold for one section only, 1½m both banks. Fourteen year waiting list for membership. Permits £10 to £20 depending on season, weekdays only, from Mrs Curwen, Greenup Cottage, Hornby Rd, Caton LA2 9JB. No dt Saturdays and Sundays, though Sunday fishing is allowed to members. Fly only when water level 1ft 6in or below, Worm prohibited in October, except at water level of 3ft. No maggot, shrimp, prawn or grub fishing. No boat fishing, no dogs. Prince Albert AS also have water, and at **Killington**. Bank House Fly Fishery, Low Mill, Caton LA2 9HX, has 2 acres stocked brown and rainbow trout fishing. Day and half-day tickets obtainable; fishing lodge, with all facilities, piers for disabled. Contact Mrs Jan Dobson, Low Mill, Lancaster Rd, Caton LA2 9HX (Tel: 01524 770412).

Hornby (Lancs). Salmon, sea trout, trout. Lancaster AA has Claughton stretch (see *Caton*). No dt. From Wenning Foot (North) for 3/4m, Southport Fly Fishers, members only.

Whittington (Lancs). Salmon, sea trout and brown trout. Apply to H G Mackereth & Son, Whittington Farm, Tel: Kirkby Lonsdale 71286/72375.

Kirkby Lonsdale (Cumbria). Salmon, sea trout, trout. Trout and sea trout fishing are very good; average 1½lb; sea trout up to 8lb. Kirkby Lonsdale AA has approx 4m of water, upstream and downstream of town. Limited 5 day visitors permit (except Oct) from Tourist Information Centre, 24 Main St, LA6 2AE (Tel: 015242 71437). Clitheroe AA has water commencing 10yds from Stanley Bridge d/s, on left bank past water board pipe bridge. Dt obtainable from Tourist Information Below Kirkby Lonsdale & Dist AA water, Lancaster & Dist AA has water. Lancashire FFA has fishing here and at Tebay. Entrance fee £250, annual subscription £250, half sub for youths 16–21. Redwell Carp and Coarse Lakes: 4 lakes of stocked fishing, dt £5, conc. Contact Ken and Diane Hall, Kirkby Lonsdale Rd, Arkholme LA6 1BQ (Tel: 015242 221979). Hotels: Royal, Red Dragon, King's Arms, Sun, Orange Tree. Pheasant Hotel at Casterton, 1m upstream, is convenient for association waters. Salmon (best August, September); sea trout (June onwards), trout.

Barbon (Cumbria). Lune, 1m W Barbon Beck. Barbon is good centre for Kirkby Lonsdale AA water. Hotel: Barbon Inn.

Sedbergh (Cumbria). Sedbergh AA has approx 3m on Lune and tributaries, 9m **Rawthey**, from source to Lune, 2m **Dee** and 1m **Clough**. Brown trout; salmon and sea trout from July. Visitors st £150 from Visitors Hon Sec; dt £10, wt £50, from "Three Peaks" Ltd, 25 Main Street (Tel: 015396 20446). Mr Metcalfe, Holme Open Farm, Sedbergh LA10 5ET (Tel: 015396 20654) has stretch of R Rawthey; tickets at the farm. Hotels: The Bull, The Dalesman.

Low Gill (Cumbria). Trout, sea trout and salmon (salmon and sea trout best at back end); about 2½m both banks preserved by A Barnes, Nettlepot, Firbank, Cumbria LA10 5EG, Tel: 015396 20204. Dt £10 or £15. Blackburn AA also has water.

Tebay (Cumbria). Salmon and sea trout (August onwards best), trout (average 3 to lb). Telbay AA has 15m of good water; wt £30, OAP £25, Oct £45. Juv £5. Limited dt from Cross Keys Inn. Occasional season permits, from Secretary. Other club, Lancashire FFA has water. Hotel: Cross Keys.

Orton (Cumbria). Trout (all season), salmon, sea trout. Pinfold Lake, **Raisbeck**; r trout, dt £14 (4 fish) from tackle shop J Pape, Market Place, Appleby. Accommodation at George Hotel. Licences: Davies, 8 North Terrace, Tebay.

Tributaries of the Lune

RAWTHEY: Trout, with sea trout and occasional salmon late in season. Sedbergh AA has virtually whole of river from its source at Fell End down to Lune, and tributaries Dee 2m, and Clough, 1m; visitor's st £150, wt £50, dt £10.

WENNING: Sea trout (good), brown trout, few salmon (late). Best latter part of season. Fishing station:

High Bentham (Yorks). Bentham AA has about 3½m of water; fast stream, good sport; visitors' tickets: st, wt, dt (jun ½) from Hon Sec. Ingleborough Estate holds 5m. st £25, wt £10

(both limited); apply Estate Office, Clapham via Lancaster LA2 8DR, Tel: 015242 51302; trout run 3 to 1lb. Prince Albert AS has stretches of Wenning at Hornby Castle and Robert Hall Estate. Accrington FC has Hazel Hall Farm fishing, near Clapham, stocked with 11in browns. Bait fishing, spinning and fly, members only. Barnoldswick AC have two stretches of Wenning, upstream from Farrars Viaduct, downstream from Clintsfield Viaduct. Bentham Trout Farm and Fishery is at Low Mill, Bentham LA2 7DA (Tel: 015242 61305); dt £12, 4 fish limit, to £6, 2 fish, conc. Hotels: The Coach House, Black Bull. Punch Bowl Hotel also has 3/4m private trout and sea trout fishing and issues dt £5. Clapham accom: Flying Horseshoe Hotel; New Inn, Arbutus House.

GRETA: Trout (4 to 6lb) and late run of salmon and sea trout. Nearest towns: **Ingleton** and **Burton-in-Lonsdale** (Yorks). Trout. Accrington FC has 2m, Burton, Wrayton and Cantsfield, stocked with 11in browns, members only. Hotel: Punch Bowl, Burton-in-Lonsdale (licences).

MEDWAY
(For close seasons, licences, etc, see Southern Region Environment Agency, p12)

Kentish river joining estuary of Thames at Sheerness through estuary of its own. Coarse fish (abundant bream, record barbel, 1993) with few trout in upper reaches.

Maidstone (Kent). Free on E.A. licence from Maidstone to East Farleigh, North Bank, except new mooring area. Maidstone Victory Angling and Medway PS have first class fishing from Yalding down to Maidstone, **R Rother** and **R Beult** fishing, and various stillwaters. Membership from Hon Sec and local tackle shops. Free fishing on Brookland Lake, Snodland Council, Tel: 01634 240228. **Monk Lake**: carp fishery, every species, fish to 28lb, also chub, tench, etc; dt £6, 24 hours, £10. Contact J Knight, 2 Port Close, Bearstead, Maidstone. **Johnsons Lakes**, Larkfield; large bream, carp and pike. Temporary membership from bailiff on bank. Mallaras Way Lake, details from Len Valley A & PS. **Abbeycourt Lake**, Sandling; coarse fishing, dt. Tel: 01622 690318 after 6 pm. Sittingbourne AC has 4 coarse lakes in vicinity, membership from Maidstone Angling Centre. Tackle shops: Maidstone Angling Centre, 15 Perryfield St, ME14 2SY (Tel: 01622 677326); Nicks Tackle, Knightrider St; Mid Kent Tackle, Milton St; all Maidstone. Medway Bait and Tackle, 64B St Johns Road, Gillingham. Inns: Medway, West Kent, Rose and Crown, Queen's Head.

East Farleigh (Kent). Free fishing as described under Maidstone; thence mostly Maidstone Victory Angling and Medway Preservation Soc water; weekday dt from Maidstone tackle shops. Inn: Victory.

Wateringbury (Kent). Large carp and tench, chub, bream, roach. Maidstone Victory Angling and Medway Pres Soc has most of towpath bank here and at **Teston**, incl Teston Bridge Picnic site, dt. Medway Wharf Marina, Bow Bridge, has fishing for boat and caravan owners using their services. Dt £4. Tel: Maidstone 813927. Barking AS has a meadow; members only but open to visiting clubs. Inn: King's Head.

Yalding (Kent). Chub, bream, perch, rudd, dace, roach, eels, and pike. Free fishing on E.A. licence u/s from Yalding Sluice 200m, south bank. Maidstone Victory Angling and Medway Preservation Soc has towpath bank downstream of Railway Inn, also Medway at **Nettlehead**, **Teston**, **Barming** and Unicumes Lane, weekday tickets from tackle shops, on bank for Teston fishing. Yalding AS has water; dt (weekdays only). Orpington and Dist AA has water on **R Teise** here, members only. Central Assn of London and Prov AC has one meadow at junction of Medway and **Beult**; members only, membership open. Other CAL-PAC stretch, 1,200 yds Yalding Medway, dt £4, conc, from bailiff on bank. No night fishing on CALPAC water. Inns: Railway (tackle, but no accommodation); George; Anchor (boats).

Tonbridge (Kent). Tonbridge and Dist A & FPS has 9m of Medway, 1½m of Eden and gravel pits of 4 to 8 acres. Dt for parts of Medway and one pit, only. Contact Sec for details. Vacancies for membership; £20 + £5 joining fee, concessions for OAP. Paddock Wood AC offer dt for **Gedges Lake**, coarse fishing. Tel: 01892 832730. **Mousehole Lake**, 3 acre fly only trout fishery, on B2015 at Nettleshead Green. Dt on site all year. Orpington and Dist AA fishes Medway and Eden, near Tonbridge. Members only. Tackle shops: Tonbridge Rod and Line, 17a Priory Road; Medway Tackle, 103 Shipbourne Road.

Tunbridge Wells (Kent). Royal Tunbridge Wells AS has coarse fishery at **Ashurst** and **Fordcombe**, trout waters on **Medway** from

Withyham to Ashurst, and coarse fishing from Ashurst to Poundsbridge (4m), also on **Teise** below Finchlock's Bridge to Hope Mill, **Goudhurst**. Grayling and barbel in places. Fishing on three ponds also. Membership limited. Annual subscription £60, joining fee £15, concessions for married couples and jun. Coarse fishing dt for Court Lodge Down, Neville Golf Course. Pembury 2388. Crowborough AA have a dozen ponds and lakes local to **Crowborough**, with large pike, carp, tench, bream; st £40, conc, from tackle shop Tackle shop: Crowborough Tackle, White Hill Rd, Crowborough, E Sussex. Other tackle shops: MA Wickham, 4 Middle Row, E Grinstead; Wadhurst Rod & Line, Highbury Place, Wadhurst.

Ashurst (Kent). Coarse fish, some trout, grayling, barbel to 12lb. Tunbridge Wells AS has water *(see above)*. Limited tickets for members' guests only.

Fordcombe (Kent). Trout, coarse fish, barbel to 16¼lb, large carp. Tunbridge Wells AS has water, limited tickets for members' guests.

Tributaries of the Medway

BEULT: Excellent coarse fishing; lower reaches noted for chub, bream and tench; trout higher. Gravesend Kingfisher A & PA (stretches at **Smarden**, **Hunton**, **Headcorn** and **Staplehurst**; members only); London AA has water at **Hunton** and **Linton**; members only. Dartford AA has fishing. CALPAC has 400 yds at Medway junction, members only. ACT Fisheries Ltd issue tickets for fishing between Linton and **Yalding**. 170 Sydenham Road, London SE26. Coarse fishing dt for Brogues Wood, Biddenden from Tel: 015806 4851.

EDEN: Coarse fish.

Penshurst (Kent). On Eden and Medway; coarse fish. Penshurst AS has rights from Ensfield Bridge to Pounds Bridge and from The Point on Medway to weir on Eden; members only. No dt.

Edenbridge (Kent). Coarse fish. 8m controlled by Edenbridge AS (members only) also a mile at Penshurst. Short stretches rented by Holland AS, also Crawley AS.

TEISE: Joins Medway at Yalding. Trout, coarse fish.

Laddingford (Kent). London AA has water for members only at Mileham Farm and Hunton Bridge right bank.

Goudhurst (Kent). Teise Anglers' and Owners' Association holds water from Goudhurst to Marden; brown and rainbow trout; mainly fly only, and winter grayling fishing. Members only (£175 sub, joining fee £50). Ass. also has stocked farm reservoir for trout fishing at Marden. Apply to B Wait, 101 Stanhope Grove, Beckenham, Kent. Season, April 3 to Sept 30.

Lamberhurst (Kent). Tunbridge Wells AS has trout and coarse fishing water d/s of the Chequers Hotel for approx 4½m; members and guests only. Mixed coarse fishery at Lamberhurst with limited permits offered, from Norwood Angling Centre, 100 Portland Rd, South Norwood SE25 4PJ. Tackle shop: Glyn Hopper Angling, High St.

MERSEY
(For close seasons, licences, etc, see North West
Region Environment Agency, p13)

Forms Liverpool Channel and seaport. Main river polluted and of no account for fishing except in higher reaches. Some tributaries contain trout.

Liverpool (Merseyside). Liverpool and Dist AA has stretch **Leeds and Liverpool Canal**. Northern AA has stretches on **R Dee** at **Worthenbury**, **Ribble** at **Salmesbury**; Worthenbury and Emral Brooks; and also fishes Bridgewater and Macclesfield Canals and **R Weaver** at **Vale Royal**, **R Glaze** at Glazebrook. Dt £2.50 on rivers, £2 canals, conc. For **Shropshire Union Canal**, see *English Canal Fishing*. Tackle shops: Johnsons', 469 Rice Lane; Taskers Tackle, 25 Utting Avenue, Liverpool 4 (Tel: 0151 260 8027); Hoppys, 14 Sefton Street, Litherland 21.

Wirral (Cheshire). Assn of Wirral Angling Clubs comprises 13 clubs, and actively promotes lake and pond fishing on Wirral. Club coarse fishing waters include Birkenhead Park Upper and Lower Lakes; Central Park Lake, Wallasey; Arrow Country Park Lake. Annual and monthly permits from bailiffs and tackle shops. Caldy Anglers have Caldy Ponds, Wirral, also 43m canal fishing. Members only.

St Helens (Merseyside). Two NNW coarse fisheries in vicinity: **Leg O'Mutton Dam**, controlled by St Helens AA, and **Paddock Dam**,

Holme Rd, Eccleston, with bream, roach, tench, perch, carp, pike. St Helens Ramblers AS, Hon Sec, Alec Twiss, 47 Exeter St, St Helens WA10 4HS. Good carp, roach, chub, tench and dace in **St Helen's Canal** (Church Street length) and in Blackbrook stretch. Lymm AC offer dt on Sankey St Helens Canal at Halton and Warrington. St Helens Tackle shops: Star Angling, 101 Duke St (Tel: 01744 738605); Angling Centre, 196 Islands Brow.

Stockport (Cheshire). Stockport & Dist AF has widespread coarse fishings, incl Combs Reservoir, Chapel-en-le-Frith (noted winter pike fishery); Ashton Canal, Manchester to Ashton under Lyne; **Rochdale Canal**, Rochdale, and Compstall Reservoir, Romiley. Dt on several waters, on bank or from local tackle shops and post offices in Staylbridge, Romiley and Stockport. Stockport Waltonians AA also has private waters; coarse fish and trout. **River Goyt**, Marple to Stockport, dt available on both banks from tackle shops. Tackle shop: Angling Centre, 145 Wellington Rd North, Stockport.

Whaley Bridge (Derbyshire). River here known as Goyt; polluted. Dt (not Sundays), for one bank only. **Cote Lodge Reservoir**, High Peak. Trout water, Old Glossop AC, dt obtainable. **Errwood Reservoir**, High Peak, Trout water, Errwood Flyfishing Club. Dt from tackle shops in Whaley Bridge, Buxton and Stockport. For further information on both these waters contact Peter Sharples, Team Leader, NW Water Ltd, Woodhead Rd, Tintwhistle, Hadfield via Hyde, Cheshire SK13 1HS, Tel: 01457 864187. **Peak Forest Canal** starts here; coarse, sport patchy. Lock pools at **Marple** stocked with carp and tench. Canal to Ashton Junction being opened and dredged. Tackle shops: J Hallam & Sons, Market St.

Tributaries of the Mersey

NEWTON BROOK (tributary of Sankey Brook):

BOLLIN:
Heatley (Cheshire). Occasional trout, roach, dace, pike. Lymm AC has several lengths of Bollin at Reddish and Little Heatley, near Lymm, part double bank, mostly single. Club also controls a large number of fisheries on Severn, Vyrnwy, Dane, Sankey St Helens Canal, and many lakes and ponds about the north of Cheshire with trout and coarse fishing. Some of

these are dt waters, membership costs £27 per annum, joining fee £12, conc, apply to N Jupp, Secretary (Tel: 01925 411774).

Ashley (Cheshire). Bollin, 1m N; trout, roach, dace, pike; Bollin and Birkin AA; private.

BIRKIN (tributary of Bollin):

Knutsford (Cheshire). Birkin, 4m; Bollin and Birkin AA has water; private. **Tabley Mere**, 3m, is let to Lymm AC; no permits. Toft Hall Pool, 1½m S; occasional permits. **Tatton Mere**, Knutsford, coarse fishing; let to Lymm AC. Dt on bank **Redesmere** and **Capesthorne Lakes** (6m S of Wilmslow on A34 road); Stoke-on-Trent AS waters. Capesthorne Hall stock pond: very good carp fishing, dt £6–£4 on bank, or from Keith Whalley, Bailiff, East Lodge, Capesthorne Hall, Macclesfield SK11 9JY (Tel: 01625 861584). Tackle shop: Trevor Allen, 16 Altrincham Rd, Wilmslow.

IRWELL:
Manchester. River polluted, but some waters have been leased to clubs. At **Poynton**, 10m out, Stockport & Dist FA has pool. St only. 18m from Manchester, at Northwich is coarse fishing in Weaver (see Weaver). Bolton & Dist AA has **Manchester, Bolton & Bury Canal,** from Hall Lane to Blue Wall length, 6 reservoirs, and other fisheries. No day tickets, but st from tackle shops in district. Warrington AA has a 20 mile stretch of **Bridgewater Canal** as well as water on Dee, **Ribble**, **Severn** and tributaries and **Dane**, reservoirs, meres, etc. Apply Hon Sec. Victoria AC controls **Turks Head Reservoir**, members only. Moss Side AS has water (see Whaley Bridge). Altrincham and District AC has stillwater and river fishing in south Manchester area. Membership £23 per annum, £15 joining fee, conc for juv and OAP. Victoria Planets Ltd, 25 Capitol Close, Moss Lane, Smithills, Bolton: 6 acre and 2 acre lakes, stocked with carp to 24lb, bream, roach, etc. Dt £4–£3, on site. Chorlton Water Park, Maitland Ave, Chorlton: dt and st fishing for large carp and pike. Tackle shops: David Marsh Tackle, 79 Long Street, Middleton; Trafford Angling Supplies, 34 Moss Rd, Stretford; Kear's, 1 Market St, Droylsden. **Bolton** tackle shops: V Smith, Highfield Road, Farnworth; Anglers Corner, Haliwell Road.

ROCH:
Bury (G. Manchester). Brooks polluted. Accrington and Dist AA has water on **Ribble**,

Greta, Wenning and **Calder**. Dt fishing. Bury and Dist AS has stretches of R Irwell, several small ponds and reservoirs including **Elton**; mostly coarse fishing. Bury AS mem £15 + £5 joining fee, concessions. Trout fishing at Entwistle (Entwistle FFC) and Dingle (Dingle FFC). **Haggs Reservoir**, Hyndburn Rd, Accrington, Accrington FC water. Tackle shop: Fishing Tackle, 12–14 Southworth Street, **Blackburn**.

Rochdale (G. Manchester). Rochdale Walton AS. **Buckley Wood**, 1m N (coarse and trout), also Healey Dell Lodge, dt only on application to Hon Sec. Rochdale and Dist AS has trout and coarse fishing at Castleton (dt 50p; visitors must be accompanied by member), and coarse fishing on **Rochdale Canal**, 3m from town; st, dt from tackle shops. Length of canal also held by Dunlop Cotton Mill Social Club; tickets from local tackle shop. **Hollingsworth Lakes**, Littleborough; coarse fish; dt from tackle shops: Towers of Rochdale, 52 Whitworth Road; Kay's, 18 St Marys Gate; Rochdale Angling Centre, 161 Yorkshire Street OL12 0DR (Tel: 01706 527604), who issues tickets for Todmorden AS and Bury AC. For Rochdale Canal see also Calder (Yorks) – Hebden.

TAME:
Ashton-under-Lyne (G. Manchester). River polluted. NWW reservoir **Walker Wood**, 2m NE; trout. Tackle shop: Pet Man, 142 Stamford Street.

COMBS RESERVOIR:
Chapel-en-le-Frith (Derby). **Combs Reservoir**, 2m W; 57 acres, a variety of coarse fish including pike to 27lb, carp to 20lb, roach, bream, tench, perch; dt £3.50; Bailiff collects on bank; enquiries to C N Farley, Lakeside, Combs Rd, Chapel-en-le-Frith, Tel: 01298 812186.

MIDLANDS
(reservoirs and lakes)

BARKER'S LAKE, **Ringstead**, 25 acres stocked with carp to 20lb, bream to 6lb, good pike in winter; part of Ringstead Island complex, with Brightwell's Lake, backwater and main R Nene. Wellingborough Nene AC water.

BLENHEIM LAKE. **Woodstock**, Oxon; excellent tench, perch, roach, bream in summer, small head of large carp; pike winter. Boat fishing only for visitors. Apply to the Estate Office, Blenheim Palace, Woodstock, Oxon 0X20 1PS for details of current charges. Tel: (during normal office hours) 01993 811432, Fax: 813108). Tackle shop: Predator Angling Centre, 6 The Kidlington Centre, Kidlington OX5 2DL.

BODDINGTON RESERVOIR, Byfield, (Northants). 65 acres; carp from 12oz to 4lb, plus roach perch and pike, opening April 2000. £5 per day on bank, no night fishing. 24-hour information line: 0113 281 6895. Or contact Fisheries and Environmental Manager, British Waterways, Southern Region, Brindley Suite, Willow Grange, Church Rd, Watford WD1 3QA (Tel: 01923 208717).

CARSINGTON WATER, nr **Ashbourne**, Derbyshire. Owned by Severn Trent Water Ltd, 2297 Coventry Rd, B'ham B26 3PU, Tel: 0121 722 4000. Opened as brown trout fishery in 1994. Season 29 Mar–7 Oct. Up to 8,000 browns stocked during 1999. Day and part-day tickets for bank and boats, plus concessionary for bank only; dt £12.50, evening £9. Rowing boats £9 day, £6; petrol boat £18 day, £4 evening. Disabled boat £6 day, must be pre-booked. Facilities, licences and catering on site. Enquiries to the Fishery Office, Carsington Water, Ashbourne, Derbys DE6 1ST (Tel: 01629 540478).

CASTLE ASHBY LAKES. Northampton 7m. Coarse fishing in 3 lakes, two carp and one mixed coarse, leased to Mr M Hewlett, 176 Birchfield Rd East, Abington NN3 2HG, Tel: 01604 712346. Dt waters. **Menagerie Pond** (specimen carp fishery). Membership £150; Details from Estate Office, Castle Ashby, Northampton NN7 1LJ, Tel: 01604 696232.

CLATTERCOTE RESERVOIR, Banbury (Oxon). 20 acres, principally carp to 20lb, chub, roach, perch, tench. Dt £5, night fishing permitted. match bookings welcome (Tel: 01923 208717). 24-hour information line: 0113 281 6895. Night fishing by arrangement, Tel: 01295 255158. Fisheries and Environmental Manager, British Waterways, Southern Region, Brindley Suite, Willow Grange, Church Rd, Watford WD1 3QA.

CLAYDON LAKES. Buckingham, 6m. Upper and Middle Lakes at Middle Claydon, near Winslow, are Leighton Buzzard AC water; Danubian catfish, pike-perch, big carp. Members only.

CLUMBER PARK LAKE. National Trust property, 4½m from **Worksop**; coarse fish

(including pike); st £40, dt £3 (jun and dis £1.50) from bailiff on bank.

CORNBURY PARK. Charlbury, nr Oxford. Rainbow trout fishing over 3 beautiful marl lakes set in an historic deer park. Day tickets over 2 lakes, membership only on remaining water. For further details and day ticket prices contact Cornbury Park Fishery, Southill Lodge, Cornbury Park, Charlbury, Oxon OX7 3EH. Tel/Fax: 01608 811509. Instruction on site. Accom at The Plough, Finstock.

COSGROVE LEISURE PARK Milton Keynes, 2m (Bucks). Coarse fishing on 10 lakes from 2 to 25 acres, and Rivers Tove and Great Ouse. 2 lakes members only, otherwise dt £3 , £1.50 juv from Manager, Cosgrove Leisure Park, Milton Keynes MK19 7JP, Tel: 01908 563360 Tackle and bait shop on site, food and refreshments, camping, caravan site.

CRANFLEET CANAL. Roach, perch, gudgeon. Trent Lock held by Long Eaton Victoria AS, also Erewash Canal, Long Eaton Lock to Trent Lock. Membership £13, concessions.

DENTON RESERVOIR. Denton (Lincs). Excellent mixed coarse fishing with large carp; held by Grantham AA; st £16, conc, from Hon Sec (Tel: 01476 575628), bailiffs and tackle shops. No day tickets.

DRAYCOTE WATER, near **Rugby** (Warks) 600 acre reservoir, brown and rainbow trout. Owned by Severn Trent Water Ltd, 2297 Coventry Rd, B'ham B26 3PU, Tel: 0121 722 4000. 46,000 rainbows stocked weekly, Mar–Oct. Dt £15, 8 fish limit; Evenings £10.50, 5 fish limit. OAP, jun, dis, £10.50. Boats £11.50, motor boats £20, evening £13. Bank anglers limited to 300. Disabled facilities, catering and courses. Optional catch and release. Information from Fishing Lodge (Tel: 01788 812018).

DRAYTON RESERVOIR, Daventry. 18 acres, principally carp to 6lb, also roach, perch and tench. Average catches, 50lb plus, with 200lb per day often recorded, record 304lb. Permits £5 per day from patrolling bailiff, £3, conc. Match bookings welcome, 120 pegs, food on site. 24-hour information line: 01132 816895. Fisheries Officer, British Waterways, Southern Region, Brindley House, Lawn Lane, Hemel Hempstead HP3 9YT (Tel: 01442 278717).

DUKERIES LAKES, Worksop. Welbeck

Estate fisheries controlled by Welbeck Estate Office. Clumber Lakes are fished by Worksop & District AA, members only. The Association has rights on **Sandhills Lake** and Steetley Pond (30 pegs), at Shireoaks near Worksop, with roach, rudd, perch; dt £2.50 on the bank.

EYEBROOK RESERVOIR. Caldecott (Leicestershire), off A6003 Uppingham to Corby Rd, south of Caldecott village, follow AA signs. 400 acres of excellent trout fishing. Well-stocked water, mostly rainbows, a few browns and occasional brook trout. Fly only, good bank and boat fishing. Season 27 Mar–1 Nov. Season and day tickets and E.A. licences obtainable from new, purpose-built fishing lodge with disabled access (Tel: 01536 770264). All bookings and inquiries to Fishing Lodge, Eyebrook Reservoir, Great Easton Road, Leics LE16 8RP (Tel: 01536 770256. Hotels: Falcon, High St East, Uppingham, Tel: 01572 823535; Vaults, Uppingham, 5m N; Strakis Carlton Manor, Corby. B & B at Mrs J Wainwright, Homestead House, Ashley Rd, Medbourne LE16 8DL (Tel: 01858 565724).

FOREMARK RESERVOIR. nr **Repton**, Derbys DE65 6EG. 230 acres, owned by Severn Trent Water Ltd (*See Draycote*). Season last Thursday in Mar–31 Oct. 25,000 rainbows stocked throughout season. Dt £12, 8 fish, afternoon £10, evening £6, 4 fish. Conc, £7.25, 4 fish. Rowing boats £10.50 to £4.50. Motor boats £19 to £9. Disabled facilities, catering and courses. Permits on site from Fishing lodge (Tel: 01283 703202).

GRAFHAM WATER. St Neots (Hunts). 1,560-acre reservoir stocked with brown and rainbow trout. Now managed by Anglian Water Services from the lodge at Mander Car Park, West Perry PE18 0BX. Records include b trout 19lb 12oz, r 13lb 13oz. Full st £519, midweek £435. Dt £14, 8 fish limit, evening £9, 4 fish. Beginners dt £4, 1 fish. Motor boats £9 to £18. It is advisable to book these in advance. New fishing lodge on site with tackle shop, restaurant, access for disabled. Tel: 01480 810531, Fax: 01480 812488.

GRIMSBURY RESERVOIR. Banbury (Oxon). Coarse fishery leased to Banbury AA. Dt £4 for non-members, concessions for juniors, from local tackle shops (see *Banbury*).

HARLESTHORPE DAM. Clowne, Derbys. Coarse fish, with pike to 22lb, carp to 32lb. St

£100, dt £5, £4 after 3pm, on site; night fishing £12 by arrangement, also tackle and bait. Enquiries to owner Carol Sibbring (Tel: 01246 810231).

LADYBOWER RESERVOIR, Ashopton Rd **Bamford**, S33 0AZ (Derbyshire). Season 6 Mar–31 Oct. St £250, midweek st £206. Dt £10.90, afternoon £7.70, conc dt £6.90. Boats £9.80 to £6.60, petrol motor £9.20. Disabled facilities. Limited permits from warden for fly fishing on R Derwent below Ladybower Dam. All prices include VAT. Enquiries to Fishery Office, Tel: 01433 651254.

NANPANTAN RESERVOIR. 2m S of **Loughborough**. 8 acre coarse fishery.

NASEBY RESERVOIR, Northants. 85 acres. Carp to 19lb, tench to 5lb, rudd. Leased by BW to Naseby Water AC, sec I A McNeil, Bufton, Walcote, nr Leicester LE17 4JS.

OGSTON RESERVOIR, near **Chesterfield**, Derbyshire. 203 acre trout fly fishery owned by Severn-Trent Water Plc, and fished by Derbyshire County AC, day tickets are obtainable from owners. Membership £185, annual subscription £145.

PACKINGTON FISHERIES, Meriden (Warks). Excellent trout fishing on 100 acres of pool, 2½m of river. Dt £16, boats £6.50. Dt for 2 in a boat, £38.50. Flexi 5-hour ticket £11. Fishing on **Somers** fishery for carp, tench, roach, perch, pike, bream and rudd. St £140–£70, dt £6.50–£3. Concessions for juniors and OAP. Reduced rates for evenings. Details from Packington Fisheries, Broadwater, Maxstoke Lane, Meriden, nr Coventry CV7 7HR (Tel: 01676 22754).

PATSHULL PARK FISHERIES, nr Pattingham, **Wolverhampton** WV6 7HY (Tel: 01902 700774). 75 acre lake, well stocked with b and r trout; fly only. St £240, incl boat hire, dt £16 for 4 fish, other fish £2.30 each. Afternoon £12, inc 2 fish. Boats £6. Permits from Fishing Lodge. Regular fly fishing contests held. Pike fishing is allowed during winter months. Small stocked coarse pool.

PITSFORD RESERVOIR, Northampton 5m. 750 acres, owned and managed by Anglian Water Services. Rainbow and brown trout, fly only, 42,000 fish released during season. Good fly hatches all season. Dt (8 fish) £14, conc £10.

Evening £9 (4 fish). Beginners £4. Boats £18 to £9. Pike fishing in Nov. Permits from Pitsford Lodge, Brixworth Rd, Holcot NN6 9SJ, Tel: 01604 781350.

RAVENSTHORPE RESERVOIR, Northampton 8m. 100 acres, the home of modern reservoir trout fishing, established 1891; owned and managed by Anglian Water. Brown and rainbow trout, fly only. Rod average '99, 5 fish. 2 fish limit, catch and release. Dt £15, £12 conc, evenings: £10. Beginners £5. Boats £10, £6 eve. Boat for disabled, and instructor on site. Apply to Pitsford Fishing Lodge, Brixworth Rd, Holcot NN6 9SJ (Tel: 01604 781350). Hotels: White Swan Inn, Holcot; Poplars Hotel, Moulton.

RUTLAND WATER, Leics. **Stamford** & A1 5m, **Oakham** 3m; managed by Anglian Water Services; Normanton Fishing Lodge, Rutland Water South Shore, Edith Weston, Oakham LE15 8HD, Tel: 01780 86770. 3,100 acres, 17m of fishing bank, largest stocked trout fishery in Britain. Browns to 15lb and rainbows to 13lb, 130,000 released per season. Pike fishing in late Oct–early Nov. 65 motor boats. Competition facilities, accommodation list. St £475 full, mid-week £435, 8 fish limit, conc £260. Dt £14, £10 conc, boat hire £18–£11. Full restaurant facilities, and tackle shop on site.

SHELSWELL LAKE, Buckingham 7m. Tench, perch, roach and pike, winter best; st £8, conc £3, from Hon Sec, Bicester AS and Allmonds Sports, Market Square, Bicester; boat at no extra charge. Bicester AS also has two stretches on **River Ray**; coarse fish; no tickets.

SHUSTOKE RESERVOIR. Shustoke; Coleshill 3m. Leased to Shustoke fly fishers by STW. St £255 to £305, dt £12, 5 fish limit, £7 for 4 hours, 2 fish, boat £3; t on site from 12 Apr. Tel: 01675 81702.

STAUNTON HAROLD RESERVOIR, near **Melbourne**, Derbys. Severn-Trent W coarse fishery, 209 acres, leased to Swadlincote AC. Tackle shop, Melbourne Tackle and Gun, 52/54 High St, Melbourne. Tel: Derby 862091

SULBY RESERVOIR. 1m **Welford**, 14m **Northampton**. Coarse fishing; exclusive syndicate fishery of 100 anglers, with specimen carp to around 35lb. Limited st only, £150. Contact MEM Fisheries Management Ltd, Bufton House, Walcote Lutterworth, Leics LE17 4JS.

SYWELL RESERVOIR. Northampton 6m. Now a Country Park. Tench to 10lb, pike (over 20lb), perch, roach and carp; members of Wellingborough and Dist Nene AC only.

THORNTON RESERVOIR. Cambrian Fisheries, Fishing Lodge, Reservoir Rd, Thornton, **Leicester** (Tel: 01530 230807). STW reservoir, 76 acres. Open 5 Feb–14 Nov. Trout, annual stocking of 15,000, fly only. St range from £329 to £141; dt £15 to £7, according to limit, which varies from 6 fish to 2 fish. Boats £6.50 and £4.50. Tickets on site, also tuition.

TITTESWORTH RESERVOIR, near **Leek** (Staffs). 184 acre trout water now leased by STW to Tittesworth Fly Fishers Ltd. St, long waiting list. Dt £8.75–£6.25, and boats £7.75–£4.75, 6–4 fish limit, advance bookings from fishing lodge at reservoir, Tel: 01538 300389, Dave Naylor, Karl Humphries. Concessions to jun, OAP and regd disabled.

TRIMPLEY RESERVOIR, near **Bewdley**, Worcs. Trout, fly only, from early March–July 31. Aug 1–Oct 15, mixed fishery; then coarse fishing until Feb 28. St £110 weekday, £75 weekend; mixed £40; coarse £15. There is a £15 joining fee. Dt for guests of members only. Write for details to sec, Trimpley AA.

WELFORD RESERVOIR, near **Welford**, Northants, 20 acre coarse fishery. Many specimen bream, pike, carp, tench, perch and roach. St £30 to fish 2 rods, (Jun half price) from BW or bailiff W Williams, Welford Grange Farm, Welford, Northants.

NENE

(For close seasons, licences, etc, see Anglian Region Environment Agency, p14)

Rises in West Northamptonshire and flows to Wash. Good, all-round coarse fishery slow-running for most part. Roach and bream predominate, the bream in particular running to a good average size. Excellent sport with carp in Peterborough and Northampton areas.

Wisbech (Cambs). Centre of intricate system of rivers and drains, including the Nene-Ouse Navigation Link; all waters well stocked with pike, bream, roach, perch and some good tench. Fenland Assn of Anglers is centred in Wisbech. Wisbech and Dist AA sub hires sections of **Pophams Eau**, **Sixteen Foot River** and **Middle Level Main Drain** (12 miles of fishing). Assn wt required. **Great Ouse Relief**

Channel provides 11m of good fishing from Downham to King's Lynn. Algethi Guest House, 136 Lynn Rd (Tel: 01945 582278), caters for anglers. Tackle shops: Brian Lakey, 12 Hill St; March Angling Centre, 88A High St, March. Hotels: Queens, Rose and Crown, Marmion House.

Peterborough. Excellent centre for roach, bream, chub, tench, carp, rudd, eels and pike. Peterborough AA now controls most of the N bank of the Nene from **Wansford** to the Dog in a Doublet and some fishings on the S bank in the same area. The Association also has water on the **Welland** from **Spalding** to u/s of Crowland. St £16, dt £3, conc. Dt **Ferry Meadows Lakes**, £3, from bailiffs. Whittlesey AA has local fishing on fenland dykes: **Bevilles Loam** from Ponders Bridge to Goosetree Corner; and **Whittlesey Dyke** from Ashline Sluice to Floods Ferry. Dt £3, juv £1, from bailiff. Yearly club card £10, conc, from Sec, or local tackle shops. Wansford AC waters now members only. At **Wansford** A1 road bridge, Stamford Welland AAA have ½m of south bank, downstream. First-class sport in fen drains and brick pits, but many pits being filled in. For Yarwell Mill, mixed coarse and carp lake nr Wansford, K Usher, Tel: 01780 221860. Eldernall Carp Lake, Coates, Whittlesay: £5 dt on bank for carp, tench, roach, etc. Barbless hooks only, no groundbait, hemp. Licences, st, wt and dt from tackle shop Webbs (below), for North Bank Trout Fishery (£12, 6 fish), and local coarse fisheries **Gerards Pit** at **Maxey**, **Werrington Lakes**, **Tallington Lakes**. Sibson Fisheries, New Lane, Stibbington PE8 6LW, have coarse lakes with large carp, tench, bream. Dt usually in advance. Tel: 01780 782621. Tackle shops: Webbs, 196 Newark Avenue PE1 4NP (Tel: 01733 566466), information and permits on various local waters; Sheltons of Peterborough Ltd (Tel: 01733 5652287), all local handbooks available; Wade, Peterborough; Angling Centre, Whittlesey (Tel: 01733 205775). Hotel: Newark.

Cotterstock (Northants). One mile of excellent fishing for roach, chub, bream, perch, tench, dace and pike held by Cotterstock AA here and at **Tansor**. St £5, conc, and dt £2 from B Wing, Manor Farm Cottage. Jun, OAP, clubs welcome. Deeping St James AC has Nene fishing here. All dt £3.50.

Elton (Northants). Leicester and Dist Amal Soc of Anglers has extensive stretches here and at **Nassington** and **Fotheringhay**. Dt from Hon Sec or bailiffs. Coventry AA has 55 pegs at Fotheringhay. Good head of tench, roach and bream. Dt £2.50.

Warmington (Northants). Warmington AC has 2 to 3 miles from d/s of Fotheringhay to u/s of Elton, members only. £10 pa, no dt. Water let to clubs for matches, of up to 50 pegs. Bluebell Lakes, Tansor, Oundle PE8 5HN (Tel: 01832 226042): fishery consists of Kingfisher, Swan and Bluebell Lakes, 1½m stretch of Nene, and Willow Creek, a backwater of 750 yds. Good coarse fishing with large carp, chub, bream, tench and pike. Membership and dt sold at fishery. Deeping St James AC fishes two stretches of Nene and coarse lake at **Stibbington**.

Oundle (Northants). Roach, bream, carp, tench, dace, etc. Oundle AA has water on both banks; limited st £10, dt £2. OAP free. Oundle AA has local Nene fishing. Coventry AA has 70 peg stretch with good head of tench and bream and roach, also large carp. St £7, night st £11. Wellingborough Nene AC has 3m at Barnwell, just upstream of Oundle and 2 acre gravel pit (tench, pike, perch and rudd). Members only. **Elinor Trout Fishery**, Aldwincle, 50 acre lake stocked weekly with browns and rainbows, fly only. Dt £14.25 (6 fish), evening £9, (3 fish), boats £7 or £5. Conc. Full st £410, boat, £305 bank. Enquiries to E Foster, Lowick Rd, Aldwincle, Kettering (Tel: 01832 720786). Coarse lake also on site, with tench, bream and roach. Perio Mill, Tel: 018326 241/376, has trout stream stretch of 1 km, fly only, £30, 4 fish limit. Hotels: Talbot, caters for anglers, Tel: 01832 273621; Ship; Chequered Skipper, Ashton (Oundle HQ).

Thrapston (Northants). Roach, dace, perch. Wellingborough Nene AC control backwater from Thrapston to Dentford. (See *Wellingborough.*) Kettering and Thrapston AA has **Aldwinkle Pits**. Earls Barton AC controls ½m R Nene at Ringstead, nr Thrapston; 1m at Cogenhoe; and 1½m at **Earls Barton**. Also Hardwater Lake, Earls Barton. Members only, membership £16, conc. Tackle shop: W Jaques, High Street.

Rushden, **Higham Ferrers** and **Irchester** (Northants). Coarse fish. With new sewage works completed, fishing now showing marked improvement. Rushden, Higham Ferrers AC have water at **Turvey** and **Sharnbrook** on

Ouse: barbel and chub, also three stretches of **R Nene** in Ditchford vicinity, and **Ditchford Lakes**. Information, tackle and Rushden club cards (membership £13, conc) from Dave Walker (*below*); Rushden and Webster, Corn merchant, Irthlingborough. Excellent trout fishery at **Ringstead Grange**, Kettering NN14 4DT (Tel: 01933 622960); 36 acres, well-stocked with large fish. Record brown 10lb 6oz, record rainbow, 14lb 4oz. Dt £14.25, limit 6 fish, conc £8.50; evening £9, 3 fish; boat for one or two £7 extra, evening £5. Tackle shop: D Walker, Rushden Angling Centre, 26 Church St, Rushden. Hotels: Rilton; Westward, both Rushden.

Wellingborough (Northants). Wellingborough Nene AC from Ditchford Weir to one meadow below Hardwater Crossing, plus 9 other Nene stretches. Other club waters: **Great Ouse** at Harrold; **Sywell Country Park Reservoir**, Ditchford, good tench fishing; Grendon Carp Ponds; **Barker's Lake**, pond, and backwaters at Barnwell, Ringstead, Denford and Ditchford. These fisheries contain many large carp, chub, bream, pike, etc. Membership £18, conc £6, from Hon Sec. Kettering and Thrapston AA has Nene fishing between Denford and Pilton, also **Islip Lake**, mixed coarse fishing, **Aldwinkle Pits** nr Thrapston. Northampton Nene AC has from Doddington up to paper mills, excluding Earls Barton AC water (1m) and water at **Billing** (*see Castle Asby, Billing and Northampton*). Ringstead Carp Fishery, 5 acre gravel pit with catfish, carp, etc. Contact P Holroyd, 10a Longfield Green, Honington, Suffolk IP31 1LH. Tackle shops: Ron's Tackle, 5 Church Way; Colin's Creel, 26A Hill St, Raunds, Wellingborough.

Castle Ashby (Northants). Pike, perch, bream, tench, roach; preserved for most part by Northampton Nene AC, which issues dt. Lakes on **Castle Ashby Estate** (1¼m S); pike, bream, tench, perch, roach; dt from bailiff at waterside or estate office. *(See also Midlands Reservoirs).* Hotel: Falcon.

Billing (Northants). Pike, roach, perch, bream, tench, chub: preserved by Northampton Nene AC (Tel: 01604 757589), which issues dt for 1½m on both banks of river and Ecton Gravel Pits off A45. Good coarse fishing at Billing Aquadrome. Seven lakes open from June 16 to Oct 16. St £15, wt £4, dt £1. All on site. Tel: Northampton 408181 or 01933 679985. At Earls Barton, Hardwater Lake, large mixed coarse gravel pit. Earls Barton AC, Tel: 01604 812059, or 812433.

Northampton (Northants). Pike, perch, bream, chub, roach, carp, etc; Nene AC controls north bank from Weston Mill to Clifford Hill Lock. Castle AA fishing includes Nene at Victoria Park, Barnes Meadow (north bank), Midsummer Meadow, Becket's Park, and lakes at Canons Ashby. Membership £23, conc, dt on some waters. Northampton good centre for lake and reservoir fishing. **Heyford Fishery**, Weedon Rd, Nether Heyford NN7 4SF (Tel: 01327 340002): a purpose-built match fishery, 1,200m long, 127 pegs, with annual stocking of 800lb of carp, roach, bream, and other coarse species. Dt £5, conc, on bank. Long Buckby AC has Nene fishing at Nether Heyford. Towcester and Dist AA has water on Nene at Kislingbury. Northampton Britannia AC controls much local canal fishing, members only. Affiliated with Leicester & Dist ASA, cards from local tackle shops: Gilders, 250/2 Wellingborough Road; Angling Centre, 85 St Leonards Rd; Sportsmans Lodge, 44 Kingsthorpe Rd.

Weedon (Northants). Pike, perch, bream, roach. **Grand Union Canal**. Northampton Nene AC has rights from Weedon to Yardley Gobion (16m); dt. At **Fawsley Park** are two lakes with pike, roach, rudd, etc; dt from Nene AC. Nene and Ouse licences needed for canal. **Hollowell Reservoir**, 140 acres, pike to 35lb, large roach and rudd. St £55, dt £5, conc. The Fishery Warden, c/o Pitsford Water, Holcot, NN6 9SJ, Tel: 01604 781350.

Tributaries of the Nene

OLD RIVER NENE:
March (Cambs). Pike, perch, bream, rudd, roach, tench. Fen drains. **Old River Nene** mostly free to licence-holders. **Reed Fen** (south bank) is now private fishing. **Twenty Foot** controlled by March and Dis AA (tickets). **Popham's Eau**, **Middle Level** are Wisbech AA waters. **Forty Foot** is now leased by Chatteris WMC. Dt £1 are sold on bank. **Mortens Leam**, 5m from March, 7m of river fishing from Rings End to Whittlesey. Wide variety of coarse fish. Dt on bank. Tackle shop: Mill View fishing Tackle, 3 Nene Parade, March. Hotels: Griffen, Wades, Temperance.

Ramsey (Hunts). Pike, perch, bream, etc. Ramsey AS has fishing on **Forty Foot Drain**, and **Old River Nene** at Ramsey St Mary's and Benwick: roach, bream, perch, tench, pike, zander. Dt waters. Contact Mr P E Aldred, 9

Blackmill Road, Chatteris PE16 6SR, Tel: 01354 2232. To the east and north of **Sawtry**, Holme and Dist AA have fishing on both banks of **Kings Dyke**, **Yaxley Lode**, **New Dyke**, **Monks Lode** and **Great Ravely Drain**. Contact Mr K Burt, 55 Windsor Rd, Yaxley, Peterborough, Tel: 01733 241119. Tackle shop: H R Wade, Great Whyte, Ramsey.

WILLOW BROOK: Trout, coarse fish; preserved.

King's Cliffe (Northants). Willow Brook. Welland, 3m NW.

ISE:
Kettering (Northants). **Cransley Reservoir**; roach, perch and tench. For st and dt on **Wicksteed Lake**, also preserved water on Nene at **Thrapston**, apply Kettering and Thrapston AA. Tackle and licences from Alans Angling Mart, 86 Rockingham Rd, Corby, Northants NN17 1AE, Tel: 01536 202900.

Geddington (Northants). Preserved to Warkton.

STRECK:
Crick (Northants). Streck, 2m S. Dunsland Reservoirs (pike, perch, etc) 3m SW; private.

Daventry (Northants). **Daventry Reservoir**, Daventry Country Park, Northern Way, Daventry NN11 5JB, Tel: 01327 877193. Coarse fishery, good pike fishing in winter, bream in late summer and autumn. Dt on bank. **Drayton Reservoir**, see *Midlands reservoirs and lakes*. Hellidon Lakes Hotel, Hellidon NN11 6LN has fishing, Tel: Daventry 262550.

NORFOLK AND SUFFOLK BROADS
(Bure, Waveney and Yare)
(For close seasons, licences, etc, see Anglian Region Environment Agency, p14)

Rivers Bure, Waveney and Yare, their tributaries and Broads are among the finest coarse fisheries in England. They contain pike, perch, roach, dace and large chub. Some banks of tidal water which may be fished free. For details, contact Environment Agency Fisheries, Tel: 01603 662800. Some Broads are preserved and can be fished on payment. Rivers and most Broads very busy with boating traffic in summer, so early morning and late evening fishing advised. Best sport in autumn and winter. Boats are essential.

BURE

Strong current from Yarmouth to little above Acle; upper reaches gentle and ideal for float fishing. The river contains a good head of coarse fish. Excellent roach, bream and pike etc, at Thurne Mouth, St Benets, Horning, Wroxham. Several Broads are connected and can be fished as well as tributaries Thurne and Ant.

Stokesby (Norfolk). Bream, roach, pike, perch. Strong tides and sometimes brackish; legering best; free.

Acle (Norfolk). Bream, roach, pike, perch. Tides often strong. River traffic heavy in summer. Acle and Burgh Marshes free fishing on E.A. licence. Inns: East Norwich Inn, Old Rd, Acle (Tel: 01493 751112); Travel Lodge, A47 By Pass, Acle.

South Walsham and **Upton**. 3¾m R bank below **Ant** mouth, and 1m right bank from S Walsham Broad to Bure confluence free to licence-holders.

St Benets Abbey, bream and roach. North bank from Ant d/s, Norwich & Dist AA. Dt for St Benets abbey and Cold Harbour from A T Thrower & Son, Ludham PO NR29 5QQ. Accommodation at Holly Farm, and Olde Post Office.

Horning (Norfolk); ns Wroxham, 3½m. Good coarse fishing; free to licence-holders; boat almost essential; roach, rudd, bream, perch, pike, tench; river very busy in summer, hence early morning and late evening fishing gives best results. At **Woodbastwick** Environment Agency has ¾m of right bank, tidal; free to licence-holders. Broads: **Ranworth** (tickets for Inner Ranworth from store on Staithe); **Decoy** (club water), **Salhouse** (dt issued); and **Wroxham**, small charge, upstream. Tackle shop: Granary Stores, The Staithe, Ranworth. Several boat yards. Hotels: Swan, Kepplegate and Petersfield House Hotel.

Wroxham (Norfolk). Roach, rudd, bream, pike, perch, tench; good pike and bream in winter; boats only. Much river traffic, summer. Broads: **Bridge Broad,** boats only. **Salhouse Broad**, right bank, dt issued. **Alderfen Broad**, specimen tench. Boats £5 per day from Wroxham Angling Centre, Station Rd, Hoveton. Hotels: Broads, Hotel Wroxham.

Coltishall (Norfolk). Boats in vicinity. Hotels: King's Head, Risings, Norfolk Mead.

Buxton Lamas (Norfolk). All banks now private.

Abbots Hall (Norfolk). Ingworth. Brown trout, stocked 4 times during season. 1m both banks, dry fly, or upstream nymph only, open to Salmon and Trout Assn members. Applications to Simon Dodsworth, The National Trust, Blickling, Norfolk (Tel: 01263 733471).

Bure Valley Lakes, nr **Aylsham** NR1 16NW, Tel: 0126358 7666. Three lakes of 3, 2 and 5 acres with trout to 15lb, fly only, carp to 30lb, roach and tench. Dt £12.50, trout, £5 coarse, £7.50 two rods. Instruction on site.

Blickling (Norfolk). Trout upstream from Ingworth Bridge. Abbots Hall, R Bure at Ingworth, 1m both banks, Salmon and Trout Assn members fishing. Tel: 01603 620551. Dt for **Blickling Lake** (20 acres), from bailiff at 1 Park Gates, Blickling NR11 6NJ; £3.50, conc. No night fishing. Tickets on bank in summer. Pike season Oct 1 to Mar 14.

Tributaries of the Bure

THURNE: Slow-flowing, typical Broadland river; tidal below Potter Heigham. Coarse fish, good bream and roach. Environment Agency water at **Potter Heigham**, **Martham**, **Thurne Marshes**.

Thurne Mouth (Norfolk). Good roach, bream, perch and eels. Hedera House, Tel: 01692 670242, has ½m of river, with fishing for guests at self-catering chalets. Contact Miss C Delf.

Potter Heigham (Norfolk). Popular centre; good roach and bream; fair-sized eels. Bure. 3m, S. Broads: **Womack**, 1½m; **Hickling Broad** and **Heigham Sound** (tench, bream, roach, perch). Approx 3½m left bank, Martham to Repps and 4½m right bank Martham to Coldharbour free to licence-holders. Access points at Ferry Rd, Martham; Potter Heigham Bridge and Repp's Staithe. Hotels: Broads Haven, Cringles, Broadland House. Boats from Whispering Reeds Boatyard, Hickling, Tel: 01692 598 314; Arthur Walch, Nurses House, Martham. Licences, tackle, etc. from Q/D Tackle, Bridge Road, Potter Heigham.

Martham (Norfolk). Rudd, tench, bream, roach, perch, pike; very little bank fishing; **Heigham Sound** 1m free on E.A. licence. Martham and Dist AC fishes **Martham Pits**, 3½ acres good coarse fishing, with tench to 6lb, bream over 7lb, carp to 17lb, good stock of silverfish. Tickets £3 from Broadland Fuels Garage, 2 Rollesby Rd, Martham. Membership £40 pa. Boats, all the year round: Whispering Reeds Boatyard, Staithe Rd, Hickling NR12 8BJ (Tel: 01692 598314). Tackle shop: Latham's, The Bridge, Potter Heigham.

ANT:
Ludham. Roach, bream, eels, perch, pike. 2¼m of the river, upstream and downstream of Ludham Bridge, free to licence-holders.

Irstead and **Neatishead** (Norfolk). Good bream, perch, rudd, pike; also tench and roach. Fishing free.

Stalham (Norfolk). River clear, slow-running and weedy in summer; roach, rudd, bream, perch, pike and few tench. Broads: **Barton**, 1m; bream, roach, eels, perch and big pike; free fishing. Boats from Barton Angler Country Inn, Neatishead NR12 8XP, or Cox's Boatyard Ltd, Staithe Rd, Barton Turf NR12 8AZ (Tel: 01692 536206). **Hickling**, 3m by road; good pike, bream, etc. Sutton Broad overgrown. Tackle shop: Broadland Angling and Pet Centre, 24–26 High Street NR12 9AN. Hotel: Sutton Staithe Hotel and Kingfisher. Nearest tackle shop, Wroxham.

Wayford Bridge (Norfolk). Upper Ant; head of navigation; fishing free to licence-holders; roach, rudd, perch, pike, tench, bream; boat advisable; river is narrow and fairly busy at times in summer; weedy and clear. Bait and tackle from Stalham. Good fishing also above the head of Ant Navigation in Dilham and North Walsham Canal, navigable to rowing boats as far as Honing Lock. Caravan site and food at Wood Farm Inn. Houseboat accom. from George Mixer & Co Ltd, Catfield, Gt Yarmouth, Tel: 01692 580355, who reserve ½m downstream.

North Walsham (Norfolk). Several coarse fisheries in locality. Gimmingham Lakes, with carp to 30lb; Roughton, with carp, tench bream, roach, and perch; Felmington, with roach, perch, tench, carp. Dt for all of these, and other local tickets and information from tackle shop Country Pursuits, 49 Market Place NR28 9BT (Tel: 01692 403162). Inns: Ockley House, Toll Barn.

SAW MILL LAKE: Fishing station: **Gunton** (Norfolk) near Cromer. 16 acre lake in Gunton Park, 3m; coarse fish; dt from bailiff, on bank. Tackle shop: Marine Sports, New St, Cromer NR27 9MP.

Horning (Norfolk). **Salhouse Broad**; too much traffic in summer, but good fishing in early mornings and from Oct to March. Dt issued. **Ranworth Broad** (tickets for Inner Ranworth from store on Staithe). **Malthouse Broad**; free. **Decoy Broad**; now open only to clubs. Tackle shop: Horning Fishing Tackle. Licences from Post Office.

Ormesby, **Rollesby** and **Filby**. Fishing by boat only, from Filby and Eels Foot Inn. These Broads are connected and undisturbed by motor cruisers and yachts, but electric out-boards may be used. Fishing good everywhere. Excellent pike in winter. Wt £27.50. **Little Ormesby Broad**, free fishing by boat only.

Salhouse (Norfolk). Salhouse Broad, 1m NE; few pike in winter.

Broads connected with the Bure

Wroxham Broad, 1m N; (see Wroxham); Information and boat-hire from Wroxham Angling Centre, Tel: Norwich 782453. **Decoy** or **Woodbastwick Broad**, 2m NE; fishing on payment. **Little Ranworth Broad**, 3m E; good for bream. These three are controlled by Norwich & Dist AA. **South Walsham Broad**, 5m E; private; good bream and pike fishing.

Wroxham (Norfolk). **Wroxham Broad**, boat fishing only. Dt from Tom Boulton, 175 Drayton Rd, Norwich, Tel: 01603 426834, and Norwich Angling Centre, 476 Sprowston Rd, Norwich. **Bridge Broad**, boat fishing only. **Salhouse Broad**, right bank, 2m SE. **Alderfen Broad** has specimen tench and bream; dt £5 from Wroxham Angling Centre, Station Rd.

Broads connected with the Thurne and Ant

Potter Heigham (Norfolk). **Heigham Sounds**; fine fishing in summer; pike fishing, roach and bream in winter (free). Pike fishing on Horsey (no live-baiting). Womack Water dredged and cleared of weed, and may be

fished from quay below. (For hotels, boats, etc, see entry under Thurne.)

Hickling (Norfolk). **Horsey**, **Barton** and **Hickling Broads**, bream, roach, pike, perch. All free except Horsey: dt from keepers. Licences from Post Office and stores; boats for hire.

Martham (Norfolk). R Thurne. Bream.

WAVENEY

Flows along Norfolk-Suffolk border. Fishing from tidal limit at Ellingham. Between Geldeston Lock and St Olaves, the tidal river gives some wonderful sport with bream in summer, winter roach at Beccles Quay.

Lowestoft (Suffolk). Oulton Broad and Waveney, which connects with Broad; bream, perch, roach, pike, etc; boats at Broad. Flounders and smelts in harbour. Good sea fishing in Oct, Nov and Dec from boats and beach for whiting, cod and flatfish. Several Broads within easy reach. Much of **River Hundred** is Kessingland AC water. **Oulton Broad** (Suffolk). Broad gives good sport with eels to 5lb, bream, roach, etc, but crowded with boats in summer. Bank fishing from Nicholas Everitt Park. Waveney near; 2m of free fishing at Puddingmoor Lane, **Barsham**; 170 yds at **Worlingham**; best from boat. Good perch and pike (best Oct–March); roach (good all season, best Jan, Feb, Mar), bream (moderate, best June–Nov); dace. **North Cove**; 400 yards with bream to 7lb, big pike, st from Post Office. **Oulton Dyke** (north side only); bream (excellent Aug, Sept, Oct); perch, roach, eels. Club: Oulton Broad Piscatorial Society. Tackle shops: Ted Bean, 175 London Rd; P & J Fishing Tackle, 52 High St, Kessingland. Hotels: Wherry, George Borrow, Broadlands.

Haddiscoe (Norfolk). **New Cut**: good coarse fishing; free. **Fritton Lake**, Countryworld, Fritton, Gt Yarmouth NR31 9HA (Tel: 01493 488288). 163 acres; well known for bream in summer, and pike in winter, also perch, roach, rudd, tench, eel, carp. Open all year. Dt, boats for hire, Wheelyboat for disabled; holiday cottages to let, with fishing included.

Worlingham (Suffolk). 170 yds of Suffolk bank; free fishing via Marsh Lane.

Beccles (Suffolk). Good roach, bream, pike,

etc; best early or late in summer but especially good Oct onwards, when river traffic eases off. Free fishing from Beccles Quay. 400 yds stretch at **Aldeby** is George Prior AC water. **Aldeby Pits** coarse fishery is 5m from Beccles, on Waveney. Tackle shop (see below) is helpful, and issue st and dt for waters belonging to Beccles, Bungay Cherry Tree, and Harleston and Wortwell clubs, on river and lakes. Charges range from st £17 to £5; dt from £1.50 to 50p. Tackle shop: Beccles Angling Centre, 27 Blyburgate. Hotels: King's Head, Waveney House, Ship House.

Geldeston (Norfolk). Good pike, roach, perch, bream, etc; free. Inns: Wherry (licences) and Geldeston Lock. Tackle shop in Beccles (3m).

Barsham (Suffolk). 2m free fishing on Suffolk bank from Puddingmoor Lane.

Bungay (Suffolk). Good roach, chub, bream, perch, pike and tench; fishes best at back end. Bungay Cherry Tree AC has from Earsham to Geldeston, 2m between Wainford and Ellingham, mostly roach, and **Ditchingham Pits**. Members only on all waters except **Broome Pits**, dt £2.50 on bank (Tel: 01986 895188). Club Hon Sec, Mr Gosling (Tel: 01986 892982). Membership £24, conc, from Bungay Angling Centre, Outney Meadow Caravan Park, who also offer fishing on private stretch of river. Suffolk County AAA has Bungay Common stretch. Dt, tackle and bait from N R Sports Shop, 4A Market Place.

Homersfield (Suffolk). Pike, perch, roach (large), dace, tench. 300 yds of free fishing. There is also excellent specimen carp fishing locally here and at **Wortwell** RMC Angling gravel pit. (For RMC Angling, see Chertsey.) Hotel: Black Swan, Homersfield IP20 0ET.

Harleston (Norfolk). Waveney, 1m S; coarse fish. Harleston, Wortwell and Dist AC has fishing on Weybread Pits, 6 lakes stocked with most coarse species. Waveney Valley Lakes, Tel: 01986 788676; Highfield Fishery, 3 lakes coarse, Tel: 01986 874869, dt on site; Mendham Trout Lakes, fish to 15lb, Tel: 01379 852328. Dts and information on all these local waters from Waveney Angling, 5 London Road, Harleston IP20 9BH, Tel: 01379 853034.

Eye (Suffolk). **Dove Brook**; large dace. Fishing in Waveney at Hoxne, 3m. **Weybread Pits,** permits from Mr Bowman, Tel: 01379 852248.

Diss (Norfolk). **Waveney** and **Dove**. Diss & Dist AC has good quality stocked water on Waveney at Scole, Billingford, Hoxne, Brockdish, 6m total, best end Sept onwards; Dove at Oakley, d/s of bridge, roach, rudd, bream, pike, tench; **Diss Mere**, 5 acres, mirror carp, tench, roach and crucian carp. No dt. St £17.50, conc £8.50, for all fisheries from P Peg, Tackle shop, 133 Victoria Rd, Diss ID22 3JN. Hotel: Saracens Head.

YARE

Rises few miles from East Dereham and flows through Norwich to Yarmouth. Tidal, still one of the best Broads rivers for roach and bream, the main species; specially good for roach in middle reaches, bream in lower.

Great Yarmouth (Norfolk). Broads and rivers. Rivers Yare, Bure and Waveney fall into **Breydon Water** (Bure joined in upper reaches by Thurne and Ant). In all, some 200 miles of rivers well suited to boat and bank angling are within easy reach; some Broads are landlocked, strictly reserved for angling and free from river traffic; others connected to rivers, but mostly best fished from boat. Many Broads easily accessible; also rivers **Bure**, **Thurne**, **Ant** and **Waveney**. Trout in Bure. Also good sea fishing. Tackle shops: Dave Docwra, 79 Churchill Rd; Pownell and Son, 74 Regent Rd; Greensteads Tackle, 73 High Street, Gorleston-on-Sea; Dyble & Williamson, Scratby Rd, Scratby, Great Yarmouth NR29 3PQ (Tel: 01493 731305).

Reedham (Norfolk). Strong tide; legering best; roach, perch, bream, eels; free at Langley on E.A. licence. Hotel: Ship.

Cantley (Norfolk). Roach, bream, perch; bream and perch plentiful; fishing free to licence-holders; mostly by leger. Inn: Red House.

Buckenham (Norfolk). Bream, roach, perch; pike; fishing free to licence-holders here and at Claxton, Rockland and Langley, 2,900 yds left bank and 5,200 right bank. Mouth of Hassingham Dyke is good spot. Lakes Strumpshaw Broad, 1m NW. Buckenham Broad and Hassingham Broad, 1m SE; preserved. Rockland Broad, 1½m SW on other bank of river; free.

Brundall (Norfolk). Roach, bream, perch in Yare. Several reaches between Coldham Hall and Surlingham Ferry can be fished by boat.

Surlingham Broad belongs to National Trust; fishing only fair in summer; water shallow and weedy; pike in winter.

Norwich (Norfolk). Free fishing at Earlham Bridge to Cringleford Bridge, 2m of left bank, with dace, roach, chub, bream, pike. **Wensum** above city holds fine roach, perch, dace, chub and pike. Good roach and bream fishing at **Rockland Broad**; 7m from Norwich; but poor access to banks. 10m from Norwich, Haveringland Hall Park, Cawston NR10 4PN, has excellent coarse fishing lake, open most of year on permit, from manager's office (Tel: 01603 87 1302/Fax 9223). Norwich AA has water on **Bure**, **Thurne**, **Ant** and **Yare**, **Ranworth Inner Broad** and **Woodbastwick Decoy** (fishing by boat only on last two waters); dt from Hon Sec and tackle shops. Anglian Water coarse fishery: **Taverham Mills**, Taverham, Norwich NR8 6TA (Tel: 01603 861014); lake, with carp, roach, pike, bream, etc; and stretch of R Wensum with barbel, chub, roach, dace; tackle shop, self-catering accom on site. Dt for lake, st only on river. Tackle shops: Norwich Angling Centre, 476 Sprowston Rd (Tel: 01603 100757); Gallyons Country Clothing and Fishing Tackle, 7 Bedford St NR2 1AN; John's Tackle Den, 16 Bridewell Alley; Tom Boulton, 173 Drayton Rd. Hotel: Maid's Head. Simon Lister, Riverside House, Brundal, NR13 5PY, large mail order tackle shop.

Tributaries of the Yare

CHET:
Loddon (Norfolk). Free coarse fishing in Chet at Loddon Staithe: roach, bream. This water now navigable and fishes best in autumn and winter when traffic finishes. Tackle from P Clemence, 22 High St, Loddon. Hotels: Swan, and Angel Inn, Loddon; Hardley Floods preserved; White Horse, Chedgrave.

WENSUM: Coarse fish (good chub and barbel).

Norwich (Norfolk). Tidal. Riverside Rd, Oak St and Hellesdon Mill controlled by City Amenities Dept. Free fishing at Fye Bridge Steps, Cow Tower, Bishop Bridge, Yacht Station and d/s of Foundry Bridge to apprx 100yds d/s of Carrow Bridge.

Costessey (Norfolk). Chub, roach, dace, bream and pike. Norwich & Dist AA have 600 yds u/s of Costessey Mill. Membership from

local tackle shops. At **Taverham**, 5 gravel pits known as the Ringland Pits, large carp, pike, roach, bream, and 480m R Wensum. St, conc. ½ price. From RMC Angling (see Chertsey). Dt from bailiff at lakes. **Costessey Pits**, 100 acres AW coarse fishery, dt from Taversham Mill tackle shop (Tel: 01603 861014). Shallowbrook Lake, 2¼ acres, coarse fish, st water, Martin Green, Tel: 01603 747667/1741123.

Drayton (Norfolk). Free fishing at Drayton Green Lane for half mile, with roach, chub, bream, dace and pike.

Attlebridge (Norfolk). Good trout fishing here, some miles of water being preserved. Tud, 4m S; private. **Reepham Fishery**, Beck Farm, Norwich Road, Reepham NR10 4NR: 3½ acre spring-fed lake, with carp to 28lb, tench to 6lb, roach, rudd. Dt £5 from bailiff on bank. Disabled swims, facilities on site. Open 6.30 to dusk.

Lenwade (Norfolk). Fishing in 3 old gravel pits set in 25 acres, administered by the trustees of two Great Witchingham charities. There is a lake with carp to 20lb. plus mixed coarse fishing. Permits £4 day, £8 night (conc. jun, OAP) from bailiff. Enquiries to Mrs D M Carvin, Blessings, The Street, Lenwade, Norwich NR9 5SD, Tel: 01603 872399.

Swanton Morley (Norfolk). Dereham & Dist AC has water, see Lyng, below. Swanton Morley Fishery, bream roach, rudd, tench, perch, pike, carp, Tel: 01362 692975. Permits and information from F W Myhill & Sons, 7 Church St, East Dereham NR19 1DJ (01362 692975). **Whinburgh Trout Lakes**, East Dereham, 4 acres of stocked b and r trout fishing. Tel: 01362 850201, Mr Potter. Accom with free fishing on R Wensum: J Carrick, Park Farm, Swanton Morley NR20 4JU (Tel: 01362 637457). Fishing and shooting parties welcome at Wensum Valley Golf Club, Beech Avenue, Taverham, Norwich NR8 6HP (Tel: 01603 261012). Permits for local fishing from Mr Marsham, Waterfall Farm, Swanton Morley.

Hellesdon (Norfolk). Roach, chub, dace, carp, pike. Free fishing from Mill Pool to New Mills.

Lyng (Norfolk). Fine roach, dace and some trout. Dereham and Dist AC has Wensum here, at **Swanton Morley** and at **Worthing**; chub, pike, roach, dace, etc; **Lyng Pit**; carp, tench, bream, pike, roach; **Worthing Pit**, specimen bream, tench, pike, carp; **Billinford Pit**, tench, bream, carp, roach; 6 pits at Swanton Morley with pike, bream, tench, roach and carp, perch, chub; and stretch of **Blackwater**, coarse fish. Membership £30, £15 conc, from Myhills (*below*), or from Secretary D Appleby (Tel: 01362 637591). London AA has water for members only. Mr Rogers, Lakeside Country Club (Tel: 01603 870400) has 26 acres of coarse lakes, carp to 30lb, Norfolk record bream 14lb, pike to 40lb. Accom and catering on site. Tackle Shop, Myhills, 7 Church St (Tel: 01362 692975). Other tackle shop: Churchills, 24 Norwich St, both Dereham. Accom: Park Farm, Swanton Morley, Tel: 01362 637457.

Elsing (Norfolk). Environment Agency has 1,270 yards of right bank.

North Elmham (Norfolk). Fishing in Wensum for pike, roach, perch, dace and few trout. Fakenham AC has Railway Lake, 1 acre, mixed coarse, members only. **Roosting Hills**, 6 acre lake at Beetley. For details of fishing contact P Green, Two Oaks, Fakenham Rd, Beetley, Tel: 01362 860219.

Fakenham (Norfolk). Trout, dace, roach, perch, gudgeon, eels. Fakenham AC has 2m, dt water, also **Willsmore Lake**, Hayes Lane, with carp, bream, tench, etc; 4 tickets daily on lake, £5, Mon–Sat from Dave's Fishing Tackle, Millars Walk (Tel: 01328 862543).

TASS or **TAES:**
Swainsthorpe (Norfolk). Yare, 3m N. **Taswood Lakes**, good carp and other coarse fish. Dt £4, night £4.50, conc. Tel: 01508 470919.

BASS:
Wymondham (Norfolk). Yare, 4m N at Barford and 6m N at Marlingford; roach. Club: Wymondham AC. Season tickets £5 from Sec, or Myhills Tackle, Queens Square, Attleborough. Tackle shop: F W Myhill & Son, Fairland St (branches at Dereham and Diss). Hotel: Abbey.

BLACKWATER: Trout; preserved.

Booton (Norfolk). Booton Clay Pit, with carp to 30lb, bream to 10lb and large roach, tench, etc; stocked by Cawston Angling Club. 24-hour dt £3.50 from bailiff on bank. Under 16, 50p. For further details contact S Brownsell, 3 Purdy Way, Aylsham NR11 6DH, Tel: 01263 732263.

Broads connected with the Yare

Buckenham. **Rockland Broad**, 1½m SW; good roach fishing and pike fishing in winter.

Brundall. Belongs to National Trust; shallow water grown up in summer, but good for pike in winter. C Bettell, 96 Berryfields, Brundall NR13 5QQ, runs guided pike fishing trips on the Broads.

NORFOLK (small streams)
(For close seasons, licences, etc, see Anglian Regional Environment Agency, p14, unless otherwise stated.)

BABINGLEY RIVER. Fishing station: **Castle Rising**, ns North Wootton, 2m. Rises in the lake at Hillington Hall, and is 9m long. King's Lynn AA has water; no tickets. See *King's Lynn – Ouse (Great)*.

GLAVEN. Rises 3m E of **Holt** and joins sea at **Cley**, 6m down. 1m at Cley. Fishing now held privately. No permits. There are several small coarse lakes in this area. **Letheringsett**, **Booton** at **Cawston**, **Selbrigg** at **Hemstead**; dt on bank, £2.50.

NAR. Rises above **Narborough** to enter the Wash at **King's Lynn**. Chalk stream brown trout fishing; private. 1m both banks below Narborough Mill, stocked, fish 11in upwards, dry fly and upstream nymph fishing only, reserved for Salmon and Trout Assn members. Applications from out-of-area members to David Burrows, Apple Tree Lodge, Squires Hill, Upper Marham PE33 9PJ (Tel: 01760 337222). Waiting list. At Narborough, 5 trout lakes. Enq to Narborough Mill (Tel: 01760 338005).

TASS. Rises N of **Wacton**, 11m S of **Norwich**, to enter Yare on outskirts of city.

OTTER
(For close seasons, licences, etc, see South West Region Environment Agency, p12)

Noted Devonshire trout stream flowing into English Channel immediately east of Exe. Mullet in estuary and some sea trout, with brown trout of good average size for West Country higher up, where hotels have some excellent dry-fly water.

Budleigh Salterton (Devon). Tidal. Free fishing from river mouth to Clamour Bridge (about 1½m, both banks) to visitors staying in East

Budleigh or Budleigh Salterton. Sea trout, brown trout, grey mullet plentiful but difficult to catch. Fishing on both banks from Clamour Bridge to Newton Poppleford. Sea fishing; bass, flatfish, etc, from extensive beach. *(see Sea Fishing Stations under Sidmouth)*.

Ottery St Mary (Devon). Some good trout water in vicinity.

Honiton (Devon). Deer Park Hotel, Buckerell Village EX14 0PG (Tel: 01404 41266), has 3m (both banks) of wild brown trout fishing; trout up to 2lb, average 1lb. Dt £30, £25 after 4pm, at hotel. Hotel also has 2 acre lake. 3 lakes with rainbow trout at Otter Falls, Rawbridge, nr Honiton. Otter Inn, **Warton**, has trout fishing on 100 yds of Otter. Coarse fishing on 3 acre lake at Fishponds House Hotel, Dunkeswell, EX14 0SH (Tel: 01404 891358). Carp, rudd, tench, and roach. Day and season tickets sold at hotel. Hollies Trout Farm and Fisheries, Sheldon EX14 0SQ (Tel: 01404 841428), trout pond of 1½ acres, spring fed. Open all year.

OUSE (Great)
(For close seasons, licences, etc. see Anglian Region Environment Agency, p14)

Rises in Buckinghamshire and flows north-east through Northamptonshire, Bedfordshire, Cambridgeshire, Huntingdonshire and Norfolk, entering the North Sea by The Wash. Coarse fishing throughout. Slow, winding river for most part. Roach and dace are to be found in quantity, together with barbel and bream. Between Newport Pagnell and Bedford there are large chub and barbel.

King's Lynn (Norfolk). Coarse fish of all kinds except barbel. King's Lynn AA has water on the Ouse from Modney Court to Denver Sluice east bank; Denver Sluice to Danby's Drove, west bank; on the Wissey, from Dereham Belt to R Ouse; on the **Relief Channel Drain**, King's Lynn to Denver Sluice; on the **Middle Level Drain** from St Germans to aqueduct, 8m; Engine Drain, Ten Mile Bank, and pits. Senior st £25, junior £5, conc £12, wt £10, dt £3.50, from bailiffs. Gatton Water, Hillington, nr Sandringham: coarse fishing in 8 acre lake, for visiting campers, and caravans. Tel: 01485 600643, Mr Donaldson. Woodlakes Holiday Park, Holme Rd, Stow Bridge, PE34 3PX (Tel: 01553 810414), 8m south of King's Lynn, coarse fishing on 5 lakes, the largest 12 and 10 acres; carp to 30lbs, pike, roach, tench, bream, rudd, perch, etc. Dt £5, 12 hrs, £10, 24 hrs, conc for juv, OAP. Contact Mary

Allen. Willow Lakes Trout Fishery, Mr Pat Gregory, Ash Farm, Chediston, Halesworth (Tel: 01986 785392): 2 lakes of total 4 acres, stocked, fly only, brown and rainbow trout; dt £15, 4 fish limit, half day £8.50, 2 fish. Swaffham AC has Bradmoor lakes, Narborough, stocked with carp, bream, etc. St £16.50, conc. Tackle shops: Anglers Corner, 55 London Rd; Geoff's Tackle Box, 38 Tower St, King's Lynn (Tel: 01553 761293). Hotel: Park View.

Downham Market (Norfolk). Coarse fish, sea trout; tidal. Tackle shop, Howlett Cycles and Fishing, 53 High St PE38 9HF (Tel: 01366 386067).

Hilgay (Norfolk). King's Lynn AA water on Ouse and **Wissey** (see *King's Lynn*). London AA has water on Ouse; dt from bailiffs.

Littleport (Cambs). Ouse and **Lark**; coarse fish, except barbel, good pike and bream, with roach, perch, zander. Littleport AC has fishing on Ouse: Littleport A10 Bridge u/s to Sandhills Bridge, both banks, except Boat Haven on west bank. Bream to 7lb, roach, rudd, perch, eels, pike, zander, carp. Permits £3 from bailiff on bank or £2 from tackle shop in village. Full membership £8, conc. London AA controls 14m of water from Littleport Bridge to Southery (Norfolk), both banks. Dt from bailiffs. Ely Beet Sports and Social Club has fishing on both banks of Ouse and Lark, at confluence. Contact Mr R J Oakman, Tel: 01353 649451. Tackle shop: Coleby's Tackle, Granby St.

Ely (Cambs). Free fishing from Lincoln Boatyard upstream to Newmarket Railway Bridge. Ely Highflyers have about 5m downstream from this and last mile of River Lark (Queen Adelaide stretch). Cambridgeshire and Isle of Ely Federation of Anglers: a body with no water under its own jurisdiction, but is comprised of some 24 angling clubs and societies. See club list for address. Rosewell pits hired by Ely Beet Sugar Factory FC; dt on bank. Dt for Borrow Pit from Cambridge FPS.

Earith (Hunts). Histon & Dist AC has apprx 1m opposite village, members only st £25. **Old West River**. Earith Bridge to Pope's Corner (Cambs); partly hired by Cambridge Albion AS; good coarse fishing. **Old Bedford River** from Earith to Welches Dam and **New Bedford Level** or **Hundred Foot** (tidal) from Sutton Gault to Ox Willow Lode controlled by Cambridge Albion AS and Shefford AS; members only but dt issued by Hon Sec for Ivel. Ploughman's Pit (good carp, bream, pike. The Hundred Foot (Earith to Sutton Gault), rented by Cambridge FPS, tidal; practically all coarse fish, except barbel; **Borrow Pit** nr Ely, coarse fish, dt £1.50, in advance, from Hon Sec or local inns for Cambridge FPS water. Cambridge Albion AS has stretch on **Delph** from Welches Dam to Chequers, Purls bridge. Great Ouse Fishery Consultative Association rents water on **Counterwash Drain**, **Old Bedford River**, **Pingles Pit** (Mepal) and the **Hundred Foot**. Affiliated clubs have rights. Members of Sheffield AAS may fish these waters, the **Delph** at Manea (Manea AC water) and the **Bedford River** from Purls Bridge to **Welches Dam**.

Over and **Swavesey** (Cambs). Bream, perch, chub, rudd, tench, pike, dace and zander. Sea trout runs up to the locks; fish over 12lb taken. Occasional salmon. St from Cambridge tackle shops.

Holywell Ferry (Hunts). Hotel: Ferry Boat. Pike, bream, roach, rudd, chub, etc; free; boats; good fishing, especially roach.

St Ives (Hunts). All coarse fish, bream, dace, perch, chub, gudgeon in quantity; also carp, barbel, rudd and tench. Ample bank fishing, but boats for hire. St Ives FP & AS has 3m water; st £12, dt £2, conc, from tackle shop. Adjoining water held by London AA. Histon & Dist AS has Holywell stretch. Tackle shop: St Ives Angling Centre, 5 Crown St PE17 4EB. Hotels: Golden Lion, Slepe Hall, Firs.

Godmanchester (Hunts). Good bream, roach, chub and chance of carp. Godmanchester A & FPS has about 10m. Tickets from Hon Sec or tackle shop. St £6, dt £1. London AA has Portholme Meadow, Berry Lane Meadows and 1¼m Old West River at Stretham (members only). Boats from Huntingdon; no free fishing. Tackle shop: Stanjay Sports, who manage **Woolpack Fishery**, Cow Lane, 60 acres of well stocked coarse fishing. St £35, £20 jun, OAP. Dt £2.50. Hotels: Black Bull, Exhibition, Bridge and George.

Huntingdon (Cambs). Chub, bream, roach and tench; good when boat traffic declines. Huntingdon AFPS has water from Town Bridge to Hartford Church. Platforms for disabled. Permits, st £10, conc £5, dt £3, juv st £5, from tackle shops. London AA (see *Clubs*) has 4½m of

Ouse, stretch of **Alconbury Brook**, **Brampton Mill Pool** and millstream, and other water at **Brampton**; members only. Tickets issued for some waters. Brampton AS has two stretches of Ouse, 4 brooks and 4 lakes. Mainly st (£15) but dt on river and one lake. Tackle shops: Sports & Fashion, 51 High St PE18 6AQ (Tel: 01480 454541); Kelly's Discount Angling Centre, 188 High St; Stanjay Fishing Tackle, 7 Old Court Wall, Godmanchester; Ouse Valley Angling, 25/31 Huntingdon St, St Neots.

Offord Cluny (Hunts). Stocked by Environment Agency. Chub, roach, bream, tench, carp, barbel, catfish. Offord and Buckden AS has 3½m of Great Ouse between St Neots and Huntingdon, incl 2 weir pools; dt £3, conc, from bank by car park. Several sections are free of boat traffic at all times. Coach-party enquiries from E Blowfield, 4 Monks Cottages, Huntingdon, Tel: 01480 810166.

St Neots (Hunts). St Neots and Dist Angling & FPS has 6 sections from Nuffield down to Wray House, Chawston Lake, carp over 20lb, Wilden Reservoir; good tench, chub to 7lb, bream, roach and big carp. St £25 from tackle shop. Dt £3, conc, on most of R Ouse fishing, from bailiffs. Letchworth and Dist AA has water at **Offord D'Arcy**. No dt, membership £33 conc. London AA has water at **Tempsford** and **Blunham** (see *Ivel*). Tackle shop: Ouse Valley Angling, 25/31 Huntingdon St, St Neots.

Biggleswade (Beds). Ouse, Ivel, Biggleswade, Hitchin & Dis. AC AA has 7m on mid Ouse at Wyboston, and 15 acre lake at Eaton Socon with large carp, tench, rudd, bream. St £18, conc, from sec of local tackle shops. Blue Lagoon, **Arlesey** (4m S); large coarse lake, Letchworth and dist AA. No dt, membership £33, conc. Tackle shop: Rods Tackle, Arlesey.

Bedford (Beds). Approx 4m water in town centre and above, free to E.A. rod licence-holders. Council controls 3 lakes at Priory Country Park, dt £2 on bank. Bedford AC has fishing and issues limited dt at £5, obtainable from Dixon Bros, along with tickets for 7 other local fishing clubs. Vauxhall AC controls Radwell complex, 6m of Ouse, and 6 gravel pits of total 100 acres, members only; club also holds stretch of R Ivel, and 6 gravel pits at Sharnbrook; st £25, conc £8. Membership details from R Morris (Tel: 01582 571738). At **Kempston**, Vauxhall AC lease west bank, Kempston AC has 2½m on

Biddenham side, dt from Bleak Hall Sports or on bank. Blunham and Dist AC has stretches at Gt Barford, 1,000 yds; Willington, 2,000 yds; and Oakley, 1,500 yds, good mixed coarse fishing with roach, chub, bream, barbel, etc; members only, £25, £7 conc. Ampthill FPS fish Ampthill Reservoir, and Marston Pits, membership £18. Hotels: Embankment, Swan, Lion. Tackle shops: Dixon Bros, 95 Tavistock Street MK40 2RR (Tel: 01234 267145); Sportsman Lodge.

Felmersham (7m N of Bedford). Ampthill FPS stretch here, at Pavenham and at Goldington Storm Drain. Membership, £18. Concessions. Vauxhall AC fishes ¾m here and ¼m at **Willington**, membership £25. Letchworth and dist AA has left bank d/s of road bridge. No dt, membership £33, conc.

Sharnbrook (Beds). Wellingborough & Dist Nene AC has ¾m upstream of **Harrold**. Leighton Buzzard AC has water on left bank here. Ampthill AC has 1½m stretch on river at Dairy Farm, Renhold, with Gadsey Brook and Westminster Pool, and Stafford Bridge stretch. St £18, (½ price conc.) for RMC Angling **Harrold Fishery** (1,500m Ouse, 1,200m Ivel and Lower Caldecott), with carp, chub, roach, dace, pike, catfish, barbel. No dt. Apply to RMC Angling (see Chertsey).

Newton Blossomville (Bucks). Coarse fish. Northampton Nene AC has water; strictly limited dt £2 from Hon Sec.

Olney (Bucks), Coarse fish, good bream. Leighton Buzzard AC has ¾m stretch at **Stoke Goldington**, from Gayhurst Spinney to brook, st £14.50; jun, OAP £4.

Newport Pagnell (Bucks). Good barbel, roach, bream, chub, perch. Stretch fishes well in winter. RMC Angling has 3m of river above town at Tyringham Estate, offering large barbel, chub, bream, roach and dace. St £20, conc. (For RMC Angling, see Chertsey.) Newport Pagnell AA leases Newport Pagnell Lakes from AW. At **Great Linford** there is a complex of gravel pits holding bream, roach, tench and pike on which the fishing rights are now held by ARC. **Vicarage Spinney** is 8 acre trout fishery at **Little Linford**, stocked with large r, 11lb to 18lb. St £200, dt £10, 4 fish, and boats £5. 6 acre b trout lake, large fish. Tel: 01908 614969. Hotel: Bull Inn (club HQ).

Stony Stratford (Bucks). Deanshanger and Stony Stratford AA has 6m of Ouse, bream, roach, perch, chub and pike, plus Grand Union Canal at **Castlethorpe**, st £15, dt £4 on bank, or £4 from Lake Bros, Church St, Wolverton, Milton Keynes. Milton Keynes AC also has fishing here, and between Wolverton and Haversham. **Cosgrove Lodge** lakes at Cosgrove (Northants): noted for roach, tench, bream, pike; dt on water. Kingfisher Sporting Club, Deanshanger, has lakes of 36 acres. Trout, fly only. Dt £25.60 or £17.40 (non members), £18.40 to £10.25 (members), 4 fish and 2 fish. Tel; 01908 562332. Hotels: Cock; Bull.

Buckingham (Bucks). Chub, roach, perch, dace, bream, pike. Buckingham and Dist AA has several miles of fishing on Ouse and tributary Padbury Brook, plus two stillwaters in area. Good quality coarse fishing throughout, with increased water flows of winter months bringing out best in the river. Assn records include carp 39lb 4oz, pike 27lb 4oz, bream, chub and tench over 7lb. Adult membership £30, dt £4, conc, from Jakeman Sport, 5 Bourbon St, Aylesbury; J & K Angling, Sheep St, Bicester; Tingewick PO; Londis, 41 Nelson St, Buckingham. Mounthill Angling Syndicate has 2m between Beachampton and Deanshanger, mostly double bank, with large perch, pike, roach, dace, bream, barbel; membership limited, contact P Welling, 1 South Park Gardens, Berkhamsted HP4 1JA. Leighton Buzzard AA, Claydon Lakes, 6m; no dt. At **Mursley**, Church Hill Fishery, Swanbourne Rd MK17 0RS: 3 lakes of 15 acres stocked with r and b trout. Dt £25, evening £15, 4 and 2 fish. Tel: 0129672 0524. Pimlico Farm Pools, Tusmore, Bicester (Tel: 01869 810306): 3 lakes with carp, perch, roach, rudd, tench; 50 pegs, open dawn till dusk; disabled access, matches, self-catering accom.

Tributaries of the Ouse (Great)

WISSEY:
Hilgay (Norfolk). King's Lynn AA have 2m of both banks down to Ouse. St £14, wt £5, dt £2.50. London AA issues dt for Five Mile House Farm.

LITTLE OUSE: Good bream and roach.

Brandon (Suffolk). The above species, plus dace, perch, pike (good), a few chub and zander. Brandon and Dist AC has 2 ponds and ¾m river at Recreation Park, and 1½m L Ouse at Weeting, Norfolk. No dt, membership £11 annually with concessions, from Recreation

Centre. Thetford and Breckland AC has water above bridge. Hotel: The Ram.

Thetford (Norfolk). Little Ouse and Thet. Roach, rudd, tench, chub and pike; and dace to specimen size. Fishing free for 7 miles through town centre out to Santon Downham.

LARK: Trout and coarse fish.

Mildenhall (Suffolk). Trout, carp, rudd, roach, perch, tench, bream, pike, dace, gudgeon, eels, chub, bream. Mildenhall AC has several stretches excellent coarse fishing on Lark at Mildenhall, u/s and d/d at Isleham Lock, and West Row Drains, around West Row village. For £10 st, contact Hon Sec, Tel: 01638 718205. From Bury St Edmunds to Lackford controlled by Bury St Edmund's AA; trout water; no permits. Lark APS has water between Lackford Bridge and West Row, with 5 mile coarse section containing roach, rudd, carp, pike, bream, eels, perch. Trout membership £100, coarse £12, conc £3–£1 from Hon Sec. Disabled facilities at Barton Mills and Mildenhall. Tackle shops: Colbys, Littleport; Little Downham Tackle; Matthews Garden Centre, Lakenheath. Hotels: White Hart, High St; Riverside, Mill St.

Bury St Edmunds (Suffolk). Coarse fish. Bury St Edmunds AA has L Ouse, Blackbourne and Stour stretches, and lakes at Rougham, Sicklemere, and Thetford, mainly carp. St £32.50, jun £15, OAP £12.50, from John Easdown (Tel: 01284 753602). Tackle shop: Tackle Up, 49a St John's Street, IP33 1SP (Tel: 01284 755022). Tackle Up has information on a variety of coarse fisheries in area, incl Weybread Fishery, with large carp, roach etc; Marsh Farm Lakes, Saxmundham; Barway Lake, nr Ely; Cross Drove Fishery, Hockwold-cum-Wilton; Swangey Lakes, Gt Ellingham.

CAM: Excellent fishery, with good roach and pike. Best catches between Baitsbite Lock and Clayhithe Bridge.

Waterbeach (Cambs). Waterbeach AC has fishing on both banks here, and on Bottisham and Swaffham Bulbeck Lodes. Contact H Reynolds, Tel: 01223 351696. Cambridge FP & AS has Reach, Burwell and Wicken Lodes.

Cambridge. R Cam can fish well, with roach, chub, dace, and many other species. Some good stretches of free fishing on common land, but disallowed on college property. University

Sports and Social Club controls R Cam at Cantelupe Farm. Permits from club. Cam from near Pike and Eel Pub, Chesterton, d/s through Baitsbite Lock to Clayhith Bridge, Cambridge FP & AS; st £16, conc, dt £3 in advance, from Hon Sec or Coopers (below). Society also has about 4m of the **Hundred Foot River** from Earith Bridge to Sutton Gault and sole rights on whole of **Burwell Lode** and **Reach Lode**, stretch of **Great Ouse** at **Great Barford**, 1m of **Lark** below **Prickwillow Bridge**; and lakes; inquire Hon Sec for permits. Waterbeach AC controls Cam, Baitside Lock area, also at **Upware**, Humphreys Wash and Wests Wash. Club also has rights on **Swaffham Bulbeck Lode**, and Leland Water, which is for members only. Cambridge Albion AS controls Cam at Wicken; Dimmocks Cote to Upware; and d/s towards Fish & Duck Pub. St £17, dt £3, from Coopers. Club also controls stretch of Hundred Foot from Sutton Gault to Ox Willow; the Old West River at Stretton Bridge; and **Old Bedford River** from **Earith** to Welches Dam, a good pike water. Histon and Dist AS controls **Old West River** from Hermitage Lock to old pump engine, and two other stretches, should be fished early in season, owing to boat traffic. St £18, conc, dt £3 in advance, a surcharge on bank. Club also fishes lake complex at **Milton**, excellent carp, no dt, st only, £38; and Counterwash Drain from Earith to Manea on both banks, tench, roach, rudd, pike, etc. R Ouse nr **Over** controlled by Over and Swaverley AS. St £15, conc, from Coopers. Agrevo ASC controls **Drayton Fen**, 80 acres, with good carp, tench, pike, also Holywell and Swavesey Lakes and Gt Ouse. Dt £5 from Coopers (below). London AA has water for members only at **Swaffham Prior**. Cambridge Albion AS has two stretches at Wicken Fen, and Dimmocks Cote, also **Barnwell Lake**, Barnwell Bridge. Tackle shops: Cooper & Son, 12 Milton Rd; Farrington, 2/4 Ferry Lane; Beecrofts, 207 Cherry Hinton Rd, Cambridge.

OLD WEST RIVER: Good stock of coarse fish. **Milton Lake**. Large carp and other coarse fish.

IVEL: Dace, roach and perch.

Tempsford (Beds). Ouse and Ivel. Biggleswade AC, now merged with Hitchin and District AA, has water on both rivers. London AA has several miles on Ouse here and at Blunham; members only.

Blunham (Beds). Ouse (1m W). Blunham and Dist AC controls 1,000 yds local fishing; also Gt Ouse at Oakley, Willington and Gt Barford; Halls Pit, nr Sandy; Barford Lake, Gt Barford; Willington Gravel Pits. Members only, £25, £7 conc. Below Blunham Bridge to Ouse held by Biggleswade and District AC. Club also has right bank of Ivel from Langford Mill to Broom Mill; no dt. Shefford AC has left bank, at **Shefford**, shared with The Tring Anglers. Members only. Nearest tackle shops, Bedford.

Lower Caldecote (Beds). RMC Angling has ¾m stretch, with trout, dace, chub, mirror carp and barbel to 3lb. *(For RMC Angling, see Chertsey.)*

Langford (Beds). Letchworth and dist AA has fishing opposite garden centre, and at Langford Mill. No dt, membership £33, conc. Assn fishes most of Ivel through its membership of the Ivel Protection Society.

Henlow (Beds). Letchworth and dist AA fishes Henlow complex, 4 lakes and river at Henlow Village, entry via Park Lane.

HIZ (tributary of Ivel): Controlled by Biggleswade, Hitchin and District AA who have 15 acre coarse fishery nearby, and 7m increase of water on Middle Ouse. Membership £25 pa, specimen perch, etc. Club also has water on **Ouse**, River **Oughton** (trout, few chub, restocking under consideration; members only), and fishes waters of Great Ouse FCA and Ivel Protection Assn. St £25. Tackle shop: Alan Brown, Nightingale Road, **Hitchin**.

OUZEL: Coarse fish.

Leighton Buzzard (Beds). Leighton Buzzard AC preserves various stretches above Leighton Buzzard and at Stoke Hammond, Water Eaton, Bletchley and Newport Pagnell. Club also has several stretches on **Gt Ouse** (3 at **Emberton** and others at **Stoke Goldington)**, 5 on **Thame Shabbington**, 3m of **Oxford Canal** and 3m of **Grand Union Canal**. Also **Claydon Lakes**, **Tiddenfoot** and other pits. Concessions to jun & OAP. Berkhamsted AS controls Bridigo Pond, Linslade, nr Leighton Buzzard; mixed carp and coarse fishery; also Steat Farm, Cublington, carp fishery, both members only. RMC Angling has 3 gravel pits stocked with large pike, carp and catfish. St £32 (conc. ½ price). *(For RMC Angling, see Chertsey.)* The Tring Anglers have water near Newport Pagnell, members only, *see Tring.*

RELIEF CHANNEL: not strictly a tributary but included here because of its traditional status as an excellent coarse fishery in its own right, now re-established as such, after a difficult period with zander, by an intensive programme of investigation and re-stocking by AWA. Now rented to Wisbech & Dist AA which issues dt.

TOVE: Coarse fish.

OUSE (Sussex)
(For close seasons, licences, etc, see Southern Region Environment Agency, p12)

Rises few miles south-east of Horsham and flows for 33 miles to enter English Channel at Newhaven. Tidal for 12 miles from mouth to point 4m upstream of Lewes. Coarse fish and trout, but notable for run of big sea trout.

Lewes and **Barcombe Mills** (E Sussex). Sea trout (good), barbel, perch, bream, roach, dace, chub, carp and pike. Ouse APS has west bank from Hamsey to Barcombe Mills (about 4m) and certain stretches of non-tidal water above the mills. Sea trout from May to Oct, but June to August best, given rain. Permits. Contact John Goodrick, Applegarth, School Lane, Barcombe BN8 5BT (Tel: 01273 406389). Barcombe Mills Pool and side streams reserved for sea-trout fishing and open to permit holders at £3 a day (2 rods daily) bookable in advance from Bailiff Jim Smith (Tel: 01825 750366). Old Mill Farm, Barcombe, has Ouse fishing. Dt at farm. Decoy Wood Fisheries, 1 Decoy Cottages, Laugthon Rd, Ringmer BN8 6DJ (Tel: 01273 814344): coarse fishing in 4 acre lake; good stock of carp, rudd, roach, tench, perch, the odd pike; book 24 hours in advance. Tackle shop: Percy's, 9 Cliffe High Street; Uckfield Angling Centre, 212A High St. Hotels: Shelleys, White Hart, Crown (all Lewes); for Barcombe Mills: Angler's Rest, Anchor Inn.

Isfield (E Sussex). Coarse fish, trout and sea trout. Isfield and Dist AC has sections of Ouse at Isfield. Club also has stretches of **Cuckmere** at Upper Dicker, **Uck** at **Uckfield**. and lakes around **E Grinstead**, **Uckfield**, **Horsted Keynes** and elsewhere, 24 fisheries in all. Large carp, tench, bream, perch, eels and pike. St £40 plus £10 joining fee, conc, from Memb Sec (sae). No dt. Exchange ticket system with other clubs. Free fishing on Piltdown Pond, 2m west of Uckfield, which is owned by golf club. Hotels: Laughing Fish, Isfield (club HQ); Maiden's Head, Uckfield. *(Tackle, see Lewes.)*

Haywards Heath (W Sussex). Coarse fish

and trout. Haywards Heath & Dist AS has 11½m bank of **Ouse** from **Linfield** down to **Newick**, and several lakes, including **Balcombe Lake**, **Slaugham Mill Pond**, **Valebridge Mill Pond**. Fishing coarse mainly, trout in river, and is for members only. Membership open to approved applicants, with concessions. Tackle shops: Sporting Chance, 29 Boltro Rd; Angling Centre, 143 Church Rd, Burgess Hill.

UCK: mainly coarse fishing below Uckfield with occasional sea trout. Joins Ouse at Isfield.

Isfield (E Sussex). Coarse fish and trout. Isfield and Dist AC has water from here to **Uckfield** (members only), with excellent coarse fishing and trout to 3lb. **Colin Godman's Trouting**, Furners Green, TN22 3RR, Tel: 01825 74 322; 3 lakes, 7 acres, browns and rainbows to 4lb, members only.

OUSE (Yorkshire)
(For close seasons, licences, etc, see North East Region Environment Agency, p13)

Forms with Trent the estuary of the Humber. Coarse fish, with some trout. Dunsforth, Beningbrough and Poppleton reaches noted for barbel and chub. Large bream present but difficult to catch. Most water held by Leeds and York clubs. Tributaries give excellent trout and coarse fishing.

Goole (N Humberside). Don enters Ouse here. Goole AA has water on **Selby Canal** near Selby, from Burn Bridge to Paperhouse Bridge, with roach, skimmers, perch, chub. Dt £2.50 at R.S. Tackle and Gun, Goole; Anchor Inn, on bank. Carlton AC has dt £1.25 for several fishings around Selby and Goole, including R Derwent at Bubwith, West Haddlesey Lake, and Selby Canal, from local tackle shops. Selby Miners Welfare AC offers dt £2.50 on bank at Selby Canal between Brayton and Burn Bridges, with roach, chub, carp, dace and other species. Selby tackle shops: Selby Angling Centre, 69 Brook St; Field Sports, 24/26 New St, Selby N Yorks YO8 0PT.

Acaster (N Yorks). Coarse fishing. Controlled by the Leeds Amalgamation. Tickets at Blacksmith's Arms, Naburn, and Manor Guest House, Acaster Maibis. Castleford Anglers fish on 150 yds below old salmon hut. Dt £1. Fish include barbel; above dam, trout and coarse fish. Accommodation: Manor Guest House.

Naburn (N Yorks). Below dam, right bank to

old salmon hut, York Amalgamated. Left bank, tickets £3 from lock keeper, or tackle dealer G E Hill, of York.

York (N Yorks). Coarse fish; some free fishing on public waters. On left bank nearly all free except 8m from Rawcliffe Ings and Clifton Ings up to Aldwark. York Amalgamation has fishing on 80m of **Ouse**, **Derwent**, **Nidd**, **Rye**, **Seven**, and several still waters. St £25, conc, dt £3 from local tackle shop for lower Nidd. 4m on Rivers Rye and Seven; very good grayling and trout; ½m on Derwent, all three fisheries members only. Tackle shops: G E Hill, 40 Clarence Street; Anglers Corner, 41 Huby Court, Walgate.

Poppleton and **Newton** (N Yorks). Good barbel, pike, etc. York and Leeds Amalgamations have extensive stretches. Dt from Fox Inn, Nether Poppleton, and Post Office.

Aldwark (N Yorks). Coarse fish. York Amal have 2½m above and ½m below Aldwark Bridge with exception of short stretch. Hotels: Three Horseshoes and Crown, Great Ouseburn; Bay Horse, Aldwark.

Low Dunsforth. From Low Dunsforth to Aldwark Bridge (about 4m right bank) fishing is in hands of Leeds Amal. Dt from Angler Inn, Low Dunsforth. Leeds Amal also has good length at **Hunterslodge** on opposite side below Aldwark bridge (left bank). Tickets as above.

Tributaries of the Ouse (Yorkshire)

DON: Rises on Wike Head and flows through Sheffield and Doncaster to the estuary of the Ouse; after 150 years of pollution from the Sheffield steel industry, this river is once more fishable. The E.A-Environment Agency has stocked over past 12 years, and 30lb nets of roach have been caught. Hemp and tares are best summer baits, maggots and casters in winter.

Doncaster (S Yorks). Doncaster & Dist AA has much widespread coarse fishing, including water on the canalised Don and **South Yorkshire Navigation Canal** at **Sprotsborough**, 4m d/s to and Doncaster Prison; 5m of **Idle** from Newington to Idle Stop; 10m of the **Torne**; the 6m of **New Junction Canal** from Barnby Dun to the **Aire & Calder** junction; 5m **Warping**

Drain; also **BW Southfield Reservoirs**, **Cowick**, 110 acres total, 40lb bags of roach and bream. Dt on the banks at many of these fisheries. **Thrybergh Reservoir**, 34 acres, near **Rotherham**; Rotherham MBC trout fishery. Permits on site. Rotherham MBC also has **Fitzwilliam Canal**, Rotherham 1m, dt. Tinsley & dist AA offer £2 dt for canal fishing in the area. Tel 01709 366142. BW Castleford Anglers have **Woodnook Reservoir**. St from Assn HQ and tackle shops. Barnby Dun Social AC have dt £1 on bank at S Yorkshire Navigation Canal between **Barnby Dun** and Kirk Sandall, with chub, roach, perch, bream, gudgeon. Tel: 01302 886024 for match bookings. Hayfield Fina Lakes, Hayfield Lane, Auckley, DN9 3NP (Tel: 01302 864555); 2 lakes with 157 pegs, mainly carp, roach, rudd, tench, gudgeon, etc; dt £5, conc. Tackle shops: Anglers Supplies, 148 High St, Bentley, Doncaster; Doncaster Angling Centre, 207 Carrhouse Rd. R & R Sports, 40 High St, Bawtry DN10 6JE (Tel: 01302 711130); has dt for a variety of coarse fisheries in area, incl Hayfield Lakes; Tyram Hall; Woodhouse Grange; Hatfield Marina; Hallcroft Fishery; and stretches of Chesterfield Canal, R Idle, Warping Drain.

Sheffield (S Yorks). **Damflask**, YW reservoir, 5m W; trout. **Underbank**, corporation reservoir, coarse fishing and a few large trout. Tickets from attendant's office. Further information under 'Yorkshire Lakes'. Sheffield Amal AS (membership books from Lord Nelson, Arundel Street) has three waters on Trent, at Besthorpe, Girton and North and South Clifton. Dt from bailiff on bank. Sheffield and Dist AA has water on Rivers **Trent**, trout fishing at Thurgoland on **Don**, and **Chesterfield Canal** from A631 to Trent junction. Dt issued for most waters. **Stainforth and Keadby Canal** controlled by joint committee including Rotherham, Doncaster, Sheffield Amal, and British Railways clubs. Dt on bank. At **Staveley** Urban District Council have 5 acre lake stocked annually with coarse fish; dt and st. Also **Foxtone Dam**; dt. Chapeltown & Dist AA fish **Westwood** and **Howbrook Reservoirs**, and ponds, various coarse species. St £9, dt £2, from G Hamstead, Tackle Shop, Station Rd, Chapeltown, or bailiffs. Tackle shops: Terry & John's, 297 Buchanan Rd; Concord Fishing, 283 Hatfield House Lane; Kerfoot Fishing Tackle, 6 Southey Green Rd (Tel: 0114 2313265); Bennett's, 1 Stanley Street, Sheffield; Ernest Stamford, 419 Attercliffe Common; W G Dawson, 70 Holme Lane; Park Angling

Centre 181 Middlewood Rd; Gunnies, 279 Buchanan Rd; Angling Centre, 34 Chester St, Brampton, both Chesterfield.

Oughtibridge (S Yorks). Sheffield 6m; free fishing, mainly roach, trout, dace, chub, barbel, with some grayling, perch. Mainly shallow, some pools and disused weirpools.

DEARNE (tributary of Don):

Barnsley (S Yorks). Dearne; free fishing on length within Hoyle Mill Country Park. Mainly free, between here and **Darfield**, and through common near Wombwell. Stocked at **Haigh**, where Wakefield AC has water. Club also has lakes near **Wakefield**, fishing on R Calder, and Calder & Hebble Navigation. Membership from Wakefield tackle shops. Barnsley MBC owns Cannon Hall Lake, Barkhouse Lane, Cawthorne (tickets from machine); and Dearne Valley Park Lake, Hoyle Mill (free fishing on selected sections of river and lake bank). Barnsley AA fish **Brampton Canal**, B Swift (Tel: 01226 712853). Worsbrough Country Park fishing, Worsbrough Bridge; Barnley Amalgamated Anglers (Tel: 01226 203090. **Worsbrough Canal**, White Rose AC (Tel: 01226 750659). **Barnsley Canal**, fishing on north bank only, Mr Brian McGraw Jnr (Tel: 01226 247131). Tackle shops: Tackle Box, 7, Doncaster Rd; Wombwell Angling Centre, 25 Barnsley Rd.

Claycross (Derby). Lakes: Williamthorpe Ponds, 2m NE. Wingerworth Hall Lakes (2), 2½m NW. Great Dam, 3½m NW.

ROTHER (tributary of Don):

Killamarsh (Derby). Short Brook. Lakes: Woodhall Moor Dams, 2m E. Barlborough Hall Lake, 3m SE. Pebley Dam, 3m SE. Harthill Reservoir, 3m E. Woodhall Pond, 3m E.

AIRE: Issues from ground at Aire Head, half a mile south of Malham village. Its upper reaches contain quality trout and grayling, which give place to coarse fish between Steeton and Keighley. Keighley AC has stretch at Marley and several more at Keighley and Skipton, with trout, chub, roach, pike, plus other fishing on ponds and 3m Leeds and Liverpool Canal; st £18, dt £2, conc. Tackle shop in Keighley. *(For Malham Tarn, see Ribble-Settle).*

Leeds (W Yorks). Contains roach, bream, chub, trout, perch. Adel Beck and Dam (private). **Roundhay Park Lakes**, 4m NE. Leeds and Dist ASA have fishing; dt from local tackle shops. Larger lake (Waterloo) contains pike, perch, roach. tench, carp, etc; no fishing on small lake. Leeds Amal has extensive fishing on Ouse and tributaries, canals and lakes, dt for many waters; full details from Hon Sec. Also trout at Pool and Arthington (see Ouse (Yorks)-Wharfe). Castleford & Dist SA fish Fairburn Ings and Fairburn Cut. Dt £1 on site. At **Swinsty** and **Fewston**, 7m from **Otley**, are YWS reservoirs, containing trout; visitors' dt can be had at Reservoir Lodge, Fewston. Fly only. Tackle shops: Abbey Match Anglers, 38 Commercial Rd; Kirkgate Anglers, 95 Kirkgate; Bob's Tackle Shop, 1A Chapel Lane, Garforth; Headingly Angling Centre, 58 North Lane, Headingly LS6 3HU (Tel: 0113 278 4445), agents for Leeds & Dist ASA, and four other local clubs.

Bradford (W Yorks). Aire, 7m N. Bradford City AA has extensive rights here and on water on the canals at **Apperley Bridge** and near Skipton; on **Wharfe, Ure** and **Swale**, reservoirs and lakes. Assn fishes Saltaire's length of **Leeds and Liverpool Canal**. Bradford No 1 AA has water on **Wharfe** at **Addingham**, Denton and Ben Rhydding, **Aire** near **Skipton**, **Swale** at **Gatenby, Ure** at Middleham, **Nidd** at Ramsgill and Nun Monkton, **Derwent**, also **R Calder** at Elland, and reservoirs. Membership £27, entrance £18, conc. Addingham AA have water on 3 reservoirs holding trout and perch. Members only st £85. Waiting list. Tackle shops: Watercraft Products, 899 Harrogate Rd; Westgate Anglers, 63 Westgate; Wibsey Angling Centre, 208 High St, Wibsey, Bradford; Richmonds, 71 Park Rd, Bradford.

Bingley, Saltaire (W Yorks). Trout, coarse fish; Bingley AC has 1m through Bingley, coarse fish; restocked annually with trout; 2m of Leeds and Liverpool Canal, with large carp and others. St £17 and dt £2, from tackle shop. Club has good trout fishing on **Sunnydale Reservoir**, Eastmorton; trout and coarse fish, dt £3.50; also two dams and beck. Trout waters are for members only. Bradford No 1 AA has two lengths, left bank, along Bingley Cricket and Football Fields, d/s. Members only. Excellent trout preserve in **Myrtle Park**; water restocked; dt 75p. Dt £1 for **Leeds and Liverpool Canal**. Saltaire AA (HQ Ring of Bells, Bradford Rd, Shipley) has 4m stretch of Aire, mixed fishery, dt water, best match bag 1997, 29lb chub; and **Tong Park Dam**, brown and rainbow trout, dt £4 from

Shipley Angling Centre. From Bankfield Hotel downstream to Baildon Bridge (both banks, except Roberts Park) is Saltaire AA water.

Keighley (W Yorks). Trout, grayling, coarse fish, chub plentiful. Sport improved after restocking. Keighley AC has 14m, trout to 5lb; best May–June and Sept. Club also has fishing on the **Leeds and Liverpool Canal**; Calden Canal; **Huddersfield Narrow Canal**; Lancaster Canal; Llangollen Canal; Macclesfield Canal; **Shropshire Union Canal**; **Whitefields Reservoir**, stocked with carp, tench, roach and perch, and, for members only; **Roberts Pond** (large tench, carp, pike); **Sugden End Reservoir**, Crossroads (large trout, roach, perch, and tench, dt £3.50) and the **R Worth**, trout. Dt for R Aire only. (See also Yorkshire lakes, reservoirs, etc). Tackle shops: K & L Tackle, 131 Mornington St; Willis Walker, 109 Cavendish Street, Keighley.

Cononley (W Yorks). Trout, perch, chub, roach, dace, bream, grayling; dt after June 1, for Bradford City AA water, dt £2 from Post Office, 2/4 King St BD20 8LH, or tackle shops from 16 June. Dt from tackle shops.

Skipton (N Yorks). Trout, grayling, pike, chub, roach, perch, dace and bream. At Skipton, Skipton AA has three miles of fishing, mainly both banks; st £40 (entrance fee £15), dt £3, from Hon Sec. or tackle shops. Association also has rights on **Embsay Reservoir** (trout), **Whinnygill Reservoirs** (trout and coarse fish) dt, and beck fishing on Eller Beck at Skipton. Bradford City AA water begins on both banks below Skipton water; about 7m in all. Near Skipton at **Kilnsey Park** are 2 trout lakes of 3 acres. Tel: 01756 752150. Dt £13, £9.50. Bradford No 1 AA has **Bradley, Broughton** and **Sandbeds** fisheries, left bank. Members only. Hotels: Highfield, Devonshire.

Bellbusk (N Yorks). Trout; preserved by owners. Lakes: **Conniston House**; trout. **Eshton Tarn**, 2m NE; pike. **Malham Tarn**, 8m N; trout and perch; tickets (see Ribble-Settle).

CALDER (tributary of Aire): Good coarse fishing from Brighouse to Sowerby Bridge.

Halifax (W Yorks). Calder 2m S. Clubs: Halifax and Dist AC (dams); Dean Clough & Ryburn AS has 2½m good coarse fishing on Calder,

Sowerby Bridge to Salterhebble; **Calder And Hebble Navigation**, same length; and some good brown trout fishing at Sowerby Bridge. St £14, conc, dt £1.50, from Jewsons (*below*), and other local tackle shops. Other societies: Brighouse AA has stocked coarse fishery with barbel and dace; st £15 plus joining fee £5, conc; Friendly AC, The Friendly Inn, Ovenden. Ripponden Flyfishers have good trout fishing in **Ryburn Reservoir**, Ripponden. Brighouse AA and Bradford No 1 AA controls 14m on Calder above and below **Brighouse**; heavily restocked and now provides sport with good-quality roach. St £27 + £18 joining fee from J Sparks, 12 Fairway Walk, Wibsey, Bradford. No dt. Brighouse AA also has water on canal and gravel pits. Hebden Bridge AC has canal fishing and brown trout fishing in area. Tackle shops: A J Jewson, 28 Horton St HX1 1PU (Tel: 01422 354146); Calder Angling Supplies, Gooder Lane, Brighouse. Hotels: Imperial Crown; Calder & Hebble Inn; Black Horse Inn, Brighouse.

Hebden (W Yorks). At **Todmorden** (Yorks, postal address Lancs), Todmorden AS has mixed coarse fishing which includes the **Rochdale Canal**, within the Todmorden boundary; **New Mill Dam**; **Grove Fishery**, Littleborough; **R Calder**; **Portsmouth Reservoir**; Croft Head Fishery; **Littleborough**. Dt £3 on the following: Cliviger Fishponds; Grove Fishery; Rochdale Canal, Locks 36–51 only; Croft Head and Lower Townhouse. Annual membership, £20, plus £10, conc, from local tackle dealers. **Calder and Hebble Navigation**: from Salterhebble Top Lock, through Brighouse, Lower Hopton Bridge, Thornhill, to upstream of Ganny Lock, the following clubs have water: Dean Clough & Ryburn AS (2½m, dt), Mackintosh AC, Brighouse AA, Bradford No. 1, Thornhill C & BC. Unity AC has fishing on R Calder; Milby Cut, **Boroughbridge**; Dyehouse Dam, Oakenshaw; all waters contain coarse fish, roach, rudd, bream, tench, perch, etc, members only on most, but dt for good coarse fishing on **Leeds and Liverpool Canal**, £2, conc. Membership £11, conc. Tackle shop: Watercraft, Greengates; or Bradford shops. Hotel: Queen.

COLNE (tributary of Calder):

Huddersfield (W Yorks). Holme Valley PA fishes **R Calder** from Battyeford to Mirfield, Magdale Dam and pond at Holmfirth. Dt on river and pond from tackle shops. Facilities for the disabled. **Hill Top**, **Sparth**, and

Longwood Compensation Reservoirs, **Huddersfield Narrow Canal**, all Slaithwaite & Dist AC waters, dt obtainable. Tickets from Chris Roberts Fishing Tackle, 22 Chapel Hill; Marsden Post Office; Holme Valley Sports, Holmfirth. Hotel: Huddersfield and many others.

Slaithwaite (W Yorks). Slaithwaite and Dist AC has fly only trout fishery from Marsden to Slaithwaite, no fishing in village centre, then east stretch from Linthwaithe Steps, all members only, no dt; **Narrow Canal**, Slaithwaite to Bargate and 3 other stretches, 3 reservoirs, dams and ponds; trout, coarse fish; st £18 + £5 joining, conc, enquiries to D Rushforth, 122 Longwood Gate, Longwood, Hudds HD3 4US. Tackle shop: Chris Roberts, 22 Chapel Hill, Huddersfield.

HOLME (tributary of Colne):

Holmfirth (W Yorks). River has wild brown trout, as well as usual coarse species. Holme Valley PA has water from Holmfirth to steps Mill, Honley, except 50 yard stretch by old Robinson Mill Dam, and Honley Village Trust land. Assn also controls stretch of R Calder; Magdale Dam, members only, and Cinderhills Pond; all waters coarse fishing, with roach, tench, perch, etc; dt on pond and on Calder, from Sec or Holmfirth Information Centre. Membership £18 plus £15 joining, conc. Slaithwaite & Dist AC fishes most of stretch from Holmebridge to Bottoms Dam, river is extremely shallow and overhung, with many small wild trout. Members only. **Holmstyes Reservoir**; trout (Huddersfield 8m) preserved by Huddersfield AA. St £38. **Boshaw Reservoir** (Huddersfield 8m); preserved as above.

DERWENT: Rises in high moors and flows almost to coast near Scarborough where it turns south and enters estuary of Ouse. Its upper reaches, most easily reached from Scarborough, are trout and grayling waters (*see Ayton*). Lower down coarse fish predominate, barbel included.

Wressle (N Humberside). Coarse fish free, some access.

Breighton (N Humberside); ns Wressle 1m. Bubwith 1m. Chub, dace, pike, etc; fishing free.

Bubwith (N Humberside). Coarse fish; Howden and Dist AC: 4m controlled by Mike

Redman, 2 Meadowfield, Breighton Rd, Bubwith YO8 7DZ (Tel: 01757 288891).

Ellerton; roach, perch, dace, bream, chub, eels and pike; flatfish lower down. For Ellerton Landing, 2m, Aughton, 1m, Bubwith, 1m, dt from V G Shop; Mike Redman, 2 Meadowfield, all Bubwith, or Boot and Shoe, Ellerton.

East Cottingwith (N Yorks); ns High Field, 4m. Coarse fish (pike and chub very good). York AA controls East Cottingwith Water (2m) and 10m of good coarse fishing on **Pocklington Canal**. Dt from secretary. At **Thorganby**, on other side of Derwent, Ferry Boat Inn has day tickets for approximately 1½m of river. Very good pike fishing.

Pocklington (N Yorks). **Pocklington Canal**. Well stocked with bream, roach, perch, pike, etc. York AA water.

Ellerton Landing (N Yorks). Hotel: White Swan, Bubwith YO8 6LT (Tel: 01757 28809).

Kexby (N Yorks). Pike, chub, etc. York and Leeds Amalgamated Societies have water; members only.

Low Catton (N Yorks). Coarse fish. Bradford No 1 AA has good length of water on left bank; members only.

Stamford Bridge (N Yorks). Excellent for roach, pike, chub, dace. York and Dist Amal has fishing on good length down to Kexby Brickworks and length at Stamford Bridge Bottom, acquired from Leeds ASA; also pits. Dt at cafes in Stamford Bridge.

Howsham (N Yorks). Coarse fishing. York and Dist AA has water on Derwent and Barton Hill Beck; Bradford No 1 AA has left bank at Howsham Wood; members only.

Kirkham Abbey (N Yorks). Coarse fish, some trout. Leeds and York Amalgamations have water; members only. Scarborough Mere AC has approx 1,300 yds north bank u/s from bridge. Members only.

Castle Howard (N Yorks). **Castle Howard Great Lake** contains specimen coarse fish, including pike, perch, tench, bream, roach and bank fishing only. For further details, see 'Yorkshire Lakes.'

Huttons Ambo (Yorks). Roach, pike, dace, eels, gudgeon, grayling, perch and few trout. South bank, 1m down and 1m up, held by Malton and Norton AC, no dt, membership £15 pa. North bank held by Huttons Ambo AC for 2m down and 2m up; membership, for people resident within 10m Malton, £5 pa. Dt £1.50 from village post office. 1,500 lbs bream stocked in Nov 1996, 1lb–6lb. Upper Derwent Preservation Society stocked 3,000 6in–10in roach in April 1997 and intend to repeat this over the next few years.

Malton (Yorks). Coarse fish, mainly roach. Malton and Norton AC. Waters extend to 1m below Huttons Ambo. Membership discretionary, issued by Hon Sec, and N & C Swift, Castlegate, Malton. York and Dist AA has 5½m at Old Malton to Ryemouth. Contact John Lane, 39 Lowfields Drive, Acomb, York YO2 3DQ, Tel: 01904 783178. Good deal of free water on Derwent and Rye. Tackle shops: J Anderson & Son, Market Place; and C Swift, Castlegate (tickets for Malton & Norton AC waters). Hotel: Green Man.

Rillington (Yorks). Derwent, 1m N. Coarse fish; Leeds Amal water. Scampston Beck, 1m E, private. Rye, 2m N. Costa Beck, 3m N.

Yedingham (Yorks). Coarse fish. Dt at Providence Inn, Station Rd YO17 8SL, for Leeds Amal waters. Inn also has private stretch.

Ganton (Yorks). Chub, pike, dace, grayling; dt for 1m each way from Hay Bridge, from Mr and Mrs Seller, Bogg Hall Farm YO12 4PB (Tel: 01944 710391), at first house across railway crossing at Ganton. Ruston Beck, 2m W. Dt waters at **Seamer** (Malton Rd), from house by stream.

Ayton (Yorks). Some good trout water. Scarborough Mere AC has **Scarborough Mere**, just outside town; coarse fish; dt £2; mere restocked regularly. About 2m trout fishing from Ayton towards Ganton controlled by Leeds Amal; no tickets.

Hackness (Yorks). Derwent AC controls 10m of trout (brown and rainbow) and grayling fishing down to **East Ayton**, for part of which dt are obtainable from July 1 to Sept 30. Farther up, above Langdale End Bridge (3m both banks), dt from April 1 to Sept 30. Fishing one fly only, wet or dry, is club rule on all water. Tickets from Grange Hotel (rod for residents on 8m of Derwent). Sunday fishing reserved for members and guests on lower club water, and all fishing between Hilla Green bridge and Langdale End bridge exclusively reserved to members and guests. Size limit for trout 10in; limited two brace per day. Wading allowed.

FOSS BECK (tributary of Derwent). Fishing station: **Fangfoss** (Yorks); fishing private.

SPITTLE BECK (tributary of Derwent):

Barton Hill (Yorks). Derwent, 2m E. Whitecarr Beck, 4m SE. Loppington Beck, 4m SE. Swallowpits Beck, 5m SE at Scrayingham. York and Dist AA have trout water **Barton Hill Beck**.

RYE (tributary of Derwent): Trout, grayling, other coarse fish.

Ryton (Yorks). Scarborough Mere AC has 5 fields at Ryton Bridge: trout, grayling and coarse fish, including barbel. Members only.

Butterwick (Yorks). Trout, coarse fish. Scarborough Mere AC has stretch, members only.

PICKERING BECK (tributary of Rye) and Costa Beck (chalk stream): Trout, grayling.

Pickering (Yorks). About 1m of free fishing in town; private above, preserved below (3m) by Pickering FA; fly only; membership limited to 120. Water also on **Costa Beck** and **Oxfold Becks**, trout and grayling, and Duchy of Lancaster water, **Newbridge**. Two trout lakes. Dt for members' guests only. Club HQ: Bay Horse Hotel. Brown and rainbow trout fishing at Hazelhead Lake, Newgate Foot, Saltersgate, Pickering YO18 7NR (Tel: 01751 460215); open 15 Apr–31 Oct; tickets from farmhouse B & B. Pickering Trout Lake, Newbridge Rd, Pickering YO18 8JJ (Tel: 01751 474219): open all year, dt from £4. Tackle shop and flies on site. Scarborough Mere AC has 6m on **Rye** near Pickering. Hotels: White Swan, Black Swan, Forest and Vale, Crossways.

SEVEN (tributary of Rye): Trout, grayling; some coarse fish.

Newsham Bridge (Yorks). York and Dist AA has water on Seven and Rye; no dt.

Marton (Yorks). Private from mill to Marton; below Marton some free water; grayling, pike,

chub, dace and a few trout. Tackle shop in Malton, 12m.

Sinnington (Yorks). Seven AC has 2½m downstream from the main road; brown, rainbow trout, some grayling; members only, long waiting list. Coarse fishing mainly below large weir and bottom farm.

WATH BECK (tributary of Rye):

Slingsby (Yorks). Trout; preserved. Rye, NE.

DOVE-IN-FARNDALE (tributary of Rye):

Kirby Moorside (N Yorks). Dove-in-Farndale, 1m E; trout; private. Dt for stretches downstream of Kirby Moorside from some of the farms. Hodge Beck, in Sleightholme Dale, 1m W, trout only. Hotel: King's Head.

THORNTON BECK (tributary of Derwent):

Thornton-le-Dale (N Yorks). Trout and grayling; preserved. Pickering Beck, 3m W. Derwent, 3m S. Hotels: The Hall; The Buck; all Thornton-le-Dale.

WHARFE: Rises on Cam Fell and flows 60m south-east to join Ouse near Cawood. Trout in upper reaches, with coarse fish downstream.

Ryther (N Yorks); ns Ulleskelf, 3m. Castleford and Dis ASA has water; mainly coarse fish. Hotel: Ryther Arms.

Ulleskelf (N Yorks). Coarse fish; preserved by Leeds Amal; dt £1.50 and B & B from Ulleskelf Arms LS24 9DW (Tel: 01937 832136).

Tadcaster (N Yorks). Trout, chub and dace, good head of barbel, perch and bream; preserved by Tadcaster Angling and Preservation Association on both banks downstream from road bridge, ¾m east bank, and 1½m west bank Grimston Park; st £15; dt £2, jun 50%. Tickets from Hon Sec; The Bay Horse; newsagent; or Pet and Aquatic Centre.

Boston Spa (W Yorks). Trout, grayling, other coarse fish (chub, barbel and pike good; bream introduced). Most rights held by Boston Spa AC. Dt £2 from Lower Wharfe Anglers, Boston Spa. Club members (who must live within 3m of Boston Spa Post Office) allowed guests at current cost of dt and guest must fish with member on non-ticket waters. Club stocks water with trout and grayling of 12in or over. Limit two trout, one grayling, or vice-versa; trout 12in. May best month for trout and August for barbel and chub.

Wetherby (W Yorks). Wetherby and Dist AC water (stocked with trout and coarse fish) extends from Collingham Beck to Wetherby Weir, south bank (about 350 yards in Collingham Wood, south bank is private). Club also has 4 fields between golf course and playing fields, north bank. This water is open for visitors on st (above weir), and dt. Members only below and on weir, but visitors may fish if accompanied by a member. Same charge as above. Dt from: The Paper Shop, Market Place, Wetherby; Star Garage, Collingham Bridge. No legitimate bait or lure barred. Trout limit 11in. Tackle shops: J R Country & Pet Supplies, Horsefair; Lower Wharfe Angling Centre, 236 High St, Boston Spa.

Collingham (W Yorks). Wetherby AC has water here; trout and coarse fish including barbel, grayling and good dace.

Pool (W Yorks). Trout, dace, chub; preserved by the Leeds and Dist ASA which has 5m of fishing from River **Washburn** to Castley Beck on left bank. Dt £2.50 from Leeds and Otley tackle shops. Members of Leeds AA, small private club, may fish Harewood Estate preserves, 3m right bank, 2m left bank.

Otley (W Yorks). Otley AC hold 2m left bank and 2½m right bank below Otley Bridge. Fishing for members only, no dt. Bradford No 1 AA fish two lengths on left and right bank, members only. Dt £2.50 for Leeds & Dist ASA **Knotford Lagoon**, near Otley; large carp and other coarse fish; stocked. Also some r trout. Bradford No 1 AA has second Knotford Lagoon. At Yeadon (6m) Airboro' and Dist AA has **Yeadon Tarn**, Cemetery Rd. Good catches of roach, perch, carp, tench. Dt £1.50 from newsagent in same road. Tackle shop in Otley: Angling and Country Sports, 36 Cross Green, Pool Road, Otley, Tel: Otley 462770.

Burley and **Askwith** (W Yorks). Trout, grayling, chub, dace. Bradford clubs have rights for members only.

Addingham (W Yorks). Trout, grayling; Bradford City AA has water here. Bradford No 1 AA has four lengths on left and right bank, and

Steven Bank Fishery, no dt obtainable. Bradford Waltonians have water at **Denton** and **Ben Rhydding**; also 4 reservoirs including **Chelker Reservoir** near here. Tickets £8 to members' guests, only; membership £205, subscription £205. Bradford No 1 AA has some left bank at Denton and right bank at Ben Rhydding, members only. Keighley AC has water; dt from Hon Sec. Addingham AA has from High Mill caravan site to Farfield Cottages on left bank, and right bank from Stephen Bank to Kexgill Beck, with trout (stocked twice a year with browns 1¼ to 2½lb) and grayling. Dt £10 from Addingham PO. Membership limited to 50, hence waiting list; apply Hon Sec. Tackle shops at Keighley and Harrogate.

Ilkley (W Yorks). Ilkley and Dist AA have water from Old Bridge to Stepping Stones, both banks, with trout, grayling dace and chub. Dt £6.50 (April 15–Sept 30 inc) from Tourist Information Centre, Station Rd, Ilkley LS29 8HA. Membership: st £55 + £38 joining, jun, OAP ½, some vacancies. Club also has 2 coarse ponds. Contact B Moore, Sec (Tel: 01943 430606). Hotels: Riverside, Craiglands, Cow and Calf.

Bolton Abbey (N Yorks). Trout and grayling. 5 miles stretch (both banks) on R Wharfe, fly only. Bailiffed, concentrating on wild trout fishery, light stocking only. Trout April 1–Sept 30. Grayling if caught to be released. St £250, wt £70, dt £15. Limit 2 fish of not less than 10in. Fishing not recommended on Sundays and Bank Holidays. Apply direct to River Bailiff, Strid Wood (Tel: 01756 710391); or Estate Office, Bolton Abbey, Skipton, BD23 6EX (Tel: 01756 710227). Hotels: Devonshire Arms, Bolton Abbey; Devonshire Fell, Burnsall.

Burnsall (N Yorks). Trout (av ½lb–1lb; many large fish), grayling; preserved by Appletreewick, Barden and Burnsall AC from Linton Stepping Stones, below Grassington, to Barden Bridge, some 7m. Dt for trout, June–Sept (excluding June and Sept week-ends) £18; wt £90, fly only; limit three brace; grayling dt £10 Nov–Jan (fly only). Waters re-stocked regularly with trout from ½ to 1lb and over. Tickets from Red Lion Hotel, Burnsall, and Burnsall Village Store. Half price juvenile tickets are available for those under 17 years, and those under 15 must be accompanied by an adult. Bradford City AA has water at **Appletreewick**; members only.

Grassington (N Yorks). Trout (av ¾lb),

grayling (av ¾lb); preserved by Linton, Threshfield and Grassington AC for 2½m both banks (also in Captain Beck and Linton and Threshfield Becks until August 31); wt £50, dt £12 for fly-fishing only. Long waiting list for membership. No night or Sunday fishing. No canoeing. Trout season: April 1 to Sept 30 inclusive. Grayling only from Oct 1 to Feb 28; st £20, dt £5; fly only during Oct. Fly only tickets £16, excl Sunday, from Dales Book Centre, 33 Main St, or Black Horse Hotel, Grassington. Saltaire AA also has left bank at **Linton**, no dt. Fishing best in May. **Eller Beck, Hebden Beck**, 2m E. Lakes: **Blea Beck** dams 4m NE. Hotels: Black Horse (Saltaire AA HQ), and others.

Kilnsey (N Yorks). Brown trout. Preserved by Kilnsey AC of 65 members, from Beckamonds to Yockenthwaite and from 1m above Starbotton down to Netherside 2m below Kilnsey; artificial fly only, limit three brace over 10in. St £420 + £75 entrance fee, from Hon Sec; wt £100, dt £20, daily, between 9am and 10am (number limited, and none on Sundays or Bank Holidays), from Keeper, C S Nesbitt, Tennant Arms, Kilnsey, via Skipton BD23 5PS, Tel: 01756 752310. Hotels: Tennant Arms, Falcon.

Buckden (N Yorks). Trout. Bradford City AA has 2m; dt £3.45 from Dalesgarth Holiday Cott. Other fishing for guests at Buck Inn; dt issued.

SKIRFARE (tributary of Wharfe): well stocked with brown trout, average 1lb.

Arncliffe (N Yorks). Some Skirfare Fishing preserved by Kilnsey AC, dt water (see Kilnsey). 2½m on Skirfare and 1½m on **Cowside Beck** open to guests at Falcon Inn Dt £7, no Sunday fishing.

FOSS (tributary of Ouse): Trout.

Earswick (N Yorks). Free fishing on right bank. Owners are Joseph Rowntree Trust.

Strensall (N Yorks). Foss Navigation Cut, 1m NE. **Whitecar Beck**, 1m NE. York and Dist Amal has coarse fishing here and at **Towthorpe**; members only.

NIDD: Trout and grayling, with coarse fish from Birstwith downstream in increasing numbers.

Nun Monkton (N Yorks). Coarse fish.

Bradford No 1 AA has 1m good coarse fishing here on left bank, both banks at **Ramsgill** and left bank at **Summerbridge**, for members only. Also 2½m right bank at **Cowthorpe**.

Moor Monkton (N Yorks). Leeds ASA has 1m mixed fishery, members only.

Kirk Hammerton (N Yorks). Coarse fish. Following on Harrogate AA water (see Goldsborough) almost all fishing downstream to where Nidd joins the Ouse controlled by Leeds and York Amalgamations. York Amal holds York side of river from Skip Bridge on Boroughbridge Road upstream for about 2m and also for about 1m above Hammerton Mill dam. Tickets from York tackle shops; and Aykroyd, Skip Bridge Filling Station, Green Hammerton.

Goldsborough (N Yorks). Trout, grayling and mixed coarse fishing, including pike and barbel. Left hand bank at Goldsborough, Knaresborough Piscatorials. From Little Ribston downstream through Walshford Bridge to first meadow below Cattall Bridge belongs to Harrogate AA. Association also has both banks of **Crimple Beck** from confluence with Nidd above Walshford Bridge up to Spofforth. Waiting list for membership. Dt issued by Hon Sec to members' guests only. Water otherwise strictly preserved.

Knaresborough (N Yorks). Trout, grayling and coarse fish, including barbel. Practically all fishing in vicinity controlled by Knaresborough AC and Knaresborough Piscatorials. Former issues st £25 and dt £4 for good stretch upstream from Little Ribston village. Club also owns fly only trout lake in Knaresborough area, members only. Full membership £180 plus £200 entry fee. Knaresborough Piscatorials fish 8 miles of Nidd, plus various stretches of Wharfe, Ure, Ouse, and Swale, mostly in area of Knaresborough, Skipton and Overton. Trout, chub, barbel, roach, bream, perch, rudd, dace, pike may be caught in club waters. Fees, £59 pa, conc. York Amal has good stretches here. Tickets from M H & C Johnson, 2 Briggate HG5 8BH (Tel: 01423 863065). **Farmire Trout Fishery**, 12 acres, at Farmire House, Stang Lane, Farnham, Knaresborough HG5 9JW, Tel: 01423 866417, has b and r trout fishing. Dt £18 4 fish, £12 2 fish, boats £10.

Ripley, Nidd Bridge (N Yorks). Trout, grayling and coarse fish. Knaresborough AC holds left bank d/s to Scotton, fly only, members only.

Birstwith (N Yorks). Trout and grayling above Birstwith Dam upstream to upper reaches of Nidd. Below Dam there are also coarse fish. Knaresborough AC has about 1,000 yds of right bank downstream from Hampsthwaite Bridge. Members and their guests only.

Darley (N Yorks). Trout and grayling water, preserved by Harrogate Fly Fishers. No tickets.

Pateley Bridge (N Yorks). Trout and grayling. From 1½m above Pateley Bridge down to **Summerbridge**, 11m total, owned and rented by Nidderdale AC, who hold nearly all water, both banks, except short pieces here and there which are private; also Scar House Reservoir. Permits, wt £30, dt £8–£6, for three lengths of river and Scar House, at Royal Oak (*below*); or local post offices in Lofthouse, Pateley Bridge, Glasshouses and Summerbridge. Anglers must obtain tickets before fishing. Disabled platform on one length of dt water. Royal Oak Hotel, Dacre Banks, Harrogate HG3 4EN (Tel: 01423 780200), offers two-day fishing breaks, with en-suite B & B, packed lunches, evening meals, and trout fishing on R Nidd and Scar House Reservoir, £99 per head.

Gouthwaite (N Yorks). River enters **Gouthwaite Reservoir**, privately owned and fished; no permits. Below reservoir Nidd private.

CRIMPLE (tributary of Nidd): This river is now private fishing.

Harrogate (N Yorks). Trout and coarse fishing, within easy reach of town in Nidd, Wharfe and Ure, and stillwaters. Tickets, tuition and guiding services from Orvis Co (*see below*). Harrogate & Claro CAA run matches, visitors welcome. Harrogate Flyfishers preserve excellent trout and grayling water at Darley. Coarse fishing at Newby Hall, **Skelton-on-Ure**, st £23, dt £2. Tel: 322583. Hotels: Crown, Majestic, Old Swan, St George, Cairn, Prospect. Tackle shops: Linsley Bros, 55 Tower St; Orvis, 17 Parliament St, Harrogate (Tel: 01423 561354).

KYLE: Coarse fish.

Tollerton (N Yorks). Coarse fishing free down to Alne. Ouse at Aldwark, 4m W, and Linton Lock, 3m S and 7m NE, at Stillington.

URE (or **YORE**): Noted for grayling, but also holds good trout. Coarse fish from Middleham downstream.

Boroughbridge (N Yorks). Fine coarse fishing (especially chub and roach, bream increasing); few trout and grayling; Boroughbridge and Dist AC, issues dt £2 (weekdays only, from June 1–Feb 27) sold at Post Office and Horsefair Grocers. At **Aldborough** Bradford City AA has 6m (roach, perch, dace, pike, chub); no dt, limited privilege tickets for members only. Bradford No 1 AA has Langthorpe stretch, left bank, and Roecliffe, right bank. Unity AC has water here, no dt, st £10, conc, from Wibsey Angling Centre, Main St, Wibsey; or Richmonds. Hotel: Boroughbridge Social Club.

Ripon (N Yorks). Trout, dace, pike, perch, chub, barbel, roach; preserved for 6m both banks by Ripon Piscatorial Assn. Assn also has **Ripon Canal** (barbel, roach, bream, perch); Racecourse Lake (carp, gudgeon, rudd and grayling); and 6m **R Laver** (brown trout, dace, chub, etc). Visitors dt £4, wt £12, st £45, from Ripon Angling Centre. Ripon AC has 1½m both banks **R Skell** at Ripon and 1m on Ure, 2m u/s of Ripon. Members and guests only, no dt. Waiting list for membership. Lakes: Queen Mary's Ponds; coarse fish; Bradford No 1 AA. Roger's Pond, coarse dt £4 from Angling Centre. **Leighton Reservoir**, Swinton Estate Office, Masham, Ripon HG4 4JR, Tel: 01765 689224; 100 acre trout fishery, dt £13–£7, from fishing hut. Tackle shop: Ripon Angling Centre, 58/9 North Street HG4 1EN.

Tanfield (N Yorks). Trout, grayling; preserved for about 5m, mostly both banks, by Tanfield AC. Guests must be accompanied by member. Full time bailiff employed. Long waiting list. Two trout fisheries at West Tanfield: Bellflask, brown and rainbow, dt £20, 4 fish. Run as fishery and nature reserve, barbless hooks. Michael Moreland, Tel: 01677 470716; Tanfield Lodge Lake, West Tanfield, Ripon (Tel: 01677 470385). Brown and rainbow, 11½ acres, disabled access. Dt £10, 4 fish, £5 evening, juv, 2 fish.

Masham (N Yorks). Trout (stocked), grayling. 6½m west bank belongs to Swinton Estate. Limited st. Details from Estate Office, Swinton, Masham. Well stocked 2½m stretch of Swinton water fished by Masham AC; brown trout and grayling; waiting list. St £125 + £30 Joining. Jun conc. Grayling membership Oct–end Feb, £40. Apply to Mr A R Proud, River Keeper, Park St, Masham, Tel: 01765 689361. Yorkshire Flyfishers hold Clifton Castle water (about 2m left bank) above Masham. No tickets. Tackle, information, and large selection of flies, from A

Plumpton, Hairdresser, Silver St. Hotel: King's Head. **Leighton Reservoir** near here. *See Yorkshire Lakes.*

Cover Bridge (N Yorks). Trout, grayling. East Witton Estate issue dt on **R Cover** from Hullo Bridge to Cover Bridge. Mostly both banks, fly only, dt £3 from Cover Bridge Inn, East Witton. Leyburn DL8 4SQ (Tel: 01969 623250).

Middleham (N Yorks). Trout, chub, grayling. Bradford No 1 AA has right bank here, left bank at **Langthorpe**, and right bank at **Roecliffe**, members only. Fishing may be had in Leeds ASA waters at Middleham Deeps and 1m downstream from Middleham Bridge, left bank. Excellent barbel, chub, grayling, a few large trout, and the odd salmon. Dt £3 from Cover Bridge Inn (above). Inn has further £3 dt for trout and grayling fishing on **R Cover**.

Leyburn (N Yorks). Grayling, trout, coarse fish. Two dt from Blue Lion, E Witton, for E Witton Estate water on Ure from Ulshaw Bridge to Harker Beck, 1¾m S bank, fly only. Hotels: Bolton Arms, Golden Lion.

Redmire (N Yorks). Trout, grayling; preserved. Restocked; fly only. All fishing now by st only (£150); numbers limited; apply Estate Office, Leyburn DL8 5EW. Trout best April, May and June; grayling Oct and Nov. Hotels: King's Arms, Redmire; White Swan, Middleham; Rose and Crown, Bainbridge; Wensleydale Heifer, West Wittom.

Aysgarth (N Yorks). Trout, grayling. Bradford City AA has approx 2m from footbridge, both banks, 3¾m both banks at **Worton Bridge**; Palmer Flatt Hotel has short stretch. Wensleydale AA water extends from 2m west of Hawes to Worton Bridge, plus ¾m beyond on north bank only. Tickets are obtainable, £6, conc. HQ, Rose and Crown Hotel, Bainbridge.

Askrigg (N Yorks). Trout, grayling; preserved by Wensleydale AA, *see above.* Tickets from King's Arms or Victoria Arms, Worton. Hotel: King's Arms.

Bainbridge (N Yorks): Wensleydale AA water includes 6m on Ure, all 2m on west bank of **R Bain**, and first mile from confluence with R Ure on east bank. For permits, *see above.*

Hawes (N Yorks). Trout, grayling; preserved with tributaries, from headwaters to 2m down-

stream of Hawes, by Hawes and High Abbotside AA. The fishing is pleasant, peaceful and not crowded. Sunday fishing, no ground bait, platforms for disabled. Visitors welcome: st £48, wt £24, dt £8, conc, from "Three Peaks Ltd", Riverside House, Bridge End, Hawes DL8 3NH (01969 667443); The Gift Shop; or Board Hotel Main St. Assn also has rights on Cotterdale, Hardraw, Duerley and Snaizeholme Becks, all both banks, trout and grayling. Below Hawes Wensleydale AA has several miles of excellent water. Disabled anglers may fish Widdale Beck at Apperset, near Hawes. Hotel: White Hart.

SWALE: Good chub and barbel water. Trouting best in upper reaches, water improving.

Helperby (N Yorks). Coarse fish; right bank from Swing Bridge to Myton Plantation controlled by Leeds Amal. Helperby & Brafferton AC have left bank from footbridge d/s for ¾m, also **Fawdington Fishery**, from ½m above Thornton Bridge, approx 1½m u/s to Fawdington Beck mouth. Chub, barbel, dace, pike, roach, perch. Dt for both these waters, 16 Jun–14 March, £3, conc, from Plowman-Render Groceries, Main St; Oak Tree Inn, Helperby (Tel: 01423 360268); or from Mr Moverley, Fawdingham Lodge Farm (Tel: 01423 360260). B & B also offered at farm.

Topcliffe (N Yorks). Noted coarse fishing centre; especially good for chub and barbel. Thirsk AC has Skipton and Baldersby fishing, dt from Thirsk Anglers Centre, Town End, Thirsk. Bradford No 1 AA has 900 yds at **Catton**, and further water at Topcliffe, members only. Black Bull Hotel, Topcliffe YO7 3PB (Tel: 01845 577 219/900) has water. Assn of Teeside and Dist Acs has 1½m at **Sand Hutton**; members only **Cod Beck**; trout; preserved by Bradford City AA; apply Hon Sec for permits.

Pickhill (N Yorks). Coarse fish; trout. Bradford No 1 AA fishes 1,800 yards at Scarborough farm, right bank. Members only. Leeds Amalgamation has a ¾m stretch at **Ainderby**.

Maunby (N Yorks). Bradford No 1 AA has two lengths left bank, members only.

Gatenby (N Yorks). Bradford No 1 AA has three stretches of right bank here, and at Old Hall Farm. Members only.

Morton-on-Swale (N Yorks). Roach, chub,

dace, barbel; fishing good. Northallerton AC has 2½m left bank downstream from A684 road bridge.

Great Langton (N Yorks). Trout, grayling, coarse fish; Kirkby Fleetham AC has both banks for 2m downstream from Langton Bridge, linking up with Northallerton AC's water at Bramper Farm; fly only; no tickets. Membership limited, with preference given to local residents.

Catterick (N Yorks). Good mixed fishing; trout, grayling, dace, chub, barbel, few roach and pike. Trout from 8oz to 1lb; fast takers. Richmond & Dist AS has 14m of water on both banks, Richmond being the centre. Ferryhill AC also has 1½m trout and coarse fishing above and below village, good barbel, chub, grayling, no dt. Hotels: Farmers' Arms; Angel Inn.

Richmond (N Yorks). Richmond and Dist AS preserves 14 miles above and below town centre, stocked with trout, plus most coarse species. St £25, wt £15, dt £5, conc. From tackle shop, 5 Market Place or Richmond Angling Centre, 8 Temple Square, Graven Gate, Richmond.

Reeth (N Yorks). Swale; trout. Black Bull Hotel has water for residents £1 day.

Muker (N Yorks). Trout; strictly preserved. Muker Beck; trout; Thwaite Beck, 1m W; trout; free. Summer Lodge Beck, 5m E; trout; preserved.

Keld (N Yorks). Trout; plentiful but small; preserved.

GUN BECK (tributary of Swale):

Husthwaite (N Yorks). Centre for good trout fishing on **Husthwaite Beck**; dt from York tackle shops.

Coxwold (N Yorks). Hole Beck and Gun Beck preserved.

BEDALE BECK (tributary of Swale):

Leeming (N Yorks). Swale, 2m NE; preserved by Black Ox AC from A1 road to confluence with Swale, excepting only two small fields above Leeming Bridge. Trout and coarse fish. St £6 from R M Wright, 5 Lascelles Lane, Northallerton.

COD BECK (tributary of Swale): good trout water, but recent pollution of lower reaches has affected sport.

Thirsk (N Yorks). Good local fishing for barbel and chub. Thirsk AC has water on Swale and Cod Beck; dt from tackle dealer. York and Dist AA have 5½ acre lake at **Sand Hutton**, Park View. Hotels: Royal Oak, Three Tuns. Tackle shop: Thirsk Anglers Centre, 7 Sowerby Rd YO7 1HR (Tel: 01845 524684) has river and stillwater tickets, for coarse and trout fishing, also instruction in fly fishing and fly tying. Free information on a variety of day ticket waters.

Sessay (N Yorks). Cod Beck, 2m W; Thirsk AC, Swale, 2m SW; Bradford club now has fishing on P J Till's farm (The Heights). The Oaks Fishery, David and Rachel Kay, The Oaks, Sessay, nr Thirsk YO8 3BG (Tel: 01845 501321): 3 lakes with carp and other coarse species. Disabled access. Inn: Railway, Dalton; Horsebreakers Arms, Sessay.

Brawith (N Yorks). Trout; preserved.

Topcliffe (N Yorks). Bradford City AA has water here, and on **Cod Beck**.

WISKE (tributary of Swale): River still troubled by pollution.

Otterington (N Yorks). Cod Beck, 2m E. Broad Beck. Sorrow Beck, 4m E.

Northallerton (N Yorks). Roach, dace, chub pike; preserved; fishing good. Northallerton AC has fishing on Wiske (members only) and on several miles of water on the Swale at Morton Bridge. *See also Morton-on-Swale*.

PARRETT

(For close seasons, licences, etc, see South West Region Environment Agency, p12)

Rises in hills on border of Somerset and Dorset, and flows into Bristol Channel near Bridgwater. Roach, bream and dace predominate. Thorney-Middle Chinnock stretch and some of tributaries hold trout. Occasional salmon and sea trout run through into Tone.

Bridgwater (Som). River tidal here. Now a Marina. Bridgwater AA fisheries are as follows: **King's Sedgemoor Drain** from ¾m above Greylake Bridge, where 18ft Rhyne enters Cary River to A38 Road bridge at Dunball. Good roach, rudd, pike, tench, bream, carp and perch. **North Drain** (jointly held with North

Somerset AA), **South Drain** (jointly held with Glaston Manor AA); **Huntspill River**; **Bridgwater and Taunton Canal**; **Dunwear**, **Screech Owl**, and **Combwich Ponds** (carp, bream, roach, rudd, tench, perch). Assn also has access to Wessex Federation waters on Rivers **Parrett** and **Isle**. St £20, wt £7, dt £4, from tackle shops in area or Hon Sec, with concessions for jun, OAP. Permits cover all waters. Pocket maps from Hon Sec. Day/night coarse fishing on Westhay Lake, 3½ acres, large tench and carp. Tel: 01278 456429. Pawlett Ponds, River Rd, **Pawlett**, 5 lakes, BB&WAA water, with carp, bream, tench, large roach, perch etc; dt £4 from Brickyard Farmhouse (below). Tackle shops: Somerset Angling, 74 Bath Rd; Waynes Tackle, 61 Eastover. Accommodation with special facilities for anglers: Brickyard Farmhouse, River Rd, Pawlett TA6 4SE (Tel: 01278 685709); Crossways Inn, West Huntspill (Tel: 01278 783756).

Langport (Som). Parret; pike to 30lb, large perch, carp, bream, roach, hybrids, tench, chub, rudd, eels. Langport AA has rights to 6½m; Assn is member of Wessex Fed; ticket holders may fish Fed waters on Parret and Isle, incl newly acquired 1½m stretch at **Hambridge**. Ass also owns 2¼ acre Coombe Lake, stocked with carp, bream and others. St £11, wt £5.50 and dt £3, conc, obtainable from tackle shop (below). Stoke-sub-Hamdon AA has stretches at **West Chinnock** and **Thorney**. Thorney Lakes, Muchelney, Langport TA10 0DW (Tel: 01458 25011) has coarse fishing, with carp to 21lb, and other species, dt £4. Tackle shop: The Tackle Shop, 1 Old Market Square, North St, Langport TA10 9RP (Tel: 01458 253665). Accommodation at Dolphin Hotel, Bow St (Tel: 01458 250200); 'Alls Well' Farmhouse B & B, Dibsbury, Langport (Tel: 01458 241465).

Crewkerne (Som). Trout, coarse fish. Stoke-sub-Hamdon AA has trout fishing (with restocking) from Bow Mills to Hurdle Pool (trout av ¾lb); members only; coarse fishing, 12 different species including 3 types of carp, from Hurdle Pool to Thorney Mill. St £4, concessions to jun & OAP, from local tackle shops and committee members.

TONE: Trout and coarse fish above Taunton, below, most species of coarse. Weedy in summer below **Taunton** but provides first-class coarse fishing in winter.

Taunton (Som). Good coarse fishing free on

town stretch. Taunton Fly Fishing Club has water on the Tone, trout and grayling, fly only. St £50 and dt for restricted areas of Tone from Topp Tackle. Taunton AA has water on **Bridgwater Canal** at Taunton; **West Sedgemoor Drain** from Pincombe Bridge, Stathe; **R Tone** fast stretch at Taunton, Creech and Ham; ponds at Walton, Norton and Wych Lodge. St £19.50, wt £10, dt £4, conc, from tackle shops (below). Quantock Fishery, Stream Farm, Bloomfield TA5 2EN (Tel: 01823 451367): 2 acre stocked rainbow trout, av 2lb. Viaduct Fishery, Cary Valley, Somerton TA11 6LJ (Tel: 01458 74022) has trout fly fishing in 25 acres of clear spring water, dt £19, 5 fish. Additional coarse fishing, dt £3. Frog Lane Fishery, **Durston**, Taunton: new carp fishery of 4 acres, easy access, good parking, open 24 hrs; permits £3.50 from Topp Tackle (below). Enterprise Angling have tickets £3.50 for British Telecom pond, nr Taunton, carp, roach, skimmers. No night fishing. Tackle shops: Topp Tackle, 63 Station Rd TA1 1PA (Tel: 01823 282518); Enterprise Angling, 1 Grays Rd, Taunton TA1 3BA, Tel: 01823 282623. Hotels: Castle (which advises visiting anglers on local facilities); County.

Hillfarrance Brook (a Tone tributary, from Hillfarrance to confluence with Tone). Trout, grayling, fly only, Taunton FFC water, members only. Axe (Chard Junction) ¾m single bank fishing below the village, fly only, Taunton FFC, members only. Axe (Axminster) ½m single bank fishing both sides of Cloakham Bridge, fly only, Taunton FFC members only. Annual subscription £50. Tickets for restricted areas from Topp Tackle.

Wellington (Som). Trout, roach, dace; trout average ½lb. Wellington AA has water from Fox Bros' works 2m up stream, and ¾m below, brown trout, grayling, roach, dace. Members only. Thereafter preserved by owners through Bradford to Taunton FFC water. Dt £2 for trout and coarse on R Tone at **Nynehead**: Mr R E Darby, Hornshay Farm, Nynehead, Wellington. **Langford Lakes**, Langford Budville, Wellington TA21 0RS (Tel: 01823 400476): 4 stocked coarse fishing ponds on conifer plantation, with mixed, carp to 25lb, tench and bream fishing. Barbless hooks only. Tackle, tickets and licences from Wellington Country Sports, 5 Lancer Court, High Street TA21 8SG (Tel: 01823 662120).

Wiveliscombe (Som). Tone, Milverton Brook and Norton Brook; trout; banks bushed.

NORTON BROOK (tributary of Tone):

Bishops Lydeard (Som). Trout; banks overgrown.

MILVERTON BROOK (tributary of Tone):

Milverton (Som). Trout; private; banks bushed.

YEO: Coarse fish, some trout.

Long Load (Som). Good coarse fishing.

Ilchester (Som). Mainly roach, dace, good chub fishing. St and wt for 6m stretch u/s and d/s of Ilchester, plus Long Lode Drain, from A D Goddard (see Yeovil). Club: Ilchester AC, who have fishing on **Yeo** and **Cam** above Ilchester. Viaduct Fishery, Somerton, 2 lakes, 4 acres, mixed coarse, dt on site. Tel: 01458 74022.

Yeovil (Som). Roach, dace, chub. Yeovil and Sherborne AA have water downstream of **Sherborne Lake**, **Sutton Bingham Stream** from Filter Station to Yeovil Junction and R Wriggle from Yetminster to R Yeo; trout. Tackle shop A D Goddard, 27/29 Forest Hill (Tel: 01935 476777) has tickets for local river and stillwater fisheries. Lyons Gate Caravan Park has 2 good lakes with carp, roach, tench. Dt £4, conc. Hotels: Mermaid; Manor; The Choughs.

ISLE: Prolific chub water; also roach, dace, etc. First ½ mile from junction with Parrett held by Wessex Federation of Anglers.

Isle Brewers (Som). Roach, chub, dace, some trout from Fivehead Road to Hambridge; Newton Abbott FA has R Ilse at Hambridge, and many coarse lakes and ponds. See Newton Abbot. **Ilminster** (Som). Roach, chub, dace. Chard & Dist AA water, members only, £10 membership from Chard Angling Centre. From below Ilminster to just above Fivehead River, Ilminster AA water; dt £2.50 from Hon Sec or Chard Angling Centre, 2 Holyrood St, Chard. Bathampton AA obtain fishing through exchange tickets. Contact Hon Sec.

RIBBLE

(For close seasons, licences, etc, see North West
Region Environment Agency, p13)

Rises in the Pennines and flows 69 miles into the Irish Sea between St Anne's and Southport.

Good coarse fishing lower down, between Great Mitton and Preston. Also coarse fishing in Church Deeps. Best salmon, sea trout, brown trout and grayling fishing is between Settle and Great Mitton. Tributary Hodder has good salmon, sea trout and brown trout fishing throughout length but much affected by water abstraction. Upper waters impounded in Stocks Reservoir. Its main tributary, the Loud, also provides good trout and sea trout fishing.

Preston (Lancs). Coarse fish, few salmon and sea trout. 2m Preston Federated Anglers water through town; st £10, dt £1.50, including other waters on **Ribble** and **Wyre**, and **Rufford Canal. Twin Lakes Trout Fishery, Croston** (Tel: 01772 601093): 12 acres, stocked fly only rainbow and brown trout, best rainbow 16lbs 7ozs. Dt £20 (4 fish), ½ day £12.50 (2 fish), boats from £6, double. Other local fishing: Greenhalgh Lodge Fishery, Greenhalgh Lane, nr Kirkham PR4 3HL (Tel: 01253 836348). Hudson's Farm, Rawcliffe Rd, St Michaels PR3 0UH (Tel: 01995 679654): mixed coarse fishery of 2 ponds and 2 lakes, large carp, bream, tench. Dt £4, one rod only, £3 conc; from farm. R Crossens, 1m from Southport, fished by Southport & Dist AA. Dt from Robinsons Tackle Shop, 71 Sussex Road, Southport. Tackle shop in Preston: Ted Carter, 85/88 Church Street (Tel: 01772 253476) has information on much Lancashire fishing.

Samlesbury (Lancs). Coarse fish, few salmon and sea trout. Several miles preserved by Ribble and Wyre FA, dt from Hon Sec. Members only. Assn also has stretch of R Wyre at St Michaels on Wyre. Northern AA have water, dt £2.50 from bailiffs or tackle shops.

Balderstone (Lancs). Northern AA have 2¼m at Balderstone Hall Farm to Lower House Farm. Fishing 4am to 11pm. Coarse, with game fish (Mar 15–Jun 15). Dt £2.50 on bank, conc. 30p, OAP, juv.

Longridge (Lancs). Ribble, 3m SE. Hodder, 5m NE. Salmon, sea trout and trout. Loud 2m N. Most of right bank preserved by Loud and Hodder AA. Visitors' tickets issued if accompanied by member. Prince Albert AS, Macclesfield, own several miles above M6 bridge. Warrington AA has short stretch at **Hurst Green**.

Ribchester (Yorks). Lancashire FFA have 4m

here, and water at **Gisburn**; also **Hodder** at **Newton and Chaigley, Lune** at Kirkby Lonsdale and Tebay; **Irt** at Santon Bridge, all with salmon, sea trout, some browns. Tickets only to members' guests. Other local body is Ribchester AC, Ribchester Arms, Ribchester. Dt £4 for good barbel fishing at Ribchester from Spar shop or White Bull.

Mitton (Yorks); ns Whalley, 2m. Salmon, sea trout, trout and coarse fish. Environment Agency controls left bank d/s from Mitton Bridge. Salmon fishing open Feb 1–Oct 31; brown trout Mar 15–Sept 30; coarse June 16–Mar 14. Permits Mrs Haynes, Mitton Hall Farm, Mitton Rd, Mitton, nr Whalley, Clitheroe BB7 9PQ, Tel: 01254 826002. Mid-Ribble AS has over 2.6m right bank of **R Hodder** above and below Lower Hodder bridge, nr Stonyhurst, down to Hodder Foot, also right bank Ribble from Hodder Foot to Starling Brook (½m below Dinckley Bridge), and left bank of Ribble at **Long Preston**. Waters stocked annually with trout, good returns for migratory fish, also coarse fishing. Members only, limited guest tickets. Details from Secretary.

Clitheroe (Lancs). Trout, salmon, sea trout. Clitheroe AA Ltd fishes 3m of Ribble, mostly double bank, and 1m of **Lune**, at **Kirkby Lonsdale**. Members only, no dt. The Inn at Whitewell, in the Forest of Bowland, offers fishing to guests (see *Whitewell*). By the A59 between Clitheroe and Accrington, Pine Lodge Coarse Fishery, dt £6–£5 on bank. Phone 01254 822208 for details. Blackburn and Dist AA have several miles on Ribble and other fisheries on **Lune**, **Wenning**, **Aire**, **Gilpin** and reservoirs. Some dt; apply Hon Sec. Ribble Valley Borough Council, issues st £26.80 to residents for water at Brungerley and below Edisford Bridge. Wt £18 for visitors, also dt £7.75 for Edisford alone, from T I Centre, Market Place, Clitheroe. Two rods on Hodder for residents of Red Pump Hotel, Bashall Eaves; dt issued. Tackle shops: Ken Varey's Outdoor World, 4 Newmarket St, Clitheroe BB7 2JW (Tel: 01200 423267); Fishing Tackle, 12–14 Southworth Street, Blackburn. Hotels: Inn at Whitewell, Old Post House; Calf's Head, Gibbon Bridge; Parkers Arms.

Chatburn (Lancs). **Ribble**, 1m W; good trout, occasional salmon and sea trout. Several miles of river preserved by Clitheroe AA; limited visitors' tickets through members only. Hotels: Pendle; Manor House Cottage.

Sawley (N Yorks). On Ribble. Salmon, sea trout, trout and grayling. Trout and salmon fishing good. Several miles preserved by Yorkshire FFC (visitors' tickets through members only). Inn: Spread Eagle.

Gisburn (N Yorks). Trout, salmon. Lancashire FFA have water at Ribchester and Gisburn, and at Walton le Dale. Fly fishing for members only. Hotels: Park House; Stirk House.

Long Preston (N Yorks). Ribble, 1m W. Trout, grayling, odd salmon, coarse fish. Left bank is preserve of Padiham & Dist AS. Members only. Staincliffe AC also have water, members plus 5 tickets for their guests. Hotels: Boar's Head; Maypole.

Settle (N Yorks). Settle AA has 7½m of good trout and grayling fishing in Ribble between Langcliffe, Settle and vicinity of Long Preston. Wt, dt at Royal Oak Hotel, Tel: 01729 822561, during licensing hours. Fly only; limit 1½ brace. Water stocked yearly. **Malham Tarn** is 6m from Settle and holds large trout. Dt water *(see Yorkshire lakes, reservoirs, etc)*. Further north are Manchester AA's waters. Licences from post offices. Other hotels at Settle: Falcon Manor and Golden Lion.

Horton in Ribblesdale (N Yorks). Trout; preserved from source to Helwith Bridge, including all tributaries, by Manchester AA. Assn also has **Newhouses Tarn** (fly only); stocked b and r trout. No tickets.

Tributaries of the Ribble

HODDER: Good salmon and trout water.

Higher Hodder Bridge (Lancs and Yorks). Salmon, sea trout, trout, grayling and coarse fish.

Chipping (Lancs). Hodder, 1½m E. Salmon, sea trout and grayling. Loud, 1m SE. Trout and sea trout. About ½m of Hodder below Doeford Bridge on right bank and several miles of **River Loud** are preserved by Loud and Hodder AA; tickets if accompanied by member. Hotel: Derby Arms.

Whitewell (Lancs). Salmon, sea trout, trout, grayling. The Inn at Whitewell, Forest of Bowland BB7 3AT (Tel: 01200 448 222, Fax: 298) has 4 rods for residents on 7m of Whitewell FA water. Dt £6 Nov–Mar, £12.50 15 Mar–31 Jul, £28 Aug–Oct incl. The Red

Pump Hotel, Bashall Eaves, has 2 rods 8m further down the river.

Newton (Lancs); Lancashire FFA have water downstream from Newton to Dunsop Bridge. At **Chaigley**, Southport FF have water, and Edisford Hall Estate; contact Townson Bros, Pendle Trading Estate, Chatburn, Clitheroe BB7 3LJ. Also at Chaigley.

Slaidburn (Lancs); ns Clitheroe, 8½m. Hodder; salmon, sea trout and trout. Tickets for several miles of Hodder from The Jam Pot Cafe, Slaidburn. Stocks Reservoir in vicinity. Hotel: Bounty.

CALDER: Coarse fishing. Some club water.

Elland (Yorks). Bradford No 1 AA fishery extends u/s of Elland Road Bridge for approx 1,800 yds. Members only.

Whalley (Lancs). West Calder. Ribble, 2m W; salmon, sea trout and coarse fish. Hodder, 2m W; salmon, sea trout and trout. Accrington FC have fishing on three stretches of Calder, members only. Contact non Sec.

Barrowford (Lancs). Pendle Water; trout. Colne Water (polluted) and Pendle join near Barrowford to form Calder (polluted). **Leeds and Liverpool Canal** from Barnoldswick to East Marton (10m), and 3½m at Keighley leased to Marsden Star AS. Dt £2.

Burnley (Lancs). Local waters mostly polluted. Burnley AS leases **Lea Green Reservoir**, at Hapton, but tickets only to local ratepayers; trout. **Hapton Lodges Reservoir** at Hapton stocked with rainbow trout; Blythe A C. Marsden Star AS fishes Gawthorpe Hall Pool at Padiham, members only, tench, carp, roach, perch fishing. Tackle shop: Macks Tackle, 33a Parliament Street.

COLNE (tributary of Calder): Much pollution but holds some trout and coarse fish.

Colne (Lancs). Colne; trout. Water held by Colne Water AS. **Leeds and Liverpool Canal** held by Marsden Star AS (10m from Barnoldswick to Bank Newton, and 3½m Howden to Morton); pike, trout, tench, bream, roach, rudd, carp and perch; st and dt for waters held by both clubs. Marsden Star AS also fishes Knotts Lane Ponds at Colne, coarse fish, members only. Ballgrove Fishery, Laneshawbridge,

Colne: coarse dt on bank, or from Pendle Leisure Services. For more information, contact Jackson's (*below*). Tackle shops: Anglers All, Colne; Jackson's Fishing Tackle, 27 Albion Street, Earby, Yorks BB1 6QA; Boyces, 44 Manchester Road, Nelson.

Foulridge (Lancs). Four British Waterways reservoirs: **Lower Foulridge** (or **Burwains**), **Upper Foulridge**, **Slipperhill**, **White Moor**. Let to clubs: coarse fishing dt on bank at Lower Foulridge from Pendle Leisure Services.

ROTHER

(For close seasons, licences, etc, see Southern Region Environment Agency, p12)

Rises near Rotherfield and reaches the sea at Rye Bay. Mostly coarse fish, with trout in upper reaches and tributaries but runs of sea trout increasing. Mullet and bass in estuary.

Rye (E Sussex). Near mouth of Rother; coarse fish. Free fishing from roadside bank between Iden and Scots Float, nr Rye. Clive Vale AC has 1m of **Tillingham River** above Rye and **Rother** at Wittersham to Iden Bridge; south bank footpath for 2 fields on **Royal Military Canal** at Winchelsea. Romney Marsh is close by. Several clubs have water, including Hastings, Bexhill and Dist Freshwater AA; st £35, dt £5, conc.

Wittersham (Kent). Roach, chub, bream, perch, pike, tench, bleak, eels, and other species. Rother Fisheries Association has 7m of Rother, accessible at Robertsbridge, Salehurst, Udiam, Bodiam, Newenden, Potmans Corner and Blackwell Bridge at Wittersham, also 3m of Royal Military Canal from Iden Lock to Appledore. Membership open to clubs, not individuals. Mostly members only, but £3 dt on canal, £1.50 juv, from bailiff on bank. Clive Vale AC have 2 good stretches at Blackwall Bridge and Otter Channel junction. Dt £3, only in advance, from Hon Sec or Hastings tackle shops. Hastings, Bexhill and Dist FAA has **Rother and Hexden Channel** between Rolveden and Wittersham. St £35, with concessions.

Newenden (E Sussex). Large bream, chub and roach; Rother Fishery Assn has fishing rights, terms described under *Wittersham*. Maidstone Victory Angling & Medway PS fish Rother here and at **Blackwell and Salehurst**. Membership on application.

Bodiam (E Sussex). Trout (small), coarse fish. Maidstone Victory Angling & Medway PS fish Rother here. Hastings, Bexhill & Dist FAA has 500 yds fishing on south bank with prime chub and dace, membership £35, conc. Hotels: Castle, Justins.

Etchingham (E Sussex). Hastings, Bexhill and Dist FAA has many miles of dykes and drains noted for pike, bream, tench and rudd on **Romney Marsh** between **Gulderford** and **Appledore**, **Wishing Tree Reservoir**, lakes and ponds, dt £5, conc, on some waters from Hon Sec or local tackle shops. CALPAC control **Speringbrook Sewer**, Snargate, nr **Appledore**, fen-like fishing of about 2,000 yds, with chub, roach, bream, dace, perch, pike. No night fishing on CALPAC water. At **Burwash** is **Lakedown Trout Fishery**, 4 lakes, 5 acres each, b and r trout from 1½lb to 16lb. Dt £28.50, 5 fish, ½ day £23.50, 3 fish. May–Aug evenings, £14.50. Contact A Bristow, Lakedown Fishery, Broad Oak, Heathfield TN21 8UX, Tel: 01435 883449.

Stonegate (E Sussex). Wadhurst AS has trout water; dt to members' guests only. Hotel: Bridge.

Tenterden (Kent). Tackle & Gun, 3 Eastwell Parade, High St TN30 6AH, have tickets for a large number of local fisheries. These include Rother FA (see Wittersham), Tenterden AC (incl various ponds, Dowels Sewer, Hexden Channel, Rother at Potmans Heath); Northiam AC (carp lakes and several miles of Rother); Rye AC (R Tillingham and R Brede, good coarse fishing); Headcorn AC (carp ponds in Biddenden area); also tickets for **Hawkhurst Fishery** (Tel: 01580 754420), 11 lakes, with trout and coarse fishing; Tenterden Trout Waters, Combe Farm, Tenterden TN30 6XA (Tel: 01580 763201): 3 lakes of 5 acres total, stocked with brown and rainbows, for fly fishing. Day and half-day permits from 8.20am to dusk.

BREDE: Rother tributary. Coarse fish, a few small trout; approx 6 miles controlled by Clive Vale AC. Members only, st £23, from Hon Sec or local tackle shops. Fishing station **Rye**, **Winchelsea**.

SEVERN

(For close seasons, licences, etc, see Midlands Region Environment Agency, p14)

Longest river in England. Rises in Wales (N Powys) and flows 180m into Bristol Channel.

Fair salmon river, with commercial fisheries near mouth; spring salmon in January/April and May. Average size good. Some trout and grayling in upper reaches, but river noted chiefly for coarse fishing, especially for chub in the upper reaches and barbel in the middle river. Shad run up river in May and are taken on rod and line, principally at Tewkesbury Weir.

Sharpness (Glos). Coarse fishing in the **Gloucester and Berkeley Canal** from Severn Bridge to Hempstead Bridge, Gloucester (about 16m); bank licence from any bridge house.

Gloucester (Glos). Gloucester United AA controls several miles of Severn from Hawbridge u/s and d/s, and Stank Lane. Dt £2, from bailiffs. (Assn also has water from **Lower Lode** to **Deerhurst**, on gravel pit at **Saul** and **Gloucester Sharpness Canal**). Red Lion Inn, Wainlode Hill, Norton (Tel: 01452 730251) has Severn fishing with facilities for disabled; tickets from hotel. **Witcombe Reservoirs**: 3 lakes of 12, 9, and 5 acres, fly only; a Troutmasters water, stocked rainbow trout of 2lb av. St £480–£220, dt £26–£15, depending on limit. Boats bookable in advance. Mrs M Hicks Beach, Witcombe Farm, Great Witcombe GL3 4TR (Tel: 01452 863591). Staunton Court, Ledbury Rd, Staunton GL19 3QS (Tel: 01452 840230), has stocked coarse fishing on Match Lake, Dovecote Lake and Pleck Pool (25 acres), with carp to 28lb, roach to 2lb, rudd, tench to 8lb, etc. £5 dt and tackle shop on site. Tackle shops: Allsports, 126/128 Eastgate Street (dt for Wye salmon fishing); Rod & Gun, 67 Alvin St; Tredworth Tackle, High St, Tredworth; D & J Sports, 75 Cricklade Street, Cirencester; Ian Coley 442/444 High St, both Cheltenham. Hotels: New County, Fleece, New Inn.

Tewkesbury (Glos). Salmon, twait and coarse fish. Avon: coarse fish. Below weir shoals of big bream. Birmingham AA has 38 stretches on Severn including those at Bushley, Ripple, Uckinghall, Severn Stoke, Deerhurst, Chaceley, Apperley (2 pools at Apperley, also) and Maisemore; also Church End Trout Fishery. Tewkesbury Popular AA has 80 pegs on Severn from mouth of Avon to Lower Load, with bream, chub, barbel, eels, gudgeon, pike and bleak, and salmon, and **Avon** from Healings Mill to Abbey Mill Ham side; bream, roach, chub, skimmer, bleak, gudgeon. Membership £14, conc, from R Danter. Only limited number of salmon permits issued each year. Gloucester

United AA have water at Drirhurst and Lower Lode. Dt from bailiff, tackle shops and Hon Sec. Trout fly fishing at Witcombe Waters Fishery, Great Witcombe (Tel: 01452 863591). Dt £25, 6 fish limit; half-day £15, 3 fish; evening £10, 2 fish. Tackle shop: R Danter, Tackle Shop, 31 Barton Street Tewkesbury GL20 5PR; Cheltenham Angling Centre, Tewkesbury Rd, Cheltenham. Hotels: Abbey, Malvern View, many others.

Ripple (Worcs). Bream, pike, perch, chub, dace, roach. Environment Agency fishery, 1,900 yds free to licence-holders, is on left bank, at M50 viaduct.

Upton-on-Severn (Worcs). Chub, barbel, bream, roach, dace, perch and pike. Environment Agency has 1,200 yds of west bank above old railway embankment, free to licence-holders, mainly bream and roach fishing. Upton-upon-Severn AA has 10 pegs at Hanley Rd, 42 pegs at Upper Ham. Free parking. Dt £2 from G Shinn, tackle shop, 21/23 Old Street, WR8 0HN. Birmingham AA has 7 meadows, members only. Hotels: King's Head, Swan, Star.

Worcester (Worcs). Barbel, bream, chub, roach. Free fishing behind cricket ground. Worcester & Dist United AA has stretches at Kempsey below Worcester, 350m I bank; Pixham Ferry, 800m r bank; West Diglis, 900m r bank; East Diglis, 350m I bank; Pitchcroft, 800m I bank. Assn also has stretches of **Avon**, and 2,500m I bank **Teme** at Knightwick. Dt through Hon Sec (Tel: 01905 424505) or through tackle shop (*below*). Dt on bank for 12 pegs at Bevere Lock (Tel: 01905 640275). Birmingham AA has stretches at Severn Stoke, Hallow, Kempsey, Grimley and Holt Fleet, rights on Worcester and Birmingham Canal from King's Norton to Blackpole (near Worcester); bream, roach, perch, pike. Bank House Hotel Lake, 40 acres, has carp fishing. Tel: 01886 833557. Tackle shop: Alan Reynolds, Worcester, Tel: 01905 422107, has tickets for Evesbatch Fisheries, 2 lakes with carp and roach.

Lincombe and **Holt** (Worcs). Wharf Inn (Tel: 01905 620289) has section at Holt Fleet, 19 pegs with carp and bream. Disabled access, dt from inn. Holt Fleet Restaurant (Tel: 01905 620286) has 550m r bank with barbel and chub. Dt on bank. Dt for Lincombe Lock, 180m I bank, from keeper on site (Tel: 01299 822887). Ockeridge Lakes, 6 Green Lane, Lower Broadheath WR2 6QH: 4 coarse lakes 7m from Worcester. Stocked with roach, gudgeon, rudd, bream, carp, perch, etc. Dt £4, £3.50 conc. Barbless hooks only.

Stourport-on-Severn (Worcs). At confluence of Severn and Stour: barbel, chub and large roach; also **Staffordshire and Worcestershire Canal**: coarse fish. Lyttelton AA has 80 pegs right bank u/s of Stourport. Tickets from Mark Lewis only. Birmingham AA has ½m both banks. Hampstall Hotel (Tel: 01299 822600) has 225m r bank, perch and roach. Tackle shop: Mark Lewis, Raven Street, where Lyttelton AA tickets are sold. 1¼m both banks downstream of **Cilcewydd Bridge** is Environment Agency fishery, free to licence-holders.

Bewdley (Worcs). Chub, roach, dace, barbel. Telford AA has 2,000m I bank, dt from Rod & Gun, Dawley, information from Hon Sec (Tel: 01952 590605). Harbour Inn, Arley (Tel: 01299 401204) has 2 meadows. Dt from bailiff. Kidderminster AA has 125 pegs, 2½m water, above and below town; 70 pegs below Stourport at **Winnalls**, and water at **Buildwas** and **Alveley**. Membership cards £19.50, conc, from all local tackle shops. Birmingham AA has six stretches in vicinity. Cards for both Assns from Stan Lewis, (*see below*). Stan Lewis runs riverside guest-house with B & B and clubroom, and issues tickets for 1½m Severn at Bewdley and 9 local pools under his own supervision, with excellent roach, chub, and pike to 26lb 8 oz; also section of **R Teme**, with large barbel and chub. Tackle shops; Stan Lewis, 3/4 Sevenside South, Bewley (Tel: 01299 403358); Mal Storey, Sutton Rd, Kidderminster; Mark Lewis, Raven St, Stourport.

Upper Arley (Worcs). Salmon, trout, grayling, chub, dace, pike, etc. Dowles Brook, 3m S. Birmingham AA has stretches at **Arley Stanley**, **Arley Kinlet**, **Arley**, **Aveley** and **Rhea Hall**. Hotels: Valentia, Harbour and Unicorn (last two issue dt).

Hampton Loade (Salop). Barbel, roach. Dt on bank for 1,875m I bank at Hampton Lock; contact Wolverhampton AA (Tel: 01902 457906). 350m, r bank, dt on bank, or from Caravan Site, Old Forge House, Hampton Loade. Birmingham AA has extensive fishing here, on both banks, and at **Alveley**.

Bridgnorth (Salop). Barbel, roach. Ship Inn (Tel: 01746 861219) has 270m west bank, dt on bank. Birmingham AA has stretches at

Knowle Sands, Danery, Quatford and **Eardington. Willey Park Pools** at **Broseley** (5m) and pools at **Ticklerton** are also on club card; rainbow, brown and some American brook trout. Membership limited. Boldings Pools, 6 lakes with carp and tench, dt on bank. Tel: 01746 763255. **Poole Hall**, nr Kidderminster, 5 coarse lakes with carp and other species. Dt on bank. Tel: 012997 861458. **Shatterford Lakes**, Bridgenorth Rd, Shatterford DY12 1TW (Tel: 01299 861597): one trout lake, "Masters", catch and kill at £15.50, 4 fish, £10.50, 2 fish; catch and release dt £8; OAP conc, Mon and Wed; also 3 coarse lakes with carp, catfish, roach, perch etc; dt £4.50, or £5.50, 2 rods. Masters lake and Stella Lake (coarse) accessible to disabled. Small tackle shop at fishery. 100 pegs at Townsend Fisheries, Tel: 01746 780551; carp and roach, tickets on bank. Kingsnordley Fisheries, **Kingsnordley**, Bridgnorth WV15 6EU (Tel: 01746 780247): 12 day ticket pools, with bream, barbel, tench, roach, chub, and large carp. Dt £3 on bank, specimen pool £5, extra rods £1 each. Astbury Falls Fish Farm (Tel: 01746 766797) has £12 dt, 5 hours, 2 trout; £18 full day, 3 trout; also coarse dt £5, for large carp. Fishing holidays at Bandon Arms, Mill St, 01746 763135. Accommodation with facilities for anglers at The Woodberry Down, Victoria Rd, Tel: 01746 76236. Kidderminster tackle shops: Storey's Angling Centre, 129 Sutton Rd. Hotels: Severn Arms; Falcon; Croft; Kings Head.

Coalport (Salop). Chub, barbel, pike, etc, fewer roach and dace than are found farther downstream. Some free water. Rowley Regis and Dist AS has stretch on right bank. No tickets.

Ironbridge (Salop). Barbel, chub, roach, perch, etc. Birmingham AA has ¼m. Environment Agency has 600 yds of fishing on left bank free to licence-holders. Tel: 01743 272828, for information. Dawley AS has right bank d/s from power station fence to Free Bridge, also pools at **Telford**, **Broseley** and **Dawley**. Dt £2.50, conc, on all waters from bailiffs. Telford AA (Tel: 01952 590605) has Sweeneycliffe House fishery near Dawley, 700m l bank. Dt on bank, or from Rod & Gun. Queens Arms AC (Tel: 01952 592602) has 3 stretches, total 51 pegs u/s and d/s of Free Bridge. Dt from bailiff on bank. Little Dawley Pools: 3 pools with carp, roach, bream, carp, Tel: 01952 590605; dt on bank or from tackle shop, Rod & Gun, High St, Dawley. Hotel: Tontine.

Atcham (Salop). Barbel, chub. Environment Agency has 2,895m r bank. Macclesfield Prince Albert AS has members only fisheries here, at **Bicton**, **Melverley**, **Longnor**, **Royal Hill**, **The Isle**, **Welshpool**, **Newton**, and elsewhere, a total of 29 Severn beats. Also fishings on the rivers **Gam**, **Vyrnwy** and **Banwy**. **Shrewsbury** (Salop). Chub, roach, barbel. Town waters, 1,800m both banks, dt on bank or from all tackle shops. Wingfield Arms Inn SY4 1EB (Tel: 01743 850750), 4m west of town, has a mile of river at Montford Bridge with barbel and eels, and good pike fishing. Seven Oaks Log Cabin Park (Tel: 01743 884271) has 350m, dt from warden on site. **Weir** fishery controlled by council, Tel: 01743 231456 for fishery; 356046 for bailiff. St £29.60 to £26.64, salmon; £14.30 to £6.60 coarse. Old LMS SC has fine stretches at **Emstry**, with fords and runs. Dt from all local tackle shops. St Helens Ramblers AS, Hon Sec, Alec Twiss, 47 Exeter St, St Helens, have two stretches at Shrewsbury. Permits. Birmingham AA has stretches at **Underdale**, **Pool Quay** and **Buttington Bridge**. Warrington AA has **Severn** at **Loton Park**, Alberbury. Lymm AC has dt water at Atcham and Rossall (nr Montford Bridge) with very large chub and barbel, members only. Tackle shops: Ebrall Bros, Smithfield Road; Kingfisher Angling Centre, 8 New St; Sundome Fishing Tackle, 1 Sundome Avenue; Shrewsbury Bait Centre, Whitchurch Rd.

Melverley (Salop). Chub, dace. Environment Agency has two meadows on left bank, about 500 yds, free to licence-holders. Tel: 01743 272828, for details. Chester AA has 800 yds immediately d/s of Environment Agency stretch. At **Crewgreen**, Fir Tree Inn, SY5 9AT (Tel: 01743 884243) is HQ of Fir Tree AC, with excellent fishing for large barbel, dace, roach, and pike. Limited dt from Inn; B & B also available.

Llandrinio (Montgomery). Chub, dace, trout, barbel, salmon; leave from farmers. Lymm AC has water on Severn and Vyrnwy, members only. Montgomery AA has 2,290 yds left bank, upstream from bridge to Lower Farm. Cheshire AA has Haughton Farm and Pentre stretches. St £10. Canal; coarse fish, tickets (see *Welshpool*). **Maerdy Brook**, 2m SW. Arddleen Brook, excellent trout, dace and chub. Hotel: Golden Lion.

Welshpool (Powys). Salmon, trout, coarse fish (incl grayling). Trout small in streams, few but big in river. Welshpool and Dist AC now in

Montgomeryshire AA which has 60m of coarse and game fishing in **Severn**, **Camlad**, **Vyrnwy**, **Banwy**. Also **Shropshire Union Canal** (coarse fishing). Their 2 Welshpool stretches are at **Coed-y-Dinas** and **Lower Leighton**, 750m and 1,500m. Dt from tackle shops in Welshpool. Black Pools trout fishery, fly only, is 1m from Welshpool on Llanfair Rd; Montgomery AA water. Some permits are sold for **Maesmawr Pool** (5m NW). Bank and boat fishing (dt £9 and £4) on Marton Pool, Marton, 5m SE. Good coarse fishing. Apply to Site Manager, Marton Pool Caravan Park. Warrington AA has Hope Farm stretch, Welshpool. Hotels: Westwood Park, Salop Rd, Welshpool, who have Montgomery AA tickets; Bear, Newton; Black Lion, Llanfair Caereinion.

Forden (Powys). Montgomery, 3m. Trout, salmon, chub, dace, etc. Birmingham AA has 3m. Camlad; trout, grayling. Montgomeryshire AA and Cheshire AA have water on river; tickets.

Montgomery (Powys). Severn, 2m; trout, salmon, grayling, chub, pike and perch. Lion Hotel, Caerhowell has 400 yards of Severn; st £25 dt £1.50. **Camlad**, 2m N; good trout, grayling, chub. Montgomeryshire AA has water; tickets. Warrington AA has waters at Caerhowell Hall, **Dolwen**, **Fron** and **Llanidloes**. Also **Vyrnwy**, **Dee**, canals and pools. Herbert Arms, Cherbury, has 1½m; dt. Caerhowel Cottage (Tel: 01686 668598) has dt for 80m r bank, mixed coarse. Tackle shops in Welshpool and Newtown.

Abermule (Powys). **Severn** and **Mule**; salmon, trout, grayling, coarse fish; mostly private but dt for some lengths. Water not always fishable in summer. Montgomeryshire AA has 1¼m of Severn and water at Mule junction; dt from Hon Sec. Warrington AA has stretch; Lymm AC has 1,000 yds, members only, trout and grayling.

Newtown (Powys). Salmon, trout, grayling, pike, chub, dace. 6,000m, mainly right bank, beginning at municipal car park, with bream; tickets from Mike Williams, Valeting, Kerry Rd, Newtown. Information from Severnside and Newtown AC (Tel: 01686 62871). Environment Agency has free fishery of 500 yds north bank beside sewage farm at **Penarth**, with chub and dace. Tel: 01743 272828 for details. Newtown and Dist FC, Llanfair Caerinion FC and Welshpool AC form Montgomeryshire AA, who

have waters here as follows: the old free stretch from above Halfpenny Bridge, both banks; Newtown recreation ground; **Vaynor Estate**; **Penstrowed** and **Dolwerw**; also **Fachwen Pool**, fly only r trout fishing. St and dt from M Cakebread's Garage, Pool Rd, Newtown. Severnside AC has extensive Severn fishing at Newtown, Penstrowydd, Vaynor, Glan Hafren Hall, Dolerw Park, also 4 meadows at **Abermule**, and pools. Prince Albert AS has stretch here. Penllwyn Lodges (Tel: 01686 640269) offers self-catering log cabins with fishing in 1m of canal plus small lake; tench, chub, carp. Tackle shop has dt for canal at **Abermule** and **Nettershiem Trout Lake**, 4½ acres. Tackle shop: Newtown Angling. Hotels: Elephant and Castle, Maesmawr Hall, Dolforwyn Hall.

Caersws (Powys). Maesmawr Hall Hotel has 3½m on Severn free to guests. Trout, coarse fish, some salmon. Caersws AA has 5m water in vicinity of Caersws and Llandinam with good brown trout and grayling; fly, spinning and worm. St £60, dt £7, conc, (also covers Llandinam fishery) from Spar shop or Buck Hotel, Main St, Caersws SY17 5EL.

Llandinam (Powys). Trout and grayling fishing on both banks. Caersws AA controls Dinam Fishery, fly only, st £60, dt £7, conc; from Llandinam P O, or see *Caersws*.

Llanidloes (Montgomery). Trout, salmon, pike, chub, dace, grayling. Llanidloes AA has about 20m fishing on upper **Severn**, **Afon Clywedog** and other tributaries. St and dt from Hon Sec. Warrington AA has Dolwen Bridge to Llanidloes. Upper Penrhyddlan, 1,125m r bank, grayling fishing, dt on bank. Tel: 01686 412584 for information. Environment Agency has 805m on right bank beginning at sewage works, which is free fishing to licence-holders, mostly chub, dace, with grayling, Tel: 01743 272828 for details. O S Evans, Dol Llys Farm, SY18 6JA has 300 yds right bank, Tel 015512 2694. Warrington AA, has water downstream. At **Trefeglwys** (4m N) is caravan park with fishing (trout and coarse) on **Trannon**. Best months for trout April–July. Llyn Ebyr, 30 acre coarse lake with perch, pike, tickets from J Williams, Llyn Ebyr, Tel: 01686 430236. Hotels: Lloyds, Unicorn, Queen's Head, Angel, Temperance, Royal Oak, Red Lion.

Tributaries of the Severn

LEADON: Trout, coarse fish (some barbel introduced).

Ledbury (Hereford). Ledbury AA has trout water, no dt. Castlemorton Lake; coarse fishing; free, but licence necessary. Three Counties Fisheries have 25 peg carp pool here, with roach, tench and rudd. Management also runs pool fishing at **Bromsberrow**, **Grandison** and **Leominster**. Contact Field Cottage, Ryton, nr Dymock, Glos GL18 2DH, Tel: 0531 890455. Hotel: Royal Oak, The Southend, Tel: 0531 632110, caters for anglers.

AVON: The principal tributary of the lower Severn. Roach, chub, dace and perch dominate higher reaches; bream and pike, the latter patchily distributed.

Tewkesbury (Glos). Confluence of Avon and Severn, connected also by 'Mill Avon'. Weirs and weir-pool fishing, including twaite shad during the spawning run. Cheltenham AC controls 2m of Avon at Corpus Christi by **Strensham** village. Good coarse fishing, chub, roach, bream, perch, pike included. Membership £11, dt £2, conc, (Mon to Sun only) from Hon Sec, Cheltenham tackle shops or the Bell Inn, Eckington. Mythe Pool, Tewkesbury: 10 acre coarse lake with bream, roach; tickets from Alan Reynolds Tackle Shop, Worcester, Tel: 01905 422107

Twyning (Glos). Chub, dace, roach, pike, perch, bream. Birmingham AA has ½m stretch. Pittville Park, Cheltenham: park lake of 50 pegs, carp to 30lb, roach, rudd. Dt £4 from Prince of Wales Stadium. Information from S Read, 4 Folly Lane, Cheltenham.

Eckington (Worcs). Most species of coarse fish, principally bream, big head of roach. Bailiff for Lower Avon, S R Spencer, Butchers Shop, Eckington, Pershore WR10 3AW (Tel: 013867 50235). Hotel: Bell Inn (Tel: 01386 750205), 1/4m from river, is HQ of Eckington AC, which controls over 4m, 200 pegs of lower Avon, with many coarse species. Permits obtainable, £2.50, contact bailiff S R Spencer (*above*).

Pershore (Worcs). Roach, bream. Worcester & Dist United AA has 900m at Burlington, and 1,000m at Pensham. Information from Assn, Tel: 01905 424505; dt from Alan Reynolds Tackle Shop, Worcester. Fox Inn AC has water 1½m below Pershore, Tel: 0121 458 2797 or 0121 327 3113. Birmingham AA has water here, both banks and at Pensham, Birlingham, **Nafford**, **Eckington**, **Bredon**, **Twyning**, **Bredons Hardwick** and at Mythe Farm.

Some free water in recreation ground. Tackle shop: Browns Tackle, Pershore, who sells Pershore AC permits. Hotel: Angel.

Evesham (Worcs). Pike, perch, bream, roach, dace, gudgeon, chub, bleak. Evesham AA has 60 pegs in town, and 26 pegs behind football club, dt £2.80 from bailiff on bank. Club has free fishing for jun and disabled at Workman Gardens, Waterside. Dt on bank for Crown Corp Meadows, 57 pegs: C Thompson (Tel: 01386 458800). At **Hampton Ferry**: E W Huxley & Son, Hampton Ferry Fishery, has 104 pegs. Dt £3 (incl car park) from bailiffs or Raphael's Restaurant. Hampton Ferry, WR11 4BP (Tel: 01386 442458). Anchor Meadows, **Harvington**: 500m right bank with barbel and chub, dt on bank, or The Bungalow, Anchor Meadows (Tel: 01386 48065). Birmingham AA has fisheries at Swifts, **Wood Norton**, **Chadbury**, **Charlton**, **Cropthorne**, **Fladbury**, **Lower Moor** and **Wick**. Manor Farm Leisure (caravan holidays), Anchor Lane, Harvington, Tel: 01386 870039, has 1,200m coarse fishing on Avon. Waterside and Workman Gardens (overnight only), reserved for local and disabled anglers. Twyford Farm, Evesham, has 1,000m right bank, chub, roach, tickets on bank. Tel: 01386 446108. Licences from post office. At Twyford Farm, Evesham WR11 4TP, 1½m R Avon, and coarse fishing lake, with carp, bream, etc. Dt £3 river, £3.50 carp pool, conc. Contact May Vince, Tel: 01386 446108, day, 01789 778365 evening. **The Lenches Lakes**, Hill Barn Orchard, Evesham Rd, Church Lench, Evesham WR11 4UB (Tel: 01386 871035): stocked rainbow trout, fly fishing on two lakes of 3½ acres each; fish av 2lb–2½lb, record 11lb 6oz; dt £35, 6 fish, half-day £20, evening £15, conc, tackle sold on site. Tackle shops: Bait Box, High St; Woof's, Mill Bank. Alcester tackle shop: Sports and Tackle, 3A High St, Alcester.

Stratford-upon-Avon (Warwick). A stretch of the Avon preserved by District Council, Elizabeth House, Church St, CV37 6HX, Tel: 01789 267575. Royal Leamington Spa AA has Lido and Recreation Ground fishing, dt £2; reservoir and two pools at Snitterfield, River Avon and pool at Wasperton, members only. Local club, Stratford-upon-Avon AA has 500 pegs on R Avon from Hampton Lucy to Luddington, and **R Stour** at Preston-on-Stour, with good variety of coarse fish in both; also 12m fishing in **South Stratford Canal**, Stratford to Wilmcote, and Grand Union Canal,

Hatton; membership £17, conc, dt £2.50 from tackle shops. Lifford AC has North Stratford Canal, Lifford Lane to Brandwood Tunnel, 60 pegs. Worcester & Dist United AA has Alveston Hill fishery, 1,500m both banks, with roach, chub. Tickets from Reynolds Tackle Shop, Worcester. Birmingham AA has stretches at **Avon Meadows**, **Welford**, **Barton**, **Bidford**, **Marlcliff**, **Cleeve Prior** and **Salford Priors**. Good chub and dace and also water on **Stour** (2m S). Alveston Village AC has 47 pegs on Avon at **Alveston**, with chub, bream, roach, carp, barbel. Dt £3 from Secretary (Tel: 01789 268110). At **Moreton in Marsh**, Lemington Lakes: 4 small pools with carp, rudd, roach, tench, bream, dt water, Tel: 01608 650872. Park Farm, Compton Verney, 20 acre coarse fishery with bream, tench, dt on bank; Tel: 01926 6402415. Tackle shop: Stratford Angling Centre, 17 Evesham Rd. Hotels: Welcombe, Falcon, Arden and many others.

Leamington (Warwick). Bream, chub, dace, roach, pike, perch. Avon at **Wasperton** and **Stratford** Lido and Recreation Ground preserved by Royal Leamington Spa AA Assn also has 12½m in Grand Union Canal, Warwick to Napton, coarse fish (good carp and tench in June, July, Aug); R **Leam**, **Offchurch** to outfall of Avon, several ponds. Dt £2, conc, for most of these at Stratford; annual membership £19, conc, from The Tackle Cellar (*below*). **Chesterton Mill Pool**, Chesterton Green, **Harbury** CU33 9NL, Tel: 0831 137277, has dts £19 to £11 on site, for 4½ acres, fly only, brown and rainbow trout, 1 Mar–30 Nov. Tackle shops: The Tackle Cellar, 24 Russell Terrace Leamington Spa CV31 1ZE; Baileys, 30 Emscote Rd, Warwick.

Rugby (Warwick). Chub, roach fishing. Environment Agency has free fishery at Avon Mill, 640m north bank beside B4112 road. Tel; 01684 850951, for details. Avon Ho AC have water on Oxford Canal nr Barby. Club also has 3 pools at Kings Newsham and stretch of upper Avon. Membership from Banks and Burr (*below*). Aces AC have water on North Oxford Canal, contact C Bower (Tel: 01788 656422). Knightley AC fishes 4m of Grand Union Canal, from Crick Tunnel to **Yelvertoft**. Large carp, eels, bream, and good stocks of smaller fish. Dt on bank, or from Yelvertoft PO.

Foxholes Fishery, Crick, Northampton-shire NN6 7US (Tel: 01788 823967): 4 pools fishable on season ticket, £50–£120; and 1 dt

pool, £5, or £10 two rods. All species stocked. One lake is specialist water with carp to 32lb. Contact Roger Chaplin. Barby Mill Pool is fish-able on dt, good carp and all species, contact R Bubb (Tel: 01788 579521). Spring Pools are 3 pools close to Rugby at Newton. All species, dt on bank, or Tel: 0467 834873. Clifton Lakes on A5 offer 8 pools and 1 lake plus length of R Avon. Dt on bank. Contact Barry Entwhistle (Tel: 0956 634079). **Newbold Quarry**, old established water for good tench and roach fishing, run by Severn Trent. Water close by Dunchurch, dt from lodge on site. **Stemborough Mill**, Stemborough Lane, Leire, nr **Lutterworth**, Leics LE17 5EY (Tel: 01455 209624). 4 acre trout fishery on upper reaches of Soar. Dt £15, part day £12 from lodge; drinks from self-service. Tackle shops: Banks & Burr, 25/27 Claremont Road, CV21 3NA (Tel: 01788 576782); Donalds, 155A Bilton Rd. Hotels: Grosvenor; Three Horseshoes, both Rugby; Post House, Crick.

ARROW joined by the **Alne** at Alcester: flows into Avon at Salford Priors. Coarse fish, some trout.

Salford Priors (Worcs). Arrow and Avon; coarse fish. Birmingham AA has ¾m.

Wixford (Warwick). Pike, perch, roach, dace, chub and bream; dt £3 for about 1m of water on Ragley Park Estate from Fish Inn, Wixford B49 6DA (Tel: 01789 778593), or from bailiff on bank. Lakes: Ragley Park, 1m NW. B & B next door to inn.

Redditch (Worcs). Redditch & Dist FA are local federation who fish **Arrow Valley Lake**, with carp to 25lb, large roach and other coarse fish. Dt £2.80 on site, Avon at Wick nr **Pershore** and **Birmingham – Stratford Canal**. Contact S Mousey, Tel: 01527 854160. 3m SW of town, Powell's Fishery on 3½ acre **Norgrove Pool**. R trout to 6lb, av 1½lb. Dt £8 + £2 per fish, 5 fish limit. Barbless hooks, no tandem lures. 12 rods per day. Contact Powell's (*see below*). Good fishing in **Lodge Pool**, tench and carp. Tackle shops: Powell's, 28 Mount Pleasant, Tel: 62669; Corn Stores, Headless Cross. Hotels: Royal, Southcrest.

Alvechurch (Worcs). Barnt Green FC has rights on **Upper and Lower Bittell Reservoirs**, **Arrow Pools** and **Canal feeder**. **Lower Bittell** and **Mill Shrub** trout (fly only), remainder coarse fish. Fishing for members and their guests.

STOUR (tributary of Avon): Coarse fish, trout, mostly preserved.

Shipston (Warwick). Shipston-on-Stour AC has water; members only. Birmingham AA has Stour fishing at Milcote. Hotel: George.

LEAM (tributary of Avon): Coarse fish.

Eathorpe (Warwick). Coventry Godiva AS has fishery here; coarse fish. Good winter fishing; st. Dt for fishing at Newbold Common, Avon confluence, from Frosts, Bath St, Leamington. Red Lion waters, **Hunningham**, from Red Lion, Tel: 01926 632715. Warwick DC (Tel: 01926 450000) has 750m at Pump Room Gardens, Leamington Spa. Dt on bank; and Leamington Mill Gardens, 350m l bank; both with roach, perch.

HAM BROOK (tributary of Leam): Coarse fish.

Fenny Compton (Warwick): Good pike, bream, tench, roach in **Oxford Canal**. **Claydon**.

SOWE (tributary of Avon): few fish.

Coventry (W Midlands). Excellent trout and coarse fishing on **Packington Estate**. **Meriden**. More than 5 miles of river fishing and 160 acres of lakes. Rainbow and brown trout; also coarse fishery 2m off. *(For details see Midlands (reservoirs and lakes)).* Coventry AA has extensive fishing on rivers, canals and reservoirs and coarse fishing in **Trent** and **Soar** at Thrumpton, **Ouse** at Turvey, **Nene**, **Thames** and **Anker**, 30 acres of coarse pools nr **Atherstone**; day tickets for some of this fishing may be had from tackle shops in Coventry area or Hon Sec. Canal waters include stretches on **Coventry Canal** and **Oxford Canal**. Dt £5 from bailiffs for Assn's **Napton Reservoirs**, noted bream, carp (to 29lb), tench and roach water, also pike to 22lb. 6m from town, Hopsford Hall Fishery, Shilton Lane, nr Withybrook. Carp to 20lb and other coarse species. Good access for disabled. Dt from bailiff on bank. Royal Leamington Spa AA control Jubilee Pools, at Ryton-on-Dunsmore. For membership, see *Leamington*. Meadowlands Fisheries, A423 Oxford Rd, Ryton-upon-Dunsmore (Tel: 024 7655 0638): 2 lakes, 13.5 and 3.5 acres, large stocks of bar-

bel, tench, carp, bream, roach and rudd. Opened 1995. Lavender Hall Premier Fisheries, Lavender Hall Lane, Berkswell (Tel: 01676 534814, or 0468 464299): 5 well stocked lakes with carp, tench, bream, roach, etc. Tackle shops: W H Lane & Son, 31/35 London Road, Coventry CVI 2JP, Tel: 024 7622 3316 (assn cards); Tusses Fishing Tackle, 360 Aldermans Green Rd. Brandon Hall Hotel, Brandon (Tel: 024 7654 2571) offers details and instruction on local angling.

TEME: Trout and coarse fish, with a few salmon; grayling. Very large barbel, strong tackle recommended. Trout in upper reaches.

Worcester (Worcs). Barbel, chub. St John's AS (Tel: 01905 358263) has 1,500m right bank at Powick Hams. Worcester and Dist UAS has 2,500m l bank at Knightwick. Dt for both from Reynolds Tackle, Worcester. Talbot Hotel (Tel: 018868 21235) has 135m both banks.

Leigh (Worcs). Trout, chub, dace, grayling, pike, perch, salmon. Bransford AS and local clubs rent Leigh to Powick; members only.

Broadwas (Worcs). Trout, grayling, chub, dace. Birmingham AA has stretch of left bank here and at Eardiston, 1¼m.

Knightwick (Worcs). Salmon, trout, barbel. Permits for one mile with large barbel and chub, from Stan Lewis, 3/4 Sevenside South, Bewley, Tel: 01299 403358.

Tenbury (Worcs). Barbel, chub. Peacock Waters (Tel: 01584 881411) has 900m l bank, tickets on bank. Tickets for Little Hereford, 500m right bank d/s of bridge, A Jones, Westbrook Farm, Tel: 01584 711280. Tenbury FA has approx 4m of Teme above and below town and 1m of **Ledwyche Brook**, trout, salmon and grayling, and barbel, chub, pike etc. Membership £80. Dt £7 game, £3 coarse; from Hon Sec (Tel: 01584 810 345/695), or from Mr Bill Drew, Oak Tree Cottage, Berrington Rd, Tenbury Wells WR15 8BB. St Michaels Pools, New House Farm, St Michaels, Tenbury (Tel: 01568 750245: brown and rainbow trout, fly only. Hotels: Crow; Royal Oak; B & B at Deepcroft Farmhouse (Tel: 01584 781412).

Stourport on Severn (Worcs). Barbel, chub. Ham Bridge fishing, 1,500m l bank, dt from Ham Bridge Farm (Tel: 01866 812228). Tackle shop; Mark Lewis.

Ludlow (Salop). Chub, dace. Ludlow AC (Tel: 01584 873577) has 1,000m right bank u/s of Dinham Weir; Saltmore fishery, 500m below bridges, r bank dt from Ludlow tackle shops. Birmingham AA has 1m here, Ashford Carbonnel, Eastham and Lindridge. Delbury Hall Trout Fishery, Diddlebury SY7 9DH (Tel: 01584 841267): dt £18, 2 fish limit. Tackle shop: Ludlow Tackle, Bromfield Rd SY8 1DW (Tel: 01584 875886) controls 5 stretches of dt water with good coarse fishing on Severn and on Teme, and local stillwaters. **Walcot West Lake**, 18 acres with bream and tench; tickets from Ludlow tackle shops. Hotels: The Feathers, Angel, Bull, Bull Ring Tavern, Charlton Arms, and Exchange.

Knighton (Powys). Mainly trout; preserved except for 1m free to licence-holders. Accom with fishing, Red Lion Inn, Llanfair Waterdine, on Teme (Tel: 01547 528214). For brown and rainbow trout, fly fishing pool nr **Llangunllo**, G Morgan, Gefnsuran, Llangunllo LD7 1SL (Tel: 01547 550219). Farmhouse accom on site. Hotels: Swan, Norton Arms.

ONNY: Good trout, chub, etc.

Plowden (Salop). Trout, chub; private water. Plowden Club has 4m trout fishing at Plowden Estate, members and guests only, no dt. Occasional membership, £120 plus joining fee. Contact S J Finnegan, The Old School, Brimfield SY8 4NZ.

Craven Arms (Salop). Water owned by Border Holidays (UK). Quinney and Byne Brooks, preserved and strictly keepered by Midland Flyfishers; trout, grayling; members only; no tickets; club also has water from Stokesay Castle Bridge to Bromfield. Stokesay Pool; pike, chub. Bache Pool, Bache Farm; carp; dt from farm. Dt for trout and grayling fishing on 150 yards of Onny from Mrs Maund, 1 Onny Cottage, The Grove.

SALWARPE: Trout, coarse fish. Birmingham AA has 1,300 yds at **Claines**.

Droitwich (Worcs). Trout above, coarse fish below. Severn 6m W. Droitwich and District AS has water at **Holt Fleet**. Noted chub waters. Society also has **Heriotts Pool** (large carp). Two sections of Droitwich Canal at Porters Mill: 36 pegs, stocked with carp, chub, roach and rudd: dt £2.50 on bank; match bookings and other enquiries, Tel: 01562 754809/630355. Astwood Fishery: 2 acre pool with carp and bream; dt on bank. Tel: 01905 770092.

Bromsgrove (Worcs). Tardebigge Reservoir rented to Bourneville Club (Messrs Cadburys) for many years. Limited st for local anglers. Upper and Lower Bittel Reservoirs owned by Barnt Green FC; members only (see also Arrow-Alvechurch). Hewell Grange Lake; permits for local clubs. (See also Worcester and Birmingham Canal.) Upton Warren Lake, 18 acres with carp, bream, roach etc. Dt on bank for 12 pegs; contact Outdoor Education Centre, Upton Warren B61 7ER (Tel: 01527 861426). Boat and several pegs for disabled. Tackle shops; Bromsgrove Angling, 54 Broad St, Sidemoor; Roy Huin, 138 Worcester Rd.

STOUR: Once heavily polluted, but fish now returning in some areas, principally lower river.

Stourbridge (Worcs). **Staffordshire and Worcestershire Canal**; coarse fish. Tackle shop: Riley's, Lower High Street (see also canal).

Brierley Hill (W Midlands). Stour, 3m S, polluted. Clubs: Brierley Hill AC (no water) and various works clubs.

Dudley (W Midlands). Lakes: Pensnett Grove Pool, Middle Pool, Fenns Pool, 3m SW (see Brierley Hill). **Netherton Reservoir**; Himley Park Lakes (Tel: 01902 324093); 16 acres good coarse fishing with carp and tench, dt on bank. Swims accessible to disabled. Plenty of fishing in canals within 6m radius. Lodge Farm Reservoir; Dudley Corporation. At Parkes Hall, **Coseley**, 2½m away, is good pool for which dt can be had; coarse fish (Dudley Corporation). Some local clubs are: Dudley AS, Tel: 01384 831924; Cross Keys AC, Tel: 01384 259147. Licences from Val's Pets, 100 Childs Avenue, Sedgley. Tackle from Hingley's, 46 Wolverhampton St, Dudley.

SMESTOW (tributary of Stour): Polluted.

Wolverhampton (W Midlands). Smestow, 2m W; polluted. Some fishing in **Penk** at Penkridge. Most local water on Severn held by Birmingham AA; permits from tackle shops. Patshull Park, nr Pattingham, trout and coarse, dt at lodge; Pool Hall, Compton, carp and other coarse, dt on bank. Lakes at Himley Park have dt. Swan Pool, **West Bromwich**, Tel: 0121 553 0220: 20 acres with carp and pike, tickets on bank. **Staffordshire Worcester Canal** is

Wolverhamton AA water. Tickets from local tackle shops: Fenwicks, Pitt Street, Tel: 01902 24607; Catchers Angling, 386 Bilston Rd; Fenwick's, Pitt St.

TERN: Coarse fish, some trout.

Telford (Salop). Tickets from Telford Angling Centre, Church St, St Georges TF2 9JU (Tel: 01952 610497), for Telford AA and other local clubs, including a good stretch at Ironbridge for barbel, pools, flashes and lakes. Uppington Estate Waters, 3,000m single bank from above Wroxeter, past site of Roman fort; tickets on bank or from Estate Office (Tel: 01952 740223). Baylis Pool, 10 acres with carp, bream. Dt on bank. Tel: 01952 460530.

Crudgington (Salop). A few trout and coarse fish. Cheshire AA have ¾m.

Hodnet (Salop). Tem. 1m E; a few trout and coarse fish. Strine Brook, 2m E. Lakes: Rose Hill Ponds, 4m NE. **Hawkstone Park Lake**, 3½m; excellent tench and carp water (40lb bags not uncommon) and large roach, rudd, pike and eels; private preserve of Wem AC, membership closed.

Market Drayton (Salop/Staffs). Trout and coarse fish. Environment Agency has free fishery of 1,200 yds on right bank, mainly d/s of Walkmill Bridge, around sewage works. Details from E.A., Tel: 01742 272828. For stocked section, Tern Fisheries Ltd, Broomhall Grange, M Drayton TF9 2PA Tel: 01630 653222, (Fax: 657444). Dt £20, 5 fish, ½ day £10, 2 fish, eve £6, 1 fish. At **Great Sowdley**, 7m SE, are canal reservoirs; perch, pike, roach, tench, carp. Market Drayton AC fishes Shropshire Union Canal at Knighton, Bridges 45–47, dt £1.50 on bank. Stoke City & Dist AA controls Sutton Lake, brown and rainbow trout, Tyrley Pool, coarse, both Market Drayton, and **Roden** at **Shawbury**, u/s and d/s of Poynton Bridge; also stretch of Shropshire Union Canal. No dt, membership from Stoke tackle shops or Hon Sec.

MEESE (tributary of Tern): Trout, coarse fish.

Newport (Salop). Meese, 1m N; trout; private. Lakes: Chetwynd Park Pond, 1m N. Minton's, Limekiln and Wildmoor Pools, 3m S. Moss Pool, 1½m NE. Park AC has good coarse fishing water on Grand Union Canal, with carp to 20lb, bream to 5lb, perch to 4lb: dt £2 on bank.

Tackle shop, Newport Tackle, 91A High St. Hotels: Bridge Inn; Fox & Duck.

REA: Trout, grayling; preserved.

Minsterley (Salop). Trout, grayling, Minsterley Brook. Habberley Brook, 3m SE. Lake: Marton Pool, 7m SW. **Lea Cross**; Warrington AA fishes on 1,000 yds stretch.

SHELL BROOK (tributary of Roden):

Ellesmere (Salop). Shell Brook, 2m NW; preserved. Halghton Brook, 4m N. Roden, 6m SE. Lakes: **Ellesmere Meres**, noted for bream (12lb plus). Ellesmere AC (st £10), issues wt £5, dt £1.50 for **Whitemere** and **Blakemere** (bank fishing only). Sunday fishing is allowed. Boats on most assn waters for members only. Ellesmere AC members may fish 4m stretch of **Shropshire Union Canal**; coarse fish. Hotels: Black Lion, Bridgewater, Red Lion (Ellesmere AC HQ); tickets *(see also Shropshire lakes).*

PERRY: Trout, preserved.

Ruyton Eleven Towns (Salop). 300m stretch on 1 bank with chub and pike; dt from Bridge Inn (Tel: 01939 260651).

VYRNWY: Provides sport with trout, grayling, coarse fish and salmon.

Llanymynech (Salop). Trout, salmon, grayling, roach, perch, pike, eels, chub, barbel, etc. Oswestry AC has water here, members only, £10 st, conc. For Lord Bradford's water at Lower House Farm inquire of agent, Llanymynech. Phoenix AC has ¾m at Domgay Farm; **R Lugg** at Moreton, and Kidderminster Captains Pool, coarse fishing. Tackle shop: Brian's Tackle, North Rd, Canalside, Tel: 01691 830027, which supplies Montgomery AA tickets. Other hotels: Bradford Arms, Cross Keys, Dolphin. Good trout fishing at **Lake Vrynwy** *(see lakes in Welsh section).*

Llansantffraid (Powys). Warrington AA has water here on Vyrnwy and **R Cain**, on Vrynwy at **Four Crosses**, and **Cross Keys**. Cheshire AA has Myliniog Farm stretch.

Meiford (Powys). Montgomeryshire AA (Tel: 01938 553867) has 750m 1 bank at Great Dufford Farm, with barbel and chub. Dt from Welshpool tackle shops.

MORDA (tributary of Vyrnwy): mostly trout, but some coarse fish in lower reaches.

Oswestry (Salop). Most river fishing preserved. Lloran Ganol Farm, **Llansilin** (Tel: 01691 70286/7) offers accommodation with fishing; also Woran Isaf, **Llansilin** SY10 7QX, with trout lake (Tel: 01691 70253). Oswestry AS has coarse fishing pools, st £10. Fawnog Fishing Lake, **Porthywaen**, well stocked with r and b trout. Tel: 01691 828474. Turfmoor Fishery, mixed, **Edgerley**; Tel: 0174381 512. Trewalyn Fly Lakes, Deythaur, Llansantffraid (Tel: 01691 828147): trout fishing. Stoke-on-Trent AS controls **Colemere**, 70 acre coarse lake nr Welshampton, with roach, bream. Tickets from Shropshire County Council. West Lake Trout Fishery, 2½ acres, stocked r and b trout fishing, fly only. Dt £20; 2 acre coarse lake, dt £5. Permits from The Lodge, Domgay Rd, Four Crosses, **Llandrinio** SY22 6SJ (Tel: 01691 831488). B & B, tearoom and tackle on site. Two coarse fisheries: Pentre Ucha Hall, Maesbrook, nr Llanymynech and Knockin on B4398 road; ¾ acre pond stocked with roach and carp; Trench Farm, Redhall Lane, Penley (Tel: 01978 710098); carp fishing on 3 pools, dt £3. Tackle shops: Guns and Angling Centre, G & A Building, Beatrice St, Oswestry SY11 1HL (Tel: 01691 653761); Brian's Angling Supplies, North Rd, Llanymynech. Accom. with fishing: Hand Hotel, Llanarmon, Tel: 01691 76666. Five coarse fishing ponds with accommodation: Sontley Farm Cottages, Middle Sontley, Wrexham LL13 0YP (Tel: 01978 840088).

TANAT (tributary of Vyrnwy): Trout (good average size), chub and grayling.

Llan-y-Blodwel (Salop). Horseshoe Inn has 1½m (dt £3), 3 rods per day, fly only, and Green Inn, Llangedwyn, has short stretch; dt issued (3 rods only); fly only.

Llanrhaiadr-y-Mochnant (Powys); trout; free. Tanat, 1m; trout, grayling, chub, etc; 6m from Llangedwyn to Llangynog strictly preserved. No dt.

CAIN (tributary of Vyrnwy): Trout, coarse fish.

Llansantffraid (Powys). Trout. Warrington AA has two stretches.

BANWY (tributary of Vyrnwy): Trout, grayling, chub, pike, dace and chance of salmon here and there.

Llanfair-Caereinion (Powys). Montgomeryshire AA has right bank downstream from town bridge to boundary fence; mainly trout, some chub and dace. At **Cyffronydd** Warrington AA has 610 yds, 700 yds right bank at **Neuadd Bridge**; dt from Mr Edwards, Neuadd Bridge Farm, Caereinion. Hotel: Wynnstay Arms.

Llangadfan (Powys). Trout; Montgomeryshire AA has good stretch; dt from Hon Sec.

SHROPSHIRE LAKES

ELLESMERE LAKES. Fishing station: **Ellesmere**. Excellent coarse fishing in Ellesmere (noted for bream), **Crosemere**, **Newton Mere**, **Blakemere**, **Whitemere** (bream of 12lb 4oz taken). Controlled by Ellesmere AC who issue dt £1, bank fishing only, on **Blakemere**. Dt also for **Hardwick Pool** (1m) noted tench water from Clay, 5a Scotland Street.

WALCOT LAKES. Lydbury North, 3m NE of Clun. Two extensive lakes, one controlled by Birmingham Anglers' Assn. Tench, pike and other coarse fish.

SOMERSET
(streams, lakes and reservoirs)
(For close seasons, licences, etc, see South West Region Environment Agency, p12)

AXE. Rises on Mendips and flows 25m NW to Bristol Channel near Weston-super-Mare. A few trout in upper reaches and tributaries, but essentially a coarse fish river, containing a mixture of the usual species, with roach now predominating.

Weston-super-Mare and Bleadon (Som). Weston-super-Mare & Dist AA fishes Old R Axe, Hobbs Boat to Cowbridge, and Lympsham to Crab Hole; South Drain, Gold Corner to Edington Junction; North Drain, pumping station to Blakeway Bridge; R Brue, at Manor of Mark. Assn waters contain roach, bream, carp, perch, rudd, pike, eels. No night fishing. Active junior section. St £20, conc, wt and dt from Thyers Tackle, and Weston Angling Centre. North Somerset AA has water on **Brue** near **Highbridge**, **Old River Kenn (Blind Yeo)**, **Congresbury Yeo**, and **North Drain**, Newtown and Apex Lakes, and Walrow Pond (jointly with Bridgwater AA), together with some smaller rivers. Membership £16, conc. Clevedon & Dist Freshwater AC fish

Old River Kenn and R Kenn (Blind Yeo) at **Clevedon**, also Congresbury Yeo in Congresbury. Mainly bream, roach, tench, pike, a few trout. Dt £3 from tackle shops. Wessex Federation have **Parrett** from Thorney to Yeo, and below Langport. Two coarse fisheries near Clevedon: Plantations Lakes, Middle Lane, Kingston Seymour, 2½ acres, stocked with 12 species, carp to 22lbs tea room on site; dt £5, conc; Bullock Farm Fishing Lakes, Kingston Seymour (Tel: 01934 835020), 3 lakes with 60 swims, heavily stocked with large variety of species. Tackle shops: Thyers Tackle, 1A Church St, Highbridge TA9 3AE; Weston Angling Centre, Locking Rd, Weston-s-M; Richards Angling, Regent St, Burnham-on-Sea; Tackle Box, 15 Station Rd; both Clevedon.

BRICKYARD PONDS: Pawlett. BB&WAA tench fishery. St from Hon Sec or tackle shops *(see Bristol).*

BRISTOL RESERVOIRS:
Chew Valley, **Blagdon** and **Barrow** reservoirs provide some of the best lake trout fishing in Europe, with a total annual catch of 46,000 fish of high average size. Season and day tickets obtainable. All fishing is fly only. Limits are four brace per day, two brace per evening bank permit. Details as follows:

Barrow Reservoirs – Barrow Gurney; brown and rainbow trout; from Bristol Water *(see Chew Valley Lake)*, bank fishing, fly only, No. 1 brown trout only.

Blagdon Lake – Blagdon; noted brown and rainbow trout water, bank fishing and rowing boats only, boat for disabled at reduced price.

Chew Valley Lake – Chew Stoke. Open April to November; noted brown and rainbow trout water where fish run large. For all waters apply to: Bristol Water Plc, Recreations Department, Woodford Lodge, Chew Stoke, Bristol BS18 8XH (Tel: 01275 332339). Bank dt and part dt from self-service kiosk. Motor boats from Woodford Lodge office (advance booking recommended). Season and day tickets are obtainable on all waters; disabled boat anglers catered for. Concessions for jun (under 17), OAP and registered disabled. Tackle shop and restaurant at Woodford Lodge, tackle on sale at Blagdon. Tackle hire and tuition arranged.

Cheddar Reservoir, Cheddar. Coarse fishery managed by Cheddar AC. Season and day permits, £30 and £15, from Broadway House Caravan Park, Axbridge Rd BS27 3DB (on main Cheddar to Axbridge road, opposite reservoir); Veals Fishing Tackle, Bristol; Thyer's Fishing Tackle, Highbridge; Thatcher's Pet & Tackle, 18 Queen St, Wells.

WESSEX WATER RESERVOIRS: Grosvenor House, The Square, Lower Bristol Road, Bath BA2 3EZ. Brochure enquiries, Tel: 0345 300600. St from above address; dt from dispensing units at reservoirs. There is a season ticket covering Clatworthy, Sutton Bingham, Hawkridge: £310, £249 conc. Dt £11, conc £9. Boat £10 (2 anglers max). Limits: 4 fish on st, 5 fish on dt, 2 fish on evening ticket. Concessions for jun and OAP.

Clatworthy Reservoir. 12m from **Taunton** in Brendon Hills; 130 acres brown and rainbow trout; fly only; 21/4m bank fishing. Season Mar 25–Oct 18. Tel: 01984 623549.

Durleigh Reservoir. 2m W of **Bridgwater.** 80 acres; coarse fishing, carp, roach, bream, pike. Biggest recently, pike 27lb, carp 18lb, bream 7lb. Dt £4, eve £2.50. Tel: 01278 424786 for more information.

Hawkridge Reservoir. 7m W of Bridgwater. 32 acres. Brown and rainbow trout; fly only. Season Mar 18–Oct 11. Boat or bank. Tel: 01278 671840.

Otterhead Lakes. About 1m from **Churchingford** nr Taunton. Two lakes of 2¾ and 2 acres; brown and rainbow trout; fly only; no boats. Season Mar 18–Oct 11.

Sutton Bingham Reservoir. 3m S of **Yeovil.** 142 acres. Brown and rainbow trout; average 1¼lb; fly only, bank or boat; season Mar 18–Oct 11. Tel: 01935 872389.

CHARGOT WATER, Luxborough. 3 ponds. Trout; fly only.

DONIFORD STREAM (Swill River at Doniford) and **WASHFORD RIVER**, **Taunton.** Trout; preserved.

HORNER WATER. On National Trust Holnicote Estate, Selworthy TA24 8TJ; upstream from Packhorse Bridge, Horner, to Pool Bridge, approx 2½m; fly fishing, small wild trout. Dt £1 from Horner Tea Garden.

WIMBLEBALL LAKE, Dulverton. 374 acres. SWW, fly only, well-known stocked rainbow trout fishery. Season Apr 1–Oct 31, boats from May 1. Dt £13, boats £7.50, (Allenard boat for disabled), conc, from self-service kiosk at Hill Farm Barn. Wimbleball Flyfishers Club obtains discount permits for members. Tackle shop: L Nicholson, High St, Dulverton TA22 9HB (Tel: 01348 323409). Hotel: Carnarvon Arms.

YEO. Fishing station: **Congresbury**. Tidal, good fly water for trout; a few coarse fish. North Somerset AA has various short stretches in area. Clevedon & Dist Freshwater AC fishes here, roach, bream, a few trout. Dt £3 from Clevedon tackle shops (see Weston).

STOUR (Dorset)
(For close seasons, licences, etc, see South West Region Environment Agency, p12)

Rises in Wiltshire Downs and flows through Dorset, joining Hampshire Avon at its mouth at Christchurch. Noted coarse fishery throughout year (large barbel, chub, roach, dace and pike are common).

Christchurch (Dorset). Avon and Stour. Pike, perch, chub, roach, tench, dace. Christchurch AC has many miles of Stour, Avon, plus numerous gravel pits, lakes and ponds. Limited dt for lower Stour and harbour, and Lifelands stretch of Hants Avon, Ringwood, from Davis (address below). Club membership, £80 pa, conc, juv and OAP. **Hordle Lakes**, 1m from New Milton; 5 lakes of total 5 acres, coarse fishing. Dt £2–£6 from Davis (below). Coarse fishing can be had on Royalty Fishery waters (see Avon), and Winkton Fishery. Sea fishing from Mudeford in Christchurch Bay is fair. Tackle shops: Pro Fishing Tackle, 258 Barrack Road; Davis Fishing Tackle, 75 Bargates. Hotel: King's Arms, Christchurch.

Throop (Dorset). Throop fisheries; 5½m of top quality coarse fishing; now Ringwood AC water.

Hurn Bridge (Dorset). Stour and Moors; no angling. Preserved now as a bird sanctuary.

STOUR (Dorset) – Tributaries

Wimborne (Dorset). Good chub, roach, bream, barbel, dace and pike. Some trout in Stour, also in R Allen. Small runs of salmon and sea trout. Red Spinner AS has water at Barford and Eyebridge; about 5m in all; members only. Wimborne & Dist AC has approx 10m of Stour in Wimborne, Longham to Child Okeford; 8 coarse and 4 trout lakes, and stretch of Avon at Fordingbridge. Membership £60 pa, plus joining fee; contact Sec (Tel: 01202 382123). Some guest tickets obtainable from Wessex Angling Centre, below, and from Bournemouth Fishing Lodge, Wimborne Rd, Bournemouth. Environment Agency own Little Canford Ponds, Wimborne, coarse fishery with good access for disabled. Leaflet from Conservation Officer at Rivers House, Sunrise Business Park, Blandford Dorset DT11 8ST. Tackle shops: Minster Sports, Wimborne; Wessex Angling Centre 321 Wimborne Rd, Oakdale, Poole. Hotels: King's Head, Three Lions, Greyhound.

Sturminster Marshall (Dorset). Southampton PS has about 2m here. Coarse, a few trout; dt £3 from Minster Sports, Wimborn Minster; 10 venues on offer. The Old Mill Guest House, Corfe Mullen, now lets to Wimborne AC, day tickets £5 from local tackle shops. Dt on site for Dorset Springs, Sturminster Marshall, Tel: 01258 857653, 3 acre stocked coarse fishery.

Shapwick (Dorset). Coarse fish. Southampton PS has several miles of fishing here; dt £3, conc, from Minster Sports, Wimborne Minster.

Blandford Forum (Dorset). Roach, chub, dace, perch, bream, carp, grayling, eels, and pike; good all year. Some tench. Durweston AC has Stour from Durweston Bridge u/s to Enford Bottom, also lake at Cann Common, Shaftesbury. St £25, conc, dt £3, river, £6 lake. Contact F Starks (Tel: 01258 451202). Blandford and Dist AC has Stour fishing from Durweston Bridge d/s to Charlton Marshall. Membership £27.50, conc; dt £4, conc, from tackle shop, A Conyers, 3 West Street (Tel: 01258 452307).

Sturminster Newton (Dorset). Chub, roach, dace, pike, perch, tench, bream; fishing very good. Sturminster and Hinton AA has 7m above and below town; 2 lakes at Stoke Wake, with tench; lake at Okeford Fitzpaine, mixed fishery, members only, St £17.50. For wt £10 and dt £4 apply to Harts Garden Centre, or Kev's Autos, both Sturminster Newton. Tackle and baits from Harts, Station Rd, Sturminster Newton. Hotel: White Hart.

Stalbridge (Dorset). Chub, roach, tench, dace, pike. Stalbridge AS has 2m of Stour, 2m on **Lydden** and 2 lakes for members only at **Buckland Newton**.

Gillingham (Dorset). Trout and coarse fish. Gillingham and Dist AA has 7m fishing from here to Mamhull; **Turner's Paddock Lake** and Mappowder Lakes, dt £4 from tackle shops or club treasurer; Loddon Lakes, members only. Turners Paddock, suitable for disabled. Membership £22, conc. Tackle shops: Sydenhams, High St, Gillingham; Todber Manor Fisheries Shop, Todber, nr Mamhull (Tel: 01258 820384); Stalbridge Angling, High St, Stalbridge (Tel: 01963 362291). Hotel: Royal (Tel: 01747 822305).

Stourton (Wilts). **Stourhead New Lake** on Stourhead (Western) Estate at Stourton, near Mere. Now a fly fishing syndicate water. Rods from April to September. Contact Malcolm Bullen, Tel: 01747 840624.

MOORS:
Verwood (Dorset). Trout in parts, otherwise mainly roach; Ringwood club has water.

STOUR (Kent)
(For close seasons, licences etc, see Thames Region Environment Agency, p15)

Rises in two arms north-west and south-east of Ashford, where they join. From junction river flows about 30m north-east and east to sea beyond Sandwich. Below Canterbury, good roach fishing with fish to 2lb common, bream to 6lb and pike over 20lb. Trout fishing restricted to club members in upper reaches.

Sandwich (Kent). River fast-flowing from Minster to Sandwich (Vigo Sluice); good fishing for bream and roach; few perch and tench; sea trout and grey mullet. Free fishing from quay and from Ropewalk, carp, tench, roach. Private fishing from Richborough Road, upstream. Sandwich and Dist AA has Reed Pond and Swallowbrook Water; **Stonar Lake** (stocked, carp and rudd), dt £5 from tackle shop; and North and South Streams, **Lydden**. Tackle shop: Brian Bayliss, Sandwich Bait and Tackle, 13 The Chain, CT13 9RA (Tel: 01304 613752) has information or tickets on a number of small coarse fisheries in vicinity of Rye, Bethersden, Kingsnorth, Whitstable and elsewhere, and also for Sandwich and Dist AA fishing. Hotel: Bell.

Grove Ferry. Stour and Little Stour. Betteshanger Colliery Welfare AS has 6m on Stour from **Plucks' Gutter** to **Stonar**. Roach, bream and mullet (Red Lion stretch, June–Aug). Society also has stretch at **Minster**. Tickets from Hon Sec, Red Lion or bailiff on bank.

Canterbury (Kent). Trout, tench, bream, roach, rudd, pike, etc. Free within city boundary for residents, except for municipal gardens stretch. Canterbury & Dist AA hold water from city boundary d/s to Plucks Gutter, 9m both banks; brown trout stocked, run of sea trout; dt £3 on stretch from Grove Ferry bridge to Plucks Gutter, from bailiff on bank; Assn also has Stour and Trenchley Lakes, fine coarse fishing, and **Fordwich Lake**, trout pool, members only. Membership £39, ½ price conc, from local tackle shops. For more information, contact Hon Sec. (Tel: 01227 710830). Mid Kent Fisheries, Chilham Water Mill, Ashford Rd, Chilham CT4 8EE (Tel: 01227 730668) control 18 lakes and 2 rivers, one being chalk stream trout fishing, also **Royal Military Canal** from Appledore to Kennardington Bridge. Limited dt on some waters. Fly fishing is £35–£18 per day, strictly in advance. **Honeycroft Fisheries**, 7 acre coarse lake, large carp. Tel 01732 851544. Tackle shops: Greenfield's Rod and Gun Store, 4/5 Upper Bridge Street; Sandwich Bait and Tackle, 13 The Chain, Sandwich. Hotels: County; Falstaff; George and Dragon.

Ashford (Kent). Ashford AS holds **River Stour** between **Ashford** and **Wye** (members only). Cinque Ports AS controls 4½m of Royal Military Canal from Seabrook Outfall, Hythe, to Giggers Green, Ashford. St £15 (+ entrance fee £7.50, conc), dt £2, conc 50p, from bailiff. Ashford Working Men's Club has a pit; good tench, carp, rudd; members only; no dt. Chequer Tree Trout Fishery is at **Bethersden**, Tel: 01233 820078. Dt £15 to £7. Licences, tuition, tackle hire and camping facilities on site. Coarse dt £2. Tackle shops: Ashford Angling Centre, 36 Stanhope Square; Denn's Tackle, Dymchurch Rd, Hythe. Hotels: County, Kent Arms.

LITTLE STOUR: Same fish as main river but overgrown in places. Most fishing now private.

WANTSUM. Carp, tench, bream, perch, roach, rudd, gudgeon. Wantsum AA has water from sea wall between Reculver and Minnis Bay to Chambers Wall Farm at St Nicholas-at-Wade, and 2m on Stour at **Minster**. Left of car park at R Wantsum members only, otherwise dt £2, conc, on bank. Membership £17 plus £5 enrolment, conc £5. Tackle shop: Kingfisheries, 34 King Street, Margate.

STOUR (Suffolk)
(For close seasons, licences etc, see Thames Region Environment Agency, p15)

Coarse fish river forming border between Suffolk and Essex. Enters sea at Harwich via large estuary. Some sea trout in semi-tidal waters below Flatford.

Harwich (Essex). Harwich AC has several coarse fisheries in area: Dock River; Oakley Lodge Reservoirs, Great Oakley; The Dykes, Harwich, with roach, rudd, pike, perch, carp, eels, bream. Members only; weekly membership sold at Dovercourt Aquatics and Angling Centre, Main Rd, Dovercourt, Harwich.

Manningtree (Essex). Tidal; roach, dace, perch, pike and occasional sea trout (fish of 9lb caught). Lawford AC has stretch at **Cattewade** (A137 bridge). Tickets. Dt from bailiff for Elm Park, Hornchurch and Dist AS stretch between club notices at **Flatford Mill**. Hotel: White Hart.

Nayland (Suffolk). Bream, chub, dace, perch, pike, roach, tench. Colchester APS has water here and at **Wiston**, **Boxted**, **Langham** and **Stratford St Mary**. New membership £43 incl £4 entry, to Box 1286, Colchester CO2 8PG. No dt. Colnes AS has stretches at **Little Horkesley**. Dt from P Emsom, Tackle Shop, Earls Colne.

Bures (Essex). Colnes AC has stretch. Dt from Emson, Tackle Shop, Earls Colne. London AA controls a good deal of water here and in **Clare**, **Cavendish** and **Sudbury** areas. Also **Bures Lake**; members only, but some waters open to associates at Bures. Moor Hall and Belhus AS has 2 excellent coarse lakes of 5 and 7 acres at Hill Farm Fishery and Little Belhus Pits, **South Ockenden**. Members only, details on application.

Henny Bridge (Essex). Great Cornard AC fishes from Henny Bridge to Henny Weir. Book a month in advance, dt £1.50.

Sudbury (Suffolk). Bream, roach, chub, dace, tench, carp, perch, pike, gudgeon. Sudbury & Dist AC has 7 stretches of Stour; Doneylands Lake, Colchester; Old Hall Farm Lakes, Wakes Coln; Stantons Farm Reservoir; membership £33, conc. Information from Tackle Up, 49a St Johns Street, Bury St Edmunds IP33 1SP (Tel: 01284 755022). Hadleigh & Dist AS have various stretches on Stour, R Brett and 6 local stillwaters. Restricted membership £24, conc, guest tickets offered on rivers. Contact D R Warner (Tel: 01473 626368). Long Melford

and Dist AA has water from Clare to Sudbury, with coarse species incl large chub, bream, roach, pike to 37lbs; and Suffolk Glem. Membership from tackle shops or Hon Sec. Tackle shops: Sudbury Angling, No 1, Unit 2, Acton Square Sudbury CO10 6HG; Stour Valley Tackle, 20 East St, Sudbury CO10 2TP (Tel: 01787 377139).

Haverhill (Suffolk). Lake Haverhill Floodpark; shallow lake with roach, rudd bream, tench, carp; several stretches of upper river at Baythorne End and Stoke By Clare, with various species incl barbel, chub, roach, dace, pike, and wild brown trout. membership for these waters £20, £10 conc, from David Sharpe, 19 Boxford Court, Haverhill CB9 8JB.

SURREY (Lakes)

BURY HILL FISHERIES. Nr Dorking. Well known coarse fishery of 3 lakes, the largest of which is 12½ acres. Particularly known for its tench, roach, carp, bream, pike and zander fishing, all of which run to specimen size. Also good stocks of rudd, perch and crucian carp. Open all year, bank and boat fishing; tuition courses, full facilities include sit-down cafe, all of which are suitable for disabled anglers. Dt £9, one rod, second rod £4 extra. Boat: £5 per person. Evening £4 per rod. Concessions to jun, OAP. Match bookings and corporate days organised. Further details from Fishery Manager, Estate Office, Old Bury Hill, Surrey RH4 3TY, Tel: 01306 883621/877540.

ENTON LAKES. Petworth Rd, **Witley**, nr Godalming GU8 5LZ (Tel: 01428 682620). Trout fishery of 2 lakes total 16 acres, bank and boat fishing. Dt £25 (4 fish), boat £5 per person extra. Chalet accommodation on site.

FRENSHAM PONDS. Farnham (4m). 60 acres and 30 acres. Farnham AS has rights on Great Pond, and Little Pond, leased from NT; coarse fishing; members of Farnham AS only.

FRIMLEY, nr **Camberley**. 4 RMC Angling lakes totalling 47 acres stocked with large carp and all other coarse species. St £28, £14 conc. *(For RMC Angling, see Chertsey.)*

RIPLEY. **Papercourt** fishery, Sendmarsh. Large carp, pike, bream, tench, chub, perch, eels, roach. An RMC Angling restricted permit fishery. St £24, ½ price conc. No day ticket. *(For RMC Angling, see Chertsey.)*

SOUTH LAKE, Yateley. 8 acre lake heavily stocked with carp to 30lb. Dt only, £6 or £10. From Yateley Angling Centre, 16 the Parade (Tel: 01252 861955) An RMC Angling fishery. *(For RMC Angling, see Chertsey.)*

SWAN VALLEY, Pond Farm Lane, **Yateley**. Four lakes with carp to 26lb, tench to 8lb, pike to 27lb. Dt £5, night £6, 24 hours £10, conc £2, from Academy Angling Centre, Sandhurst (Tel: 01252 871452).

TRILAKES. Sandhurst, Berks GU47 8JQ (Tel: 01252 873191). Mixed fishery; well stocked with tench, very large carp (common, mirror, crucian, ghost), bream, rudd, roach, perch, pike, eels, trout. Open 8am to 7.30pm or sunset if earlier. Purchase dt on entry, £7.50. Car park, cafe, access for disabled.

VIRGINIA WATER. Virginia Water, Johnson Pond and Obelisk Pond, Windsor Great Park fishable by season ticket only; coarse fish; st £50 (incl VAT). Early application advised in writing, to Crown Estate Office, The Great Park, Windsor, Berks SL4 2HT (Tel: 01753 860222) (sae).

WILLOW PARK, Ash Vale, nr Aldershot. Three lakes of 15 acres, mixed fishery stocked with a variety of species. Dt £6, £12 double rod, from bailiff. Night permit £15 from fishery, Youngs Drive, Shawfields Rd, Tel: 01252 25867.

WINKWORTH LAKES. Winkworth, nr Godalming. National Trust property. Trout fishery (fly fishing and boats only) managed by Godalming AS. St £175, plus entry fee of £80. Details from Hon Sec.

WIREMILL POOL. Nr **Lingfield**. Coarse fish include tench up to 6lb, bream up to 7lb, roach up to 3lb, carp up to 6lb.

YATELEY. Nr Camberley. Thirteen RMC Angling lakes totalling 73 acres stocked with pike, carp, tench, roach and perch, bream, rudd, catfish, crucian carp. Large specimens recorded, carp to 50lb. A restricted permit fishery. St £40. No dt. Concessions to jun, OAP, dis. *(For RMC Angling, see Chertsey.)*

SUSSEX
(lakes and streams)

ARDINGLY RESERVOIR. Ardingly, nr Haywards Heath. 198 acre coarse fishery with excellent pike, fish to 30lb, also good stocks of bream, roach, tench etc; coarse season 1st June–1st June; 16 June; pike season 1 Oct–1 May, dt 1 Nov–31 Mar. (Only very experienced specialist pike anglers allowed, 18+.) Enq to The Lodge, Ardingly Reservoir, Ardingly, W Sussex RH17 6SQ. Tel: 01444 892591.

ARLINGTON RESERVOIR, South East Water, Fishing Lodge, Berwick, Polegate, BN26 6TF (Tel: 01323 870810). Excellent rainbow trout fishery. Dt at water, on the day; special membership rates on request. Disabled boat and platform, by year 2000.

BARCOMBE RESERVOIR, Nr Lewes. 40 acres, South East Water, fly fishing for rainbow trout only. Information from Fishing Lodge (Tel: 01273 814819). Dt in advance.

BUXTED. Uckfield. Buxted Oast Farm, Lephams Bridge, TN22 4AU (Tel: 01825 733446): coarse pond, with carp and roach, dt at farm shop. Mr Greenland. Cyprus Wood Trout Fishery, Tallanmoor Cottage, Howbourne Lane TN22 4QD, contact Mr & Mrs Cottenham, Tel: 01825 733455. Tackle, B & B on site. Boringwheel Trout Fishery, **Nutley**, Tel: 01825 712629. Tackle shop: Uckfield Angling Centre, High St, Uckfield.

CHICHESTER CANAL. Chichester (W Sussex). Chichester Canal Society has 2½m from Chichester to Donnington Bridge, with roach, rudd, perch, carp, tench, bream, pike, eels, chub and dace. No fish to be removed. St £21, dt £2.40, conc, from bailiffs on bank. Southern Anglers have 1¾m south from A27 road, with tench, carp, roach, perch, pike. 24 hr fishing. Annual subscription £39, conc. Mixed fishery at Lakeside Village, Tel: 01243 787715. Tackle shops: Southern Leisure Centre, Vinnestrow Rd; Southern Angling Specialists, 2 Stockbridge Place. Selsey tackle shop: Raycrafts, 119 High Street Selsey PO20 0QB (Tel: 01243 606039) sells canal angling tickets.

DARWELL WATER. At Mountfield, **Robertsbridge** (Tel: 01580 880407), bookings between 8.30 and 9.30; brown and rainbow trout to 6lb; 180 acres; leased from Southern Water by Hastings Flyfishers Club Ltd; membership £220, st £250, dt £13.50, self-vending service at fishing lodge; boats £10 day extra, to be booked 48 hrs in advance from bailiff. Fly only; limit 6 fish; season: mid Mar–Oct 31. Take precise care over approach route down small lanes.

FRAMFIELD PARK FISHERY, Brookhouse Rd, Framfield, nr Uckfield TN22 5QJ, Tel: 01825 890948. Three coarse fishing lakes totalling over 17 acres. Good match weights, with large tench, bream and carp. Shop on site. Bailiff will give instruction, free to juniors.

FURNACE BROOK TROUT FISHERY nr Herstmonceux. Brown and rainbow trout from 2lbs up. Dt £10. St water. Phone 01435 830298 or 830151 for details.

POWDERMILL WATER. **Sedlescombe**. 52 acres, brown and rainbow trout to 6lb. Hastings Flyfishers Club Ltd. (See *Darwell Water*.) Bookings, Tel: 01424 870498, between 9.30 and 10.30am.

MILTON MOUNT LAKE. Three Bridges (W Sussex). Crawley AS water (st £20); carp; dt, Crawley AS also has Tittermus Lake (pike, tench, carp, roach, perch) and **Sandford Brook** (trout; fly only) in Tilgate Forest; Roffey Park Lake, near Colgate (carp, roach, tench, perch, gudgeon); New Pond, Pease Pottage (carp and crucian carp, tench); the Mill Pond, Gossops Green; Buchan Park lakes, nr **Crawley**, carp, pike etc. Dt £6 on some waters, from Jack Frost Tackle, 52/54 Ewhurst Rd, West Green, Crawley WSX RH11 7HE (Tel: 01293 521186).

CLIVE VALE RESERVOIRS. **Harold Road**: mixed coarse fishery, Clive Vale AC; st £23, junior £10; dt £4.50, junior £2.50.

ECCLESBOURNE RESERVOIR. Hastings. Good carp, tench, roach, bream pike and rudd. Tickets issued by Clive Vale AC. St £23 from Hon Sec. Dt £5 on bank, or from local tackle shops, which include Redfearns, Castle St, Hastings.

PEVENSEY LEVELS. Marshland drained by various streams into **Pevensey Haven** and **Wallers Haven**; good coarse fishing on large streams (pike, roach, rudd, perch, bream, carp and tench), most of best waters rented by clubs. Fishing stations: **Eastbourne, Hailsham, Pevensey**. Southdown AA has major stretches of Pevensey Haven between Pevensey and Rickney, also Railland's Ditch and Chilley Stream (tench, bream, rudd, perch, carp and eels); both banks of Wallers Haven (renowned pike, tench and bream); water on **R Cuckmere** on both banks between Horsebridge and Alfriston, Abbots Wood and three other small lakes at Arlington, stocked with large carp, and other species. Tickets, st £25, dt £3 from Hon Sec at Polegate Angling Centre, 101 Station Rd, Polegate BN26 6EB; or from Anglers Den, 6 North Rd, Pevensey Bay.

SCARLETTS LAKE. 3 acres, between E Grinstead and **Tunbridge Wells**. Good coarse fishing, carp incl (free st offered to any angler beating record carp, 23lb 4oz). Dt £5 at lakeside. St £50 from lakeside or Jackson, Scarletts Lake, Furnace Lane, Cowden, Edenbridge, Kent TN8 7JJ (Tel: 01342 850414). F/t students, OAP, jun, dis, unemployed, 50%.

WEIR WOOD RESERVOIR. Forest Row (W Sussex), 1½m; **East Grinstead**, 4m; 280 acres. Trout fishery with an emphasis on natural fishing. Fly fishing suspended between Jul 9 and Sept 8 for coarse fishing, thereafter fly until Dec 2. St £380, 25 visits £165 (3 fish per visit), dt £14.50 to £7.50, evenings; full permit 6-fish limit, conc. Enquiries to The Lodge, Weir Wood Reservoir, Forest Row, East Sussex RH18 5HT, Tel: 01342 822731 (24 hour). Tackle shop: Mike Wickams Fishing Tackle, 4 Middle Row, E Grinstead.

TAMAR

(For close seasons, licences etc, see South West Region Environment Agency, p12)

Rises in Cornwall and follows boundary between Devon and Cornwall for good part of course, emptying finally into Plymouth Sound. Holds salmon, sea trout, brown trout to the pound not uncommon.

Milton Abbot (Devon). Endsleigh FC has 9m, salmon and sea trout. Limited wt £140–£364, and dt £20–£52, for guests at the historic Endsleigh House, PL19 0PQ (Tel: 01822 870248). Average salmon catch 230; 90% taken on fly. Good car access to pools, tackle shop, and tuition on site by Bob Wellard, APGAI and STANIC. Apply to Manager for accommodation details, and to M D S Healey, 52 Strode Rd, Fulham, London SW6 6BN (Tel: 020 7610 1982) for fishing and courses.

Lifton (Devon). Tamar, **Lyd, Thrushel, Carey, Wolf** and **Ottery**; trout, sea trout (late June to end Sept), salmon (May, to mid-October). Hotel: Arundell Arms, Lifton, Devon PL16 0AA (Tel: 01566 784666, Fax: 784494) has 20m of excellent water in lovely surroundings; 23 individual beats, also 3-acre trout lake, brown and rainbow trout to 9lb. Licences and tackle at hotel, fly fishing courses (beginners and semi-advanced) by two resident instructors. Dt (when there are vacancies) for S & ST £15.50–£25, according to date; lake trout £17, brown trout £16. (See advt).

Launceston (Cornwall). Salmon, sea trout, trout. Permits can be obtained for 7 miles of Tamar, also **Ottery**, **Kensey**, **Inney** and **Carey** from Launceston AA, which has about 16m of fishing in all. Lakes and ponds: **Stone Lake**, 4½ acres coarse fishing (Tel: 0183786 253). **Tredidon Barton Lake**, dt £2 (Tel: 0156686 288). **Alder Quarry Pond**, Lewdown, Okehampton EX20 4PJ (Tel: 01566 783444), 4½ acres, coarse, dt water. **Dutson Water**, coarse fishing, Tel: 01566 2607. Hotels: White Hart; Eagle House; Race Horse Inn, North Hill. Launceston Publicity Committee issues booklet listing accommodation.

Bridgerule (Devon). **Tamar Lakes** here: SWW waters for which tickets are issued, (See Cornwall lakes). 14 acres coarse fishing lakes, with various carp species, orfe, tench, and others; J Ray, Clawford Vineyard, Holsworthy EX22 6PN (Tel: 01409 254177). B & B on site. Hotel: Court Barn, Clawton, Holsworthy.

Tributaries of the Tamar

TAVY: A moorland spate river, rises in Cranmere Pool on Dartmoor and flows about 17m before entering Tamar estuary at Bere Ferrers. Excellent salmon and sea-trout river.

Tavistock (Devon). Tavy, Walkham and Plym FC; limited membership. Salmon, sea trout and brown trout permits for visitors on main river, **Meavy**, **Plym** and **Walkham**. Spinning allowed but no natural baits. Salmon and sea trout st £100, dt £15. Brown trout st £40, mt £20, wt £15, dt £5, from Tavistock Trout Fishery (below); Yelverton Garage, 1 Moorland Villas (Tel: 01822 853339); DK Sports, The Barbican, Plymouth. **Tavistock Trout Fishery** Parkwood Rd, PL19 9JW (Tel: 01822 615441); 1m from A386 towards Oakhampton; fishing on 5 lakes beside R Tavy. Dt 7 days a week; rods for hire, only £3, plus permit; well stocked children's fishing lake; fly tackle shop Fishery owns Trout 'n' Tipple Hotel (Tel: 01822 61886). Other Hotels: Bedford (salmon and trout fishing on Tamar and Tavy); Endsleigh.

Mary Tavy (Devon). Brown trout; late run of salmon and sea trout. Fishing mostly privately owned. Plymouth & Dist Freshwater AA has rights at **Peter Tavy** (members only, st £80 from D L Owen, Tel: 01752 705033).

Yelverton (Devon). Good centre for Tavy, Walkham and Plym FC waters. Salmon, sea trout. Ticket suppliers listed under Tavistock. Coombe Fisheries, Miltoncombe: two 1 acre lakes with rudd, roach, tench, bream, ghost carp in top lake; various carp in bottom lake. Open all year, dawn till dusk, barbless hooks only. Contact S Horn, New Venn Farm, Lamerton, Tavistock PL19 8RR (Tel: 01822 616624).

WALKHAM (tributary of Tavy): rises northwest of Princetown, and joins the Tavy below Tavistock. Upper reaches rocky and overhung, but downstream from Horrabridge there are many fishable pools. Peal run from July onwards.

INNY: Trout, sea trout.

LYD: Trout, sea trout, some salmon.

Lifton (Devon). Arundell Arms (see advt) has fishing for salmon, sea trout and brown trout, also on main river and other tributaries.

TAW
(For close seasons, licences etc, see South West Region Environment Agency, p12)

Rises on Dartmoor and flows 50m to Barnstaple Bay, where it forms estuary. Salmon with sea trout (peal) from May onwards. Excellent brown trout always available and good coarse fishing in places.

Barnstaple (Devon). Bass and mullet in estuary. Salmon, trout, peal, roach and dace. Salmon best March, April, May; peal July, August. Barnstaple and Dist AA has water immediately below New Bridge (d/s of this, 300 yds free water), on **Yeo** (trout and sea trout), and on pond at **Lake Venn** (carp, tench, bream, rudd, perch). Visitors' tickets for salmon, trout and coarse fisheries from local tackle shop or Hon Sec. Visitors may become assn members which entitles them to coarse fishing in ponds (Mon–Fri only). Tickets limited and not weekends or Bank Holidays. Riverton House and Lakes, **Swimbridge**, EX32 0QX (Tel: 01271 830009) has coarse fishing on two 2 acre lakes with large carp, bream, tench, roach, perch, rudd. Night fishing by prior arrangement. Dt £5, evening £3.50. Self-catering cottages and B & B on site. At **Braunton**, coarse fishing with carp over 20lb. Dt £5–£3 (Tel: 01271 812414). Self catering and B & B. C L and Mrs Hartnull, Little Bray House, **Brayford**, have about 1m (both banks) of Bray; small trout only; dt £2. Also at Braunton, Little Comfort Farm (Tel: 01271 812414) has fishing for carp, perch, roach, bream, etc. Dt £5, accommodation. For other trout fishing see tributary Yeo. East and West Lyns, Badgeworthy Water and Heddon are accessible, as well as fishing on Wistlandpound and Slade Reservoirs. Tackle shop: The Kingfisher, 22 Castle St, supplies local tickets and information.

Chapelton (Devon). Salmon, peal, trout, dace. Taw mostly private down to New Bridge. Barnstaple and Dist AC water below (see Barnstaple).

Umberleigh (Devon). Salmon, peal, trout; preserved. Rising Sun has almost 4m of water (8 beats) for which dt are issued when not required for residents; fly only after April 30. Sunday fishing is allowed; salmon best March, April, May, August and September; sea trout June, July, August and September. Brochure, giving charges, etc, on request. Dt £25 non-residents, £21.50 residents only. Other Hotel: Northcote Manor, Burrington.

South Molton (Devon). Oaktree Fishery, Yeo Mill, EX36 3PU (Tel: 01398 341568) has three well-stocked lakes: two match, one specimen, large carp, tench, roach, open all year. Dt £4, £5 two rods, conc, at fishery.

Eggesford, **Chulmleigh** (Devon). Eggesford Country Hotel, EX18 7JZ (Tel: 01769 580345), has 7m of private salmon, sea trout and brown trout fishing on Taw. Spinning March to Apr. Fly only from Apr 1. No fishing in Feb. St £600–£350, wt £100, dt £20 and £12. Resident ghillie, tuition; licences and limited tackle on sale; 3-day fishing packages. Full details from hotel.

Coldridge (Devon). Taw Fishing Club has water from Brushford Bridge to Hawkridge Bridge; very good trout fishing; complimentary for members' guests only. St £40 + joining fee £40. Limited to 30.

Chenson (Devon). Chenson Fishery, salmon from 1 Mar, sea trout from Apr, trout. St only, £150–£250. Contact M Nicholson, Schoolmasters Cottage, Chenson, Chulmleigh.

North Tawton (Devon). Trout. Burton Hall

Hotel has about 4m of water here; trout; occasional sea trout and salmon. Free to guests; dt issued subject to hotel bookings. K Dunn, The Barton, also issues dt for about 1m.

Sticklepath (Devon). Trout. Dt £1 from Mr & Mrs P A Herriman, Davencourt, Taw Green, S Tawton for ½m downstream. Accommodation: Taw River Inn.

YEO (Barnstaple): Sea and brown trout. Barnstaple and Dist AA has water on Yeo, wt and dt from Barnstaple tackle shop. (See Barnstaple).

BRAY (tributary of Mole):

South Molton (Devon). South Molton AC has right bank from Brayly Bridge u/s to Newton Bridge, with salmon, trout and peal, fly only; £5 dt issued, from Hon Sec. Tackle shop: Sports Centre, 130 East St, South Molton, EX36 3BU. Hotels: The George, The Tiverton.

North Molton (Devon). Trout, sea trout, few salmon; ns South Molton 2m. Poltimore Arms Hotel has 2m of fishing on Bray; fishing good. C and M Hartnull, Little Bray House, **Brayford**, issue dt for about 1m of river.

TEES
(For close seasons, licences etc, see North East Region Environment Agency, p13)

Rises below Cross Fell in Pennines, flows eastward between Durham and Yorkshire and empties into North Sea near Middlesbrough. The Tees Barrage was completed in June 1995, and has already created a much cleaner river, upstream. Fish are being caught throughout all previously tidal stretches, from the new Princess of Wales Bridge to Thornaby and above. Well stocked from Middleton-in-Teesdale down to Croft.

Middlesbrough (Cleveland). NWA reservoirs **Lockwood** and **Scaling Dam** in vicinity. Stocked with trout; dt on site. Middlesbrough AA have R Tees at Over Dinsdale, Thornaby and Preton Park, **Stockport**; trout, salmon and usual coarse fish, 8 stretches of **R Swale** at Ainderby, Gatenby, Maunby, Skipton, Kirby Wiske, Danotty Hall, Holme and Baldersby, Marske Reservoir (stocked with carp) and ponds, all good coarse fishing. Local tackle shops: Anglers Choice, 53 Clive Rd, who has st £23 (+ £10 entry), conc, for Middlesbrough AA waters, and tickets for Middlesbrough stillwaters; Cleveland Angling Centre, Thornaby.

Stockton (Cleveland). Trout; grayling, coarse fish on one of best stretches of river. Stockton AA has over 10m at **Gainford, Winston, Dinsdale Middleton-on-Row**, nr Darlington, **Aislaby**, nr Yarm, and on **Swale**, nr **Ainderby** (Moreton-on-Swale) and above Great Langton, lower reaches of Tees and Swale fishings. **Hartlepool Reservoir** is coarse fishery run by Hartlepool & Dist AC. Contact Mr J Hartland, 7 Chillingham Ct, Billingham, Teeside. Tackle shop: F Flynn, 12 Varo Terrace, Stockton; Tackle Box, Station Rd, Billingham, Stockton. Stockton Tees permits are sold at Anglers Choice, 53 Clive Rd, Middlesbrough TS5 6BH.

Eaglescliffe, (Cleveland). Yorkshire bank in Yarm free fishing. **Leven** joins just below Yarm. Trout and coarse fish. Middlesbrough AA to above falls; Thornaby and Yarm AA together up to Hutton Rudby. Excellent brown trout fishing; occasional sea trout.

Yarm (Cleveland). Tidal good coarse fishing; chub, dace, roach, occasional trout. Some free fishing inside of loop surrounding town, ½m, on E.A. licence. Mixed fishery, deep, slow moving water. Yarm AA, strong team club with 15m of Tees fishing at Low Middleton, Yarm, Over Dinsdale, Sockburn and Piercebridge; members of Assn. of Teeside & Dist Angling Clubs, with 10m water; st £29, dt £1.50; limited dt from Yarm AA headquarters, 4 Blenavon Court, Yarm, Tel: 0164278 6444.

Neasham (Durham). Free fishing for 300 yards behind Fox and Hounds pub (mixed fishery).

Sockburn (Durham). Chub, dace, roach. Approx 3m controlled by Assn of Teesside & Dist Angling Clubs, which consists of Thornaby AA, Yarm AA, Darlington Brown Trout Anglers and Stockton Anglers.

Croft (Durham). Fair head of trout, grayling and coarse fish. Free fishing for 200 yds upstream of road bridge. Several miles controlled by Thornaby Anglers, members only, application forms from W P Adams (see *Darlington*).

Darlington (Durham). Trout, grayling, coarse fish. Council water free to residents. Darlington AC fish 10½m between Croft, Darlington and High Coniscliffe, and 1m of **Clow Beck**, 3m S of Darlington; north bank. Strictly for members

only. Darlington Brown Trout AA has water between Middleton and Croft, also on **Swale**. Dt for members' guests only. Stockton AA has water at **Winston**. At **Whorlton**, T J Richardson, Whorlton Farm, issues limited permits for stretch. Woodland Lakes, Carlton Miniott, nr Thirsk, Tel: 01845 522827, has good carp fishing in 5 lakes. Dt £5. Tackle shops: W P Adams Fishing Tackle & Guns, 42 Duke Street, DL3 7AJ, Tel: 01325 468069 (has permits for several small coarse ponds in vicinity, and for R Tees fishing); Darlington Angling Centre, 341 North Rd DL1 3BL.

Piercebridge (Durham). Trout, grayling, dace, chub, gudgeon. Tickets for Raby Estates water, £32 trout, £23 coarse; Estate Office, Staindrop, Darlington DL2 3NF, Tel: 01833 660207. Otherwise preserved. Forcett Park Lake, 8m SW; pike, perch; private, occasional winter permits. Hotel: George.

Gainford (Durham). Trout, grayling, coarse fish. Up to Winston, most of the water held by Stockton AA. No tickets. Alwent Beck, 1m W; trout; private. Langton Beck, 2m N.

Barnard Castle (Durham). Trout, grayling. Free fishing on south bank d/s from stone bridge to Thorngate footbridge. Taking of salmon prohibited. M Hutchinson, Thorngate Mill, has fishing offered. Barnard Castle FFC has from Tees Viaduct to Baxton Gill, near **Cotherstone**, private club water; stretch above Abbey Bridge to beyond Tees Viaduct on south bank, and from Lendings caravan park to Tees Viaduct on south bank. Barnard Castle AC has from a point below Abbey Bridge to Tees Viaduct on north bank; private club water, but some dt to visitors staying locally. Darlington FFC has 2½m above and below Abbey Bridge, 1m below Barnard Castle. Water holds trout and grayling; members only. Grassholme, Selset, Balderhead, Blackton and Hury reservoirs, 5m NW; dt obtainable (see *Tees Valley Reservoirs*). Langlands Lake fly fishing, Langlands Farm, **Barningham**, Richmond DL11 7ED (Tel: 01833 621317), rainbow trout, dt £5–£9, joint father and son dt £12. All local permits from R T Oliver, 40 Horsemarket, Barnard Castle DL12 8NA. Hotel: King's Head, Market Place.

Mickleton (Durham). Trout. St £15, wt £6, dt £3 for S bank between Cronkley Bridge and Lune Fort from Teesdale Hotel; J Raine & Son 25 Market Place; both Middleton-in-Teesdale.

Hotel: Teesdale DL12 0QG.

Middleton-in-Teesdale (Durham). Trout (plentiful but small), a few late salmon. Several miles open to dt on Raby Estate water, Tel: 01833 40209 (office hours). Teesdale Hotel (Tel: 01833 40264) offers dt on several miles of south bank. Strathmore Estate water, 7m north bank, fly only, dt £7.50, wt £20, st £50, salmon £100. Contact J Raine & Son, 25 Market Place, Middleton-in-Teesdale DL12 0QA (Tel: 01833 640406).

GRETA: Trout.

Bowes (Durham). All private fishing.

TEIGN
(For close seasons, licences etc, see South West Region Environment Agency, p12)

Rises from two sources high on Dartmoor, which form the North and South Teign, joining west of Chagford while still small streams. Between Chagford and Steps Bridge river runs through a wooded gorge, which is best fished around Fingle bridge. Upper Teign contains trout, sea trout and salmon. Principal tributary is Bovey. Salmon, sea trout (peal) and brown trout. Teign usually fishes best for salmon from late May to September. River flows to sea through an estuary beginning below Newton Abbot

Newton Abbot (Devon). Salmon, sea trout, trout; preserved by Lower Teign FA from Sowton Weir to Teignbridge (stretch from New Bridge to Preston Footbridge members only). Three separate beats. Dt (3 per beat) £10, valid for 24 hrs from sunrise. Spinning by day, at night fly only. Assn also has 3m on Bovey, members only (see Bovey). Tickets from Drum Sports (see below). Newton Abbot FA has 6 lakes at **Rackerhayes**, 5 at **Kingsteignton**, 2 ponds at **Coombe-in-Teignhead**, 2 at **Chudleigh**, newly acquired pond beside Stover Canal, and **R Isle** at **Hambridge**. Fisheries contain carp to 36lb, pike to 20lb, large tench, roach, rudd, perch, bream. Dt £4, conc, on some of these waters. Full membership £30, conc. Coarse fish, including carp. **Watercress Farm**, 4 acres trout fishing, Tel: 01626 852168. **Trago Mills** has 600 yds coarse fishing, dt £3, OAP, jun £2. G Mole, Tel: 01626 821111. Decoy Lake, small coarse lake open all year, stocked. Tackle shop: Drum Sports, 47a Courtenay Street.

Chudleigh (Devon). Salmon, sea trout, trout; Lower Teign FA has water (see Newton Abbot). 2½ acre coarse lake at Finlake Woodland Village. Open 31 Mar to 31 Oct. Newton Abbot FA has 2 ponds here.

Chagford (Devon). Trout, sea trout, Upper Teign FA preserves about 14m in all, on left and right bank, fly only before June 1 on some parts and whole season elsewhere; size limit 8in. Full annual sub £135, trout membership £45. Brown trout tickets from Bowdens, The Square, Chagford, also limited sea trout dt on 2 short stretches, Chagford Weir, £6. Limited non-members salmon and sea trout tickets £15, from Anglers Rest, Fingle Bridge, Drewsteignton, Exeter EX6 6PW (Tel: 01647 281287). Halfstone Sporting Agency offers salmon and sea trout fishing and instruction; 6 Hescane Park, Cheriton Bishop EX6 6SP, Tel: 01647 24643. Fernworthy Reservoir, 3½m.

Tributary of the Teign

BOVEY: Salmon, sea trout, trout.

Bovey (Devon). On Bovey and Teign. Fishing above Bovey preserved by landowners and below by Lower Teign FA. No tickets. Lakes: Tottiford and Kennick Reservoirs; trout (see Devon lakes, streams, etc). Hotels: Manor House, one mile from North Bovey (water on Bovey and Bowden, and salmon and trout fisheries on Teign); Glebe House, North Bovey.

TEST
(For close seasons, licences etc, see Southern Region Environment Agency, p12)

Rises from springs in the chalk near Overton, above Whitchurch and flows via Stockbridge and Romsey to enter Southampton Water. Brown and rainbow trout, salmon run as far as Romsey. The Test and Itchen Association represents virtually all riparian owners and many who wish to fish these rivers and their tributaries. The secretary maintains a register of rods to let. (See clubs list.) Roxton Bailey Robinson let beats on a daily, weekly and seasonal basis. 25 High St, Hungerford RG17 0NF (Tel: 01488 683222, Fax: 01488 682977).

Romsey (Hants). Trout and grayling fishing good; salmon fishing good below the town, all preserved by the different landowners. Test Valley Angling Club has various lakes and river stretches in vicinity, and also water from Eastleigh across to Romsey, covering

Marchwood and Totton. Subscriptions are £58, family £83, conc £31 juv, £23 OAP. An entrance fee is also chargeable. Contact Membership Sec (Tel: 0123 8086 3068). **Broadlands Estates** has salmon fishing on 3 beats of ¾m each, and trout fishing on three ¾m beats of Test and on 3m carrier stream. Average season salmon catch, 35 fish, average weight 6lb. Salmon rods and 1/2 rods, a named day per week for two for £925 and a named day per fortnight for two for £465. Trout fishing st for one rod (1 day per week) is £1,235 and £640 (1 day per fortnight), 2 brace, dry fly only. Trout fishing in carrier stream, st £1,005. There is also an excellent stillwater coarse fishery with large carp, roach, bream, tench. Enquiries: Estate Office, Broadlands, Romsey S051 9ZE. Tel: 01794 518885. Fisheries Manager, John Dennis, Tel: 023 8073 9438. Dt for residents from Council Offices, Duttons Road, for Romsey Memorial Park; limited to two rods daily. Salmon, few small trout, grayling, coarse fish. For Tanyard beat, opp Broadlands, contact 1 Donaldson, 9 Oatlands Chase, Weybridge, Surrey KT13 9RF. Good trout fishing at **Two Lakes**, near Romsey (**see Hampshire, streams, lakes, etc**).

Stockbridge (Hants). Greyhound Hotel has water stocked with brown and rainbow trout; Dry fly and nymph only. Fish average 3lb. St (2 rods) (one day per month) £425. Dt £50 May/June, £40 otherwise; 4 fish limit. Instruction, £30 per day. Early booking advisable as rods are limited. Special fishing/accommodation package can be arranged. Roy Gumbrell, Tel: 01264 810833. Tackle from Orvis, High St.

Awbridge (Hants). Fishing Breaks, 23 Compton Terrace, London N1 2UN (Tel: 020 7359 8818/Fax: 4540) has rods here, and on **R Itchen**, **Avon** above Amesbury, and **R Dever**, **R Piddle**, **R Coln**, and **R Frome**.

Houghton (Hants). Bossington Estate, Stockbridge SO20 6LT lets rods by season. Long waiting list.

Fullerton Bridge (Hants). Trout (av 2lb 8oz). Season mid-April to end of Sept.

Tributaries of the Test

ANTON: Trout, grayling.

Andover (Hants). Anton joins Test at Testcombe Bridge. Trout and grayling; all pre-

served. At **Rooksbury Mill**, Rooksbury Road, a first-class trout fishery (2 lakes and river fishing), st £375, dt £28 (5 fish), river £36. Boats on Mill Lake. Well stocked game fishing tackle shop on site. Tel: 01264 352921, Fax: 333449) for full details. Andover AC owns Foxcotte Lake at **Charlton**, 50 to 60 pegs approx. Usual coarse species; also has access to Broadlands at **Romsey** and **Basingstoke Canal**. Dt from tackle shop John Eadies, 5b Union St or Charlton PO. **Dever Springs Trout Fishery**, 2 lakes, 7 acres and river: contact Tel: 0126472 592. Other Tackle shop: Cole & Son, 67 High Street, who also supply st £18, which includes Broadlands Lake fishing. Hotels: Star and Garter, White Hart, Junction, George, Anton Arms, Globe Central.

PILL HILL BROOK: Trout, grayling.

Amport and **Monxton** (Hants). Trout and grayling. Nearly as long as Anton, but pure chalk-stream. Monxton Mill reach greatly improved and contains full head of locally bred brown trout averaging 14oz, with occasional heavier fish. Fishing preserved by landowners. Dry-fly only.

DEVER: Trout, grayling. Dever joins Test at Newton Stacey.

Bullington. Fishing Breaks Ltd has rods here, see *Awbridge, above*. For trout fishing on 1,000 yds at head of river, and 3 lakes, D Henning, Chapel Cottage, Old Lane, Ashford Hill RG19 8BG. Day and season rods offered.

BOURNE:
St Mary Bourne (Hants). Strictly preserved. Bourne joins Test above Longparish.

THAMES
(For close seasons, licences, etc, see Thames Region Environment Agency, p15)

Second longest river in England. Tidal reaches much recovered from pollution and fish returning in considerable numbers. The occasional salmon and sea trout in river, together with dace, roach, flounder, bream, perch, carp and smelt; rainbow trout are caught quite regularly in the freshwater tideway. River worth fishing from Southwark Bridge upstream. Downstream of this point, estuarine species such as eel, flounder, bass and even whiting may be caught. Above Teddington Lock boat traffic largely spoils sport in summer, except in weir pools, but fishing can be good early and late. River fishes well from October to March. Holds good stock of coarse fish, with excellent bream and barbel in some stretches. Perch seem to be making a welcome return to the river throughout its length. However, the tremendous dace fishing of recent years has declined. Bream, roach and perch now dominate the lower river, above Teddington, with chub becoming more numerous the further up the river one goes. Among famous tributaries are Kennet, which comes in at Reading and is one of best mixed fisheries in England. Trout and coarse fish run large. Higher up, Coln, Evenlode and Windrush are noted trout streams, but for most part are very strictly preserved and fishing difficult to obtain. Fishing on Thames open up to City Stone at Staines. Above, permission often necessary and lock-keepers and local tackle shops should be consulted. Thames Environment Agency issues annual permits on 18 locks and weirs, and these are entered below, in the appropriate section of the text. The Thames Angling Preservation Society, founded in 1838, has restocked 7 tributaries – now keeps close watch on water quality and fish stocks in whole Thames basin. It is not a fishing club, but a fishery preservation society supported by anglers, membership details from secretary, A E Hodges, The Pines, 32 Tile Kiln Lane, Bexley, Kent DA5 2BB. London Anglers Association (LAA) HQ, Izaak Walton House, 2A Hervey Park Road, London E17 6LJ, has numerous shings on Thames and elsewhere. Permits issued for some waters. Several reservoirs in which fishing is allowed (coarse fish and trout). *(See London – Reservoirs, etc).*

London Docklands. Redevelopment has led to increased angling facilities at **Shadwell**, **Millwall**, **Royal Docks** and **Southwark**, each locality with its own angling society. Details from Docklands Watersports Club, Unit 1, Royal Victoria Dock, Mill Rd, E1 6XX Tel: 020 7511 7000.

Isleworth to **London Bridge** (G London). Tidal. Dace, flounder, eel, roach, perch, with some carp and bream. Juvenile bass common at seaward end of this stretch; free from towpath or boats and foreshore throughout Central London 2 hrs each side of low tide. Fly-fishing for dace on shallows when tide is down. Reach down past Chiswick Eyot can be good for roach, dace; towpath only; free. Tackle shops: Hounslow Angling Centre, Bath Road also Colne-Wraysbury).

Richmond (G London). Tidal below Teddington Lock, non-tidal above. Down to Isleworth is fishing for roach, dace, bream, perch, eel, the odd chub; free from towpath or boats. Barnes and Mortlake APS are local club, with water on Grand Union Canal at Brentford from Thames Lock to Clitheroe Lock (dt on bank), and "Clockhouse Pool" at Bedfont Country Park. In Richmond Park **Pen Ponds** hold perch, carp, bream, roach and pike. Open 16 Jun–14 Mar. St £11, conc £5.50 (I.D. required). Apply to Park Superintendent at Holly Lodge, Richmond Park, Richmond TW10 5HS (enclose sae). Tickets on bank day and night for coarse fishing in Potoma Lake, Gunnersbury Park. Tackle shop: Ron's Tackle, 465 Upper Richmond Rd West, East Sheen SW14 7PU.

Twickenham (G London). Coarse fishing; free from boats and towpath. Deeps hold barbel, roach, bream, eel, carp. Corporation allow fishing from Radnor, Orleans and Terrace Gardens. Syon Park Trout Fishery, Brentford, managed by Albury Estate Fisheries, Estate Office, Albury, Guildford GU5 9AF, Tel: 01483 202323. Tackle shop: Guns and Tackle, 81 High Street, Whitton. Hotels: Bird's Nest, White Swan.

Teddington (G London). Thames holds dace, roach, bream, eel, perch; free fishing from towpath. **Molesey Lock** is fishable on special Environment Agency annual permit, which covers 18 locks and weirs; contact Kings Meadow House, Kings Meadow Rd, Reading RG1 8DQ (Tel: 0118 953 5000). Hotels: Anglers', Clarence, Railway.

Kingston (G London). Canbury Gardens is very popular stretch and has yielded large carp, bream, perch and roach.

Hampton Court (G London). Thames, Mole; coarse fish. Gardens and Estate Manager, Hampton Court Palace Gardens, Surrey KT8 9AU (Tel: 020 8781 9610), issues permits for Hampton Court: Long Water and Rick Pond, also Bushy Park: Diana Pond, Heron Pond and Leg of Mutton Pond. Coarse fish. St £13, juv and OAP conc, £6.50. No night fishing. Tackle shop: Fishing Unlimited, 2 Hampton Court Parade, East Molesey.

Hampton (G London). Hampton Deeps hold bream, pike, perch and sometimes a good trout; free fishing from towpath and boats.

Sunbury (Surrey). Excellent for all-round angling; free. Fine weir and weir shallows fishable on Environment Agency permit, Tel: 019327 82089; barbel, chub, dace, bream and occasional trout may be taken. Tackle shop: Tackle Up, 357 Staines Rd West, Ashford Common TW15 1RP, sells tickets for local fisheries, trout and coarse. Hotel: Magpie.

Walton-on-Thames (Surrey). Bream, perch, dace, chub, carp and pike; perch and pike in backwater.

Shepperton (Surrey). Pike, barbel, perch, bream and carp; free; boats for hire. Shepperton Lock is Environment Agency fishery, see Molesey Lock for permit details. Sheepwalk Lakes: 2 lakes, 7 acres, with carp to 30lb, tench to 9lb, bream to 11lb, good pike fishing; access for disabled; dt £5 for two rods, from Ashford Angling Centre (see Chertsey). Two RMC Angling gravel pits, 16 acres, coarse fishing for carp, roach, chub, pike, eels, etc. No night fishing. St £22, ½ price conc. No dt. (For RMC Angling, see Chertsey.) Hotel: Anchor.

Weybridge (Surrey). There is local free fishing in Thames and **R Mole**. Members of Weybridge AC and other clubs have fishing on 6 sections of **Wey Navigation** Canal between Town Lock and Walsham Lock and have formed Wey Navigation Angling Amalgamation; dt £1.50 from bailiff. Weybridge AC also fishes 1,000 yards d/s and 1,000 yards u/s of Wey Bridge on R Wey. Dt £2 from tackle Shop: Weybridge Guns & Tackle, 137 Oatlands Drive, Weybridge KT13 9LB (Tel: 01932 842675). Hotels: Ship, Thames St; Lincoln Arms, Thames Street; Oatlands Parks; Blue Anchor.

Chertsey (Surrey). Pike, perch, chub, roach, bream, occasional trout; free fishing from boats and towpath. Between Chertsey Weir and Penton Hook, Staines, good nets of bream caught all year, also perch. Chertsey Bridge is very popular for piking, with fish to 25lb. RMC Angling (see below) have 4½ acre gravel pit and 1,000m of River Bourne. Excellent tench, bream, carp, roach and pike in pit, chub, roach, dace and perch in river. St £24, ½ price jun, OAP, dis. Club: Addlestone AA, which has water at **New Haw**, **Wey** and **Bourne** and a gravel pit at Laleham; dt to members' guests only. RMC Angling have two stretches of Wey at **Addlestone**, 600m total, with pike, barbel, chub, carp, roach, bream, dace, perch. St only, £20. RMC Angling run many other fisheries

throughout southern England, and they may be contacted at The Square, Lightwater, Surrey GU18 5SS (Tel: 01276 453300). Free fishing on Shortwood Common, Ashford: 3 acre lake with carp to 20lbs, tench, etc. Ashford Lakes: three lakes of 1 acre each, with large carp, tench, bream, good head of roach and pike. Disabled access. Dt £3 per rod, from tackle shop: Ashford Angling Centre, 357 Staines Road West, Ashford Common, Middlesex TW15 1RP.

Staines (Surrey). Good coarse fishing; free from boats and towpath. Environment Agency fisheries at Penton Hook Lock, and Bell Weir Lock, **Egham**; see Molesey Lock for permit details. Club: Staines AS, stretch opposite Runnymede; members only. One mile free water in **R Colne** at Staines, with good roach, dace, chub, barbel and perch. Tackle shop: Davies Angling, 47/9 Church St.

Wraysbury (Berks). RMC Angling **Kingsmead Fishery**, 2 lakes of 50 and 30 acres with carp to 45lb, and other coarse species. St £32. RMC Angling also have fishery at **Horton** nr Wraysbury; syndicate membership, specimen carp, bream, tench and catfish; and Wraysbury One Fishery, 120 acre specimen carp fishery which holds current British record carp 56lb 6oz. (For RMC Angling, see Chertsey.) Berkshire Fisheries Assoc. has Slough Arm of G Union Canal from **Cowley** to Slough Basin, approx 5m, excellent fishery in summer, very little boat traffic. Specimen tench and other species, and good pike fishing in winter; dt from bailiff. Tackle shop: Stows Tackle, Wexford Rd, Slough.

Windsor (Berks). Chub, barbel, bream, roach, dace, perch, pike. Fishing from south bank below Windsor Bridge and north bank to Eton-Windsor road bridge, by E.A. licence only. Dt issued for club waters near Maidenhead; enq tackle shops. Salt Hill AC has Clewer Meadow, Windsor, dt on bank. Old Windsor AC has Romney Island and Meadow fishing to east of Windsor, and Albert Bridge, Datchet, all river species. Junior trophies and tuition available. Tickets £3 at Romney and Albert Bridge on bank, from Windsor Angling Centre (below), or Maidenhead Baits, 11-13 Station Parade, Station Hill, Cookham. Free public fishing on right bank from Victoria Bridge u/s to railway bridge. Royal Berkshire Fishery, North St, Winkfield, Tel: 01344 891101: 3 small lakes with coarse fish. Dt on bank. Fishing can be had in Windsor Great Park ponds and Virginia Water *(see Surrey lakes)*. Tackle shop: Windsor Angling Centre, 153 St Leonard's Rd, Windsor, Tel: 01753 867210.

Boveney (Bucks). Coarse fish. Backwater good for pike, and weir pool for trout and barbel. Towpath free. London AA Eton Wick fishery here. Hotels: Clarence, Royal Windsor.

Bray (Berks). Weir pool good for trout, and free from boat or punt. Bray Mill tail from 1m above lock to lock cut private. Towpath free. Monkey Island Hotel caters for anglers. Tel: 01628 23400. Environment Agency fishery at Bray Lock, *see Molesey Lock* for permit details.

Maidenhead (Berks). Roach, pike, perch, barbel, dace, chance of trout. Some free fishing right bank, Maidenhead Bridge to Boulter's Lock. Hurley Lock, Environment Agency fishery, *see Molesey Lock* for permit details. Maidenhead and District AS has left bank u/s from Boveney Lock to gardens at Dorney Reach. Permits from Hon Sec. Dt for clubs stretch from My Lady Ferry to gardens at Maidenhead from bailiff. Tackle shops: Kings, 18 Ray St; Jack Smith, 4 High Street.

Cookham (Berks). Cookham & Dist AC has right bank u/s of Cookham Bridge to Railway Bridge. London AA has water at Spade Oak Ferry, members only. Hotels: Ferry, Royal Exchange, King's Arms, Bell and Dragon, Crown.

Bourne End (Bucks). Wide, open water with some shallow stretches, good for fly fishing. London AA has water here. Stretch also open to associates.

Marlow (Bucks). Usual coarse fish, including barbel. Free fishing d/s from Marlow Lock to end of Riverside Drive, ½m stretch. Marlow AC has water from Riverswood Drive to opp. first islands and left bank u/s from Marlow Bridge opp. Temple Island, and pits; Secretary, Jeff Woodhouse (Tel: 01494 523988). Tickets from Kings Tackle, 1 Ray St, Maidenhead. The Compleat Angler Hotel, Marlow Bridge SL7 1RG (Tel: 01628 484444), has fishing from grounds, free for residents, non-residents on temporary permit. Ghillie supplied, if required.

Hurley (Berks). London AA has fisheries at Frogmill Farm and Hurley Flats. Dt issued for 1½m. Members and associates only. Hurley Lock, Environment Agency fishery, *see Molesey Lock* for permit details.

Henley (Oxon). Pike, roach, perch, tench, bream, eels. Free fishing u/s from Promenade to Cold Bath Ditch. Environment Agency fishery at Marsh Lock, *see Molesey Lock* for permit details. Oxon and Bucks bank water controlled by society for members only. Also from end of Henley Promenade upstream to Marsh Lock, bridges and meadows upstream from Marsh Lock. London AA has stretches for members. Reading & Dist AA has Aston Ferry fishing, about 4m d/s of Henley, 25 swims stretching nearly to Hambledon Lock. Tackle shops: Alf Parrot, 15 Thameside; Sports Centre, Greys Rd. Boats: Hobbs, Parrott. Good accommodation for anglers at Flower Pot Hotel, Aston RG9 3DG.

Wargrave (Berks). Thames and Loddon; good coarse fishing.

Sonning (Berks). Much fishing from **Shiplake** to Sonning Bridge on Oxfordshire bank controlled by Shiplake and Binfield Heath AS; members only. Guests at White Hart can fish private stretch of ½m on Berkshire bank towards Shiplake. London AA has water for members only at Shiplake, Lowfield and Mapledurham. Reading & Dist AA has Sonning Eye fishery (lake and river). Members only. Environment Agency fishery at Shiplake Lock, *see Molesey Lock* for permit details.

Reading (Berks). Most coarse fish. Reading Borough Council controls length from opposite Caversham Court Gazebo to 1½m u/s of Caversham Bridge. The fishing from Thameside Promenade to Scours Lane is controlled by Thames Water. There is some free water on the **Kennet** from Horseshoe Bridge to County Weir (adjacent to Inner Distribution Road). Reading and District AA, comprising about 40 affiliated clubs, control 28 miles of river and canal, plus 14 lakes in Berkshire and Oxfordshire. Subscription £30, with concessions. Supplementary permits on three specimen waters, £25–£80. £3 dt offered for Wylies Lake, stocked, with good tench and bream fishing in Reading vicinity. Farnborough AS has good trout and coarse fishing on **Whitewater** at Heckfield (8m), also 2m fly only stretch. St £30, joining fee £10. dt £4, conc. Countryside Club, 109 Upper Woodcote Road, Caversham Heights, Reading, has trout and carp fishing let on a family st basis; At Bradfield, **Pang Valley trout lake**, approx 6 acres, stocked with rainbow trout. Dt £25, 4 fish limit, £15 2 fish, from tackle shop T Turner *(see below)*. RMC Angling has coarse fisheries on permit at **St Patrick's**

Stream, **Twyford** and **Theale** (52 acres). *(For RMC Angling, see Chertsey.)* Tackle shops: Reading Angling Centre, 69 Northland Avenue; Thames Valley Angling, 258 Kentwood Hill, Tilehurst, Reading; Tadley Angling, Padworth Rd, Padworth. Hotels: Thameside; Thames House; Pennyfarthings, Swallowfield.

Tilehurst (Berks). Reading and District AA control the fishing at Purley, and on the Oxfordshire bank. Free fishing from towpath to Caversham *(see restrictions under Reading).* Beethoven Hotel has private stretch on south bank. Tackle shop: Thames Valley Angling, 258 Kentwood Hill, Tilehurst.

Goring (Oxon). Pike, bream, roach, chub, perch and (in weir pool especially) barbel and a few trout; weir pool Environment Agency fishery, *see Molesey Lock,* for permit details. Other fishing can be had from towpath above and below lock.

Pangbourne and **Whitchurch** (Berks). Thames and **Pang**. Trout, perch, pike, roach, bream, chub, dace. River fishes well in winter; free fishing 1½m above and below Whitchurch Bridge; good coarse fishing; boats for hire. Weir pool private. Pang holds trout, especially near Tidmarsh, but is strictly preserved; trout at its mouth. Pangbourne and Whitchurch AS is affiliated with Reading & Dist AA, and fishes in a number of localities, including 3m of R Kennet with good chub, barbel, roach and dace. St £23 from Hon Sec.

Moulsford (Berks). All coarse fish. London AA has water here; members only. Hotel: Beetle.

South Stoke (Oxon). London AA controls the water from footbridge above railway bridge down to Beetle and Wedge ferry and second meadow below the ferry down to Runsford Hole; members only.

Wallingford (Oxon). Reading & Dist AA has Severals Farm fishing: two sections, above and below Bensons Lock, with barbel, chub, roach, perch. Local club: Jolly Anglers, who have four stretches (good bream in summer, chub in winter); st £10, wt £7, dt £3 (concessions for juniors), from Rides on Air, 45 St Mary's Street and Wallingford Sports Shop, 71 High Street.

Cleeve (Oxon). Usual coarse fish. London AA has right bank from Beetle and Wedge Hotel to Cleeve Lock; Gatehampton Farm fishery.

Members only, but ¾m open to associates.

Benson (Oxon). Usual coarse fish. Benson AS has water from Benson to Wallingford. Wt £5, dt £2 from Benson Marina or from Hon Sec. Some Sundays reserved for matches. Benson Lock is Environment Agency lock and weir fishery, *see Molesey Lock* for permit details.

Shillingford (Oxon). Wallingford AA has water upstream; dt from Hon Sec. Shillingford Bridge Hotel, nr Wallingford OX10 8LZ (Tel: 01865 858567, Fax: 858636), has good pike fishing with trout, tench, dace, etc, on ¼m (both banks) reserved for guests and members of High Wycombe AC.

Little Wittenham (Oxon). Thame comes in here.

Clifton Hampden (Oxon). Oxford & Dist AA has water here, d/s from the scenic bridge for 9 fields. Bream, chub and roach, also large barbel. Dt on part of this water from tackle shops only, no night fishing. Clifton Lock is Environment Agency fishery, *see Molesey Lock* for permit details. Inn: The Barley Mow.

Appleford (Berks). London AA controls from just above the railway bridge down to beginning of Clifton Hampden cutting; both banks, then a short stretch on right bank only; members only.

Culham (Oxon). All water except weir pools controlled by Abingdon & Dist ARA. Other clubs: Culham AC and Sutton Courtenay AC have pits. No day tickets.

Abingdon (Oxon). Bream, chub, pike and barbel good. Free fishing for residents. Tickets from Town Clerk's office for the 1½m controlled by Council, from Nuneham railway bridge to notice-board 200 yds u/s from Culham footbridge. Details from Stratton Lodge, 52 Bath Street, Abingdon. Fishery includes weir, but must be fished from bank. Abingdon & Oxford Anglers Alliance has much local fishing. The Alliance trout section has lake at **Standlake**, Oxon, st £50, entrance fee £15. Members and their guests only: R H Williams, 2 Holyoake Rd, Oxford OX3 8AE. Tackle shop: The Right Angle, Wootton Rd.

Sandford-on-Thames (Oxon). Pike, bream, roach, perch, etc. Oxford & Dist AA has water here on both banks d/s of weir to the main river, with roach, chub, dace, barbel and pike.

Abingdon A & RA have water; R Pitson, Tel: 01235 25140. Environment Agency lock and weir fishery at Sandford Lock, see *Molesey Lock* for permit details.

Iffley (Oxon). Thames (or Isis). From Botley Road Bridge d/s to Folly Bridge is Oxford & Dist AS water. Large shoals of roach, perch and chub. Dt from tackle shops. Inn: Isis Tavern.

Oxford (Oxon). Thames (Isis), **Cherwell** and **Oxford Canal**. All coarse fish. N Oxford AS has water on Thames, at **Gostow** and **Carrot's Ham**, Cherwell, canal, and carp and tench fishing in **Dukes Lake**. Their best water is **Seacourt Stream** at Carrot's Ham, with many species. Club offers dt on water between Godstow and Seacourt Overspill, and Seacourt Stream from Overspill to A420. Rose Revived Hotel, Newbridge, Tel: 0186 731 221 has tickets for 2 fields d/s on left bank at Newbridge and from road bridge to confluence with left hand bank R Windrush. **Donnington** and **Iffley** water held by Oxford & Dist AA. Good roach fishing, also chub. Heavy boat traffic here. Assn is an affiliation of clubs local to Oxford. It has excellent coarse fishing on Thames at **Medley**, **Kennington**, **Newbridge**, and elsewhere, with dt £3.50 from tackle shops only. 4½m W of Oxford, **Farmoor Reservoirs**, Cumnor Rd, Farmoor OX2 9NS. No. 1 leased by Farmoor Flyfishers. Members only. Tel: 01235 850619. Reservoir No. 2, Cumnor Rd, is 240 acre trout fishery, stocked with brown and rainbow, fly only from boat or bank. Dt and st from gatehouse. Facilities for disabled. Phone 01865 863033 for advance bookings. Day tickets for **Adderbury Lakes** coarse fishing from Old Bake House Stores, High St, Adderbury. Shimano-Linear Fisheries have 5 pools near **Stanton Harcourt** on B4449 road. Fishery records incl pike to 27lb, carp to 40lbs; also Hunts Corner Lake, dt water, close to others. Contact Fishery Manager, 10A Rackstaw Grove, Old Farm Park, Milton Keynes MK7 8PZ (Tel: 01908 645135). Tackle shops: North Oxford Tackle, 95 Islip Rd OX2 7SP; State Tackle, 19 Fettiplace Rd, Witney OX8 5AP; and others. Hotels: Swan, Islip; Prince of Wales, Cowley Rd APS HQ.

Eynsham (Oxon). Good coarse fishing; large bream. Oxford Angling and Pres Soc has water (see *Oxford*). Eynsham Lock fishing open to holders of Environment Agency lock permits, see *Molesey Lock* for permit details. Hotels: Ye Talbot Inn, Railway, Red Lion.

Bablock Hythe (Oxon). Ferryman Inn, Northmoor OX8 1BL (Tel: 01865 880028) issues dt for 3m on north bank upstream. Special fishing mini-break for two persons, any two nights, £90.

Newbridge (Oxon). Near Witney. Good coarse fishing (bream increasing), few trout in the **Windrush**. Shifford Lock is one of Environment Agency's fisheries, see *Molesey Lock* for permit details. Newland AC has water from **Shifford** to within 600 yds of Newbridge, Steadies Lane, Stanton Harcourt and Heyford Lakes, Standlake, with specimen fish. St, dt for lakes only. Non-locals membership by approval of committee, only. Hotels: Rose Revived (¾m water on Thames and Windrush; good coarse fish, some trout) and May Bush (½m water on Thames). Witney AS have Thames fishing here, R Windrush, trout only, and coarse pits; members only, £20 per annum, conc. Stroud AA have 1m of Thames (dt Batemans Sports, Stroud. Tel: 4320). Tackle shop: State Fishing Tackle, 19 Fettiplace Rd, Witney, Tel: 01993 702587, who can give further information.

Tadpole Bridge, Buckland (Berks). Coventry & Dist AA has Rushey Wier fishery. Good chub and barbel; pike in weir-pool.

Radcot (Oxon). Bream, chub, barbel, roach, perch, pike, occasional trout. Swan Hotel, OX18 2SX (Tel: 01367 810220) has ½m, dt £1.50. Radcot AC has 5m, st only, £17.50, conc. Apply Hon Sec (Tel: 01993 841645), Swan Hotel, or Turner's Tackle. Clanfield AC also has left bank, Old Man's Bridge to Rushey Lock, st only, £10, 3m fishing. Three Environment Agency lock fisheries, at Radcot; Grafton Lock; and Buscot Lock, see *Molesey Lock* for permit details. Permits for stretch from **Buscot** to Grafton Lock, season cards for Radcot AC and Clanfield AC, from Turner's Tackle and Bait, 4A Station Rd, Faringdon, SN7 7BN (Tel: 01367 241044).

Lechlade (Glos). For Thames, Coln and Leach. Phoenix AA controls 2m of Thames at Lechlade upstream from Trout Inn to Murdoch Ditch. Permits for weir pool only, from Trout Inn GL7 3HA. For Highworth AC water between Lechlade and Buscot, contact M Mills, 58 Croft Rd, Swindon. Tackle shop: Turner's Tackle, Faringdon.

Cricklade (Wilts). Thames known here as Isis. Isis No. 1 Lake at **South Cerney** (Glos), carp to 30lb. Membership £27, dt £5 from tackle shops. South Cerney AC has 5 lakes in Cotswold area, membership £25, conc, from House of Angling, 59/60 Commercial Rd, Swindon SN1 5NX.

Tributaries of the Thames

MOLE: Coarse fish.

Esher (Surrey). Pike, roach, perch, the odd big chub. Feltham Piscatorials have 'The Ledges'. Epsom AS has ½m at Wayne Flete and ½m on Wey at **Weybridge**. St £10, conc £4, from Hon Sec. Tackle shop: Weybridge Guns & Tackle, 137 Oatlands Drive, Weybridge KT13 9LB.

Cobham (Surrey). Central Association of London and Provincial Angling Clubs (CAL-PAC) has 1½m of Mole here, various coarse species, and Manor Pond, holding pike, carp, roach, tench and bream. Members only. Further CALPAC stretch, 1½ miles at **Hersham**, chub, perch, roach, dace, eels, pike, dt £4, conc, sold on bank. Cobham Court AC have water adjacent and above: large chub, pike, very big perch and eels. Some rainbows stocked.

Leatherhead (Surrey). Leatherhead & Dist AS have waters above A246 road bridge. Sunmead AS has water at Norbury Park, Leatherhead, with chub, roach, dace, perch, together with carp and pike to double figures. Dt £3 on bank. Tackle shops: S C Fuller, 28/32 South St, Dorking RH4 2HQ (Tel: 01306 882177); F.U. Tackle, Cock Lane, Leatherhead. Hotel: Bull.

Dorking (Surrey). Coarse fish. Dorking AS has about 4m of Mole and 4 lakes; large stocks of carp, tench, bream, roach, rudd, orfe. Members only except Fourwent Pond, South Holywood, dt on bank or from S C Fuller (below). Furze Farm Fishery, Knowle Lane, nr Cranleigh, 3½ acre mixed fishery. Dt £6 on bankside. Contact Stone Cottage, Ridgeway Rd, Dorking RH4 3EY. Tackle shop: S C Fuller, 28/32 South St, Dorking RH4 2HQ (Tel: 01306 882177) Hotels: White Horse, Bell, Arundel.

Brockham (Surrey). Chub, roach, carp and bream. Brockham AS water.

Betchworth (Surrey). Chub dominate below weir, anything can, and does appear above weir. Carshalton and Dist AS has water; members only.

Sidlow (Surrey). Roach dominate, together with perch, carp, chub. Horley P S fish much of this water.

WEY: Coarse fish, trout higher up.

Weybridge (Surrey). Wey Amalgamation have water here (see Thames), St £12.50, dt £1.50, jun, OAP, 50%; from bailiff.

Woking (Surrey). Roach, chub, pike, etc. Woking and Dist AS has rights on 23 miles of river bank and 2 ponds (perch, carp and tench) at Send; dt for members' guests only. New members welcome; details from Hon Sec. Tackle shop: Weybridge Guns & Tackle, 137 Oatlands Drive, Weybridge KT13 9LB.

Wisley (Surrey); ns Ripley. Ponds: Wisley Mere, Hut Pond, and several other ponds on Ripley Common and Ockham Common; carp, pike, perch, roach.

Guildford (Surrey). Guildford AS has about 9½m R Wey; lakes at Broad Street and Whitmoor Common (carp to 19lb in Britton Pond). CALPAC fishes Stoke Park Farm stretch of Wey, 1½ miles nr Guildford. Dt £4, conc, on bank or from Guildford Angling Centre. At Shamley Green **Willinghurst Trout Fishery**, Shamley Green (Tel: 01483 271005): 3 acre lake, mostly rainbow trout, ave 2¼lbs. Dt £22.50, 4 fish, to £15, 2 fish. Good mayfly hatch. **Albury Estate Fisheries**, Estate Office, Albury, Guildford GU5 9AF (Tel: 01483 202323); 8 lakes, totalling 16 acres, of brown and rainbow trout fishing; 3 dt waters: Powdermills (4lb av), Weston (2½lb) and Vale End (1lb 14oz); one syndicated: Park (2lbs av); dt waters £42–£18 per day. Limits 2–5 fish, depending on venue. One lake of 6 acres, rainbow trout dt £27, 4 fish. Instruction, if required. Brittens Pond, Salt Box Lane, Jacobs Well; big carp, perch, roach, etc. Dt £4. Tackle shops: S R Jeffrey & Son, 134 High St; Guildford; Peter Cockwill Game Angling, The Street, Albury GU5 9AG (Tel: 01483 205196). Accommodation: Drummond Arms, Albury.

Shalford (Surrey). Wey; bream, roach, pike, etc. **Tillingbourne**; trout; preserved. Inns: Parrot, Victoria, Sea Horse, Percy Arms, Chilworth.

Godalming (Surrey). Godalming AS has Wey from Eashing Bridge (Stag Inn) to Broadford Bridge (about 8m); coarse fish, some grayling and trout. Society also has Broadwater Lake (10 acres) which holds carp, roach, tench and perch; Busbridge Lake, Enton Lake and Bramley Park Lake; st £40 plus £60 entry fee, short waiting list except for residents. Peper Harow Flyfishers have 2m of Wey and 3 ponds (brown and rainbow trout); rods limited; st only. **Wintershall Waters**, Bramley, is 3 acre trout fishery. St only. Tel: 01483 275019. Hotels: Farncombe Manor, Lake, King's Arms (Godalming AS HQ).

Frensham (Surrey). Farnham AS has trout water below Frensham Mill, **Frensham, Great** and **Little Ponds**, roach, perch, carp, etc; open membership for coarse fishing. St £49 (joining fee £20), conc, from The Creel, Station Rd, Aldershot. Frensham Trout Fishery, Crosswater Lane, Churt GU10 2JN (Tel: 01252 794321): 5 lakes stocked with rainbow, brown, tiger, and also wild brown trout. Variety of dt, incl catch and release.

Haslemere (Surrey). Coarse fish. At St Patricks Lane, **Liss**, is coarse fishing on 2 lakes, plus 5 ponds at **Rake** for matches only. For dt, contact MBK Leisure, Petersfield Angling Centre, 34 Dragon St, Petersfield GU31 4JJ (Tel: 01730 266999).

Farnham (Surrey). Farnham AS offers extensive local fishing, for members only. Club coarse fishing waters include 1m R Wey at **Dockenfield** and **Elstead; Frensham Ponds**; Badshot Lea Ponds; Lodge Pond; Stockbridge Pond at **Tilford, Loddon** at **Winnersh**, lakes at **Yateley**, incl specimen water; **R Whitewater** near **Riseley**, small stream with chub, perch and roach. No day tickets; st £49, joining fee £20, conc; apply Membership Sec for details. Note: all waters heavily fished early in season.

COLNE: Coarse fish, some trout. Information about the river is obtainable from the Colne Valley Anglers Consultative, Mr R McNab, 136 Braybourne Close, Uxbridge UB8 1UL.

Wraysbury (Bucks). Blenheim AS has **Colne Brook** from Wraysbury Rd to Hythe End Bridge; coarse fish and occasional trout. Also Cargill Lake, Silver Wings Lake, and Watts Pool, members only. Twickenham PS and Staines AC have gravel pits; no tickets.

West Drayton (G London). Trout, pike, perch, bream, dace, roach, tench, chub. Grand Union Canal is near. Lizard Fisheries, Trout Rd, West Drayton (Tel: 07931 255897): all species of carp to 35lb. Dt from pay and display machine on site; £5, one rod for 12 hours. Contact Bowmans Lakes, 10/11 Pleasant Place, West Hyde, Rickmansworth WD3 2XZ.

Uxbridge (G London). Pike, perch, roach, dace and bream. Fishing free on Uxbridge Moor. London AA holds long stretches of **Grand Union Canal**, on which dt is issued. National Trust **Osterley Park Lake** holds bream, tench, pike, roach, carp. Limited st £23, conc. No night fishing. Enquiries to Head Gardener, Osterley Park, Jersey Rd, Isleworth, Middx TW7 4RB. **Farlows Pit, Iver**, holds roach, tench, carp, bream, pike; limited number of st.

Denham (Bucks). Colne; coarse fish. Blenheim AS has 6½m of **Grand Union Canal**; dt on Denham to Rickmansworth stretch, £3, from bailiff on bank.

Harefield (G London). **Savay Lake**, Moorhall Road: 52 acre gravel pit stocked with specimen fish. St £100 from P Broxup, Fishery manager, 309 Shirland Road, London W9 (Tel: 020 8969 6980). **Bowmans Lakes**, London Colney, **St Albans**: 3 lakes, 2 of which have 60 and 100 pegs, with large bream, carp and pike. St £50–£100, dt £7–£5, enquiries to 10/11 Pleasant Place, West Hyde, Rickmansworth WD3 2XZ, Tel: 01895 824455. Tackle shop: Bowmans Angling Shop, Bowmans Farm, Coursers Lane, London Colney, St Albans.

Rickmansworth (Herts). Trout, chub, dace, roach, pike, perch. Blenheim AS has 1½m of **Grand Union Canal**; good roach and bream; dt £3 from bailiff on water for length between Lock 87 and Lock 85. Limited st from Harefield Tackle. (Note: no dt on section between Springwell Lock No 83 and Black Jays Lock No 85.) Watford Piscators have 4m of canal; also two stretches of **R Gade**, with barbel, large roach, shoals of bream and chub, good perch; three stretches of R Colne; and 6 coarse lakes, incl Tolpits, Castles, Staneys, Thurlows, and Rouseburn Lakes, Cassiobury Park. Club also has 12 to 16 jun section. All waters members only, except two sections of canal, dt £2.50. Membership £85, conc. Kings Langley AS has 2m of canal at Hunton Bridge, also short stretch of R Gade. Information from Tackle Carrier (*below*). **Chess**; trout, preserved. **Croxley Hall** Trout Fishery, Rickmansworth WD3 3BQ; 4 lakes in 20 acres: trout, fly only. Tel: 01923 778290. Kings Langley Fishery, Home Park Link Rd, **Kings Langley** (Tel: 0378 030939 or 01923 269578): 4 acre dug-out pond with carp to 24lbs, tench, roach, perch, etc; dt £6, two rods, conc. Tingrith Coarse Fishery, **Tingrith** (Tel: 012525 714012): 3 pools with carp, tench, bream etc. Tackle shops: Colne Valley Angling, Money Hill Parade; Tackle Carrier, 157 St Albans Rd, Watford (Tel: 01923 232393).

Watford (Herts). Boxmoor and Dist AS has stretch of river here. **Gade** at Cassiobury is free fishing for approx 1m. Ticket waters: Elstree and Tring reservoirs and Grand Union Canal. London AA issues dt for canal from Hunton Bridge to Tring. Free fishing in Gade in Cassiobury Park. Watford Piscators have fishing in Rivers Gade and Colne, lakes, and dt water on Grand Union Canal (see *Rickmansworth*). Tackle shop: The Tackle Carrier, St Alban's Road. Hotels: Maldon, Clarendon, Rose and Crown.

CHESS: Brown and rainbow trout – one of few British streams where rainbows spawn naturally. There is free public fishing at Scotts Bridge Playing Fields, Rickmansworth.

Chorleywood (Bucks). Chess; trout.

Latimer (Bucks). Latimer Park Lakes Chesham, Bucks HP5 1TT (Tel: 01494 766 333, Fax: 555): upper river and 2 lakes (12 acres in all) open for trout fishing; brown and rainbow; average 2lb 6oz; daily restocking; boat for hire. Fly only. Season: Mar to Oct. St £576 to £186. Dt £25; any 6 hours £18; any 4 hours £14. Advance booking essential. Disabled facilities and boat.

GADE: coarse fish.

Boxmoor (Herts). Boxmoor and Dist AS has private water at Westbrook Mere, Bourne End, with large carp, bream, tench, pike, roach, rudd and perch. Club also has Upper Ouse at **Stoney Stratford**, Colne at Watford, and Stort Navigation at Harlow, all mixed fishing, matches throughout year. Boxmoor Trout Fishery, 3 acres of converted water cress farm. St £350 to £160 on flexible basis. Inquiries to R Hands, 23 Sebright Rd, Boxmoor, Hemel Hempstead, Tel: 01442 393381 or to Fishery, 81 Marlowes, Hemel Hempstead.

Berkhamsted (Herts). Visitors can fish London AA water on Grand Union Canal; coarse fish, dt £1.50 from bailiff. No free water. Hotels: King's Arms (Trust House), Crown, Swan.

LODDON: coarse fish, barbel improving, trout scarce.

Twyford (Berks). Three pits, 100 acres, with carp, bream, tench, pike, chub, dace, eels at Twyford, plus Charvil and St Patrick's stream (fine barbel), held by RMC Angling. St £20, concessions to jun, OAP, dis. (For RMC Angling, see *Chertsey*.)

Arborfield Cross (Berks). Farnham AS has a stretch at Sindlesham Mill, Winnersh; coarse fish, barbel in faster stretches (see *Wey – Farnham*). Cove AS also has water near here at **Shinfield** and on **Hart** and **Whitewater**; members only (see also *Fleet*). Farnborough AS has 2½m R Loddon at **Winnersh**, 4m R Whitewater at Heckfield, Basingstoke Canal and Shawfields Lake and Hollybush Pits. Fine mixed coarse fishing, fly fishing, membership £30 + £10 joining fee. Felix Farm Trout Fishery, Howe Lane, **Binfield**, RG42 5QL (Tel: 01189 345527). 10 acres, stocked with b and r between 2–10 lb. Dt £25, 4 fish, ½ day £19, 3 fish, evening £14, 2 fish. Boats for hire. Contact Martin Suddards at fishery for more details.

KENNET: One of England's finest mixed coarse fisheries; upper reaches noted for trout and grayling.

Theale (Berks), Water west of point 1m upstream of Bridge House (Wide Mead Lock) strictly preserved; few trout and coarse fish. Englefield Lake, 2m. Pike, and fine tench and carp (private). Reading and Dist AA has much water on lower **Kennet** at Theale, Rushey Meadow, Calcot, Lower and Upper Benyons, Ufton, Padworth Mill and elsewhere, the **Holybrook** and backwaters, together with 9 local gravel pits, 120 acres. No dt. Blenheim AS fishes Kennet and Holybrook at Southcote. Barbel, roach, dace, chub, perch. Members only, £50 pa, £10 joining fee, conc. At **Burghfield**, four RMC Angling lakes with big carp and other species, and 1m R Kennet, large chub and barbel. St £26, ½ price conc, dt £6 from Reading Angling Centre (Tel: 01189 872216). (For RMC Angling, see *Chertsey*.)

Aldermaston (Berks). Coarse fish and few

trout. Old Mill, Aldermaston RG7 4LB (Tel: 0118 9712365) issues permits for about ½m of water with four weirs, and small lake with carp to 30lb; dt £9 at door, £10 in bank. CALPAC has 750 yard stretch of Kennet at **Padworth**, with large barbel, tench, bream, pike, etc. Members only, membership £26, conc. London AA has 2m on **Fisherman's Brook**; coarse fish; members only.

Thatcham (Berks). Fishing between Reading and Thatcham controlled chiefly by Reading & Dist AA. Members only on river and Hambridge Lake, but £3 dt on site for Whylies Lake, Thatcham. Details from Hon Sec (see club list). Thatcham AA has water on canal, R Kennet plus lakes. Members only, £52.50 per annum. Tackle shops: Thatcham Angling Centre, Unit 4, 156 Sagecroft Rd RG18 3BQ (Tel: 01635 871450); Crowmead Angling Centre, 10 Crowmead, Bath Rd, Thatcham.

Newbury (Berks). On Rivers Kennet and **Lambourn** and **Kennet and Avon Canal**; trout and coarse fishing. Newbury & Dist AA, Thatcham AA and Reading & Dist AA hold water in this area. Kintbury AC owns canal and river fishing; st £12. For these and other local clubs contact Field and Stream (below). CALPAC has Kennet fishery at Bulls Lock, with large barbel and other coarse species. Some brown and rainbow trout have been caught. Members only. Tackle shop: Field and Stream, 109 Bartholomew Street RG14 5ET (Tel: 01635 43186). Foley Lodge Hotel (Tel: 01635 528770) caters for anglers.

Hungerford (Berks). Kennet and **Dunn**; trout, grayling; preserved. **Hungerford Canal** fishing in hands of Hungerford Canal AA (3m). CALPAC has fishery at **Sulhampstead**, 750 yds of river, followed by 700 yds of canal, with large barbel and other coarse species. No night fishing. Dt £4, conc, from Canal Cottage or on bank. S Wilson, 53 Einion, Llanbardan Campus, Aberystwyth, has 1½m Kennet fishing with stocked rainbows and wild browns, running to 4lb, and the odd 8lb fish. Accommodation at Red Lion, Three Swans, Bear, Lamb Hotel (Canal AA HQ).

Lockinge (Oxon). Lockinge Fishery, John Haigh, Orpwood, Ardington, Wantage OX12 8PN (Tel: 01235 833300, Fax: 820950); stocked trout fishing on lakes and streams, running through Ardington and Lockinge, nr Wantage. Av brown and rainbow, 2lb. St £570.

Nearest tackle shop: Didcot Angling Centre, 36 Wantage Rd, Didcot.

Marlborough (Wilts). Trout at Axford, Marlborough and District AA has fishing rights on **Kennet and Avon Canal** from Milkhouse Water to Burbage Wharf and Bruce Tunnel to Little Bedwyn. St £12 + £2 entry, conc. **Wroughton Reservoir**, Overtown Hill, Wroughton, Swindon. Coarse fishing, Wroughton AC: Mr Hammond, Tel: 01793 81231. Bristol, Bath and Wilts AA has **Tockenham Reservoir**, near Swindon, members only, st £25 from House of Angling (below). Tackle shop: Leathercraft, High Street. Tackle shops in Swindon: Cotswold Angling, Hyde Road, Kingsdown; Angling Centre, 5 Sheppard Street; House of Angling, 60 Commercial Road. Hotels: Aylesbury Arms, Savernake, Castle and Ball, Crown (Marlborough AA HQ).

THAME: Coarse fish.

Dorchester (Oxon). Thames and Thame. Coarse fish; good chub and dace, and carp quite numerous. Dorchester AA has water; dt from Hon Sec or Fleur-de-Lys.

Thame (Oxon). Roach, bream, perch, chub. Leighton Buzzard AC has stretches at **Shabbington**, **Worminghall**, **Ickford** and **Waterperry**. The Tring Anglers have water at Ickford, the Shabbington Island, and **Chearsley**, members and guests tickets. St £32, dt £3, conc half price.

Eythrope (Bucks). Roach, bream, perch, chub, good dace. Aylesbury Dist and Izaak Walton AA has water (4m from Aylesbury), members and friends only. Blenheim AS has water at Shabbington and Cuddington and backwaters, with roach, dace, chub, perch. Members only, annual sub £45, £10 entrance, usual conc.

CHERWELL: Coarse fish.

Islip (Oxon). Cherwell and Ray; good chub, roach, perch and pike fishing may be had in the Cherwell. Preserved by Oxford Angling and Preservation Society, st £8.50, dt £1.50. The Bicester AS has 1½m on Cherwell Northbrook, and ½ acre carp pool, 2m Bicester. St £12 from tackle shops. Oxford & Dist AA has Cherwell at Enslow and Northbrook; wt from tackle shops. Bicester AA has Kirtlington water. Tackle shops: Allmond, Bicester; J & K Tackle, 8/9 Wesley Precinct, Bicester. Inns: Red Lion, Swan.

Heyford (Oxon). Preserved by Banbury and Dist AA; members only. Oxford & Dist AA has South Oxford Canal from Enslow Bridge to Heyford Wharf. Dt £2.50 from Oxford tackle shops.

Banbury (Oxon). Banbury AA has much local R Medway and canal fishing, incl stretches at Cropedy, Nell Bridge, Clifton, Somerton, Heyford and Bletchington, also **Clattercote** and **Grimsbury Reservoirs**. Dt £4, conc, for reservoirs only from tackle shops. Coventry AA hold stretch 8m of **Oxford Canal**, with large carp, amongst other species. Dt on bank, £2. Farnborough Hall Lake is leased to Banbury AA. Coarse fishing at Butler Hill Farm, Gt Rollright, OX7 5SJ (Tel: 01608 84319); carp to 25lb, large rudd, chub, bream; dt £4. Rye Hill, Milcombe, and Chacombe Fishery, carp bream, tench, etc, dt for these and others from Castaway, see below. Cheyney Manor Fishery, Manor House, **Barford St Michael**; 5 acres, rainbow trout are fly fished in trout pond, brown trout in river. The moat contains carp, and fishpond has rudd, roach, tench, perch. Tickets from bailiff. Tel: 01869 38207. Castle AA fishes 2 lakes, 6 acres, at **Canons Ashby**: carp to 22lb, bream and roach. College Farm Fishing, Aynho (Tel: 01869 81258): lake with carp, chub, bream etc, 20 pegs, open dawn till dusk. The Goldfish Bowl, Boulderdyke Farm, off Chapel Close, Clifton, nr Deddington (Tel: 01869 338539): Carp lake, 18 pegs, disabled access. Nellbridge Coarse Fishery, Aynho (Tel: 01295 811227): 3 lakes stocked with tench, roach, carp, 100 pegs plus, open dawn till dusk. Tackle shops: Banbury Angling Centre, 12B South St, OX16 7LN; Castaway, 86 Warwick Rd OX16 7AJ; Banbury Gunsmiths, 47A Broad St OX16 8BT. Chipping Norton tackle shop: K & M, 23 West Rd.

EVENLODE: Trout, coarse fish (roach and dace especially).

Long Hanborough (Oxon). Red Spinner AS rents 9m of the Evenlode from **Fawler** to **Cassington**; trout (re-stocked annually), dace, roach, chub, pike; members only. Good fishing on **Blenheim Park Lakes**. Excellent tench, perch and roach, with pike in winter. Boat fishing only. (See Midlands lakes, reservoirs, etc). **Salford Trout Lakes**; 5 and 3½ acres stocked with r and b trout. Dt £19 (4 fish limit), ½ day and evening, £13. St £265 also offered. E A Colston, Rectory Farm, Salford, Chipping Norton OX7 5YZ (Tel: 01608 643209).

WINDRUSH: Trout, grayling, coarse fish (dace up to 1lb and 2lb roach not rare).

Witney (Oxon). Large trout; preserved below; leave must be obtained from the proprietors; good hatch of mayfly. Witney AS (HQ Eagle Vaults) has water. No dt and membership £15 pa restricted to county as a rule, but outside applications considered; apply Hon Sec. Club now has water on gravel pits at **Stanton Harcourt** (carp, tench, etc). Vauxhall AC has stretch. Members only. Newland AC has backstream from Hardwick Village downstream, and Heyford Lakes Fishery, dt £2.50. Tackle shop: Derek State, Tackle, 19 Fettiplace Rd.

Minster Lovell (Oxon). Cotswold Flyfishers have 10m at **Swinbrook** and **Stanton Harcourt**; trout (restocked yearly), fly only; membership limited; no dt. Whitney AA has water on Windrush at **Worsham** (1m above village; trout re-stocked yearly) and Thames at **Newbridge** and **Standlake**; trout, grayling, coarse fish; fishing much improved. **Linch Hill Leisure Park**, Stanton Harcourt; Willow Pool stocked with specialist carp; Stoneacres Lake mixed trout and coarse fishing. 10 acre Christchurch Lake, carp. St £25, dt £2.50 to £5.50, depending on which pool fished. Concessions. Boats for hire. Tel: 01865 882215. Hotel: Old Swan Inn.

Burford (Oxon). Burford AC holds approx 1m, with brown and rainbow trout to 5lb, grayling, large roach, perch, chub, dace, gudgeon, and pike to 14lb. All grayling to be returned. St £20, conc, from J Swallow, 8 Meadow End, Fulbrook, Burford, Oxon. Dt £5 from Highway Hotel, Burford. Club is affiliated with Oxford and Dist AA. Tackle shop: K and M Fishing Tackle, 23 West St, Chipping Norton (Tel: 01608 645435). Hotels include Cotswold, Gateway, Lamb, Highway.

COLN: notable dry fly fishing for trout of good average size; grayling.

Fairford (Glos). Trout; excellent; April 1 to Sept 30. Grayling Oct–Mar. Dry fly only upstream. Not stocked. Tickets can be had for 1½m from Bull Hotel, Market Place GL7 4AA. Catch/return; trout of 1–1½lb plentiful. Dt £22, half day £15 (reduction for residents). Whelford Pools, coarse fishery, off A417; dt on site, £5, £6 specimen lake, conc. Tel: 01285 713649. Nearest tackle shop at Lechlade, 4m.

Bibury (Glos). Coln: trout. Swan Hotel GL7 5NW (Tel: 01285 740695) has 300 yds facing hotel, day tickets from hotel: dry fly only, 3 rods on offer.

TORRIDGE
(For close seasons, licences, etc, see South West Region Environment Agency p12)

Rises on Cornwall, Devonshire border, but is also fed from Dartmoor via a tributary, the River Okement. It flows into Bideford/ Barnstaple Estuary. Salmon, sea trout, peal and brown trout.

Bideford (Devon). River for 2m on east side, and 2 reservoirs, at **Gammaton**, stocked with brown and rainbow trout, leased by Torridge Fly Fishing Club; st £100 from Hon Sec, written application only; dt £7 from Summerlands Tackle, 3 Golf Links Rd, Westward Ho!, Tel: 01237 471291. **Weare Giffard**, 1m right bank, salmon, sea trout, brown trout; dt £15 from E Ellison, Riversdale Guest House, Weare Giffard, Tel: 01237 423676. Torridge Valley Trout Farm, Halspill, Weare Giffard EX39 4RA, Tel: 01237 475797: rainbow trout dt £3.50, plus catch weight. Hotels: Royal, New Inn, Tanton's.

Torrington (Devon). Salmon, sea trout, brown trout. Fishing lodge and occasional day rods on **Beaford** stretch; contact Group Capt P Norton-Smith, Little Warham, Beaford, Winkleigh EX19 8AB, Tel: 0180 5603317. Coarse fishing at **Darracott Reservoir**, Torrington; 3 acres, Peninsula Coarse Fishery open all the year, 24 hr day, dt £3.50 from Summerlands Tackle, see above. Tackle shop: The Kingfisher, 22 Castle St, Barnstaple.

Shebbear (Devon). Devil's Stone Inn EX21 54RU, Tel: 01409 281210, has an arrangement with local farmers for 2½m of salmon, sea trout and brown trout fishing on Torridge; fly and spinning; excellent dry-fly trout water. Nearest beat 1m. Licences, tackle, and angling instruction on site. Dt sometimes issued to non-residents.

Sheepwash (Devon). Half Moon Inn EX21 5NE (Tel: 01409 231376) has 10m of private salmon, sea trout and brown trout fishing on Torridge. Season 1 Mar–30 Sept, spinning allowed in Mar, otherwise fly only; also 6 acre lake stocked with rainbow trout. Dt for non-residents £16, salmon, £12 sea trout, £8, b trout. Brochure on request from Charles Inniss. Tackle shop at hotel, also tackle for hire, and rod licences.

Hatherleigh (Devon). Torridge, Lew, Okement; salmon, sea trout, brown trout. Highhampton Trout Lakes, 6 acres, fly only, rainbow trout: Mrs S Thomas, Greenacres, Highhampton, Tel: 01409 231376 for bookings. 4 coarse lakes at **Halwill**, 'Anglers Eldorado'. Specimen fish: carp, golden tench, golden orfe, golden rudd, koi, grass carp, all on £4 dt. Mr Zyg Gregorek, The Gables, Winsford, Halwill Junction EX21 5XT (Tel: 01409 221559) offers fishing and fishing holidays as follows: Anglers Paradise: luxury accom and 12 lakes, with coarse fish incl carp to 30lb, unusual species such as golden orfe, golden rudd, golden tench, for residents only; Anglers Eldorado, 4 coarse lakes on dt; Anglers Shangri-La, 3 lakes of up to 240 pegs for match fishing; Anglers Utopia, three villas, purpose built for disabled, with lake fishing. Tackle shop on site. Hotel: New Inn, Meeth (½m on Torridge; dts for salmon and trout).

Tributaries of the Torridge

LEW: Sea trout, trout.

OKEMENT:
Okehampton (Devon). Fishing presently suspended on this stretch of Okement, to allow stocks to grow. **Highampton Trout Fishery** is accessible from Oakhampton.

WALDON: Principal tributary of Upper Torridge.

Mill Leat Fishery, Thornbury, Holsworthy EX22 7AY (Tel: 01409 261426), offers dt £5 on ½m stretch of with brown trout, and 3 acre stillwater, with rainbows. Self-catering accom at same address.

TRENT
(For close seasons, licences, etc, see Midlands Region Environment Agency, p14)

Largest river system in England. Rising in Staffordshire, Trent drains much of Derbyshire, Nottinghamshire and Lincolnshire, and empties into Humber. A hundred years ago, one of England's principal fisheries; now recovering its status following massive effort at water quality improvement. The tidal water, in particular, now fishing excellently. Some famous trout-holding tributaries, notably Dove, Wye and Derwent.

Gainsborough (Lincs). Pike, perch, roach, carp, barbel, chub. There are a few fish to 3m below Gainsborough. Tidal. Scunthorpe AA has

¾m, Coates to N. Leverton. Dt on bank. Lincoln AA has water south of Gainsborough, and at North Clifton and Laughterton. Membership £20, dt £2.50. Good local carp fishery: Daiwa Gull Pool, nr Scunthorpe; 2 lakes of 10 and 34 acres, with carp to 32lb, catfish 17lb. Syndicate only. Contact N J Fickling, 27 Lodge Lane, Upton, Gainsborough DN21 5NW. Tackle shop: The Tackle shop, Kings Court, Bridge Rd DN21 1JS.

Marton (Lincs). Tidal water. Free fishing at Littleborough. Excellent catches of roach. Doncaster and Dist AA has sole fishing rights on the land owned by Mr H R Tindale, and 4m on the Osburton Estate at Littleborough, members only, on both stretches. Lincoln & Dist AA has stretch here. Tickets from bailiff, Mr P Robinson, 37 Lincoln Rd, Fenton LN1 2EP.

Torksey (Lincs). Chub, roach. South of Laneham Waterski Zone, Lincoln & Dist AA fish right bank. White Swan AC has 15 pegs of natural bank and 15 pegs off platforms, between Lincoln and Gainsborough. Dt £2 on bank. B & B at White Swan Hotel, 400 yds from bank. Scunthorpe & Dist AA (Tel: 01652 655849) has 1,125m at North Leverton. Dt on bank. Worksop District AA (Tel: 01909 486350) fishes 15 pegs of Torksey Arm, with chub, roach, bream, skimmer; dt £3 on bank.

Dunham (Notts). Sheffield and Dist AA have a lake and left bank of Trent u/s and d/s. Rotherham and Dist AA offers dt for its fishing on right bank, u/s and d/s of Dunham.

High Marnham (Notts). Mansfield & Dist AA has 50 pegs here. Dt on bank. Worksop and Dist AA has water above the Mansfield stretch at **Normanton-on-Trent** (85 pegs). Assn also controls High Marnham Boat Club (12 pegs). Dt on bank, £3. Sheffield & Dist AA also has 40 pegs on left bank at Normanton, dt £2.50, before commencement of fishing.

Sutton-on-Trent (Notts). Tidal water. Pike, roach, dace, chub. Sheffield AA has Sutton left bank. Dt and st from The Memory Lane Inn, Sutton-on-Trent NG23 6PF (Tel: 01636 821071). Sheffield Amalgamated AS has sole right of Newcastle Fishery, about 6m. Heavily match-fished. Lincoln & Dist AA has fishing at **North Clifton** and **Laughterton**. Tickets £2.50 from tackle shops in Lincoln and Gainsborough. Sheffield ASA has **South Clifton** fishing, dt on bank

Carlton-on-Trent (Notts). Retford AA has 650 yds with barbel, bream, chub, roach, perch and gudgeon. Dt £2 on bank. Sheffield & Dist AA has right bank at **Girton**. Dt from Bridge Garage, Dunham.

Collingham (Notts). Club water. Trent 2m W; pike, carp, barbel, roach, dace, chub, perch, bream. Collingham AA has 4m from Cromwell Weir to Besthorpe parish boundary; dt £2.50 from bailiff on bank. All round coarse fishing. Worksop and Dist AA waters are from immediately above the weir to just below Winthorpe Lake (185 pegs) Dt on bank, £3. At Besthorpe Wharf is Newcastle Fishery; dt 50p. Sheffield AAA. Hotels: Royal Oak, King's Head, Grey Horse.

Muskham (Notts). Nottingham Piscatorial Society preserves from Fir Tree Corner (Kelham boundary) to Crankley Point, both sides, including gravel pits; members only.

Averham, **Kelham** (Notts). Very good coarse fishing; preserved by Nottingham Piscatorial Society for members only – roach, dace, chub (excellent fly water) – from weirs as Staythorpe to South Muskham boundary on both sides of the river.

Newark-on-Trent (Notts). Roach, dace, pike, chub, bream, barbel, gudgeon, perch, eels. Newark and Dist Piscatorial Federation (Tel: 01636 702962) has Trent at Rolleston, East Stoke, Winthrope, Kelham Hall; tidal Trent at Girton and Cottam, and **Newark Dyke** at three sections. Dt £3 on some waters. Sheffield Amal AS, 6m at **Besthorpe**, **Girton** and **South Clifton**, dt on bank or from HQ Lord Nelson, Arundel St, Sheffield. Mansfield & Dist AA have Besthorpe and High Marnham fishing, dt for latter on bank. Sheffield & Dist AA has left bank at **Cromwell**, right bank and lake at **Winthrope**. Dt from Level Crossing Cottage, Winthrope. Nottingham AA fishes from Farndon Ferry to Newark Dyke. Dt from bailiff on bank. Other dt stretches: Worksop and Dist AA controls from Cromwell Lock and Winthrope Lake to Winthrope Crossing, 225 pegs; Ness Farm, 40 pegs; Footits Marsh 25 pegs; dt on bank £2.50, conc. Holme Marsh fishing: 185 pegs n bank, dt on bank, and 40 pegs at Winthrope Crossing, contact Secretary D Brown (Tel: 01909 486350). Newark and Dist PF controls water from Crankly Point to Winthrope Crossing. Dt £3 on bank.

Hazelford Ferry, Bleasby, Mrs Mitchell, Tel: 01636 813014; Trent Lane, **Collingham**, Collingham AA. Tickets on bank. Tackle shop: Angling Centre, 29 Albert Rd, Newark.

Farndon (Notts). Nottingham Piscatorial Society has north bank (tickets as Rolleston), south bank let to Nottingham AA; dt issued.

Rolleston (Notts). Newark & Dist PF have fishing here, dt £3. Greet, trout; preserved. Nottingham AA has water at **Farndon Ferry** (opp Rolleston); dt from bailiff; matches can be arranged in advance. Sheffield & Dist AA has left bank at **Normanton**, dt.

Fiskerton (Notts). Good roach and chub fishing. Nottingham Piscatorial Society water from Greet mouth (Fiskerton) to Farndon, (excluding members field and car park); good roach, barbel and chub; dt £3 from Hon Sec (Tel: 01623 759589), Nottingham tackle shops and Pa Li Chuang, Fiskerton Rd, Rolleston, Newark (Tel: 01636 812141). No permits on bank. Barnsley Anglers have one mile of left bank. Dt £2.50 from bailiffs. Concessionary st. The Greet enters Trent at Fiskerton; trout; preserved.

Hazleford (Notts). Nottingham and Dist FAS has dt water on both banks. Nottingham AA has water south, on left bank towards Hoveringham, dt.

Hoveringham (Notts). Dt £2 for Nottingham AA stretch from Star and Garter 1¾m u/s. Midland AS has stretch to Caythorpe, barbel, roach, chub, bream, gudgeon, etc. 134 pegs, dt £2.40, conc, on bank, also 144 pegs d/s on **Dover Beck**. Dt £2 for Nottingham AA stretch from Hazelford Ferry hotel.

Gunthorpe (Notts). Good coarse fishing; roach, dace, chub. Nottingham and Dist FAS has water, dt. Good pub near water, The Anchor.

Burton Joyce (Notts). Chub, roach (mainly), dace. Nottingham and Dist FAS has good stretch for which dt issued (matches arranged, booked in advance after Nov 1 for following season); tickets from bailiff; Stoke Ferry Boat Inn.

Shelford (Notts). Stoke Weir to Cherry Orchard and Gunthorpe Bridge to Boatyard, Nottingham AA water. Dt on bank.

Radcliffe-on-Trent (Notts). Roach, chub, dace and gudgeon, with perch, pike and tench in Lily Ponds. North Bank from Stoke Weir down to **Gunthorpe**, Nottingham AA; dt. From Stoke Weir up to Radcliffe Ferry, including Lily Ponds, Nottingham FAS; dt. Fedn also holds from Radcliffe Ferry upstream (members only) and water below Radcliffe railway bridge (see Burton Joyce).

Colwick (Notts). Nottingham AA has from Viaduct downstream for one field. Colwick Country Park, Mile End Rd, Colwick NG4 2DW (Tel: 0115 987 0785), operated by Nottingham City Council, includes a 65 acre trout fishery, and coarse waters on River Trent (with 40 bookable match pegs), and lake. Permits and information from Fishing Lodge, at above address. Council also runs Newstead Abbey Park fishing. Local club: Colwick Flyfishers, D Swinscoe, 1 Nairn Mews, Carlton, Nottingham NG4 1BE.

Nottingham (Notts). Good mixed fishing. Several miles in city free. Nottingham AA (Tel: 0115 9708080) has **Clifton**, south bank; for 1,500m Clifton north bank, Royal Ordnance AS (Tel: 0115 9279241). Holme Pit Frontage; **Colwick**, viaduct d/s 600 yds; **East Bridgford**, 180 yds below weir, d/s for 1,350 yds. Dt £3 from bailiff. Nottingham Piscatorial Society has fishing at **Rolleston** and **Fiskerton**; dt from tackle shops only. Long Eaton Victoria AS has 30 pegs below Colwick sluices, left bank; dt £1.50. Raleigh AC have dt at Clifton Bridge, other clubs with Trent fishing near town are Nottingham Waltonians (right bank north of Clifton), Nottingham AA (several stretches on both banks, south of town). Nottingham and District Federation of Angling Societies comprises upwards of 68 clubs, with water at **Burton Joyce**, **Thrumpton**, **Gunthorpe**, **Carlton**, **Hazelford**, **Clifton Grove**, and **Holme Pierrepont**. Coventry AA also has R Trent fishing at Thrumpton, dt on bank, £3.50. Midland AS (Tel: 0115 9634487) has 144 pegs at **Hoveringham** and **Caythorpe**; dt on bank. Earl Manvers AC (Tel: 0115 9879994) has dt on bank for 27 pegs at **Long Higgin**, and **West Bridgford** fishing. Parkside AC (Tel: 01159 787350) has Long Higgin fishing; 67 pegs s bank, dt on bank; Pinders Ponds, West Bridgford; Grantham Canal, and Castle Marina, both near Nottingham. Dt £2 on bank on all waters except Marina, members only. Lake in **Wollaton Park** may be fished by dt from Parks Superintendent, Wollaton Park. **Sutton**

Lake (not to be confused with Sutton Lake, Shropshire): 17 acre trout fly water, fished by Derbyshire County AC. Guest tickets obtainable. Long Eaton Victoria AS has left bank below sluice at Colwick; dt £1.50 on bank. National Watersports Centre, Holme Pierrepont, Tel: 0115 9821212, offer angling on 62 acre coarse lake with roach, perch, dt on bank. Tackle shops: Meadows and Netherfield, Bunbury St, Junction Tackle, 210 Tamworth Rd; Gerry's, 96/100 Radford Boulevard, Radford, and many others.

Wilford (Notts). Rivermead to Wilford Church, Nottingham AA; dt on bank. Club also has Ironmongers Pond, dt on bank. Clifton Grove is Nottingham and Dist FAS water.

Beeston (Notts). Chub, roach, dace, bleak, gudgeon; preserved by Nottingham AA. Dt for stretch from N Bank Lock from bailiff. Assn also has water on **Beeston Canal**. Tackle shop: Beeston Angling Centre, 33 Humber Rd; Supertackle, 192 Station Rd. Hotels: Brackley House; Hylands.

Thrumpton and Long Eaton (Notts). Roach, bream, dace, chub, perch, barbel. Long Eaton Victoria AS has 2 meadows d/s of Cranfleet Lock. Full membership £13, conc. Coventry & Dist AA also has water here with large barbel and carp, dt £3.50 for Ferry Farm on bank, and for sections above weir. Soldiers and Sailors have Trent Lock, dt £1.50 on bank. Contact Mr W Walker (Tel: 0115 9721478). **Erewash Canal**. Roach, gudgeon, bream, carp, perch, chub. Dt at Sandiacre, £1 on bank, or from West End AC. Long Eaton Victoria AS has **Soar**, at Kegworth, Radcliffe, dt £1.50; canal fishing, on Cranfleet Canal (Trent Lock), Erewash Canal (Long Eaton Loch to Trent Lock), also ponds in Long Eaton, members only. Long Eaton and Dist AF has water on Trent at Long Eaton, and **Erewash Canal** fishing. Tackle shops: Wainwrights, Bridge Tackle, 30 Derby Rd; Junction Tackle, 210 Tamworth Rd, Sawley. Hotels: Elms, Europa, Sleep Inn.

Sawley (Notts). Above moorings, Olympic AC offer day tickets, purchased in advance. Pride of Derby AA has fishing on both banks above and below M1 motorway bridge, from Marina down to R Derwent, and 7m between Swarkeston and Willington on Melbourne bank; also 5 lakes and ponds of 22 acres total. St from Secretary.

Barrow-upon-Trent (Derbys). Derby AA controls 1,500m both banks, Swarkestone Inglesby, Twyford and Chelaston. Dt from Bridge Guest House, Swarkestone, and local tackle shops. Manor House Fishery: 20 pegs designed for disabled anglers, open Monday to Saturday; excellent chub, roach, barbel and perch; dt £2; D White, Practical Angling for the Disabled, 40 Rupert Rd, Chaddesden, Derby DE21 4ND (Tel: 01332 675849, evenings).

Burton-upon-Trent (Staffs). Free fishing for Burton residents, at R Dove confluence on right bank (left bank Swadlincote and Warrington Assns), and on right bank above and below Burton Bridge up to Stapenhill. Burton-upon-Trent Mutual AA have fishing which includes **Dove** at **Tutbury** to confluence with Trent, Trent at **Walton** and **Kings Bromley**, **Cuttlebrook**, Branstone Water Park; and other waters; members only. Warrington AA has **Claymills** river fishery. Wychnor Manor Stables (Tel: 01283 791056) have dt for 100m north bank, with barbel and chub. **Hartshorne Dams**, 2 coarse lakes, are 2 min off A50 at Woodville. Dt from Rooney Inn or Manor Farm, both Hartshorne. Wetmore Hall has 450m, dt from the Lodge (Tel: 01283 536041). Pride of Derby AA has 12m of Trent and Mersey Canal in vicinity. Willsley Lake, Moira, has £5 dt for carp to 30lb, good stocks of bream, etc. Contact P Chamberlain 389 Anglesey Rd, Burton-upon-Trent. Ripley & Dist AC has 1m left bank of Dove at **Scropton**; mixed fishery, members only. Tickets for canals, various stretches on the R Trent and 8 local trout and coarse venues from Alsopps Tackle, Waterloo St. Other tackle shop: Burton Angling Supplies, 30 Borough Rd. Hotels: Queen's, Station and Midland.

Alrewas (Staffs). Chub, dace, roach. Prince Albert AS has fishing on both banks, north of Alrewas, below Alrewas AC water on right bank. Birmingham AA has water here, **Wychnor, Kings Bromley** and at **Yoxall**. **Trent and Mersey Canal**, dt from keeper. All three clubs, members only. Catton Park fishing: 1,500m, and 10 acre pool with carp and roach; dt on bank. Tel: 01283 716876. Midland Game and Coarse Fisheries, P Jackson, Fisherwick Wood Lane, Lichfield, Staffs (Tel: 01543 433606); 7 lakes between Lichfield and Alrewas, all year-round fishing.

Rugeley (Staffs). Usual species. Rugeley and Brereton AS has about 1m on Trent and water on **Trent and Mersey Canal** from Armitage to Wolseley Bridge. From here to Colwich held by British Waterways (dt from them); roach, pike, perch. **Blithfield Reservoir**, 4m NE; trout; Blithfield Anglers Ltd allows fishing on season permit only. Inquiries to Fishery Office, Blithfield Reservoir, Abbots Bromley, Staffs.

Stone (Staffs). Stone & Dist AS (Tel: 01785 819035) fishes 750m Trent left bank here. Cookston AC fishes right bank at Weston, and Hanley AS has a stretch of double bank between Sandon and Burston. Heronbrook Fisheries, Slindon, nr Eccleshall (Tel: 01785 513666), 3 lakes, one specimen, stocked with carp, tench, bream; one match pool with mixed coarse species; third lake and canal with carp, tench, golden tench, chub, roach, bream. Dt on bank, match bookings, professional instruction from Neil Dale. Crown AC has pools at Eccleshall and Market Drayton, as well as Shropshire Union Canal. Dt £1.50 from tackle shop: Cooper Sports, Queen St, Market Drayton.

Stoke-on-Trent (Staffs). Stoke City & Dist AA has Longwaste fishing on **R Tern, R Roden** at Poynton Bridge, **R Meece** at Norton Bridge, **Trent & Mersey Canal**, from Aston Lock to Burston and in city between Wieldon and Etruria Road Bridges; **Shropshire Union Canal** (200-peg match venue, enq invited) and **Knighton Reservoir**, **Cheswardine**. Also pools at Stoke, Market Drayton and Eccleshall. Coarse fish, members only on all waters. Subscription £20, conc. £9, for ladies, jun, OAP, from mem sec D Deaville, 1 Churston Place, Sneyd Green. Tel: 267081. Club also has 6 and 4 acre trout lakes, 36 rod syndicate, extra cost. Apply to Hon Sec. Fenton & Dist AS has fishing on **R Dove** (barbel, chub and grayling); **R Churnet**, trout and coarse; **R Blithe**, Stoke Overflow, with large carp; Trent & Mersey Canal fishing; Sutton Brook, Hilton, and pools at Cheadle; st £20, conc, dt £2 for Trent & Mersey Canal stretch only, from Dolphin Discount, *below*, and other tackle shops. At **Newcastle-under-Lyme**, Cudmore Fishery, 6 pools with carp, barbel, bream, tench, chub, incl specimen pool; tickets from the Lodge (Tel: 01782 680919). Tackle shops: Abbey Pet Stores, 1493 Leek Road, Abbey Hulton; Dolphin Discount Tackle Shop and Warehouse, Old Whieldon Road, Stoke ST4 4HW (Tel: 01782 849390); Mellors Tackle, 30/32 Brunswick St, Hanley ST1 1DR; Horsley's 63/7 Church St, Audley; and many others.

Trentham (Staffs). Village about 3m from Stoke-on-Trent on main road London to Manchester. Lake of 80 acres at Trentham Gardens Coarse Fishery, Stone Rd, Trentham ST4 8AX (Tel: 01782 657341). Bream, carp, roach, rudd, pike and perch; dt from Caravan Reception (Tel: 01782 657519), some ideal pegs for disabled.

Weston-on-Trent (Staffs). Coarse fishing in **Trent and Mersey Canal**; chub, roach, bream, perch.

Tributaries of the Trent

IDLE: Excellent coarse fishing in parts, with bream, roach, chub, predominating.

Misterton (Notts). Scunthorpe & Dist AA (Tel: 01652 655849) has 2,200m from Haxey Gate to Trent confluence. Dt on bank. Gate Inn AC (Tel: 01427 891106) has 1,500m at Haxey Gate, dt £2 from HQ, Gate Inn, Haxey Rd, Misterton DN10 4BA (Tel: 01427 890746). No fishing on right bank from Misterton to West Stockwith, or on right bank from Langholme parish boundary to West Stockwith.

Misson (Notts). Doncaster and Dist AA has from Newington to Idlestop, about 10m on the Misson side. Good roach, bream, perch, pike; st and dt from tackle dealers. Assn also has Warping Drain and R Idle and ponds at Idle Stop, with carp, pike, tench, roach, eels. Dt on bank.

Bawtry (Notts). Chub, roach main species. Environment Agency has 500 yds of left bank free to licence-holders, Tel: 0115 9455722. Doncaster & Dist AA has 100 pegs at Newington, both banks; Idlestop, 170 pegs, both banks; Cornley Lane, 2,200m both banks; dt on bank.

Retford (Notts). Poulter, 4m S. Meden, 4m S. Maun, 4m S. Idle above Retford private. Derbyshire County AC has 6½m, Lound to East Retford, with chub, roach, dace, bream, pike. Membership £185, annual sub £145. Club also controls coarse fishing on R Trent at Willington, 1½m, 5m on Derwent, and trout fishing on Dove, Manifold, and Ogston Reservoir. Worksop and Dist AA controls a stretch of the **Chesterfield Canal** from Drakeholes Basin to West Retford bridge, 10½m, famous for chub and roach, match weights up to 50lb. Limited membership. dt £2.50 on bank, conc. Retford &

Dist AA fishes 5½m Chesterfield Canal at Retford, **R Trent** at Fledborough (1,200yds), and **Carlton**, also 2m **R Till, Saxilby**, various coarse species. Woodside Lake, Lound, further Retford AA coarse fishery, with bream, tench, roach. Dt on bank, £2.50, membership £8.50, conc. For £14.50 permit to fish **River Idle**, also dt on **Halsthorpe Dam**, Clowne; Welbeck Lakes, and other fisheries, apply to Mr B's Expert Angling, 2 Mansfield Rd, Creswell, Worksop, (Tel: 01909 721322). **Daneshill Lakes**, 30 acres with carp and pike, tickets on bank or from local newsagents. Information from Daneshill Lakes (Tel: 01909 770917). Hallcroft Coarse Fisheries, Hallcroft Rd, Retford DN 22 7RA, (Tel: 017777 10448): 4 lakes total 16 acres with bream, roach, carp, tench, perch, chub, and river fishing. Tickets at cafeteria. Tackle shops: Retford Angling Centre, Hallcroft, Retford; Worldwide Angling, Hallcroft, Retford.

TORNE and **NEW IDLE**: Doncaster and Dist AA has 10m from Candy Farm to Pilfrey Bridge and water on **Stainforth and Keadby Canal**; dt from Doncaster and Bawtry tackle shops.

Althorpe (S Humberside). **Stainforth & Keadby Canal**; coarse fish; about 14m of water above and down to Trent; good fishing; rights held by Sheffield, Rotherham, Doncaster, Scunthorpe and British Rail associations. Other fishing stations for canal are **Thorne** and **Crowle. Lindholme Lakes, Sandtoft**, Doncaster, S Yorks, mixed fishery on 3 lakes, 1 trout, 1 carp and a general coarse lake. Dt water, Tel: 01427 872015/872905.

Crowle (S Humberside). Excellent centre for coarse fishing. **Stainforth and Keadby Canal**, and **Torne** are ½m from Crowle Central Station; Doncaster AA; roach, tench, bream, perch, carp, pike. Three Drains on A18; Sheffield and Dist AA; roach, perch, tench, carp. Licences, association books and dt from hotels or Hon Sec (enclose s/a envelope). Tackle shop: Thorne Pet & Angling, 5 The Green; also many in Doncaster and Scunthorpe. Hotels: South Yorkshire, Crowle; Friendship Inn, Keadby. Tackle shops in Doncaster (17m) or Scunthorpe (10m).

RYTON (tributary of Idle): Coarse fish.

Scrooby (Notts). Ryton. From Bramshall's Farm to junction with Idle, 2m; dt from Pilgrim Fathers and the garage, Scrooby.

Worksop (Notts). On Ryton and **Chesterfield Canal**; coarse fish. Worksop and Dist AA has 10½m of canal from W Retford Bridge to Drakeholes Basin. Assn also fishes Trent at various locations; Coronation Channel, Spalding; **Clumber Park Lake** (National Trust), where dt and st can be had; Woodsetts Quarry Pond, 8 acres; Steetley Pond, Oakshires; and **Sandhill Lake**; coarse fish. Dt £2.50–£3 on all water except Clumber Park. Grafton AA fishes 4m of Chesterfield Canal in and around town; predominantly large bream, chub, rudd, ruffe, carp, skimmer bream, gudgeon, plenty of roach. St £8, conc, (limited). Dt from bailiff. For **Langold Lakes**, 14 acres with bream and carp, north of Worksop, contact Site Office (Tel: 01909 730189) or Bassetlaw Leisure Centre, Eastgate, Worksop (Tel: 01909 480164). Tackle shops: Angling Supplies, 49 Retford Rd (Tel: 01909 482974); Ken Ward Sports, Carlton Rd (Tel: 01909 472904); Gateford Angling Supplies, Gateford Rd.

MAUN (tributary of Idle): Polluted, but fish returning in some parts.

Mansfield (Notts). Field Mill Dam; coarse fish, dt. Vicar Water, Clipstone; coarse fish, dt. Kings Mill Reservoir, Sutton Rd: Nottingham AA water, with carp, roach, bream, dt £2 on bank. Mansfield & Dist AA has water at High Marnham on **Trent**, and Bleasby Gravel Pits; st £18, conc; dt £2 from Hon Sec and tackle shops. Permits for local coarse ponds also from Forest Town Angling, 113 Clipstone Road NG19 0BT; Mansfield Angling, 20 Byron Street NG18 5PR.

Sutton-in-Ashfield (Notts). Lakes: Lawn, Dam. King's Mill Reservoir, 1m NE; tickets on bank. Hardwick Lakes, Hardwick Hall, are 6m W. Tackle shop: H Burrows, 91 Outram Street NG17 4AQ, Tel: 01623 557816. Hotels: Nag's Head, Denman's Head.

DEVON: Coarse fish.

Bottesford (Notts). Smite, 3m NW at Orston. Car Dyke, 5m NW. Bottesford AA preserves 5m of **Grantham Canal** at Bottesford, Muston Bridge and Woolsthorpe-by-Belvoir; st and dt from Bull Inn and Rutland Arms, Woolsthorpe-by-Belvoir (on canal bank); and from Hon Sec and from bailiffs on bank. Good coarse fishing, with pike over 20lb. Other Assn waters are **River Witham** at **Westborough**, members only; **River**

Devon at Cotham Grange, right bank d/s of Wensor Bridge to Pack Bridge, 1½m, members only. Tackle shop: Abbon and Watts Ltd, 96 Westgate, Grantham, and 39 Sherrard St, Melton Mowbray.

Belvoir Castle (Leics). Between Melton Mowbray and Grantham, Belvoir Lakes and Knipton Reservoir (coarse fish); open 1 Jun–31 Mar; st £50, ½ st £30, dt £4.50 (£6 on bank), conc £3.50, from Estate Office, Belvoir Castle, Grantham NG32 1PD (Tel: 01476 870262, Fax: 870443), also from Knipton Shop, or Keepers Cottage, Knipton Reservoir. **Nottingham and Grantham Canal**: Bottesford and District AA has water. Other stations on canal are **Long Clawson**, **Harby**, **Hose** and **Stathern**.

GREET: Trout; coarse fish; preserved.

Southwell (Notts). River private. Trent, 3m SE at Fiskerton. At Oxton, 5m SW, Nottingham Fly Fishers' Club has a trout lake at Gibsmere; strictly members only, long waiting list. Greet FC, too, has trout fishing. Cromwell Fly Fishers, 20 Norwood Gardens, Southwell, has a lake north of Cromwell.

NUT BROOK: no longer a fishery.

West Hallam (Derby). Lakes: **Mapperley Reservoir**, 2m N, **Shipley Park Lakes**, **Lescoe Dam** and stretch of Erewash Canal all NCB waters. St £12. jun, dis, £3 from D Allsop, 27 Hardy Barn, Shipley, Derbys. Dt £1 from park rangers.

SOAR: Very popular coarse fishery with anglers in the Leicester area. Environment Agency fishery at **Thurmaston**, nearly 1,000 yds right bank free to licence-holders, west of A46 road.

Radcliffe (Derby). Good coarse fishing. Long Eaton & Dist AF administrate between Kegworth and Radcliffe Flood Locks, and 1m Trent, Trent Lock, south bank. Dt £2 from tackle dealers. Soldiers and Sailors AC have water, dt £1.50, also Trent Lock fishing. Contact W Walker, Tel: 0115 9721478.

Kegworth (Derby). Roach, dace, bream, tench, chub, perch. Confluence with R Trent upstream approx 75 pegs, Zingari AC. Dt from bailiff on bank. Two meadow u/s of Kegworth Bridge held by Long Eaton Victoria AS. Dt and

st. Nottingham AA has from notice board below Kegworth Bridge to Kingston Dyke (members only). Long Eaton AF has good 2m stretch down to Radcliffe. Dt from tackle shops. Soar AS has water here. Kegworth AS has approx 400 mtrs.

Normanton-on-Soar (Leics), Good coarse fishing. Loughborough Soar AS water.

Loughborough (Leics). Loughborough Soar AS has fishing near here with large carp, chub, bream, roach, perch, plus dace and barbel on two stretches. Dt in advance from Soar Valley Tackle (*below*); for information contact Secretary Stan Sharpe (Tel: 01509 551061). Proctor's Pleasure Park, Barrow-on-Soar LE12 8QF (Tel: 0150 9412434): lake and river fishing, mainly carp, bream, tench, perch. Dt £3 from machine on site. Lake open during close season. Charnwood Leisure Centre: 11 acre lake with carp, pike. Tickets from Soar Valley Tackle. Tackle shops: Soar Valley Tackle, 7 Woodbrook Rd LE11 3QB (Tel: 01509 231817); Bennetts, 9 Market Place, Mountsorrel. Hotels: King's Head and Railway Inn.

Quorn (Leics). Roach, bream. Quorn AS has rights on stretches of river and 1m of canal; they now have joint ticket with Leicester & Dist AS, st £6, jun £2.50; inquire Hon Sec. River fishes best in autumn and winter.

Barrow-upon-Soar (Leics). About 3m river and canal fishing; good roach and bream; recently restocked. Fishes best autumn and winter. Loughborough Soar AS has water. (See *Loughborough*), also Quorn AC. Proctor's Park has about 1m fishing (see *Loughborough*).

Leicester (Leics). Coarse fish. 6,000m between Leicester and Barrow on Soar, towpath side held by Leicester and Dist Amal Soc of Anglers (Tel: 0116 2666911); also 4,500 l bank **Wreake** at **Melton Mowbray**, **Nene**, and canals. Membership £7. St and dt from bailiffs or Lakeside Marina (Tel: 0116 2640222). Leicester AC: Soar and canal; dt and st. **Leicester Canal**; some good coarse fish but boat traffic ruins summer sport. Very high quality coarse fishing in 5 lakes totalling 22 acres in **Mallory Park**, 8m from Leicester. St £180, conc, (covering all 5 lakes) from Marks and Marlow, address below. The Pool, Groby, 5m NW; bream, tench, roach, pike; dt from house at pool. Broome AS fishes Watermead Park Lakes, 50 acres, **Birstall**; good tench and bream fishing; also 4 coarse lakes at Asfordby; 2 lakes at Frolesworth with carp to 20lb, and mixed coarse; 2 acre lake at Syston with large carp, and good head of small fish, and stretches of Welland and Soar. Membership, £32 per annum, conc, from Mr G Taylor, 100 New Romnet Cres, Leicester (Tel: 0116 2202162). Tackle shops: Marks & Marlow, 39 Tudor Road LE3 5JF (Tel: 0116 2537714); The Angling Man, 228 Melton Road; J C Townsend, 394 Humberstone Road; Match Catch, Syston; Bob Berry, 8 Dunton St, S Wigston. Hotels: Grand, Royal, Hermitage (Oadby).

Narborough (Leics). Hinckley and Dist AA has water here containing trout and grayling; permits from permits sec. Broome AS has a stretch here and at **Wanlip**, roach, perch, chub, barbel.

WREAKE (tributary of Soar): An attractive coarse fishery on which Leicester and Dist ASA has extensive coarse fishing rights between Thrussington and Melton Mowbray; dt.

Asfordby (Leics). Roach, perch, dace, pike, chub. Mostly Leicester ASA water; dt £1.50 from E Edwards, G Rainbow, bailiffs. Asfordby SOA has water on Wreake and pits at **Frisby** (1m). Members only, no dt.

Melton Mowbray (Leics). Leicester and Dist AS has water at Brokesby, Hoby, Frisby on the Wreake, Pig Sties. Dt from bailiff. Local club: Asfordby and Melton Society of Anglers. Kala Lakes, Hoby Rd, Ashfordby, has carp to double figures, dt £5, conc, on bank. Eye Kettleby Lakes, off Leicester Rd, 3 lakes with large carp, etc, dt £4–£5 on bank, or contact Arbon & Watts (below). Disabled swims at both these fisheries. **Knipton Reservoir**, 8m N, at Branston. Tackle shop: Arbon & Watts, 39 Sherrard St LE13 1XH (Tel: 01664 855030).

DERWENT: Noted trout and grayling water in upper reaches; downstream coarse fish come into their own.

Sawley (Derby). Coarse fish. Pride of Derby AA has rights, also on **Trent** between Swarkestone and Willington; one mile of **R Dove** at **Scropton** and 12m of Trent and Mersey Canal between Shardlow and Burton upon Trent; and several ponds. Members only, st £30, conc, applications to Hon Sec. Long Eaton & Dist AF has 1m south bank of Trent at Sawley, very good fishing, dt £2. Soldiers and

Sailors AC has Derwent fishing nearby at **Draycott**, members only. Contact W Walker, Tel: 0115 9721478. Inn: Harrington Arms, Old Sawley, Long Eaton (permits for local waters).

Borrowash (Derby). Coarse fish. Earl of Harrington AC waters (see Derby). Derbyshire County AC has 5m from Borrowash to Sawley, mainly double bank, with barbel, chub, roach, bream, carp, tench, perch and pike. Membership £185, annual subscription £145. Apply to secretary. Nottingham and Dist FAS has fishing rights at Riverside Farm Estates, on Derwent, mill streams and lake. Strictly members only.

Spondon (Derby). Coarse fish; preserved by Earl of Harrington AC. Chaddesden Brook, 1m NW, and Locko Park, 2m N. Private.

Derby (Derby). Coarse fish, Earl of Harrington AC has Derwent from Borrowash Road Bridge u/s to Darley Park, st £12.50, conc, and from Borrowash u/s to Railway Bridge, dt £2, from Hon Sec and tackle shops. Derby City Council issues dt ½ conc, for Derwent from Darley Abbey to Derby Railway Station. Council also issues tickets for coarse fishing at **Alvaston Lake**, **Markeaton Park Lake**, **Allestree Park Lake** and **Derwent** in **Darley Abbey Park** (dts from keeper). DCC, Derby City Parks, 15 Stores St, Derby DE21 4BD. Locko Park Lake and Chaddesden Brook private, Other clubs: Pride of Derby AA (see Sawley); Derby RIFC (water on Derwent, **Trent**, **Dove**, **Ecclesbourne**; canals). Earl of Harrington AC (Derwent, 1m of **Big Shrine** at Borrowash, canal, dt).

Duffield (Derby). Coarse fish, trout and grayling. Derbyshire Angling Federation has 3m from Milford Bridge to Little Eaton, trout and coarse fish, also R Ecclesbourne from Duffield to Derwent confluence. St £20, conc, from Hendersons Tackle (see Belper).

Belper (Derby). Chub, roach, bream, perch, barbel, pike, occasional grayling, trout; Belper AC: 6m covered by st, £25, conc, incl 2½ acre Wyver Lane Pond, large carp etc. 2m covered by dt £5, conc, from Hendersons Quality Tackle, 37 Bridge Street.

Ambergate (Derby). Few trout, pike, coarse fish. Alderwasley Ponds, 2m NW. **Butterley Reservoir** and **Codnor Park Reservoir**; roach, bream, tench, carp, pike; Ripley and Dist AA waters, st £18, dt £2 from Hon Sec, bailiffs and tackle shops. Hotel: Hurt Arms.

Whatstandwell (Derby). Mostly grayling, brown and rainbow trout, with chub, barbel, some dace and odd perch. Derwent Hotel, Derby Rd, Whatstandwell, Matlock DE4 5HG (Tel: 01773 856616) has ¼m fishing; rather overhung with trees, but plenty of fish and good wading in low water; car park on bank. £2 dt for visitors, free fishing to hotel guests. At **Hartlington**, Charles Cotton Hotel has 1m double bank, dt £15, 4 fish limit, fly only. Tel: 01298 84229.

Cromford (Derby). Trout; fly only; preserved below road bridge (both banks), as far as and including Homesford Meadows, by Cromford Fly Fishers; members only, no tickets. St £100 + £200 entrance fee; 4-year waiting list. Above bridge, Derbyshire County AC water. No tickets. Hotel: Greyhound.

Matlock (Derby). Trout (some rainbows), grayling and coarse fish. Matlock AC issue wt and dt; dt from Midland Hotel (Matlock Bath); water at Matlock and Matlock Bath; trout and coarse; about 1m. Press Manor Fisheries, Birkin Lane, **Wingerworth**, nr Chesterfield, off Matlock-Chesterfield A632 Road, has 3 lakes as follows: 5 acre trout lake with stocked rainbow, brown, brook and tiger trout, qualified instruction on site. Dt £13.50 for 3 rainbows then catch and release, evening £10. Float tubing allowed; facilities and disabled platform; 3 acre mixed coarse lake, roach, bream, etc, dt £4, eve £2.50, on bank, specimen carp lake, large mirror and common, dt £6. Permits from cabin or tackle shops. Contact Mr Maher, Bentley Cottage, Matlock Green, Matlock DE4 3BX (Tel: 01629 760996, or mobile 0976 306073). Tackle shop: Lathkill Tackle, Unity Complex, Dale Rd North, Matlock DE4 2HX.

Rowsley (Derby). Haddon Estate owns **River Wye** from Rowsley to just north of Bakewell, together with Rivers Lathkill and **Bradford** for most of their length. Wye has pure wild rainbows and fine head of natural browns. Dt £25, fly only. Grayling fishing is open in the winter. For information contact Head River Keeper I Ross, Tel: 01629 636255. Two-day tickets are obtainable from the Peacock Hotel, Rowsley, to residents and non-residents. Warrington AA has fishing at Darley Abbey.

Baslow (Derby); nr Bakewell, 4m. The Cavendish Hotel, originally the famous Peacock,

has 6 rods on the Chatsworth Fishery, from Old Bridge at Baslow to Smelting Mill Brook at Rowsley (brown and rainbow trout, grayling), and Monsal Dale Fishery on R Wye, from boundary of Chatsworth Estate below Cressbrook Mill to New Bridge at Ashford marble Works (brown and rainbow trout), by courtesy of Chatsworth Estate. 4½m of the **Derwent,** 4½m of the **Wye**. Residents only. For full details, phone 01246 582311. For annual membership of Chatsworth and Monsal Dale Fisheries apply to Estate Office, Edensor, Bakewell DE45 1PJ.

Hathersage (Derby). Trout, grayling; preserved by the Derwent FFC; also at Bamford and Grindleford (members only).

Bamford (Derby). Trout, grayling. Derwent FFC has water below Bamford Mill; and from Bamford Mill to Yorkshire Bridge; members only. Peak Forest AC has **River Noe** upstream from Derwent confluence to Jaggers Clough in Edale; fly fishing for brown and rainbow trout and grayling; also Bradwell Brook and Castleton Brook, Hope, trout and grayling. Members only; subscriptions £350. Tel: 01433 621613.

Ladybower. Centre for **Ladybower** and **Derwent Reservoirs;** trout; fly only (see *Midlands reservoirs and lakes*). Hotels: Ladybower Inn, Yorkshire Bridge Inn, Ye Derwent Hotel, Bamford (1m), Anglers' Rest (1m), Marquis of Granby, Bamford (2m), Rising Sun, Bamford (2m).

AMBER (tributary of Derwent): trout, coarse fish.

Alfreton (Derby). St £18, dt £2 from Ripley AC for reservoirs at **Butterley** and **Codnor Park**: pike, perch, roach, tench, bream, and carp; dt also from keepers. Sheffield Trout Anglers have water on Amber at Wingfield. Tackle shop: Alfreton Angling, 77 Mansfield Rd. Hotels: George, Castle. Also fair fishing in Derwent at Ambergate, 5m SW.

WYE (tributary of Derwent): One of few rivers in which rainbow trout breed. Also holds good brown trout.

Bakewell (Derby). Trout. Fishing preserved by Haddon Hall Estate. Details are to be found under **Rowsley**, above.

Monsal Dale (Derby). The Chatsworth Estate

has excellent trout fishing on ¾m double bank. 4 rods per day only. Apply for day tickets at £23.50, to River Keeper, Rose Cottage, Monsale Dale, Buxton SK17 8SZ (Tel: 01629 640159).

Buxton (Derby). River private. Brown and rainbow trout fishing in **Lightwood** and **Stanley Moor reservoirs**; Buxton FFC: dt £8, conc, from Buckingham Hotel, Buxton, Tel: 01298 70481. Tackle shop: Peak Aquatics, 4 Fairfield Rd, Buxton.

DOVE: Dovedale waters, where Izaak Walton and Chas Cotton fished, are preserved, no tickets. Good sport with trout and grayling elsewhere. In lower reaches, where polluted Churnet enters Dove, angling is improving. Stretches below Uttoxeter, Doveridge, Marchington, Sudbury, etc, also improving: barbel, chub, grayling, pike present. Very limited opportunities for day tickets.

Uttoxeter (Staffs). Trout, grayling. Uttoxer AA preserves good deal of water between Rocester and Uttoxeter; no permits. Leek and Moorlands FC has water here. Membership £37. 3,000m l bank, dt on bank, or from Doveridge Sporting Club, nr Uttoxeter (Tel: 01889 565986).

Rocester (Staffs). Trout, grayling. ¼m single bank, dt £8, contact Mr Appleby (Tel: 01889 590347). Churnet; fishing spoilt by pollution, but improving; private.

Ashbourne (Derby). Several miles of **R Henmore** and **Bentley Brook**, both tributaries stocked with trout and grayling, and two small lakes controlled by Ashbourne Fly Fishers' Club. St only; no dt. In **Dovedale** 3m of good trout and grayling fishing can be had by guests at Izaak Walton Hotel, Dovedale DE6 2AY (Tel: 01335 350555). Yeaveley Estate nr Ashbourne DE6 2DT (Tel: 01335 330247), has fly fishing for rainbow and brown trout on 1½ acre lake, open all year. Dt £17, 3 fish, then catch and release, all browns to be returned. Tuition by appointment, flies for sale. Tackle shop: Fosters of Ashbourne Ltd, (mail order only, Tel: 01335 343135) publish guide to all local day ticket waters. Hotel in Ashbourne; Green Man; hotel at Mayfield, 2m SW (Staffs); Royal Oak.

Hartington (Derby). Trout. Charles Cotton Hotel has about 250 yds of the River Dove; residents only. Proprietor will give data about stretches permitted by farmers.

CHURNET (tributary of Dove): Mixed fishery spoilt by pollution for some years, but improving.

Leek (Staffs). Trout, coarse fish; preserved above Leek town by landowners. Fishing improving as pollution decreases. Leek and Moorlands FC has coarse fishing on Leek Arm of **Cauldon Canal**; Deep Hayes Country Park, Longsdon; Heron Marsh Pool, Rudyard; Crakemarsh Pool, nr Uttoxeter; also **R Dove** and **R Churnett**; tickets for Deep Hayes Country Park from Leek Pets and Fishing Centre (*below*), otherwise members only; membership £37, conc. **Turners Pool**, Swythamley, nr Rushton Spencer; coarse fish, dt £4. Mr Wilshaw, Tel: 01260 227225. Springfield Fishery, Onecote: r and b trout, 4 fish dt £7.50. Tel: 01538 300 223/452. Freshwater Trout Farm, Macclesfield Rd, Tel: 01538 33684. Dt £1.41 plus charge for fish caught. **Rudyard Lake** is 3m NW, 170 acre reservoir; very good bream, with roach, perch, and pike to 30lb; dt £2.50–£1.50, depending on season. Punts on half and full day from water bailiff Lake House, Rudyard, near Leek or from BW. Match lengths pegged. Basford Coarse Fishery, Turners Croft, **Basford** ST13 7ER; carp and other coarse fish, dt £3.50, conc, at poolside. **Tittesworth Reservoir**: 189-acre Severn-Trent W trout fishery. *(See Midlands reservoirs and lakes).* Tackle shops: John Morgan, Albion Mill, Albion St; Leek Pet and Fishing Centre, 36 St Edward St.

MANIFOLD (tributary of Dove): Offers visitors few opportunities.

Longnor (Staffs). Buxton, 7m; trout. Dove, 1m E; trout, grayling. Crewe and Harpur Arms stretch, Derbyshire County AC; members only. Part of Hoo Brook and Manifold is National Trust property; trout restocked.

MEASE. Coarse fish. Fishing stations are: **Measham** (Leics); **Snarestone** (Leics); and **Ashby-de-la-Zouch** (Leics); **Netherseal** (Derby); **Edingale** and **Harlaston** (Staffs); Birmingham AA has water at last three. Hazeldine AA has Clifton Campville fishing, membership £10, conc. Hotels: Queen's Head, Royal.

SEAL BROOK (tributary of Mease): a small watercourse with few fish.

Over Seal (Leics). Lakes: Ashby Wolds Reservoir, 1m N.

TAME: After a long history of pollution, much recovered under the care of the Severn-Trent W. Fish now present in many stretches. Further improvement scheduled.

Tamworth (Staffs). Tributary Anker holds roach, pike and perch. Town waters are all let to clubs, tickets from Tamworth Tackle. 500m double bank in castle grounds may be fished through Dosthill Cosmopolitan AC, 69 High St, Dosthill, Tamworth, Tel: 01827 280024. Chub, barbel, roach, dace, perch. Dt on bank. Birmingham AA has approx 1,300 yds here. Hazeldine AA also has stretch. Dt from Warren Farm, **Amington**. Mease; roach, chub, dace; Haunton, **Harleston**; dt from W T Ward and Harleston Mill. Local clubs: Lamb AC; Fazeley Victory AC; Birch Coppice AC; Tamworth WMC, Polesworth AC; which fishes Coventry and Birmingham Canals; some tickets on offer. Tackle shops: Tamworth Fishing Tackle, 23 Lichfield St; Hambry's Fishing Tackle, The Square, Polesworth.

Kingsbury (Warwicks). Kingsbury Water Park, Bodymoor Heath Lane, Sutton Coldfield B76 0DY (Tel: 01827 872660): nr B'ham. 2m from Junction 9 of M42; 13 fishing lakes, with specimen carp to 32lb, tench to 8lb, large bream, roach, perch and pike. Some pegs suitable for disabled. A variety of season and day permits offered, from a family st at £112, to dt £1.70, conc; contact Information Centre, at above address.

Sutton Coldfield (W Midlands). Lakes at Visitors Centre, Sutton Park, Park Rd, Sutton Coldfield B74 2YT, Tel 0121 3556370: Bracebridge Pool, Blackroot Pool, Powell's Pool. Fishing includes carp to 30lb, bream, roach, pike, and other species. Dt £2.50 (£1.05 jun) on bank. Penns Carp Fishery, Penns Hall, Wylde Green; dt from tackle shop, or on bank. Local club: Sutton Coldfield AS has fishing on rivers and lakes. Grounds Farm Fisheries, 18 Welford Grove, Four Oaks B74 4AS (Tel: 0121 351 1160): 4 pools stocked with variety of coarse fish. Dt £5, dawn till dusk, access for disabled. Tackle shop: Fosters, Kingstanding Rd, B'ham 44, Tel: 0121 344 3333. Hotel: Penns Hall, beside fishery.

ANKER (tributary of Tame): coarse fish; best sport in winter.

Amington (Warwick). Hazeldine AA has 30 pegs here, coarse fish, members only, membership £10, conc.

Polesworth (Warwick). Coventry AA has 2m plus Alvecott Pools; good head of tench and chub in river, large carp and bream in pools. Dt £2.50 on bank. St from Hon Sec. Assn also has 7m on canal; dt from Assn, bailiffs and tackle shops.

SENCE (tributary of Anker): small stream, but good trout and grayling in places, as well as chub, roach and dace.

BOSWORTH BROOK (tributary of Sence): Trout; preserved.

Market Bosworth (Leics). Bosworth Brook, 1m North; trout; preserved by owner of Bosworth Hall. Sence, 3m W. Tweed, 3m SW. Lakes: The Duckery, Bosworth Park, 1m S; pike, etc. Gabriel Pool, 3m NE.

BOURNE BROOK (tributary of Bourne). Fishing station: Plough Inn, **Shustoke**, Warwicks. Trout fishing in Avon Division STW Shustoke Reservoir.

BLYTH (tributary of Tame): Coarse fish. Centres: **Coleshill** (Warwicks). Chub, perch, pike, roach. **Hampton-in-Arden** (Warwicks). Chub, dace, roach. **Solihull** (Warwicks). Earlswood Lakes, 6m SW; ticket for 3 coarse lakes on bank from bailiff. **Olton Mere** coarse fishing; apply to sec, Olton Mere Club.

REA (tributary of Tame): Polluted and fishless.

Birmingham (W Midlands). Birmingham AA, formed from a number of local clubs, controls extensive water on river, canal and lake throughout the Midlands and into Wales. The club-card gives details of all fishing rights, which include numerous fisheries on **Severn and tributaries**, **Trent and tributaries**, **Wye and tributaries**, canals, lakes and ponds. A detailed guide with excellent maps is issued from Assn HQ, see *clubs list*. White Swan Piscatorials own or rent waters on the **Severn**, **Avon**, **Teme**, **Mease**, **Tern**, **Rea**, **Lugg**, **Ithon**, **Herefordshire Arrow** and numerous pools. St £32 + £32 entrance fee; limited. Day permits to members' guests only. Reservoir at **Edgbaston** fishable on permit. **Park Lakes**: coarse fishing on 14 lakes and pools in city. Dt from park keepers. Special st for pensioners. Tackle shops: William Powell, 35 Carrs Lane, City Centre B4 7SX (Tel: 0121 643 0689); Triplex Angling, 213 Monyhullhall Rd, Kings Norton; Barry's, 4 School Rd, Hall Green;

John's, 42 Kitsland Rd, Shard End; and many others. Many hotels.

Lifford (Birmingham). Lifford Reservoir. Good coarse fishing. Dt from park keeper. Tackle shop: Clissets, Pershore Rd, Cotteridge.

FORD BROOK (tributary of Tame). Fishing stations: **Pelsall** and **Walsall** (W Midlands). Brook polluted. Lake: Hatherton Lake; pike. Swan AC leases **Sneyd Pool**, Bloxwich, Essington Wyrley and Shropshire Union Canals, coarse fishing. Dt £2 on bank. Match booking. Walsall and Dist AS has **Hatherton Canal**. **Park Lime Pits**; carp, bream, roach, perch, pike; dt and st for small charge. **Aboretum Lake**; bream, tench, roach, perch, pike; dt. Tackle shop: Bentley Bait Box, 197 Wolverhampton Rd.

SOWE: Coarse fish, some trout.

Stafford (Staffs). Upstream of town; perch, pike, dace, roach, chub. Downstream; perch, roach, bream, chub, occasional trout. Free for about ¼m upstream of town on left bank only; remainder preserved by Izaak Walton (Stafford) AA. This association has fisheries on the Sowe, the **Penk**, **Trent & Mersey Canal**, **Shropshire Union Canal** and **Hopton Pools**, carp, tench and other coarse fish. Apply Hon Sec for annual membership, wt and dt. White Eagle Anglers have North End Pool, on B5066. Carp to 20lb, st £8, conc. Hotels: Swan, Station, Vine, Royal Oak, Garth, Tillington Hall.

Great Bridgford (Staffs). Sowe. Izaak Walton (Stafford) AA has about 1½m (see Stafford).

Eccleshall (Staffs); Trout; preserved. Stoke City & Dist AA fishes Garmelow Pool, 4 rods per day; bookings to E Gardner, Tel: Stoke-on-Trent 818380. Stone & Dist AS fishes Ellenhall Pools. Dt water.

PENK (tributary of Sowe):

Penkridge (Staffs). Coarse fish. **Staffordshire and Worcestershire Canal**. Stafford AA has water (see Stafford). Radford Bridge (Staffs). Izaak Walton (Stafford) AA has water here. **Gailey Upper Reservoir**, Cannock, 34 acres, trout fishery managed by Tern Fisheries, Broomhall Grange, Market Drayton. Stocked rainbows, browns, American brook trout; open all year, pike fishing Nov–Mar. Apply to Gailey Fishing, Gailey Lea Lane, Penkridge, Staffs ST19 5PT, Tel:

01785 715848, or booking, Tel: 01384 836955. Tackle shop: Tight Lines, Market Place, Penkridge.

TYNE

(For close seasons, licences, etc, see North East Region Environment Agency p13)

Formed by junction of North and South Tyne at Hexham, and empties into North Sea at Tynemouth (Northumberland). Since recovery from pollution this river is considered by some to be the best salmon river in England; trout fishing fair. Pike are increasing in lower reaches (below Hexham) and dace in the North and South Tyne.

Newcastle upon Tyne (North'land). **Whittle Dene Reservoirs**, nr Stamfordham, trout fishery. Dt £16 from fishing hut at reservoir, 6 fish limit, self service. Swallow George Hotel, **Chollerford**, NE46 4EW (Tel: 01434 681611) has fishing. Free fishing at Killingworth Pond, N Tyneside. **Killingworth Lake** is dt coarse fishery (Tel: 0191 266 8673). Felling Flyfishing Club has reasonably priced fishing on the following: **North Tyne**, approx 5.5m through Bellingham; 4m of **R Rede**, through West Woodburn, incl Ingram pool, salmon and sea trout; 2.5m of **Coquet**, d/s from Weldon Bridge; 1.5m of **R Till**, on Fenton Estate nr Milfield; 2.5m of **R Wear** between Durham City and Franklin, under-fished stretch, with browns ad grayling; **Tumbleton Lake**, 10 acres, in grounds of Cragside Estate, 2m from **Rothbury**, good fishery stocked with rainbows. Contact either Brian Tindle, Membership Sec (Tel: 0191 4151977); or Stuart Hurst, Club Sec (Tel: 0191 4190281); or Robertson (*below*). Tackle shops: Angling Centre, 123/5 Clayton St West; J Robertson, 101 Percy Street NE1 7RY (Tel: 0191 2322018); Bagnall & Kirkwood, 28 Grey St NE1 6AE (Tel: 0191 2325873). Whitley Bay tackle shop: W Temple, 43 Ocean View (Tel: 0191 252 6017).

Ryton (Tyne and Wear). Occasional salmon; trout, coarse fish. Federation water. Ferryhill AC have 1½m stretch, which can be reached via Heddon on the Wall.

Wylam (North'land). Federation water. Salmon; trout, coarse fish.

Prudhoe (North'land). Trout, coarse fish; occasional salmon; water here and at **Ovingham** and **Wylam** preserved by the Northumbrian Anglers' Federation; also Coquet at Warkworth, Felton and Rothbury. St £55 salmon from Head Bailiff, Thirston Mill, Felton

NE65 9EH (Tel: 01670 787663); £35 trout, from most Newcastle tackle shops and Alto Outdoors, 72A Front St, Prudhoe.

Mickley (North'land). Trout, coarse fish; occasional salmon; Federation water *(See Prudhoe)*. Lakes: Whittle Dene Reservoirs, 5m N.

Bywell (North'land). Salmon, sea trout. Limited day rods for 3m double bank from Reeltime Fishing Services, Stocksfield NE43 7HP, Tel: 01661 843799.

Corbridge (North'land). Trout and dace; trout plentiful but small with runs of sea trout and salmon. Corbridge Riverside Sports Club has 3m on south bank; membership restricted to persons living locally; dt to members' guests only.

Hexham (North'land). Trout (av ¾lb), coarse fish; salmon improving. Tynedale Council, Prospect House, Hexham NE46 3NH (Tel: 01434 652200) owns ½m on south bank off Tyne Green from Hexham bridge upstream. St £28.50, dt £5, conc for residents, OAP, etc, from Hexham House, Gilesgate, Hexham, or Dept of Leisure and Tourism, Prospect House *(above)*. All other salmon water preserved. Langley Dam, 8m west of Hexham: 14 acre lake stocked weekly with r trout. Fly only. Dt £15, 5 fish; £9, 3 fish. NWW Derwent Reservoir, 10m east, 1,000 acres; dt for brown and rainbow trout, £16, conc, 6 fish, eve £6. Dam and north bank fly only, south bank fly and worm. Tel: 01207 255250. Club: Hexham AA has water; no tickets. 4 miles south, Linnelwood Lake, fly only trout lake of 4½ acres. Dt £20, 4 fish. Tel: 01434 609725. Licences from Blair, Post Office, Allendale. Tackle shop: Mr Tackle, Market St, (Tel: 01434 606988).

Tributaries of the Tyne

DERWENT: Stocked brown trout, average about 1lb, with fish to 3lb, some grayling.

Swalwell (Durham). Derwent Haugh to Lintzford is now pollution free, held by Axwell Park and Derwent Valley AA; dt for b and r trout, fly only until June 1, then limited worm. Enquiries to PO Box 12, Blaydon NE1 25TQ.

Shotley Bridge (Durham). Derwent, 1m W; trout and grayling. Derwent AA preserves about 14m of river from Lintzford to **Derwent Reservoir** *(see Durham reservoirs)* and one

bank above reservoir to Baybridge; worming allowed after July 1, except one bank above reservoir to Bay Bridge, fly only. Open membership, £35. Dt £5 from Royal Derwent Hotel, Allensford, Durham DH8 9BB (Tel: 01207 592000). Licences from Post Office, Shotley Bridge. Hotels: Crown; Cross Swords.

NORTH TYNE: trout water, with one or two salmon.

Chollerford (North'land). Trout, coarse fish. The George Hotel, Chollerford NE46 4EW, Tel: 01434 681611, has ¾m bank fishing upstream of bridge for residents and non-residents. Trout average ½lb. Dt £4.80 £2.40, conc, free to guests.

Bellingham (North'land). Trout, salmon sea trout; best July–Oct. Felling Flyfishing Club has approx 5½m from Low Carriteth u/s of Bellingham to Tail of the Eels pool d/s, several excellent named pools. Best salmon to date 23lb, best sea trout 12lb, and brown to 3½lb. Contact either Brian Tindle, Membership Sec (Tel: 0191 4151977); or Stuart Hurst, Club Sec, (Tel: 0191 4190281); or Robertson *(see Newcastle)*. Ferryhill AC have 800 yds d/s from Burn, dt £5 from Town & Country Shop in town centre. Riverdale Hall Hotel, NE48 2JT, Tel: 01434 220254, has 3m salmon and trout fishing for residents, on Tyne (3 beats) and Rede. Licences; Bellingham Hardware, Park Side Place. Hotels: Rose and Crown, Cheviot, Black Bull, Riverdale Hall.

Falstone (North'land). Forest Enterprise offers dt £3, wt £12 for stretch between **Butteryhaugh** and **Deadwater**. The permit also covers Akenshaw, Lewis, Kielder and Ridge End Burns, and is sold at Kielder Castle Forest Centre, Tel: 01434 250209. Falstone FC issues permits for 2m of North Tyne, £10 per day, £20 between 1 Sept–31 Oct, £75 per season, from Blackcock Inn (Tel: 01434 240200), or from A Banks, 5 Hawkhope Rd, Falstone.

Kielder (North'land). Major NW reservoir of 2,700 acres. Stocked with browns and rainbows, also contains a good head of wild brown trout. 'Explorer' season ticket, covering other NW waters £479, conc £399. Six fish permit £11, £9 conc, motor boats for hire, £22 weekend, £15 midweek. Fly, trolling and worm. Tickets on site. Tel: 01434 250312. Hotels: Riverdale Hall, Bellingham; Percy Arms, Otterburn.

REDE: Trout and pike, with few autumn salmon.

Otterburn (North'land). The Tower, NE19 1NS (Tel: 01830 520620) has 3½m on Rede, south of Mill Bridge. Trout dt £10. **Sweethope Lake**, Lough House, Sweethope, **Harle** NE19 2PN, Tel: 01830 540349: trout fishing for natural b, stocked r; dt £19, 6 fish, boat £8 extra. Otterburn Towers Hotel distributes licences. Other hotel, Percy Arms. Self-catering accom from Ray Demesne Office, Kirkwhelpington NE19 2RG, Tel: 01830 540341.

SOUTH TYNE: A spate river, usually fishes well by September. One or two clubs issue tickets for trout and salmon fishing.

Fourstones (North'land). Trout and occasional salmon. Newbrough and Fourstones AA has 2½m of north bank only; no visitors' tickets.

Haydon Bridge (North'land). Trout and occasional late salmon. South Tyne AA preserves 5m of water. Enquiries to Clarke Newsagents, Church St (Tel: 01434 684303). Hadrian Lodge Trout Fishery, North Rd, Above Haydon Bridge, NE47 6NF (Tel: 01434 688688); 1¾ acre upland water, well stocked rainbow and browns 1–6lb; no booking reqd; £10 permit, 2 fish, then catch and release, £6 after 6 pm, one fish. Hotel: Hadrian Lodge, overlooks fishery.

Haltwhistle (North'land): Brown trout, sea trout, salmon. Haltwhistle and Dist AA has visitors wt £50, conc, for 7m around Haltwhistle, sold at Four Seasons Shop, and Greggs Sports, both Main St. Hotels: Manor House, Wallace Arms.

Alston (Cumbria). Salmon, sea trout, trout. Alston & Dist AA has 10m of water from Lambley Viaduct to Alston weir, with wt £25 to £55 and dt £7.50 to £17.50, ½ price conc, from Sandra Harrison, News and Essentials; Alston Post Office; or from Secretary (Tel: 01434 381260); st £85 from Little Gill Cottage, Ashgill CA9 3HB (Tel: 01434 381270).

EAST ALLEN: Allendale AA water. Licences from Allendale Post Office (Tel: 01434 683201).

WANSBECK
(For close seasons, licences, etc, see North East Region Environment Agency p13)

Northumberland trout stream which fishes well under favourable conditions of water, but opportunities for visitors are few.

Morpeth (North'land). Brown trout; preserved by Wansbeck AA for 5m; members only, st £10 + joining £10. Water in town free to licence-holders. **Fontburn Reservoir**, NW fishery of 87 acres, with stocked rainbow and brook trout, dt £13 on site, 6 fish limit, fly and worm permitted. Fishing lodge (Tel: 01669 621368). Licences obtainable from D Bell, 9 Biltons Court, Morpeth. Tackle shop: McDermotts Fishing Tackle, Station Rd, Ashington. Hotels: Waterford Lodge, Queen's Head, Angler's Arms, Weldon Bridge.

Tributary of the Wansbeck

BROOKER BURN:
Longhirst (North'land). Wansbeck, 2m S; trout. Lyne, 2m N.

WAVENEY
(see Norfolk and Suffolk Broads)

WEAR
(For close seasons, licences, etc, see North East Region Environment Agency p13)

Rises on Kilhope Moors in extreme west of Co Durham and enters North Sea at Wearmouth. After history of pollution, river now contains salmon, sea trout, brown trout, dace, chub, roach and barbel, perch and bream. Tributaries Browney and Rookhope are improving. Bedburn preserved.

Chester-le-Street (Durham). Sea trout, brown trout (stocked by club) excellent coarse fish. Chester-le-Street AC has 12m good water with the above species plus salmon, dace, chub, barbel, eels, roach. St £44 + £10 joining, conc, dt £1.25, from O'Briens, North Burns (Market Place). Dunelm City AC fishes Chester Moor and Frankland stretches. Contact G Hedley Tel: 0191 386 4603. Tackle shop: Chester-le-Street Angling, 21 North Burns (Market Place).

Durham (Durham). Trout, sea trout. Free fishing on E. A. licence from ice rink to sewage works, also ice rink to Kepier Farm boundary. Last stretch to Orchard Wall is strictly private. Durham City AC has more than 1½m on river, and stillwater fisheries stocked with coarse fish. St £34, conc. Dt for guests of members only. Enquiries to M J Hall, 21 Northumbria Place, Stanley, Co Durham, Tel: 01207 232401. Grange AC has stretch of river at Kepier Woods, migratory fish, good head of brown trout, grayling, chub, dace, large pike; and Brasside Pond; membership £12, game dt £5 from Belmont Pets, Blue House Buildings, Sunderland, and K9 Fishing Tackle and Guns, Sunderland City Centre (Tel: 01915 100005). Bear Park, Cornsay and New Branspeth Assns all have water on **Browney**, 4m W of Durham; limited dt; restocking. Ferryhill & Dist AC have Wear fishing, also Browney, both banks to Wear junction, and R Gaunless, 1½m from West Auckland, with brown trout. Tackle shop: Turners Fishing Tackle, Sacriston, Durham.

Willington (Durham). Willington & Dist AC has fishing at Sunnybrow to Page Bank. Dt from Bonds Tackle Shop, Tel: 01388 746273.

Bishop Auckland (Durham). Sea trout, brown trout, grayling, salmon. Bishop Auckland & Dist AC controls some 20m of water on Wear, between Witton le Wear and Croxdale. Also Witton Castle Lakes, trout stillwater. Dt at lakes or tackle shop. Dt £5 for grayling fishing, 1 Nov–31 Jan, from Windrow Sports, Fore Bondgate; hotels, post offices and other tackle shops in the area. Further details from Hon Sec. Ferryhill & Dist AC has fishing at **Croxdale**, **Tudhoe**, **Witworth Estates**; **Byers Green** and **Old Durham** fisheries, also **Newfield** and **Page Bank**. Club waters also include Rivers **Browney**, **Tees**, **Swale**, **Skern**, **Gaunless** and various coarse fishing ponds. Some dt waters; membership £25, plus £5 entrance fee, conc. Hotel: Manor House, West Auckland.

Witton le Wear (Durham). Bishop Auckland AC, see above.

Wolsingham (Durham). Trout, sea trout (good). Wolsingham AA has water; members only (limited st £29 + £10 joining, for visitors). Long waiting list. No dt. At Hagbridge, **Eastgate** (about 8m W), Northumbrian Environment Agency has stretch; dt water. North-West Durham AA has trout fishing on **Hisehope**, **Waskerley** and **Smiddy Shaw Reservoirs**. Contact Gordon Byers, Tel: 010207 501237. **Tunstall** a NWW fishery.

Frosterley (Durham). Trout, sea trout. About 1½m water belongs to Frosterley AC; members only, who must reside in area.

Stanhope (Durham). Trout, sea trout and salmon. About 2m water (both banks) belongs to Stanhope AA; members only, limited mem-

bership £20, when available. Sec, J Lee (Tel: 01388 528906). Sea trout June onwards. Northumbrian Water has 2m. Dt (limited) from Bell's Service Station. Salmon and rainbow trout in Quarry Ponds, contact Ian Fisher. Tackle from Ian Fisher Communications, 4 Market Place DL13 2UJ (Tel: 01388 528464). Hotels: King's Arms; Packhorse. For **Eastgate** fishing: Miss Bell, (Tel: 01388 528414).

Upper Weardale (Durham). Trout, sea trout (Sept and Oct). Upper Weardale AA has 6m in total of Wear and tributaries from Westgate to Cowshill; st £30, wt £10 (not obtainable Sept/Oct), dt £5 (Sept/Oct £7), jun 50%, from The Post Office, St John's Chapel (Tel: 01388 537214). Water re-stocked 3 times per annum with fish up to 12in. Hotels: Cowshill, Cowshill; Golden Lion, St John's Chapel.

Tributary of the Wear

BROWNEY; now free of pollution; trout and sea trout.

Langley Park (Durham). Langley Park AA lease river here. Assn. also has R Wear at Durham, trout and coarse, and coarse ponds.

Burn Hill (Durham). Waskerley, Tunstall Hisehope and Smiddy Shaw Reservoirs close together on moors between Stanhope and Consett. (See above and under Durham Reservoirs.)

WEAVER
(For close seasons, licences, etc, see North West Region Environment Agency, p13)

Rises south-west of Cheshire and flows into Mersey estuary. Most species of coarse fish, trout in the upper reaches. British Waterways have a cooperative scheme, the Weaver Waiters, which invites fishing clubs to partake in the management of the River Weaver Navigation between Saltisford and Weston, and represents a long-term strategy of improvement and development of the lower reaches of the river. Contact Regional Manager for further details (See English Canal Fishing).

Northwich (Cheshire). Good coarse fishing held by Northwich AA. Water on **Weaver**, **Dane**, **Trent and Mersey Canal** (about 17m); **Billinge Green Pools**; **Great Budworth Mere**; **Petty Pool Mere** (limited access); **Pickmere Lake**. Comprehensive st (all waters); St £15, wt £5. Exceptional concessions to OAP and regd disabled, from Box 18,

Northwich. No tickets sold on bank. Tackle shop: Scotts of Northwich, 185/7 Witton St, Tel: 01606 46543. Hotels: Moulton Crow Inn, Moulton; Mayfield Guest House, London Rd.

Winsford (Cheshire). Roach, bream, perch, carp. Winsford & Dist AA have stretch from New Bridge upstream to Church Minshull, several pools around Winsford and R Dane at Middlewhich, with barbel and perch. St £20, conc, dt £2.50 on bank for Dane, Mon–Fri and Weaver, Newbridge to Bottom Flash. Stockport & Dist AF has water on Rochdale Canal, Weaver and the lake in Drinkwater Park. Dt on bank. Crewe LMR Sports AS has Sandhole Pool (coarse fish) and good tench water at **Warmingham** (½m). Tackle shops: Weaverside Angling Centre, Wharton Road, Winsford; Daves of Middlewich, Lewin St, Middlewich.

Crewe (Cheshire). Weaver 2½m W. No fishing in Crewe, but Crewe LMR Sports AS has 3m of Weaver near Nantwich (4m away) on Batherton Estate. **Sandhole Pool** (1m), and **Doddington Hall Pool** (5m), rights on **Shropshire Union Canal** and stretches of **Severn**, **Weaver** and **Dane**, as well as good bream, tench and pike fishing on **Hortons Flash**. Guest tickets are not issued for any of these waters. Dt for Macclesfield Canal; coarse fish (see also Congleton). Tackle shops: Tilleys Tackle Shop, 10 Edleston Road.

Nantwich (Cheshire). Trout, grayling, dace, roach, chub, Nantwich AS controls nearly all Weaver near Nantwich; st only; water starts on Reasenheath Estate and stretches SE of town for 7m mainly on both banks, broken at Batherton Mill. Society also has stretch on **Severn** at Trewern. Other clubs with water near Nantwich are Pioneer AA, Amalgamated Anglers and LMR Sports (all Crewe) and Wyche Anglers; Winsford and District AA control **Dane** (Croxton Lane to King Street), **Weaver**, from Newbridge to Church Minshull; flashes; pools; st from Hon Sec. These 4 clubs are members of Cheshire AA. Winsford Club's pools contain fine tench, carp, bream and pike. Weaver is chalk stream here; well stocked with roach, dace and chub. **Shropshire Union Canal** controlled by BW: dt from bank ranger; st from tackle shop. Other waters within 10m of Nantwich are: Big Mere, Osmere, Blakemere (boats), Combermere (boats). Egerton Lake, Egerton Fruit Farm, Cholmondely; carp water of 50 pegs, dt £5, from bailiff. Information from

Secretary, Caldy Anglers. Hotels: Lamb, Crown, Three Pigeons.

Audlem (Cheshire). Adderley Brook. Birchall Brook, 2m NE. Lake: Woolfall Pool, 2m NE. Hotels: Lamb, Crown. (For club water, see Nantwich.)

Wrenbury (Cheshire). Nantwich AS has water in area; no tickets. Marbury Brook. Sale Brook, 2m S. Baddiley Brook, 2m N. Hotel: Combermere Arms, Burleydam, Whitchurch.

Tributaries of the Weaver

DANE: Trout in upper reaches, but difficult to come by. Coarse fishing, with odd trout and grayling lower down.

Northwich (Cheshire). Chub, dace and roach. Northwich AA have fishing, dt offered.

Davenham (Cheshire). Trout, barbel, roach. Davenham AC have fishing, members only, Davenham to Leftwich.

Middlewich (Cheshire). Trout, dace, roach, chub. Winsford and Dist AA have fishing from Croxton Lane to King St, dt water, also right bank d/s to Bulls Wood. Middlewich Joint Anglers have Trent and Mersey Canal and Shropshire Canal stretches, and pool and river fishing, which includes R Dane, left bank u/s from Byley Bridge, approx 2m; right bank u/s approx ½m, both banks between Byley and Ravenscroft Bridge, and from Wheelock confluence on left bank d/s; also **R Wheelock**, right bank u/s from R Dane confluence, and left bank d/s to Bullswood, Bostock, approx 4m. Chub, dace, roach, gudgeon, barbel and other species. St £28, conc. Dt £3 at some waters, on bank or from tackle shop: Dave's, Lewin St, Middlewich. Hotel: Boars Head, Kinderton St (Tel: 01606 833191).

Swettenham (Cheshire). Prince Albert AS has much of R Dane; here, and at Allgreave, Congleton, Byley, and Wincle.

Congleton (Cheshire). Dace, roach, chub, gudgeon and occasional grayling and perch. 5m of prolific water in and around Congleton controlled by Congleton AS, plus excellent carp and coarse fishing in Goodwins Pool and Castle Pits. Disabled pegs at Goodwins. Membership £23, plus £5 joining fee. Guest dt £3, from Terry's, below. From Radnor Bridge towards

Holmes Chapel partly controlled by Prince Albert AS, Cheshire AA, Grove and Whitnall AA and Warrington AA. St for Cheshire AA stretch at **Somerfordbooths** from secretary or Crewe tackle shops. Assn also has water on Severn. Buglawton Trout Club have fly only water from Eaton to Havannah, and at Holmes Chapel, Saltersford. Dt, mainly coarse fish. Moreton Coarse Fisheries, New Rd, Astbury, nr Congleton (Tel: 01260 272839): fishing on 3 lakes, dt from bailiff. Carp to 28lb, large bream and tench. Barbless hooks only, bays for disabled. Westlow Mere Trout Fisheries, Giantswood Lane, Tel: 01260 270012. **Macclesfield Canal**: Warrington AA; roach, perch, tench, bream, pike; recently dredged; st and dt at small charge from bailiff. Winsford AA and Lymm AC also have stretches of Dane. Astbury Meadow Garden Centre, Newcastle Rd, has new coarse fishery on **Astbury Mere**, with large pike, carp, roach, bream, perch; dt on site. Tackle shop: Terry's of Congleton, 47A Lawton St (Tel: 01260 273770), has club memberships for Congleton AS, Mow Cop Anglers, Cheshire Anglers.

Bosley nr **Macclesfield** (Cheshire). Roach, chub, carp, bream, pike; private. Lake: **Bosley Reservoir**; Prince Albert AS water, members only.

Macclesfield (Cheshire). Extensive fishing controlled by Prince Albert AS, a nationally famous club with many rivers, lakes and reservoirs in the NW of England and in Wales. These include many stretches on the R Dane, the **Severn**, the **Ribble**, **Wye**, **Wenning**, **Wharfe**, **Towy**, **Teifi**, **Cothi**, **Banwy**, **Twymyn**, **Trent**, **Dove**, **Winster**, **Vyrnwy**, **Lledr**, **Dulas**, **Dysinni**, **Dee**, **Dovey**, **Mawddach** and **Lune**; **Marbury Mere**, Whitchurch, **Isle Lake**, Shrewsbury, **Langley Bottoms** and **Lamaload Reservoirs**, Macclesfield and others. Long waiting list for membership. Dt issued for a few of their waters. Danebridge Fisheries has small trout lake at Wincle, fish to 16lb, dt £14–£9, 3 or 2 fish limit; instruction on site. Tel: 01260 227293. Marton Heath Trout Pools, Pikelow Farm, School Lane, Marton SK11 9HD (Tel: 01260 224231); 7 acres of stocked trout fishing, rainbow and brown; tuition; barbless hooks reqd, coarse pool on site, well stocked with common, mirror and crucian carp, roach, etc; and tackle. Macclesfield Waltonian AS has **Teggsnose Reservoir**, coarse fish, carp to 20lb; dt £5–£3 from Barlows (*below*). Other clubs: Macclesfield

Fly-fishers' Club (12m on Dane and **Clough**, preserved; no tickets), and Macclesfield and District Amalgamated Society of Anglers. **Macclesfield Canal**; good carp, pike, roach, etc. Prince Albert AS has approx 6m, from Buxton Rd Bridge to Robin Hood Bridge. Dt from Barlows (*below*). Macclesfield Waltonians also fish stretch, at Buglawton, dt from Maccl. Tile Centre, Windmill St. **Redesmere** and **Capesthorne**; roach, bream, tench, perch, pike, mirror and crucian carp; dt from bailiff. East Lodge, Capesthorne (*see Cheshire lakes, meres, etc*). Other waters in area: **South Park Pool**; carp, roach, perch, pike; dt. **Knypersley Reservoir** controlled by Cheshire AA; dt from bailiff. No night fishing. Tackle shop: Barlows Tackle, Bond St, Macclesfield.

WHEELOCK (tributary of Dane):

Sandbach (Cheshire). Clubs with fishing in vicinity are Northwich AA, Winsford & Dist AA, Middlewich Joint Anglers.

WELLAND

(For close seasons, licences, etc, see Anglian Region Environment Agency, p14)

Rises near Market Harborough and flows through Lincolnshire Fens to The Wash. Coarse fishing very good, much of it controlled by clubs. Upstream of Market Deeping river is renowned for large winter catches of chub and roach. Downstream, river is much wider, with regular banks and excellent access, and slow flowing with bream, roach, tench and eels, also a popular match and pike venue. Fen Drains hold roach, bream, tench and pike, North and South Drove Drains improving, especially in winter.

Spalding (Lincs). Welland, from Spalding to The Deepings, provides 12m of good fishing for pike, perch, chub, roach, dace, bream and tench; controlled by Peterborough AA to Crowland. Dt £2 from D T Ball. **Lincolnshire Drains**; good coarse fishing. At South Holland Drain, Foreman's Bridge Caravan Park, Sutton Rd, Sutton St James PE12 0HU (Tel: 01945 440346) has permits for Holbeach & Dist AC water in South Holland and Little Holland Main Drains; £3 dt, £10 wt. 90 disabled pegs. Spalding FC preserves Counter, North, South and Vernatts Drains; pike, perch, roach, carp, rudd, bream, tench; also **River Glen** from Guthram Gowt to Surfleet village bridge and **New River** from Spalding to Crowland. **Coronation Channel** also fishable. Worksop and Dist AA lease 2½m, both banks, at Spalding. Tickets on bank.

Cowbit (Lincs). Pike, perch, dace. Spalding FC water (see Spalding).

Crowland (Lincs). Pike, perch, dace. Nene, 2m SE at Black Horse Mills. New River from Spalding to Crowland preserved by Spalding FC; pike, roach, perch, dace, rudd, bream, tench; tickets from D T Ball, or M Tidwells (see Spalding).

Deeping St James (Lincs). Chub, dace, roach, bream, rudd, pike. Deeping St James AC controls much water in vicinity, including Several Fishery, above town at junction of old river; Greatford Cut, also Welland at Market Deeping and **Tallington**; Folly Bridge Peakirk, National Grid waters, Bainton; **Nene** fishing; the **Bourne Eau**; **R Glen**; **Redlands Lakes**, with good access for disabled. All mixed fisheries, dt obtainable. Tackle shop: P D's Tackle, 721 Lincoln Rd, Peterborough (Tel: 01733 344899).

Market Deeping (Lincs). Several Fishery controlled by Deeping St James AC. It extends 6½m from Market Deeping to Kennulph's Stone, on Deeping high bank. Notice boards erected. Dt £3.50 on most club waters, from bailiffs or tackle shop: P D's Tackle, 721 Lincoln Rd, Peterborough (Tel: 01733 344899). Accom at Broughtons B & B, 44 Halfleet.

Stamford (Lincs). Chub, dace, roach, pike, perch; fishing free to licence-holders on N bank between Town and Broadeng Bridges; approx 1¼m. Elsewhere preserved by Stamford Welland AAA. Approx 18m of water, stretching from Barrowden to confluence of R Gwash and w bank of Gwash to Newstead road bridge, 8 stretches in all. Chub to 5lb, bream to 7lb. St £13, jun £3, OAP free, from Hon Sec or tackle shop. Other local assn, Stamford & Dist AA. **Burghley Park Lake**, 1m SE (bream and tench, some rudd), Monday to Saturdays; dt £5 to fish island side of Burghley Lake from Burghley Estate Office, 61 St Martins, Stamford, PE9 2LQ (Tel: 01780 752075). Tackle shop: Bob's Tackle, 13A Foundry Road.

Ketton (Leics). Oakham AS has water here and on **River Chater**; members only; coarse fish. Broome AS has 1m at **Duddington**, with roach, chub, perch, bream, dace. St £32, half price for juv, OAP, etc, from Mem Sec Mr G Taylor, 100 New Romney Cres, Leicester (Tel: 0116 2202162).

Rockingham (Northants). 400 acre Eyebrook Reservoir is only 2m distant, just south of Caldecott; good trout fishing (see Midlands reservoirs and lakes). At **Corby**, District Council runs coarse fishery on Corby Boating Lake, with specimen carp. Tel: 01536 402551. Hotels: Falcon, High St East, Uppingham, Tel: 01572 823535; Vaults, Uppingham, 5m N; Strakis Carlton Manor, Corby. B & B at Mrs J Wainwright, Homestead House, Ashley Rd, Medbourne LE16 8DL (Tel: 01858 565724).

Market Harborough (Leics). **Saddington Reservoir** is Saddington AA water. Enquiries to Hon Sec. Broughton and Dunton AC has **Grand Union Canal** stretch, and members only lake at Liere. Dt for canal, £2.50, on bank. Market Harborough and District Society of Anglers has about 1½m of **Grand Union Canal**, good for tench, bream, carp early in season; roach Nov–March, also local Folly Pond, with roach, tench, bream, roach, rudd, carp. Membership cards £14, dt £4–£2, conc, from tackle shop or bailiffs on bank. Permits for 2m stretch of Foxton Canal at Tungsten, with good roach fishing, from local tackle shop, or contact M Tate, 22 Welland Ave, Gartree, M H. 1½ acre coarse lake with carp, roach, tench and other coarse fish, in grounds of Welland Lodge Public House, Market Harborough. Dt £5 on bank, conc £3; Nick Bale (Tel: 01858 433067). At Leire, near Lutterworth is **Stemborough Mill Trout Farm,** well stocked with r trout. Open all year. Tel: Leire 209624. Tackle shop: Bait Box, Nelson St. Hotels: Angel, Grove.

Tributaries of the Welland

GLEN: River free from Surfleet village to reservoir, coarse fish; trout above Bourne.

Surfleet (Lincs). Glen free below village. Preserved above by Spalding FC.

Pinchbeck (Lincs). Permits issued by Welland and Nene RD. River Welland, 2m SE at Spalding; also Coronation Channel.

Counter Drain (Lincs). Counter Drain; coarse fish; Spalding FC.

Bourne (Lincs). Glen holds trout upstream.

GWASH: Fair trout and grayling stream. Private fishing. Stamford Welland AA have confluence with Welland to Newstead road bridge, west bank.

CHATER:
Ketton (Leics). Roach and dace. Stamford Welland AA has stretch from junction with Welland to Ketton road bridge, both banks.

EYE BROOK: Good head of roach, dace and chub; trout upstream.

WITHAM

(For close seasons, licences, etc, see Anglian Region Environment Agency, p14)

Rises south of Grantham and flows northward to Lincoln, then south-eastward to Boston, where it enters the Wash. Above Grantham noted mainly for trout and grayling, mainly private. Between Grantham and Lincoln it is a good mixed coarse fishery, with chub, dace and barbel, mainly private clubs. Winter areas include Kirkstead and Tattershall Bridge sections. From Lincoln to Boston it is entirely embanked with excellent roach and bream fishing. The fishing rights for the majority of this length are leased to the Witham and District Joint Anglers' Federation. Members of the following affiliated associations have free fishing: Grimsby ASA; Boston AA; Sheffield AAS; Rotherham UAF; Lincoln AA; Worksop AA; Newark PF. Otherwise, temporary members, day-permits from their bailiffs on the bankside or local tackle shops. Main fishing accesses are **Washingborough**, **Bardney**, **Southrey**, **Stixwold**, **Kirkstead Bridge** to **Tattershall Bridge** (road alongside), **Chapel Hill**, **Langrick Bridge** and **Boston**. **Woodhall Spa** is another good centre for Witham angling, with several hotels catering for anglers, including Kings Arms, Kirkstead Bridge LN10 6XZ, Tel: 01526 352633, who also sell local permits; Railway, 01526 352580.

Boston (Lincs). Angling facilities exceptionally good; at least 100 miles of good coarse fishing (pike, perch, dace, tench, roach and bream) in Witham; Witham and Dist JAF holds 30m between Lincoln and Boston, also tributaries. Boston & Dist AA waters: **South Forty Foot Drain**, **Sibsey Trader**, **Bargate Drain** (Horncastle Rd), **River Glen** at Guthrum and Tongue End, the **Bourne Eau**, and **East and West Fen Catchwaters**. Disabled pegs on Trader Drain. St £10, conc, dt £2. Tackle shops: Hooked, High St; Vanguard Fishing Tackle, 25 Wide Bargate; Boston Angling Centre, Horncastle Rd. Accom at Fairfield Guest House, 101 London Rd; Kings Arms, Horncastle Rd.

Lincoln (Lincs). Good coarse fishing. Witham fishes best from Aug–Oct with bream predominant. Lincoln is HQ for Lincolnshire Anglers Fedn and Lincolnshire Rivers Anglers Consultative Assn. Witham and Dist JAF has Witham from Stamp End Lock to Boston West on right bank, with exception of a few short stretches, Witham left bank, Lincoln 1,500 yds d/s of Stamp End Lock to Bardney, with exception of 1,200 yds in Willingh Fen, Witham at Stixwould to Kirkstead Bridge; **Sincil Drain/South Delph** between Stamp End Lock and point 630 yds u/s of Bardney Lock; **North Delph**, **Branston Delph**, **Sandhill Beck**, **Timberland Delph**, **Billinghay Skerth**, **Kyme Eau**. Dt £1.75 from bailiffs, local inns or Secretary. Lincoln AA has excellent coarse fishing on **Trent**; 5m **Upper River Witham** to R Brant confluence; **Till** at Lincoln, **Saxilby** and **Sturton by Stow**; drains, dykes, **Boulton Park** and **Hartsholme Lakes** (good bream, eels, pike, carp and others species). Membership books £20 from tackle shops, concessions to jun, OAP. 11m **Fossdyke Canal** between Torksey and Lincoln, mainly roach and bream; BW managed: address in Canal section. **North Hykeham**; **Richmond Lakes**, 40 acres, coarse; dt £1.50, on bank. Apex Lake, Hykeham: Witham and Dist JAF water; pike to 30lb, bream to 10lb, roach, carp, etc; members only. Tel: Lincoln 681329. **Butterley Aggregates Lake**; 200 acre coarse; dt 80p on site. Lincoln tackle shops: South End Pet Stores, 447 High Street LN5 8HZ; G Harrison, 55 Croft Street LN2 5AZ; Boundary Pet Stores, 6 Bunkers Hill LN3 4QP; Newport Tackle Shop, 85 Newport, Lincoln LN1 3DW; Feed 'n' Weed, 22 Birchwood Centre LN6 0QQ. Hotels: Barbican, Brickmakers Arms, Branston Hall, Red Lion, many others.

Grantham (Lincs). Grantham AA has good coarse fishing on Witham, **Grantham Canal,** and **Denton Reservoir**; dt £3 for canal only from Arbon and Watts, *below*. Membership £16, conc £6. Assn is a member of the federation of Midlands clubs, which includes Boston, Oakham, Newark, Asfordby and Deeping St James Clubs, and has been established to protect fisheries in area and leases waters on **Bourne Eau** and the **Glen**. Woodford Waters, Willoughby Rd, Ancaster, Grantham NG32 3RT (Tel: 01400 230888) has match lake, with large head of tench, and specimen lake, with carp over 30lb. Holiday camping on site. Tackle shops: Arbon & Watts, 96 Westgate, (Tel: 01476 400014) has many local permits, and sole supplier for Grantham AA.

Long Bennington (Lincs). Chub, roach, perch, grayling, etc. No dt. Trout lakes at Lakeside Farm, Caythorpe (Tel: 0400 72758). Pickworth Hall, Folkingham, has fishery, Tel: 015297 257.

Tributaries of the Witham

SOUTH FORTY FOOT DRAIN:
Good coarse fishing. From Boston to Hubbert's Bridge, and from Swineshead Bridge to Donington, Boston and Dist AA. Matches booked through Match Sec Mr Rob Mottram (Tel: 01205 365386). Centres are **Boston**, **Wyberton**, **Hubberts Bridge**, **Swineshead, Donington**.

RIVER BAIN:
Tattershall (Lincs). Good stretch of river with large chub, occasional barbel, also good bream, perch, and pike to 25lb.

Horncastle (Lincs). Rivers Bain and Waring; trout, roach; preserved. Some good chub water, free fishing. Tupholme Brook 7m NW. Horncastle AA has Bell Yard Pit and about 1½m on Horncastle Canal; st £8, conc, from Hon Sec. **Revesby Reservoir**, 35 acres, coarse fish; contains big pike, roach, tench, bream, perch, eels; apply to Estate Office, Revesby, Bolton, Tel: 01507 568395. Other water on site, the Wong, 4 acres, syndicate water with carp. Tickets for local fishing from tackle shop: F & D Grantham, Synchro Sports, Market Place. Hotels: Bull, Red Lion, Rodney.

FOSSDYKE NAVIGATION:
Fossdyke held by BW. Centres: **Lincoln**, **Saxilby** and **Torksey**. Good coarse fishing, especially noted for bream. Match bookings to BW, Tel: 01522 530762, dt on bank from patrolling bailiff.

HOBHOLE DRAIN, EAST AND WEST FEN DRAINS:
All canalised lengths of river forming part of fen drainage system. Hold good stock of coarse fish (bream, roach, perch, pike, tench), and include following waters: **Maud Foster**, **Sibsey Trader**, **East Fen Catchwater drains**, **West Fen**, **Kelsey** and **Bellwater drains**. St £5 and dt £1 from Boston tackle shops and D G Wootton, Myyom, Hall Lane, Spilsby, Lincs PE23 4BJ. Match pegs 80p. Hobhole and West Fen drains may be fished free on E. A. licence only. St covers also fishing on **Witham, Steeping**,

Steeping Relief Channel, **Glen**, **Bourne Eau** and **South Forty Foot**.

SLEA: Rises west of Sleaford and enters Witham at Chapel Hill. Trout in upper reaches. Coarse fish, particularly roach, elsewhere. Private fishing throughout length. Tackle shop: Slingsby. Hotel: Carr Arms.

WYE
(For close seasons, licences, etc, see Welsh Region Environment Agency, p15)

Most famous of English salmon rivers. Rises on south side of Plynlimon near source of Severn and enters estuary of Severn 2m south of Chepstow. Most of rod fishing in private hands, but there are several hotels and one or two associations with rights on river. Sea trout fishing is of no account, but coarse fishing in middle and lower reaches exceptionally good. No free fishing. Licences may be obtained from local post offices and sub-post offices and have usually to be produced when obtaining tickets or other permits to fish. Good brown trout fishing in Upper Wye and tributaries, very little trout fishing in Middle Wye. Carter Jonas, 22 Broad St, Hereford HR4 9AP (Tel: 01432 277174) have more than 30m of river under management. Lettings usually for season on one day per week basis, but a few permits on every and any day basis.

Tintern (Gwent). Tidal; mostly eels and flatfish, though salmon sometimes taken. Contact J Jones, The Rock, Tintern, Gwent. Rose and Crown Inn.

Redbrook (Gwent). Chub, dace, pike, perch, salmon. Contact the Post Office, Redbrook. For Whitebrook fishing, V Cullimore, Tump Farm, Whitebrook, Gwent. At Fairoak Fishery, The Cot, St Arvans, Chepstow, Monmouth NP16 6HQ (Tel; 01291 689711), fly only fishing for trout on three waters. Various tickets on site, incl £28, 5 fish, £15, 2 fish. Lodge on site, with good facilities for anglers, incl disabled.

Monmouth (Monmouthshire). Wye holds salmon, pike, trout, grayling, chub, dace; preserved. Town water is fishable on day, week and annual permit, coarse and salmon, from Council Offices, Monmouth. Monmouth Dist AS own or rent 7m of three rivers: **Wye**, coarse fishing during salmon close season, on both banks from Wye Bridge downstream; **Monnow**, with trout, grayling, chub, dace, carp, 3m of single or double bank trout fly fishing;

Troddi at Dingestow, over 5m of single or double bank trout fishing, all methods. Contact Hon Sec Mr Dodon (Tel: 01600 713821). Skenfrith AS also has local water, members only, details from Bob Forrest-Webb, 1 Trelasdee Cottages, St Weonards, Hereford HR2 8PU (Tel: 01981 580497). Trothy, trout; preserved. Brockweir to Livox Quarries, trout and coarse fish; St £20, dt £6 from Tourist Information Centre, Shire Hall, Monmouth (Tel: 01600 71399). Tackle shop: Monnow Angling Supplies, Monnow St, Monmouth NP5 3EG (Tel: 01600 719056).

Symonds Yat (Hereford). Salmon, trout and coarse fishing all preserved. 1½m both banks between **Goodrich** and Symonds Yat controlled by Newport AA. Good S water; members only. For Lower Lydbrook, contact G H Crouch, Greenway Cottage, Stowefield Rd, Lower Lydbrook, Glos, Tel: 01594 60048.

Kerne Bridge (Hereford). Chub, dace, pike, perch, salmon, trout; preserved. Castle Brook, Garron, 2m; trout. Luke Brook, 2m. Lammerch Brook, 5m.

Ross (Hereford). Salmon, trout, barbel, bleak, carp, bream, roach, large pike, chub and good dace. Ross-on-Wye AC has fishing on town water, Weir End, Netherton and Benhall, approx 5m. Permits £4 for town water on bank or from G B Sports (below). Ebbw Vale Welfare AC has 2½m at **Foy**, with chub, dace, roach, barbel. Members only, membership open to application. Hotels: Royal, Radcliffe Guest House. Ross-on-Wye AC will be pleased to help visitors; send sae if writing. Foy Bridge Fishery, Lyndor has 250 metres double bank, spinning and fly fishing. Boats for hire. Tel: 01989 63833. Wye Lea County Manor, **Bridstow** HR9 6PZ (Tel: 01989 562880, Fax: 768881) has 1m single bank from Backney to Wye Lea. Salmon (4 rods), mixed coarse, ghillie, boat and tackle on site. Licences and tackle from G B Sports, 10 Broad St, Ross HR9 7NY (Tel: 01989 563723).

Hereford (Hereford). Salmon, trout, grayling, other coarse fish incl big chub, and more recently barbel. Hereford and Dist AA holds 11½m bank on Wye and 8m **Lugg**, 2m intended as brown trout fishery, with £12 dt; in addition, three stillwater fisheries with trout and coarse fish. Three types of membership offered. Salmon members may fish some 18 named pools, fishable at various heights. Salmon dt

£15, trout £12, brace limit, coarse £3.50. Membership applications to Hereford & Dist AA, PO Box 35, Hereford, or Perkins of Hereford, 23 Commercial Rd. 40 pegs at Monte Bishop, 12 Old Eign Hill HR1 1TU, Tel: 01432 342665. Permits from Mordiford PO. Letton Court, Hereford HR3 6DJ, has salmon fishing on 1½m of Wye, dt £20–£25; also coarse fishing on 1½m of river and 2 lakes with chub, tench, carp, pike, dt £5. Ghillie, R F Pennington, Tel: 01544 327294, day; 01497 831665, evening. Birmingham AA has water on Lugg at Dinmore and Moreton. Longworth Hall Hotel, **Tidnor**, has coarse fishing on Wye, and a short stretch on the Lugg. For other fishing inquire Garnons Estate Office, Bridge Sollars, who sometimes have salmon dt, in advance only, also coarse dt; phone bailiff on 01981 590270. W Jones, Carrier Cottage, Whitney-on-Wye; and Red Lion, Bredwardine. Local tackle shops: Hattons (also fishery agent, pleased to give information), 64 St Owen Street (Tel: 01432 272317); Woody's Angling Centre, Hereford (Tel: 01432 344644). Hotels: City Arms, Green Dragon, Farm Hand, Firkin, Booth Hall. Red House Farm, Eaton Bishop, caters for anglers.

Bredwardine (Hereford). Red Lion Hotel HR3 6BU, Tel: 01981 500303, has tickets for 8m, salmon, trout, coarse fishing.

Hay-on-Wye (Hereford). Salmon, trout, pike, perch, chub. Hay-on-Wye Fishermans Assn has local fishing, with trout, grayling and coarse, not salmon. Waiting list for membership, Tel: 01497 820545. E. A. licences from post office. Tackle and permits (£25 to £3) for Hay Town Council water from H R Grant & Son, 6 Castle Street. Swan at Hay Hotel, Church St HR3 5DQ, Tel: 01497 821188, has permits for fishing on Wye, £25 non-residents, £15 residents. For R Llynfi and Ford Fawr, Wye confluence, contact Mrs Lloyd, Bridgend Cottage, Glasbury-on-Wye, Tel: 01497 847227. **Llangorse Lake** can be fished from here. Griffin Inn, Llyswen, Brecon, has 7½ miles u/s from Hay-on-Wye. Tackle shop: Sportfish, Winforton, nr Hay-on-Wye HR3 6EB.

Glasbury-on-Wye (Hereford). Salmon, trout, chub, dace, grayling, pike. Fishing in Wye and Llynfi preserved. Llangorse lake is accessible.

Builth Wells (Powys). Salmon (best April, May, June and Oct); good head of grayling, wild brown trout declining. Groe Park & Irfon AC has 2m on Wye incl ½m double bank, 1m on Irfon, incl ½m double bank, with 9 salmon catches on Wye and 4 late season catches on **Irfon**. Fly fishing only during trout season on Irfon and 2 sections of Wye. Club stocks heavily with brown trout. 3-day salmon permit £25, trout £18, trout dt £9, juv £3, coarse dt between 1 Nov–27 Feb, £4, from The Park Hotel; Nibletts, Ironmongers; or M Morgan, 27 Garth Rd, Builth. No keep nets for grayling on club waters, prawn and shrimp for salmon banned. Club also owns Llyn Alarch, 1½ acres, nr Builth, stocked rainbows. Platforms for disabled anglers. 4 fish limit, dt £16, conc, from Mrs Morgan (above). A few country memberships available, salmon £64, trout £32, contact Secretary (Tel: 015978 22404 day, 23119 evening). **Elan Estate Reservoirs** accessible (see Rhayader). Cueiddon, Duhonw, Baili and Edw preserved. Tackle shop: N J Guns, High St, Builth. Hotels: Park Hotel, Lion, Caer Beris Manor Hotel.

Newbridge-on-Wye (Powys). Salmon, trout, grayling, chub, dace, pike, roach; preserved, Ithon, trout; preserved.

Rhayader (Powys). Wye; trout (av ½lb; Wye record, 10½lb, caught at Rhayader Bridge), salmon. Rhayader AA has 4m on Wye, 3m on Marteg to St Harmon, 1.5m on R Elan, and 16-acre **Llyngwyn** at Nant Glas, rainbow trout to 6lbs; fly only. River dt £4, lake dt £12, st £90, conc, from Nant-y-Mynach Farm, nr Llyngwyn, or D Powell, newsagent, Rhyader. Brown trout fishing in **Elan Valley** (Caban Coch, Garreg Ddu, Pen-y-Garreg and Craig Goch), all fly only, st £55, dt £7, conc, from Visitors' Centre below Caban Coch dam (10am–6pm), and Mrs Powell, newsagent, West St. Rhayader. Dt £4 for local Wye stretch. **Llngwyn Fishery**. Dt £10, st £65, conc, from J and L Price, Nant Y Mynach Farm, Nantmel, Tel: 01597 810491. Tickets also from newsagents. Spinning on Craig Goch; other waters fly only. Elan Valley AA (Tel: 01597 811099) fish **Dolymynach Reservoir (3–6m W) Claerwen Reservoir** (650 acres), controlled by WW. Elan Valley Hotel, LD6 5HN (Tel: 01597 810448), caters for anglers, and has various fishing permits. Mr and Mrs C Easton, Glanrhos, Llanwrthwl, Llandridod Wells LD1 6NT (Tel: 01597 810277) have accom for anglers, and 3/4m west bank of Wye north of Llanwrthwl Bridge, several named pools, with plentiful trout and grayling, salmon late season, fly only. Dt £7, wt £35 by arrangement.

Tributaries of the Wye

TROTHY: Trout, some assn water.

Dingestow (Gwent). Trout; preserved. Glamorgan AC, Cardiff, has 6m fishing. Inquiries to the Hon Sec. Monmouth and Dist AS has 4m, mostly double bank. Trout and eels, excellent mayfly. St £20, dt £6 from Information Bureau, Agincourt Sq, Monmouth.

MONNOW: Good trout and grayling stream. The Game Fishers' Club has water on **Lugg**, **Rea**, **Monnow** and several brooks. Trout and grayling. Day permits to members' guests only. Annual membership £100, entrance fee, £75, conc. Monmouth & Dist AS has 3m of Monnow, see Monmouth.

Skenfrith (Hereford). Trout, chub, dace. Birmingham AA has fly fishing here.

Pandy (Gwent). Trout, grayling; preserved. Honddu: trout; preserved. Hotel: Pandy Inn.

HONDDU (tributary of Monnow): Trout.

Llanfihangel Crucorney (Gwent). Permits for trout fishing here may be purchased at local post office.

Llanthony. River fishing has deteriorated; recently opened Grywne Fawr Trout Fishery provides reservoir fishing. Contact Simon Holland (Tel: 01873 890271). Hotel: Abbey, Llanthony NP7 7NN (Tel: 01873 890487).

LUGG: Trout and grayling, with coarse fish in some stretches.

Mordiford (Hereford). Trout, grayling, etc; and Leominster AC has water; Birmingham AA also has good stretch here, also water at Tidnor, Lugg Mill, Bodenham, Dinmore, Marden and Moreton. The Moon Inn, HR1 4LW (Tel: 01432 870236) is HQ of fishing club, and has permits for two beats at Old Lacey. Tickets for Sufton Estate fishing, both banks between Mordiford Bridge and Wye junction, also for Leominster AC, from Post Office & Stores, Mordiford HR1 4LN (Tel: 01432 870235).

Longworth (Hereford). Longworth Hall Hotel has trout and coarse fishing, and on **Wye**, outside salmon season. Mt £34, wt £9, dt £1.50. Advance booking recommended.

Lugwardine (Hereford). 8½m preserved by Hereford and District AA. Dt for right bank d/s starting some 150 yds below the Worcester Rd.

Leominster (Hereford). Trout, grayling, pike, perch, dace. Above town Lugg preserved by landowners. White Swan Piscatorials also have water; otherwise preserved by landowners. **Pinsley Brook**; trout, grayling; landowners sometimes give permission. Mr T Brooke, Brimstone Cottage, Nicholson Farm, Docklow HR6 0SL (Tel: 01568 760346) has coarse pools at Docklow: dt £6, and holiday cottages to let. Hotels: Royal Oak (where fishing can be arranged for guests); Talbot.

Kingsland (Hereford). Lugg. Arrow, and Pinsley Brook; trout, grayling. Fishing generally preserved by landowners. 2m from Kingsland is River Arrow at Eardisland. Accommodation: Angel and Mortimer Cross.

Presteigne (Powys). Lugg, Arrow and Teme afford excellent trout and grayling fishing, generally dry fly; preserved. The Gamefishers Club has Lugg here, as well as Monnow and Honddu near Pontrilas; Rea, Cradley Brook and Leigh Brook near Worcester; and Severn tributaries Tanat and Cound Brook near Shrewsbury; all brown trout waters, fly only, members only. Subscription £100 + £70 entrance: Mr Dick Steele, 56 Poolfield Drive, Solihull, West Midlands B91 1SH (Tel: 0121 704 9234). Near Presteigne, holiday flat in Georgian farmhouse, with fly fishing for trout on 4-acre Hindwell Lake; stocked annually with 300–400 rainbows and browns; boat on water. Details from Mrs A Goodwin, Hindwell Farm, Walton, Presteigne LD8 2NU (Tel: 01544 350252).

FROME (tributary of Lugg): Trout, preserved.

Ashperton (Hereford). Frome, 2½m Leddon, 2½m. Devereux Park Lakes, 4m.

ARROW (tributary of Lugg): Trout, grayling, dace; but few opportunities for visitors.

Pembridge (Hereford). Trout, grayling, dace; preserved by landowners. White Swan Piscatorials have a stretch at Ivington. No tickets. Inn: New Inn.

Kington (Hereford). Trout; preserved. Inns: Swan, Royal Oak.

LLYNFI: Trout, grayling, etc; preserved.

Glasbury-on-Wye (Hereford). Lynfi enters Wye here. Trout, grayling, chub. Fishing good, but mostly preserved. Hotel: Maesllwch Arms, Tel/Fax: 01497 847637, located on R Wye, has day tickets for local fishing.

Talgarth (Powys). Llynfi. Dulais brook. Rhiangoll; trout. Treffrwd, 2m. **Llangorse Lake** (pike, perch) can be fished from here (4m); boats for hire. Hotel: Castle. Visitors' tickets from local association.

IRFON: limited salmon, trout few unless stocked; good grayling.

Llangammarch Wells (Powys). Lake Country House Hotel, LD4 4BS (Tel: 01591 620202, Fax: 620457) has about 5m of Irfon and nearby streams (**Garth Dulas**, **Chwefri**, etc), and some rods for salmon fishing on Wye negotiated each year and charged accordingly. Also 2½ acre trout lake in grounds, brown and rainbow; fish to 3½lb. Lake and rivers restocked annually. Fly only, wading sometimes essential. Wt and dt offered. Salmon dt £25, trout and grayling £15. Limit 2 brace from lake, £2.75 per lb caught. Seasons on Irfon: trout 3 Mar–30 Sept; salmon 26 Jan–25 Oct; grayling 16 Jun–14 Mar. Lake open all year.

Llanwrtyd Wells (Powys). Trout. 3m of Association water. Lakes. Riverside Guest house has accom. with fishing, Tel: 429. Victoria Wells Mountain Centre has accom. with fishing, Tel: 334. Hotel: Neuadd Arms has 1½m of fishing.

ITHON: Trout, chub, few salmon. Good hotel and Assn water.

Llandrindod Wells (Powys). Trout, grayling, chub, some eels and salmon. Llandrindod Wells AA controls 5m of trout fishing close to town, mainly between Disserth and Llanyre Bridges. Limit 2 brace per day. Sunday fishing; no spinning for trout allowed, 9in size limit; waders essential. Open to visitors on st £25, wt £20, dt £6.50, conc, from Wayfarers, Ddole Rd Enterprise Park (Tel: 01597 825100). Accom with private fishing at Disserth Caravan and Camping Park, LD1 6NL (Tel: 01597 860277). Hotel: The Bell, Llanyre.

Penybont (Powys). Trout, chub, grayling, dace, eels, pike. Hotel: Severn Arms LD1 5UA (Tel: 01597 851224/344) has 6m of trout fishing on Ithon, free to residents, otherwise dt £4. Fish run 3 to lb average. Licences at post office in village, tackle from Wayfarers, Llandridod Wells.

Llanbadarn Fynydd (Powys). Upper Ithon. New Inn, LD1 6YA, Tel: 01597 840378, has 3½m trout fishing; free to guests (fly only).

WYRE
(For close seasons, licences, etc, see North West Region Environment Agency, p13)

From Churchtown downstream coarse fish and brown trout. Above Churchtown limited amount of salmon, sea trout and brown trout fishing.

Fleetwood (Lancs). Sport in estuary improving as pollution lessens; flatfish mostly. Licences and sea baits from Langhornes, 80 Poulton Road, Tel: 01253 872653.

St Michael's (Lancs). Mainly brown trout and coarse fish. Ribble and Wyre FA have fishing at St Michaels, some sea trout. Hotel: Grapes.

Churchtown (Lancs). Salmon, sea trout, trout and coarse fish. Warrington AA has fishing here.

Garstang (Lancs). Salmon, sea trout, trout and coarse fish. Garstang AA preserves 3m both banks. Fly only. No dt, members only. Hotels: Royal Oak, Eagle and Child, Crown.

Scorton (Lancs). Salmon, sea trout, trout, coarse fish. Wyresdale Anglers have 7m water; no tickets.

YARE
(See Norfolk and Suffolk Broads)

YORKSHIRE
(lakes, reservoirs, canals and streams)
(For close seasons, licences, etc, see North East Region Environment Agency p13)

BRANDESBURTON PONDS. Several ponds offering varied sport to leisure anglers and specialists. Hull and District AAA, membership from local tackle shop or secretary. No dt.

BURTON CONSTABLE LAKES. 25 acres, at caravan park in grounds of Burton Constable Hall; excellent coarse fishing for roach, bream, perch, tench, carp and pike. St £40, wt £10, dt £4 from Warden, Old Lodges, Sproatley, nr Hull HU11 4LN (Tel: 01964 562508). Season 1 Mar–31 Oct.

CASTLE HOWARD GREAT LAKE. Near **Malton**. 78 acres, noted for specimen pike over 40lb, perch, tench to 10lb, bream to 14lb, roach, and eels to 8lb+. Fishing 6am to sunset. Ground bait allowed in moderation. Peat and leam banned. Close season 1 Apr–31 May. Sunday fishing.

CHELKER, SILSDEN, LEESHAW and **WINTERBURN RESERVOIRS**. Trout; let to Bradford Waltonians; no tickets. Waiting list. Near Silsden and Ilkley.

DAMFLASK and **UNDERBANK RESERVOIRS**. YW Services Ltd. Damflask (Tel: 01274 372742), 5m from Sheffield. Underbank, 10m from Stocksbridge. Both coarse fisheries, bank fishing only. Disabled access at high water (with caution). Day and monthly tickets sold from machines at reservoirs. Further enquiries to Yorkshire Water, PO Box 500, Western House, Western Way, Halifax Rd, Bradford BD6 2LZ (Tel: 01274 691111).

DOE PARK RESERVOIR, Denholme. 20 acres. Trout, coarse fish; let to Bradford City AA; dt £5, Mon–Fri incl, 7am (8.30 weekends) until 1 hour after sunset.

EMBSAY, and **WHINNYGILL RESERVOIRS**. Let by YW to Skipton AA, jointly with Barnoldswick AC. St £40 + £15 entrance fee. Dt £6 (Embsay, trout), £3.95 (Whinnygill, trout, roach, bream and perch). £2 winter coarse fishing. Assn also has fishing on R Aire, dt £3.50. Tickets obtainable from Paper Shop, Embsay, and Earby tackle shops.

FEWSTON and **SWINSTY RESERVOIRS**. YWS Ltd trout fishery, 153 acres each, fly only, barbless hooks. Regular stocking, 1lb 6oz av, 3lb rainbows. Dt (limit 4/2 fish), from machine at Fishing Office at Swinsty Moor Plantation. Area for disabled only, at Swinsty Lagoon where worm or fly may be used. Av catches for 1994, 2 fish per rod. Near **Harrogate** and **Otley**.

HORNSEA MERE. Hornsea HU18 1AX. Yorkshire's largest inland water (350 acres). Very good pike, carp, bream, rudd, perch, roach, tench. Hornsea Mere Marine Co (Tel: 01964 533277). Dt £2, evening and junior £1, punts £7 day (limited boat and bank fishing).

LEEMING RESERVOIR. Fishing station: **Oxenhope**. 20 acres; good trout fishing, brown and rainbow. Bradford City AA; dt £3, Mon–Fri.

LEIGHTON RESERVOIR. Masham, N Yorks. 105 acre water-supply reservoir on the Swinton Estate stocked with rainbow trout (some very large) for season and day ticket fishing. Barbless hooks. Dt £13 (4 fish), evening £7 (2 fish), concessions, from fishing hut in car park. Catch and return allowed after limit reached. Swinton Estate Office, Swinton, Masham, Ripon, N Yorks HG4 4JR. Phone 01765 689224 for further details.

LEVEN CANAL. Beverley 6m. 3m of good coarse fishing.

LINDHOLME LAKE FISHERIES, Sandtoft. 4 acre fly only trout lake; 13 acre mixed coarse lake; 3 acre match lake, and 1½ acre carp pool. Day tickets £16.50, 4 fish, to £11, 2 fish, trout; £4 coarse, at fishery. Enquiries to Lindholme Leisure Lakes Ltd, Don Farm House, West Carr, Epworth, Doncaster DN9 1LF (Tel: 01427 872 905/281 Fax).

MALHAM TARN. 6m from **Settle**. A Nature Reserve owned by the National Trust. Boat fishing only, for trout with fly, and for perch with worm. Barbless hooks only. Fish may run large. Dt £7 boat, £6 rod. Weekends, £12 boat, £6 rod. ½ price conc, except weekends and public holidays. No outboard motors allowed. Bookings and detailed information from Warden or Secretary (Tel: 01729 830331). Phone bookings recommended. Seasons May 1 to Sept 30 for trout. Accommodation locally.

MARKET WEIGHTON CANAL. Fishing stations: **Newport** and **Broomfleet**. 6m long; bream, perch, roach, pike. Match fishing leased from Environment Agency. Dt sold locally.

MORE HALL RESERVOIR. Sheffield 7m. YW Services Ltd, leased by Bentham Trout Farm, Low Mill, Bentham (Tel: 01524 261305). Trout, fly only; dt £14, 4 fish, £10, 2 fish, conc, from machine at reservoir. Barbless hooks. Bailiff (Tel: 07808 175882).

NOSTELL PRIORY LAKES. Foulby, nr Wakefield. Well-stocked with perch, pike, eels, large carp, bream, tench and roach. St £35, dt £4, ½ day £2.25. Various concessions. Details from Fisheries Office, Foulby Lodge. Tel/Fax: 01924 863562. Open from 7.00am daily.

SCOUT DIKE, Penistone. 16m from Sheffield. YW (Southern Division). Trout, 2 fish limit; st £17.50. Dt £3.50 sold from machine at reservoir.

SHIPTON LAKE. Shipton-by-Beningbrough. Tench, perch, roach, trout, pike. Bradford City AA, members only.

STAINFORTH AND KEADBY CANAL. Controlled by joint committee including following clubs: Rotherham, Doncaster, Sheffield Amal, Scunthorpe AA and British Railways. Usual coarse fish.

THORNTON STEWARD RESERVOIR, Bedale. 35 acre YW trout fishery, fly only, barbless hooks. Regularly stocked, 11lb 6oz av, together with many 3lb rainbows. Season: Mar 25 to Nov 30. 4 or 2 fish limit. Dt from Joan Hainsworth, Hargill House, Finghall, Leyburn DL8 5ND (Tel: 01677 450245).

TILERY LAKE, Faxfleet, nr Goole. 60 acres of water with carp to 30lb, bream, pike and roach. Controlled by Hull AA, st from Hon Sec or tackle shops in Hull and Goole locality. No night fishing without special permit, from Night Permit Sec.

ULLEY COUNTRY PARK, nr **Sheffield**. Rotherham MBC. 33 acre coarse fishery with bream, roach, perch, pike, rudd. Disabled platform. No closed season at present, but this may be subject to change. St £42, conc. Dt £3, conc, from ticket machine at fishery. Tackle shop on site, and maggot vending machine. Enquiries to Ulley C P, Pleasley Road, Ulley S26 3XL. Tel: 01709 365332.

WORSBROUGH RESERVOIR, Barnsley. Coarse fish, all species, open all year. Barnsley AS has rights and on ½m of canal. St £15, ladies, juniors, disabled £8. Dt £2 from bailiffs walking the bank. Sunday fishing to assn members only; hempseed and bloodworm barred, no keep nets.

NORTHUMBERLAND, Co DURHAM, and CLEVELAND RESERVOIRS. These groups of reservoirs, managed or leased by Northumbrian Water, include both stocked and wild trout fishing. **Fontburn**; **Grassholme** (140 acres); **Cow Green**; **Scaling** (105 acres); **Blackton** (66 acres); **Hury** (125 acres); **Derwent**; **Hanningfield**, managed by Essex and Suffolk Water. For **Kielder**, see *North Tyne*. Prices are as follows: 'Explorer' Permit, covering all waters, £479, £399 conc. 'Twelve fish' permit £7, conc £6, from fishing lodges, or self-service, or local post offices. Bank fishing only, except Kielder. For information: Kielder: (Tel: 01434 250312); Fontburn: (Tel: 01665 830619); Grassholme, Blackton and Hury: (Tel: 0191 383 2222); Scaling Dam: (Tel: 01287 660974); Hanningfield: (Tel: 01268 710101, shop), or (Tel: 01245 212031, office), Derwent: (Tel: 01207 255250). **Lockwood Beck**, 60 acres, is under new management; stocked fortnightly with 2–14lb rainbows, open 8am till after sunset. Tuition, bank and boat fishing. Dt £16, 3 fish, plus catch and release. Evening £10, 2 fish. Boat £12, £8 evening. The Fishing Lodge, Lockwood Beck, Lingdale, Saltburn by the Sea, TS12 3LQ (Tel: 01287 660501).

English Canal Fishing

British Waterways own 1,100 miles of canal, and 92 operational supply reservoirs. The large majority of these fisheries are leased to fishing clubs, but the B W retains direct control of fishing on a number of canal sections, and several reservoirs (shown below) or in the appropriate geographical section of the book, with season or day tickets easily obtainable.

100,000 anglers over the age of 12 fish British Waterways fisheries regularly. They form an important part of the coarse fishing on offer in England and Wales. Roach, perch, bream, gudgeon, eels, pike, dace, chub, and other coarse fish are to be found. Carp to 38lb have been reported from Middlewich Branch Canal, and in some Grand Union stretches, a good head of tench, larger bream and crucian carp. Stocking levels are extremely good and surpass the EU designated standard. The fishing is governed, as elsewhere, by water quality and natural food supply. Facilities for anglers in wheelchairs have been introduced in places; competitions can be arranged on directly controlled waters on application to the Fisheries Manager. The North West Region has introduced both the Waterways Anglers Scheme, by which a number of fishing clubs share the leasing of 43m of Shropshire Union Canal, 40m of Llangollen Canal, 45m of Leeds and Liverpool Canal, 55m of Lancaster Canal, and a further 30m on 8 additional waterways: clubs participating are able to fish all waters for a year at less than half the day ticket charge; also the Waterway Wanderers permit on the same fisheries. The latter is offered as a £15 season, or £2 day ticket, with concessions, and covers all fishing under the scheme. A further permit is the Waterways Permit, offered on a monthly basis, and income from it is used for restocking. Contact Regional Fisheries Manager for further details. **Anglers should take special care to avoid overhead power lines above rural canals**.

There are at present three administrative areas of British Waterways Fisheries: North West Region, Navigation Road, Northwich, Cheshire CW8 1BH (Tel: 01606 723800, Fax: 01606 871471); North East and Midlands Regions, Peel's Wharf, Lichfield Street, Fazeley, Tamworth, Staffordshire B78 3QZ (Tel: 01827 252000, Fax: 01827 288071); Southern Region, Brindley Suite, Willow Grange, Church Road, Watford, Hertfordshire WD1 3PA (Tel: 01923 208717, Fax 01923 208717). Some of the fishing clubs mentioned below are, for reasons of space, not in the club lists of this edition. The Regional Fisheries Manager at the appropriate office will supply addresses and other information.

Southern Region

Grand Union Canal; Osterley Lock to Hayes leased by London AA. Hayes to West Drayton, Central Assn of London & Prov AC. West Drayton to Denham, London AA. Denham to Batchworth, Blenheim AS. Sabeys Pool and part of R Chess, West Hampstead AS. Batchworth to Lot Mead Lock, Sceptre AC. Lot Mead to Cassionbury Park, Watford Piscators, and to Hunton Bridge, Kings Langley AS. Hunton Bridge to Tring, London AA. Tring to Cheddington, Tring Anglers. Cheddington to Stoke Hammond. Luton AC. From Stoke Hammond to Great Linford, Milton Keynes AA. Great Linford to Wolverton Bridge, North Bucks Div. SE Midlands, CIU Ltd. Old Wolverton to R Ouse Aqueduct, Galleon AC. 400m Canal and Broadwater at Cosgrove, Mr & Mrs M Palmer, Lock House, Cosgrove. Cosgrove to Castlethorpe, Deanshanger & Old Stratford AA. Castlethorpe to Yardley Gobion, Britannia AC. Yardley Gobion to Dodford, Northampton Nene AC. Brockhall to Watling Street Bridge, Daventry AC. Norton Junction to southern end of Braunston Tunnel, AM-PRO UK Ltd AC.

Grand Union: Arms and Branches
Paddington Arm; Bulls Bridge Junction to Lock Bridge at Paddington, London AA. **Paddington Basin**; Westminster AC.

Regents Canal; Little Venice to Islington, Raven AC. Islington to Mile End, London AA. Mile End Lock to Commercial Road, Brunswick Brothers AS. **Hertford Union Canal**; Junction with Regents Canal nr Victoria Park to Lee Navigation at Old Ford, London AA. **Slough Arm**; Whole of Arm from junction with Main Line at Cowley to Slough, Gerrards Cross & Uxbridge AC. **Wendover Arm**; Main Line to Tringford Pumping Station, Tring Anglers. **Aylesbury Arm**; Main Line to Red House Lock, Tring A. Red House Lock nr Aston

Clinton to u/s of Aylesbury Basin, Aylesbury & Dist AF. To the Basin Terminus, Aylesbury Canal Society. **Northampton Arm**; Main Line to Milton Malsor, Northampton Britannia AC. Milton Malsor, Northampton Castle AA. Milton Malsor to Hardingstone, and Hardingstone to Duston Mill Lane, Northampton Castle AA. Bridges 13 to 14, Glebe AC, Bridges 14 to 18, Northampton Castle AA. Gayton Marina, Gayton AC. **Leicester Branch**; Norton Junction to Crick Tunnel, Towcester & Dist AA. North end of Crick Tunnel to Bridge 20, Knightley AC. Bridges 20 to 22 at Yelverton, Eldon Sports and SC. Bridges 31 to 33, Lutterworth AC. Bridges 34 to 37, and 39 to 41, White Hart Match Group. Bridges 37 to 39, Bostrom AC. Bridges 41 to 45, Brixworth AC. North Kilworth to southern end of Bosworth Tunnel, White Hart Match Group. To Bridge 47, Broughton & Dunton AC. Bridges 47 to 51, White Hart MG. Bridges 54 to 57, Wellingborough Nene AC. Bridges 57 to 60, Broughton & Dunton AC. Whole of **Welford Arm**, Bostrom AC.

Lee Navigation; Limehouse Basin to Blackwell Tunnel, Brunswick Brothers AS. Bow Lock stretch, Lee Anglers Consortium. Cheshunt, off-side bank plus Cadmore Lane Gravel Pit, Metrop Police AS. West bank Old R Lee, Kings Weir, W E Newton, Slipe Lane, Wormley. Carthegena Lock, Mr P Brill, Carthagena Lock, Broxbourne, Herts. Above Kings Weir to below Aqueduct Lock, London AA. Dodds Wier, L.V.R.P.A. Weir Pool at Feildes Weir, and Feildes Weir Lock to Rye House Station Bridge, plus stretch ½m u/s of Ryehouse Bridge, Lee Anglers Consortium. Ryehouse Bridge for 1,020 metres, London AA. Offside bank between Hardemeade and Stanstead Locks, Ware AC.

Oxford Canal (South); Dukes Cut, Wolvercote Pool, Hythe Bridge Street to Kidlington Green Lock, North Oxford AS. Kidlington Green Lock to Bullers Bridge, N. Oxford AS. Bullers Bridge to Langford Lane, Kidlington AS. Langford Lane to Bridge 221, Tring Anglers. Bridge 221 to end of moorings at Thrupp, Thrupp Canal Cruising Club. Thrupp to Bridge 216, Tring Anglers. Bridges 216 to Lower Heyford, plus River Cherwell at Enslow, Kirtlington, and Northbrook, Oxford & Dist AA. Lower Heyford to Aynho, Banbury & Dist AA. Aynho to Banbury, Coventry & Dist AA. Banbury to Cropredy, Banbury & Dist AA. Cropredy Lock to Bridge 148, Standard-Triumph Recreation C. Bridge 148 to Claydon, Sphinx C. Claydon to Fenny Compton, Ford (Leamington) AC. Fenny Compton Marina to Bridge 136, Cowroast Marina AC. Folly Bridge to Napton Junction, Leamington Liberal AC. Napton Junction to Bridge 103, and Bridges 101 to 102, Coventry & Dist AA. Bridge 102 to Bridge 103, Northampton Castle AA.

River Stort; From junction with Lee Navigation to Lower Lock, Lee Anglers Cosortium. From Road Bridge 6 to Railway Bridge 7, Roydon, Two Bridges AS. To Hunsdon Mill Lock, Globe AS. Stort and Stort Navigation at Burnt Mill, Harlow FA. Burnt Mill Lock to Parndon Lock, Stort Valley AA. Spellbrook Backwater, O J Smith, Spellbrook Lane East, Bishops Stortford. Bishops Stortford and to Spellbrook Lock, Bishops Stortford & Dist AS. Further stretch to Sawbridgeworth AS.

Oxford Canal (North); Bridges 101 to 97, Warwick & Dist AA. Bridges 97 to 85, Willoughby, Braunston Turn and Braunston Tunnel, Braunston AC. Willoughby Wharf Bridge to Bridge 83, George AC. Bridges 80 to 77, Avon Ho AC. Bridge 76 to Hillmorton Top Lock, Avon Ho AC. Hillmorton Bottom Lock to Bridge 9, Aces AC.

Bridgwater and Taunton Canal; Bridgwater to Durston, Bridgwater AA. Durston to Taunton, Taunton AA.

Gloucester & Sharpness & Stroudwater Canals; Hempsted Bridge, Gloucester, to Sharpness, leased to Gloucester Canal Angling on the towpath side. Frontage of Borrow Silos (150 yds), Babcock AC. Tanker Bay Area, MEB AC. Offside bank at Two Mile Bend, nr Gloucester, and Rea Bridge to north of Sellars Bridge, Gloucester United AA. Stroudwater Canal; Walk Bridge to 'Feeders', Frampton & Dist AA, also from Ryalls Farm to 'Stone' near Frampton. Walk Bridge to Whitminster, Whitbread AC.

Kennet and Avon Canal; Eight stretches from Bear Wharf, Reading, to Kennet Junction, Reading & Dist AA, with the exception of stretch near Sulhampstead Lock, Central Assn of London & Prov AC. Woolhampton Lock to Heales Lock and stretch near Oxlease Swing Bridge to Heales Lock, Glendale AC. Heales Lock to Midgham Bridge, Reading & Dist AA. Junction with Kennet at Northcroft, 2 stretches at Midgham Lock, Reed Thatcham AA. Thatcham to Widmead Lock, Thatcham AA.

Bulls Lock to Ham Lock, Newbury AA. Ham Mill (offside bank) I Fidler, Ham Mill, London Road, Newbury. Whitehouse Turnover Bridge to Greenham Lock, Twickenham PS. Greenham Lock to Greenham Island, Newbury, and Northcroft to Guyers Bridge, Newbury AA. Two sections at Kintbury (560 yds), Civil Service AS. Ladies Bridge near Wilcote to Milkhouse Water Bridge, Pewsey and District AA. Ladies Bridge to Semington Bridge, Devizes AA. Semington Bridge to Avoncliffe Aqueduct, and Bradford Lock to Winsley Bridge, Bradford on Avon Dist AA. Winsley Bridge to Limpley Stoke Bridge, Kingswood Disabled AC. Limpley Stoke Bridge to R Avon confluence, Bathampton AA.

Monmouthshire and Brecon Canal; from Pontypool to Brecon, BW directly controlled fishery. Goytre Marina, Red Line Boats. Cattle Upper Bridge to Llanfoist Bridge, Cwmcelyn AC. Stretch nr Llanfoist, Mr R Tod, Boat House, Llanfoist, Abergavenny. Auckland Bridge to Haunted House Bridge, Gilwern & Dist AC. Haunted House Bridge to Penpedair Heal Bridge, Gwent Avengers. Workhouse Bridge to Fro Bridge, Ebbw Vale Welfare AC. Brynich Lock to Canal Terminus at Brecon, BW directly controlled. **River Usk**; at Llanfrynach and Brynich, private fishing.

River Severn Navigation; Island bank at Upper Lode Lock, Diglis, BW directly controlled. Belvere Lock, G H Drake, 30 Dunstans Close, Worcester. Cock Island, left bank 350 yds d/s, Shoulton AC. East bank at Diglis, Punchbowl AC. Bevere Lock, Mrs M E Smith, Bevere Lock, Grimley. Holt Lock u/s and d/s, A S Portman, Holt Lock, Holt Heath, near Worcester. Salmon rights, Lincomb Lock, P Gough, Courtnay House, Feiashill Road, Trysull, WV5 7HT. Coarse rights, B Turner, Lincomb Lock, Stourport. West bank, Lincomb Lock, Carter Jones, 20 St Owen St, Hereford (Severn Valley Sand & Gravel Ltd).

Midland Region

Ashby Canal; Stretches leased by Birchmoor AC, Shackerstone & Dist AC, Measham AC.

Birmingham and Fazeley Canal; Tyburn to Curdworth Tunnel, Fosters of Birmingham, Dams and Lock AC, BRS (Midlands) AC, Stirrup Cup AC. Curdworth Tunnel to Whittington is Birmingham AA, Fazeley Victory AC, Lamb AC and Hope and Anchor AC. Whittington Bridge to Huddlesford Junction, Whittington Social AC.

Birmingham Canal Navigation (BCN), **Wyreley and Essington Canal; Cannock Extension**; Yates AC, Chase Social AC. **BCN Rushall and Daw End Branch Canal**; leased to Pelshall Social AC, Trident AC, Fletchers Tackle AC, Hawkins AC, WMTS AC, Conex AC. **BCN Soho Loop**, Fisherman of England AC.

Coventry Canal; Coventry to Polesworth, Coventry & Dist AA. The remaining sections leased by Birchmoor AC, Amington AC, Tamworth Progressive AC, Weddington Social Club AS, Dordon AC. Huddlesford Junction to Fradley Junction, Lamb AC, Lichfield Marina AC, Pirelli AC, Drayton Manor AC, Belgrave AS.

Grand Union Canal, Main Line; North Napton Junction, through Calcutt Bottom Lock to Junction Bridge, Warwick, Royal Leamington Spa AA. Junction Bridge to Ugly Bridge, Warwick & Dist AA. **Saltisford Arm**; Saltisford Canal (Trading) Ltd. Hatton Top Lock to south end of Shrewley Tunnel, Stratford-upon-Avon AA. Shrewley Tunnel to Rowington, Tunnel Barn AC. Rowington to Chessets Wood and Small Arm at Kingswood Junction, Massey Ferguson Recreation C. Knowle, Civil Service AC. Knowle Top Lock to Birmingham, Tavern AC, Crown Leisure AC, Wild Manufacturing AC, Hay Mills AC, Lode Mill AC.

Staffordshire and Worcester Canal, Southern Section; York Street Stourport to Botterham Lock, Birmingham AA. Botterham Lock to Dimmingsdale Lock, Wolverhampton AA. **Stratford-upon-Avon Canal**; leased by Olton AC, Raven AC, Redditch FA, Solihull AC. **South Stratford Canal**; Stratford AA, Evesham AA, Alcester AC, Studley Rd AC. **Worcester and Birmingham Canal**; Diglis Basin to Blackpole Bridge, Worcester UA. Blackpole Bridge to Kings Norton Tunnel, Birmingham AA.

Staffordshire and Worcester Canal, Northern Section; stretches held by Lilleshall & Dist AS, Marston Palmer AS, Goodyear AS, New Invertion WMC, Littleton & Mid-Cannock AC, Union Locks Anglers, Staffs Co Council AC, Four Ashes FC, Whitmore Reans CAA. Roseford Bridge to

Milford Aqueduct, Izaac Walton (Staffs) AA. Milford Aqueduct to Great Haywood Junction, Potteries AS.

Trent and Mersey Canal; Derwent Mouth to Weston-upon-Trent, Pride of Derby AA. Weston-upon-Trent, Derby Railway AC. Weston-on-Trent to Clay Mills, Pride of Derby AA. Clay Mills Bridge to Wychnor Lock, Burton Mutual AA. Findern Crossing Pond, Derby RAC. Wychnor Lock – south west, Alrewas AC. Section to Woodend Turn, Woodside Caravan Park AC. Handsacre Bridge to Wolseley Bridge, Rugeley & Brereton AS. Wolseley Bridge to Colwich Lock, Norton Lido AC. Three stretches between Great Haywood Lock and Ingestre Bridge, Evode AC. Ingestre Bridge to Weston Lock, Cadbury AC. Next beat, Hazeldine AA to Salt Bridge. Salt Bridge to Sandon Lock, Universal Sports C. Sandon Lock to Flute Meadow Bridge, Olditch AC. Flute Meadow Bridge to Long Meadow Bridge, Stone AS. Middlewich Junction to Preston Brook Tunnel, Trent and Mersey AA. Booth Top Lock to Middlewich Junction, Cheshire AA. Bridge No 159 to Booth Lane Top Lock, Middlewich JA. Bridge No 149, Hassall Green to Middlewich Junction, Cheshire AA. Bridge No 138, Rode Heath to Bridge No 149, Hassall Green, Waterway Wanderers. Lawton Lock No 52, to Bridge No 138, Rode Heath, Waterway Wanderers. Bridge 135 to Lock No 50, Royal Doulton AC. Bottom Lock 46 to Bridge No 135, Church Lawton, Alsager A. Harecastle Tunnel North to Bottom Lock 46, and Bridge 129 to Harecastle Tunnel (South), Waterway Wanderers. Bridges 126, Longport to 129, Tunstall, Red Lion Anglers. Whieldon Road Bridge to Stoke Summit Lock, Stoke City & Dist AA. Trentham Lock to Stoke Basin, Fenton & Dist AC.

Shropshire Union Canal; in Wolverhampton area Wolverhampton AA have section, also Post Office AC, Dawley AC, then British Rail AC, George Carter Ltd AC. Further sections leased by Codsall Legionnaires AC, Penkridge Anglers; section to Stretton Aqueduct, Swan AC Stretton, Brewood AC. Next two sections are leased by Hazeldine AA. Section to Cowley Tunnel, Izaac Walton (Stafford) AA. To Gnossal, Marston Palmer AS. The leased sections to Tyreley are held by the following clubs: Market Drayton AC, Fusileer AC, Park AC, Stafford Hospital AC, Hodnet WMC AC, Palesthorpes AS, Crown AC. Tyreley Locks to Audlem, Crewe Pioneers AC.

Audlem Bottom Lock to Ellesmere Port is BW managed, except stretch from Bridges 82 to 83, Audlem FC.

North East Region

Chesterfield Canal; Stockwith to Drakeholes Low Wharf, Sheffield & Dist AA. Clayworth Church Lane Bridge to Retsford Bridge, Worksop & Dist. AAA. West Retford Bridge to Chequer House Bridge, Retford & Dist AA. Chequer House to Bracebridge Lock, Worksop United AA. Bracebridge Lock to High Grounds Farm Bridge, Grafton AA.

Erewash Canal; Trent Lock to Long Eaton Lock, Long Eaton Victoria AS, also **Cranfleet Canal**. Long Eaton Lock to Sandiacre Lock, Long Eaton & Dist FA. Sandiacre Lock to B5010 Bridge, West End AC. B5010 to Pasture Lock, Lace Webb Spring Co Sports & SC. Pasture Lock to Stanton Lock, Draycott AC. Stanton Lock to Greens Lock, and on to A6096, Middleton WMC. A6096 to Common Bottom Lock, Durham Ox FC. Common Bottom Lock to Shipley Lock, Cotmanhay AC. Shipley Lock to Langley Mill Lock, NCB No 5 Area FC. **Grantham Canal**; Grantham to Woolsthorpe-by-Belvoir, Grantham AA. Lady Day Bridge to Gamston Bridge, Matchman Supplies AC. Other sections, Nottingham AA. Very little of this canal is fishable. **River Soar Navigation**; Sections at Thurmaston and Wreake Junction, Leicester & Dist ASA. Barrow Shallow to Kegworth Old Lock, Loughborough Soar AS. 400 metres at Lock Island, Kegworth AS. Kegworth Flood Lock to Ratcliffe Lock, Long Eaton & Dist AF. Canal in Loughborough, Quorn AS. **River Trent**; Hazelford Island, BW directly managed. Lenton, Raleigh FC. Beeston Canal, Nottingham AA. Trent at Gunthorpe, Nottingham & Dist FAS. These are small fisheries.

Grand Union Canal: Arms and Branches; Market Harborough Arm; Junction, Foxton Boats Ltd. Foxton to Mkt Harborough, Tungstone FC, Desborough and Rothwell AC, Mkt Harborough AC. Foxton to Leicester, Wigston AS.

Huddersfield Broad Canal; section from Apsley Basin entrance, Holme Valley PA. Red Doles Lock to Deighton Mill, Huddersfield Broad Canal Alliance. **Pocklington Canal**; Pocklington to Derwent junction, East Cottingwith, York & Dist AA. **Ripon Canal**; terminal to R Ure junction, Ripon Canal Fisheries (T Welbourne, 116 Stonebridgegate, Ripon). **Selby Canal**; wide commercial waterway. Selby Basin to Bawtry Road bridge, Wheatsheaf AC. Bawtry Bridge to Brayton Bridge, Knottingley Conservative Club AS. Brayton Bridge to Burn Bridge, Selby AA. Burn Bridge to Paperhouse Bridge, Goole & Dist AA. Paperhouse Bridge to Tankards bridge, Carlton AC.

Sheffield and South Yorkshire Navigation (Stainforth and Keadby Canal); Keadby Lock to Mauds Bridge, Stainforth & Keadby Joint AC. M18 to Dunston Hill Bridge, Hatfield Colliery AC. Dunston Hill to Stainforth High Bridge, Stainforth AA. Bramwith Lock to Barnby Dun Swing Bridge, Northfield Bridge to aqueduct on New Junction Canal, and on past Sykehouse Lock, Doncaster & Dist AA.

Sheffield and South Yorkshire Navigation; wide commercial section. Barnby Dun to Kirk Sandal, Barnby Dun SAC. Kirk Sandal to Railway Bridge, Pilkington (Kirk Sandal) Rec C. Rotherham to Sprotborough (9 miles), all Rotherham AA, except short lengths controlled by Group 35 AC, Conisborough AC, E Hemingthorpe S & SC, and Guest & Chrimes Ltd AS. Sprotborough to Kirk Sandall (6 miles), all Doncaster AA.

Remainder Length; Tinsley & Dist ACA have two sections; Tinsley Canal junction with R Don, and R Don to Holmes Lock. Tinsley Wire Sports & SC have two basins, as do Firth-Derihon (Tinsley) FC. Broughton Lane to Tinsley, BSC (Tinsley) Sports & SC. To Coleridge Road, Tuffnells AC. Between bridges at Coleridge Road and Darnall Road, Fox House Social Club AS. Darnall Road to Shirland Road, Ranmoor Dept AC. Shirland Rd to Staniforth Rd, Firth Park WMC. Staniforth Road to Bacon Lane, Stocks AC. Bacon Lane to Bernard Road, Hogs Head AC. Bernard Road to Cadman Street, Woodseats WMC. **River Ure**; Ure and Milby Cut at Boroughbridge, Plus Milby Lock to Tinkers Lane; Harrogate & Claro Conservative AA. Also on Ure and Milby Cut at Boroughbridge, Unity AC.

North West Region

Caldon Canal; very good water quality. Bedford St Double Lock to Planet Lock No 3, Waterway Wanderers and Adderley Green AC. Planet Lock No 3 to Lichfield St Bridge,

Fenton & Dist AS. Lichfield St Bridge to Abbey Rd Bridge 15, Waterway Wanderers. Abbey Rd Bridge 15 to Foxley Lift Bridge 172, Corbridge Coronation CIUC. Foxley Lift Bridge 17 to Stockton Brook Bridge 25, Waterway Wanderers. Stanley Rd Bridge to Post Bridge 28, Abbey Hulton Suburban AS. To Hazlehurst Junction, and from Hazlehurst Bottom Lock to Cheddleton Top Lock Bridge 43, Waterway Wanderers. From Cheddleton Top Lock Bridge 43 to Consall Forge Bridge 49, Embreys Bakeries AC; Basford Bridge 44 to Bridge 47, Stoke Telephone AG. Bridges 49 to 53, Waterway Wanderers. 53 to 54, TBJ AC. Froghall Tunnel Bridge to Bridge 55, Stoke on Trent Disabled AC. Bridge 55 to terminus, Frognall Wharf. **Leek Branch**; Hazlehurst to Horse Bridge, Waterway Wanderers. Horse Bridge to end, Leek & Moorlands FC.

Llangollen Canal; Hurleston Locks to Hampton Bridge No 50, Waterway Wanderers. Bridges 50 to 51, Fernwood FC. Bridges 51 to 55, Waterway Wanderers. Bridge No 59, Ellesmere through Bridge No 62, Tetchill, to Bridge No 68, Waterway Wanderers. Nichola Bridge No 2 to Bridge No 49A, Waterway Wanderers. **River Dee**, Berwyn, Waterlog AC.

Macclesfield Canal; Hardingswood Junction to Hall Green Stop Lock, Kidsgrove & Dist AA. Five sections to Watery Lane Aqueduct, Alsager A, Warrington AA, Middleport WMC, Warrington AA, Victoria AC. To Henshalls Bridge 80, Warrington AA. From Henshalls Bridge to Lamberts Lane Bridge 77, Victoria and Biddulph AS. To Lamberts Bridge, Bridges 72 to 77, Warrington AA. Porters Farm Bridge to Buxton Road Bridge, Congleton, Macclesfield Waltonian AS. To Congleton Bridge 61, Waterway Wanderers.

Montgomery Canal; Rednal Basin, Redwith, day permit on sale. Burgedin Locks to Bridge 106, incl Wern Clay Pits, Churchstoke AC. Bridges 131 to 133, Waterway Wanderers. Bridge 134 To Tan-y-Fron Bridge 136, Penllwyn Lodges AC. Tan-y-Fron to Bridge 153, Waterway Wanderers. **River Severn** at Penarth Weir, Potteries AS. Penllwyn AC have stretch at Tan-y-Fron. R Severn at Penarth Weir, Potteries AS. **Peak Forest Canal**; Dukinfield Junction to Whaley Bridge Terminus, Stockport & Dist AF.

Trent and Mersey Canal; Trentham Lock to

Stoke Basin, Fenton & Dist AS. Whieldon Road Bridge to Stoke Summit Lock, Stoke City & Dist AA. To Longport, Middleport WMC. Longport to Tunstall, Red Lion A. Tunstall to S end of Harecastle Tunnel, Waterway Wanderers. N end of Harecastle Tunnel to Red Bull Bottom Lock 46, Waterway Wanderers. Church Lawton to Lawton Lock 50, Royal Doulton AC. Lawton Lock to Rode Heath Bridge, Waterway Wanderers. Rode Heath Bridges 138–139, Knutten British Steel AC. 139–141, Waterway Wanderers. 141 to Middlewich Junction, Cheshire AA. Rookery Bridge to Booth Lane Top Lock, Middlewich Joint A. Rookery Bridge to Booth Lane Top Lock, Cheshire AA. Middlewich Junction to Preston Brook Tunnel, Trent & Mersey Canal AA.

Middlewich Branch Canal; From Barbridge Junction to Cholmondeston Lock, Waterway Wanderers. Cholmondeston Lock to Railway Bridge 5A, Venetian Marine AC. Railway Bridge 5A to Bridge 22 Clive, Waterway Wanderers. Bridge 22 Clive to Bridge 32, Middlewich Junction, Middlewich Joint Anglers.

River Weaver; at Saltersford, Frodsham Cut, Sutton Pool, Warrington AA.

Weaver Navigation; Saltersford to Sutton Weaver, elver fishing.

Ashton Canal; Junction with Rochdale, to Whitelands Road Bridge, and Ashton New Bridge 10 to Clayton Bridge 11, Stockport & Dist AF. Between Fairfield Bottom and Top Locks, Water Sports Adventure Centre. Guide Bridge 26 to Bridge 28, Tootal AC. Bedford St Dble Lock to Planet Lock No 3, Corbridge Coronation CIU Club. Planet Lock No 3 to Lichfield St Bridge No 8, Waterway Wanderers. Stanley Rd Bridge 26 to Hazlehurst Junction, Waterway Wanderers. Hazlehurst Junction to Hazlehurst Bottom Lock, to Bridge 47, Waterway Wanderers. Bridge 47, 400m past Bridge 48, Embreys Bakeries AC. Bridge 54 to 55, Stoke on Trent Dis AC. Bridge 55 to terminus, Frognall Wharf. **Leek Branch**: Hazlehurst Junction to Bridge 6, Waterway Wanderers. Bridge 6 to canal end, Leek and Moorlands AC.

Huddersfield Narrow Canal; water tends to acidity, but contains trout. Huddersfield to Lock No 11, Milnsbridge, Waterway Wanderers. Locks 11 to 17, Linthwaite, and to Lock 21 Slaithwaite, Slaithwaite & Dist AC.

Locks 23 to 24, Waterway Wanderers. Locks 24 to 26, Scholes AC. Locks 26 to 27, Waterway Wanderers. Locks 27 to 28, Sefton Hall PAC. Lock 28 to West Slaithwaite Rd Bridge, Waterway Wanderers. West Slaithwaite Rd Bridge, to Lock 34 Marsden, Slaithwaite & Dist AC. Lock 34 to Stannedge Tunnel, Waterway Wanderers. Ward Lane, Diggle to Lock 24 Saddleworth, Saddleworth & Dist AS. Lock 24 to Lock 19 Greenfield, Diggle AC. Lock 19 to Milton Mill Bridge, Mossley, Medlock Bridge Match Group. To Scout Tunnel, Border Anglers & Naturalists. Scout Tunnel to Bridge 95, Waterway Wanderers. Bridges 95 to 99, Croft AS. Caroline St Stalybridge to Lock no 1, Stockport & Dist AF. Bayley St to Caroline St, Waterway Wanderers.

Lancaster Canal; Stocks Bridge, Preston to Stainton, Waterway Wanderers.

Leeds and Liverpool Canal (East); Bank Newton Top Lock to Scarland Lock 34, Waterway Wanderers. Lock No 34 to Anchor Lock No 33, Starbeck Working Men's AC. Anchor Lock 33 to Milking Hill Swing Bridge 184, Waterway Wanderers. Milking Hill Swing Bridge 184 to Brunthwaite Bridge 192, Keighley AC. Brunthwaite Bridge 192 to Bridge 194, Waterway Wanderers. Bridge 194 to Granby Swing Bridge 197A, Marsden Star AS. Bridge 197A to Swine Lane Bridge 198, Waterway Wanderers. Swine Lane to Dowley Gap Top Lock, Bingley AC. From Downey Gap Bottom Lock to Bridge 210, Saltaire AC. Bridge 210 to Field Lock, Thackley, Waterway Wanderers. Thackley to Idle Swing Bridge 212, Unity AC. Idle Swing Bridge to Thornhill Bridge, Idle and Thackley AA. Bridges 214B to 215, Waterway Wanderers. Bridges 215 to 216A, Listerhill Old Boys AA. Horseforth Rd Bridge 216A to Rodley Swing Bridge, Rodley Boats AC. Bridges 217 to 219, Waterway Wanderers. Bridge 219 to Newley Lock, Leeds & Dist ASA. To Redcote Bridge 224, Waterway Wanderers. 224 to Spring Garden Lock 6, Leeds & Dist ASA. To Bridge 225H, Waterway Wanderers.

Leeds and Liverpool Canal (West); Liverpool to Halshall Bridge 24, Liverpool & Dist AA. Halsall to Moss Lane, Wigan & Dist AA. Johnson's Hillock Bottom Lock to Jacksons Bridge 87, Waterway Wanderers. From Jacksons Bridge to Bridge 89, Deane AC. Bridge 89 through Foulridge Tunnel to Park Bridge 151A, Waterway Wanderers. Park Bridge 151A to Long Ings Bridge 152, Marsden Star AS.

Leigh Branch; Dover Lock to Plank Lane Bridge, Ashton & Dist Centre Northern AA. To Leigh Wharf, Leigh & Dist AA.

Manchester, Bolton and Bury Canal; Canal Wharf Bury to Ladyshore Road Bridge, Waterway Wanderers. To Canal End at Paper Mill, Tongue AC. Hall Lane to Nob End, Bolton & Dist AA. Road Bridge to Ringley Lock, Prestolee, Waterway Wanderers. Park House Road to Canal End, Agecraft, Salford AC

St Helens Canal; Section leased by St Helens AA; Carr Mill End to Old Double Locks.

Reservoirs and Lakes in English canal system:

Halton Reservoir, Wendover. Coarse fishery leased from BW by Prestwood & Dist AC. Enquiries to Hon Sec.

Wormleighton Reservoir, near **Banbury**. Tench to 9lb. Contact Mr Roe (Tel: 01926 853533).

Gayton Pool, Gayton, near Northampton. Carp fishery; Gayton AC members only.

Tardebigge Reservoir, Bromsgrove, now BW directly controlled, season ticket only.

Upper and **Lower Bittell Reservoirs** (near **Bromsgrove)**. Rights owned by Barnt Green FC, who stock Lower Bittell and adjacent Arrow Pools with trout; other pools hold coarse fish, including pike and bream. Tickets for coarse fishing to members' personal guests only (see also Arrow tributary of Warwickshire Avon).

Lifford Reservoir. Birmingham Parks. Dt from park keeper.

Caldon Canal Reservoirs. Stanley, let to Stoke on Trent AS. **Rudyard**, day permit on site.

Earlswood Lakes. BW direct managed fishery. Three lakes totalling 85 acres. Engine Pool, commercial carp fishery; Windmill Pool, stocked with roach, perch, bream, pike; Terry's Pool, roach, bream. Dt on bank from bailiff. Match booking enquiries, Tel: 01827 252066.

Stockton Reservoir. Excellent coarse fishery, tickets from Blue Lias public house, near

site. Match booking enquiries, Tel: 01827 252066.

Sneyd Pool, Walsall. Excellent carp and tench fishing, leased by Swan AC. Dt on bank.

Harthill, near **Worksop**. Coarse fishing leased by Handsworth AC.

Gailey Lower Reservoir, near **Wolver-hampton**. 64 acre coarse fishery. Management under review, fishing temporarily closed.

Calf Heath Reservoir, nr **Wolver-hampton**. Good coarse fishery with carp, tench, big bream. Leased to Blackford Progressive AS.

Lodge Farm Reservoir, Dudley. Coarse fishery. Enquiries to Dudley Corporation.

Himley Hall Lake, Himley. Trout, coarse fish. Enquiries to Dudley Corporation.

Trench Pool, Telford. 16 acres, coarse fishing.

Elton Reservoir, Greater Manchester. Leased to Bury AA.

Wern Clay Pits, Montgomery. Leased by Mid-Wales Glass AC.

Stanley Reservoir, Stoke-on-Trent. Coarse fishery leased by Stoke-on-Trent AS.

Sulby Reservoir, Northants. Specimen carp to 36lb, numerous 20lb fish. Limited dt. Unique platforms designed exclusively for carp fishing. Contact Southern Region. Annual permits only.

Huddersfield Narrow Canal Reservoirs. **Brunclough**, Saddleworth & Dist AS water; **Tunnel End**, vacant; **Redbrook**, Cairo Anglers; **March Haigh**, vacant; **Black Moss**, vacant; **Swellands, vacant**; **Slaithwaithe** and **Sparth**, Slaithwaite & Dist AS waters. **Diggle**, Pennine Shooting and sports AS.

Welford Reservoir, Northants. Bream, tench and pike to 20lb plus. Permits from Mr Williams (Tel: 01858 575394).

Lower Foulridge Reservoir, Borough of Pendle Council, Town Hall Pendle BB8 0AQ (Tel: 0282 865500).

English Sea Fishing Stations

In the following list the principal stations are arranged in order from north-east to south-west and then to north-west. Sea fishing can, of course, be had at many other places, but most of those mentioned cater especially for the sea angler. Clubs secretaries and tackle shops are usually willing to help visiting anglers either personally or by post on receipt of a stamped and addressed envelope. Details of accommodation, etc, can generally be had from the local authority amenities officer or information bureau of the town concerned. Those fishing the Devon and Cornwall estuaries should be aware of prohibitions on the taking of bass in some areas.

Seaham (Co Durham). Cod, whiting, flounder (winter); coalfish, flounder, plaice, dab, mackerel, cod (summer). Excellent fishing from North and South Piers, open only to members of Seaham SAC, Clifford House, South Terrace, SR7 7HN. Club has 500 members, and well equipped HQ; promotes annual competitions and active junior section. Membership £12, conc. Further information from Mr Norman Conn, Competition Sec (Tel: 0191 5810321). There is disabled access on both piers, and promenade. Tackle shop: Bait Box, 5 North Terrace, Seaham (Tel: 0191 5819585).

Sunderland (Co Durham). Fishing from river, pier, beaches and rocks, for codling (best Oct–Apr), whiting (best Sept–Feb), coalfish, flounders, eels, throughout year. Roker Pier provides good sport with cod and flatfish. North Pier is free of charge to anglers, good access for disabled. Several small-boat owners at North Dock will arrange fishing parties, but there are also good beaches. R Wear banks at entrance good for flounders throughout year. Bait can be dug in Whitburn Bay and bought from tackle shops. Clubs: Sunderland Sea AA, membership £7 per year; Ryhope Sea AA (both affiliated to Assn of Wearside Angling Clubs). Tackle shop: Rutherfords, 125 Roker Ave, SR6 0HL (Tel: 01915 654183). Hotels: Parkside, 2 Park Ave; Parkview, 25 Park Ave.

Saltburn (Cleveland). Flatfish, coalfish, codling, whiting, mackerel, gurnard, some bass in summer and haddock late autumn. Float-fishing from pier in summer gives good sport; good codling fishing Oct to March.

Redcar (Cleveland). Five miles of fishing off rock and sand. Principal fish caught: Jan–April, codling; April–June, flatfish; summer months, coalfish (billet), whiting, mackerel, gurnard.

Larger codling arrive latter part of August and remain all winter. South Gare breakwater (4m away); good fishing, but hard on tackle, spinning for mackerel successful. Good fishing from beach two hours before and after low tide. Competitions every month. Tackle shops: Redcar Angling Centre, 159 High St, Redcar TS10 3AH; Anglers Services, 27 Park Rd, Hartlepool.

Whitby (N Yorks). A popular centre for boat fishing on hard ground and wrecks, with charter boats travelling up to 60 miles from Whitby. Cod taken from boats, British record cod, 58lb 6oz caught here, as well as catches of haddock, coalfish, whiting, flatfish, sea bream, catfish, ling, mackerel, etc. Boat festival in July. West Pier: fishing only from lower part of pier extension. Mainly sandy bottom, but weeds and rock towards end. Billet, codling, flatfish, mackerel and whiting in season. East Pier: mainly on rocky bottom, weed off pier extension. More and bigger codling off this pier. Beach fishing from the sands either to Sandsend or Saltwick: billet, codling, flatfish, whiting, mackerel, a few bass. Small area at end of New Quay Rd for children only. No fishing allowed in harbour entrance. Best baits are lugworm, mussel, peeler crab. Local assn: Whitby Sea Anglers, meets in winter only, at Pier Inn, Pier Rd. Boats to accommodate 8 to 12 persons on hire at quays: Mermaid, P O Box 38, Whitby YO22 4YH (Tel: 01947 603200); Achates (Tel: 01947 605535); Chieftain, (Tel: 01947 820320), and others. For boats, accom, rod hire, contact Skipper of Enterprise: Tony Stevens, 7 Vicars Croft, Northallerton DL6 1JQ (Tel: 01609 780412). Tackle shop: Rods and Reels, 67 Church St (Tel: 01947 825079).

Scarborough (N Yorks). Sea fishing good from boat or harbour piers most of year.

Autumn whiting very good in bay. West Pier fishes on sandy bottom, East Pier on rock, with better chances of bigger codling. Marine Drive good all year round cod fishing. Codling most plentiful Aug onwards. Winter codling fishing from First or Second Points to south of Scarborough and the Marine Drive. Mackerel, June–Sept, float or spinning. Various boats take out parties; bags of 3–4,000lb of cod in 12hr sessions sometimes taken. Many over 20lb, ling also, 20lb plus from wrecks. Festival in Sept. Tackle shops: at 56 Eastborough, and Buckley's Angling Supplies; 6 Leading Post Street YO11 1NP, Tel: 01723 363202 (who issue dt for the Mere; coarse fish). Charter boats for hire, taking 8–12 anglers. Charge: approx £2.50 per person for 4 hrs but longer trips to fish reefs and wrecks now popular. Valhalla (Tel: 01723 362083); Wandering Star (Tel: 01723 374885); Sea Fisher, (Tel: 01723 364640); Linda Maria, (Tel: 01482 823644); Eva Anne, (Tel: 01723 352381). Harbour Master: Harbour Dept, 18 West Pier, YO11 1PD (Tel: 01723 373530).

Filey (Yorks). Cod, coalfish, ling, mackerel, flatfish, bass, pollack. Famous Filey Brigg, ridge of rocks from which baits can be cast into deep water, is fishable in most weathers and tides. Ledgering with crab and mussel baits (summer), worm and mussel (winter) can produce good catches of cod, coalfish and wrasse. Use of a sliding float with mussel, and mackerel bait is effective technique for coalfish, pollack and mackerel (Jul–Sept). At Reighton Sands, ledgering with mussel, rag, lug and mackerel baits can produce flounders, some dabs, and occasional plaice or bass. Preferred method for bass is spinning. Local bait digging prohibited, good supplies from local tackle shop. One charter boat operating, ideal launching site for small privately owned boats. Local clubs: Filey Brigg AS (st £3) organises fishing festival every year (first week of Sept), with 6 boating and 8 shore events. Filey Boat AC. Good flyfishing for coalfish (billet) from Brigg. Tackle and bait from Filey Fishing Tackle, 12 Hope St YO14 9DL (Tel: 01723 513732). Hotel: White Lodge, The Crescent YO14 9JX.

Bridlington (N Humberside). South Pier may be fished free all year and North Pier in winter only. Sport in summer only fair – small whiting, billet, flatfish mainly – but good codling from Dec–March. Launches and cobles sail daily from Harbour at 06.30, 09.30, 13.30, 18.00 during summer. They operate from 3 to 60 mile radius around **Flamborough Head**, or wrecks.

Catches include cod, haddock, plaice, ling and skate. Rock fishing from shore at Thornwick Bay. Bait: lugworm may be dug in South Bay and small sand eels caught by raking and digging on edge of tide. Sea angling festival Sept 18–23. Boats: D Brown, 81 Queensgate (Tel: 676949), I Taylor (Tel: 679434), (British record ling caught from this vessel); J Jarvis (Tel: 604750); Cobles: R Emerson (Tel: 850575). Tackle shop: Linford's, 12 Hilderthorpe Road. Hotels: Windsor, Lonsborough and others.

Hornsea (N Humberside). Tope, skate, flounders, occasional bass from shore; cod, haddock, plaice, dabs, tope, skate from boats. May to Oct. Whiting, dabs, codling, Oct to May.

Grimsby (NE Lincs). Sea fishing along Humber bank free, and along foreshore to Tetney Lock; plaice, codling, dabs, flounders, eels. West Pier: st from Dock Office. Boat fishing: 12 hour trips, mainly around oil rigs. Tel: 01472 885649 or 72422. All boats and persons in charge of boats must be licensed by N.E. Lincolnshire Council. Enquiries to Municipal Office, Town Hall Square DN32 7AU (Tel: 01472 324770, Fax: 324785). Good centre for fens and broads. Clubs: Humber SAC, Cromwell Social Club (SA section). Tourist Information: Alexandra Rd, Cleethorpes (Tel: 01472 323111). Tackle shops: Fred's Fishing Tackle, 413 Weelsby St; Lightwoods, 172 Cleethorpe Rd; Garden & Pet Centre, 25 Louth Rd; Sparks Bros, 43 Cromwell Rd; M.T.S. Tackle, 168E Sutcliffe Ave, all Grimsby; Tight Lines, 51 Cambridge St, Cleethorpes. Many hotels and B&B.

Mablethorpe (Lincs). Good sea fishing from Mablethorpe to Sutton-on-Sea. Beach all sand; mainly flatfish, but some bass, skate, mackerel, tope from boats. Cod in winter. Sept–Dec best. Boat fishing limited by surf and open beach. Good flounders in Saltfleet Haven; also sea trout in Sept. Local club: Mablethorpe, Sutton-on-Sea and Dist AC (water on Great Eau for members only). Tackle shop: Bela's, 54–56 High Street. Hotels at Mablethorpe, Trusthorpe, Sutton-on-Sea.

Skegness (Lincs). Beach fishing for cod, dab and whiting in winter; silver eels, dabs and bass in summer; whiting and dab in Sept and Oct. Chapel Point (producing many cod over 4lb), Huttoft Bank and Ingoldmells the best beaches in winter, 3 hrs before high tide until 2 hours after. Lugworm best bait. No charter boats operate in Lincolnshire. Club: Skegness SAC.

Tackle and bait from Skegness Fishing Tackle, 155 Roman Bank; Palmers, 11 High St (Tel: 01754 764404).

Salthouse, near **Sheringham** (Norfolk). Sea here is deep quite close in shore, and fishing considered good. Good flatfish, Oct–Jan. Occasional bass and mackerel in summer. Guest house: Salthouse Hall.

Sheringham (Norfolk). Flatfish all year; cod autumn and winter, mackerel June–Sept. Beaches good all year, best months April and May. Best sport west of lifeboat shed towards Weybourne or extreme east towards Cromer. Centre beaches too crowded in season. Bait can be ordered from tackle shops. Boat fishing best well off shore. Tope to 40lb and thornbacks to 20lb; plenty of mackerel. Blakeney: good launching ramps.

Cromer (Norfolk). Good all-year fishing; mainly cod (Sept–April), whiting and dabs, with odd tope (summer); skate and bass (summer) from pier (50p) and beaches. Around the third breakwater east of the pier the water is deeper, last three hours of flood tide best time. Occasional mackerel from end of pier. Boat fishing in calm weather (beach-launching). Fresh lugworm baits, and dt for local coarse fishing, obtainable from tackle shop: Marine Sports Shop, 21 New St, Cromer, NR27 9HP (Tel: 01263 513676); open Sundays. Hotels: Cliftonville, Red Lion, Hotel de Paris, Cliff House, Western House, recommended for anglers.

Great Yarmouth, (Norfolk). All styles of sea fishing catered for, including two piers, several miles of perfect shore line for beach angler, two miles of well-wharved river from harbour's mouth to Haven Bridge, and boat angling. To north are Caister, Scratby, Hemsby, Winterton, Horsey, Sea Palling, Weybourne etc, and to south, Gorleston-on-Sea and Corton. The riverside at Gorleston from the lifeboat shed leading to the harbour entrance, and Gorleston Pier are popular venues. Sport very similar in all these places; Sept–Jan, whiting, dabs, flounders, eels, cod from latter end of Oct. From Apr–Sept, Winterton known for good bass fishing. Most successful baits are lugworm, herring or mackerel; lug, peeler crab and squid for bass, flatfish etc, Apr–Sept. Boats: Bishops, Tel: 01493 664739; Dybles: (*below*). Tackle shops: Dave Docwra, 79 Churchill Rd; Gorleston Tackle Centre, 7/8 Pier Walk; Dyble & Williamson, Scratby Rd, Scratby, NR29 3PQ (Tel: 01493 731305).

Gorleston-on-Sea (Norfolk). Whiting, cod, dabs and flounders from beaches and in estuary (best Oct to March); good skate Aug and Sept. Sport good in these periods from boats, pier or at Harbour Bend in river and on beaches. Baits: lugworm, crab and ragworm. Freshwater fishing (coarse fish) within easy reach on rivers and broads. Boats: Bishop Boat Services, 48 Warren Rd, Tel: 664739. Tackle shops: Gorleston Tackle Centre, 7/8 Pier Walk; Greenstead Tackle Centre, 72 High St.

Lowestoft (Suffolk). Noted centre for cod, autumn–May. Also whiting, flatfish, pollack and coalfish, with bass, tope, ray from charter boats and mullet in warmer months. Lugworm best bait. Good sloping beaches to north and south. Hopton, Pakefield, Kessingland are best. North best on flood, south on ebb. Club: Lowestoft SA (Tel: 01502 581943). Baits from tackle shop: Sam Hook (Lowestoft) Ltd, Bevan Street East, (Tel: 01502 565821). Further information from Tourist IC, The Esplanade (Tel: 01502 523000).

Southwold (Suffolk); ns Halesworth. Good codling, whiting, bass, plaice, flounder, dab, pollack, mackerel, mullet fishing from beach, October to March. Bass main species in summer from harbour or shore; soles and silver eels also provide sport May to Sept. Reydon Lakes are local freshwater fishery. Licences from Purdy's Newsagents, High St. Hotels: Swan, Crown, Red Lion, Avondale.

Felixstowe (Suffolk). Fishing in autumn and winter for cod and whiting. Excellent bass fishing in recent years, with fish well into double figures from sea front and Rivers Orwell and Deben; garfish by day and sole at night, and with eels in the estuaries, May–Sept; flounders from Oct–Jan from the Orwell towards Ipswich. Skate fishing good in May, June and July, especially in harbour. Other species: pouting, plaice, tope. Good sport from boats, good fishing in evenings from Manor Terrace to Landguard Point, Sept onwards. Pier closed, pending restoration. Wrecking trips obtainable locally. Felixstowe SAS organises matches, beach festivals, and caters for the needs of boat anglers, with a compound of 50 dinghies adjacent to club HQ. Tackle shop: Castaway Tackle, 20 Undercliffe Rd West, IP11 8AW (Tel: 01394 278316).

Harwich and **Dovercourt** (Essex). Bass, mullet, eels, garfish, flatfish, sting-ray, thornback, skate, soles (all May to Sept), whiting, pouting, codling (Sept to March). Best fishing from boats, but Stone Breakwater, Dovercourt is good. Several good boat marks in estuary of Stour and Orwell and in harbour approaches. Best baits: lug, king rag, soft and peeler crabs. Boats: Bartons Marina, 8 West St, Tel: 01255 503552, or V Caunter, Tel: 01255 552855. Club: Harwich AC (freshwater). Tackle shop: Dovercourt Aquatics and Angling Centre, Main Rd, Dovercourt, Harwich. Copy of Borough Guide supplied by Town Clerk on request.

Walton (Essex). Cod, skate, mullet and dab are species most commonly caught, best fishing is from pier, Frinton Wall and Frinton Sea Front. Cod fishing begins about second week in Sept and runs to end of March. Club: Walton-on-Naze Sea AC. Boats may be chartered in Walton: S Murphy, Tel: 01255 674274. Tackle shop: J Metcalfe, 15 Newgate St. Hotels: Elmos, Queens.

Clacton (Essex). Mainly autumn and winter fishing for whiting and cod. Summer fishing from beach, pier and boats for dabs, plaice, bass, eels, thornback, dogfish, tope, sting ray to 50lb (Walton-on-Naze). Matches arranged by Clacton Sea AC, membership £7 p.a. Tackle shop: Brian Dean, 43 Pallister Road, Tel: 01255 425992; baits, permits and information. Hotels: Frandon, Kingscliff, many others, from Tendring T.I., Clacton, Tel: 01255 423400.

Southend-on-Sea (Essex). Mullet, bass, mackerel, scad, garfish, plaice and flounders are the main catches from the pier during the summer, with cod, codling and large flounders in the winter. A fleet of registered charter boats operate from the Pierhead, but prior booking is essential. Thornback, stingray, smoothhound, bass, tope, plaice and cod can be caught. Pier: st day £41.46, night £37.40; dt £2.60. Application form from Southend Council, Directorate of Leisure Services, Civic Centre, Victoria Ave SS1 3PY. Off season shore fishing in vicinity, with all year round facilities at the Thorpe Bay and Westcliff bastions, also the river Crouch. Numerous open, pier, shore and boat events organised. Charter boats: "Predator" operates 7 days a week, for parties and individuals; bait and tackle supplied; D Godwin, 70 Sutton Ct, Pantiles SS2 4BJ; Skerry Belle, Colin Bond (Tel: 01702 308043). Tackle shops: Southend Angling Centre, 5/6 Pier Approach SS1 2EH, has a variety of local freshwater fishing permits on sale; Jetty Anglers; Essex Angling Centre (Westcliff).

Sheerness (Kent). Venue of British Open in Nov. Popular marks around Sheerness are Bartons Point; New Sea Wall, Garrison; East Church Gap; cod and whiting plentiful from beaches in autumn. Tackle shop: Island Bait & Tackle Shop, 57 High St (Tel: 01795 668506). Fresh baits always obtainable.

Whitstable and **Tankerton** (Kent). Good fishing in spring and summer on shore between Swale and Whitstable. Dabs, plaice, bass, skate, flounders, eels, etc. Lugworm and white ragworm are to be found in shallow areas. Peeler crabs are plentiful in Swale estuary. Cod in winter from Tankerton beach. Boats for hire. Freshwater fishing on Seasalter Marshes, near Whitstable; roach, rudd, tench, pike, eels. T I Centre: Horsebridge, Whitstable.

Herne Bay (Kent). Excellent spring fishing for flounders, bass and eels, bags of up to 20lb may be expected on peeler crab bait, which can be collected locally or bought at tackle shops in April and May. In June, bass move into the shallow warm water of the estuary. These may be caught with the last of the peeler crab, ragworm, and by spinning. In July and August bass are plentiful, black bream, lesser spotted dog, smoothhound and stingray may be caught with ragworm on beaches between Bishopstone and Reculver. Local record stingray, over 40lb. Whiting in autumn and winter on main beaches: just after dark is the best time to fish for them. Excellent facilities for anglers with own dinghies to launch and recover from new slipway. Local information on best marks, etc, from tackle shops. Club: Herne Bay AA, HQ 59/60 Central Parade. Tackle, bait and licences: Ron Edwards, 50 High Street; Herne Bay Angling, 224 High St. Hotels: Victoria, Adelaide and Beauville Guest Houses, all Central Parade.

Margate (Kent). Noted for mixed catches. Fine bass often taken from shore on paternoster, and boat by spinning. Stone pier good for cod and whiting in winter. Bass and cod from rocks at low water. Cod best Nov to May; fish up to 20lb. April and May mixed bags of bass and eels. Most popular rock marks are at Foreness, Botany Bay, Kingsgate, Dumpton Gap. Skate at Minnis Bay, Birchington. Tope fishing from boat from June on through summer. Also dogfish and conger. Tackle shop: Kingfisheries, 34 King Street.

Broadstairs (Kent). Bass, plaice, flounders eels, from beaches or stone jetty. Best in winter months. Lugworm usual bait, dug in Pegwell Bay. T I Centre: Pierremont Hall, High St.

Ramsgate (Kent). Good sport along 2m of shore, harbour piers (free fishing), and Eastern and Western Chines. East Pier gives ample scope, best in winter. Beaches crowded in summer, so night fishing best. In spring and summer good bass fishing (from shore), also soles, flounders, dabs and thornbacks. In autumn and winter; cod in large quantities, whiting. Pegwell Bay Foreness and Dumpton Gap are good boat marks for mackerel, bass and pollack. Five boats operate at harbour. Goodwin Sands produce skate, bass, dogfish, spurdog, tope and plaice. The Elbow and Hole in the Wall, also marks for boat fishing. Lugworm may be dug in Pegwell Bay. Licences, baits, fishing trips and freshwater angling information from tackle shop: Fisherman's Corner, 6 Kent Place. Charter boat for wreck fishing: A Booth, 6 St Augustines Park, CT11 0DE (Tel: 01843 595042). Hotels in Thanet too many to list.

Sandwich (Kent). Bass at the mouth of the haven; sea trout and mullet run up the river; flounders, grey mullet, plaice, dabs, codling and pouting more seaward. Entry to Sandwich Bay by toll road, 9am to 5pm. For winter cod fishing, deep water off yacht club end of bay is best. Local club: Sandwich and Dist AS. Hotels: Bell, Haven Guest House. *For freshwater fishing, see Stour (Kent).*

Deal and **Walmer** (Kent). Excellent sea fishing throughout the year from beaches and Deal Pier, open 8am to 10pm, all night Friday and Saturday. Winter cod fishing, from Sandown Castle, Deal Castle, Walmer Castle. Charter boats take anglers to the Goodwin Sands and the prolific waters of the Downs. Cod, skate and whiting in winter; plaice, dabs, sole, mackerel, eels, flounders, dogfish and garfish throughout summer. Strong tidal currents. Tables from local tackle shops. Deal & Walmer Inshore Fishermen's Assn supplies list of boats: David Chamberlain (Tel: 01304 362744). T I Centre: Town Hall, Deal. Clubs: Deal and Walmer AA; Deal 1919 AC. Tackle shops: The Foc'sle 33 Beach St; Channel Angling, 158/160 Snargate St, Dover CT17 9BZ (Tel: 01304 203742). B & B: Fairways (Tel: 01304 374387); Cannon Gate (Tel: 01304 375238); Malvern (Tel: 01304 372944).

Dover (Kent). Excellent boat and beach fishing in the area; cod taken from wrecks and sand banks; good fishing for bass, codling, whiting and flatfish. Good beach fishing from Shakespeare Beach. Prince of Wales Pier suitable for all anglers, incl junior and handicapped. Admiralty Pier controlled by Dover Sea AA: open 8am to 4pm, and 6am to 9pm Fri and Sat. £2.50 dt, conc. Access to Sandwich Bay is by toll road, £2.50. Boat trip (Dover Motor Boat Co, Tel: 01304 206809) to fish Southern Breakwater departs 9am from Dump Head, Wellington Dock, £3 + £3.50 fishing charge. Tackle shops: Bill's Bait & Tackle, 121 Snargate St; Brazils, 162 Snargate St (Tel: 01304 201457). Hotels: Ardmore, Beaufort, many others.

Folkestone (Kent). Good boat, beach and pier fishing. Conger, cod, bass, bream, flatfish, whiting, pouting and pollack, with mackerel in mid-summer. Pier open to anglers, £2.50 per day, £1 conc. Cod caught from boats on the Varne Bank all through the year, but from the shore, Oct–Feb only. Beach fishing best dusk onwards for bass and conger. The Warren produces good catches of cod in winter and bass in summer. Good sport from pier. Some good offshore marks. Popular rock spots are Rotunda Beach, Mermaid Point, Sandgate Riviera. For tickets, boats and bait apply: Folkestone Angling, 12 Tontine Street (Tel: 01303 253881). Tourist Information Centre, Harbour St CT20 1QN (Tel: 01303 258594, Fax: 259754). Hotels: Burlington, Windsor and others.

Sandgate (Kent). Very good fishing from beach and boats. There is a ridge of rock extending for over a mile 20 yds out from low-water mark. Bass good July–October; codling, whiting, pouting, conger March–May, August–Nov; good plaice taken May–June, especially from boats. Best months for boat fishing, Sept–Nov. Hotel: Channel View Guest House, 4 Wellington Terrace.

Hythe (Kent). Fishing from boat and shore for bass, codling, pouting, whiting, conger and flats. Princes Parade, Seabrook, is popular for cod fishing, between Sept and Jan, lugworm is the best bait. Open storm beach, giving pouting, whiting, mackerel, sole, dab and flounder in summer and cod (up to 25lb), whiting and pouting in winter. Few bass. Clubs: Seabrook Sea AS; Castaways Sea AS. Tackle shops: Hythe Angling, 1 Thirstane Terrace; Romney Tackle, 19 Littlestone Rd, Littlestone (Tel: 01797 363990). Hotels: Nyanza Lodge, 87 Seabrook Rd; Romney Bay House, New Romney.

Dungeness (Kent). Cod fishing around the

lighthouse, with whiting, and dab in winter, pout, bass, dab, eels and sole in summer. Best baits in winter are black or yellowtail lugworm. Denge Marsh is a top venue for sole, marks are at Diamond and towards Galloways, ragworm and lugworm for bait. Best months: May to Oct for boat fishing; Oct to Feb for shore fishing.

Hastings (Sussex). Sea fishing from pier and boats. Tope, bass, conger, plaice, codling, whiting, etc. Boats from local fishermen. Hastings and St Leonards SAA has its own boats on beach opposite headquarters; club boundary, Beachy head to R Rother at Rye. Guests £1 per day in boats. Winching facilities. Association also has clubroom on Hastings Pier. Annual International Sea Angling Festival in October. Bait, tackle: S.H. Tackle, Bohemia Rd; Steve's Tackle Shop, 38 White Rock TN34 1JL (Tel: 01424 433404); Redfearn's, 8 Castle Street, who have good knowledge of local coarse fishing, and have dt.

St Leonards (Sussex). Good sea fishing all the year round from boats and beach for flatfish, bass, mackerel, conger, tope, whiting, cod, bull huss, turbot. Boats and boatmen from Warrior Square slipway. St Leonards Sea Anglers' club house at 16 Grand Parade. Competitions run throughout the year, boats and beach. Annual subscription £9 + £2 joining fee. Concessionary £4.

Bexhill (Sussex). Boat and shore fishing. Cod, conger, whiting (Sept to end Dec). Dabs, plaice, mackerel, tope (July–Sept). Bass, best months May, June and July. Club: Bexhill AC (Hon Sec will help visitors, enclose sae). Freshwater fishing in Pevensey Sluice, Pevensey Haven and dykes; coarse fish. Tackle shop: Tight Lines. Hotel: Granville.

Eastbourne (Sussex). Boat, pier and shore fishing. Dabs, huss, pouting and conger (all year), cod in winter and skate (May to Dec). Best for plaice and bream from June to Nov. Also soles, whiting, flounders, mullet. Good bass and mullet in warmer months. Notable tope centre, many around 40lb; June and July best. Some of the best beach fishing for bass around Beachy Head (up to 17lb). Pollack from rocks. Flatfish off Langney Point and from landing stages of pier. Best marks for beach fishing are on east side of pier. West side can be rocky in places. Club: Eastbourne AA, Club House, Royal Parade, Tel: 723442. Membership £32 pa. Boats available to members, £42 pa. Tackle

shops: Anglers Den, Pevensey Bay; Tony's, 211 Seaside.

Seaford (Sussex). Beach and boat fishing. Bass, cod, codling, conger, flats, huss, mackerel and few ling and pollack. Good night fishing off beach. Catches of tope few miles offshore. Seaford AC has freshwater fishing on five local waters, members only (Tel: 01323 897723). Tackle shop: Peacehaven Angler, Coast Rd, Peacehaven.

Newhaven (Sussex). Centre for deep sea fishing. Beach fishing for bass excellent May–Oct, mackerel and garfish. Flounders from Tide Mills Beach. Good cod fishing from beaches between Seaford Head and Newhaven's East Pier, late Oct to early March. Breakwater gives good all-round sport, with bass, and cod all running large. Boat fishing excellent for cod in winter, large Channel whiting also give good sport. Monkfish off Beachy Head late August and Sept. Boats from Harbour Tackle Shop, Fort Rd (Tel 514441). Other tackle shops: Dennis's, 107 Fort Road; Book & Bacca, 8 Bridge Street. Hotel: Sheffield.

Brighton and Hove (Sussex). Very good bass fishing from boats, trolling with variety of plug baits, Apr–Oct. Charter boats operate from Shoreham, Newhaven and Brighton Marina, for deep sea and wreck fishing. In spring and summer boat fishing produces bream, bass, conger, tope, plaice and dabs; shore fishing: mackerel off marina wall, bass at night or l/w surf, mullet. Winter boat fishing for large cod, whiting, bull huss; shore for whiting, flounders and cod. Most dealers supply bait. Hove Deep Sea AC members launch boats from beach, and generally fish inshore marks. Membership £35 pa plus £30 joining, allows free use of boats, equipment, car park. Active social club. Tel: 01273 413000 for details. Marina arms for mackerel, garfish, pollack, occasional bass, fishing fee, £1.50 per rod per day. Tackle shop: Brighton Angler, 1/2 Madeira Drive BN2 1PS (Tel: 01273 671398).

Shoreham and **Southwick** (Sussex). Boat and harbour fishing. Bass (July and August); grey mullet, skate and huss (June to Sept); cod and whiting (Sept to Dec); dabs, plaice, pouting, black bream, mackerel and flounders (May onwards). Mullet fishing in River Adur near Lancing College very good July–August; light paternoster tackle and red ragworm recommended. Baits: white rag, red rag and lugworms may be dug from beach and mud banks of river. Mussels and other baits can also be obtained.

Worthing (Sussex). Beach and pier fishing. Flounder, bass, whiting, codling, plaice, mullet, eels. Mixed catches from boats. River Adur, east of Worthing, noted for flounders, mullet and eels. Bait digging in Adur restricted to between toll bridge and harbour. Local association: Worthing Sea AA (HQ, Worthing Pier). Tackle shops: Ken Dunman, 2 Marine Place BN11 3DN (Tel: 01903 239802), opp Pier entrance; Prime Angling, 74 Brighton Rd, Worthing, Tel: 01903 821594. Boats from harbours at Shoreham and Littlehampton. Popular one-day pier festival held in early September. Reduced fee to OAP and juniors.

Littlehampton (Sussex). Noted for black bream, which are taken in large numbers during May and early June, but wide variety, including skate, smoothound (spring), whiting and cod (winter best) and plaice. Mid-channel wrecking for cod, pollack, ling and conger (spring onwards). Well known marks are Kingmere Rocks for black bream, West Ditch for smoothound, Hooe Bank for conger. A large fleet of boats caters for sea anglers, and there is good fishing from beaches and in harbour. Boats from P Heaslewood, 100 Clun Rd BN17 7EB (Tel: 01903 730229); and others, full list from Harbour Master, Harbour Office, Pier Rd, BN17 5LR (Tel: 01903 721215). Tackle shop: Tropicana, 5 Pier Rd. B&B: Quayside, Pier Rd; Bunkhouse, Pier Rd.

Bognor Regis (Sussex). Good sea fishing at several marks off Bognor. Tope, bass, pollack, mackerel, whiting, wrasse. From May to July bream are plentiful. The conger, skate and sole fishing is very good. Grey mullet abound in the shallow water between Felpham and Littlehampton Harbour. Good cod fishing between September and November. Bass weighing 5–10lb and more caught from pier and shore. Good shore fishing for bass, mackerel, cod, smoothhounds off East and West Beaches at **Selsey**. Club: Selsey Angling & Tope Club. Tackle shops: Suttons, 7 Shore Rd, East Wittering; Raycrafts Angling Centre, 119 High St, Selsey (Tel: 01243 606039) who has tickets for Chichester Canal fishing.

Hayling Island (Hants). From the South Beach of Hayling Island good fishing can be had with a rod and line for bass, plaice, flounders, dabs, whiting, etc, according to season. Fishing from boats in Hayling Bay for tope, skate, bass, mackerel, etc, is popular and a much favoured area is in the vicinity of the Church Rocks and in Chichester Harbour. Portsmouth AS has coarse lake in area. Tackle shop: Paige's Fishing Tackle, 36 Station Rd, Hayling Island.

Southsea (Hants). Over 4m of beach from Eastney to Portsmouth Harbour provide good sport all year. Bass fishing especially good from spring to September. Flatfish and rays numerous, large mackerel shoals in midsummer. Best sport from boats. Boom defence line from Southsea to IoW, although navigational hazard, is probably one of the best bass fishing marks on the South Coast. Vicinity of forts yields good bags of pollack, bass, black bream, skate, etc. Tope fishing good during summer. Portsmouth, Langstone and Chichester within easy reach and provide good sheltered water in rough weather. Boats can be hired from Portsmouth boatmen. Club: Southsea SAC. Tackle shops: A & S Fishing Tackle, 147 Winter Rd, Southsea PO4 8DR (Tel: 023 92739116); Allan's Marine, 143 Twyford Ave, Portsmouth.

Southampton (Hants). Fishing in Southampton Water really estuary fishing; thus not so varied as at some coastal stations. However, flounders abound (float and/or baited spoon fishing recommended), and whiting, pouting, silver eels, conger, bass, grey mullet, soles, dogfish, thornback, skate, stingray, plaice, dabs, scad, shad, mackerel have all been caught. At the entrance to Southampton Water, in Stokes Bay and the Solent generally, excellent tope fishing may be had. Angling from Hythe Pier, and from Netley and Hamble shores, but best fishing from boats. Southampton Water is rarely unfishable. Good sport in power station outflow. Tackle shops: Eastleigh Angling Centre, 325 Market St, Eastleigh (Tel: 023 8065 3540); Angling Centre of Woolston, 6 Portsmouth Rd, Woolston (Tel: 023 8042 2299). Rovers, 135A High St, Lee on Solent.

Lymington (Hants). Sting-ray, smoothound, bass, eels in summer; cod, whiting, flounder, rockling, in winter. Hurst Castle and Shingle Bank good fishing all year round for bass, cod, garfish, mackerel, rays; Lymington and Pennington sea walls for flounders, eels, bass, mullet. For further information, W Ward (Tel: 0973 269745). Lymington and Dist SFC fishes areas from Eastern boundary of Emsworth to western side of Lyme Regis, including Solent and all round I of Wight. Charter skippers oper-ate from Lymington and Pennington Sea Wall. Around Needles area, good fishing for black bream, tope and bass in summer months; large cod, Oct–Feb. Tackle shop: Forest Sports and Tackle, 23 High St, Milford on Sea, Lymington, Hants SO41 0QF (Tel: 01590 643366).

Mudeford (Dorset). Christchurch Harbour at Stanpit is good for bass and grey mullet. All-round sea fishing in Christchurch and Poole Bay, the vicinity of the Ledge Rocks and farther afield on the Dolphin Banks. Fishing is free below Royalty Fishery boundary (a line of yellow buoys across harbour). Tope, dogfish, conger, bream, pout, pollack, whiting and good sport spinning for mackerel and bass. Plaice off Southbourne; flounders, dabs, skate and sole off beaches at Highcliffe, Barton and Southbourne; flatfish, bass, whiting, etc, from quay, beach, groyne or shore at Hengistbury Head; large tope, stingray, skate and occasional thresher shark off The Dolphins. Fairly good cod fishing in winter, Needles-Christchurch Ledge, Pout Hole and Avon Beach (off Hengistbury Head). Whole squid favourite bait, but large baited spoons and jigs also successful. Good sole from Taddiford and Highcliffe Castle (best after dark). Groyne at Hengistbury good for bass in summer; sand eels by day and squid by night. Best months for general sport, mid-June to mid- or late Sept. Most local fishermen now take parties out mackerel fishing in summer. Flounders, eels, bass and mullet taken inside the harbour. Boats from R A Stride, The Watch House, Coastguards Way, Mudeford. Hotels: Avonmouth, Waterford Lodge, The Pines Guest House. For tackle shops and freshwater fishing, see Christchurch under Avon (Wiltshire) and Stour (Dorset).

Bournemouth (Dorset). Fishing good at times from the pier yielding bass, grey mullet, plaice, dabs, etc. Excellent catches of plaice, dabs, codling, silver whiting, mackerel (spinning), tope up to 40lb, conger, skate, from boats. Shore fishing, when sea is suitable, for bass and other usual sea fish. Bait supplies fairly good. Club: Christchurch & Dist FC. Tackle shops: Christchurch Angling Centre, 7 Castle Parade, Iford Bridge, Bournemouth. Good accommoda-tion for anglers at Edelweiss Guest House, 32 Drummon Rd; Bournemouth Fishing Lodge, 904 Wimborne Rd, Moordown. For freshwater fishing, see Avon (Wiltshire) and Stour (Dorset).

Poole (Dorset). Boat, beach and quay fishing in vast natural harbour. Great variety of fish, but now noted for deep-sea boat angling and bass fishing. Conger, tope, bream, etc, are caught within three miles of the shore. Bass, plaice, flounders, etc, caught inside the harbour at Sandbanks and Hamworthy Park in their sea-sons. Local tackle shops should be consulted for up-to-the-minute information. Boat fishing facil-ities largely controlled by Poole Sea Angling Centre (Tel 676597), which has over 20 boats for hire. Sea Fishing (Poole) Ltd, Fisherman's Dock, The Quay BH15 1HJ, also cater for bass and deep-sea angling (Tel: 01202 679666). Baits favoured locally: mackerel, squid, sand eel and ragworm. Tackle shops: Poole Sea Angling Centre, 5 High Street; Sea Fishing Poole, Fisherman's Dock, The Quay.

Swanage (Dorset). Double high tide in Swanage and Poole Harbour. Species taken from pier and beach incl bass, mullet, pollack, mackerel, flounder, wrasse and pouting. Beach here too crowded for daytime fishing, but boat fishing is very good, with skate, conger, bream, huss, dogfish, pollack, large wrasse, tope and other species. Good cod fishing in winter, a few miles offshore, and boats are on hire at Poole and Weymouth. In summer, boats operate from Swanage Angling Centre, just off quay, or from Angling Club House, Peveril Boat Park. Local knowledge is essential, as tides and races are very dangerous for small boats. Several open angling competitions are held each year. Swanage T I Centre is at The White House, Shore Rd, Swanage BH19 1LB. Tackle and boat hire from Swanage Angling & Chandlery Shop, 6 High St. Many hotels.

Weymouth (Dorset). Centre for the famous Chesil Beach, Shambles Bank, Portland and Lulworth Ledges. The steeply sloping Chesil Beach provides year-round sport for many species, but autumn and winter best for mackerel, codling, whiting, bream and dogfish; beach fishes best at night; fairly heavy tackle required. Good conger fishing at the Chesil Cove end, Ringstead Bay, Redcliffe and round the piers. Piers yield good sport with grey mul-let. Good bass from Greenhill beach in heavy surf, with variety of flatfish at most times. Ferrybridge and the Fleet noted for bass, mullet and flounders. Boat fishing. In the area around Portland Bill some big skate and stingray give good sport, while the notable Shambles Bank continues to yield turbot and skate, etc. Lulworth Ledges have a large variety of fish including tope, blue shark, conger, skate, dogfish, black bream, pollack, whiting, etc. Best baits are lugworm, ragworm, soft crab, mackerel and squid. No boats from Chesil Bank, but 16 boatmen operate from Weymouth throughout year. Angling Society booklet from Weymouth Publicity Office, Weymouth Corporation and Hon Sec. Tackle shops: Anglers' Tackle Store, 56 Park Street; Denning Tackle & Guns, 114 Portland Road, Wyke Regis.

Portland (Dorset). Good bass fishing in harbour; live prawns for bait. Mullet, mackerel, whiting and conger are plentiful. Boats from fishermen at Castletown (for the harbour), Church Ope, The Bill and on the beach. Near the breakwater is a good spot, where refuse from the warships drifts up.

Bridport (Dorset). Beach fishing yields bass, pouting, flatfish, thornback rays and conger, with whiting and cod in winter and large numbers of mackerel in summer. From boats: black bream, conger, pollock, whiting, pout, dogfish, bull huss, rays, cod and wrasse, West Bay the angling centre. Burton Bradstock, Cogden, West Bexington and Abbotsbury are popular venues on Chesil Beach. Eype and Seatown favoured to west. Bait: lugworm, ragworm, squid, mackerel favoured. Boat hire from West Bay: Duchess II (Tel: 01308 425494); licensed for offshore wreck fishing trips. Club: West Bay Sea AC has thriving junior section with special competitions, etc. Tackle shops: West Bay Water Sports, 10A, West Bay, DT6 4EL (Tel: 01308 421800), boat fishing trips arranged; The Tackle Shop, Clarence House. Hotel: The George, West Bay.

Lyme Regis (Dorset). Bass may be caught from the shore. Best baits are live sand eel, fresh mackerel, (sometimes obtainable from motorboats in harbour), or ragworm from tackle shop. Mackerel may be caught from May to October. Pollack plentiful in spring months. Conger and skate can be caught from boats about 2m from shore. Deep sea day and half day trips from Charter boats bookable. Self-drive motor boats are on hire at the Cobb Harbour, also tackle, mackerel lines free of charge, salted bait available (Tel: 0976 528234). Information from Harbour Master, The Cobb, Lyme Regis DT7 3JJ (Tel: 01297 442137). Tackle shop: Chris Payne, The Tackle Box, Marine Parade (Tel: 01297 443373).

Seaton (Devon). Boat fishing. Pollack, pouting, conger, wrasse (March to Sept), bass (virtually all year, but best Sept–Nov), bream, mackerel,

dabs, skate, plaice, dogfish. Axe estuary good for bass, mullet and sea trout: dt from Harbour Services Filling Station, Seaton. Boat for disabled: (Tel: 01297 20194). Local Club: Beer and Dist Sea AC, c/o V Bartlett, 9 Underleys, Beer, Devon EX12 3LX. Tackle shop: Royal Clarence Sports, Harbour Rd, Seaton EX12 2LX (Tel/Fax: 01297 22276). Hotel: Seaton Heights (Tel: 01297 20932).

Sidmouth (Devon). Sea fishing in Sidmouth Bay. Mackerel (May to Oct), pollack (excellent sport spring and summer east and west of town), bass (to 13lb in surf at Jacob's Ladder beach during summer), wrasse, large winter whiting (July–Oct on rocky bottom), skate to 105lb and conger to 44lb have been taken; bull huss to 19lb, and tope. Also plaice, dabs, flounders and occasional turbot. Club: Sidmouth SAC. At **Budleigh Salterton**, a few grey mullet in river, but fairly uncatchable; beach best fished at night for flat-fish.

Exmouth (Devon). Main species caught here in summer are pollack, wrasse, pout whiting, garfish and mackerel. Favourite baits are lugworm, ragworm, peeler crab and sand eel. Pollack are caught on artificial sand eels. Popular places are: car park near Beach Hotel, docks area, estuary beaches, where flounders are caught, mid-Sept to Jan. Deep Sea fishing trips can be booked, with chances of big conger eel, or small cuckoo wrasse, from W Means, skipper of Cormorant. Details from tackle shop: Exmouth Tackle & Sport, 20 The Strand. Other charter boats: Foxey Lady (Tel: 01404 822181); Trinitas (Tel: 01626 865768), Pioneer (Tel: 01404 822183).

Dawlish (Devon). Dabs and whiting in bay off Parson and Clerk Rock and between Smugglers' Gap and Sprey Point. Mackerel good in summer. Conger eels and dogfish about ¾m from shore between Parson and Clerk Rock and Shell Cove. Good fishing sometimes off breakwater by station and from wall of Boat Cove. Boats from Boat Cove.

Teignmouth (Devon). Sea fishing ideal (especially for light spool casting with sandeels for bass). Bass, pollack, flounders in estuary. Mackerel, dabs and whiting in the bay. Good flounder fishing from the shore. Deep sea, wreck and offshore trips are possible. The town has an annual sea fishing festival. Club: Teignmouth SAS (HQ, River Beach). Fisherman's & Waterman's Assn, Mrs Joyce

Boyne, Talgarth, Higher Yannon Drive (Tel: 776716). Tackle shops: McGeary Newsagents, Northumberland Place (bait for sea angling, information); The Rock Shop, Northumberland Place. Boats and bait obtainable on river beach. Details of accommodation from Tourist Information Centre, The Den. It should be noted that the estuary is a bass nursery area between May and October.

Torcross, nr **Kingsbridge** (Devon). Hotel: Torcross Apartment Hotel, offering both self-catering facilities and high-class catering beside the Slapton Ley nature reserve and coarse fishery. Slapton Sands; ns Kingsbridge. The sea fishing is very good, especially the bass fishing. Hotel can make arrangements. For coarse fishing see *Slapton Ley.*

Torquay (Devon). Excellent centre for sea fishing, most species found. Base for famous Skerries Bank and Torbay wrecks; conger, cod, pollack, turbot, flatfish, whiting, etc. Hope's Nose peninsula provides best venue for shore angler, with bass and plaice mainly sought. Other species caught are dabs, wrasse, mullet, flounder, gurnard. Babbacombe Pier good for mackerel. Bass and pollack off the rocks. Natural bait hard to come by, but tackle dealers can supply. Local association: Torbay and Babbacombe ASA (membership £10, jun £3). Tackle shops: Quay Stores, Vaughn Parade. Details of accommodation from Local Authority Publicity Dept, 9 Vaughan Parade. *For freshwater fishing, including Torquay Corporation reservoirs, see Teign and Dart.*

Paignton (Devon). Summer and autumn best. Bass, mackerel and garfish can be taken from beaches between Preston and Broadsands and from harbour, promenade and pier respectively. Mullet also present, but very shy. Fishing from rock marks, too. Club: Paignton Sea AA, who have information service and social centre for anglers at HQ at Ravenswood, 26 Cliff Road, The Harbour (open 7.30pm onwards); annual membership £6; Mr Holman (Tel: 01803 553118). 5-day fishing holidays aboard Our Joe-L, from Parkholme Hotel, £199, contact Simon and Sandra Pedley, 5 Garfield Rd, TQ4 6AU (Tel: 01803 551504); Wreck fishing: Our Jenny (Tel: 857890); Sea Spray II (Tel: 851328); Gemini (Tel: 851766). Tackle shops: The Sportsman, 7 Dartmouth Rd; H Cove Clark, 45-47 Torbay Road; Venture Sports, 371 Torquay Rd, Preston. Details of accommodation from Tourist IC, Esplanade TQ4 6BN. Trout fishing 2½m away at

New Barn Angling Centre, a series of lakes and pools, £3 per day, fish caught extra, Tel: 553602.

Brixham (Devon). Boat fishing in bay for plaice, dabs, mackerel. Good pollack off East and West Cod rocks of Berry Head. Neap tides best; baits: worms or prawn. Farther out is Mudstone Ridge, a deep area, strong tide run, but good general fishing with big conger. Local boats take visitors out to deep water marks (wreck fishing) or to Skerries Bank, off Dartmouth, for turbot, plaice, etc; advance bookings (at harbour) advisable. Shore fishing: bass, pollack, wrasse, conger, mackerel from Fishcombe Point, Shoalstone and the long Breakwater. Grey mullet abound in the harbour area (bait, bread or whiting flesh). Bass from St Mary's Beach (best after dark) and south side of Berry Head (bottom of cliffs) for flat fishing. Sharkham Point good for mackerel and bass (float with mackerel, strip bait or prawn for bass). Mansands Point good for bass and pollack (float). Night fishing from Elbury or Broadsands beach for bass, flatfish or conger (use thigh boots). Club: Brixham SAA. Quayside Hotel has boats. Tackle shop: Quay Stores, 10 The Quay.

Dartmouth (Devon). River holds large conger, record around 60lb; thornback ray to 15lb: best bait, prawn; also dabs, flounder, mullet, pollack, pouting. Baits, squid, ragworm, peeler crab. Shore angling is best from late Sept. Good marks are Warfleet Creek, mullet; rocks at castle, with garfish, mackerel, scad, wrasse, bass and other species caught; Leonards Cove, bass, mullet, wrasse, pollack in summer, whiting and codling in winter; Combe Rocks, boat fishing for wrasse, pollack, dogfish, bass, garfish, mackerel, rock pouting, ling, conger; Western Black Stone, best at night for bass: Homestone Ledge and Mewstone are boat locations. Charter boats: Steve Parker (Tel: 01803 329414); Lloyd Sanders, (Tel: 01803 554341). Association Club House is at 5 Oxford St. Tackle shops: Sport 'n' Fish, 16 Fairfax Place, Dartmouth TQ6 9AB (Tel: 01803 833509); Sea Haven, Newcomen Road. Hotels: Castle, Victoria, Dart Marina. *For freshwater fishing, see Dart.*

Salcombe (Devon). Mackerel June to Sept and turbot, dabs, flounders, plaice, skate and rays rest of year. Entire estuary is a bass nursery area, and it is illegal to land boat caught bass between April–December. Plenty of natural bait. Beaches crowded in summer, but fishable in winter. Wreck fishing for conger, bream, etc. June–Oct. Turbot numerous. Boats:

Whitestrand Boat Hire, Whitestrand Quay TQ8 8ET (Tel: 01548 843818); Tuckers Boat Hire, Victoria Quay; both sell tackle and bait; Salcombe Boat Hire (Tel: 01548 844475). Club: Salcombe and Dist SAA (HQ: Fortesque Inn, Union St.); annual membership £6 (jun £3); annual festival, four weeks from mid-August; special prizes and trophies for visitors throughout season.

Newton Ferrers (Devon). Noted station on Yealm Estuary. All-year bottom fishing; bass, flounders, pollack (from rocks), with mullet, conger, mackerel and flat fish from boats; shark June–Oct. Good base for trips to Eddystone. Boats from D Hockaday (Tel: 359); L Carter (Tel: 210). Abundant bait in estuary. Hotels: River Yealm, Family, Anglers, Yachtsmen.

Plymouth (Devon). One of finest stations in country for off-shore deep water fishing at such marks as East & West Rutts, Hands Deep and, of course, famous Eddystone Reef. Specimen pollack, conger, ling, whiting, pouting, cod, bream and mackerel plentiful. Fishing vessels for charter are Decca and Sounder equipped – fast exploring numerous wrecks within easy steaming of port; outstanding specimens taken. Inshore fishing for same species off Stoke Point, The Mewstone, Penlee, Rame and The Ledges. Sheltered boat and shore fishing in deep water harbour and extensive estuary network – at its best in autumn for bass, pollack, flounders, thornback and mullet. Shore fishing from rocks at Hilsea, Stoke, Gara Point, Rame Head, Penlee and Queeners for bass, pollack and wrasse, etc. Beach (surf) fishing at Whitsands and sand bar estuaries of Yealm, Erme and Avon rivers for bass, flounder and ray. All angling associations in city – British Conger Club (affiliated with 97 sea angling clubs), Plymouth Federation Sea AC and Plymouth SAC – now under one roof, on waterfront, at Plymouth Sea Angling Centre, Vauxhall Quay. Visiting anglers cordially welcomed. Tackle shops: D K Sports Ltd, 88 Vauxhall Street; Osborne & Cragg, 37 Bretonside; Clive's Tackle and Bait, 182 Exeter St. Charter boats are all moored on Sea Angling Centre Marina, Vauxhall Quay, and ownership is as follows; D Brett (Tel: 01752 551548); G Hannaford (Tel: 500531); Mac (Tel: 666141); R Street (Tel: 768892); D Booker (Tel: 666576); R Strevens (Tel: 812871), G Dickson (Tel: 201572). Plymouth Angling Boatman's Assn (Tel: 01752 666576).

Looe (Cornwall). Important centre for all-round sport. Bass, pollack and mullet from 'Banjo Pier' breakwater, October to March. Excellent bass fishing in Looe River when fish are running, and mullet. Good rock fishing from White Rock, Hannafore, and westwards to Talland Bay, where pollack, bass, conger and wrasse can be taken. Eastwards, flatfish from beaches at Millendreath, Downderry and Whitsand Bay. Bass, flounders, eels, pollack and mullet from river at quayside and upriver. Excellent sport from boats on deep-sea marks; porbeagle, mako, blue and some thresher shark taken, and wide variety of other fish. Clubs: Looe is HQ of Shark AC of Gt Britain, Tel/Fax: 01503 262642, and is official weighing-in station for British Conger Club. Local club: Looe Sea AA. Deep sea boats and information from Colin Cotton, The Tackle Shop, The Quay, East Looe, PL13 1AQ (Tel: 01503 262189); Looe Chandlery, Millpool Boatyard, West Looe, PL13 2AE (Tel: 01503 264355); Fishing Co-operatives, The Fish Quay, East Looe, PL13 1DX (Tel: 01503 265444). Boat charges are £30 per head shark; £20 bottom fishing; £8 inshore. Looe Information Bureau is at The Guildhall, Fore St, PL13 1AA (Tel: 01503 262072).

Polperro (Cornwall). Few boats, shore fishing weedy. Bass, whiting, pollack, mackerel are most likely catches. Hotels: Claremont, Noughts & Crosses, Ship, Three Pilchards; also farm accommodation.

Fowey (Cornwall). Excellent sport with bass (June to Oct) in estuary and local bays from Udder to Cannis. Pollack numerous and heavy (20lb and more). Good bream, cod, conger, dogfish, ling, mullet, mackerel, wrasse, whiting and flatfish (big flounders and turbot). Bass, mullet and flounders taken from river. Par Beach to west also good for bass. Rock fishing at Polruan, Gribben Head and Pencarrow. Sandeel, rag and lugworm obtainable. Clubs: Polruan Sea AC, 9 Greenbank, Polruan; Foye Tightliners SAC, 20 Polvillion Rd, Fowey. Boats: Fowey Diving Services, 21 and 27 station Rd PL23 1DF (Tel: 01726 833920) has boats for 2 to 7 anglers, for day, half-day, or weekly hire. Tackle shops: Leisure Time, 10 Esplanade; Fowey Marine Services, 21/27 Station Rd.

Mevagissey (Cornwall). Excellent sea fishing, boat and shore, especially in summer. Shark boats are based here (local club affiliated to the Shark AC of Great Britain). Tackle Box will make arrangements for shark and deep-sea trips. £17 per day, £9 half day. Shore fishing quite productive, especially bass from beach. Good night fishing at Pendower and Carne beaches, near Veryan, in Gerrans Bay area; best on falling tide and at low water, best bait squid and lug worm. Rock fishing productive at Blackhead near St Austell, dogfish, pollack, wrasse, gurnard, garfish, plaice, flounder. Good pollack off Dodman Point and from marks out to sea. Bass in large numbers were at one time taken at the Gwinges, but few have been caught in recent years. Excellent sport with large mackerel at Gwinges and close to Dodman from late Aug. Sport from the pier can be very good at times, especially with mullet. Boatmen can be contacted through The Tackle Box, 4 Market Sq (Tel: 01726 843513). Club: Mevagissey SAC (HQ, The Ship Inn, Pentewan; visitors welcome). Annual sub £3.

Gorran Haven (Cornwall). Same marks fished as at Mevagissey. Rock fishing in area. Bass from sand beach. The Gorran Haven fishermen offer some facilities for visitors wishing a day's fishing. Excellent pollack fishing from boat with rubber sandeel off Dodman Point. Limited accommodation at the Barley Sheaf (1½m); also Llawnroc Country Club and houses.

Falmouth (Cornwall). Excellent estuary, harbour (pier, shore and boat) and offshore fishing, especially over Manacles Rocks. Noted for big bass and pollack, latter taken off wreck and rock marks. Pendennis Point for wrasse and pollack; St Anthonys Head for wrasse, black bream at night in autumn. Porthallow for coalfish and conger; Lizard for wrasse, mackerel, and conger at night. Bait in estuary or from tackle shops. For boat fishing: Blue Minstrel (Tel: 01326 250352); from Helford Passage, deep water wrecks; Gamgy Lady (Tel: 01326 375458); K&S Cruises (Tel: 01326 211056), MV Seaspray from Prince of Wales Pier; 2½ hr or 4 hr wreck fishing trips. Boats in St Mawes: M E Balcombe (Tel: 01209 214901). Tackle shops: Tackle Box, Arwenack St; AB Harvey, Market Strand. For wreck and shark fishing apply: Frank Vinnicombe, West Winds, Mylor Bridge, near Falmouth (Falmouth 372775). Charter-rates per rod £25, Per boat £180. Details of hotel accom from Town Information Bureau, Killigrew Street. *For freshwater fishing, see River Fal.*

Porthleven (Cornwall). Bass are to be taken from the rocks in Mount's Bay. Best bass fishing from Loe Bar, 1½m E. Good pollack and mackerel fishing outside the rocks. Nearly all

fishing is done from the Mount's Bay type of boat in deep water. For charter boats, contact Harbourmaster. Hotel: Tye Rock.

Penzance (Cornwall). Excellent boat, pier, rock and shore fishing for pollack, mackerel, mullet and bass. Long Rock beach recommended, best Jun–Nov; bass, ray, flatfish. Marazion beaches offer flatfish and ray. Pier at Lamorna, turbot, gurnard and dogfish. Breakwater at Sennen, the same. Boat trips can be arranged with The Shell Shop, Tel: 68565. Shark fishing also possible. Best months: June–Nov. Club: Mount's Bay AS (headquarters: Dolphin Inn, Newlyn). Annual fishing festival, five weeks, Aug–Sept. Tackle shop: Newtown Angling Centre, Newton Germoe.

Mousehole, via **Penzance** (Cornwall). Good station for fishing Mount's Bay. Excellent mackerel, bream, pollack, conger, whiting, bass close to harbour according to season. Sheltered from west. Rock fishing in rough weather. Bell Rock between Newlyn and Mousehole has produced record catches. Between Mousehole and Lamorna, Penza Point, Kemyell Point and Carn Dhu are marks. Charter boat: Talisman, contact S Farley, Tel: 01736 731895/731154. Best grounds: Longships and Runnel Stone. Good results with sharks. Hotels: The Ship, Old Coastguards, The Lobster Pot.

Isles of Scilly. From shores and small boats around islands, wrasse, pollack, mackerel, conger and plaice; farther off in deep sea, particularly on The Powl, south-west of St Agnes, big catches made of cod, ling, conger, pollack, etc. Mullet pay periodical visits inshore, but usually caught by net; bass rare in these waters. Some shark fishing, but visitors advised to take own tackle. Peninnis Head and Deep Point on St Mary's are good rock marks for pollack, wrasse and mackerel. Boating can be dangerous, so experience essential. Accommodation limited, early bookings advisable between May and Sept. Full information from Tourist IC, Porthcressa, St Mary's TR21 0JL (Tel: 01720 422536, Fax: 01720 422049). For boats inquire of St Mary's Boating Assn, "Karenza", Ennor Close, St Mary's. Several shops stock tackle.

St Ives (Cornwall). Bass, flounder, turbot, plaice, mackerel and garfish plentiful in St Ives area. Surf fishing from shore, especially from island, Aire Point, Cape Cornwall, Portheras, Besigrau, Man's Head, Clodgy Point; Godrevy Point offers mackerel, pollack and wrasse, which are also found at Navax Point. Chapel Porth good for ray and turbot. Boat fishing gives sport with mackerel (summer months) and large pollack (off reef from Godrevy Island). For boats contact Harbourmaster, Tel: 01736 795081. Bass, tope, mullet, flatfish and occasional sea trout taken in Hayle river estuary. Trout fishing on Drift Reservoir, Penzance and St Erth Stream (4m). Symons of Market Place, TR26 1RZ, sells tackle and bait, also local coarse permits. Tel: 01736 796200. Hotels: Dunmar, Demelza, St Margarets, and many others.

Newquay (Cornwall). Boat, beach; rock and estuary fishing. Mackerel (April to Oct); school bass (June–Sept); larger fish July onwards, including winter; pollack (May–Nov); flatfish, wrasse (May–Sept); whiting in winter. Mullet good from June–Sept. Beach fishing at Perranporth, Holywell Bay, Crantock and Watergate Bay: ray, turbot and plaice. Off-peak times only. Shark and deep sea fishing possible. For boats, contact Boatmans Assn (Tel: 01637 873585); Anchor Sea Angling Centre, (Tel: 01637 877613/874570), or Dolphin Booking Office (Tel: 01637 878696/877048). Trout fishing in Porth Reservoir. Sea trout and brown trout in Gannel estuary. Tackle Shop: Beach Rd; Goin Fishin, 32 Fore St. Numerous hotels.

Padstow (Cornwall). Trevose Head, Park Head and Stepper Point are good marks in summer for float fishing and spinning for mackerel, pollack, garfish, bass, wrasse, rays, dog fish, plaice, turbot, occ. tope, and in winter for whiting, codling, dogfish, conger. Carneweather Point nr Polzeath is recommended for all-year-round fishing with cod in winter, but beware of dangerous ocean swells. The beaches at Trevone, Harlyn, Mother Ivys, Boobys, Constantine, Treyarnon, Porthcothan, Mawgan Porth, provide surf casting for bass, plaice, turbot, rays. The estuary has good flounder fishing in winter. Clubs are Padstow AC, Social Club, Padstow; St Columb Club, The Red Lion, St Columb; Glenville Fishing Club, Social Club, St Dennis; or contact Treyarnon Angling Centre (Ed Schliffke), Treyarnon Bay, St Merryn, Padstow PL28 8JN, Tel: 01841 521157. Tackle shop: Treyarnon Angling Centre, provides shore fishing guide. Hotel: Treyarnon Bay.

Bude (Cornwall). Codling, flatfish, mackerel, whiting and dogfish from breakwater and Crackington Haven. Northcott Mouth Crooklets, Maer, for skate and flatfish. Widemouth Bay is good venue. Rays may be taken from shore in late summer and autumn. Rock fishing is to be had from Upton, Wanson and Millock. Several boats work from Port Isaac in summer. Club: Bude and Dist SAC, annual subscription, £3.50. Tackle shop: 'Tackle shop', The Wharf, Bude.

Hartland (Devon); ns Barnstaple, 24m. Good all-round sea fishing, especially for bass at times with india-rubber sandeel, prawn or limpet from beach or rocks according to tide (bass up to 11½lb have been caught); whiting, mullet, conger and pouting also taken. Hotels: Hartland Quay, New Inn, King's Arms.

Lundy (Bristol Channel). Good mackerel, conger, pollack and wrasse inshore. Ray, plaice, dabs, tope and bass at East Bank. 1¼ to 2½m E. Good anchorage at Lundy, but no harbour. Boats occasionally on hire for 8 persons fishing. For accommodation write to The Agent, Lundy, Bristol Channel, N Devon EX39 2LY.

Clovelly (Devon); W of Bideford. Whiting, cod, conger, bull huss, dogfish and the occasional plaice caught all the year round; ray in spring, bass and mackerel in summer. Few inshore boats; fishing from the breakwater forbidden from 9am to 6pm in summer. Hotels: New Inn, Red Lion.

Bideford (Devon). Bass (from the bridge, in summer) flounders, mullet higher up the river. Tackle shop: B & K Angling Supplies, 14 The Quay.

Westward Ho! (Devon). Extensive beach and rocks from which bass, dogfish, smooth-hounds, bull huss, tope and mackerel may be taken in summer; codling to 10lb in winter. Tackle Shop: Summerlands Tackle, 16–20 Nelson Rd, Westward Ho, EX39 1LH (Tel: 01237 471291). Baits, and advice offered to anglers.

Appledore (Devon), north of Bideford in Torridge estuary, in summer has good bass fishing from rocks. Cod and whiting in winter. Lugworm beds at Appledore and Instow. Few boats.

Ilfracombe (Devon). From pier: conger, pollack, whiting, dabs; key from Variety Sports (below). Capstone Point, bass, wrasse. Capstone Rocks, similar species; Watermouth Cove, mixed bag; pollack, coalfish, wrasse, bass, a few flatfish. From boat, conger, skate, ray; mackerel Jun–Sept. Cod Dec–Feb. Bait: mackerel, squid, sand eel. Boat hire: (Tel: 863460), (Tel: 864625), (Tel: 863849), or (Tel: 01271 867947). Club: Ilfracombe and District AA, c/o Variety Sports. Reservoir trout fishing (see freshwater section). Details of accom from Tourist Information Centre, The Promenade EX34 9HN (Tel: 01271). Tackle and bait from Variety Sports, 23 Broad St EX34 9EE (Tel: 01271 862039).

Lynmouth (Devon). Good harbour and boat fishing. Grey mullet and bass from harbour arm. Drift fishing for pollack and mackerel. Tope, skate and conger in Lynmouth Bay and off Sand Ridge, 1m. For motor boats with skipper (Tel: 015987 53207). Best months: June to Oct. Several hotels in Lynton and Lynmouth; details from Lynton Tourist Office, Town Hall, Lynton EX35 6BT (Tel: 01598 752225). (For freshwater fishing see Lyn).

Minehead (Som). Beach, boat and rock fishing, principally for tope, skate, ling, thornback ray, conger, cod, bass and flatfish (Dunster to Porlock good for bass from beaches). Dogfish in bay. Mackerel in summer. Harbour and promenade walls provide sport with mullet, codling and some bass. Boats: through the tackle shop named below, all year round. Bait from sands at low water. Club: Minehead and Dist SAC. Tackle shop: Minehead Sports, 55 The Avenue. For further information and for boats contact Information Centre, Market House, The Parade.

Watchet (Som). Watchet and Dist Sea Angling Society fishes all the year round, covering coast from St Audries Bay to Porlock Wier. Monthly competitions from piers and shore. Codling, bass, whiting, conger and skate, according to season. Good boat fishing. New members welcomed by AS.

Weston-super-Mare (Avon). Record list of the Weston-super-Mare Sea AA includes conger at 25lb, sole at 2lb 8oz, bass, 13lb, skate 16lb 8oz, cod at 22lb, silver eel at 4lb, whiting and flounder at 2lb. Best venues 2 hours either side of low tide are Brean Down, conger, skate; Weston Beach, whiting, flatfish; Knightstone, the same. Woodspring is fishable throughout year, best at autumn. Boat fishing, Tel: 01934 418033, or through Weston Angling Centre. For baits, beds of lugworms are to be found along the low water mark of the town beach and off Kewstoke Rocks. Also from Tackle shop: Weston Angling Centre, 25A Locking Rd, Weston-s-Mare BS23 3BY (Tel: 01634 631140).

Southport (Merseyside). Dabs and flounders, with whiting and codling in winter, chief fish caught here; also skate, mullet, dogfish, sole, plaice, conger, gurnard and some bass. Shore flat and sandy, and fishing mainly from pier. Local clubs: Southport SAS. Good coarse fishing on River Crossens run by Southport AS. Tackle shops: Robinsons, 71 Sussex Road.

Liverpool, Mersey is cleaner nowadays, and cod and whiting are taken at Alexander Dock.

Blackpool (Lancs). Seven miles of beach, and fishing from North Pier, but boat fishing is the best option, although fewer boats are now operating. Tickets for certain parts of Wyre from tackle shops. Chater boat: Steve Averdel (Tel: 07971 203607). Coarse fishing in Stanley Park Lake. Dt. Tackle shop: Howarth, 128 Watson Rd. Many hotels.

Morecambe and **Heysham** (Lancs). Beach and stone jetty fishing throughout year. Beaches yield plaice, flounders, dabs, bass and eels from June to October, and dabs, codling, whiting and flounders in winter. Estuary catches up to 100 flounders to 2lb weight at Arnside. Stone Jetty has been extended, angling free; good catches of plaice, flounders, codling, whiting. At Heysham Harbour and North Wall whiting, cod, flounders, dabs, pouting, conger and mullet can be taken. Storm Groynes is producing good flatfish. Club: Heysham AC. Tackle shops: Morecambe Angling Centre, Thornton Rd, Morecambe; Charlton & Bagnall, 3/5 Damside St, Lancaster.

Fleetwood (Lancs). Plaice, whiting, skate, codling, tope, etc, from boats and shore. Club: Fleetwood and District AC. Sea baits from tackle shop: Langhorne's, 80 Poulton Road, Tel: 01253 872653.

Barrow-in-Furness (Cumbria). Boat and shore fishing for tope, bass, cod, plaice, whiting, skate. Good marks include Foulney Island, Roa Island, Piel Island, Scarth Hole and Black Tower (Walney Island) and Roanhead. Good beach areas are Priory Point to Canal Foot, bait may be dug here, also, and Greenodd from sea wall alongside A590 and from car park.

ISLE OF WIGHT

The Island provides a wealth of shore and boat fishing, and sheltered conditions can always be found, Bass are the main quarry for beach anglers, but pollack, conger, mackerel, pouting, thornback rays, flatfish and wrasse, with occasional tope, are also taken. Black bream, skate and shark are caught by boat anglers as well as the species already mentioned. Cod run regularly to 20lb in autumn. Due to strong tides on the north coast and lack of harbours on the south coast, the visiting angler would be best advised to arrange boat trips with one of the local charter skippers working out of Yarmouth or Bembridge. Strong tides also mean heavy leads and sometimes wire line. There are a large number of fishing clubs on the island. T I centres provide information about them.

Alum Bay. This necessitates a steep descent from the car park down the steps provided. From March to October there is a chair lift in operation. Fishes well after dark for large conger, bass, rays and sole, especially when rough. From the old pier remains to the white cliffs is the main area, although the rocks to the east, towards Totland, make a good station from which to spin for bass in the tide race, or to light ledger with squid or mackerel. Deep water at all states of tide.

Atherfield. A number of record fish have been taken from this stretch. The beach is of shingle with scattered rock, easily reached via path alongside holiday camp. Bass, rays, pout, etc after dark, to mackerel, squid and cuttle baits. Crab bait produces smoothhounds. Ragworm fished over the drying ledge to the left of this mark produces large wrasse and bass, day or night. Large cod in late autumn.

Bembridge. Species to be caught include bass, pout, conger, ling, bream, dogfish, turbot, brill, pollack, skate and ray. The shore from Whitecliff to Bembridge is mainly rock formation with stretches of shingle and is good ground for bass and conger although not fished a great deal. Bass, mullet, eels, among the rocks. Here, the beach turns to fine flat sand and flatfish and bass are taken. Bembridge Harbour is a wide inlet with St Helens on the opposite bank. Shark fishing, July–August, drifting from St Catherines Light to Nab Tower. Boats and bait obtainable on shore. A sand gully near the "Crab and Lobster" can be fished from the rocks. Fine bream may be taken from boats on Bembridge Ledge, early May to June, plenty of mackerel, also. A good number of fish are taken in the harbour: flounders, eels, bass. Many large mullet can be seen but are seldom fished for. Very strong tide in narrowest part of entrance.

Kingrag and lugworm are good baits for ledgering and small mud ragworm on light float tackle is successful. Baited spoon or wander tackle works well for flounder and plaice. Sea wall at St Helens is a convenient place to park and fish over the top of the tide. Club: Bembridge AC, holds 12 competitions pa. Membership £12 annually.

Bonchurch. Bass, conger, wrasse and pout from beach. Good fishing in gulleys between the extensive rocks at flood tide, after dark, especially after a south westerly gale.

Brooke. A shallow water mark that fishes well when the sea is coloured. Expect conger, bass, pout, plus cod in late autumn. One good spot is to be found in front of easy cliff path, 200 yds to left of point.

Chale. Best beach for rays on island, reached by steep cliff path. Specimen small-eyed rays are taken on frozen sand eel, day or night, from Mar–Sept, when sea is coloured after a storm. Some bass and conger, plus mackerel in summer.

Colwell Bay. A shallow sandy beach with easy access. Bass, sole, wrasse after dark, when crowds have gone home.

Compton Bay. 1m west of Brooke. Long flat sandy beach with patches of flat rock. Occasional bass when the sea is rough. Avoid the rocks under the cliff at the west end, where there is a danger of major cliff falls.

Cowes. The River Medina runs from Newport to Cowes Harbour and offers flounder fishing throughout the year with the best sport from the late summer to autumn. The shoals move about the river with the tide and location is often a matter of local knowledge. As a general guide the fish may be expected further upstream on the stronger spring tides. Weights average up to a pound. Bass also move into the river and have been taken to 4lb, often on flounder tackle. Rowing boats may be launched from the Folly Inn on the East bank, reached by turning off the main Newport to East Cowes road. Kingston power station about a mile down from Folly is a good boat mark for school bass, plaice, sole. Mullet and silver eels may be caught anywhere. Ragworm is usually used in preference to lugworm.

Cowes Harbour. Bass, flounder, plaice and sole may be taken by the boat angler from either side of the fairway above and below the floating bridge and during the summer there are many large mullet within the harbour. Inside the breakwater to the east, flounder and plaice are taken on the bottom from along the edge of the hovercraft channel to inshore towards the East Cowes Esplanade. Flounder and plaice are also taken from the mud-flats outside the East Cowes breakwater.

West Cowes Esplanade to **Gurnard**. Float fishing and spinning from the slipways and jetties for bass and mullet. Along the Princes Green to Egypt Light, bass and conger can be found and in late summer bass often venture close in under the walls in search of prawns and may be taken by trailing a worm over the balustrade and walking it quietly along. At Egypt Light, the shingle slopes steeply so long casting is unnecessary, and tope have occasionally been landed here as well as bass to 8lb, and cod to 20lb in late autumn. The sandy patches among the rocks may yield sole and plaice in season. Free car parking here.

Freshwater Bay. Pouting, bass, small pollack and few conger. Fish from middle of beach when rough. Survey at low tide, then fish after dark. Very easy access.

Newport. Nearest sea fishing in River Medina; flounders, school bass, mullet, plaice, eels. Tackle/boat hire from Scotties, branch at 11 Lugley St, Tel 522115.

Newtown. Bass and flounders in Newtown River. Clamerkin reach is best, using light gear and ragworm. Limited access, as large area is nature reserve.

Ventnor to **St Catherines**. Series of rocky ledges and gullies, best surveyed at low water. Bass, conger, pout, wrasse etc after dark and some mullet during calm days.

Yarmouth. Flounder and mullet and school bass in harbour. Bass, rays and mackerel from pier in summer. Notable cod venue in late autumn but strong tides prevail.

Ryde. A very shallow, sandy beech, popular with holidaymakers. Bass, small pollack, plaice, flounders, eels, bream and grey mullet from pier. Conger, dogfish, dabs, skate, mackerel from deep water marks, and plaice, flounder, bass and sole fishing inshore. Cod up to 24lb taken in autumn. Sheltered resort giving ideal

fishing conditions all year. All beaches fishable. King rag and lugworm plentiful. Vectis Boating and Fishing Club offers annual membership. Details from Hon Sec (enclose sae). Boats can be hired along shore.

Sandown. Fishing from end of pier (daytime only) produces plaice, rays, bass and bream on sandy ground. Float fishing produces mackerel, scad, small pollack and mullet. Local club: Sandown and Lake AS, organising frequent open competitions. Visitors welcome. Membership £10 annually (£5 juveniles), dt £1 from pier. Boat hire and tackle: Scotties, 22 Fitzroy Street; Castaways, Clarendon Rd, Shanklin.

Seaview. From St Helens to Seaview the coast is a mixture of rocks and sand and shingle. Priory Bay is reached by boat and provides very good mackerel and bass fishing. Plaice may be taken to 3lb from early April, with lugworm. During the summer months bream can also be taken from this spot. From June onwards, bass and mackerel are shoaling and large catches from boats are common. Cod are also taken late in the year.

Shanklin. Pier has been demolished. Various other venues exist which fish well for specific species, such as sting ray, but require very detailed directions re access, times to fish, etc. Contact Scotties of Newport for such details, and to obtain a wide variety of suitable baits. Norfolk House Hotel, The Esplanade, PO37 6BN, offers fishing holidays of two or three nights, for experienced angler and novice, with two full days at sea with all bait and tackle supplied. Contact Alan Davis, Tel: 01983 863023.

Totland. Bass off shingle bank from boat. Bass, conger from shore. Fishing also from pier. Boats from Fair Deal Amusements, The Pier. Hotels: Chalet, Sentry Mead.

Totland Bay. Next to Colwell Bay, deeper water. More chance of bass, especially when rough. It's possible to fish straight from a car on the sea wall. Fishing is good beside the disused pier.

Ventnor. The western end of the beach is good for bass, skate, pout and conger and the sea wall in front of the canoe lake is a good bass spot. Boat (from Blakes) for pollack and mackerel. Club: Ventnor AC (associate members welcome). Tackle and bait: Bates & Son, 5 Spring Hill; J Chiverton 70 High St. Beach fishing *(see also Bonchurch)*.

Wootton. School bass and flounders.

Yarmouth. Bass, small pollack; pier fishing.

CHANNEL ISLANDS

Wide variety of sport from beaches, rocky headlands and boats. Many specimen fish landed from deep-sea marks. Shark fishing growing in popularity. Boats easy to come by.

Guernsey. No fewer than 52 different species are recorded in Bailiwick of Guernsey rod-caught record list. Guernsey is 15 miles from the Hurd Deep, near major shipping lanes, and hundreds of wrecks yield high catches. Inshore, many headlands offer first-class spinning, and a flat, sandy, west coast gives good surf-casting for bass and a few flatfish. Several Guernsey fish accepted as new British records. The most common species are bass, bream, conger, dog-fish, garfish, mackerel, mullet, plaice, pollack and wrasse. Anglers may fish anywhere from the shore except for marinas, the fisherman's quay, and the land reclamation to the south of St Sampson's Harbour. Bottom fishing is produc-tive in spring, late autumn and winter; spinning in summer. Long casting is no advantage, on westerly rocks. Baits: ragworm is found in the rocky bays on west coast, Grand Havre, Bordeaux North, to Beaucette Marina, Bellgreve Bay; lugworm in sandy bays, especially, Grand Havre, Cobo and Vazon. Crabs, prawns and white rag can also be obtained. In north east, Fort Doyle is one of the best marks; south east, Soldiers Bay. South west cliffs are fishable but dangerous. There are 9 different fishing competitions between June and December. Boat charter: D Lane, Mon Desir, Les Hautes Mielles, L'Ancress, Vale GY3 5JU (Tel: 01481 45444); Brian Blondel (Tel: 04481 101288); R Taylor (Tel: 37959); Belle de Serk, Fishing and Charter (Tel: 724677); G Le Tisseier, (Tel: 52620). Local clubs: Guernsey SAC; Guernsey Freshwater AC; Guernsey Mullet Club; Castaways AC, and others. Tackle shops: North Quay Marine, St Sampson's Harbour (Tel: 46561); Marquand Bros, North Quay, **St Peter Port** (Tel: 01481 720962); Western Tackle Supplies, Castel (Tel: 56080); Micks Fishing Supplies, Les Canns, Capelles (Tel: 700390); Tackle and Accessories, Wet and Wild Leisure, Mallard Complex, Forest (Tel: 66621). Baits, rod hire: Boatworks & Castle Emplacement, St Peter Port (Tel: 726071). For further information about Guernsey fisheries contact States of Guernsey Department of Fisheries, Raymond Falla House, PO Box 459, Longue Rue, St Martins, Guernsey GY1 6AF (Tel: 014812 35741, Fax: 35015). Tourist Information publishes official sea angling guide, £1, widely obtainable.

Jersey. Winter fishing yields pollack, ray and other flatfish, conger, a few bass, cod fishing can be good. Spring: garfish, early mackerel off such points as Sorel and La Moye; grey mullet, por-beagle, blue shark and other species. Summer is good for all forms of fishing, by boat on offshore reefs, which is 80% of charter angling. Excellent fishing for bream commences in May and con-tinues to Oct, fish up to 5lb. Rays (incl blonde rays, over 30lb) are caught in good quantities on inshore sandbanks, as well as brill and turbot, especially early and late season. In autumn, white-bait concentrates at places such as Belle Hougue bring in large mackerel and bass, and flatfish move into shallow waters in the Islands bays. Venues: St Helier's harbour heads; Noirmont Point; St Brelade's Bay; La Corbiere; L'Etacq; Plemont; Greve de Lecq; Bonne Nuit Bay har-bour; Bouley Bay harbour; Rozel Bay harbour; St Catherine's breakwater; St Aubin's Bay. Charter boats: "Anna II", from St Helier Marina, contact A Heart, Highview Farm, Rue de la Hauteur, Trinity (Tel: 01534 863507); "Theseus", D Nuth, Tel: 01534 858046). Local club: Jersey SFC. Jersey Freshwater AA has coarse and trout dt: R A Mallet (Tel: 01534 23882). Tackle shops: P.J.N. Fishing Tackle, 7 Beresford Market, JE3 4WN C.I. (Tel: 01534 74875); I S Marine, 15/16 Commercial Buildings (Tel: 01534 877755); J F S Sport, Green St; all St Helier.

ISLE OF MAN

The Island's coastline is extremely varied. The long, flat, surf beaches of the North contrast sharply with the sheer faces of the South. Similarly, its fishing methods and species of fish are equally diverse. Despite the Island's location, coastline and clean waters, saltwater angling from both shore and boat remains unexploited and largely undiscovered. Information is obtain-able from Isle of Man Tourist and Leisure Department, Information Bureau, Sea Terminal, Douglas, Tel: 01624 686766.

Castletown. Conger, pollack, cod, wrasse, tope, flatfish from beach and boat; best months, June to Oct. Big skate from boats 600 yds off Langness; best Aug–Sept. Boats for hire locally.

Douglas. Plaice, sole (British record lemon sole), coalfish, pollack, flounder from Victoria Pier; best months, May to Oct, coalfish, wrasse, cod, plaice, dabs, sole from boats in Douglas Bay. Rock fishing off Douglas Head; float or spinner (good for pollack). Cod, wrasse, red gurnard, plaice, Little Ness Head to Douglas Head; skate from boats 2m out, and large tope, conger, cod, etc. Club: Douglas (IOM) and District AC, annual membership fee £12 (£4 discount before 28 Feb), jun £3 (membership includes trout fishing rights in **R Glass**). Club sec/treasurer, Mrs Sue McCoubrey, 47 Hildesley Rd, Douglas, takes applications for membership. Tackle shops: Hobbytime, Castle St; Intersport, 58 Duke St. Also, Tackle Bow, at Foxdale.

Kirk Michael. Beach fishing from here to Point of Ayre is excellent for bass, flatfish, dogfish.

Laxey. Plaice, dabs and bass from March to Oct from beach. Cod, mackerel, flatfish, offshore from boats at Garwick Bay. Clubs: Garwick Sailing and Fishing Club.

Peel. Breakwater: cod, coalfish, dogfish plentiful all year round; mackerel, dogfish, coalfish, plaice, flounder, dabs (July to Oct). Beach: similar. Rock fishing: from Castle rocks and headlands plenty of pollack. Sand eel best bait all season. Limited lugworm on beach. Boat fishing, but hire limited: cod and haddock in winter. In spring and summer spur dogfish common.

Rock fishing off St Patrick's Isle for mackerel, wrasse, coalfish; float and spinner. Local club; Peel Angling Club.

Port Erin. Good sport from pier and breakwater for pollack, mackerel, wrasse, grey mullet, coalfish, angler fish and conger. The bay yields flatfish and mackerel, with cod in the colder months. Tackle shop: Henry Crellin, IOM Sea Sports Ltd, Strand Road. Hotels: Balmoral, Falcons Nest.

Port St Mary. Probably best centre on island. Pollack, coalfish, wrasse from rocks, pier, boats (most of year). Flatfish and mackerel offshore and pier during herring season. Tope, skate, cod, conger, ling from boats. Boats from J Williams, Beach Cliff, Bay View Rd and W Halsall, Lime Street PSM. Several competitions. Inquiries to Hon Sec, Southern AC. Visitors welcome. Tackle shop: The Tackle Box, Foxdale. Hotels: Station, Albert.

Ramsey. Free fishing from pier, dogfish, codling, whiting, flounder, dab, coalfish, plaice, mackerel, rockling; from Ramsey beach to Point of Ayre, same as pier, plus bass (Aug–Sept), tope, bull huss. Pollack also taken by spinning with artificial sandeel. For help with bait and boats, contact officials of Ramsey AC (Tel: 01624 812279, after 6pm); annual membership fee £10, conc 50p. Tackle shop: The Ramsey Warehouse, 37 Parliament Street. Hotels: Viking, Sulby Glen.

Fishing Clubs & Associations in England

The English fishing clubs and associations listed below are by no means the total number of those existing. Club secretaries retire or change address, often after a comparatively short term of office, making it all too probable that the address list is out of date by the time it is issued. This regrettable fact also applies to the club lists in the other national sections of the book. Please advise the publishers (address at the front of the book) of any changed details for the next edition. The names and addresses of countless more fishing clubs and associations may be obtained from the various regional offices of the Environment Agency, from British Waterways, and from such federated bodies as the British Conger Club, see below.

National Bodies

Anglers' Conservation Association
Jane James, Director
5H Alford Dairy
Aldermaston
Berks
RE7 4NB
Tel: 01476 61008
Fax: 01476 60900
Angling Foundation
Federation House
National Agriculture Centre
Stoneleigh Park
Warwickshire
CV8 2RF
Tel: 024 7641 4999
Fax: 024 7641 4990
Internet: www.british-
sports.co.uk
Association of Professional Game
Angling Instructors
Michael Evans, Secretary
Little Saxbys Farm
Cowden, Kent
TN8 7DX
Tel: 01342 850765.
Fax: 01342 850926.
Association of Stillwater Game Fishery
Managers
Packington Fisheries
Meriden, Coventry
West Midlands
CV7 7HR
Tel: 01676 522754
Fax: 01676 523399

Atlantic Salmon Trust
Director:
J B D Read
Moulin, Pitlochry
Perthshire PH16 5JQ
Tel: 01796 473439
Fax: 01796 473554
British Conger Club
Tom Matchett
112 Bearsdown Road
Eggbuckland
Plymouth
Devon PL6 5TT
Tel: 01752 769262
HQ: Sea Angling Centre,
Vauxhall Quay
Sutton Harbour,
Plymouth
Devon
Affiliated with 97 sea angling
clubs
British Record (rod-caught) Fish
Committee
David Rowe
Acting Secretary
c/o National Federation of Sea
Anglers
51A Queen Street
Newton Abbot
Devon TQ12 2QJ
Tel/Fax: 01626 331330
British Waterways
All fishery enquiries to
Fisheries Manager:
Brindley Suite, Willow Grange
Church Road, Watford
Hertfordshire WD1 3PA
Tel: 01923 208717
Fax: 01923 208717

Countryside Alliance
Robin Hanbury-Tenison
59 Kennington Road
London SE1 7PZ
Tel: 020 7928 4742
Fax: 020 7793 8484 (8899)
Freshwater Biological Association
The Director
The Ferry House
Far Sawrey, Ambleside
Cumbria LA22 0LP
Tel: 015394 42468
Fax: 015394 46914
Internet:
wiua.nwi.ac.uk/idm/fba.html
E-mail: CSR@wpo.nerc.ac.uk
Grayling Society
R Cullum-Kenyon
Hazelwood
The Green
Fairford, Glos. GL7 4HU
Tel: 01285 712530
Fax: 01285 713636
Handicapped Anglers' Trust
Taigh na Iasgair
Russell Close
Little Chalfont
Bucks HP6 6RE
Tel/Fax: 01494 764333
International Fly Fishing Association
Ian Campbell
Secretary and Treasurer
Cruachan
16 Marindin Park
Glenfarg
Perth & Kinross PH2 9NQ
Tel/Fax: 01577 830 582

Marine Biological Association of the United Kingdom
The Secretary
The Laboratory
Citadel Hill
Plymouth
PL1 2PB
Tel: 01752 633100
Fax: 669762/633102

National Federation of Anglers
Halliday House
Egginton Junction
Nr Hilton
Derbyshire DE65 6GU

National Federation of Sea Anglers
D Rowe
NFSA Development Officer
NFSA Office,
51A Queen Street
Newton Abbot,
Devon T12 2QJ
Tel/Fax: 01626 331330

Register of Experienced Fly Fishing
Instructors and Schools
Chairman
Richard Slockock
Lawrences Farm
Tolpuddle
Dorchester
Dorset DT2 7HF
Tel: 01305 848460
Fax: 01305 849060

Ribble Fisheries' Association
Keith B Spencer,
Chairman/Secretary
36 Heap street
Burnley BB10 1LR

Salmon and Trout Association
C W Poupard, Director
Fishmongers' Hall
London Bridge
London EC4R 9EL
Tel: 020 7283 5838
Fax: 020 7929 1389

Shark Angling Club of Great Britain
Linda Reynolds
The Quay
East Looe
Cornwall PL13 1DX
Tel/Fax: 01503 262642

The UK Fly Fisherman & Tyers' Federation
Keith Bartlett
1 Claremont Avenue
Bishopston
Bristol
BS7 8JD
Tel/Fax: 0117 983 3661
E-mail: info@fly-fisherman.org.uk

CLUBS

Abbey Cross Angling Club
P Jourdan
12 Burnside
Hertford
SG12 2AW

Accrington and District Fishing Club
A Balderstone
42 Townley Avenue
Huncoat
Lancashire
BB5 6LP

Addingham Angling Association
H D Sutherland
51 Moor Park Drive
Addingham
Ilkley
LS29 0PU

Aln Angling Association
L Jobson
Tower Showrooms
Alnwick
Northumberland

Alston and District Angling Association
J Pullin
Nether Leys
Wardway
Alston
Cumbria CA9 3AP

Altrincham and District Angling Club
P O Box 70
Altrincham
WA15 6HD

Alveston Village Angling Club
M A Pitcher
62 Avon Crescent
Stratford-upon-Avon
Warwickshire
CV37 7EZ

Ampthill and District Angling Club
R Ward
15 Kingfisher Road
Flitwick
Bedfordshire
MK45 1RA

Annan and District Angling Club
D Carse
24 Port Street
Annan DG12 6BN

Appletreewick Barden and Burnsall Angling Club
J G H Mackrell
Mouldgreave
Oxenhope
N Keighley
West Yorks
BD22 9RT

Asfordby and Melton Society of Anglers
M Smith
63 Victoria Street
Melton Mowbray
Leicester

Ashmere Fisheries
Mr & Mrs K Howman
Felix Lane
Shepperton
Middlesex

Avon Fishing Association (Devon)
J E Coombes
19 Stella Road, Preston
Paignton
South Devon TQ3 1BH

Aylsham and District Angling Club
K Sutton
17 Town Lane
Aylsham
Norfolk NR11 6HH

Banbury and District Angling Association
G V Bradbeer
7 Bentley Close
Banbury, Oxon
OX16 7PB

Barnsley and District Amalgamated Anglers' Society
T Eaton
60 Walton Street
Gawber
Barnsley
Yorkshire S75 2PD

Barnstaple and District Angling Association
S Toms
1 Maysleary Cottages
Filleigh, N Devon
EX32 7TJ

Barnt Green Fishing Club
Mrs J Lunt
Square Cottage
Cherry Hill Drive
Barnt Green
Worcs B45 8JY

Barrow Angling Association
J R Jones
69 Princes Street
Dalton in Furness
Cumbria LA15 8ET

Basingstoke Canal Angling Association
R Jenkins
26 Tinern Close
Basingstoke
Hampshire
RG24 9HE

Bathampton Angling Association
D Crookes
25 Otago Terrace
Larkhall
Bath
Avon BA1 6SX

Bedford Angling Club
Mrs M E Appleton
18 Moriston Road
Bedford
MK41 7UG

Bedlington and Blagdon Angling Association
S Symons
8 Moorland Drive
Bedlington
Northumberland
NE22 7HB

Belper and District Angling Club
P Smith
11 Lander Lane
Belper
Derbys

Bembridge (IOW) Angling Club
P Knight
Berrylands
Heathfield Road
Bembridge IOW
PO35 5UW

Benson Angling Club
D Cook
24 The Cedars
Benson
Wallingford
Oxon OX10 6LL

Berkhamsted and District Angling Society
P Welling
1 South Park Gardens
Berkhamsted
Herts HP4 1JA

Bexhill Sea Angling Club
J Boston
17 St James Street
Bexhill-on-Sea
Sussex

Bicester Angling Society
W H Bunce
Tel: Bicester 44653

Bideford and District Angling Club
Mrs Joan Ash
42 Clovelly Street
Bideford, N Devon

Billingshurst Angling Society
J Hitchin
12 West Lark Lake
Goring-by-Sea
Worthing

Birmingham Anglers' Association Ltd
J Williams
100 Icknield Port Road
Rotton Park, Birmingham B16 0AP

Bishop Auckland and District Angling Club
J Winter
7 Royal Grove
Crook
Co Durham DL15 9ER

Blandford and District Angling Club
Mr Gordon
Arthur Conyers
3 West Street
Blandford
Dorset

Blenheim Angling Society
F W Lancaster
Briarwood, Burtons Lane
Chalfont St Giles
Buckinghamshire
HP8 4BB

Blunham Angling Club
G Palmer
5 Brockwell
Oakley
Bedfordshire MK43 7TD

Bodmin Anglers' Association
R Burrows
26 Meadow Place
Bodmin
Cornwall
PL31 1JD

Bolton and District Angling Association
Terence A McKee
1 Lever Edge Lane
Great Lever
Bolton
Lancs BL3 3BU

Boston and District Angling Association
Mrs Barbara Clifton
1 Kings Crescent
Boston
Lincolnshire PE21 0AP

Boston Spa Angling Club
A Waddington
The Cottage
17 The Village
Thorp Arch
Wetherby
Yorkshire LS23 7AR

Bottesford and District Angling Association
N Chenoweth
Holme Farm
Shelford
Nottingham

Boxmoor and District Angling Society
41 Crofts Path
Leverstock Green
Hemel Hempstead
Herts HP3 8HB

Bradford No 1 Angling Association
Membership Secretary
J Sparks
12 Fairway
Wibsey
Bradford BD7 4JW
or Secretary
H M Foster
6 Moorclose Lane
Queensbury
Bradford BD13 2BP

Bradford Waltonians'
Angling Club
H J B Swarbrick
43 Hawksworth Drive
Menston, Ilkley
West Yorkshire
LS29 6HP

Brampton (Cambs)
Angling Society
Kevin Medlock
1 Stanch Hill Rd
Sawtry, Huntingdon
Cambs PE17 5XG

Brandon and District
Angling Club
P Cooper
16 High Street
Feltwell, Thetford
Norfolk IP26 4AF

Bridgwater Angling
Association
B Hill
28 Sedgmoor Road
Highbridge
Somerset
or
Secretary
M Pople
14 Edward Street
Bridgwater
Somerset TA6 5EU

Brighouse Angling
Association
D W Noble
1A Church Lane
Brighouse
West Yorks HD6 1A7

Bristol, Bath and
Wiltshire Anglers'
Amalgamation
Jeff Parker
16 Lansdown View
Kingswood
Bristol BS15 4AW

Bristol and West of
England Federation of
Anglers
B Williams
157 Whiteway Road
Bristol BS5 7RH

Brixham Sea Anglers'
Society
A Halliday
94B The Post House
Drew Street
Brixham
Devon

Bromley and District
Anglers' Society
M Sale
13A Charlesfield Road
Horley Road
Horley
Surrey RH6 8BJ

Broome Angling Society
A Smith
10 Lords Avenue
Benskins Croft
Leicester LE4 2HX

Brunswick Brothers
Angling Society
Terry Taylor
40 St Andrews Road
Cranbrook
Ilford
Essex IG1 3PF

Buckingham and District
Angling Association
Mrs J Begley
20 Vicarage Close
Steeple Claydon
Bucks MK18 2PU

Bude Angling Association
Mrs P Casson
29 West Park Road
Bude
Cornwall EX23 0NA

Bude Canal Angling
Association
K M Harris
9 Quarry Close
Bude, Cornwall

Bude and District Sea
Angling Association
D Harris
3 Quarry Close
Bude
Cornwall EX23 8JG

Bungay Cherry Tree
Angling Club
I Gosling
37 St Mary's Terrace
Flixton Road
Bungay, Suffolk
NR35 1DW

Burford Angling Club
J Swallow
8 Meadow End
Fulbrook, Burford
Oxon OX18 4RG
HQ
The Highway Hotel
117 High Street
Burford OX18 4RG

Burnley Angling Society
P J King
16 Croasdalk Avenue
Burnley
Lancs BB10 2DN

Burton-on-Trent Mutual
Angling Association
D J Clark
7 Denton Rise
Burton-on-Trent,
Staffordshire DE13 0QB

Caersws Angling
Association
D Corfield
2 Maes-y Dre Flats
Caersws
Powys SY17 5HU

Caldy Anglers
N Hopper
2 Raeburn Avenue
West Kirby
Merseyside
L48 5JE

Calne Angling
Association
Miss J M Knowler
123A London Road
Calne
Wiltshire
SN11 0AQ

Cambridge Albion
Angling Society
R Gentle
34 Ramsden Square
Cambridge CB4 2BL

Cambridge Fish
Preservation and Angling
Society
G Tweed
27A Villa Road
Impington
Cambridge
Cambs

Cambridge Izaak Walton
Society
T J Sawyer
6 Pump Lane
Hardwick
Cambridge
CB3 7QW

Canterbury and District
Angling Association
R D Barton
14 Mill Road
Sturry
Canterbury
Kent CT2 0AF

Carlisle Angling Association
G Proud
39 Borland Avenue
Carlisle
Cumbria CA1 2SY

Castaways Angling Club
P Dunne
Dieu Donne
La Bellieuse
St Martins
Guernsey

Central Association of London and Provincial Angling Clubs
A J Jenkinson
68 Taynton Drive
Merstham, Surrey
RH1 3PT

Cheddar Angling Association
A T Lane
P O Box 1183
Cheddar
Somerset BS27 3LT

Chelmsford Angling Association
Membership Secretary
61 Readers Court
Great Baddow
Chelmsford
Essex CM2 8EX
or
Mrs I Lewis
60 Delamere Road
Chelmsford
Essex CM1 2TG

Cheshire Anglers' Association
Graham Tompkinson
31 Wareham Drive
Crewe, Cheshire
CW1 3XA

Chester-le-Street and District Angling Club
G Curry
62 Newcastle Road
Chester-le-Street
Co Durham
DH3 3UF

Chichester And District Angling Society
Mrs C Luffham
17 Arun Road
Bognor Regis,
West Sussex

Chichester Canal Society
Edward Hill
9 Marden Avenue
Chichester
West Sussex
PO19 2QZ

Chippenham Angling Club
J Duffield
95 Malmesbury Road
Chippenham
Wilts SN15 1PY
Club HQ
Liberal Club
Gladstone Road
Chippenham

Christchurch Angling Club
Mr Andrews
4 Marley Close
New Milton
Hants BH25 5LL

Clevedon and District Freshwater Angling Club
S Bonwick
13 Tennyson Avenue
Clevedon
North Somerset BS21 7OQ

Clitheroe Angling Association
B Jacques
24 Rylstone Drive
Barnoldswick
Lancs BB8 5RG

Clive Vale Angling Club
J Greenhalf
33 Hollington Park Road
St Leonards-on-Sea
E Sussex TN38 0SE

Colchester Angling Preservation Society
M K Turner
29 Lodge Road
Braintree, Essex CM7 1JA

Colchester Piscatorial Society
R J Moore
66 The Willows
Colchester
Essex CO2 8PX

Collingham Angling Association
P Thomas
61 Station Road
Collingham
Nottinghamshire
NG24 7RA

Colnes Angling Society
P Empson
16 Station Road
Colne Engain,
Colchester, Essex
CO6 2ES
Suffolk Stour

Compleat Angler Fishing Club
T Lelliott
Polegate Angling Centre
101 Polegate Road
Polegate, E Sussex
BN26 6EB

Congleton Angling Society
N J Bours
8 Norfolk Road
Congleton, Cheshire
CW12 1NY

Coquet Angling Club
J Engles
80 Castle Terrace
Ashington,
Northumberland

Cotterstock Angling Association
Mrs Joan E Popplewell
40 North Street
Oundle,
Peterborough
Cambs PE8 4AL

Coventry and District Angling Association
A J Hyde
1 Oak Tree Avenue
Green Lane
Coventry CV3 6DG

Crediton Fly Fishing Club
Keith Hicks
372 Pinhoe Road
Exeter EX4 8EB

Croydon Sea Angling Club
9 Hurstbourne,
Claygate
Surrey KT10 0NG
(01372 803907)
Inshore and offshore Fishing,
including
Jersey, Alderney, Ireland

Danby Angling Club
F Farrow
11 Dale End, Danby
Whitby, N Yorkshire
Y021 2JF

Darlington Anglers' Club
I Ablott
58 Swaledale Avenue
Darlington
DL3 9AL

Darlington Brown Trout Angling Association
G Coulson
5 Grange Avenue,
Hurworth Place
Darlington

Darlington Fly Fishers' Club
W D Holmes
39 Barrett Road
Darlington
DL3 8LA

Dart Angling Association
D H Pakes
Holly How
Plymouth Road
South Brent
Devon
TQ10 9HU

Dartford and District Angling Preservation Society
Lake House
Walnut Tree Avenue
Dartford
Kent DA1 1LJ

Dartmouth Angling and Boating Association
Headquarters
5 Oxford Street
Dartmouth
Devon

Darwen Anglers' Association
F W Kendall
45 Holden Fold
Darwen
Lancashire
BB3 3AU

Dawley Angling Society
Mike Tuff
18 New Road
Dawley,
Telford
Shropshire TF4 3LJ

Deal and Walmer Angling Association
c/o Channel Angling
158/160 Snargate Street
Dover
Kent CT17 9BZ

Deal and Walmer Inshore Fishermen's Association
D Chamberlain
34 The Strand
Walmer, Deal
CT14 7DX

Dean Clough and Ryburn Angling Society
T Hooson
4 Chester Terrace
Boothtown
Halifax
West Yorks HX3 6LT

Deanshanger and Stratford Angling Association
T Valentine
34 Mallets Close
Stony Stratford
Milton Keynes
MK11 1DQ

Deeping St James Angling Club
K W Allum
5 Conway Avenue
Walton
Peterborough
Lincs PE4 6JD

Derbyshire Angling Federation
S W Clifton
14 Highfield Road
Little Eaton
Derbys

Derbyshire County Angling Club
O W Handley
Osprey House, Ogston
Higham, Alfreton
Derby DE55 6EL

Dereham and District Angling Club
D Appleby
6 Rump Close
Swanton Morley
Norfolk NR20 4NH

Dingle Fly Fishing Club
G Roscoe
8 Kiln Brow
Bromley Cross
Bolton

Diss and District Angling Club
Mr D Gladwell
5 Martin Road
Diss
Suffolk IP22 3HR

Doncaster and District Angling Association
W Sams
28 Pipering Lane
Scawthorpe
Doncaster DN5 9NY
or c/o
The Good Companions
Haslemere Grove
Bentley
Doncaster

Dorchester and District Angling Society
HQ
Dorchester Bowling Green
Sandringham Sports Centre
Armada Way
Fordington Fields
Dorchester

Dorchester Fishing Club
J Grindle
36 Cowleaze
Martinstown
Dorchester, Dorset
DT2 9TD

Dunelm City Angling Club
G Hedley
3 Hawthorne Crescent
Gilesgate Moor
Durham DH1 1ED

Durham City Angling Club
M J Hall
21 Northumbria Place
Co Durham
DH9 0UB

Durweston Angling Association
V Bell
Endcote
Durweston
Dorset

Earl Manvers Angling Association
G R Dennis
11 First Avenue
Carlton
Nottingham
NG4 1PH

Earls Barton Angling Club
P Tipler
70 Station Road
Earls Barton
Northampton
NN6 0NT

**Eastbourne Angling
Association**
The Club House
Royal Parade
Eastbourne
East Sussex
BN22 7AA

**Eastfield Angling
Association**
J Ford
3 Newby Court
Eastfield
Northampton

**Eastleigh and District
Angling Club**
J Remington
121 Desborough Road
Eastborough
Hants
SO5 5NP

**Edenbridge Angling
Club**
Mr Fishlock
3 Locks Meadow
Dormansland
Surrey

**Egremont Angling
Association**
Clive Fisher
8 North Road
Egremont
Cumbria
CA22 2PR

Ennerdale Lake Fisheries
D Crellin
3 Parklands Drive
Egremont
Cumbria
CA22 2JL

Errwood Flyfishing Club
T Speake
11 Cliffmere Close
Cheadle Hulme
Cheshire

**Evesham and District
Angling Association**
C Leeming
44 Coronation street
Evesham
Worcs
WR11 5BD

**Exeter and District
Angling Association**
B Luca
Mayfield
Cheriton Bishop
Exeter EX6 6JP

Fakenham Angling Club
G Twite
16 Back Street
Hempton
Fakenham
Norfolk
NR21 7LR

Farnham Angling Society
Mr Borra
The Creel
Station Road
Aldershot
Hants

Faversham Angling Club
N Prior
1C St Nicholas Road
Faversham
Kent ME13 7PG

**Felixstowe Sea Angling
Association**
End Manor Terrace
Felixstowe
Suffolk IP11 8EL
Secretary:
K M Tompkins
11 High Road East
Felixstowe
Suffolk IP11 9JU

**Fenton and District
Angling Society**
C Yates
The Puzzels
5 Gatley Grove
Meir Park
Stoke-on-Trent
Staffs ST3 7SH

**Ferryhill and District
Angling Club**
Secretary
B Hignett
74 Grasmere Road
Garden Farm Estate
Chester-le-Street
Co Durham

Filey Boat Angling Club
H Cammish
11 Ravine Top
Filey
North Yorkshire
YO14 9HA

**Filey Brigg Angling
Society**
Mrs K Marshall
87 Scarborough Road
Filey
North Yorkshire
YO14 9NQ

Flyfishers' Club
Commander T H Boycott
OBE RN
69 Brook Street
London W1Y 2ER
Private members club, no
fishery.

**Framlingham and District
Angling Club**
R Boon
16 Horseman Court
Martlesham Heath
Nr Ipswich
Suffolk IP5 7SZ
or
D R Smith, Vice Chairman
11 Lark Rise
Martlesham Heath
Nr Ipswich
Suffolk IP5 3SA

**Frome and District
Angling Association**
R J Lee
51 Welshmill Lane
Frome
Somerset BA11 3AP

Gamefishers' Club
J H Andrews
Meadow View
Dinedor
Hereford HR2 6LQ

**Gillingham and District
Angling Association**
S Hebditch
5 Ham Court
Shaftesbury Road
Gillingham
Dorset SP8 4LU

**Gipping Angling
Preservation Society**
George Alderson
19 Clover Close
Chantry, Ipswich
Suffolk IP2 0PW
Gipping. Tickets

Glebe Angling Club
C Broome
2 Crockett Close
Links View Estate
Northampton

**Godalming Angling
Society**
M R Richardson
87 Summers Road
Farncombe
Godalming
Surrey GU7 3BE

Goole and District Angling Association
L Rogers
39 Clifton Gardens
Goole
North Humberside
DN14 6AR

Gosforth Anglers' Club
G Thomas
11 Fell View
Gosforth
Seascale

Grafton Angling Association
G D Williams
9 Edward Street
Worksop
Notts S80 1QP

Grange Angling Club
Paul Hutchinson
26 Hereford Road
Hillview
Sunderland
SR2 9LE

Grantham Angling Association
W J C Hutchins
28 Cottesmore Close
Grantham
Lincolnshire
NG31 9JL

Great Cornard Angling Club
P Franklin
48 Queensway
Gt Cornard
Suffolk

Great Yarmouth and Norfolk County Angling Association
K Ford
2 Parana Close
Sprowston
Norwich

Grenville Sea Angling Club
Social Club
St Dennis
Padstow
Cornwall

Groe Park and Irfon Angling Club
J L Burton
Angle House
Pentrosfa Crescent
Llandrindod Wells
Powys LD1 5NW

Guernsey Freshwater Anglers' Society
A Bradley
Les Tracheries Cottage
Les Tracheries
L'Islet
Guernsey

Guernsey Mullet Club
M Weyson
La Cachette
6 Clos des Caches
St Martins
Guernsey

Guernsey Sea Anglers' Club
P Le Lacheur
Santa Ana
Les Emrais Estate, Castel
Guernsey

Hadleigh and District Angling Society
D R Warner
5 Churchill Avenue
Hadleigh, Ipswich
Suffolk IP7 6BT

Haltwhistle and District Angling Association
Chris Wilson
Melkridge House,
Melkridge
Haltwhistle,
Northumberland NE49 0LT

Harleston, Wortwell and District Angling Club
P Brown
15 Pine Close
Harleston
Norfolk

Harwich Angling Club
G Shields
5 Gordon Way
Dovercourt
Harwich
Essex CO12 3TW

Hastings and St Leonards Sea Angling Association
Marine Parade
Hastings
East Sussex TN34 3AG

Hastings, Bexhill and District Freshwater Angling Association
P T Maclean
37 Colliers Road
Hastings
East Susses TN34 3JR

Hastings Flyfishers' Club Ltd
D E Tack
23 Wealden Way
Little Common
Nr Bexhill-on-Sea
E. Sussex TN39 4NZ

Hawes and High Abbotside Angling Association
G Phillips
Holmlands, Appersett
Hawes,
North Yorks
DL8 3LN

Hawkshead Angling Club
J L Locke
Flat 1 The Croft
Hawkshead
Ambleside
Cumbria LA22 0NX
Limited to 100 members.

Hay-on-Wye Fishermans' Association
B Wigington
Flat 2, Pembertons,
4 High Town
Hay-on-Wye
Herefords HR3 5AE

Haywards Heath and District Angling Society
J Kenward
60 Franklyn Road
Haywards Heath
RH16 4DH

Hazeldine Anglers' Association
J W Hazeldine
8 Dudley Road
Sedgley
Dudley
Staffordshire
DY3 1SX

Hebden Bridge Angling Club
C N Pickles
17 Undershot Avenue
Hebden Bridge
West Yorks

Helperby and Brafferton Angling Club
F Marrison
Gardener's Cottage
York Road
Helperby, York
North Yorkshire
YO6 2PJ

Herne Bay Angling Association
Honorary Secretary
c/o HQ, 59 Central Parade
Herne Bay
Kent

Heron Angling Society (Herne Bay)
Red Shelter
Spa Esplanade
Herne Bay
Kent

Histon and District Angling Club
Colin Dodd
122 Rampton Road
Willingham
Cambs
CB4 5JF

Holmesdale Angling and Conservation Society
Mrs E M Divall
PO Box 248
Orpington
Kent BR6 6ZG

Holme Valley Piscatorial Association
P Budd
39 Derwent Road
Honley
Huddersfield
Yorkshire HD7 2EL

Horizon Angling Club
P Bradbury
The Bungalow
12A Petworth Road
Milton
Portsmouth
Hampshire PO3 6DH
Angling opportunities for registered disabled.

Horncastle Angling Association
G Alder
The Cottage
Sandy Lane
Woodhall Spa
Lincs LN10 6UR

Horsham and District Angling Association
PO Box 22
Horsham
West Sussex RH12 5LN

Hull and District Angling Association
PO Box 188
Hull HU9 1AN

Huntingdon Angling and Fish Preservation Society
Mrs Anne W Wallis
8 Clayton's Way
Huntingdon
Cambridgeshire
PE18 7UT

Huttons Ambo Angling Club
Paul Thompson
Firby Hall
Firby
North Yorkshire YO6 7LH

Idle and Thackley Angling Association
Charles Taylor Hardaker
24 Park Avenue
Thackley
Bradford
West Yorkshire BD2 4LP

Isle of Man Fly Fishing Association
Ray Caley
Caley's Stores
Sulby
Isle of Man

Isle of Wight Freshwater Angling Association
Ian de Gruchy
66 Merrie Gardens
Lake, Sandown
Isle of Wight

Jersey Rodbenders Sea Angling Club
E Read
3 Clos Des Pas
Green Street
St Helier
Jersey

Jersey Sea Fishing Club
T Jones
9 Valley Close
St Saviour, Jersey

Keighley Angling Club
Treasurer/Secretary
D Freeman
62 Eel Holme
View Street
Beechcliffe
Keighley
West Yorks

Kelvedon Angling Association
B Pike
11 Keene Way
Galleywood
CM2 8NT

Kempston Angling Club
K Green
24 The Elms
Kempston
Bedford
Beds
MK42 7JW

Kent Angling Association
D Aldworth
Helm Drive
Kendal
Cumbria

Keswick Angling Association
J D Thompson
15 Low Mill
Greta Side
Keswick
Cumbria
GA12 5LL

Kettering and Thrapston Angling Association
L R Garret
10 Naseby Road
Kettering
Northants

Keynsham Angling Association
W Bates
158 Park Road
Keynsham
Bristol
Avon
Chew, Avon. Tickets

Kidderminster and District Angling Association
M Millinchip
246 Marlpool Lane,
Kidderminster
Worcestershire
DY11 5DD

King's Lynn Angling Association
M R Grief
67 Peckover Way
South Woonton
King's Lynn
Norfolk
PE30 3UE

Kirkby Fleetham Angling Club
M L Smith
26 Eden Grove
Newton Aycliffe
Co Durham
DL5 7JG

Kirkham and District Fly Fishers' Club
D Wardman
65 Longhouse Lane
Poulton-le-Fylde
Lancashire FY6 8DE

Knaresborough Piscatorials
P Davies
26 Kendal Drive
Harrogate
N Yorks HG1 4SH
Membership Secretary
M Johnson
2 Briggate
Knaresborough
N Yorks HG5 8BH

Knightley Angling Club
c/o Knightley Arms
High Street
Yelvertoft
NN6 6W

Lamorbey Angling Society
Membership Officer
PO Box 56
Sidcup
DA15 9ZQ

Lancashire Fly-Fishing Association
J P Shorrock
Plane Tree House
Lomas Lane
Balladen
Rossendale BB4 6HH

Langport and District Angling Association
Dennis Barlow
'Florissant'
Northfield
Somerton
Langport
Somerset TA11 6SJ

Lanhydrock Angling Association
B Muelaner
The National Trust Estate Office
Lanhydrock Park
Bodmin
Cornwall PL30 4DE

Lark Angling Preservation Society
E T West
8 Arrowhead Drive
Lakenheath
Suffolk IP27 9JN

Lee Anglers' Consortium
T Mansbridge
7 Warren Road
Chingford
London E4 6QR

Leeds and District Amalgamated Anglers' Association
Derek Taylor
75 Stoney Rock Lane
Beckett Street
Leeds
West Yorkshire
LS29 7TB

Leek and Moorlands Angling Club
Roy Birch-Machin
53 Novi Lane
Leek, Staffs
ST13 6NX

Leicester District Amalgamated Society of Anglers
R T Bent-Fossey
431 Gleneagles Avenue
Rusheymead
Leicester LE4 7YT

Leigh and District Angling Association
C Hibbs
417 Nabchester Road
Lewigh
Lancashire
WN7 2ND

Leighton Buzzard Angling Society
H Holliday
54 Pebble Moor
Eddlesborough
Leighton Buzzard
Beds LU7 8EF

Letchworth and District Angling Association
P N Jones
79 Howard Drive
Letchworth
Herts S96 2BO

Lewisham Piscatorials Association
D J Head
75 Riverview Park
Catford
London SE6 4PL

Lifford Angling Club
P Taylor
E-mail:
Petetaylor@connectfree.co.uk

Lincoln and District Angling Association
Colin W Parker
4 Pottergate Close
Waddington
Lincoln
LN5 9LY

Liskeard and District Angling Club
W E Eliot
64 Portbyhan Road
West Looe, Cornwall
PL13 2QN

Littleport Angling Club
David Yardy
168 High Barns
Ely
Cambs

Liverpool and District Angling Association
James Browne
33 Eleanor Road
Bootle
Liverpool
Merseyside
L20 6BP

Llandrindod Wells Angling Association
B D Price
The Cedars
Llanyre
Llandrindod Wells
Powys
LD1 6DY

London Anglers' Association
A E Hedges
Isaak Walton House
2A Hervey Park Road
Walthamstow,
London
E17 6LJ
(LAA offices)

Long Buckby Angling Club
M Hill
33 South Close
Long Buckby
Northants
NN6 7PX

Long Eaton and District Angling Federation
E Ainsworth
37 Dovecote Lane
Beaston
Nottinghamshire
NG9 1HR

**Long Eaton Victoria
Angling Society**
D L Kent
2 Edge Hill Court
Fields Farm
Long Eaton
Notts, NG10 1PQ

**Long Melford and District
Angling Association**
N Meacham
6 Springfield Terrace
East Street
Sudbury
Suffolk CO12 2TS

**Looe and District Sea
Angling Association**
c/o Cotton's Tackle Shop
The Quay, E Looe, Cornwall
PL13 1AQ

**Lostwithiel Fishing
Association**
G Rogers
(Tel: 01637 872872)

**Loughborough Soar
Angling Society**
S Sharpe
16 Edward Street
Loughborough
Leicester LE11 1QF

**Lowestoft Sea Angling
Society**
57 Lorne Park Road
Lowestoft
Suffolk NR33 0RB

**Luton and District
Angling Club**
Mrs B A Bunnage
33 Kingsdown Avenue
Luton
Beds LU25 7BU

**Lymington and District
Sea Fishing Club**
Mrs G Moody
'Gina-Mia'
Hundred Lane, Portmore
Lymington
Hants

Lymm Angling Club
Neil Jupp
P O Box 350
Warrington WA2 9FB

**Macclesfield Flyfishers'
Club**
W F Williams
1 Westwood Drive
Brooklands, Sale
Cheshire M33 3QW

**Macclesfield Waltonian
Angling Society**
Michael E Bowyer
7 Ullswater
Macclesfield
Cheshire SK11 7YN

**Maidstone Victory
Angling and Medway
Preservation Society**
J Perkins
33 Hackney Road
Maidstone
Kent ME16 8LN

Maldon Angling Society
T Lazell
14 Barn View Road
Coggeshall
Essex CO6 1RF

**Malton and Norton
Angling Club**
M Foggins
123 Wellram Road
Norton, Malton
Yorks

**Manchester and District
Angling Association**
c/o 1 Chapel Lane
Horton in Ribblesdale
N Yorks

**Mansfield and District
Angling Association**
A Quick
158 Huthwaite Road
Sutton-in-Ashfield
Nottinghamshire NG17 2GX

Manx Game Fishing Club
P O Box 95
2A Lord Street
Douglas, Isle of Man

Marazion Angling Club
Tickets from: County Angler
39 Cross Street
Camborne
Cornwall TR14 8ES

**Market Harborough and
District Society of
Anglers**
N Bale
27 Rainsborough Gardens
Market Harborough
Leicestershire LE16 9LN

**Marsden Star Angling
Society**
Jeff Hartley
3 Duerden Street
Nelson
Lancs BB9 9BJ

**Martham and District
Angling Club**
Liz Carpenter
15 Repps Road
Martham
Norfolk
NR29 4SU

**Melksham and District
Angling Association**
D Branton
16 Ingram Road
Melksham
Somerset

**Mevagissey Sea Angling
Club**
The Ship Inn
Pentowan,
Cornwall

**Middlesbrough Angling
Club**
R Thompson
25 Endsleigh Drive
Acklam, Middlesbrough
Cleveland
TS5 4RG

Middlewich Joint Anglers
C Bratt
13 Elm Road
Middlewich
Cheshire
CW10 0AX

**Mid-Ribble Angling
Society**
J W Whitham
Pendleside
58 Lingmoor drive
Burnley
Lancashire BB12 8UY

Mildenhall Angling Club
M Hampshire
63 Downing Close
Mildenhall
Suffolk
IP28 7PB

**Millom and District
Angling Association**
D Dixon
1 Churchill Drive
Millom
Cumbria
LA18 5DD

**Milton Keynes Angling
Association**
c/o 52 Jenkinson Road
Towcester
Northamptonshire
NN12 7AW

Montgomeryshire Angling Association
(formed by Newtown & District Fishing Club, Llanfair Caereinion Fishing Club & Welshpool Angling Club)
P Hulme
306 Heol-y-Coleg
Vaynor Estate, Newtown
Powys SY16 1RA

Moor Hall and Belhus Angling Society
M Tilbrook
46 Mill Road
Aveley
South Ockendon
Essex RM15 4SL

Moreton Angling Club
Bill McKenzie
"Lyndale", Landown
Burton on the Water
Cheltenham
Glos GL54 2AR

Nelson Angling Association
H Hargreaves
171 Reedley Road
Briarfield
Nelson
Lancs

Nene and Welland Angling Consultative Association
G Bibby
5 Ermine Way
Sawtry
Cambs

Newark and District Piscatorial Federation
J N Garland
58 Riverside Road
Newark, Notts
NG24 4RJ

Newport Pagnell Angling Association
R Dorrill
7 Bury Road
Newport Pagnell
Milton Keynes
MK16 0DS

Newton Abbot Fishing Association
David Horder
Mistlemead, Woodlands
Higher Sandygate
Newton Abbot
Devon TQ12 3QN

Nidderdale Angling Club
T Harpham
PO Box 7
Pateley Bridge, nr Harrogate
North Yorks, HG3 5XB

Norfolk and Suffolk Flyfishers' Club
E A Fenn
White Horse House
White Horse Common
North Walsham, Norfolk

Northampton Britannia Angling Club
G H Richmond
34 Ilex Close
Hardingstone
Northampton NN4 6SD

Northampton Nene Angling Club
Mrs P Walsh
363 Kettering Road
Northampton NN3 6QT

Northern Anglers' Association
A G R Brown
10 Dale Road
Golborne
Warrington
Cheshire WA3 3PN

North Durham Angling Association
ÚįAarhus'
View Lane
Stanley
Co Durham DH9 0DX

North Oxford Angling Society
L Ballard
70 Blackbird Leys Road
Cowley
Oxford 0X4 5HR

North Somerset Association of Anglers (Embracing Highbridge and Clevedon clubs)
R Newton
64 Clevedon Road
Tickenham
Cleveden
Somerset BS21 6RD

Northumbrian Anglers' Federation
P A Hall
3A Ridley Place
Newcastle upon Tyne
Northumberland
NE1 8LF

Northwich Anglers' Association
J Clithero
High Acres
Hartford Bridge, Hartford
Northwich
Cheshire CW8 1PP

Norwich Anglers' Association
C Wigg
3 Coppice Avenue
Norwich NR6 5RB

Nottingham Anglers' Association
I Foulds
95 Ilkeston Road
Nottingham

Nottingham and District Federation of Angling Societies
W Belshaw
17 Spring Green
Clifton Estate, Nottingham

Nottingham Piscatorial Society
P F Olko
63 Forest Road
Annesley Woodhouse
Nottingham NG17 9HA

Offord and Buckden Angling Society
John Astell
154 Eastrea Road
Whittlesey
Cambs
PE7 2AJ

Old Glossop Angling Club
R North
1 Morpeth Close
Ashton-under-Lyne
Lancs OL7 9SH

Old Windsor Angling Club
A Beaven
88 St Andrews Way
Slough, Berks SL1 5LJ

Orpington and District Angling Club
Membership Officer
PO Box 7
Kent BR6 7ZW

Oswestry Angling Club
L Allen
30 Brookfields
Weston Rhyn
Oswestry
Shropshire

**Oundle Angling
Association**
D Laxton
31 St Peters Street
Oundle
Peterborough

**Ouse Angling
Preservation Society**
Permit Secretary
Keith Potter
3 Orchard mews
Heighton Road
Denton, Newhaven
W Sussex BN9 0RB

**Over and Swaverley
District Anglers' Society**
D Cook
75 Willingham Road
Over
Cambs CB4 5PE

**Oxford and District
Anglers' Association**
Secretary
D H Witham
15 Broad Close
Botley, Oxford
OX2 9DR

**Padstow Sea Angling
Club**
Social Club
Padstow
Cornwall

**Paignton Sea Anglers'
Association**
26 Cliff Rd
The Harbour
Paignton, Devon

Parkside Fishing Club
D Fallows
27 Woodstock Avenue
Radford
Nottingham
NG7 5QP

**Peak Forest Angling Club
(Derbyshire)**
Colin Jones
Greenwood
Edale Road
Hope Valley
Derbys S33 6ZF

**Penrith Angling
Association**
Miss E Lomas
3 Newtown Cottages
Skirwith
Penrith
Cumbria CA10 1RJ

**Peterborough Angling
Club**
R Warr
24 Whitmore Court
Whittlesley
Cambs

**Petersfield and District
Angling Club**
Ash Girdler
3 Chase Plain Cottages
Portsmouth Road
Hindhead, Surrey
GU26 6BZ

Petworth Angling Club
R Haenaire
25 Station Road
Petworth
GU28 0EX

**Pewsey and District
Angling Club**
D Underwood
51 Swan Meadow
Pewsey
Wilts SN9 5HP

Plowden Fishing Club
S J Finnegan
The Old School
Brimfield
Salop SY8 4NZ

**Plymouth and District
Freshwater Angling
Association**
D L Owen
39 Burnett Road
Crownhill
Plymouth
Devon PL6 5BH

**City of Plymouth Sea
Angling Club**
c/o Osborne and Cragg
Fishing Tackle
37 Bretonside
Plymouth
Devon PL4 0BB

**Portsmouth and District
Angling Society**
R Snook
86 Caernarvon Road
Copnor
Portsmouth PO2 7NL

**Portsmouth Services Fly
Fishing Association**
Captain F Hefford OBE, DSC,
AFC, RN (Retired)
20 Stoatley Rise
Haslemere
Surrey GU27 1AF

**Pride of Derby Angling
Association**
A Miller
16 Mercia Drive
Willington,
Derby
DE65 6DA

**Prince Albert Angling
Society**
J A Turner
15 Pexhill Drive
Macclesfield
SK10 3LP
or
Membership Secretary
C Swindells
37 Sherwood Road
Macclesfield
Cheshire SK11 7RR

**Pulborough Angling
Society**
M Booth
5 South Lane
Houghton
Arundel
W Sussex BN18 9LN

Radcot Angling Club
Secretary
9 Thorpesfield
Alvescot
Oxfordshire OX18 2QF

**Ramsey Angling Club
(Cambs)**
P E Aldred
9 Blackmill Street
Chatteris
Cambs PE16 6SR

**Ramsey Angling Club
(I.O.M.)**
Chris Culshaw
Parkhill
Coburn Road
Ramsey
Isle of Man IM8 3EH.

**Reading and District
Angling Association**
W Brown Lee
47 Calbourne Drive
The Orchard, Calcot
Reading
Berkshire RG31 7DB

**Red Spinner Angling
Society**
K Stabler
9 Marlborough Road
London
N9 9PT

**Retford and District
Angling Association**
H Wells
31 Ainsdale Green
Ordsall
Retford
Nottinghamshire DN22 7NQ

**Rhayader Angling
Association**
Alan Lewis
Crown Inn
Rhayader, Powys
LD6 5BT

**Ribble and Wyre
Fisheries Association**
S A Gray
10 Lord Street
Wigan
Lancs WN1 2BN

**Richmond (Yorks) and
District Angling Society**
P Bennett
Tel: 01748 824894.

**Ringwood and District
Angling Club**
K J Grozier
11 Merlin Close
Hightown
Ringwood
Hants BH24 3RB

Ripon Angling Club
Roger Trees
43 College Road
Ripon
N Yorks HG4 2HE

Ripon Fly Fishers
C Clarke
9 Moorside Avenue
Ripon
N Yorks HG4 1TA

**Ripon Piscatorial
Association**
C M Morrison
12 Princess Road
Ripon
North Yorks HG4 1HW

**Rochdale Walton Angling
Society**
R Pealin
723 Whitworth Road
Rochdale
Lancashire

Rochford Angling Club
L Dorey
231 Kents Hill Road
Benfleet
Essex SS7 5PF

**Ross-on-Wye Angling
Club**
T Gibson
10 Redwood Close
Ross-on-Wye
Herefordshire
HR9 5UD

Rother Angling Club
C Boxall
Innisfree
Ashfield Road
Midhurst
West Sussex GU29 9JX

**Rother Fishery
Association**
Steve Crowley
9 Haydens Close
Orpington, Kent
BR5 4JE

**Royal Leamington Spa
Angling Association**
E G Archer
9 Southway
Leamington Spa
Warwickshire CV31 2PG

**Royston and District
Angling Club**
P R Harrow
46 Greengage Rise
Melbourne
Herts SG8 6DS

Rudgwick Angling Society
C Wood
16 Waldy Rise
Cranleigh
Surrey GU6 7DF

**Rushden and Higham
Ferrers Angling
Association**
J Boswell
49 Washbrook Road
Rushden
Northants NN10 9UY

**Saddleworth and District
Angling Society**
John Cox
3 Rhodes Avenue
Uppermill
Saddleworth
Oldham OL3 6ED

**St Helens Angling
Association**
D Fishwick
4 Sherwell Grove
Sutton Leach
St Helens
Merseyside

**St Ives and District Fish
Preservation and Angling
Society**
H Pace
48 Fairfields
St Ives
Cambridgeshire
PE17 4QF

St Leonards Sea Anglers
HQ, 16 Grand Parade
St Leonards
East Sussex

St Mawgan Angling Club
T J Trevenna
Lanvean House
St Mawgan
Newquay
Cornwall TR8 4EY

**St Neots and District
Angling and Fish
Preservation Society**
Mrs D Linger
Skewbridge Cottage
Great Paxton
Huntingdon
Cambs PE19 4RA

**Salcombe and District
Sea Anglers' Association**
Headquarters
Victoria Inn
Fore Street
Salcombe
Devon TQ8 8BT

**Salisbury and District
Angling Club**
R W Hillier
29 New Zealand Avenue
Salisbury
Wilts SP2 7JK

**Sandown & Lake Angling
Society**
G Davis
17 Lake Green Road
Lake
Isle of Wight PO36 9HW

**Sandwich and District
Angling Association**
J Heyburn
15 Fords Hill
Ramsgate
Kent CT12 5EL

**Sawbridgeworth Angling
Society**
Miss D Barnes
10 The Crescent
Old Harlow
Essex CM17 0HN

Saxmundham Angling Club
A Firman
46 Barhams Way
Wickham Market
Woodbridge
Suffolk IP13 0SR

Scunthorpe and District Angling Association
M Storey
74 Appleby Lane
Brougham, Brigg
South Humberside

Sedbergh and District Angling Association
G Bainbridge
El Kantara, Frostrow
Sedbergh
Cumbria LA10 5JL

Selsey Angling and Tope Club
Mike Bell
19 Littlefield Close
Selsey
West Sussex PO20 0DZ

Services Dry Fly Fishing Association (Salisbury Plain)
Major (Retd) C D Taylor
c/o G2 Headquarters
43rd (Wessex) Brigade
Picton Barracks
Bulford Camp
Salisbury SP4 9NY

Seven Angling Club
Mrs B J Stansfield
Sun Seven
Sinnington, Yorkshire
YO6 6RZ

Seven Stars Angling Club
The Seven Stars
Birchfield Road
Headless Cross
Redditch
Worcs

Severnside Angling Club
H Rodway
Fairview
Bryn Gardens
Newtown, Powys
SY16 1NP

Sheffield Amalgamated Anglers' Society
A D Baynes
HQ Lord Nelson
166/8 Arundel Street
Sheffield

Sheffield and District Anglers' Association
142/4 Princess Street
Sheffield S4 7UW
or
G Woods
1 Everingham Road
Longley
Sheffield S5 7LA

Sheffield Piscatorial Society
Mr Anderson
Farm House
Retford
Notts

Shefford and District Angling Association
J Leath
3 Ivel Close
Shefford
Beds SG17 5JX

Shropshire Anglers' Federation
Ian Moorhouse
22 Pendle Way
Shrewsbury
Salop SY3 9QN

Slaithwaite and District Angling Club
D Rushforth
122 Longwood Gate
Longwood
Huddersfield
HD3 4US

Southern Anglers
B D Smith
3 Cheriton Close
Havant
Hants
PO9 4PU
or
T Irons
7 Nelson Crescent
Horndean
Portsmouth PO8 9LZ

Southsea Sea Angling Club
c/o
42 Granada Road
Southsea
Hants

Stalbridge Angling Society
T Cairns
35 Blackmore Road
Stalbridge
Dorset DT10 2NU

Stalybridge (Fox) Angling Society
I S Warton
17 Coneymead
Stalybridge
Cheshire SK15 2LJ

Stamford Welland Amalgamated Anglers' Association
G E Bates
16a Austin Street
Stamford
Lincs PE9 2QP

Stanhope Angling Association
J J Lee
6 Cowgarth Hill
Stanhope
Bishop Auckland
Co Durham

Stockport and District Anglers' Federation
H Ollerenshaw
133 Manchester Road
Hyde
Cheshire
SK14 2BX

Stoke City and District Anglers' Association
P Johansen
31 East Crescent
Sneyd Green
Stoke-on-Trent
ST1 6ES

Stoke on Trent Angling Society
A Perkins
Muirhearlich
Fowlers Lane
Light Oaks
Stoke on Trent
ST2 7NB

Stratford-upon-Avon Angling Association
A Bruce
Lower Lodge Farm
Bishopton Lane
Stratford-upon-Avon
Warwickshire
CV37 0RJ

Sturminster and Hinton Angling Association
S Dimmer
38 Grosvenor Rd
Stalbridge
Sturminster Newton
Dorset DT10 2PN

Sunderland Sea Angling Association
Tom Parkin
c/c 125 Roker Avenue
Roker
Sunderland
SR6 0HL

Sunmead Angling Society
P Tanner
24 Ryebrook Road
Leatherhead
Surrey KT22 7QG

Sutton Coldfield Angling Society
100 Rectory Road
Sutton Coldfield
West Midlands
B75 7RP

Swan Angling Club
J Stanhope
4 High Road
Lane Head
Willenhall
West Midlands
WV12 4JQ

Swanage and District Angling Club
Peveril Slipway
Swanage
Dorset

Taunton Angling Association
M Hewitson
56 Parkfield Road
Taunton
Somerset
Tone, Taunton Canal, Drains

Taunton Fly-Fishing Club
J Greene
2 Old Vicarage
Bradford on Tone
Taunton
Somerset TA4 1HG

Tavy, Walkham and Plym Fishing Club
John Soul
Trevenevow
Crapstone Road
Yelverton
Devon PL20 6BT

Taw Fishing Club
J D V Michie
Wheel Barton
Broadwoodkelly
Winkleigh
Devon
EX19 8ED

Tebay Angling Association
H Riley
White Cross House
Tebay
Via Penrith
Cumbria

Teignmouth Sea Angling Society
Mrs L Hexter
1 Headway Rise
Teignmouth
Devon
TQ14 9UL
or
D Lawer
19 Inverteign Drive
Teignmouth
Devon

Telford Angling Association
M Kelly
14 Sycamore Close
Wellington
Telford
Salop
TF1 3NH
Tel: 01952 244272

Tenbury Fishing Association
Mrs L M Rickett
The Post House
Berrington Road
Tenbury Wells,
Worcestershire WR15 8EN

Test and Itchen Association Ltd
Jim Glasspool
West Haye
Itchen Abbas
Winchester
Hants
SO21 1AX

Test Valley Angling Club
Membership Secretary
1A Rumbridge Street
Totton
Southampton
Hants

Tewkesbury Popular Angling Association
Terry Smith
25 Milne Pastures
Ashchurch
Tewkesbury
Gloucestershire
GL20 8SG

Thetford and Breckland Angling Club
S J Armes
Kings Croft
Shropham Road
Great Hockham
Thetford
Norfolk IP24 1NJ

Tisbury Angling Club
Treasurer:
E J Stevens
Knapp Cottage
Fovant
Salisbury
Wiltshire SP3 5JW
Secretary
R Frogerty
10 Catherine Crescent
Dinton
Salisbury
Wiltshire SP3 5HE

Tiverton and District Angling Club
R Retallick
21 Alstone Road
Canal Hill
Tiverton
Devon
EX16 4LH

Todmorden Angling Society
R Barber
12 Grisedale Drive
Burnley
Lancs
BB12 8AR

Torbay And Babbacombe Association of Sea Anglers
Mrs C Wilden
100 St Marychurch Road
Torquay
Devon TQ1 3HL

Towcester and District Angling Club
Mr Pannet
30 Bickerstaff Road
Towcester
Northants

Trent and District Anglers' Consultative Association
N Walsh
5 Derby Road
Homesford
Matlock
Derbyshire

The Tring Anglers
R Gibbs
PO Box 1947
Tring
Herts HP23 5LZ

Ulverston Angling Association
J A Baldwin
24 Springfield Park Road
Ulverston
Cumbria
LA12 0EQ

Unity Angling Club
E K Mann
19 Busfield Street
Bradford
W Yorks BD4 7QX

Upper Tanat Fishing Club
R R Hall
Melyniog
Llansantffraid
Powys SY22 6AX

Upper Teign Fishing Association
J Getliff
22 The Square
Chagford, Devon
TQ13 8AB
or Chairman
M Weaver M.B.E.
Pippin Cottage
Drewsteignton
Devon

Upper Thames Fisheries Consultative Association
R Knowles
360 Banbury Road
Oxford OX2 7PP

Upper Weardale Angling Association
H C Lee
7 Westfall
Wearhead,
Co Durham DL13 1BP

Uttoxeter Angling Association
I E Davies
Three Oaks
Hollington Lane
Stramshall
Uttoxeter, Staffordshire
ST14 5AJ

Vauxhall Angling Club
R W Poulton
20 Leeches Way
Cheddington
Beds LU7 0SJ

Victoria Angling Club
John Rowley
98 Franklin Road
Penkhull
Stoke on Trent
Staffordshire
ST4 5DS

Victoria and Biddulph Angling Society
Philip R Moston
4 Stile Close
Brown Lees, Biddulph
Stoke on Trent
Staffordshire
ST8 6NL

Wadebridge Angling Association
A Gill
Jasmine Cottage
Kelly Park
St Mabyn
Bodmin
Cornwall PL30 3BL

Walkham, Tavy and Plym Fishing Club
I H Parker
36 Upland Drive
Derriford
Plymouth PL6 6BD

Wansford, Yarwell, Nassington and District Angling Club
S Longfoot
2 Dovecote Close
Yarwell, Peterborough
PE8 6PE

Wareham and District Angling Society
M Spiller
G Elms and Sons
St Johns Hill
Wareham
BH20 4NB

Warmington Angling Club
R Bosworth
2 Buntings Lane
Warmington
Peterborough
PE8 6TT

Warrington Anglers' Association
F Lithgoe
PO Box 71
Warrington
Cheshire WA1 1LR
Lancashire

Waterbeach Angling Club
H Reynolds
3 Crosskeys Court
Cottenham
Cambs BB4 4UW

Watford Piscators
Press and Public Relations Officer
S Terry
27 Wood Rise
Pinner HA5 2JE
or
A J Huntley
37 Oaklands Avenue
Oxhey
Watford WD1 4LN

Wath Brow and Ennerdale Angling Association
D F Whelan
11 Crossing Close
Cleator Moor
Cumberland

Wellingborough and District Nene Angling Club
R Blenkharn
66 Redland Drive
Kingsthorpe
Northampton
NN10 8TU

Wellington Angling Association
M Cave
60 Sylvan Road
Wellington
Somerset TA21 8EH

Wensleydale Angling Association
Mrs P A Thorpe
Grange Farm
High Birstwith
Harrogate HG3 2ST

Wessex Federation of Angling Clubs
J J Mathrick
Perham Farmhouse
Wick, Langport
Somerset
TA10 0NN

West Bay Sea Angling Club
A Neal
116 Gerrards Green
Beaminster
Dorset

Weston-super-Mare and District Angling Association
K Tucker
26 Coniston Crescent
Weston-super-Mare
Somerset BS23 3RX
or
R Stark
17 Ashcroft
Brompton Road
Weston-super-Mare

Westwater Angling
3 Crossways
East Boldon
Tyne & Wear NE36 0LP

Wey Navigation Angling Amalgamation
Secretary
c/o Village Hall
Byfleet
Surrey

Weybridge Angling Club
Howard Whitney
Guns and Tackle
137 Oatlands Drive
Oatlands Village
Weybridge, Surrey
KT13 9LB

Weymouth Angling Society
S Atkinson
Angling Centre
Commercial Road
Weymouth, Dorset

Whitby Sea Anglers' Association
D Johnson
14 Runswick Avenue
Whitby YO21 3UB

White Eagle Anglers
R A M Skelton
339B Stone Road
Stafford
Staffs ST16 1LB

White Swan Angling Club
N Barratt
Three Trees
Newark Road
Torksey, Lock
Lincoln LN1 2EJ

Whittlesey Angling Association
J Warren
55 Bellmans Road
Whittlesey
Cambs PE7 1TY

Wigan and District Angling Association
G Wilson
11 Guildford Avenue
Chorley
Lancs PR6 8TG
Membership Secretary
K Hogg
95 Holme Crescent
Wigan WN1 2HF

Wimbleball Fly Fishers' Club
Unavailable as we go to press

Wimborne and District Angling Club
G E Pipet
12 Seatown Close
Canford Heath
Poole
Dorset BH17 8BJ

Windermere, Ambleside and District Angling Association
Hon Treasurer
C J Sodo
Ecclerigg Court
Ecclerigg
Windermere
Cumbria LA23 1LQ
or Secretary
J Newton
Brackenthwaite Lodge
Black Beck Wood
Bowness
Cumbria LA23 3LS

Winsford and District Angling Association
J Stewart Bailey
22 Plover Avenue
Winsford CW7 1LA

Association of Wirral Angling Clubs
Chairman
D Billing
2 Patterdale Road
Bebington
Wirral
Secretary
S Ross
17 Greenville Road
Bebington
Wirral

Wisbech and District Angling Association
B Lakey
28 Hill Street, Wisbech
Cambridgeshire

Witham and District Joint Anglers' Federation
Stewart Oxborough
6 Ormsby Close
Cleethorpes
South Humberside
DN35 9PE

Woodbridge and District Angling Club
D N Abbott
17 Prospect Place
Leiston, Suffolk

Worksop and District Anglers' Association
D Brown
4 Dove Close
Worksop
Notts S81 7LG

Worthing and District Piscatorial Society
B Scholes
23 The Lawns, Sompting
Lancing BN15 0DT

Wroxham and District Anglers' Association
R Westgate
31 The Paddocks
Old Catton
Norwich
Norfolk NR6 7HF

Yarm Angling Association
c/o 4 Blenavon Court
Yarm
Co Durham

Yeldington Piscatorial Society
Hon. Secretary
8 Elm Quay Court
London SW8 5DE

York and District Angling Association
John Lane
39 Lowfields Drive
Acomb
York YO2 3DQ

Fishing Stations in Wales

In the pages that follow, the catchment areas of Wales are given in alphabetical order, being interspersed with the streams and the lakes under headings such as "Powys (streams)"; "Gwynedd (lakes)", etc. The rivers of each catchment area are arranged in the manner described under the heading English Fishing Stations, on p.16 and the other notes given there apply equally to Wales. The whole of the Wye and the Severn, it should be remembered, are included in the section on England, while the whole of the Dee is listed among the Welsh rivers.

Note: Sea trout are commonly referred to as "sewin" in Wales although some associations define sewin as immature sea trout returning to the river for the first time.

AERON
(For close seasons, licences, etc, see Welsh Region Environment Agency, p15)

Rises in Llyn Eiddwen, 7m north-west of Tregaron, and flows about 17m to sea at Aberaeron. Excellent run of sewin from June onwards with smaller salmon run. Brown trout plentiful but small.

Aberaeron (Dyfed). Salmon, sea trout and brown trout. Aberaeron Town AC has a 2½m stretch on R Aeron; 3m on **Arth**, a stream to the north, which holds fine brown trout and has an excellent run of sea trout; and 3 stretches on **Teifi**, north of Lampeter. Permits from Ceilee Sports, Bridge St. Tackle shop: F K Moulton & Son, Aeron Sports & Fishing Tackle, Bridge St, Aberaeron, Tel: 01545 571209.

ANGLESEY (streams)
(For close seasons, licences, etc, see Welsh Region Environment Agency, p15)

ALAW. **Llanfachraeth** (Anglesey). Rises above Cors y Bol bog and flows some 7m to sea beyond Llanfachraeth, opposite Holyhead. Fishes well (trout) for first three months of season and again in September when good run of small sea trout expected; usually too low in summer. Permission of farmers.

BRAINT. **Llangeinwen** (Anglesey). Small stream which flows almost whole width of the island, parallel with Menai Straits, to sea at Aber Menai, beyond Llangeinwen. Trout, some sea trout, but usually fishable only first three months of season. Permission of farmers.

CEFNI. **Llangefni** (Anglesey). Rises above Llangwyllog, flows through Llyn Frogwy, on to Llangefni and Cefni Reservoir, and then to sea in 6m. Lower reaches canalised. Only fair-sized river in island. Brown trout and chance of late salmon or sea trout. Permission of farmers.

CEINT. **Pentraeth** (Anglesey). Small stream entering sea at Red Wharf Bay; some trout; permission of farmers; summer conditions difficult.

FFRAW or GWNA. **Bodorgan** (Anglesey). Under the name of Gwna rises 4m above Bodorgan and waters Llyn Coron just below village. Stream then takes name of Ffraw and runs to sea at Aberffraw in 2m. Little more than brook. One or two pools fishable early on, but overgrown June onwards. Trout, some sea trout.

WYGYR. **Cemaes** (Anglesey). Small stream falling into sea at Cemaes Bay. Trout; restocked. Wygyr FA has about 2m (both banks); permits from Treasurer. Good sea fishing in bay. Hotel: Harbour, Cemaes Bay; Cefn Glas Inn, Llanfechell.

ANGLESEY (lakes)

Bodafon Lake. **Llanallgo** (Anglesey). Rudd and tench; contact Trescawen Estate, Anglesey, Gwynedd.

Cefni Reservoir. **Llangefni** (Anglesey), 172 acres: brown and rainbow trout, fly only; good wading; boats. Leased by Welsh Water plc to Cefni AA. Permits from D G Evans (Treasurer), Wenllys, Capel Coch, Llangefni; dt and wt from Ken Johnson, Tackle and Guns, Devon House, Water St, Menai Bridge; and Peter Rowe, Jewellers, Above Mon Properties, Glanhwfa Rd, Llangefni. Hotels: Nant yr Odyn Country, Tre Ysgawen Hall.

Cwn Reservoir. Holyhead (Anglesey). Coarse fishing on 2 acre reservoir; carp, rudd, bream, roach and tench; open all year round. Dt from Tackle Bar Shop, William St, Holyhead.

Llyn Alaw. Llantrisant (Anglesey). Situated in open lowland countryside this productive 777 acre reservoir offers fly fishing, spinning and worming, for brown and rainbow trout. Season 20 Mar–17 Oct for brown. Mid Sunday in Mar–last Sunday in Oct for rainbow. Dt £12, evening £10, st £380, from Visitor Centre at reservoir (dt and evening from machine in car park). Concessions to OAPs, juniors and disabled. Boats (rowing or with engine) for hire. Boat for disabled at no extra charge. Worms, flies, line, weights, spinners and a wide variety of other tackle for sale at Visitor Centre. Further information from Llyn Alaw Visitor Centre, Llantrisant, Holyhead, Anglesey, LL65 4TW, Tel: 01407 730762. Accommodation: caravans and camping, and bed and breakfast at Bodnolwyn Wen Farm, Llantrisant, Holyhead, Anglesey LL65 4TW, Tel: 01407 730298; and caravans and camping, plus meals, at The Ring (Public House), Rhosgoch, Anglesey LL66 0AB, Tel: 01407 830720.

Llyn Bryntirion. Dwyran (Anglesey). Carp, tench, roach and perch fishing on 3 ponds (3 acres of water); season Mar–Oct; no barbed hooks or keepnets; only one rod per angler. Dt from J Naylor, Bryntirion Working Farm, Dwyran, Anglesey LL61 6BQ, Tel: 01248 430232.

Llyn Coron. Bodorgan (Anglesey). Trout, sea trout; fly only. St £95, wt £35, dt £10 and evening tickets £4, after 4pm. St from Bodorgan Estate Office, Anglesey LL62 5LP (Tel: 01407 840197); or from Bailiff, Mr C Girling, at lakeside (Tel: 01407 810801). Holiday cottages are available.

Llyn Dewi. Llandeusant (Anglesey). Coarse fishing on 1 acre lake; carp, roach and rudd; open all year. Dt from Mr & Mrs Hughes Fferam Uchaf Farm, Llandeusant, Anglesey, Tel: 01407 730425.

Llyn Jane. Llandegfan (Anglesey). Trout fishing on 4 small, man-made lakes including pool for juniors. Contact Dewi & Linda Owen, Llyn Jane, Llandegfan.

Llyn Llwydiarth Fawr. Llanerchymedd (Anglesey). Coarse and game fishing on 1½ acre lake; rudd and brown trout. Fishing is only available for guests at Llwydiarth Fawr (guest house); contact R & M L Hughes, Llwydiarth Fawr, Llanerchymedd, Anglesey LL71 8DF, Tel: 01248 470321.

Llyn Maelog. Rhosneigr (Anglesey). Roach, perch, rudd, bream, eels. Permission to fish from various landowners. Information, licences and tackle (not bait) from K D Highfield, 7 Marine Terrace, Rhosneigr. Hotels: Maelog Lake, Cefn Dref, and Glan Neigr.

Llyn y Gors. Llandegfan (Anglesey). 10 acres coarse fishery, 4 lakes. Mixed lake with carp, tench, roach, rudd and perch; carp lake with carp to 27lb; match lake and children's lake. Permits, large tackle shop and bait on site. Self-catering cottages, tents and tourers. Further information from Llyn y Gors, Llandegfan, Menai Bridge, Anglesey, LL59 5PN (Tel: 01248 713410, Fax: 01248 716324).

Parc Newydd Trout Fishery. Llanerchymedd (Anglesey). Llyn Edna is 5 acre, man-made lake; stocked with brown and rainbow trout. Accommodation in self-catering cottages. For further information contact Andrew Gannon, Parc Newydd, nr Llanerchymedd LL71 7BT, Tel: 01248 470700.

Plas-y-Nant Trout Fishery. Mynydd Mechell (Anglesey). Fishing on 2½ acre lake; American brook, rainbow and brown trout; fly only, max fly size 10 and no boobys are allowed. Fishing hut and 2–5 berth caravans for hire. Also tuition and tackle hire. Permits from Plas-y-Nant Fishery, Mynydd Mechell, Amlwch, Anglesey LL68 0TH.

Ty Hen Carp Lake. Rhosneigr (Anglesey). 1½ acres of natural spring water (Ph 7.8, nitrate 0.01) for specimen carp, tench, roach and rudd. Dt £7 at lake. All fish to be returned to water. Caravan self-catering family holidays with fishing. Contact Mr Bernard Summerfield, Ty Hen Farm, Station Road, Rhosneigr, Anglesey LL64 5QZ, Tel: 01407 810331.

Tyddyn Sargent. Benllech (Anglesey). Coarse fishing on 1½ acre lake; common carp, ghost carp, crucian carp, roach, rudd, tench and bream; barbless hooks only. Fishing by appointment only; contact K Twist, Tyddyn Sargent, Tynygongl, nr Benllech, Anglesey, Tel: 01248 853024.

CLEDDAU
(EASTERN AND WESTERN)
(For close seasons, licences, etc, see Welsh Region
Environment Agency, p15)

East Cleddau rises on the east side of Prescelly Mountains and flows 15m south-west, partly along old Carmarthenshire border, to north branch of Milford Haven. West Cleddau rises in the hills and valleys south-west of Mathry and flows east towards Castle Morris. It is joined by streams such as the Afon Cleddau and Nant-y-Bugail and then flows south-east to Wolf's Castle. Here it is joined by the Afon Anghof and Afon Glan Rhyd. It then flows south to Haverfordwest and on to join the E Cleddau in a creek in the Haven. Fishing for sewin and trout is mainly in June, July and August; for salmon in August.

WESTERN CLEDDAU: Salmon, sewin and trout.

Haverfordwest (Pembrokeshire). Pembrokeshire AA has 15m stretch from Wolf's Castle to Haverfordwest; salmon, sea trout, brown trout; st £40, wt £40, dt £10: permits from County Sports, 3 Old Bridge, Harvordfordwest, Pembrokeshire; facilities for disabled in field at Nan-y-Coy. Accommodation: The Rising Sun Inn, Caravan and Camp Site, St David's Road, Haverfordwest, SA62 6EA (Tel: 01437 765171). Hamdden Ltd manages 2 reservoirs in the area on behalf of Welsh Water plc. **Llys-y-Fran Reservoir** (212 acres), rainbow trout reared on in cages within the reservoir and brown trout. Season Mar–31 Oct; limited winter fishing only until mid-Dec; catch limit 6 fish (half-day 3 fish); size limit 10in; boats; permits and tackle from Visitor Centre Shop. **Rosebush Reservoir** (33 acres) brown trout fishery in Prescelly Hills. Now operated by local syndicate but bank and boat rods from Llys-y-Fran Reservoir; advanced booking advisable. For further information contact J Waddington, Visitor Centre, Llys-y-Fran Reservoir, Clarbeston Road, nr Haverfordwest, Pembs SA63 4RR, Tel: 01437 532732/532694. **Hayscastle Trout Fishery**, 3 acre, stocked trout lake; fly only. Booking advisable. Permits from Hayscastle Trout Fishery, Upper Hayscastle Farm, Hayscastle, Dyfed, Tel: 01348 840393. Riparian owners may give permission elsewhere. Sewin fishing good June to August. Tackle shop: County Sports, Bridge Street. Hotels: Mariners.

EASTERN CLEDDAU: Trout in all rivers and tributaries in E Cleddau area; stocks mostly small fish under 7½in. Trout, sewin and salmon in **Syfynwy**, a tributary of E Cleddau.

Llanycefn (Pembrokeshire). Fishing in E Cleddau controlled by individual syndicates as far as the ford at Llandissilio; day tickets are sold by T & P J Murphy, Llangwm Farm, Llanycefn, Clynderwen, SA66 7LN, Tel/Fax: 01437 563604. U/s seek farmers permission. D/s fishing is expensive and it is necessary to join syndicates. Glancleddau Farm, Felinfach and Landre Egremont have holiday caravan parks where visitors enjoy some of the best fishing in the area. Rod licences from Post Office, Felinfach.

CLWYD
(For close seasons, licences, etc, see Welsh Region
Environment Agency, p15)

A celebrated sea trout and salmon river which has its source in the high ground to the north of Corwen and runs down through Ruthin, passes Denbigh, St Asaph and Rhuddlan and finally enters the Irish Sea at Rhyl.

Best fished for sea trout from June onwards as these fish tend to run during latter part of the month. The native brown trout population is composed of small fish, though stocking of larger specimens is undertaken annually by most of the angling clubs. There are no coarse fish species in this area.

Rhyl (Clwyd). Salmon, sea trout, brown trout. No permits needed for stretch from sea to railway bridge, however, no holding pools therefore salmon and sea trout tend to run straight through; for salmon, trout and eels, rod licence needed; close season 30 Sept–31 May. Rhyl and District AA is one of the oldest fishing clubs in the Vale of Clwyd; the majority of its waters are rented, but the club is fortunate in owning the fishing rights on 2 substantial stretches on the **R Elwy** known as Maes Elwy and Pont y Ddol; it rents 2 further stretches at Dolganed and Bron Heulog; all beats on the **R Clwyd** (Bryn Clwyd, Wern Ddu and Bryn Polyn, and Bodfair) are rented. About 10m fishing in total; all stretches contain pools which give good fishing, holding salmon, sea trout and trout. Members only, limited membership. St £80 + £100 joining fee; apply to Hon Sec (Tel: 01745 854390). Waiting list approx 1 year, conc for juv. **Tan-y-Mynydd Lake**, rainbow, brown and brook trout from 1½ to 10lb; purpose-built trout lakes, total 4 acres. Permits from A Jones, Moelfre, Abergele, Clwyd. Self-catering cottages also available. Tackle shop: Wm Roberts Ltd, 131 High St.

St Asaph (Clwyd). Salmon, sea trout and brown trout. St Asaph AA has excellent and various fishing: 6 beats on Clwyd; 3 beats on **Elwy**, 4m in St Asaph area; a beat on **Aled**, 1½m double bank at **Llansannan**; and an excellent beat on **Conwy** at Bettws-y-Coed. St £60 (OAP £38, jun £22, family £82) + £60 joining fee (no joining fee for juniors). Day permits for Elwy; and dt £10 on Gypsy Lane beat (limited rods), from Foxon's Premiere Angling Centre, Lower Denbigh Rd, St Asaph LL17 0ED (Tel: 01745 583583) which, in addition to a comprehensive range of tackle, sells various permits, and offers expert advice on all aspects of fishing both game and coarse. Hotel: Oriel House.

Denbigh (Clwyd). Clwyd, 2m E; salmon, sea trout, brown trout. Denbigh & Clwyd AC has extensive water on Clwyd, **Ystrad**, **Elwy**, **Wheeler**, and also on small stocked trout lake; members only. Tickets from Hon Sec. **Llyn Brenig** and **Alwen Reservoir**, 11m SW; trout. **Llyn Aled**, 11m SW; coarse. Permits for Llyn Brenig, Alwen Reservoir and Llyn Aled; from Llyn Brenig Visitor Centre, Cerrigdrudion, Corwen, Conwy LL21 9TT, Tel: 01490 420 463. Boat for disabled on Llyn Brenig. Coarse fishing at **Lleweni Parc**, Mold Road, Denbigh. Hotel: Fron Haul.

Ruthin (Clwyd). Trout, salmon, sea trout. Denbigh & Clwyd AC has water on Clwyd and on **River Clywedog**; members only. Hotel: Ruthin Castle.

Tributaries of the Clwyd

ELWY: Brown trout, sea trout (June onwards), salmon. No coarse fish.

St Asaph (Clwyd). St Asaph AA has Gypsy Lane Waters: dt £10 from Foxon's Tackle, Penrhewl, St Asaph. Capenhurst AC has water; salmon and trout; member only.

Bodelwyddan (Denbighshire). Bodelwyddan Angling Club has 2 small beats on the Elwy; day tickets for small beat on lower Elwy; permits from Foxon's Tackle, Penrhewl, St Asaph. **Felin y Gors Fisheries**, stocked brown and rainbow trout; 4 lakes; 10½acres; fly only. Day ticket fishery with various prices from £6 to £17 (fullday). Children's bait fishing on 3 separate

waters. Tuition, tackle hire, tackle shop and self-contained accommodation. Bookings in advance from Robert Monshin, St Asaph Road, Bodelwyddan, Denbighshire LL18 5UY, Tel: 01352 720965 (day), 01745 584044 (evening).

Llansannan (Clwyd). St Asaph AA has 1½m double bank on **Aled**. **Dolwen** and **Plas Uchaf Reservoirs**, a few miles SW of St Asaph; well stocked with brown and rainbow trout; fly, spinning and worming; 6 fish limit. Season 14 Mar–31 Oct. Permits from Shirley Anne's Newsagents, 2 Church View, Bodelwyddan, St Asaph, Tel: 01745 582206. Booking advised as rods limited to 16. Concession OAP and jun.

WHEELER: Trout.

Afonwen (Clwyd). Denbigh & Clwyd AC has 2m; some fly only. Mold Trout A has 1¼m. Mold Kingfishers AC has fishing on Wheeler and on lake at Afonwen.

CLYWEDOG: Salmon and sea trout (very late), trout. All water strictly preserved.

Ruthin (Clwyd). Denbigh & Clwyd AC has stretch from confluence with Clwyd to Rhewl; and has water in Bontuchel and Llanrhaeadr areas; member only. Capenhurst AC has stretch at Bontuchel; salmon, sea trout and trout; members only. Members children (under 18) may fish free of charge, but must be accompanied by adult.

CONWY
(For close seasons, licences, etc, see Welsh Region Environment Agency, p15)

Rises on Migneint, in the County of Conwy and flows between the old Caernarvonshire and Denbighshire boundaries for much of its course, emptying into the Irish Sea near Conwy. The upper part of its valley is noted for its beauty. Spate river with salmon runs throughout season (May and June usually best); grilse early July; sea trout late June to September.

Conwy (Gwynedd). Tidal; sea fishing only. Codling, dabs, plaice, bass and mullet above and below suspension bridge. Boats for hire. Salmon and sea trout; Prince Albert AS has Belmont fishery, at Meenan Abbey. **Llyn Gwern Engan**, a small lake on Sychnant Pass Common; rudd, tench, carp, gudgeon; also free fishing, contact Snowdonia National Park

Committee, Penrhydeudraeth, Gwynedd. **Llyn Nant-y-Cerrig**, Brynymaen, 1½ acres; carp, bream, tench, perch; tickets at lakeside or local tackle shops. For further information contact N Roberts, Goleugell, Eglwysbach, Colwyn Bay, Clwyd LL28 5UH, Tel: 01492 650314. **Clobryn Pool**, Clobryn Rd, Colwyn Bay; tench, crucian carp, roach, rudd, perch. **Glas Coed Pools**, Bodelwyddan, set in grounds of Bodelwyddan Castle, carp, tench, roach, rudd. **Trefant Pool**, newly opened; stocked with tench, carp, roach, rudd and perch. Permits for Llyn Nant-y-Cerrig, Clobryn Pool, Glas Coed Pools and Trefant Pool from The Tackle Box, 17 Greenfield Rd, Colwyn Bay LL29 8EL, Tel: 01492 531104; the shop offers a full list of trout, coarse and specialist waters in the area and the proprietor (a previous Welsh bass champion) can also advise on all aspects of local sea fishing. Other tackle shops: North Wales Bait Supplies, 4 Parc Ffynnon, Llysfaen; and Llandudno Fishing Tackle, 14 Mostyn Ave, Llandudno.

Dolgarrog (Gwynedd). Salmon, sea trout and brown trout; deep tidal pools. Dolgarrog FC has tidal water. Club also has rainbow and brown trout fishing on **Llyn Coedty**; and trout fishing on **Llyn Eigiau**. Permits from Hon Sec. **Llyn Melynllyn**, 5m E; **Llyn Dulyn**, 6m E; **Llyn Cowlyd** (5m W Llanwrst); all trout reservoirs belonging to Welsh Water plc; free to licence-holders. **Llanrwst** (Gwynedd). Salmon and good sea trout; brown trout poor. Llanrwst AC has various beats on R Conwy at Llanrwst and Trefriw; some sections members only. Limited wt £45 (to 12 Sept only) and dt £15 from Hon Sec. Sunday fishing allowed. Permits from Forestry Commission, Gwydyr Uchaf, for left bank of **Machno** from junction with Conwy and portion of right bank. Dt 60p, from P Haveland, Manchester House, Penmachno, Betws-y-Coed LL24 0UD, Tel: 01690 760337. Hotels: Maenan Abbey Hotel and Victoria Hotel (both have salmon and trout); and Eagles Hotel, Bridge St.

Betws-y-Coed (Conwy). Salmon, sea trout, brown trout. Betws-y-Coed AC has 4½m of salmon, sea trout and brown trout fishing on Conwy and **Llugwy**; on the Conwy, from the Waterloo Bridge (left bank) downstream to the confluence of the **Llugwy**. The club also has 3 trout lakes: **Elsi Lake**, stocked with some American brook trout and brown trout; **Llyn Goddionduon**, stocked with brown trout; and **Llyn Bychan**. St £135 (£65 for partially disabled) from Hon Sec; dt £30 and £18 (river),

and £15 (lake) from Mr G Parry, Tan Lan Café (nr Post Office). Concessions juniors. St Asaph AA has ¾m stretch. Gwydyr Hotel has 8m of salmon and sea trout fishing; season 20 Mar–17 Oct; tickets for residents only. For further information contact Owen Wainwright, Gwydyr Hotel, Bangor Road, Betws-y-Coed LL24 0AB, Tel: 01690 710777. Tackle at hotel. Bryn Trych Hotel has salmon, trout and sea trout fishing on Conwy, tributaries and lakes. Other hotels: Craig-y-Dderwen Country House, Waterloo.

Ysbyty Ifan (Conwy). Brown trout. National Trust has stretch at Ysbyty Ifan and Dinas Water on upper Conwy; fly, worm and spinning. Permits from National Trust, Trinity Square, Llandudno, Conwy LL30 2DE; National Trust, Estate Office, Dinas, nr Betws-y-Coed, Gwynedd LL24 0HF; and R Ellis, Bron Ryffydd, Padog, Betws-y-Coed, Conwy LL24 0HF, Tel: 01690 710567. For holiday cottages contact The National Trust Holiday Booking Office, PO Box 536, Melksham, Wiltshire SN12 8SX, Tel: 01225 791199.

Tributaries of the Conwy

ROE: Trout.

Rowen (Gwynedd). Fly fishing impossible on lower reaches **Conwyn Valley Fisheries**, Glyn Isa, Rowen, nr Conwy LL32 8PT, Tel: 01492 650063; 2 acre, spring-fed lake, rainbow trout, fly only, all year round. Tackle hire and instruction arranged. Shop stocks flies and accessories; cafe; good access for disabled; permits sold on bank. Accommodation at Glyn Isa in 4 self-contained cottages with free fishing on Conwy Valley Fisheries.

DDU: Trout.

Pont Dolgarrog (Gwynedd). Trout. Ddu enters Conwy ½m below village; drains Llyn Cowlyd. **Llyn Cowlyd**, brown trout and Arctic char; fly only; free permits from Welsh Water plc.

CRAFNANT: Trout.

Trefriw (Gwynedd). Trout fishing on Llyn Crafnant, one of the most beautiful lakes in Wales, 63 acres, stocked rainbow trout supplementing wild brown trout. Sunday fishing. Day tickets, rod licences, boats, cafe, self-catering accommodation, toilets, car parking and information from Mr & Mrs J Collins, Lakeside Café,

Llyn Crafnant, Trefriw, LL27 0JZ, Tel: 01492 640818. Hotel: Princes Arms and Fairy Falls.

LLEDR: Trout, sewin, salmon.

Dolwyddelan (Gwynedd). Dolwyddelan FA fishing on River Lledr both above and below the village, and at Pont y Pant; salmon, brown trout and sea trout; good late season salmon runs; sea trout from 1st July. Wt (Mon–Fri) and dt for visitors, although wt only for visitors resident in village. Permits and tackle, including locally tied flies, from Post Office, Dolwyddelan, Gwynedd LL25 0NJ, Tel: 01690 750201. Prince Albert AS has 2 stretches, at Bertheos and Hendre; enquire Hon Sec. Hotel: Elen's Castle Hotel, Dolwyddelan.

LLUGWY: Salmon, sea trout, brown trout.

Betws-y-Coed (Conwy). Betws-y-Coed AC has a stretch, both banks, from Swallow Falls downstream to the confluence of Conwy on right bank and to railway bridge on left bank. Permits from Tan Lan Café, Betws-y-Coed, Tel: 01690 710232.

MACHNO: Trout.

Penmachno (Conwy). National Trust has water on Machno; no salmon fishing above Conwy Falls; brown trout only. Permits from National Trust, Trinity Square, Llandudno, Conwy LL30 2DE; National Trust, Estate Office, Dinas, nr Betws-y-Coed, Conwy LL24 0HF; and Robin Ellis, Bron Ryffydd, Padog, Betws-y-Coed, Conwy LL24 0HF, Tel: 01690 710567.

DEE (Welsh)

(For close seasons, licences, etc, see Welsh Region Environment Agency, p12)

Usually has a spring run of fish up to 30lb. Grilse enter in June and there is a run of grilse and summer fish until the end of the season as a rule. In spring most fish are taken from Bangor to Corwen. Trout from Bangor upstream and grayling above Llangollen. Coarse fish predominate downstream of Bangor. River holds good bream, roach, dace, perch and pike.

Holywell (Clwyd). **Forest Hill Trout Farm**, Mostyn, nr Holywell, CH8 9EQ (Tel: 01745 560151): fishing on 3 lakes fed by spring water, stocked with home-reared rainbow and brown trout; fly or bait. Tea, coffee, homemade cakes on site, facilities for disabled.

Seven Springs Trout Farm and Fisheries, Caerwys, nr Mold, Flintshire CH7 5EZ, Tel: 01352 720511; 3 pools over 1 acre, containing rainbow trout; fly and bait; tackle hire and tuition; anglers' room, toilet and gutting room; tickets at fisheries (bookings taken), £7.50, 3 fish, £10, 5 fish, £14, 7 fish. Coarse fishing at **Gyrn Castle Fishery**, Llanasa, Holywell, Flintshire CH8 9BG; 2 lakes, 3 acres and 1 acre; well stocked with carp, rudd and tench; heaviest carp to date – 30 lb; barbless hooks only. Fishermen's hut with tea and coffee-making facilities. Closed 30 Sept–31 Jan. Dt £15, accompanied juv £7; only 8 permits per day allowed. Permits from Mr Partington, Gyrn Castle Estate, South Lodge, Glan-yr-Afon, Tel: 01745 561672. Greenfield Valley AC issue membership, £15, conc, for **Flour Mill Pool**; 4 acre fishery situated in Greenfield Valley Heritage Park; rudd, crucian carp, tench, perch, bream, ghost carp, gudgeon, common and mirror carp, roach; contact Visitors' Centre.

Connah's Quay (Clwyd). Connah's Quay and Dist AC has 2m trout fishing at **Wepre Brook**; 2½m trout and coarse fishing on **River Alyn**; no dt. Club also has coarse fishing at **Wepre Pool**, **Swan Lake** and **Cymau Pools**; st and dt from Deeside Tackle & Sport, Chester Road, Shotton, Deeside. Tackle shop: Mrs I M Williams, 316 High Street, Connah's Quay.

Chester (Cheshire). Coarse fish. Little permit-free fishing. No licence for coarse fishing in tidal waters. Most fishing on River Dee controlled by Chester AA. Assn also has fishing on **Rivers Vyrnwy** and **Severn**. No day tickets. St £10 (OAP and jun £4) for trout and coarse fishing only from Hon Sec or Chester area tackle shops. Free fishing from Mon to Fri, on Eaton Estate from public footpath that adjoins river. **River Gowy**, which runs into Mersey, passing by Mickle Trafford about 3m from Chester; Warrington AA has water. **Meadow Fishery**, Mickle Trafford, Tel: 0124 300 236, rainbow trout; 5 acres; st and dt. Tackle shops: Henry Monk (Gunmaker) Ltd, 8 Queen Street (Tel: 01244 320988); Jones Fishing Tackle & Pet Foods, 39 Vernon Rd.

Holt (Clwyd). Salmon, trout, pike, bream. Holt and Farndon AA has stretch at Holt; bream, dace, roach, perch; st and dt from Hon Sec. Dee AA rent approx 10m of Dee from Chester AA in the Farndon and Sutton Green area. Maps can be obtained from Hon Sec, price 50p plus SAE. Assn issues salmon permits (limited) for

Sutton Green stretch; separate trout and coarse fish permits. Permits from local tackle shops and B W Roberts, 23 Alpraham Crescent, Upton, Chester, Tel: 01244 381193. All waters in the Chester area and downstream to Queensferry controlled by the Chester AA; match permits and membership cards from B W Roberts; no day tickets issued for these waters. Maghull and Lydiate AC has stretch on Dee at Lower Hall; roach, bream, chub, perch, sea trout, salmon, trout and gudgeon; members only. Instruction for juniors and competitive events for all members. Warrington AA has Shocklach Water and stretch at Almere; members only, but visiting anglers accommodated, providing they supply date of visit in advance. Lavister AC has 1m stretch (left bank) upstream from Almere Ferry; bream, dace, roach, perch, pike; members only. Kirkdale AA has 2m at Holt; members only. Cheshire AA has 1m on Dee upstream of Farndon Bridge, south bank. Waters on the **Grosvenor Estates** at Churton and Aldford downstream to Chester; free freelance fishing but matches must be booked with the Eaton Estate Office, Eccleston, Chester (Tel: 01244 684400).

Bangor-on-Dee (Clwyd). Salmon, trout, coarse fish. Bangor-on-Dee Salmon AA has 2 stretches; one downstream from town, the other near Shocklach; member only but membership available (£55 + £25 joining fee); dt £5 (coarse) and £12 (salmon). Permits from Hon Sec. Northern A has stretches on **Dee** and **Worthenbury Brook**; club also has fishing on **Shropshire Union Canal** and **River Alyn**; members only. Warrington AA has water on Worthenbury Brook. Hotel: The Buck Hotel.

Overton (Clwyd). Bryn-y-Pys AA has 7m on R Dee between Overton Bridge and Bangor-on-Dee; rainbow and brown trout, grayling and coarse fish. St £34.50, £24.50 (OAP) and £15 (junior); entrance fee £10. Dt £8 (trout season) and £4, from Deggy's Fishing Tackle, 2 Ruabon Road, Wrexham. Boat Inn, Erbistock, has salmon and trout beat. **Trench Fisheries** have 4 pools (3 acres) with carp, tench, rudd and crucian carp; day tickets only; contact Mr & Mrs M A Huntbach, Trench Farm, Redhall Lane, Penley, Wrexham LL13 0NA, Tel: 01978 710098.

Cefn Mawr (Clwyd). Trout, salmon, coarse fish (including pike and excellent grayling fishing). Maelor AA has 6m, with good autumn salmon fishing on 2 beats, coarse fishing,

stocked brown trout, and very good winter grayling; st £100 salmon, trout £50, 4 fish per day limit; contact Chairman (Tel: 01978 820608); coarse fishing good September onwards. Tickets from tackle shop. Newbridge AA has Wynnstay Estate Waters from Newbridge Old Bridge downstream on wooded bank, approx 3m; salmon, trout, grayling, dace and pike fishing; members only, except for salmon rods on top beat; members to reside within local radius of 5m. Salmon permits from Hon Sec, membership £27 per annum, £70 salmon. Tackle shop: Derek's Fishing Tackle, London House, Well St. Hotel: Wynnstay Arms, Ruabon.

Llangollen (Denbighshire). Salmon, sea trout, brown trout, grayling. Llangollen AA has 14m of bank fishing in and around the town. All waters have good access and parking provided. Downstream from Horseshoe Falls, all methods for salmon and trout; above Horseshoe Falls, all methods for salmon, fly only for trout and grayling. Trout water stocked with 5,500 trout per season, averaging 12in with larger fish up to 3lb. Both trout and grayling fishing excellent and near best on River Dee. Salmon fishing good from May to end of season, average catch for club is 65 fish. Wt £40 (S) and £25 (T), dt £15 (S) and £6 (T). No waiting list for trout membership. Permits from Hughes Newsagents, 12 Chapel Street, Llangollen, Denbighshire LL20 8NN (Tel: 01978 860155), also fishing tackle and information. Half day closing Thursday and Sunday. **Abbey Fishery**, a trout farm 1½m from Llangollen; 2 bait ponds, 1 fly pond and ½m on River Dee. Accommodation in log cabins. Contact David and Margaret Penman, Penvale Lodges, Abbey Fishery, Llangollen, Denbighshire LL20 8DD, Tel: 01978 860266. Northern A has stretch on **Shropshire Union Canal** from Hurleston Junction to Llantysilio; members only. Hand Hotel, Bridge St, Llangollen, Denbighshire LL20 8PL, Tel: 01978 860303, has own stretch of water below the bridge on right bank; fishing on hotel stretch of river for hotel residents only. Liverpool & Dist AA has salmon and trout fishing at Chain Bridge; st and dt. Tackle from Hughes Newsagents, 12 Chapel St, Llangollen, LL20 8NN (Tel: 01978 860155); Elbourns, Chapel St. Hotels: Royal, Bryn Howell.

Glyndyfrdwy (Denbighshire). Salmon, trout and grayling. Corwen and Dist AC has 1½m (mainly single bank) on Berwyn Arms Water; 5 named salmon pools; salmon, trout and grayling.

Contact Membership Sec (Tel: 01824 710609). Midland Flyfishers have 3m of salmon and trout fishing on the Dee from Groeslwyd to Glyndyfrdwy; and trout fishing on **River Onny**, **Quinney Brook**, **Byne Brook**, **River Lugg** and a trout pool. Fly fishing for trout and grayling only. Salmon fishing is reserved for members. Membership is strictly by invitation only, and there is a long waiting list. Nr Pershore, Worcs WR0 3JA. Dt £6, from Post Office, Glyndyfrdwy; Bob Jones-Roberts, Coedial, Glyndyfrdwy; Hughes Newsagents, 12 Chapel Street, Llangollen, Denbighshire LL20 8NN.

Corwen (Clwyd). Corwen and Dist AC has **Rhug Estate Water**, approx 4m mostly double bank, trout and grayling, fly only except winter grayling; ¼m stretch at **Cynwyd** including large holding pool, salmon, trout and grayling; ¾m stretch at **Carrog**, 3 named pools and runs, salmon, trout and grayling; 1½m stretch at Glyndyfrdwy; 2 stretches, 1m (double bank) and ¾m (double bank), between Cynwyd and Llandrillo, salmon, trout and grayling; and Chain Pool at Bonwn. Club also has several miles of water on **Rivers Alwen** and **Ceirw** at Bettws Gwerfil Goch and Maerdy; salmon and sea trout, mid to late season; and good trout early and late. No dt; members only. Apply to Membership Sec (Tel: 01824 710609). Capenhurst AC has stretch downstream of Carrog Bridge, Carrog; salmon, sea trout and trout; members only. **Gwyddelwern Pool**, Corwen, ¾ acre lake, stocked with coarse fish (large carp and tench); permits from D M Lewis, Maes-y-Llyn, Gwyddelwern, Corwen, Clwyd LL21 9DU, Tel: 01490 412761. Rod licences from Corwen Post Office. Hotel: Owain Glyndwr.

Cynwyd (Clwyd). Trout, grayling, salmon. Corwen and Dist AC has stretch on Dee from Glascoed to Cynwyd Bridge; plus ¾m double bank (salmon, trout and grayling) above Cynwyd Bridge; and trout fishing on **Cynwyd Reservoir**; Sunday fishing, fly only. Members only. Crown Inn, Llanfihangel, has free fishing for guests.

Llandrillo (Clwyd). Salmon, trout, grayling, perch and pike. Strictly preserved by executors of Duke of Westminster's Pale Estate. Tyddyn Llan Country Hotel arranges fishing for guests; tuition and equipment. Rod licences from Tyddyn Llan Country House Hotel & Restaurant.

Llandderfel (Gwynedd). Salmon, trout, grayling. Pale Hall Country House Hotel, Llandderfel, nr Bala, Gwynedd LL23 7PS, Tel: 01678 530285, has prime salmon and trout fishing during game season. Excellent grayling fishing provides ideal winter sport with specimens reaching 3lb. Fishing is based on 6m of **River Dee** with access to brown trout in mountain lake. Coarse fishing on **Bala Lake** included in permit. Permits from D Evans, Yr Eryr Sports & Tackle, 31–33 High Street, Bala LL23 7AF; and Bryntirion Inn, Llandderfel.

Bala (Gwynedd). Salmon, trout, perch, pike and grayling. Bala AA has water, including from confluence with Tryweryn to Bala Lake; and fishing on Bala Lake (members only). Assn also has water on **Rivers Tryweryn**, **Lliw**, and **Llafar** (dt); **Lynn Tryweryn** (trout, fly only, dt); **Llyn Celyn** (brown trout). Sunday fishing allowed. Concessions for juniors. Instruction and competitions for juniors. Permits from tackle shop and J A Jones, Post Office, Frongoch, nr Bala. **Bala Lake** or **Llyn Tegid**; trout, roach, perch, pike, grayling, eel; owned by Snowdonia National Park Authority. Permits from tackle shops and Lake Warden. Warden's Office, 24 Ffordd Pensarn, Bala, Tel: Bala 520626. Tackle shop: D Evans, Yr Eryr Sports & Tackle, 33 High Street, Bala LL23 7AF. Hotels and accommodation: White Lion Royal; Plas Coch; Mrs Shirley Pugh, 4 Castle St; Penbryn Farm Guesthouse, Sarnau (coarse fishing).

Llanuwchllyn (Gwynedd). Trout and grayling. Prince Albert AS has trout and grayling fishing on 9 stretches of Dee, here and elsewhere. and Twrch; members only; waiting list. Dolhendre Uchaf Caravan Park (Tel: 01678 540629) has private fishing for owners of caravans on site only.

Tributaries of the Dee

ALYN: Trout. Drains hills to west of Clwydian Range, runs past Mold towards Wrexham and finally opens into lower part of Dee on Cheshire Plains near Farndon at Almere.

Rossett (Clwyd). Trout. Rossett and Gresford FF has wild brown trout fishing on 2½m stretch (both banks) on well maintained and stocked section of R Alwyn between Rossett and Gresford, nr Wrexham. Members only; fly only; bag limit. St £35 and £5 (juniors). Permits from Hon Sec (Tel: 01978 854514). Warrington AA have water lower down and stretch on Dee, at

Almere. Hotel: Trevor Arms Hotel, Marford, Wrexham, Tel: 01244 570436.

Gresford (Clwyd). Trout. Griffin AC has 3 stretches; members only.

Wrexham (Clwyd). Wrexham and Dist AA has water on Alyn; trout fishing, fly only. Permits issued to guests of members only. Dee Valley Services PLC, Packsaddle, Wrexham Rd, Rhostyllen, Wrexham, Clwyd LL14 4DS, Tel: 01978 846946, manage 3 local reservoirs: **Ty Mawr Reservoir** (20 acres), **Penycae Upper Reservoir** (7 acres) and **Penycae Lower Reservoir** (5 acres). The fishing is quiet and secluded with very clear water; possible to locate and stalk individual fish (stocked up to 6 lb). Brown and rainbow trout; fly fishing only. St £228, dt £16–£11 (Penycae) and £15–£10 (Ty Mawr). At least 12 hrs' notice must be given in order to reserve a rod. Number of rods limited. Contact the bailiff, Tel: 01978 840116. Ponciau AS has **Ponciau Pool**, 2½m from Wrexham; roach, bream, tench, carp; members only. Rhostyllen AC has coarse fishing at pool near Sontley; club also has access to extensive game and coarse fisheries on **Dee**, **Vyrnwy** and **Shropshire Union Canal**. Tackle shops: Deggy's Fishing Tackle, 2 Ruabon Rd, Pen-y-Bryn, Tel: 01978 351815; and Morrison's Fishing Tackle, York Street, Wrexham. Hotel: Trevor Arms Hotel, Marford, Wrexham.

Llay (Clwyd). Llay AA has good coarse fishing on **Llay Reservoir** (tench, carp, rudd, perch, pike); and **Cymau Pool** (carp, rudd, tench, perch, roach, crucian carp and gudgeon) at Caergwrle. Members only. St £8.50 (jun £3.50 and OAP £1) from Hon Sec, local shops or bailiff on bank. Hotels: Crown Inn, Mount Pleasant.

Hope (Clwyd). Wrexham and Dist AA has trout fishing from Llong railway bridge to Pont y Delyn; fly only; permits issued to members' guests only. Brown and rainbow trout fishing at **Tree Tops Fly Fishery**; 10 lakes stocked with rainbow and brown trout. Rods to hire and basic tuition by arrangement. Cafe, tackle shop and accommodation. For further details contact Joy & Peter Price, Tree Tops Fly Fishery, Llanfynydd, nr Wrexham, Flintshire LL11 5HR, Tel: 01352 770648.

Mold (Clwyd). Mold TA has 5m on Alyn and 2m on **R Wheeler**; and fishing on **New Lake**,

Rhydymwyn. All fisheries stocked with brown and rainbow trout. Permits from Grosvenor Pet and Garden Centre, Grosvenor St, Tel: 01352 754264. Mold Fly Fishers have trout fishing on **Pistyll Pool** at **Nercwys**, 1½ acres (stocked brown and rainbow trout) and 1½m of **R Terrig** at Nercwys (brown trout); members only; day tickets if accompanied by member, conc for juv. Pen-y-Ffrith Fly Fishery, Llandeela Rd, Llanarmon-yn-Ial, Mold, CH7 4QX (Tel: 01824 780501); 3 spring-fed lakes stocked daily with rainbows from 2lb to 20lb, some brown and blue trout; 8 hours fishing, 4 fish limit, 4 hrs 2 fish; also catch and release; tackle shop on site, book in at lodge. Buckley AA has **Trap Pool**, a good mixed fishery; permits from Lionel's Tackle Shop, Pentre Lane, Buckley, Flintshire CH7 3PA, Tel: 01244 543191. Alltami AC has coarse fishing on **Alltami Clay Pits**; carp, tench, bream, roach; no dt, details from Lionel's Tackle Shop. Coarse fishing at **Gweryd Lakes**, Gweryd Lodge, Plas Lane, Llanarmon-yn-Ial, nr Mold, Denbighshire CH7 4QJ (Tel: 01824 780230). 12½ acre lake with specimen carp, 1¾ acre lakes with smaller chub, etc. Dt £5, £6 Fri/Sun, conc. Accom on site.

Cilcain (Clwyd). Cilcain FFA has 4 trout reservoirs nearby; stocked with rainbow trout; fly only. Permits from H Williams, Treasurer, 20 Maes Cilan, Tel: 01352 740924. **Nant-y-Gain Fishery**, 2 pools stocked with brown and rainbow trout, fly only. Access and facilities for disabled anglers. Tickets and refreshments available on site. Contact Glyn and Judy Jones, Nant-y-Gain Fishery, Cilcain, Flintshire CH7 5PE, Tel: 01352 740936.

Nannerch (Clwyd). **Sarn Mill Trout Fishery**, Sam Mill, Nannerch, nr Mold, Tel: 01352 720323, 5 pools; one pool wild brown trout; 2 pools stocked with brown trout and rainbow trout; 2 pools stocked with brown trout, rainbow trout, roach, rudd, tench and carp. Bait for sale, fishing tackle for hire and camp site for tents and caravans. **Wal Goch Fly Fishing**; 2 lakes (2½ and ½ acre); brown and rainbow trout. Open all year; fly only; max 20 rods; floodlights, catch-and-release, trickle stocked. Contact Philip Robinson, Wal Goch Fly Fishing, Wal Goch Farm, CH7 5RP, Tel: 01352 741378.

CEIRIOG: Trout.

Chirk (Clwyd). Ceiriog Fly Fishers have 6½m, both banks, from Dee Junction to Ladies Bridge and from Chirk Aqueduct to Pontfadog Village; good fishing, trout and grayling; fly only; keepered and stocked. No tickets; strictly members and guests only. St £150 from to Hon Sec. Chirk Trout Fishery, LL14 5BL (Tel: 01691 772420); two small lakes for fly and spinning, plus children's lake; stocked with rainbow, brown, and American brook trout; dt £20, 6 fish, £12, 4 fish, conc. Hotel: The Hand Hotel, Chirk; Golden Pheasant, Llwyn Mawr.

Glyn Ceiriog (Clwyd). Glyn Ceiriog FC has trout fishing on **River Teirw** at Pandy, nr Glyn Ceiriog; permits from Golden Pheasant Hotel, Glyn Ceiriog, nr Llangollen LL20 7BB, Tel: 01691 718281.

Llanarmon Dyffryn Ceiriog (Clwyd). Ceiriog, 2½m, brown trout. West Arms Hotel (Tel: 01691 600665) has 1½m (both banks) trout fishing; shallow clear water with some deep pools. Free to hotel residents; dt for non-residents. Limit 2 rods per day; fly only. Hand Hotel has trout and coarse fishing for guests (both hotels issue rod licences).

ALWEN: Flows out of large reservoir (trout, perch) on Denbigh Moors and enters Dee near Corwen. Very good trout fishing and some salmon.

Cerrig-y-Drudion (Clwyd). Cerrig-y-Drudion AA has river fishing on Alwen and on **R Ceirw**, parallel with A5 road. Crown Inn, Llanfihangel Glyn Myfyr, has fishing on ¼m of bank for small wild brown trout; fly and worm; permits (free to hotel residents). Welsh Water plc manage 3 reservoirs north of town. **Llyn Brenig**, 919-acre reservoir amid heather moorland and forest. Fly only, brown and rainbow trout. Llyn Brenig was the venue for 1990 World Fly Fishing Championship and regular Home Fly Fishing Internationals. St £340, dt £10.50, evening £8.50, boats £17 per day. Season: Mar–Nov. Concessions OAP & jun; block bookings offered. **Alwen Reservoir** (368 acre), moorland reservoir stocked with rainbow and brown trout, although also natural population of brown trout and perch; dt £7.50. Fly fishing, spinning and worming permitted; catch limit 6 trout. Season Mar–Nov. **Llyn Aled Reservoir** (110 acres) holds large numbers of roach, perch and pike and is a good match venue; occasional wild brown trout. No close season for coarse fish. Concessions OAP and jun. Tickets and further information from Llyn Brenig Visitor Centre,

Cerrigdrudion, Corwen, Conwy LL21 9TT, Tel: 01490 420 463; where there is also a café and well-stocked tackle shop. Coarse fishing at **Tyddyn Farm Field Centre**, Cefn Brith, Cerrig-y-Drudion, Corwen LL21 9TS. Fly fishing at **Dragonfly Fisheries**, On the A5, Cerrig-y-Drudion, Corwen, Clwyd, Tel: 01490 420530; American brook, rainbow and brown trout; dt.

TRYWERYN: Joins Dee below Lake Bala. Good trout fishing.

Bala (Gwynedd). Bala AA has 2 stretches on Tryweryn, **Llyn Celyn** and mountain lake **Cwm Prysor**. Tickets from E W Evans, Sports & Tackle Shop, 31–33 High St LL23 7AF.

DYFI (Dovey)
(For close seasons, licences, etc, see Welsh Region Environment Agency, p15)

Rises on east side of Aran Fawddwy and flows 30m south and south-west to Cardigan Bay at Aberdovey. Has long estuary and provides splendid sport with sewin (sea trout) and salmon. Many large sea trout taken. Salmon run in from July to October; sea trout from May on. Best months: July, August, September. Small tributaries hold some little trout, and permission can generally be obtained from owners.

Aberdyfi (Gwynedd). At estuary mouth; surf and estuary fishing. Free trout fishing in Happy Valley on permission of farmers; stream; trout small.

Machynlleth (Powys). Sea trout and salmon. New Dovey Fishery Association controls 15m (both banks) of river between Llyfnant stream and Nant Ty-Mawr and left bank, from opposite Llyfnant mouth to Abergwybedyn brook. Season rods available £590 when vacancies occur (long waiting list – contact Hon Sec). Upper reaches st £150 from Hon Sec. Limited visitors wt £100 (juv dt £3.50, when accompanied by adult) from T A Hughes Newsagent, Penrallt St, Machynlleth, Powys SY20 8AG, Tel: 01654 702495; Mrs L Humphreys, Post Office, Cemmaes Rd, Machynlleth SY20 8JZ (Tel: 01650 511422); and Hon Sec, Tel/Fax: 01654 702721. Dt £10 for upper reaches. No Sunday fishing. Permission from farmers for **Pennal Stream**; rapid water; trout small. Corris AC controls 7m of **N Dulas**. St £15, wt £7.50 and dt £5. Concessions for juveniles and OAPs. Permits from Hon Sec; Hughes Newsagents,

Machynlleth; and Maelor Stores, Corris. Llugwy Hotel, Pennal, has ½m on **S Dulas** free to guests. Tackle shop: Greenstiles. Hotels: Wynnstay Arms, White Lion.

Llanbrynmair (Powys). On **River Twymyn**, a tributary of **Dyfi**; sewin, salmon. Llanbrynmair and Dist AC has water on Twymyn from village to confluence with Dyfi (apart from one stretch held by Prince Albert AS); and wild brown trout fishing on **Lakes Gwyddior** and **Coch-Hwyad**, both lakes 25 acres with a boat on each. Best months Jul–Oct. Permits from Mrs D R Lewis, Bryn-Llugwy Llanbrynmair, Powys SY19 7AA, Tel: 01650 521 385. Prince Albert AS control 3m of Twymyn, and Dyfi at **Aberangell** and **Dinas Mawddwy;** enquiries to Hon Sec.

Dinas Mawddwy (Gwynedd). Sewin, salmon, trout; fishing good. Brigands Inn, Mallwyd, has some of the best pools on upper reaches and stretch on **Cleifion**; day tickets for guests only. Buckley Arms Hotel has water from the Cowarch down to hotel, for residents only. Sea trout runs (water permitting) May, July, Sept; best July to October. The Dolbrodmaeth Inn, Dinas Mawddwy, Machynlleth, Powys SY20 9LP, Tel: 01650 531333, has ½m stretch on Dyfi in grounds of hotel; sewin, salmon, trout; reserved for guests. The hotel also issues tickets for 12m of Rivers Mawddach and Wnion, and Lake Cynwch (all in vicinity of Dolgellau). Prince Albert AS has 2½m stretch of Dyfi at Gwastad Coed, Gwerhefin.

DWYRYD

(For close seasons, licences, etc. see Welsh Region Environment Agency, p15)

Rises in small, nameless pool 3m above Tanygrisiau and flows into Cardigan Bay through estuary north of Harlech. A classic spate river with deep pools which hold good numbers of fish following a spate. Sea trout enter the river towards the end of May: these tend to be large fish with the 1–3lb following in June. Fresh sea trout still enter the river in October. The first run of salmon appears in July with increasing numbers in August, September and October.

Maentwrog (Gwynedd). Dwyryd Anglers Ltd has fishing at **Tan-y-Bwlch Fishery** on River Dwyryd (north bank only), 1¾m downstream from Maentwrog Bridge. St £40 (limited), wt £20 (any 7 consecutive days) and dt £7.

Concessions for juniors and OAPs. Permits from Gareth Price, Tackle Shop, Hafan, Fford Peniel, Ffestiniog, Gwynedd, Tel: 01766 762451. Dwyryd Anglers Ltd also has 3½m (double bank) of private water on Dwyryd; a very limited number of season rods may become available, contact G. Price for information.

Blaenau Ffestiniog (Gwynedd). Principal trout lakes controlled by Cambrian AA as follows: **Dubach**, well stocked with brown trout; **Manod**, fishing rather rough due to rocky shore conditions, holds plenty of fish; **Morwynion**, most easily accessible, average weight 12ozs; **Cwmorthin**, well stocked with brown trout 8–9ozs. Other Cambrian AA lakes: **Dubach-y-Bont**, fish to 2½lb no rarity, **Barlwyd, Cwm Foel** and **Cwm Corsiog**. St £35, wt £16, dt £4, Concession for juniors. **Tanygrisiau Reservoir** (2m NW), 95 acres, stocked with brown and rainbow trout; controlled by local syndicate. Spinning and bait fishing allowed. Permits for Cambrian AA waters and for Tanygrisiau from F W Roberts, Fishing Tackle, 32 Church Street, Blaenau Ffestiniog, Gwynedd LL41 3HD, Tel: 01766 830607. Hotels: Pengwern Arms, Ffestiniog.

Tributaries of the Dwyryd

PRYSOR:

Trawsfynydd (Gwynedd). Prysor AA controls 5m on **Prysor River**, which provides good fishing towards the end of the season when lake trout run upstream; season 1 Apr–30 Sep; also 3m on upper **Eden**: salmon and sea trout July onwards. Assn also manages **Trawsfynydd Lake**, 1,200 acres; brown and rainbow trout (average 1½lb), perch and rudd; season: rainbow trout 1 Feb–31 Dec; brown trout 1 Mar–30 Sept; coarse fish 1 Feb–31 Dec; fly fishing, bottom fishing and spinning; boats with motors for daily hire; fly only from boats. St £195, wt £50 and dt £9; boats with motors per day £30 (pair) and £20 (single); conc for OAP; fly only from boats; regular trout stocking. Membership and permit enquiries to Hon Sec or to M P Atherton Newsagent, Manchester House, Trawsfynydd, Tel: 01766 540234. Hotels: Cross Foxes and White Lion, Trawsfynydd; Grapes and Oakely Arms, Maentwrog; Abbey Arms and Pengwern Arms, Ffestiniog. Accommodation at Fron Oleu and Bryncelynog Farms, Trawsfynydd and in self-catering chalets at Trawsfynydd Holiday Village.

DYSYNNI
(For close seasons, licences, etc, see Welsh Region
Environment Agency, p15)

Rises in Llyn Cau, on steep southern side of Cader Idris, then falls rather rapidly via Dol-y-Cau. Falls into Talyllyn Valley about half a mile above well known Talyllyn Lake. Emerging from lake, flows westwards as typical upland stream to Abergynolwyn where, joined by the Gwernol, it turns north through narrow valley until it enters upper end of broad Dysynni Valley. At Peniarth it becomes deep and sluggish and finally enters Cardigan Bay 1½m north of Tywyn. Trout along whole length and tributaries, and sea trout (sewin) and salmon travel beyond Talyllyn Lake and up to Dolgoch on Afon Fathew. In lower reaches good sport may be had, early and late in season, with trout and sewin; August generally best. Also excellent grey mullet and bass in estuary.

Tywyn (Gwynedd). Salmon, sewin, trout, eels, with grey mullet in tidal parts and excellent bass fishing at mouth and from adjacent beaches. Rod licence only needed for fishing on estuary. Tywyn Post Office issues permits for several beats on River Dysynni; **Penowern Water**, ½m left bank from confluence with Afon Fathew. Peniarth Estate, Llanegryn, Tywyn, Gwynedd LL36 9LG (Tel: 01654 710178) has 3 beats, permits for 1 beat and north bank of Afon Fathew from Tywyn Post Office; and Estimaner AA water near Abergynolwyn, 6m from Tywyn, day permits £7, conc, from Railway Inn, Abergynolwyn. Middle Peniarth Estate beat is private. Prince Albert AA has Upper Peniarth Estate beat; members only. Peniarth Estate also has caravan park, 3m from Tywyn. **Peniarth Uchaf Fishery**, 2½m both banks, held by Hamdden Ltd; permits from Tynycornel Hotel, Talyllyn (see below). Tackle shop: North Prom, Sandilands Rd, Twywyn.

Abergynolwyn (Gwynedd). Salmon, sea trout, brown trout. Estimaner AA has 3m on Dysynni; stocking at intervals during seasons. Membership for local residents only. Visitors permits: st £25, wt £12, dt £7 (conc for jun), from Railway Inn.

Talyllyn (Gwynedd). Salmon, sea trout, brown trout. Tynycornel Hotel and Talyllyn Fishery, Talyllyn, Tywyn, Gwynedd LL36 9AJ (Tel: 01654 782282) issues permits for **River Dysynni**, 3½m of mostly double bank fishing; **Talyllyn Lake**, 220 acres; and **Llyn Bugeilyn**, 45 acres.

Salmon, sea trout, first rate brown trout fishing. Tackle shop, ghillies, fishing tuition, boat hire (with engine) and tackle hire. Boat hire priority given to hotel residents but day tickets for bank fishing always available, £15 for Talyllyn, Afon Dysynni, £8–£10, Llyn Bugeilyn, £8. Hotel also sells permits for Estimaner AA.

GLASLYN
(For close seasons, licences, etc, see Welsh Region
Environment Agency, p15)

Rises in Llyn Glaslyn, 3m south-west of Pen-y-Gwyrd, and flows through three lakes to Beddgelert then along Pass of Aberglaslyn to lower reaches and Porthmadog, where it enters the sea. Noted sea trout river and efforts are being made to increase salmon run. Best trout fishing in upper reaches, mountain lakes and tributaries. Best spots for salmon and sewin are: Glaslyn Hotel Bridge; Verlas; and above the pass.

Porthmadog (Gwynedd). Glaslyn AA has 14m both banks of R Glaslyn between Porthmadog and Beddgelert, and far bank of **Dinas Lake**; trout, sea trout and salmon: average catches over past 5 years, 530 sea trout, 46 salmon, 18 grilse. No prawn fishing; no ground bait; no boat fishing. St £50, wt £25 and dt £10; conc for OAPs, dis and juv. Tickets from The Fisherman, (below); K Owen, Llyndu Farm, Nantgwynant, Beddgelert, Gwynedd LL55 4NL; Penrhyn Guns, High St, Penrhyndeudraeth, Gwynedd. **Llyn Cwmystradllyn**, Caernarfon Rd, wild brown trout fishery, 95 acres, 6 bag limit. **Llyn Glan Morfa Mawr**, Morfa Bychan, 8 acre lake, rainbow trout, 6 bag limit. **Bron Eifion Fisheries**, Criccieth, Gwynedd, fly-only lake and bait lake; 6 fish limit. Permits from The Fisherman, Central Buildings, High St, Porthmadog, Gwynedd LL49 9LR, Tel: 01766 512464, open 7 days a week, fresh bait sold; Penryn Guns, High St, Penrhyndeudraeth. Hotels: Royal Sportsman, High St; Madog Hotel, Tremadog.

Beddgelert (Gwynedd). Sea trout and salmon. Best for sea trout mid-May to early Sept; salmon May–Oct. Glaslyn AA has Glaslyn from Beddgelert to Porthmadog; and **Llyn Dinas**, 2m NE, sea trout and salmon. Permits – Mon to Fri; left bank (only) on Llyn Dinas, no boats, one day. Concessions jun & OAP. Permits from Beddgelert Post Office, Beddgelert, Caernarfon, Gwynedd, Tel: 01766 890201. Many good hotels, guest houses, and B & B.

GWYNEDD
(rivers and streams)
(For close seasons, licences, etc, see Welsh Region Environment Agency, p15)

ABER. Aber, nr **Llanfairfechan** (Gwynedd). Aber rises in Llyn Anafon, runs to Aber and sea in 2m. Trout (average 7–8 in). Now a nature reserve. No fishing.

ARTRO. Rises in Llyn Cwm Bychan, 6m E of Harlech, and enters sea 1m below Llanbedr. Good bass fishing in tidal waters. Noted for night fishing for sea trout. Good fly pools below village and above Dol-y-Bebin.

Llanbedr (Gwynedd). Artro and Talsarnau FA has salmon and sea trout fishing on Artro. Assn also has water on **River Nantcol**, brown trout; **Cooke's Dam**, rainbow trout; **Llyn Tecwyn Uchaf** (brown trout) and **Llyn Tecwyn Isaf** (stocked with carp, roach, rudd, tench, perch) at Talsarnau; **River Glyn** at Talsarnau, sea trout and salmon; and **Llyn Fedw** at Harlech, brown trout. St £45, wt £20, dt £7. Concessions for OAP and junior. Permits from Newsagent, Llanbedr; Post Office, Talsarnau; Barnacle Bill's Tackle, Barmouth; Tackle Shop, High St, Barmouth; and tackle shops in Penrhyndeudraeth and Porthmadog. Hotels: Victoria, Ty-Mawr.

DARON. Aberdaron (Gwynedd). Daron and Cyll-y-Felin run down two valleys and join at Aberdaron; restocked and hold good sized trout. Sea fishing for mackerel, pollack, lobster, crab, etc., from rocks or boat. Tackle and licences from R G Jones, Eleri Stores, Aberdaron LL53 8BG.

DWYFAWR. Best part of river lies 1m W of Criccieth, where there is length of 12m unobstructed and good for fly fishing. Salmon fishing has greatly improved owing to restrictions on netting. Sewin very good; late June to Oct; night fishing best.

Criccieth (Gwynedd). Sea trout and salmon. Criccieth, Llanystumdwy and Dist AA controls about 10m both banks. Assn also has about 2m on **Dwyfach**; shorter river than Dwyfawr (about 10m) and rather heavily wooded. Permits £75 season, £25 week, £10 day, from Hon Sec (Tel: 01766 523342); R T Pritchard & Son, Sheffield House, High Street, Criccieth, Gwynedd LL52 0EY (Tel: 01766 522116; Celt Roberts, Pet Companions, High St (Tel: 01766

522805). Rod licences from Post Office. Good sea fishing in this area. Hotels: Glyn y Coed, Lion, Marinewise, George, Caerwylan.

ERCH. Pwllheli (Gwynedd). Pwllheli and Dist AA has brown trout, sea trout and salmon fishing on **Rivers Erch** and **Rhydhir**. Assn also has brown trout fishing on **Llyn Cwmystradllyn**; approx 10m NW; 95-acre lake holding wild and stocked brown trout; an upland fishery, situated in the heart of the rugged foothills of Snowdonia. Bag limit 6 brown trout per day. Weekly and daily tickets. Concessions for juniors and OAPs. Permits from D & E Hughes, Walsall Stores, 24 Penlan St, LL53 5DE, Tel: 01758 613291.

GEIRCH. Nefyn (Gwynedd). Geirch, 2m W, 5m long; good sea fishing at Morfa Nefyn. Tackle shop: Bryn Raur Sports Shop, Morfa Nefyn, Pwllheli, Gwynedd.

GWYRFAI. Issues from Llyn Cwellyn, near Snowdon, and flows into Menai Strait through Betws Garmon and Llanwnda. Salmon, sea trout, trout.

Betws Garmon (Gwynedd). Seiont, Gwyrfai and Llyfni AS controls much of Gwyrfai; salmon, sea trout and brown trout. Wt £50, dt £12. Society permits and accommodation from Cwellyn Arms Hotel, Rhyd-ddu. **Bontnewydd Fishery**, salmon, sea and brown trout; dt from G J M Wills, Bryn Mafon, Caethro, Caernarfon, Tel: 01286 673379 – after 6pm).

Rhyd-Ddu (Gwynedd). Seiont, Gwyrfai and Llyfni AS offers boat and bank fishing on **Lynn Nantlle**, salmon and sea trout fishing; **Llyn Cwm Dwythwch**, Llanbers, and **Llyn Cwm Silyn**, Nantlle, both excellent wild brown trout; **Llyn Cwellyn**, brown trout, char, salmon and sea trout; **Llyn-y-Dywarchen**, regularly restocked with rainbow and brown trout, fly only, bag limit 4. Society also controls wt £50, dt £14 (Llyn Cwellyn £8 and Llyn-y-Dywarchen £10). Permits from Cwellyn Arms. Boat packages available, enquiries to Hon Sec, Tel: 01248 670666.

LLYFNI. Penygroes (Gwynedd). Rises in Drws-y-Coed, 4m E of town and runs through Nantlle Lake; salmon, sea trout (good), trout. Seiont, Gwyrfai and Llyfni AS controls most of river; wt £50, dt £14; permits from A D Griffiths, Newsagent, Snowdon St. Club also has fishing on **Llyn Nantlle**; boat only for salmon and trout; apply to Hon Sec, Tel: 01248 670666.

SOCH. **Llangian** (Gwynedd). Trout and rudd; an early stream; dry fly useful; weeds troublesome later; some sewin, late; plenty of sea fishing, bass, pollack, whiting, flatfish, at Abersoch, from which this stream can be fished. Hotels: Rhydolion (Soch runs on boundary of farm, equipment available); Coed-y-Llyn, Sarn Bach Rd, Abersoch.

YSGETHIN. River rises in **Llyn Bodlyn**. Brown trout, Arctic char.

GWYNEDD (Lakes)
(For close seasons, licences, etc, see Welsh Region Environment Agency, p15)

Bala Lake or **Llyn Tegid**. **Bala** (Gwynedd). Owned by Snowdonia National Park Authority, Penrhydeudraeth. Permits from Lake Warden, Warden's Office, 24 Ffordd Pensarn, Bala (Tel: 01678 520626), and tackle shop. Salmon may sometimes be taken and trout early in season. Pike, perch, roach, grayling, eels. Bala is largest natural lake in Wales, 4m long, ¾m wide. Here, too, is found that rare and interesting fish called the gwyniad, a land-locked whitefish. Coarse fishermen will find all their wants more than provided for; pike up to 25lb; perch and good roach. Rod licence required. Tackle shop: Eryr Sports & Tackle, 31 High St (Tel: 01678 520370).

Llyn Celyn. **Bala** (Gwynedd). Situated in the Snowdonia National Park at the foot of the Arenig Mountains; rainbow trout are stocked to supplement wild brown trout. Reservoir managed under licence by Bala AA; permits from D Evans, Tackle Shop, 31–33 High Street. Concessions for jun and OAP. Sunday fishing.

Hafod-y-Llyn. **Llanbedr** (Gwynedd). Roach, perch, eels. Permits from Lewis Bros, Tyddyn Ddu, Llanfair, nr Harlech.

Cwm Bychan Lake. **Llanbedr** (Gwynedd). Trout and sewin; good fishing. For permission to fish, apply to Farm Manager, Cwm Bychan Farm, Cwn Bychan. For **Gloywlyn Lake** apply Cwmrafon Farm. **Llyn Perfeddau**, trout, good fishing; free.

Maentwrog (Gwynedd). **Y-Garnedd**, 1m N (trout) and **Hafod-y-Llyn**, 1m NW (pike, coarse fish) are both private. Cambrian AA lakes in area: **Morwynion**, **Cwmorthin**, **Manod**, **Barlwyd**, **Dubach**, **Dubach-y-**

Bont, **Cwm Foel**, **Cwm Corsiog**. Permits from F W Roberts, 32 Church St, Blaenau Ffestiniog, Gwynedd LL41 3HD, Tel: 01766 830607.

Talsarnau (Gwynedd). Artro and Talsarnau FA has water on **Llyn Tecwyn Uchaf** and **Llyn Tecwyn Isaf**, brown trout; and on **River Glyn**, sea trout and salmon. St £45, wt £20, dt £6. Permits from Post Office. Hotels: Ship Aground; Motel.

LLWCHWR
(or Loughor)
(For close seasons, licences, etc, see Welsh Region Environment Agency, p15)

Rises some 3m east of Llandybie on Taircarn Mountain and flows 15m south-west through Ammanford and Pontardulais to Burry Inlet, north of Gower Peninsula. Fishing very good for sewin, and some brown trout and salmon (Apr–July; Aug–Oct best). Salmon and sewin runs reported to be increasing. Most fishing controlled by clubs, from whom tickets are available.

Llanelli (Carmarthenshire). Carmarthenshire County Council controls fishing on **Upper** and **Lower Lliedi Reservoirs**; with game fishing only on Upper Lliedi. Boat hire is available for members at £6 per day. The bottom Lliedi Reservoir is now a coarse fishery of 32 acres. The council also has fishing at **Furnace Pond** and **Old Castle Pond** (carp, bream and pike), and **Cwmoernant Reservoirs**, **Carmarthen**. Within Council's jurisdiction is **Gwellian Pool**, nr Kidwelly, with trout, sewin and salmon. St and dt from Tourism and leisure Office, Ty Elwyn, Llanelli, SA15 3AP (Tel: 01554 742296), and Anglers Corner, 80 Station Rd (Tel: 01554 773981).

Llangennech (Carmarthenshire). Llangennech AC has 4m on **River Gwendraeth Fach** between Llandyfaelog and Llangendeirne Bridge near Kidwelly; and 2m on **River Morlais**, a tributary of R Loughor, from the road bridge at Llangennech upstream. Season 3 Mar–17 Oct. Mainly brown trout with good runs of sea trout in both rivers. Waters stocked with average 12in brown trout at intervals during the season. Bag limit 4 fish. St £25 plus £15 joining fee, conc for juv, OAPs and disabled. Season members only, application forms from Hon Sec (Tel: 01554 820948); or Anglers Corner, 80 Station Rd, Llanelli (Tel: 01554 773981). Club offers fresh water and some sea fishing competitions; and, during the close season, runs fly-tying classes.

Pontardulais (Glamorgan). Trout and a run of sea trout; some salmon. Pontardulais and Dist AA has 6m good fishing; permits from Bridge Café. Concessions for OAP and jun. Llangyfelach AA also has water. **White Springs Lakes**, Holiday Complex, Garnswllt Rd, Pontardulais, Swansea SA4 1QG, Tel: 01792 885699; 2 trout lakes of 4 acres (fly only), and 2 acres (any method); and 3 coarse lakes with large carp, tench, golden orfe, etc; night-fishing and tents allowed on coarse lakes. Lakeside parking. Tickets on site in shop, also maggots, ground bait, tackle and rods for sale. Licensed lodge; accommodation in holiday apartments.

Ammanford (Dyfed). Ammanford & Dist AA has water on middle and upper reaches of Llwchwr and tributaries. Boat for club members at **Llys-y-Fran Reservoir**, much improved sea trout run, biggest fish 16½lb. Permits for these and other local waters, £5–£40, from Tightlines Direct, 72–74 Wind St, Ammanford, Carmarthenshire SA18 3DR, Tel: 01269 595858. Hotel: Glynhir Mansion, Llandybie, Carmarthenshire SA18 2TD, Tel: 01269 850438; guest house and self-catering cottages

Tributaries of the Llwchwr

AMMAN: Trout, sewin, few salmon. Very fast running; fishes well in spate.

Ammanford (Dyfed). Ammanford & Dist AA has water on **Llwchwr**, 5m; **Amman**, 3m; **Lash**, 3m; **Marlais**, 3m; **Cennen**, ½m; **Gwili**, 1½m. Sea trout run from May onwards. Concessions for juniors, youths and ladies. Instruction, fly-tying classes and competitions. Club boat based on Usk Reservoir, £5 to members. Permits from Tightlines Direct, 72–74 Wind St, Ammanford, Carmarthenshire SA18 3DR, Tel: 01269 595858; and John Jones, 8 Florence St, Ammanford, Tel: 01269 595770. Hotel: Glynhir Mansion.
MARLAIS BROOK: Llandybie (Dyfed). Sewin, July onwards. **Llwchwr**, 3m. **Gwendraeth Fawr**, 5m W. **Llyn Lechowen**, 5m W.

MAWDDACH
(For close seasons, licences, etc, see Welsh Region Environment Agency, p15)

Rises in hills between Bala and Trawsfynydd Lakes and flows 10m south to confluence with Wnion, 2m below Dolgellau, and thence through long estuary to sea at Barmouth. One of the best rivers in Wales for salmon and sea trout fishing, also brown trout, and is all preserved, although permits can be had for some stretches. Successful stocking with locally hatched salmon and sea trout. Salmon and sea trout may be taken up to Pistyll Mawddach.

Barmouth (Gwynedd). Rivers Mawddach and **Wnion**; lower reaches of Wnion have excellent night fly fishing for sewin and sea trout, in various named pools. Dolgellau AA has fishing on both rivers; permits, see *Dolgellau*. Run of sea trout and salmon is from beginning of June to end of season. Trout fishing on **Cregennan Lakes**, Emlyn Lloyd, Fridd Boedel Farm, Arthog, nr Fairbourne (Tel: 01341 250426); 2 natural lakes owned by the National Trust, situated on northern slopes of Cader Idris overlooking beautiful Mawddach Estuary; 27 acre lake with island, wild brown trout only, fly spin or worm; dt £8 and evening £6; 13 acre lake, regularly stocked with rainbows, plus a good head of wild brown trout, fly only. Dt £15 and evening £8. Boat for hire but booking advisable. **Penmaenpool** (Gwynedd). Salmon, sea trout. Overlooking estuary, George III Hotel, Penmaenpool, Dolgellau, Gwynedd LL40 1YD, Tel: 01341 422525, has access to Dolgellau AA permits on all waters; salmon and sea trout fishing on lower beats of Mawddach; free fishing for residents.

Ganllwyd (Gwynedd). Salmon, sea trout. Dolgellau AA has left bank of upper beat from Ganllwyd to Tyn-y-Groes Pool. Permits, see *Dolgellau* (Tel: 01341 421080). Hotels: Tyn-y-Groes, Ganllwyd, (1½m salmon and sea trout fishing on river); Plas Dolmelynllyn Country Hotel, Ganllwyd, LL40 2HP (Tel: 01341 440640), has 1½m salmon and sea trout fishing on Mawddach right bank, priority given to guests.

Tributaries of Mawddach

WNION: Salmon, sewin, sea trout. The Rivers Mawddach and Wnion are well known for the excellent salmon and sea trout fishing. Dry weather only effects the upper reaches of the two rivers, as lower beats cover tidal waters.

Dolgellau (Gwynedd). Salmon and sea trout. Wnion runs by Dolgellau and joins Mawddach

2m below town. Best months for salmon and sea trout: May–Oct. Sewin fishing: Jul–Oct. Dolgellau AA owns fishing rights on 13m of Mawddach and Wnion. Stocked with salmon and sea trout from Mawddach Trust Hatchery. Assn also has wild brown trout and rainbow trout fishing on **Llyn Cynwch**, near well-known Precipice Walk. Annual Family Fishing Competition held on Llyn Cynwch early in August; contact Hon Sec for further details. St £57, wt £35, dt £14; dt £10 lake only. Concessions for juniors. Permits from W D Pugh & Son, Garage & Motel, Ardd Fawr, Dolgellau, Tel: 01341 422681; and Tackle shop: Fish Tales, Bridge St (Tel: 01341 421080). Hotels: Fronolau Farm Hotel, Dolgellau, Tel: 01341 422361; Dolmelynllyn Country Hotel (with private fishing, see *Ganllwyd*); Dolbrawdmaeth, Dinas Mawddwy, Machynlleth, Powys; George III Hotel, Penmaenpool, Dolgellau. These hotels can arrange fishing holidays for residents on all Dolgellau AA waters.

OGWEN

(For close seasons, licences, etc, see Welsh Region Environment Agency, p15)

Rises in Ogwen Lake, halfway between Bethesda and Capel Curig, with tributaries running in from Ffynnon Lloer and Bochlwyd Lakes, and runs from lake to outlet at Menai Straits, near Bangor, about 10m in all. Excellent trout fishing; leased by Ogwen Valley AA from Penrhyn Estate. Trout, sea trout (sewin) and salmon. Autumn good for salmon.

Bangor (Gwynedd). **Ogwen**, 2m E; salmon, sewin, trout. Sea trout run starts about mid-June. Salmon best Aug–Oct. Parts of river leased by Ogwen Valley AA; visitors permits, wt £25, dt £10, conc for juv. Tackle shop: Bangor Angling Supply Stores, 21 The High St, Bangor, Gwynedd LL57 1NP, Tel: 01248 355518. Hotels: Waverly, British, Castle, Railway.

Bethesda (Gwynedd). Ogwen Valley AA has approx 5m of River Ogwen and tributaries near Bethesda; sea trout and salmon from July onwards. Assn also has brown trout fishing on 4 lakes: **Ogwen**, **Idwal**, **Ffynon Lloer** and **Bochlwyd**. Lake Ogwen stocked annually. Wt £25 and dt £10. Concessions for juniors. Permits from W Edwin (grocer), opp Victoria Hotel, High St, Bethesda; Ogwen Bank Caravan Park, Bethesda; or Ogwen Falls Cafe, nr Ogwen Cottage, Ogwen Lake.

POWYS (lakes)

Gludy Lake, Cradoc, **Brecon**, LD3 9PA (Tel: 01874 610093), (Powys). Fly fishing for brown and rainbow trout to 14lb, with boats, electric outboards, full self-catering lodge sleeps up to nine. St £198, dt sometimes obtainable. Six anglers permitted on any day.

Llyn Clywedog. **Llanidloes** (Powys). NW 3m; 615 acres; Llanidloes and Dist AA. Reservoir shared with sailing club; western half is fishery area, but fishing also permitted in much of eastern half by arrangement with sailing club. Well stocked with brown and rainbow trout averaging 1¾lb. Fly only. Boat hire. Permits from Hon Sec and Mrs Gough, Traveller Rest Restaurant, Longbridge Street, Llanidloes, Tel: 01686 412329. Rod licence required. **Dol-llys Farm** has free fishing for their caravan users; contact O S Evans, Dol-llys Farm, Llanidloes, Powys SY18 6JA, Tel: 01686 412694. Hotels: Mount Inn, Unicorn, Lloyds, Trewythen Arms.

Llangorse Lake. **Llangorse** (Powys). Holds good pike, good bream, perch, roach, eels. Fishing from boats only; can be hired. Permit needed to launch privately owned boats. Caravans for hire from Apr–Oct; some tackle from lakeside shop. Permits and boats from Ray Davies, Lakeside Caravan and Camping Park, Llangorse Lake, Brecon, Powys LD3 7TR, Tel: 01874 658226. Accommodation and fishing at Trewalter Farm LD3 0PS; equipment for hire. Llynfi runs from lake to Wye at Glasbury and holds a few trout; overgrown in places; requires short rod. Hotel: Red Lion.

Talybont Reservoir. **Brecon** (Powys). Reservoir in Brecon Beacons National Park, 318 acres, good wild brown trout fishery. Season 20 Mar–17 Oct; fly only; catch limit 6 fish; size limit 9 in. Permits from Garwnant Centre, off A470 road above Llwynonn Reservoir. Further information from C Hatch, Area Manager, Hamdden Ltd, Sluvad Treatment Works, Llandegfedd Reservoir, New Inn, Pontypool, Gwent NP4 0TA, Tel: 01495 769281.

Lake Vyrnwy. **Llanwddyn** (Powys). Lake (1,100 acres) stocked with rainbow and brown trout. Annual catch 3,000 to 3,500 averaging 1lb. Fly only. Ghillies and instructors can be arranged together with hire of rods. Apply to Lake Vyrnwy Hotel (see *advt*), Llanwddyn, via Oswestry, Shropshire SY10 0LY, Tel: 01691 870692.

SEIONT
(For close seasons, licences, etc, see Welsh Region Environment Agency, p15)

Rises in two tarns in Cwm-glas, under crest of Snowdon, and runs to Llanberis, 3m, where it enters the Llanberis Lakes, Llyn Peris and Llyn Padarn. Flows thence into Menai Straits at Caernarfon. Attractive river with long flats, nice runs and excellent pools holding salmon (May onwards), sea trout (June onwards), and brown trout. Trout rather small, but in faster water can give good account of themselves.

Caernarfon (Gwynedd). Salmon, sea trout, trout. Seiont, Gwyrfai and Llyfni AS has 40m of salmon, sea trout and brown trout fishing on **Rivers Seiont, Gwyrfai** and **Llyfni**. Assn also has boat and bank fishing on **Llyn Padarn**, brown trout, char, salmon, sea trout; **Llyn Cwellyn**, brown trout, char, salmon, sea trout; **Llyn-y-Dwarchen**, 35 acres, rainbow trout and brown trout, fly only. Season ticket on application only. Wt £50, dt £14 (£8 Llyn Padarn and Llyn Cwellyn; £10 Llyn-y-Dywarchen) from Post Bach Newsagent, 55 Pool St; A D Griffiths Newsagent, Penygroes; Garth Maelog Pet Centre, 51 High St, Llanberis, LL55 4EU, Tel: 01286 870840, which stocks tackle and bait; Cwellyn Arms, Rhyd-Ddu. Maps and information from Hon Sec, Tel: 01248 670666. Seiont Manor Hotel, Llanrug, Caernarfon, Gwynedd, Tel: 01286 673366, offers free fishing for guests on all club waters including use of boats on all lakes. B & B, Lake View, Llanberis (Tel: 01286 870422).

Llanberis (Gwynedd). Brown trout, Arctic char, salmon, sea trout. Seiont, Gwyrfai and Llyfai AS has bank and boat fishing on almost the whole of **Llyn Padarn**; dt £8 from A C Philips at Boat Hire Jetty, Tel: 01286 870717, on lake. Special boat permits allow fishing on Lakes Padarn, Cwellyn, Dywarchew, and Nantlle, by booking only (Tel: 01248 670666) for fishing. Permits, tackle and bait from Garth Maelog Pet Centre, 51 High St, LL55 4EU, Tel: 01286 870840. Hotels: Lake View, Tel: 01286 870 422; Dolbadarn, High St, LL55 4SU, Tel/Fax: 01286 870277.

SOUTH EAST WALES
(For close seasons, licences, etc, see Welsh Region Environment Agency, p15)

AFAN. Aberavon (West Glamorgan). Small trout stream (with sewin on lower reaches) on which Afan Valley AC has water from Aberavon to Cymmer. Assn has improved sport; 3 salmon caught in 1991 season; tremendous runs of sewin in last few years; regular stocking. Fly only in March; worming allowed rest of season; spinning July–Sept at certain water levels. **River Nedd** 4m away; trout, sewin. Hotels: The Twelve Knights, Aberavon Hotel, Grand Hotel, Beach.

CADOXTON STREAM. Cadoxton (South Glamorgan). Cadoxton Stream rises 6½m from Cardiff and enters the sea 2m below Cadoxton. Small trout; permission from farmers (Glamorgan RD).

Eglwys Nunydd Reservoir. Margam (West Glamorgan). British Steel plc (Port Talbot) reservoir. Excellent trout fishing, brown and rainbow. Season: 3 Mar–31 Oct. Very high stocking levels. Special terms for working and retired employees, and families. 4 boats for members. Fishing lodge for anglers. Apply Sports Club, British Steel plc, Groes, Margam, Port Talbot, Tel: Port Talbot 871111 Ext 3368 during day.

NEATH. Rises in the Brecon Beacons and flows 27m to sea. Salmon, sewin, brown trout. Tributaries of the Neath are **Dulais** and **Pyrddin**.

Neath (West Glamorgan). Neath and Dulais AA has fishing on **River Neath** from Rehola to the estuary except for a short private beat; both banks; trout, sea trout and salmon. Assn also has both banks on **River Dulais** above Aberdulais Falls to the treatment works at Crynant. St £55 and dt £10; from Gary Davies, 6 Martins Ave, Seven Sisters, Neath, Tel: 01639 701828. Limit of 100 members out of area. Concessions for juniors and OAPs. Skewen Coarse AC has fishing on: **Tennant Canal**, Aberdulais to Jersey Marine (all species); **Neath Canal**, Tonna to Briton Ferry (all species except pike); **Square Pond** at Briton Ferry (carp, roach, rudd, tench, bream, perch, eels, grass carp); and **Lower Reservoir** at Briton Ferry (carp, roach, rudd, perch, trout, bream). Close season in force on both canals but not on other waters. 2 rods only on all waters except Square Pond where 3 rods allowed. Permits available from Membership Secretary, Tel: 01639 639657; Tackle and Bait, 149 Windsor Rd, Neath, SA11 1NU (Tel: 01639 634148); and Mainwarings, Sketty, Swansea, Tel: 01792 202245. Hotel: Castle.

Glynneath (West Glamorgan). Glynneath and Dist AA has salmon, sea trout and brown trout waters on Neath and its tributaries, **Pyrddin**, **Nedd Fach**, **Mellte**, **Hepste** and **Sychryd**. Fly, worm and spinning from June only. Junior (under 12s) competition in June. Membership £30 + £10 joining fee, wt £15 and dt £8 (concessions for OAP, disabled and juniors). Coarse fishing on canal, between Tonna and Neath, also from Assn. Daily and weekly permits from Hon Sec; Dave Pitman's Hair-Stylist, 3 Avenue Buildings, Heathfield Avenue, Glynneath (Tel: 01639 720127) which also sells a large selection of fishing tackle; Tackle and Bait, and White Horse Inn, Pontneddfechan. Pyrddin AS (10m from Neath) has water; trout, salmon, sea trout; permits from Hon Sec. In headwaters of the Neath is Ystradfellte Reservoir. Tackle shop: Tackle and Bait, Stockhams Corner, Glynneath.

OGMORE

Porthcawl (Mid Glamorgan). Porthcawl SAA has coarse fishing on **Wilderness Lake** and **Pwll-y-Waem Lake**; carp, bream, tench, roach, perch and eels. Concessions for juniors. Permits from Porthcawl Angling, Dock St; and tackle shop Ewenny Angling, 11B Ewenny Rd, Bridgend CF31 4SS (Tel: 01656 662691). Ewenny Angling has permits for several coarse fisheries, and for Glamorgan AC. Hotel: Brentwood, St Mary St; Ewenny Guesthouse, 17 Ewenny Rd, Bridgend CF31 3HN.

Bridgend (Mid Glamorgan). Ogmore AA has 15m of Ogmore and tributaries **Ewenny**, **Llynfi** and **Garw**; salmon, sea trout and brown trout. Membership is restricted but weekly tickets are available from secretary. Concessions for juniors. Competitions for juniors; and fly-tying and casting lessons. Garw Valley AA has water on Ogmore and Garw. Membership restricted to residents but weekly tickets for visitors. Concessions for juniors and OAPs; Secretary (Tel: 01656 722077). Tackle shops: Ewenny Angling, Bridgend; Keens, Marine and Angling Superstore, 117–119 Bridgend Rd, Aberkenfig, Bridgend, Mid Glamorgan CF32 9AP, Tel: 01656 722448. Hotel: Heronstone.

Maesteg (Mid Glamorgan). **River Llynfi**, a tributary of Ogmore; trout and sea trout. Llynfi Valley AA has 8m (Maesteg to Tondu); trout, sea trout and salmon. Flyfishing-only stretch and no spinning until 1 Jul. Members only. St £25 + £20 joining fee from Hon Sec.

RHYMNEY. Rhymney (Mid Glam). About 30m long, rises above town. Excellent grayling, chub, roach and dace fishing run by Caerphilly AC; further information from Green's Fishing Tackle. Rhymney and Dist AS has rights on Butetown Pond, Rhymney, and Bryn Brith Pond, **Pontlottyn**; also **Cwm-Darren Lake**; Rhos-las, nr **Dowlias**; and **Brecon Canal** at Llanfoist. All well stocked with coarse fish of usual species; pike in Rhos-las, all fish except pike to be returned to water; dt on all waters. Matches run most Saturdays for juniors and Sundays for seniors Jun–Aug, plus aggregate awards. New members st £12, dt £5, conc, from Hon Sec; Cal White, 39 The Square, Pontlottyn, Mid Glamorgan CF8 9PD, Tel: 01685 841 245; Greens Fishing Tackle, Bryn Road, Pontllanfraith, Blackwood, Gwent NP2 2BU; and Tiles and Tackle, Tredegar, Gwent.

TAWE. Lower tidal reach now impounded by a barrage. Salmon and sewin runs have increased in recent years and they can be caught from Abercraf to Morriston. Upper reaches noted for scenery. Fishing controlled by clubs in all but tidal reaches.

Swansea (West Glamorgan). Swansea Amateur AA has salmon and sea trout fishing on the upper reaches of **Cothi** and a section of **Towy** at Llnwrda. Assn is a private company with a limited membership with a limited allocation of tickets for members' guests. Swansea AC has coarse fishing at Gower on **Fairwood Lake**, pike, bream, carp, perch, tench, roach, rudd, eels; and **Werganrows**, bream, carp, perch, tench, roach, rudd, eels. Members only. No day tickets. Concessions for juniors; also junior matches and match league coaching. City and County of Swansea has coarse fishing on 3 lakes. **Singleton Boating Lake**, Singleton Park, 2 acres; carp, tench, rudd, perch, crucian carp, eels; angling permitted when boats not in use. **Clyne Valley Pond**, small, very deep lake; perch, rudd, eels, trout. **Pluck Pond**, Lower Swansea Valley, 1 acres; perch, rudd. Brynmill and Dist AC have coarse fishing at **Fendrod Lake**, 15 acres, 82 pegs, with fairly good head of fish from carp up to 20lb and bream up to 8lb, with an added bonus of attractive surroundings; and at Half Round Ponds, two ponds of one acre each, with rudd, perch, tench. Permits £3.05 on bank, conc; from Mainwaring's (below); or from Leisure Services Dept, The Guildhall, Swansea SA1 4PE (Tel: 01792 635411). **Shimano Felindre**

Trout Fishery; rainbow, brown and golden trout; fly only. Tackle for sale and hire; casting lessons. Contact Jud Hamblin, Manager, Shimano Felindre Trout Fishery, Blaen-Nant Ddu, Felindre, Swansea SA5 7ND, Tel: 01792 796584; accommodation for anglers 2m from fishery at Ganol Guest Houses, contact Frank Jones, Tel: 01269 595640. Riverside Caravan Park has stretch on Tawe; bungalow accommodation and touring caravan park with all facilities. For further information contact Riverside Caravan Park, Ynysforgan Farm, Morriston, Swansea SA6 6QL. Tackle shops: Mainwaring's Angling Centre, 44 Vivian Road, Sketty, Swansea, Tel: 01792 202245, has permits for a number of lake and river fisheries within range of Swansea, both coarse and game; Hook, Line & Sinker, James Court, Swansea Enterprise Zone, Winchwen, Tel: 01792 701190; Kingfisher Sports, 25 High St, Swansea SA1 1LG; Siop-y-Pentref, Ynystawe, Swansea.

Pontardawe (West Glamorgan). Pontardawe and Swansea AS has stretch on R Tawe from Pontardawe to Morriston; brown trout, sea trout and salmon; st £50 and dt £10; concessions for OAP, disabled and juniors; tickets available by post from secretary or from tackle shops in Swansea. Llangyfelach and Dist AA has water on **River Llan**; sewin, brown trout; permits from B I Thomas, 1321 Carmarthen Rd, Fforestfach, Swansea, Tel: 01792 427449; Mainwaring's Angling Centre, 44 Vivian Road, Sketty, Swansea, Tel: 01792 202245.

Ystradgynlais (West Glamorgan). Tawe and Tributaries AA has 25m on **Tawe** and tributaries **Twrch, Gwys, Llynfell, Giedd, Lech, Gurlais** and **Cwn Du**, above Pontardawe; salmon, sea trout, brown trout and eels; trout stocked regularly up to 3lb. Assn runs its own brown trout hatchery and rearing pond complex (during 1997, stocked waters with over 15,000 brown trout measuring from 9–18in). Membership restricted to local residents but permits available to non-members. St £55 and dt £15. Concessions for juniors and OAPs. Junior river competition held annually. Fly-tying and casting tuition during close season. Permits from John Glynne Davies, Fieldsports, Station Road, Ystradgynlais, Tel: 01639 843194; Pet, Garden and Sports Centre, Ystradgynlais, Tel: 01639 843194; and Turners Newsagents, Capital Buildings, Ystalyfera. Hotels: Copper Beech; Abercrave Inn; and Gwyn Arms Public House, Craig y Nos, Swansea Valley.

SOUTH WEST WALES
(lakes)

Lake Berwyn. Tregaron (Ceredigion), 4m SE. Liming has taken place and as a result it holds excellent brown trout up to 1–2lb. Stocked periodically. Tregaron AA hold fishing rights; Assn also has wild brown trout fishing on R Teifi, and Teifi Pools, 3 remote mountain lakes with plenty of wild browns; permits: Medical Hall, Tregaron; Post Office, Pontrhydfendigaid; W Rees, London House, Llanddewi Brefi; Post Office, Llanfair Clydogau; and Alan Williams, 57 Bridge St, Lampeter. Self contained accom on river bank: Toby and Sue Jackson, Brynteify, Tregaron, with trout fishing by arrangement with Tregaron AA.

Devil's Bridge (Ceredigion). Aberystwyth AA has the Penrhyncoch lakes in the hills between Devil's Bridge and Nant-y-Moch Reservoir (**Llyn Craig-y-Pistyll, Llyn Rhosgoch, Llyn Syfydrin, Llyn Blaenmelindwr** and **Llyn Pendam**); the Trisant Lakes 2m SW of Devil's Bridge, (**Llyn Frongoch** and **Llyn Rhosrhydd**); and part ownership of **Bray's Pool** and **Llyn Glandwgan**. Some are stocked, others self-stocking. Several contain trout up to 3lb. Fly only on Rhosgoch, Frongoch and Rhosrhydd; spinning and fly only on Craig-y-Pistyll. Permits: Aber Fishing Tackle and Gun Shop, 3 Terrace Road; and Mrs Dee, Erwyd Garage, Ponterwyd, Aberystwyth (who sells small amounts of fishing tackle and has fresh live worms for sale). Hotel: Hafod Arms.

Nant-y-Moch and **Dinas Reservoirs**. **Ponterwyd** (Ceredigion). These waters are set in the hills 12m E of Aberystwyth. Dinas, 38 acres, stocked weekly with brown and rainbow trout; fly, spinning and worming. Nant-y-Moch, 600 acres, native and stocked brown trout, fly only. Boats for hire on lake. **Cwm Rheidol Dam**, native and stocked brown trout, salmon and sea trout. Boats for hire on lake. Fly spinning and worming. Permits from Mrs Dee, Erwyd Garage, Ponterwyd, Aberystwyth, Dyfed SY23 3LA, Tel: 01970 890664. Permits for Cwm Rheidol Dam also from PowerGen Visitors Centre and Fish Farm at the Power Station, Capel Bangor.

Pembroke (Pembrokeshire). Pembroke Town Mill Pool; mullet, bass, flatfish; also trout and sewin higher up. Hotel: Milton Manor.

Talybont (Ceredigion). Talybont AA has exclusive rights on **Llyn Conach, Llyn Dwfn, Llyn Nantycagal** and **Llyn Penrhaeadr.** Lakes some 7–9m into hills from village; 3 lakes stocked with brook trout; native wild brown in Penrhaeadr. Fly only on all lakes except Nantycagal. Boat hire on all lakes for holders of season tickets. Assn also has fishing rights on Forestry Commission land; 1m, both banks, on **River Leri** from Talybont to Dolybont; trout, sea trout and salmon. St £35 (junior £10) and dt £10 (bank only). Permits from Spar Store, Talybont; The White and Black Lion Hotels in Talybont; Mrs Hubbard, Compton Gift Shop, Borth, Ceredigion SY24 5JD (information and tackle also available); and Flymail Tackle Shop, Aberystwyth.

Teifi Lakes. Pontrhydfendigaid (Ceredigion). Lakes at headwaters of Teifi. Permits from Post Office, Pontrhydfendigaid.

SOUTH WEST WALES
(rivers and streams)
(For close seasons, licences, etc, see Welsh Region Environment Agency, p15)

ALUN. **St David's** (Pembrokeshire). 6m long; 4m suitable for fishing, mostly on private property with owners' permission; trout good quality but small. Boat trips and fishing tackle from R O Evans, High Street, St David's. Rod licences from Post Office, 13 New Dew St.

BRAWDY BROOK. Brawdy (Pembrokeshire). Small trout. Brook, 7m long, is mostly on private property. Licences can be purchased at Post Office, 13 New Dew Street, St David's.

CAREW BROOK. Carew (Pembrokeshire). This river, which rises by Redberth, is 4m long, joining sea water at Carew which is an inlet from Milford Haven. Although there is an element of rod fishing effort put into this river and its tributaries, the controlling interest is the farmer and the catchment is prone to agricultural pollution. The river does support a very small number of sea trout which only seem to appear in the close season.

CARNE. **Loveston** (Pembrokeshire). Carne rises 1½m W of Templeton, runs 3m to Loveston, and 1m down is joined on left bank by **Langden Brook**. Little or no rod fishing interest; fishing wiped out in 1993 with agricultural pollution; although an important spawning area for salmon and sea trout. Possible sea trout late in season, if adequate flows and no pollu-

tion. From confluence of Carne and Langden Brook into Cresswell, fishing controlled by Cresselly Estate, c/o Owen & Owen, 140 Main St, Pembroke, SA71 4HN (Tel: 01646 621500). Coarse fishing reservoir at **Roadside Farm**; common, crucian and mirror carp, bream and roach; well stocked; tranquil surroundings and ample parking. Day, week and year permits. Contact D A Crowley, Roadside Farm, Templeton, Narberth, Dyfed SA67 8DA, Tel: 01834 891283. Carp fishing at West Atherton near Narberth. Tackle shop: Bay Fishing, High Street, Saundersfoot, Dyfed.

CLARACH. Good numbers of sea trout can be found in the river late July onwards.

Aberystwyth (Ceredigion). Enters sea 1m N of Aberystwyth. Holds trout, sewin and occasional salmon; preserved. Permission from farmers. Tackle shop: Aeron Sports and Fishing Tackle, Kings Hall (Tel: 01970 624830). Flymail Fishing Flies, from 3 Terrace Rd, Aberystwyth, SY23 1NY.

GWAUN. **Fishguard** (Pembrokeshire). This 8–9m trout stream rises on lower slopes of Prescelly Mountains, and runs through a beautiful wooded valley. Trout not large but provide excellent sport with fly, and sewin also caught in season. A few salmon. **Yet-y-Gors Fishery**, Colleen and Hans Verhart, Manorowen, Fishguard, Pembrokeshire SA65 9RE, Tel: 01348 873497, has 2 adjoining lakes covering 3 acres, well stocked with rainbow trout and brownies for fly fishing. Also 2 coarse fishing lakes with common and mirror carp, bream, tench, rudd, perch and roach. Tackle for sale or hire, facilities for disabled, tickets and licences on site. Tackle shop: Thomas & Howells, Dyfed Sport, 21 West St. Hotel: Glanmoy Country House.

GWENDRAETH FACH. Kidwelly (Carmarthenshire). Carmarthen and Dist AC has 5m; very good trout fishing; occasional sea trout in lower reaches. Llangennech AC has 4m stretch from Llandyfaelog to Llangendeirne Bridge, brown trout and sea trout. **Gwendraeth Fawr** runs 1m E from Kidwelly; trouting fair. Hotel: White Lion, Pen-y-Bac Farm (river fishing for trout, sewin and salmon; tuition and equipment).

LLANDILO BROOK. Maenclochog (Pembrokeshire). Small trout. Electro-fishing surveys show very few fish of takeable size. No angling clubs. Seek permission from farmers to fish.

LLETHI. Llanarth (Ceredigion). Llethi Gido rises 3m above Llanarth, and 2m down is joined on left bank by brook 4m long. Llethi runs to Llanina and sea. One mile NE runs Drowy to sea, 4m long. Small trout. Llanarth Coarse Fishery (Tel: 01545 580598), ¾m south of Llanarth, 2 acre pool, open 7 days a week. **Nine Oaks Trout and Coarse Fishery**, John Steels, Oakford, rr Aberaeron SA47 0RW, Tel: 01545 580 482; fly and coarse fishing, 2m inland between Newquay and Aberaeron; rainbow and brown trout in 4 pools; carp to 25lb, tench and bream in coarse fishing lake. Tackle hire, beginners tuition and accommodation. Trout dt £18, 4 fish, £10 evening, 2 fish, £5 coarse.

MARLAIS. Narberth (Pembrokeshire). Gwaithnoak, 2m. Eastern Cleddau, 2m. Taf, 5m. Small trout. Rod licences from: Salmon & Son, Narberth Ltd, 28 High St; S H Davies, I St James St.

MULLOCK BROOK. St Ishmael's (Pembrokeshire). Small trout, 6m long, joining the sea at Dale Road.

NEVERN. Nevern (Pembrokeshire). River rises near Crymych and flows to sea at Newport; fast-flowing, densely wooded, deep holding pools. Nevern AA has salmon, sea trout and brown trout fishing; 6m on **Nevern**, nr Newport; and ¾m on **Teifi**, nr Llechryd. St £50, joining fee £25, from Hon Sec. Wt £30 and dt £15 from Trewern Arms, Nevern; Y Siop Lyfrau (Bookshop), Newport; The Reel Thing, Lower Market Stall, Cardigan, Ceredigion SA43 1HJ; and Castaways, Cardigan. Concessions for juniors. Coaching for beginners and juniors (fly only). There are also club outings and fly-tying lessons. Hotels: Trewern Arms; Cnapan, Newport; Salutation Inn, Felindre Farchog. Guest House, Llys Meddyg, East St, Newport (Tel: 01239 8202008).

PERIS. Llanon (Ceredigion). Peris is 6m long. Llanon, 4m long, runs ½m. Small trout. Hotel: Plas Morfa.

RHEIDOL. Aberystwyth (Ceredigion). Salmon, sea trout. Hydro-electric scheme governs flow. River almost entirely Aberystwyth AA water. Assn also has 2m stretch on **River Ystwyth**; and trout fishing on 9 lakes. Permits

from Aber Fishing Tackle and Gun Shop, 3 Terrace Road; Mrs Lee, Erwyd Garage, Ponterwyd, Aberystwyth; and Richard Rendell, Blaenplwyf Post Office, nr Aberystwyth, Ceredigion, Tel: 01970 612499. Assn has 2 caravans (6-berth) to let at **Frongoch Lake**, approx £120 per week; includes week's fishing on the whole fishery and exclusive use boat for 4 days of the week. Coarse fishing at **Cwm Nant Nursery**; 2½ acre pond; carp, roach and tench. Permits from Mr W Evans, Cwm Nant Nursery, Capel Bangor, Aberystwyth SY23 3LL. Coarse fishing at **Tair Llyn Coarse Fishery**; privately owned 9-acre lake; carp, bream, roach, tench, rudd and perch. Permits from Mrs Ruth Jones, Tair Llyn, Cwm Rheidol, Aberystwyth. Hotels: Conrah, Chancery, Bay.

WYRE. Llanrhystyd (Ceredigion). Trout (small), some salmon and sometimes good for sewin. Fishing controlled by a number of riparian owners.

YSTWYTH. A natural, gravel bed spate river. Brown trout stocked in spring; large sea trout run in first spate in June, several runs of smaller sea trout July to Sept. Salmon usually run mid-Aug to early Oct.

Aberystwyth (Ceredigion). Llanilar AA has most of river, approx 15m both banks, from Aberystwyth to Pontrhydygroes; some brown trout in Llanilar area. Best sea trout fishing is by fly at night, spinning in high water and with quill minnow as water clears; fly is also effective during the day when there is a touch of colour in the water. St £45, wt £25, dt £10, conc, from Hon Sec; Aber Tackle; Post Office, Crosswood; Llanilar Garage; Blaenplwyf Post Office, nr Aberystwyth, Ceredigion (Tel: 01970 612499); and Royal Oak, Llanfarian. Mr Tovey, Fron Farm, **Bronnant** (Tel: 01974 251392) has 3 lakes with trout fishing. **Trawscoed Estate Fishery** has over 3m stretch on the central reaches of R Ystwyth, sea trout from June onwards; **Birchgrove Reservoir** situated in Forestry Commission woodlands, 1½ acres, carp fishing; and **Maesllyn Lake**, 5 acres, stocked with rainbow and brown trout, boat available. For further information contact Mick and Nikki Skevington, Post Office Trawscoed, Aberystwyth, Tel: 01974 261 201. Accommodation can be arranged; and permits, rod licences and fishing tackle, including locally produced flies, are available at the Post Office. Tackle Shop: Aber Tackle, Terrace Rd, Aberystwyth.

TÂF

(For close seasons, licences, etc, see Welsh Region Environment Agency, p15)

Rises on Prescelly Mountains and flows about 25 miles south-east to Carmarthen Bay at mouth of Towy. Has good runs of sewin and salmon most years. Brown trout fishing good upstream of Whitland.

St Clears (Dyfed). Good salmon and sewin; brown trout fair. April, May, Sept best for salmon. Sewin mid-June onwards. Carmarthen and Dist AC have water on Tâf and stretch on **Dewi Fawr**. St Clears and District AA has 5m on Tâf, from St Clears to Llanddowror; salmon, sea trout and brown trout. Assn also has salmon, sea trout and brown trout fishing on **R Ginning**, 3m; **R Dewi Fawr**, 1½m; **R Cowin**, 1½m. Concessions for juveniles and OAPs. Permits from Hon Sec; and The Pharmacy, Pentre Road. Other waters on these rivers by permission of farmers. Hotels: Black Lion; Gardde House; Picton House, Llanddowror, St Clears. Caravan sites at St Clears and Laugharne.

Whitland (Carmarthenshire). Salmon, sewin, brown trout. Whitland AA has approx 5m of fishing, mainly double bank; all legal methods, season 1 Apr–7 Oct. St £50, conc for juv, OAP, dt £10 from Treasurer P Hunt (Tel: 01834 831304); Bay Fishing Tackle, Saundersfoot; The Fishfinder, Carmarthen; and Chwareon Gog Sports, St Johns Street, Whitland. **White House Mill Trout Fishery**, Barbara Hunt, White House Mill, Lampeter Velfrey, Whitland SA34 0RB (Tel: 01834 831304): fly fishing for brown and rainbow trout on 4 acre lake, emphasis on nymph and dry fly. Easy access for disabled, tackle for hire, self-catering cottage near lake. Dt from £10. Coarse fishing on **Llyn Carfan**; two lakes of 1½ acres each with good quality water, stocked with carp to 18lb, tench, plentiful roach, and rudd. Rods and tackle for hire. Contact Llyn Carfan, Whitland, Dyfed SA34 0ND (Tel: 01994 240819).

TAFF AND ELY

(For close seasons, licences, etc, see Welsh Region Environment Agency, p15)

Taff has its source in two headstreams on the Brecon Beacons and flows about 40m south-east to enter the Severn Estuary at Cardiff. A short and steep river, heavily polluted since the 19th century by local iron, coal and steel industries. However, by the early 1980s there had been major improvements in the water quality due to economic recession and improved pollution control; and sea trout and some salmon were again entering lower reaches of river. Since then, the Welsh Water Authority, and subsequently the National Rivers Authority, have been successfully carrying out a strategy for rehabilitating salmon in the Taff; through pollution control, building fish passes, transporting adult fish upstream, artificial propagation and control of exploitation. In the 1990s, the Taff has become a prolific salmon and sea trout river in the lower reaches; these fish can now travel as far as Pontypridd. The Lower Taff, from Cardiff to Pontypridd is also a good coarse fishery, the main species being chub, dace, roach, gudgeon and barbel. Now that the polluted legacy of the past has largely disappeared, the remainder of the Taff catchment supports good brown trout. The River Ely joins the mouth of Taff at Penarth. There are good roach in the lower reaches of the Ely; and an improvement in trout fishing throughout; salmon and sea trout have also been making a steady return since the late 1980s.

Cardiff (Glamorgan). Brown trout (stocked) and run of sea trout and salmon. Glamorgan AC has fishing on **River Taff** (chub, dace, eels, roach, salmon, sea trout, barbel, pike, perch and brown trout); 2 stretches on **River Wye**, at Monmouth (chub, dace, perch, pike, roach, bleak, gudgeon, eels and barbel) and at Clifford (chub, dace, roach, perch, pike, barbel, bleak and grayling); **River Usk** near Abergavenny (chub, dace, brown trout, salmon and sea trout); **East Dock** (roach, perch, chub, dace, carp and eels); **River Ely** at St Fagans (roach, chub and trout); **River Trothy** near Monmouth (chub, dace, trout, grayling, roach and pike); **Troes Pond** at Troes near Bridgend (bream, tench, perch, carp, roach and rudd); **Pysgodlyn Mawr** (bream, carp, roach, perch, rudd and tench); **Warren Mill** (carp, roach, bream, tench, rudd and perch); **Llantrythyd Lake** (carp, bream, roach, rudd, tench, perch and eels); and **St-y-Nyll Ponds** (pike, rudd, tench, perch and carp). For membership contact Chris Peters, 24 Llaleston Close, Barry, S Glamorgan. Bute AS, Birchgrove (Cardiff) AS and Glamorgan AC share lease of approx 3m fishing on R Taff in city limits; coarse (chub, roach, dace, gudgeon with barbel introduced recently); and game (salmon, sewin and brown trout) under auspices of combined Cardiff clubs known as Taff Fisheries. Day tickets from Gary Evans, 105 Whitchurch Rd,

Heath, Cardiff, and A E Bales & Son, 3 Frederick St, Cardiff CF1 4DB. Bute AS has fixture list fishing on **R Wye** at Builth Wells and **R Usk** at Monmouth, and on a private lake within Cardiff's city limits; all venues hold roach, dace, gudgeon, bleak; members only; club membership from secretary. Birchgrove AS has fishing on **Rivers Ely** and **Taff**; salmon, sea trout, chub, dace, grayling, roach and barbel. Through kindness of riparian owners, the society also has coarse fishing on prime stretches on **R Wye** between Glasbury and Built; chub, dace, eels, grayling, pike, roach and perch. Fishing on Wye for members only. Permits from A E Bale & Son, 3 Frederick St. **Roath Park Lake** (Cardiff Corporation) holds rudd, roach, carp, tench. **Llanishen** (59 acres) and **Lisvane** (19 acres) **Reservoirs**, located within Cardiff City boundary, approach via B4562 road; leased to Cardiff Fly Fishing Club; day tickets sold at reservoirs. **Cardiff Bay** opens 2000/2001, giving a huge freshwater lake, with dace, roach, grayling, barbel, gudgeon and carp fishing. Tackle shop: A Bale & Son, 3 Frederick Street, Cardiff CF1 4DB (information, bait, licences); Gary Evans, 105 Whitchurch Road, Heath, Cardiff; Anglers Supplies, 172 Penarth Rd, Cardiff; Ely Angling Suppliers, 572 Cowbridge Rd East, Ely Bridge, Cardiff. Hotels: Angel, Cardiff International, Clare Court, Glenmor.

Merthyr Tydfil (Glamorgan). Merthyr Tydfil AA offers a large variety of waters from wild brown trout fishing on the Upper Neuadd Reservoir in the heart of the Brecon Beacons to salmon fishing on the Usk, with ponds and reservoirs for the coarse fishing enthusiast. The assn has 17m on **Taff** and **Taf Fechan** at Merthyr Tydfil from Pontsticill Reservoir to Quaker's Yard, brown trout, regularly stocked, size limit 10in, bag limit 6 fish; **Upper Neuadd Reservoir**, wild brown trout, very lightly stocked, fly only; **Taf Fechan Reservoirs**, trout (20 Mar–17 Oct) and coarse (16 Jun–17 Mar), no pike or other coarse fish to be removed; **Penywern Ponds**, coarse fish including carp in excess of 10lb, dt. Permits from Cefn Coed Tackle, High St, Cefn Coed, Tel: 01685 379809; A Rees, Treasurer, 13 Alexandra Avenue, Tel: 01685 723520; N Morgan, 20 James St, Twynyrodyn. Assn also has 2 stretches of salmon and trout fishing on **Usk** at **Mardy Fishery**, 1¼m; and **Kemeys Commander Fishery**, ¾m. Day tickets for Usk from A Rees and N Morgan (see above). Reservoirs in Taf Fawr Valley managed by

Hamdden Ltd: **Beacons Reservoir** (52 acres) brown trout, fly only; **Cantref Reservoir** (42 acres) rainbow and brown trout, fly only; **Llwyn-On Reservoir** (150 acres) rainbow and brown trout, fly, worm and spinner. All located in Brecon Beacons National Park adjacent to A470 (T) road, 3m north of Merthyr Tydfil and 15m south of Brecon. Cater for disabled. Private boats permitted. Dt from machine at Llwyn-On water treatment works. For further information contact C Hatch, Area Manager, Hamdden Ltd, Sluvad Treatment Works, Llandegfedd Reservoir, New Inn, Pontypool, Gwent NP4 0TA, Tel: 01495 769281. Tackle shops: Cefn Coed Tackle, High St, Cefn Coed.

Tributaries of Taff

RHONDDA FAWR and RHONDDA FACH:

Pontypridd (Mid Glamorgan). At Junction of Rhondda Fawr and Fach, and Taff.

Tonypandy (Mid Glamorgan). Glyncornel AA has trout fishing on Rhondda; restocked annually with brown and rainbow trout. St £22 and wt £8, conc for juv; competitions for adults and juniors. Club also holds rights on very good coarse fishing at **Darran Lake**; carp, bream, tench, rudd, perch and silver bream; st £16 and wt £5. Contact Secretary (Tel: 01443 439961) for permit outlets.

Ferndale (Glamorgan). Maerdy and Ferndale AC has water on River Rhondda Fach; and on **Lluest Wen** and **Castell Nos Reservoirs** at Maerdy. All water are trickle-stocked throughout the season. Fly only on Lluest Wen. Day permits from David Hughes, North Road Motors, North Road, Ferndale.

ELY: Roach, chub, trout.

Ely (Glamorgan). Glamorgan AC has trout fishing on River Ely at St Fagans and coarse fishing in **St-y-Nyll Ponds** at St Brides-super-Ely.

Llantrisant (Glamorgan). **Seven Oaks Trout Fishery**, Cowbridge Road, nr Pontyclun, Mid Glam CF7 9JU, Tel: 01446 775474. Cowbridge Fly Lake, fishing for rainbow trout and dameron blues, also novice pond with rainbows and tiger trout; dt waters. Tackle hire and some tackle sold on site, bank only, good access for disabled.

TEIFI

(For close seasons, licences, etc, see Welsh Region
Environment Agency, p15)

Rises in Llyn Teifi, near Strata Florida, in Ceredigion, flows south-west and then west, entering Cardigan Bay below Cardigan Town. Association water provides salmon, sea trout (sewin) and brown trout fishing. April and May are the best months for spring salmon; summer salmon fishing through to October can also be productive given reasonable water levels. Sea trout run from May onwards. Coracle and draft nets come off 31 August. Main salmon run September onwards.

Cardigan (Dyfed). Salmon, sewin, trout. Bass, mullet and flounders below bridge to sea, 2m; boats for hire. Teifi Trout Assn has fishing for salmon, sea trout and brown trout on 20m stretch of lower River Teifi, from a few miles above Cardigan to just beyond Newcastle Emlyn, including fishing at Cenarth. Assn also has stretch, ¾m, above Henllan (salmon, sea trout and brown trout). St £125 plus £20 join-ing fee from Membership Secretary. Surcharge of £40 on Cenarth waters. Concessions for OAPs, disabled and junior. Wt £60-£70 and dt £15–£20 (junior £3) from The Reel Thing, Lower Market, Cardigan, Ceredigion SA43 2HJ; Thomas Sports Shop, Newcastle Emlyn; The Salmon Leap and Cenarth Falls Holiday Park, Cenarth; and Afon Teifi Caravan Park, Pentrecagal.

Llechryd (Dyfed). Salmon, sea trout. Castle Malgwyn Hotel has 2½m of salmon, trout and sea trout fishing on the lower reaches of Teifi; best time for salmon July and Aug; reserved for guest of hotel; special rates for parties. Nevern AA has ¾m stretch on R Teifi, nr Llechryd. Teifi Trout Assn water.

Cenarth (Dyfed). Salmon, sewin, trout. Famous falls. Teifi Trout Assn water; surcharge for Cenarth Fishery. Permits from The Salmon Leap, Cenarth, Newcastle Emlyn, Dyfed SA38 9JP, Tel: 01239 711242, where there is also a comprehensive range of fishing tackle and bait for sale; and Cenarth Caravan Park. West Wales School of Fly Fishing has its own private fisheries (clients only) on **R Cych** and **R Gwili**, and teaching beats on **R Teifi**; wild brown trout, sea trout and salmon. It also has 2 lakes stocked with brown and rainbow trout. The school runs courses for beginners and for those keen to improve their skills; free flyfishing

lessons for young people in school summer holidays. Contact Pat O'Reilly, Senior Instructor, West Wales School of Fly Fishing, Ffoshelyg, Llancych, Boncath, Pembrokeshire SA37 0LJ, Tel: 01239 698678.

Newcastle Emlyn (Dyfed). Salmon and sea trout. Good centre for Teifi. Teifi Trout Assn has water; permits from Thomas Sports Shop, Newcastle Emlyn. Riverside cottages with exclusive private fishing on an adjoining ¾m stretch of Teifi, salmon, sea trout and brown trout. Rod licences from Chwaraeon Andrew Sports, 7 Sycamore St. Hotels: Emlyn Arms.

Llandysul (Ceredigion). Salmon, sewin, brown trout. Popular centre with good fishing. Best April–May and Aug–Sept for salmon; sewin July onwards. Llandysul AA has Middle Teifi from Newcastle Emlyn to above 2m north of Lampeter; free instruction for children by qual-ified instructors from the West Wales School of Fly Fishing every Fri through Aug, including for non-members. Wt £57 and dt £17 from Gwilym Jones, The Alma Store, Wind St, Llandysul SA44 6HB, Tel: 01559 363322, and Alan Williams, Lampeter Angling, 57 Bridge St, Lampeter, Tel: 01570 422985. Cross Hands and Dist AA has stretch on R Teifi, nr Llandysul; salmon and sea trout. Rainbow trout fishing on a 2-acre lake at **Rhydlewis Trout Fishery**; stocked daily; fly only. Lakeside parking, toilets, tea & coffee-making facilities, smokery and smokery shop. Further details from, Ryd-yr-Onnen, Rhydlewis, Llandysul, Dyfed SA44 5QS (Tel: 01239 851224). Hotels: Kings Arms; Castle Howell; Henllan Falls, Henllan, Llandysul; Porth and County Gate, Llanfihangel-ar-Arth, Pencader.

Llanybydder (Carmarthenshire). Salmon, sewin, brown trout. Llanybydder AA has approx 5m of Middle Teifi, both banks, above and below Llanybydder Bridge. St £45, wt £31.50 and £36.50, dt £8.50 and £12.50. Concessions for jun. Instruction, and challenge cup for best junior angler. Permits from Hon Sec and David Morgan, Siop-y-Bont, Llanybydder. Hotels: Crosshands; Black Lion; Grannell Arms, Llannwnen, Ceredigion.

Lampeter (Dyfed). Salmon, April onwards; sewin, late June, July, August onwards; brown trout, both dry and wet fly. Both Llandysul AA and Tregaron AA have water on Teifi around Lampeter. **Hendre Pools**, rainbow trout; per-mits from O G Thomas, Hendre, Cilcennin, nr

Lampeter SA48 8RF. **Troed-y-Bryn Fisheries**, rainbow and brown trout, privately owned lakes, 3½ acres, fly only; permits from Mrs E E Edwards, Troed-y-Bryn, Cribyn, Lampeter. Rod licences from Post Office, Cribyn. Tackle shop: Alan Williams, 57 Bridge St, Lampeter, Dyfed SA48 7AB, Tel: 01570 422985.

Tregaron (Dyfed). Good fly fishing for brown trout. Salmon fishing also good when conditions right. Tregaron AA has 17m of **R Teifi** from Pontrhydfendigaid to Tregaron and down river to Cellan; **Teifi Pools**, 3 mountain lakes, with wild brown trout; and **Llyn Berwyn**, 50 acres. St £40 and dt £6. Concessions for juniors. Permits from Medical Hall Newsagent, The Square, Tregaron; Post Office, Pontrhydfendi-gaid; W Rees, London House, Llanddewi Brefi; Post Office, Llanfair Clydogau, Lampeter, Dyfed SA48 8LA; and Alan Williams, 57 Bridge St, Lampeter. Permits for **Teifi Pools**; dt £5; from Newsagent, Tregaron; Post Office at Pontrhydfendigaid; and farm on road to fishery. Further information on Tregaron AA fishing from Tregaron Development Officer, 4 Brennig Terrace, Chapel St SY25 1HA (Tel: 01974 298146). Other good fishing on Aeron, 6m. Hotel: Talbot. Accommodation: Brynawel and Aberdwr Guest Houses.

TOWY (or TYWI)
(For close seasons, licences, etc, see Welsh Region Environment Agency, p15)

Lower reaches near Carmarthen are tidal holding trout, salmon and sewin in season (May, June and July best); association waters. Above this Towy mostly preserved, but some fishing by leave, ticket or from hotels. Salmon average 12lb and sea trout up to 8lb are taken; brown trout generally small.

Carmarthen (Dyfed). Salmon, sewin, trout. April and May usually good for large sewin. Tidal up to Carmarthen and 3m above. Cross Hands and Dist AA has water in vicinity, see *Llandeilo*. Carmarthen Amateur AA has water on **Towy** at Nantgaredig, White Mill and Abergwili; sewin and salmon. Assn arranges 6 competitions a year and has 5 private car parks. Weekly permits from Secretary, or The Fishfinder (*below*). Carmarthen and Dist AC has water on **Rivers Towy** (tidal and non-tidal), **Cothi**, **Gwili**, **Taf** and **Gwendraeth Fach**; all these waters are within 5–10 miles of Carmarthen. Membership £60; dt £20, under 16 free. Permits are available from Hon Sec and The Fishfinder, 51 King St,

Carmarthen SA31 1QD (Tel: 01267 220226). Pantybedw Fishery, Nantgaredig (Tel: 01267 290315): 7½ acre fly fishing lake, catch and release only; 1½ acre lake, catch and keep only. Dt £18, 4 fish, £10, 2 fish. Hotel: Golden Grove Arms, Llanathne, Carmarthen SA32 8JU (Tel: 01558 668069). Accommodation: Farm Retreats, Capel Dewi Uchaf Farm, Capel Dewi Road, Capel Dewi, Carmarthen, Carmarthenshire SA32 8AY, Tel: 01267 290799; Old Priory Guest House, Carmarthen; Spilman Motel (Tel: 01267 237037).

Nantgaredig (Dyfed). Salmon and sea trout fishing on the Abercothi Estate; 3 beats on **Towy** and 1 beat on **Cothi**. Weekly letting on Towy for parties of up to 5 rods; seasonal letting on Cothi. Contact Hamdden Ltd, Plas y Ffynnon, Cambrian Way, Brecon, Powys LD3 7HP (Tel: 01874 614657, Fax: 01874 614526). Carmarthen Amateur AA has water on **Cothi** and **Gwili**. Cross Hand and District AA has stretches on R Towy and R Cothi in area; salmon and trout. Rod licences from Post Office Dolgoed, Station Rd. Tackle shop: The Armourers Shop, Ye Olde Post Office, Felingwm Uchaf.

Llandeilo (Dyfed). Salmon, sea trout, brown trout. Llandeilo AA preserves 4½m on Towy, about 1½m on **Lower Dulais** and about 3m on **Lower Cennen**. Season tickets, members only (waiting list), from Hon Sec; weekly and day tickets from Hon Sec and Towy Sports, *below*. Concessions for jun. Fishing good when water in condition. Cross Hands and District AA has several stretches of Towi in vicinity, also water on R Cothi, and **R Teifi** at Llandysul; access for disabled on some waters; membership £50 + joining fee £10, conc; limited dt £20 and wt £40–£50, from Towy Sports; Dyfed Guns, 7 High St Ammanford (Tel: 01269 597812); The Fishfinder, 4 Jackson Lane, Carmarthen (Tel: 01267 220226); Llanfynydd P O (Tel: 01558 668231). Salmon and sea trout fishing on Golden Grove Estate; 10m stretch on **Towy** from Llandeilo to Llanegwad, mainly double bank; best months Jun–Aug. Self-catering accommodation for anglers at Sannan Court, Llanfyndd. For further information on Golden Grove fishery and Sannan Court, contact Hamdden Ltd, Plas y Ffynnon, Cambrian Way, Brecon, Powys LD3 7HP (Tel: 01874 614657, Fax: 01874 614526). Black Lion Inn, Llansawel, has 2½m on Towy; rods also on **Teifi** and **Cothi**. **Cennen** good trout stream. Tackle shop: Towy Sports, 9 King St, Tel: 01558

822637. Hotels: Cawdor Arms, Castle, Edwinsford Arms, Plough Inn, White Hart, Cottage Inn, Ty-Isaf Fishing Lodge and Country Cottages, Trapp, Llandeilo (game fishing on rivers and reservoirs; tuition).

Llangadog (Dyfed). Salmon, sewin, trout. Llangadog AA have water. Wt, dt and limited night-fishing tickets issued.

Llanwrda (Dyfed). Salmon and sea trout. Swansea Amateur AA rents 1m (both banks), on an annual basis; access south of railway station; fly only. Members and guests only. Concessions for juniors. Glanrannell Park Country House Hotel, Crugybar, Llanwrda, nr Llandovery, Carmarthenshire SA19 8SA, Tel: 01558 685230, has agreements with a number of private owners on **Rivers Cothi, Towy** and **Teifi**; and tickets for assn waters are obtainable from nearby towns, Llandeilo and Lampeter. Hotel keeps some tackle for hire and basic instruction in fly fishing is from Dai Davies, the hotel's resident proprietor. Springwater Lakes, **Harford**, Llanwrda, SA19 8DT (Tel: 01558 650788): two 3 acre lakes, one with carp, tench, roach, bream, rudd, dt £5, 24 hr £10, conc; the other with stocked brown and rainbow trout, dt £15 2 fish, £20 4 fish; tackle hire, facilities, access for disabled.

Llandovery (Dyfed). Salmon, sewin (best June–Sept), trout. Llandovery AA has 8m on **Towy**, double and single bank, excellent fly water below Llandovery, holding pools with fish (sewin) up to 14lb, and salmon and grilse in Aug–Sep; and 10m on tributaries **R Gwydderig** and **R Bran**, good head of natural trout and sewin from July onwards. Membership occasionally available; st £150, dt £17–£18; from Secretary (Tel: 01550 7206133), and The Carmarthen & Pumpsaint Co-operative Store at main car park, Llandovery (Tel: 01267 290202). Hotels: Castle Hotel, Llandovery; Llwyncelin Guest House, Llandovery; and Cwmgwyn Farmhouse (B & B) which overlooks R Towy, Tel: 01550 720150.

Tributaries of the Towy

GWILI: Small river of 12ft to 16ft in width which joins Towy 1m north of Carmarthen. Sea trout (sewin), fish running from early June onwards, averaging 2lb and attaining 6lb. Brown trout fishing poor. A few salmon caught on Gwili, especially at the end of year.

Llanpumsaint (Dyfed). Sewin, trout, occasional salmon. Carmarthen Amateur AA and Carmarthen and Dist AC both have stretches on Gwili. Hotel: Fferm-y-Felin (18th century farmhouse with 15 acres of countryside for fishing and bird-watching, tuition and equipment for hire).

COTHI: The largest tributary of the Towy, noted for its sewin which run in late summer and early autumn. Salmon, sewin and brown trout.

Carmarthen (Dyfed). Carmarthen Amateur AA and Carmarthen & Dist AC both have stretches on Cothi. The Cothi Bridge Hotel, Pontargothi, Carmarthen, Dyfed SA32 7NG (Tel: 01267 290251) has a short stretch of salmon fishing and has arrangements for guests to fish on other private and club waters; special rates for fishermen. Two fisheries in area: Llanllawddog Lake (Tel: 01267 253436), near Llanllawddog Church, has fly only lake and 'any method' lake, dt £12 2 fish, £20 4 fish; Premier Coarse Fisheries, Ian Heaps, Holgan Farm, Llawhaden, SA67 8DJ (Tel: 01437 541285); coarse fishing on 3 lakes, with big carp and tench, tuition from former world champion angler. Dt £5, tackle sold on site. Tackle shop: Towy Sports, Llandeilo (Tel: 01558 822637).

Brechfa (Dyfed). Salmon and sea trout. Swansea Amateur AA has 2m (both banks), between Abergorlech and Brechfa. Members and guests only. Hotels: Ty Mawr.

Pumpsaint (Dyfed). **Cothi** and **Twrch**. Trout, sea trout (June onwards); salmon from early July. Dolaucothi Arms, Pumpsaint, Llanwrda, Dyfed SA19 8UW, Tel: 01558 650547, has approx 8m of fishing, made up of 12 rods. Season starts from July to August when the salmon come up. Permits from pub; and bed and breakfast. Glanrannell Park Country House Hotel, Crugybar, Llanwdra, nr Llandovery, Carmarthenshire SA19 8SA, has salmon, sea trout and trout fishing on Teifi, Cothi and Twrch. Spring Water Lakes, Pumpsaint, Llanwrda: 2 acre coarse lake with carp to 20lb, good roach and rudd.

SAWDDE: Llanddeusant (Carmarthenshire). Trout. Accommodation and fishing at Black Mountain Caravan and Camping Park, Llanddeusant, nr Llangadog SA19 9YG (Tel: 01550 740617); rainbow and brown trout fishing on **Usk Reservoir** (3m), also on Sawdde (3m) and Towy (6m).

USK AND EBBW
(For close seasons, licences, etc, see Welsh Region
Environment Agency, p15)

The River Usk is a good salmon river and first rate for trout. Geological formation is red sandstone, merging into limestone in lower reaches. Trout average from about ¾lb in the lower reaches to ¼lb towards the source. Some tributaries also afford good trout fishing: Afon Llwyd, Honddu, Grwyne, Yscir and Bran. Salmon fishing mostly private, but several opportunities for trout. The River Ebbw flows into the Severn Estuary between the mouths of the River Rhymney and the River Usk. The Ebbw has recently experienced great improvements in water quality which has been reflected in the fishery improvements, with very good trout and reports of sea trout. The Sirhowy, a tributary of Ebbw, also has good trout fishing.

Newport (Gwent). Newport AA has stretch of **Monmouthshire and Brecon Canal**, **Woodstock Pool**, **Morgans Pool**, **Liswerry Pond** and **Spytty Lake**; all providing good coarse fishing, including roach, perch, bream, carp and tench. Assn also has coarse fishing on **R Wye** at Symonds Yat; roach, dace, chub. Day tickets from bailiffs at lakes. Islwyn & Dist AC have trout fishing on Ebbw, **Sirhowy** and **Penyfan Pond**. Membership from Mrs J Meller, Membership Secretary, 7 Penllwyn Street, Cwmfelinfach. Day tickets from Pontllanfraith Leisure Centre, Pontllanfraith, Blackwood, Gwent, Tel: 01495 224562. Newport Reservoir Fly Fishing A has fishing on **Ysyfro Reservoir**, High Cross, nr Newport; rainbow and brown trout. Day permits (£11) for non-members can be purchased from hut at reservoir. **Wentwood Reservoir**, nr **Chepstow**, brown and rainbow trout. Tickets at fishing lodge, boat for disabled, for details contact Secretary, Wentworth Reservoir FFA (Tel: 01291 425158). Rainbow and brown trout fishing on **Cefn Mably Lakes**, a complex of 5 spring-fed waters on farm land lying beside the River Rhymney; one 6½ acre lake, fly only; two any method; two coarse lakes stocked with carp, roach, rudd, perch, gudgeon, bream, etc, open all year; access for disabled, bait and full facilities on site. Apply to John Jones, Cefn Mably Lakes, nr Castleton, Newport, Tel: 01633 681101. **Hendre Lake**, 10-acre coarse fishery at St Mellons; an excellent lake, especially in hot and cold weather when other lakes are struggling; permits from Garry Evans. Tackle shops:

Garry Evans, Fishing Tackle, 29 Redland St, Tel: 01633 855086; Dave Richards, 73 Church Road, Tel: 01633 254910; Pill Angling Centre, 160 Commercial Rd, Tel: 01633 267211; Richards Tackle, Duckpool Rd. Hotels: Rising Sun, High Cross, nr Newport, Gwent; Tredegar Arms, Bassaleg, nr Newport, Gwent; Tredegar Arms, Risca Road, nr Newport, Gwent.

Pontypool (Gwent). Usk private. Tributary **Afon Llwyd**, good trout fishing and regularly stocked by local clubs. Subject to periodic pollution but soon recovers due to exceptionally fast flow. Pontypool AA and Cwmbran AA have stretches. Pontypool AA also has **Allway Brook**, nr Usk, trout, dace and chub: and coarse fishing on **Monmouthshire & Brecon Canal** at Pontypool (Bridges 55 to 57), roach, perch, bream, carp and tench. Permits from Pill Angling, Orsbourne Road. **Llandegfedd Reservoir** (429 acres), Sluvad Treatment Works, Llandegfedd Reservoir, Panteg, Pontypool, NP4 0TA (Tel: 01495 755122); owned by Welsh Water plc, and a major boat fishery; stocked with 30,000 rainbow trout av 1½lbs–2lbs, small numbers of browns; season 20 Mar–31 Oct (rainbow), 20 Mar–17 Oct (brown). Fly only; st £380, dt £12, 6 fish, part day £9, 4 fish, conc OAP and juv. Permits from vending machines on site, or from Ranger's waterside office. Forty boats for hire, incl for disabled, with or without motor, £17–£10, pre-booking is recommended. Cwmbran AA has coarse fishing on **Monmouthshire & Brecon Canal**; average depth 4ft; stocked with bream, tench, crucian carp, roach, perch, good eels in parts; strict control on litter. Assn also has coarse fishing, for members only, at **Llantarnam Industrial Estates Ponds** (3 ponds stocked with roach, perch and dace, and one stocked with rudd and bream); and excellent mixed fishing on **River Monnow**, trout, grayling, bream, roach, perch, dace, chub and carp. Night fishing on canal and Monnow. Permits from Cwmbran Pet Stores and Angling Supplies, 23 Commercial St, Old Cwmbran (Tel: 01633 483051). No day tickets on Llantarnam Ponds; members only. Day ticket on bank at Cwmbran Boating Lake.

Usk (Gwent). Usk Town Water Fishery Association holds about 2m, mostly above Usk Bridge. Trout fishing only. Rod licence required. Wading advisable. Merthyr Tydfil AA has water at **Kemeys Commander**. Permits, tackle and licences from Sweet's Fishing Tackle, 14 Porthycarne Street, Usk, Gwent NP5 1RY, Tel:

01291 672552. Hotels: Three Salmons; Castle; Cross Keys; Glen-yr-Avon; Kings Head; Chain Bridge, nr Usk; Bridge Inn.

Abergavenny (Gwent). Salmon, trout. Monmouth DC holds town waters, both banks from Llanfoist Bridge to Sewer Bridge. Tickets from Bridge Inn, Llanfoist. Merthyr Tydfil AA has rights to **Mardy Fishery**, 1¼m above town. Crickhowell and Dist AS has approx 1½m u/s of Llanfoist Bridge, on left bank, see *Crickhowell*, for permits. Hotel: Wenallt; Penpergwm House. Accom information from T.I.C. (Tel: 01873 857588)

Glangrwyney (Powys). Salmon, sea trout, brown trout. Bell Inn, NP8 1EH (Tel: 01873 810247) has water here and issues tickets to residents and non-residents for salmon and trout fishing.

Crickhowell (Powys). Salmon, sea trout, wild brown trout. Crickhowell and Dist AS has approx 1m d/s of Crickhowell Bridge on both banks, except for garden of Bridgend Public House on left bank; also approx ½m u/s of bridge on left bank. Dt £12 salmon, £6 trout, from tackle shop, or general stores, 1 Standard St (Tel: 01873 810321). Gliffaes Country House Hotel, NP8 1RH, Tel: 01874 730371 *(see advt)*, has 1m on Usk adjacent to hotel and a further 1½m upstream. Excellent wild brown trout water; salmon improving and some sea trout. Primarily for hotel guests but outside rods if space. Bridge End Inn has short length below bridge. Trecastle and **Talybont Reservoirs** are within reach. Tackle shop: Crickhowell Angling Supplies, Unit 2, Riverside, New Rd (Tel: 01873 811877). Hotel: Stables. Accom information from T.I.C. (Tel: 01873 812105).

Brecon (Powys). Brecon AS has water on R Usk from Llanfaes Bridge to Boat House; salmon and trout. Left bank (Llanfaes side) members only. Promenade bank (right bank) dt £1 from Mrs Lindsey Wilding, Post Office, Llanfaes, Brecon, Tel: 01874 622739; and H.M. Supplies Ltd, Watton, Brecon, Tel: 01874 622148. Powys County Council has stretch on Usk from boathouse to Gwennies Lane, on which salmon stones and groynes have been placed, platforms for disabled, and water is stocked with brown trout. Tickets from Post Office (above), or Town Clerk's Office, Guildhall (Tel: 0874 622884). For salmon and trout fishing day tickets on Wye and Usk in the Brecon and Builth Wells area, contact Chester-Master (Chartered Surveyors & Land Agents), Dolgarreg, North Road, Builth Wells, Powys LD2 3DD, Tel: 01982 553248. Brecon FA has 1m both banks below Llanfaes Bridge; trout; fly only. Coarse fishing in pools on **Dderw Farm, Llyswen**; carp (to 12lb), roach, tench; permits from Mrs J Eckley, Dderw Farm, Llyswen, Brecon LD3 0UT, Tel: 01874 754224. **Llangorse Lake**, 6m from Brecon; pike, perch, roach and bream; no permits required only rod licence. Hotels: Griffin Inn, Llyswen, Brecon; Castle of Brecon; Nythfa, Uskview GH.

Sennybridge (Powys). Rods on **Crai Reservoir** (100 acres) owned by Cnewr Estate Ltd, Sennybridge, Brecon LD3 8SP, tel: 01874 636207. Wild trout; fly fishing from bank only. Day tickets from reservoir keeper. Self-catering accommodation is usually with the fishing. Hotels: Tir y Graig Uchaf.

Trecastle (Powys). **Usk Reservoir** (280 acres), one of the best trout fisheries in Wales, well stocked with rainbow and brown trout supplementing natural production. Fly fishing, spinning and worming. Catch limit 6 fish; size limit 9in. Anglers are permitted to use their own boats by prior arrangement. Caters for disabled. Permits from machine on site. For further information contact C Hatch, Area Manager, Hamdden Ltd, Sluvad Treatment Works, Llandegfedd Reservoir, New Inn, Pontypool, Gwent NP4 0TA, Tel: 01495 769281. Hotel: Castle.

Ebbw Vale (Gwent). Ebbw Vale Welfare AC has coarse fishing on **River Wye** at Foy, nr Ross-on-Wye, 2½m (chub, dace, roach and barbel); **Monmouthshire & Brecon Canal**, nr Crickhowell, ½m (roach, perch, bream); **Machine Pond** at Brynmawr, 5 acres (carp, roach, perch); and 10 ponds in the Ebbw Vale area (carp, pike, roach, perch and gudgeon). Members only. Membership open to all; from Hon Sec and local pet shop. Contact Hon Sec for season tickets for people on holiday. Concessions for juniors. Tackle shops: J Williams & Son, Bethcar St; Petsville, Bethcar St.

WYE
(For close seasons, licences, etc, see Welsh Region Environment Agency, p15)

The whole of the river Wye is included in the section on England, although it also flows through Monmouthshire and Powys.

Welsh Sea Fishing Stations

Those given in the following list are arranged from south to north. Sea fishing is available at other places also, but those mentioned are included because they cater specially for the sea angler. Further information may be had from the tackle shops and club secretaries (whose addresses will be found in the club list). When writing, please enclose stamped addressed envelope for reply. Local tourist information offices will help with accommodation.

Newport (Newport). Newport and District Sea Anglers operate in Magor, Redwick, Goldcliff, St Brides, Cardiff and Barry, with rover matches from Severn Bridge to Gower in West Wales; matches held every weekend; and, during the summer, Docks Summer League every Wed for 16 weeks. Tackle shops: Dave Richards, 73 Church Road, Tel: 01633 254910; Pill Angling Centre, 160 Commercial Rd, Tel: 01633 267211. Hotel: Kings Head.

Swansea (Swansea). Bass, flatfish from beaches and rocks (Worm's Head). Fish baits cast from Llanmadoc take conger, tope, thornbacks and monkfish. Mackerel caught in warmer months. Bass, mullet and flounders in estuary at Loughor Bridge. Excellent boat fishing in Carmarthen Bay and off Worm's Head. Charter boats operate from Swansea Marina, for fishing the bay and Pwlldu. Information from Roger's (*below*). Small bass, mullet, flatfish and mackerel off Mumbles Pier; no night fishing. Docks permit required for Queens Dock breakwater; good for cod in winter. Bait can be dug in Swansea Bay and estuary; squid, herring, sprats and mackerel from Swansea Market. List of clubs available from South West Wales Assn of SAC. Tackle shops: Mainwaring Angling Centre, 44 Vivian Rd, Sketty, Swansea, Tel: 017921 202245; Hook, Line & Sinker, Fishing Tackle Shop, Viking Way, Enterprise Park, Winchwen; Roger's Tackle, Pilot House Wharf, The Marina, Swansea SA2 0JB (Tel: 01792 469999).

Tenby (Pembrokeshire). Good sport from Old Pier; whiting, pollack, bass, codling and grey mullet; good bass fishing from south and north sandy beaches, and spinning from rocks. Fine mackerel fishing most seasons, and tope off Caldey Island. For boats enquire tackle shop. Shark trips also arranged. Tackle shop: Morris Bros, Troy House, St Julian Street.

Milford Haven and **Pembroke** (Pembroke-

shire). Fine surf-fishing and spinning from rocks for bass from Freshwater West and Broad Haven (Bosherton); best late summer and autumn. Kilpaison good for bass, flatfish early on; also codling and coalfish. Stone piers and jetties inside Haven provide deep water sport for pollack, skate, rays, whiting, codling, dogfish and coalfish. Hobbs Point (Pembroke Dock) excellent for conger and skate. Mackerel from rocks and boats (Stackpole Quay good). Tope from boats in Barafundle Bay and mackerel and bass from rocks. Other useful venues are Nab Head, Martins Haven and Angle Bay, Thorn, Rat and Sheep Islands and Harbour Rock. Mackerel from boats at harbour entrance. Lugworm and razor fish may be dug in several places, especially mud-flats at Kilpaison and Angle Bay. Pennar Gut and Pembroke River. Brindley John Ayers, "Antique Fishing Tackle", 8 Bay View Drive, Hakin, Milford Haven SA73 3RJ, Tel: 01646 698359, is a mail order business that collects and specialises in used high-quality fishing tackle; visitors are welcome; and bed and breakfast is available. Tackle shops: Trevor's Tackle Box, Gallery Parade, with good selection of baits stocked; Penfro Fishing Tackle, Pembroke Dock.

Fishguard (Pembrokeshire). Main captures from shore and breakwaters are flatfish, codling, conger, pouting, mackerel, bass, pollack, whiting and some tope. Sea trout and mullet near mouth of Gwaun. Tope, mackerel, conger, skate, etc. from boats. Boats from Fishguard Yacht & Boat Co, Main Street, Goodwick, Tel: Fishguard 873377, and Brooks, Lower Town. Tackle shop: Thomas and Howells, Dyfed Sports, 21 West Street. Hotel: Beach House, Fishguard Bay, Goodwick, Dyfed SA64 0DH (Tel: 01348 872085); sea fishing trips and packed lunches plus freezer for keeping catch.

Aberystwyth (Ceredigion). From the shore, May to November, bass (especially on soft crab bait), pollack, painted ray, mullet, huss, conger, wrasse. From October to January, whiting; July to September, mackerel. Dogfish, dabs and flounder throughout the year, turbot also caught. Fish caught off the rocks, off storm beaches, from the harbour and stone jetty. Borth beach and Leri estuary specially good for flounders; Tan-y-Bwlch beach particularly good for whiting. Bull huss and thornback ray form the backbone of the boat fishing, but dogfish, dabs, gurnard, pollack, tope, bream, turbot, monkfish and porbeagle shark are taken in their seasons. Boat trips are run from the harbour ranging from 2-hour sessions for mackerel to 12 hours out at sea. There are many well-equipped boats commanded by highly experienced skippers. Endeavour Deep Sea Angling Club operates from St David's Wharfe, Aberystwyth; instruction and tackle hire; specimen competitions all year. Annual membership £5 (individual) and £10 (affiliated club); visiting membership £1. Club owns fully equipped offshore boat; skipper with 30 years' experience; operating in 20m radius on day-to-day basis; long range wreck-fishing on suitable neap tides. Club, Tel: 01970 880474; boat, Tel: 0374 298240. Tackle shops: Aber Fishing Tackle & Gun Shop, 13 Terrace Road. Accommodation: Mr & Mrs Elwill, Shoreline Guest House, 6 South Marine Terrace.

Tywyn (Gwynedd). Good beach fishing for bass, turbot, and cod. Tywyn SAC, new club of 70 members, runs monthly competitions, casting lessons, and has discounts at club shop.

Barmouth (Gwynedd). Bass (large), flatfish, mullet in Mawddach estuary and from nearby beaches; also codling, mackerel, flatfish, and even tope and skate from boats. Ynys-y-Brawd island good for bass and flounders from shore and boats. Charter boat, The Viking, operates Apr–Oct; 8-hour deep sea or 2-hour short fishing, pleasure trips; licensed by the Dept of Trade for up to 60 passengers; full safety equipment and fishing tackle provided. Bookings can be made at Seafarer Fishing Tackle, Church St, Barmouth, Gwynedd LL42 1EH, Tel: 01341 280978.

Porthmadog (Gwynedd). Mackerel fishing trips (2 hrs) and deep sea fishing trips (8 hrs, 10 hrs, 20 hrs); bookings from The Fisherman, Central Buildings, High St, Porthmadog, Gwynedd LL49 9LR, Tel: 01766 512464.

Pwllheli and **Criccieth** (Gwynedd). Improved bass fishing April–October with new size limit to protect small bass; dogfish, dabs, plaice, skate, pollack and a few sole the year round; mackerel, tope and monkfish from June to September and black bream now on the increase. October to January; whiting and coalfish. Boats and bait available. Tackle shops: D & E Hughes, Walsall Stores, 24 Penlan Street, Pwllheli LL53 5DE; R T Pritchard & Son, Sheffield House, High Street, Criccieth LL52 0EY, Tel: 01766 522116.

Bangor (Gwynedd). Centre for Menai Straits and Anglesey. In Menai Straits, good mackerel and skate fishing during summer months, also plaice and flounder; good winter fishing for cod, pollack and whiting. Bait is plentiful along shores, incl crab and lugworm. Best beaches on Anglesey. Good rock marks abound for wrasse, pollack, thornback, smoothhound, mackerel, herring and bull huss. Good cod fishing in winter. Boats, for parties and clubs, apply A J Regan, 106 Orme Road, Tel: 01248 364590. Tackle shops: BASS Fishing Tackle, Unit 2, Plaza Buildings, High St.

Deganwy (Conwy). Wide variety of fish taken from boats in Gt Orme, Menai Straits and Puffin Island areas. Bass in estuary and off Benarth, Bodlondeb and Deganwy Points and Beacon Light. Wreck fishing. Bait from shore and estuary. Sea fishing trips with tackle for sale or hire from Carl Davies, Pen-y-Berllan, Pentywyn Road, Deganwy LL31 9TL (Tel: 01492 581983, mobile 0410 819747); wreck fishing for pollack, conger, cod, etc, and reef fishing for bass, around Anglesey, Conwy Bay and Great Orme area, Llandudno; accom arranged, disabled catered for.

Llandudno (Conwy). Skate, cod, codling, pollack, bass, mackerel, plaice, whiting, conger, coalfish, etc. Rocky beach at corner of Little Orme good for bass; so is west shore, especially Black Rocks area. Bait plentiful. Fishing from pier, beach, rocks and boats. Tope and mackerel taken by boat fishers. Tackle shop: Llandudno Fishing Tackle, 41a Victoria St, Craig-y-Don. Hotel: Epperstone (fishing can be organised from hotel).

Colwyn Bay (Conwy). Bass off Rhos Point and Penmaenhead. Whiting, codling in winter from beach. Dabs, whiting, some plaice from pier (dt available all year). Tope and skate from boats. For sea fishing contact Rhos Point Sea Fishing Trips, Bait and Tackle Shop, 2 Rhos

Point, Rhos-on-Sea, Rhos-on-Sea, Colwyn Bay (Tel: 01492 544829). Club: Colwyn Bay Victoria SAC, Marine Drive, Rhos-on-Sea. Tackle shop: Duttons, 52 Sea View Road (bait). Hotel: Ashmount Hotel, College Avenue, Rhos-on-Sea, Colwyn Bay LL28 4NT (a variety of activities available including sea fishing trips); Stanton House, Rhos-on-Sea (sea fishing organised by hotel).

Rhyl (Denbighshire). Skate, dabs, codling, whiting, plaice, gurnard, dog-fish, tope. From Foryd Harbour at Rhyl, east towards Dee Estuary at Prestayn, no licence or permit to fish is required, providing tackle and bait used are for sea fishing and not game fishing. Several boats, fully licensed to take fishing parties and charter booking, are available at Foryd Harbour from Blue Shark Fishing Trips, The Harbour, Quay Street, Tel: 01745 350267.

ANGLESEY

Holyhead and **Holy Island** (Anglesey). Fishing off Holyhead Breakwater, 1¾ m long, good on any tide; summer and winter fishing, many species caught. Very good fishing also on Stanley Embankment, at Cymyran, Rhoscolyn, Trearddur Bay, Porthdafarch and Holyhead Mountain. Bull huss, dogfish, pollack, wrasse, mullet, cod, plaice, dab, flounder, conger, whiting, codling, thornback ray and bass all taken in season from the various shore-marks. Boat-fishing, possible in all but the worst of weather, yields also shark, tope, ling and smoothhound. Bait readily available. Excellent boat fishing;

thornbacks, tope, etc. Bait in harbour or from tackle shop: Thos Owen, 19/20 Cybi Street. Hotel: Bull.

Amlwch (Anglesey). Tope taken to 40lb, skate, conger, herring, mackerel, etc, from boats; obtainable at Amlwch Port and at Bull Bay (1½m); charter boat from Cemaes Bay, wreck fishing for up to 8 anglers, 'Stingray', D Williams, Beach Rd, Cemaes Bay, LL67 0ES (Tel: 01407 7105100); rods on board, facilities, bait to order. At **Benllech**, the area one mile out to sea has been recommended as good boat fishing for mackerel in summer, pollack, whiting in winter, and dogfish all year round. Tackle shop: The Pilot Store and Fishing Tackle, 66 Machine St, Amlwch Port, Anglesey LL68 9HA, Tel: 01407 831 771; maggots, fresh and frozen bait, and rod hire available with flexible opening times to suit anglers. Hotel: Bryn Arfor, Amlwch Port. Hotels: Lastra Farm, Trees.

Beaumaris (Anglesey). Big bass, tope, pollack, mullet and mackerel opposite Beaumaris and along the Straits. Between Menai and the Tubular Bridge fair-sized bass and conger are caught. For boat fishing contact Stan Zalot, Starida Boats, Little Bryn, off Rosemary Lane, Tel: 01248 810251, and Dave Jones, Beaumaris Marine Services, The Anchorage, Rosemary Lane (Tel: 01248 810746, mobile 0860 811988); "Cerismar Two", fast twin-engined catamaran. Tackle shop: Anglesey Boat Co, The Shop, Gallows Point, Ttel: 01248 810359; Ken Johnson, Menai Bridge, Tel: 01248 714508. Hotels: Ye Olde Bulls Head Inn, Bulkeley, Bishopsgate.

Fishing Clubs & Associations in Wales

*Included in this list of fishing clubs and associations in Wales are some organisations which have their water on the upper reaches of the Wye or Severn, details of which are contained in the English section of **Where to Fish**. Further information can usually be had from the secretaries and a courtesy which is appreciated is the inclusion of a stamped addressed envelope with postal inquiries. Please advise the publishers (address at the front of the book) of any changed details for the next edition.*

National Bodies

Association of Welsh Anglers
John Mayers
6 Biddulph Rise
Tupsley
Hereford HR1 1RA
Tel: 01432 358334
Wales Tourist Board
Dept F108
PO Box 1
Cardiff CF24 2XN
Tel: 029 2047 5345
Fax: 029 2047 5345.
Internet: www.visitwales.com
E-mail:
liz.weekley@tourism.wales.gov.uk
Publishes an attractive guide to Welsh fishing.
Welsh Federation of Sea Anglers
G H Jones, M.B.E.
8 Moreton Road
Holyhead
Gwynedd LL65 2BG
Tel: 01407 763821
For general information
Colin Doyle
Tel/Fax: 01443 831684
Welsh Salmon and Trout Association
M J Morgan
Swyn Teifi
Pontrhydfendigaid
Ystrad
Meurig, Dyfed SY25 6EF
Welsh Tope, Skate and Conger Club
Colin Delfosse
25 Mill Place
Ely, Cardiff CF5 4AJ

CLUBS

Aberaeron Town Angling Club
D S Rees
10 North Road
Aberaeron, Dyfed SA46 0JF
Aberaeron Angling Club
Nigel R Davies
Wenallt
16 Belle Vue Terrace
Aberaeron
Dyfed SA46 0HB
Abergwili Angling Club
Eric Thomas
60 Abergwili Road
Carmarthen, Dyfed
Aberystwyth Angling Association Ltd
P W Eklund
42 Erwgoch
Waunfawr
Aberystwyth
Dyfed SY23 3AZ
Afan Valley Angling Club
M Reynolds
8 Newlands
Baglan
Port Talbot
W Glamorgan
Alltami Angling Club
A Price
69 Circular Drive
Ewloe, Clwyd
Ammanford and District Angling Association
Ron Woodland
2 Pontardulais Road
Llangennech
Llanelli
Dyfed SA14 8YF
Artro and Talsarnau Fishing Association
B Powell

3 Glandwr
Llanbedr
Gwynedd LL45 2PB
Bala and District Angling Association
David Gumbley
Llwyn Ffynnon
17 Mawnog Fach
Bala
Gwynedd LL23 7YY
Bangor City Angling Club
Mrs Pat Thomas
21 Lon-y-Glyder
Bangor
Gwynedd
Bangor-on-Dee Salmon Angling Association
P Edwards
13 Ludlow Road
Bangor-on-Dee
Wrexham LL13 0JG
Betws-y-Coed Anglers' Club
Melfyn Hughes
Cae Garw
Betws-y-Coed LL24 0BY
Birchgrove (Cardiff) Angling Association
J S Wilmot
4 Clydesmuir Rd
Tremorfa, Cardiff CF2 2QA
Bradley Angling Club
M Harper
6 Yorke Avenue
Marchwiel
Wrexham, Clwyd
Brecon Angling Society
D D Harris
66 Coryton Close
Brecon
Powys LD3 9HP
Brynmill and District Angling Club
J Clement

6 Nantyfin Road
Llansamuet
Swansea
Bryn-y-Pys Angling Association
Mrs A Phillips
2 Ruabon Road
Wrexham LL13 7PB
Buckley Angling Association
R W Jones
Cresta
35 Bryn Awelon
Mold, Clwyd CH7 1LT
Bute Angling Society
D Ramsey
46 Church Road
Rumney, Cardiff CF3 8BA
Capenhurst Angling Club
A T Howdon
24 Saughall Hey
Saughall
Chester, Cheshire CH1 6EJ
Carmarthen Amateur Angling Association
Ron Ratti
Rhydal Mount
The Parade
Carmarthen SA31 1LZ
Carmarthen and District Angling Club
Herbert Evans
25 Maple Crescent
Carmarthen SA31 3PS
Carmarthen Fishermen's Federation
Garth Roberts
Talrhyn
Tresaith Road
Aberporth
Dyfed SA43 2EB
Cefni Angling Association
G R Williams
Tyn Lon
Pentre Berw
Gaerwen
Anglesey
Ceiriog Fly Fishers
Alan Hudson
Kingfisher
96 Crogen
Lodgevale Park
Chirk
Wrexham LL14 5BJ
Cheshire Anglers' Association
Graham Tomkinson

31 Wareham Drive
Crewe
Cheshire CW1 3XA
Chester Association of Anglers
B W Roberts
23 Alpraham Crescent
Upton Cross
Chester CH2 1QX
Chirk Angling Association
Incorporated in Ceiriog Fly Fishers
Cilcain Fly Fishing Association
A E Williams
Gwynfryn
Caerwys Hill
Caerwys, Mold
Clwyd
Connah's Quay and District Angling Club
Paul Roberts
118 Wepre Park
Connah's Quay
Clwyd CH5 4HW
Connah's Quay Angling Association
R W Ambrose
25 Pinewood Avenue
Connah's Quay, Clwyd
Corris and District Angling Association
Jeremy Thomas
Foamation Products
Era Works
Ceinws, Machynlleth
Powys SY20 9HA
Corwen and District Angling Club
Gordon H Smith
Llais-yr-Afon
Bontuchel
Ruthin
Denbighshire LL15 2DE
Criccieth, Llanystumdwy and District Angling Association
William E Hughes
Kinlet, Penrallt
Llanystumdwy
Criccieth, Gwynedd LL52 0SR
Crickhowell and District Angling Society
Paul Bowen
13 Hatherleigh Road
Abergavenny
Monmouths NP7 7RG

Cross Hands and District Angling Association
Pat Kiernan
48 Waterloo Road
Penygroes
Llanelli
Carmarthenshire SA14 7NS
Cwmbran Angling Association
P M Gulliford
305 Llantarnam Rd
Cwmbran, Gwent NP44 3BJ
Cwmcelyn Angling Club
P Hunt
East Pentwyn Farm
Blaina, Gwent NP3 3HX
Cwmllynfell Fly Fishing Club
D Lloyd
73 Bryn Road
Bryn Villas
Cwmllynfell
West Glamorgan
Cymdeithas Pysgota Cefni Angling Association
G R Williams
Tyn Lon, Pentre Berw
Gaerwen
Anglesey LL60 6HY
Cymdeithas Bysgota Talybont Angling Association
I Jones
Wern
Talybont
Ceredigion SY24 5ER
Dee Anglers Association
A Hogg
6 Llwynon Close
Bryn-y-Baal
Mold
Clwyd CH7 6TN
Denbigh and Clwyd Angling Club
C P Harness
8 Llwyn Menlli
Ruthin, Clwyd LL15 1RG
Dolgarrog Fishing Club
Peter Jones
12 Hillside Cottages
Dolgarrog
Gwynedd LL32
Dolgellau Angling Association
E M Davies
Maescaled, Dolgellau
Gwynedd LL40 1UF

Dolwyddelan Fishing Association
D E Foster
The Post Office
Dolwyddelan
Gwynedd LL25 0NJ

Dwyryd Anglers' Ltd
Gareth Ffestin Price
Hafan
Ffordd Peniel
Ffestiniog
Gwynedd LL41 4LP

Ebbw Vale Welfare Angling Club
R Satterley
8 Pen-y-lan
Ebbw Vale
Gwent NP3 5LS

Elan Valley Angling Club
Noel Hughes
25 Brynheulog
Rhayader
Powys LD6 5EF

The Endeavour Deep Sea Angling Club
B Haigh
Ty-Llyn
Cwm-Rheidol
Aberystwyth
Dyfed SY23 3NB

Estimaner Angling Association
John Baxter
11 Tan y Fedw
Abergynolwyn
Gwynedd LL36 9YU

Felindre Angling Club
M Randall
77 Water Street
Kidwelly, Dyfed

Gilwern and District Angling Club
H R Lewis
27 Brynglas, Gilwern
Nr Abergavenny
Gwent NP7 0BP

Glamorgan Anglers' Club
M Roberts
4 Neol Don
Whitchurch
Cardiff CF4 2AU

Glaslyn Angling Association
J Daniel Hughes
Berthlwyd
Penrhyndeudraeth
Gwynedd LL48 6RL

Glyncornel Angling Association
John M Evans
126 Ystrad Road
Ystrad, Rhondda
Mid Glamorgan
CF41 7PS

Glynneath and District Angling Association
Gareth Evans
21 Godfrey Avenue
Glynneath, Neath
West Glamorgan
SA11 5HF

Clwb Godre Mynydd Du
203 Cwmamman Road
Glanamman
Dyfed

Greenfield Valley Angling Club
Secretary
Basingwerk House
Administrative Centre
Greenfield Valley Heritage Park
Greenfield
Holywell
Flintshire CH88 7BQ

Griffin Angling Club
A Pickles
Green Pastures
Pont-y-Capel
Gresford
Wrexham, Clwyd

Gro Park and Irfon Angling Club
Dolshedyn
15 Irfon Road
Builth Wells
Powys LD2 3DE

Gwaun-Cae-Gurwen Angling Association
P E Edwards
32 Heol Cae, Gurwen
Gwaun-Cae-Gurwen
Amman Valley
West Glamorgan
or
W Gill
6 Llwyn Nant Drive
Cwmgorse
SA18 1RP

Gwent Avengers
R Dalling
3 The Spinney
Malpas Park
Newport, Gwent

Holt and Farndon Angling Association
R Williams
4 The Cross
Holt, Wrexham
Clywd

Isca Angling Club
P Facey
357 Pilton Vale
Newport
Gwent NP9 6LU

Islwyn and District Anglers
Mrs J Meller
7 Penllwyn Street
Cwmfelinfach, Gwent
NP1 7HE

Kirkdale Angling Association
A C Hoer
61 Baythorne Road
Liverpool L4 9TJ

Lavister Angling Club
G Watkins
Rathgillan
Lache Hall Crescent
Chester
Cheshire CH4 7NE

Llanbrynmair and District Angling Club
M Jones
Craig-y-Gronfa
Mallwyd
Machynlleth, Powys

Llandeilo Angling Association
28a Rhosmaen St
Llandeilo
Dyfed

Llandovery Angling Association
Michael Davies
Cwmrhuddan Lodge
Llandovery
Carmarthenshire SA20 0DX

Llandybie Angling Association
R Jones
9 Margaret Rd
Llandybie
Dyfed SA18 3YB

Llandysul Angling Association
Artie Jones
Glas-y-Dorlan
Llyn-y-Fran Road
Llandysul, Dyfed SA44 4JW

Llanelli Angling Association
D Watkins
60 Llwyn Hendy
Llanelli, Dyfed

Llangadog Angling Association
Hafan Las
Llangadog
Dyfed

Llangennech Angling Club
D A Owen
99 Hendre Road
Llangennech
Llanelli
Carmarthenshire SA14 8TH

Llangollen Angling Association
W N Elbourn
Bwthyn Bach
2 Green Lane
Llangollen
Denbighshire LL20 8TB

Llangyfelach and District Angling Association
R L Griffiths
Cefn Cottage
Cilibion
Llanrhidian
Swansea SA3 1ED

Llangynidr Service Station Angling Club
T B Williams
Llangynidr Service Station
Llangynidr
Crickhowell, Powys NP8 1LU

Llanidloes and District Angling Association
J Dallas Davies
Dresden House
Great Oak Street
Llanidloes, Powys SY18 6BU

Llanilar Angling Association
John H Astill
Dryslwyn, Llanafan
Aberystwyth
Ceredigion SY23 4AX

Llanrwst Anglers' Club
David W P Hughes
36 Station Road
Llanrwst
Gwynedd LL26 0AD

Llanybydder Angling Association
William Wilkins

Maes-y-Fedw
Llanybydder
Dyfed SA40 9UG

Llay Angling Association
John Preston
20 Mold Road Estate
Gwersyllt, Wrexham
Clwyd LL11 4AA

Llynfi Valley Angling Association
G Thomas
39 Darren View
Llangynwyd
Maesteg
Mid Glamorgan

Llysyfran Angling Club
Peter J Eaton
18 Mount Pleasant Way
Milford Haven
Pembrokeshire SA73 1AB

Maelor Angling Association
K Bathers
Sunnyside, Hill Street
Cefn Mawr, Wrexham
Clwyd LL14 3AY

Maerdy and Ferndale Angling Club
Terry Pain
16 Highfield
Ferndale, Rhondda
Mid Glamorgan CF43 4TA

Merthyr Tydfil Angling Association
Nigel Morgan
20 James Street
Twynyrodyn
Merthyr Tydfil
Mid Glamorgan

Midland Flyfishers
Middle Moorend Farm
Much Cowarne
Herefordshire HR7 4JL

Mold Fly Fishers
A T Allcock
3 Highfield Avenue
Mynydd Isa
Mold, Flintshire CH7 6XY

Mold Kingfishers Angling Club
R W Ambrose
25 Pinewood Avenue
Connah's Quay, Clwyd

Mold Trout Anglers
Alun Powell
Makuti
Sunny Ridge

Mold
Flintshire
CH7 1RU

Neath and Dulais Angling Association
Ivor J Jones
5 Bryndulais Row
Seven Sisters
Neath SA10 9EB

Nevern Angling Association
Mrs Nica Prichard
Spring Gardens
Parrog Road
Newport
Pembrokeshire SA42 0RJ

Newbridge Angling Association
Kerry F R Clutton
28 Worsley Avenue
Johnstown
Nr Wrexham
Clwyd LL14 2TD

New Dovey Fishery Association (1929) Ltd
Ian C Rees
Leeds House
Maengwyn Street
Machynlleth
Powys SY20 8DT

Newport Angling Association
L J Clarke
14 Allt-yr-yn Ave
Newport
South Wales
NP9 5DB

Newport and District Sea Anglers
Joe Guscott (Secretary)
51 Monnow Walk
Bettws Estate
Newport
Monmouthshire NP9 6SS
or
Joe Crowley (Chairman)
55 Moore Crest
Newport
Monmouthshire

Newport Reservoir Fly Fishing Association
W G C Jones
74 Greenfield
Newbridge
Gwent NP1 4QZ
or N A Jones
Tel: 01443 812440

New Quay Angling Club
H Davies
Min-yr-Afon
Abergorlech
Dyfed SA32 7SN

**Ogmore Angling
Association**
W A Protheroe
Henllan
Coychurch Road
Pencoed, Bridgend
Mid Glamorgan CF35 5LY

**Ogwen Valley Angling
Association**
Bryn Evans
Tan y Coed
Bron Arfon
Llanllechid, Bangor
Gwynedd LL57 3LW

**Ogwr Valley Angling
Association**
F J Hughes
20 Heol Glannant
Bettws, Bridgend
Mid Glamorgan CF32 8SP

**Pembroke and District
Angling Club**
Mrs T Lustig
10 Deer Park
Stackpole
Pembrokeshire

**Pembrokeshire Anglers'
Association**
Permit Secretary
Mrs B E Summers
72 City Road
Haverfordwest
Pembrokeshire
SA61 2RR

**Pencoed and District
Angling Club**
Dr G M Gwilliam
5 Velindre Road
Pencoed, Bridgend
Mid Glamorgan

**Penllwyn Lodges Angling
Club**
Derek Thomas Field
Penllwyn
Garthmyl
Powys SY15 6SB

**Picton Waters Angling
Club**
I Richards
North Pines
Wiston
Haverfordwest, Dyfed

Ponciau Angling Society
D K Valentine
Bryn-yr-Owen
Ponciau
Wrexham, Clwyd

**Pontardawe and Swansea
Angling Association**
R H Lockyer
8 Bwllfa Road
Ynystawe
Swansea SA6 5AL

**Pontardulais and District
Angling Association**
J Gabe
20 James Street
Pontardulais, Swansea
West Glamorgan SA4 1HY

**Pontypool Angling
Association**
B J Jones
79 Robertson Way
Woodlands
Malpas, Newport
Gwent NP9 6QQ

**Porthcawl Sea Angling
Association**
(Freshwater Section)
J Lock
67 West Road
Nottage
Porthcawl, Mid Glamorgan

**Prince Albert Angling
Society**
J A Turner
15 Pexhill Drive
Macclesfield
Cheshire SK10 3LP

**Prysor Angling
Association**
Idwal W Williams
8 Pantycelyn
Trawsfynydd
Gwynedd LL41 4UH

Pyrddin Angling Society
Robert Browning
91 Main Road
Duffryn Cellwen
Nr Neath, West Glamorgan

Pysgotwyr Maesnant
D P Higgins
90 Maesceinion
Waunfawr
Aberystwyth SY23 3QQ

**Rhayader Angling
Association**
G H Roberts
Belmullet, Rhayader

Powys LD6 5BY

Rhostyllen Angling Club
J R Williams
57 West Grove
Rhostyllen
Wrexham
Clwyd LL14 4NB

**Rhyl and District Angling
Association**
Martin Fowell
Bon-Amie
28 Ffordd Tanrallt
Meliden
Prestatyn
Denbighshire LL19 8PS

**Rhymney and District
Angling Society**
J Pugh
12 Castle Field
Rhymney
Gwent NP2 5NS

Ridgeway Angling Club
R Martin
Hillcroft
Bethlehem
Cardigan Road
Haverfordwest, Dyfed

**Rossett and Gresford Fly
Fishers**
Brian Harper
7 Hawthorn Road
Marford
Wrexham LL12 8XJ

**St Asaph Angling
Association**
W J P Staines
Delamere
Coed Esgob Lane
St Asaph
Denbighshire LL17 0LH

**St Clears Angling
Association**
David J Bryan
Madras Cottage
Laugharne
Carmarthen, Dyfed SA33
4NU

**Seiont, Gwyrfai and Llyfni
Anglers' Society**
H P Hughes
Llugwy, Ystad Eryri
Bethel, Caernarfon
Gwynedd LL55 1BX

**Severnside and Newtown
Angling Club**
Michael John Thomas
253 Measyrhandir

Newtown, Powys SY16 1LB

Skewen Angling Club
Mike Doyle
58 The Highlands
Skewen, Neath
West Glamorgan SA10 6PD

**South West Wales
Association of Sea
Angling Clubs**
Mrs B Walters
279 Gwynedd Avenue
Cockett
Swansea

**Swansea Amateur
Angling Association Ltd**
J B Wolfe
147 St Helen's Road
Swansea SA1 4DB

Swansea Angling Club
Paul Cannin
9 Heol Ceri
Waunarlwydd
Swansea SA5 4QU

**Talsarnau and District
Angling Association**
I Owen
Eryri Llanfair
Harlech
Gwynedd

**Tawe and Tributaries
Angling Association**
Michael Matthews
32 Farm Road
Briton Ferry
Neath
West Glamorgan SA11 2TA

**Tawe Disabled Fishers'
Association**
R W Hale
Willow Bank
Ilston

Swansea SA2 7LD

Teifi Trout Association
W Bishop
Greenacres
Pentrecagal
Newcastle Emlyn
Carmarthenshire
SA38 9HT
or
Mike Evans (Membership
Secretary)
Llysycoed
Llandygwydd
Llechryd
Cardigan
Ceredigion

**Tenby and District
Angling Club**
Mr Bird
Primrose Villa
Narbeth Road
Tenby
Pembrokeshire

**Tregaron Angling
Association**
Moc Morgan
Swyn Teifi
Pontrhydfendigaid
Aberystwyth
Ceredigion
SY25 6EF

Tywyn Sea Angling Club
Peter Wilson
Bryn y Mor Camp Shop
Sandilands Road
Tywyn
Gwynedd LL36 0AB

**Warrington Angling
Association**
Frank Lythgoe, Secretary
P O Box 71

Warrington WA1 1LR
Headquarters
52 Parker Street
Warrington
(Open every Friday
7pm–9.30pm)

**Wentwood Reservoir Fly
Fishing Association**
D G P Jones
123 Castle Lea
Caldicot
Monmouths NP26 4HS

**Whitland Angling
Association**
Treasurer
P Hunt
White House Mill
Lampeter, Velfrey
Whiteland
Carm SA34 0RB

**Wirral Game Fishing
Club**
D Jones
31 Meadway
Upton, Wirral
Cheshire

**Wrexham and District
Angling Association**
J E Tattum
Llys Athro, King Street
Leeswood, Mold
Clwyd CH7 4SB

**Wygyr Fishing
Association**
J M Fraser (Treasurer)
Crug Mor Farm
Rhydwyn
Llanfaethlu
Anglesey

Fishing in Scotland

District Salmon Fishery Boards and Close Season for Salmon and Trout

Fishing in Scotland is under the general jurisdiction of the Scottish Executive Rural Affairs Department, Pentland House, 47 Robb's Loan, Edinburgh, EH14 1TW (Tel: 0131 244 6227, Fax: 0131 244 6313).

The annual close season for **trout** in Scotland extends from October 7 to March 14, both days included. Trout may not be sold between the end of August and the beginning of April, nor at any time if the fish are less than 8in long.

Visiting anglers are reminded that on Scottish rivers and lochs the owner of the fishing is the riparian proprietor, whose permission to fish should be obtained. The only public right of fishing for brown trout is in those portions of the rivers which are both tidal and navigable, but the right must not be exercised so as to interfere with salmon or sea-trout fishing and can be exercised only where there is a right of access to the water from a boat or from the banks. A number of rivers in Scotland including the Aberdeenshire Don are subject to Protection Orders granted by the Secretary of State for Scotland. On rivers where a Protection Order is in force, it is an offence to fish for any freshwater species without the owner's permission.

Salmon. Provision is made in the Salmon Act, 1986, for the formation and amalgamation of District Salmon Fishery Boards, composed of representatives of proprietors of salmon fisheries in each district, and co-opted representatives of anglers and tenant netsmen. These boards, the addresses of which are given on pages below, are responsible for the administration and protection of the salmon fisheries in their districts, and boards have been formed for practically all the important salmon rivers. More recently, the Boards have become increasingly involved in management, research and stock enhancement, as well as the more traditional function.

Add. Annual close time for net-fishing: From Sept 1 to Feb 15, both dates inclusive. Annual close time for rod-fishing: From Nov 1 to Feb 15, both days inclusive.
Ailort. Aug 27 to Feb 10; Nov 1 to Feb 10.

Aline. Aug 27 to Feb 10; Nov 1 to Feb 10.
Alness. Aug 27 to Feb 10; Nov 1 to Feb 10.
Annan. Sept 10 to Feb 24; Nov 16 to Feb 24.
Applecross. Aug 27 to Feb 10; Nov 1 to Feb 10.
Arnisdale. Aug 27 to Feb 10; Nov 1 to Feb 10.
Awe. Aug 27 to Feb 10; 16 Oct to Feb 10.
Ayr. Aug 27 to Feb 10; Nov 1 to Feb 10.
Baa and **Goladoir**. Aug 27 to Feb 10; Nov 1 to Feb 10.
Badachro and **Kerry**. Aug 27 to Feb 10; Nov 1 to Feb 10.
Balgay and **Shieldaig**. Aug 27 to Feb 10; Nov 1 to Feb 10.
Beauly. Aug 27 to Feb 10; Oct 16 to Feb 10.
Berriedale. Aug 27 to Feb 10; Nov 1 to Feb 10.
Bervie. Sept 10 to Feb 24; Nov 1 to Feb 24.
Bladnoch. Aug 27 to Feb 10; Nov 1 to Feb 10.
Broom. Aug 27 to Feb 10; Nov 1 to Feb 10.
Brora. Aug 27 to Feb 10; Oct 16 to Jan 31.
Carradale. Sept 10 to Feb 24; Nov 1 to Feb 24.
Carron. Aug 27 to Feb 10; Nov 1 to Feb 10.
Clayburn. Sept 10 to Feb 24; Nov 1 to Feb 24.
Clyde and **Leven**. Aug 27 to Feb 10; Nov 1 to Feb 10.
Conon. Aug 27 to Feb 10; Oct 1 to Jan 25.
Cowie. Aug 27 to Feb 10; Nov 1 to Feb 10.
Cree. Sept 14 to Feb 28; Oct 15 to Feb 28.
Creran (Loch Creran). Aug 27 to Feb 10; Nov 1 to Feb 10.
Crowe and **Shiel** (Loch Duich). Aug 27 to Feb 10; Nov 1 to Feb 10.
Dee (Aberdeenshire). Aug 27 to Feb 10; Oct 1 to Jan 31.
Dee (Kirkcudbrightshire). Aug 27 to Feb 10; Nov 1 to Feb 10.
Deveron. Aug 27 to Feb 10; Nov 1 to Feb 10.
Don. Aug 27 to Feb 10; Nov 1 to Feb 10.
Doon. Aug 27 to Feb 10; Nov 1 to Feb 10.
Drummachloy (Bute). Sept 1 to Feb 15; Oct 16 to Feb 15.
Dunbeath. Aug 27 to Feb 10; Oct 16 to Feb 10.
Eachaig. Sept 1 to Apr 30; Nov 1 to Apr 30.
East Lewis. Aug 27 to Feb 10; Oct 17 to Feb 10.
Esk, North. Sept 1 to Feb 15; Nov 1 to Feb 15.

Esk, South. Sept 1 to Feb 15; Nov 1 to Feb 15.

Ewe. Aug 27 to Feb 10; Nov 1 to Feb 10.

Fincastle. Sept 10 to Feb 24; Nov 1 to Feb 24.

Findhorn. Aug 27 to Feb 10; Oct 7 to Feb 10.

Fleet (Kirkcudbrightshire). Sept 10 to Feb 24; Nov 1 to Feb 24.

Fleet (Sutherlandshire). Sept 10 to Feb 24; Nov 1 to Feb 24.

Forss. Aug 27 to Feb 10; Nov 1 to Feb 10.

Forth. Aug 27 to Feb 10; Nov 1 to Jan 31.

Fyne, **Shira** and **Aray**. Sept 1 to Feb 15; Nov 1 to Feb 15.

Garnock. Sept 10 to Feb 24; Nov 1 to Feb 24.

Girvan. Sept 10 to Feb 24; Nov 1 to Feb 24.

Glenelg. Aug 27 to Feb 10; Nov 1 to Feb 10.

Gour. Aug 27 to Feb 10; Nov 1 to Feb 10.

Grudie or **Dionard**. Aug 27 to Feb 10; Nov 1 to Feb 10.

Gruinard and **Little Gruinard**. Aug 27 to Feb 10; Nov 1 to Feb 10.

Halladale. Aug 27 to Feb 10; Oct 1 to Jan 11.

Helmsdale. Aug 27 to Feb 10; Oct 1 to Jan 10.

Hope and **Polla**. Aug 27 to Feb 10; Oct 1 to Jan 11.

Howmore. Sept 10 to Feb 24; Nov 1 to Feb 24.

Inchard. Aug 27 to Feb 10; Nov 1 to Feb 10.

Inner (Jura). Sept 10 to Feb 24; Nov 1 to Feb 24.

Inver. Aug 27 to Feb 10; Nov 1 to Feb 10.

Iorsa (Arran). Sept 10 to Feb 24; Nov 1 to Feb 24.

Irvine. Sept 10 to Feb 24; Nov 16 to Feb 24.

Kannaird. Aug 27 to Feb 10; Nov 1 to Feb 10.

Kilchoan. (Loch Nevis). Aug 27 to Feb 10; Nov 1 to Feb 10.

Kinloch (Kyle of Tongue). Aug 27 to Feb 10; Nov 1 to Feb 10.

Kirkaig. Aug 27 to Feb 10; Nov 1 to Feb 10.

Kishorn. Aug 27 to Feb 10; Nov 1 to Feb 10.

Kyle of Sutherland. Aug 27 to Feb 10; Oct 1 to Jan 10.

Laggan and **Sorn** (Islay). Sept 10 to Feb 24; Nov 1 to Feb 24.

Laxford. Aug 27 to Feb 10; Nov 1 to Feb 10.

Leven. Aug 27 to Feb 10; Nov 1 to Feb 10.

Little Loch Broom. Aug 27 to Feb 10; Nov 1 to Feb 10.

Loch Long. Aug 27 to Feb 10; Nov 1 to Feb 10.

Loch Roag. Aug 27 to Feb 10; Oct 17 to Feb 10.

Loch Sunart. Aug 27 to Feb 10; Nov 1 to Feb 10.

Lochy. Aug 27 to Feb 10; Nov 1 to Feb 10.

Lossie. Aug 27 to Feb 24; Nov 1 to Feb 24.

Luce. Sept 10 to Feb 24; Nov 1 to Feb 24.

Lussa (Mull). Aug 27 to Feb 10; Nov 1 to Feb 10.

Moidart. Aug 27 to Feb 10; Nov 1 to Feb 10.

Morar. Aug 27 to Feb 10; Nov 1 to Feb 10.

Mullanageren. Sept 10 to Feb 24; Nov 1 to Feb 24.

Nairn. Aug 27 to Feb 10; Oct 8 to Feb 10.

Naver and **Borgie**. Aug 27 to Feb 10; Oct 1 to Jan 11.

Nell, Feochan and **Euchar**. Aug 27 to Feb 10; Nov 1 to Feb 10.

Ness. Aug 27 to Feb 10; Oct 16 to Jan 14.

Nith. Sept 10 to Feb 24; Dec 1 to Feb 24.

Orkney Islands. Sept 10 to Feb 24; Nov 1 to Feb 24.

Ormsary. Aug 27 to Feb 10; Nov 1 to Feb 10.

Pennygowan and **Aros** (Mull). Aug 27 to Feb 10; Nov 1 to Feb 10.

Resort. Aug 27 to Feb 10; Nov 1 to Feb 10.

Ruel. Sept 1 to Feb 15; Nov 1 to Feb 15.

Sanda. Aug 27 to Feb 10; Nov 1 to Feb 10.

Scaddle. Aug 27 to Feb 10; Nov 1 to Feb 10.

Shetland Islands. Sept 10 to Feb 24; Nov 1 to Feb 24.

Shiel (Loch Shiel). Aug 27 to Feb 10; Nov 1 to Feb 10.

Sligachan (Skye). Aug 27 to Feb 10; Nov 1 to Feb 10.

Snizort (Skye). Aug 27 to Feb 10; Nov 1 to Feb 10.

Spey. Aug 27 to Feb 10; Oct 1 to Feb 10.

Stinchar. Sept 10 to Feb 24; Nov 1 to Feb 24.

Strathy. Aug 27 to Feb 10; Oct 1 to Jan 11.

Tay. Aug 21 to Feb 4; Oct 16 to Jan 14.

Thurso. Aug 27 to Feb 10; Oct 6 to Jan 10.

Torridon. Aug 27 to Feb 10; Nov 1 to Feb 10.

Tweed. Sept 15 to Feb 14; Dec 1 to Jan 31.

Ugie. Sept 10 to Feb 24; Nov 1 to Feb 9.

Ullapool (Loch Broom). Aug 27 to Feb 10; Nov 1 to Feb 10.

Urr. Sept 10 to Feb 24; Dec 1 to Feb 24.

Wick. Aug 27 to Feb 10; Nov 1 to Feb 10.

Ythan. Sept 10 to Feb 24; Nov 1 to Feb 10.

District Salmon Fishery Boards

The names, addresses and telephone numbers of the clerks of the various salmon district fishery boards in Scotland are as follows. Please note that their duties are purely to operate the Acts and that they do not have fishing to let.

Annan District Salmon Fishery Board. Ms C A K Rafferty, Messrs McJerrow and Stevenson, Solicitors, 55 High Street, Lockerbie,

Dumfriesshire DG11 2JJ (Tel: 015762 202123/4).

Awe District Salmon Fishery Board. T C McNair, Messrs MacArthur, Stewart & Co, Solicitors, Boswell House, Argyll Square, Oban, Argyllshire PA34 4BD (Tel: 01631 562215).

Ayr District Salmon Fishery Board. F M Watson, D W Shaw & Company, 34a Sandgate, Ayr KA7 1BG (Tel: 01292 265033).

Beauly District Salmon Fishery Board. J Wotherspoon, MacAndrew & Jenkins WS, Solicitors and Estate Agents, 5 Drummond Street, Inverness IV1 1QF (Tel: 01463 233001).

Bladnoch District Salmon Fishery Board. Peter M Murray, Messrs A B & A Matthews, Bank of Scotland Buildings, Newton Stewart, Wigtownshire DG8 6EG (Tel: 01671 404100).

Broom District Salmon Fishery Board. G C Muirden, Messrs Middleton, Ross and Arnot, Solicitors, PO Box 8, Mansfield House, Dingwall, Ross-shire IV15 9HJ (Tel: 01349 862214).

Brora District Salmon Fishery Board. C J Whealing, Sutherland Estates Office, Duke Street, Golspie, Sutherland KW10 6RR (Tel: 01408 633268).

Caithness District Salmon Fishery Board. P J W Blackwood, Estate Office, Thurso East, Thurso, Caithness KW14 8HW (Tel: 01847 63134).

Conon District Salmon Fishery Board. Miles Larby, Finlayson Hughes, 45 Church Street, Inverness IV1 1DR (Tel: 01463 224343).

Cree District Salmon Fishery Board. Peter M Murray, Messrs A B & A Matthews, Solicitors, Bank of Scotland Buildings, Newton Stewart, Wigtownshire DG8 6EG (Tel: 01671 3013).

Creran District Salmon Fishery Board. Lady Stewart, Salachail, Appin, Argyll PA38 4BJ.

Dee (Aberdeen) District Salmon Fishery Board. George Alpine, Messrs Paull & Williamson, Solicitors, Investment House, 6 Union Row, Aberdeen AB9 8DQ (Tel: 01224 621621).

Dee (Kirkcudbrightshire) District Salmon Fishery Board. G S Scott, Messrs Gillespie, Gifford & Brown, 27 St Cuthbert Street, Kirkcudbrightshire DG6 4DJ (Tel: 01557 330539).

Deveron District Salmon Fishery Board. John A Christie, Murdoch, McMath and Mitchell, Solicitors, 27–29 Duke Street, Huntly AB54 5DP (Tel: 01466 792291).

Don Distinct Board. George Alpine, Messrs Paull & Williamson, Solicitors, Investment House, 6 Union Row, Aberdeen AB9 8DQ (Tel: 01224 621621).

Doon District Salmon Fishery Board. A M Thomson, 23 Wellington Square, Ayr KA7 2HG (Tel: 01292 266900).

Eachaig District Salmon Fishery Board, Robert C G Teasdale, Quarry Cottage, Rashfield, By Dunoon, Argyll PA23 8QT (Tel: 01369 84510).

East Lewis/Loch Roag District Salmon Fishery Board. George H MacDonald, Estate Office, North Uist Estate, Lochmaddy, North Uist HS6 5AA (Tel: 01876 500329).

Esk District Salmon Fishery Board. John Scott, Scott Alexander, 46 High Street, Montrose, Angus DD10 8JF (Tel: 01674 671477).

Ewe District Salmon Fishery Board. G C Muirden, Messrs Middleton, Ross and Arnot, Solicitors, PO Box 8, Mansfield House, Dingwall, Ross-shire IV15 9HJ (Tel: 01349 62214).

Findhorn District Salmon Fishery Board. Sir William Gordon Cumming, Altyre House, Altyre, By Forres, Moray.

Fleet (Kirkcudbrightshire) District Salmon Fishery Board. C R Graves, Carse of Trostrie, Twynholm, Kirkcudbright DG6 4PS (Tel: 01557 860618).

Forth District Salmon Fishery Board. T Mackenzie, 12 Charles Street, Dunblane FK15 9BY (Tel: 01786 825544).

Girvan District Salmon Fishery Board. S B Sheddon, Messrs Smith & Valentine, Solicitors and Estate Agents, 16 Hamilton Street, Girvan, Ayrshire KA26 9EY (Tel: 01465 713476).

Halladale District Salmon Fishery Board. G D Robertson, 29 Traill Street, Thurso, Caithness KW14 8EQ (Tel: 01847 893247).

Harris District Salmon Fishery Board. G A Macdonald, The Estate Office, Lochmaddy, North Uist HS6 5AA (Tel: 01876 500428).

Helmsdale District Salmon Fishery Board. N Wright, Arthur and Carmichael, Cathedral Square, Dornoch (Tel: 01862 810202).

Iorsa (Arran) District Salmon Fishery Board. J W Perkins, ÚjRamera, Sannox, Isle of Arran (Tel: 01770 810671).

Kanaird District Salmon Fishery Board. J Bramell, Drummond Road Stafford ST16 3HJ.

Kinloch District Salmon Fishery Board. A Sykes, Messrs Brodies WS, 15 Atholl Crescent, Edinburgh EH3 8HA (Tel: 0131 228 4111).

Kyle of Sutherland District Salmon

Fishery Board. J Mason, Bell Ingram Ltd, Estates Office, Bonar Bridge, Sutherland IV24 3EA.

Laggan & Sorn District Salmon Fishery Board, R I G Ferguson, Messrs Stewart, Balfour & Sutherland, 2 Castlehill, Campeltown, Argyll PA28 6AW (Tel: 01586 553737).

Lochaber District Salmon Fishery Board. Malcolm Spence QC, 2 Gray's Inn, Gray's Inn, London WC1R 5JH.

Loch Fyne District Salmon Fishery Board. P M Fairweather, c/o Argyll Estates Office, Cherry Park, Inveraray, Argyll PA32 8XE (Tel: 01499 302203).

Lossie District Salmon Fishery Board. Messrs Andrew McCartan, Solicitors, 145 High Street, Forres, Moray (Tel: 01309 675259).

Luce District Salmon Fishery Board. E A Fleming-Smith, Stair Estates, Estate Office, Rephad, Stranraer, Wigtownshire DG9 8BX (Tel: 01776 2024).

Mullanagearan District Salmon Fishery Board. G Macdonald, Estate Office, Lochmaddy, Isle of North Uist PA82 5AA (Tel: 01876 3324).

Nairn District Salmon Fishery Board. E M B Larby, Finlayson Hughes, 45 Church Street, Inverness IV4 1DR.

Naver and Borgie District Salmon Fishery Board. N Wright, Arthur and Carmichael, Cathedral Square, Dornoch, Sutherland IV25 3SW.

Ness District Salmon Fishery Board. F Kelly, Messrs Anderson, Shaw & Gilbert, Solicitors, York House, 20 Church Street, Inverness IV1 1ED (Tel: 01463 236123).

Nith District Salmon Fishery Board. R Styles, Walker and Sharp, Solicitors, 37 George Street, Dumfries DG1 1EB (Tel: 01387 67222).

North and West District Salmon Fishery Board. A R Whitfield, Estate Office, Achfary, by Lairg, Sutherland IV27 4BQ.

Ruel District Salmon Fishery Board. J Ferguson, 6 The Strand, Rye, E Sussex TN31 7DB (Tel: 01797 222601).

Skye District Salmon Fishery Board. Mr P R A Butler, Mile End House, Glen Hinnisdal, Snizort, Portree, Isle of Skye IV51 9UX (Tel: 01470 542331).

Spey District Salmon Fishery Board. C D R Whittle, Messrs R & R Urquhart, 121 High Street, Forres, Morayshire IV36 0AB (Tel: 01309 72216).

Stinchar District Salmon Fishery Board. Mrs A McGinnis, 6 The Avenue, Barr, nr Girvan, Ayrshire KA26 9TX.

Tay District Salmon Fishery Board. R P J Blake, Messrs Condies, Solicitors, 2 Tay Street, Perth PH1 5LJ (Tel: 01738 440088).

Tweed District Salmon Fishery Board. Mrs J Nicol, River Tweed Commissioners, North Court, Drygrange Steading, by Melrose, Roxburghshire TD6 9DJ (Tel: 01896 848 294/277(Fax))

Ugie District Salmon Fishery Board. B Milton, Masson & Glennie, Solicitors, Broad House, Broad Street, Peterhead AB42 6JA (Tel: 01779 74271).

Ythan District Salmon Fishery Board. M H T Andrew, Estate Office, Mains of Haddo, Tarves, Ellon, Aberdeenshire AB41 0LD (Tel: 01651 851664).

Note. Anglers visiting Scotland to fish for coarse fish should note that it is not, in certain districts, lawful to fish with two or more rods simultaneously. The rule is one rod only.

SCOTTISH ENVIRONMENT PROTECTION AGENCY

The Scottish Environment Protection Agency (SEPA) is the body entrusted by the Secretary of State for Scotland with the task of protecting and improving the quality of the water environment. The present structure dates from 1996, under new arrangements contained in the Environment Act 1995, but Scotland has benefitted from independent control over water pollution by the Authorities since the 1950s. SEPA's powers derive primarily from the Control of Pollution Act 1974. Its main job is to monitor discharges, to see that the necessary standards are maintained, and to be fully aware of the general conditions of Scotland's waters. As a consequence of its vigilance and that of its predecessors the River Purification Boards, pollution has been considerably reduced in such river systems as the Tweed, the Solway, the Clyde, the Tay, and the Forth, and salmon have returned to the Clyde after an absence of more than 80 years. Cases of pollution should be reported to the appropriate office.

SEPA Regional Addresses

Head Office
Erskine Court
The Castle Business Park
Stirling FK9 4TR
Tel: 01786 457700
Fax: 01786 446885

East Region
Clearwater House
Heriot Watt Research Park
Avenue North
Edinburgh EH14 4AP
Tel: 0131 449 7296
Fax: 0131 449 7277

West Region
SEPA West
5 Redwood Crescent
Peel Park

East Kilbride
Glasgow G74 5PP
Tel: 01355 574200
Fax: 01355 574688

North Region
Graesser House
Fodderty Way
Dingwall Business Park
Dingwall IV15 9XB
Tel: 01349 862021
Fax: 01349 863987

Fishing Stations in Scotland

The nature of Scotland with its many rivers and lochs, especially on the west coast, makes it impracticable in some cases to deal with each river's catchment area separately. Thus some fisheries on the west coast, north of the Firth of Clyde are grouped under the heading 'West Coast Rivers and Lochs'.

The need again arises to decide whether a river should be included in England or Scotland. The Border Esk is dealt with in the English section, together with the Kirtle and the Sark, which happen to fall within the Esk's catchment area on the map. The Tweed and all its tributaries are included in this section. All the Scottish Islands, including Shetland and Orkney, are considered as within one watershed, viz, 'The Islands', in which, for convenience, Kintyre is included. The exact position in the book of any river or fishing station can, of course, readily be found by reference to the index.

ALNESS and GLASS

Alness drains **Loch Morie**, then flows 12 miles to enter Cromarty Firth at Alness. Glass drains Loch Glass then flows into Cromarty Firth near Evanton.

Alness (Ross-shire). Salmon, sea trout, grilse and brown trout. Alness AC has water on R Alness, salmon, sea trout, brown trout; and on Loch Morie, brown trout and Arctic char. Good bank fishing on Loch Morie; worm or fly only. Permits from Hon Sec. Novar Estate, Evanton, also issues permits for fishing on R Alness; salmon, sea trout, grilse and brown trout.
Evanton (Ross-shire). Brown trout fishing on R Glass and **Loch Glass**; bank fishing on loch. Permits from Factor, Novar Estates Office, Tel: 01349 830208. Salmon, sea trout and brown trout fishing on Rivers Glass and **Skiach**; and brown trout fishing on Loch Glass. Sea trout fishing on shore of Cromarty Firth. Permits from A & M Alcock, Newsagent, 16 Balconie St, Tel: 01349 830672. Local club, Evanton A C.

ANNAN

Rises in Moffat Hills and flows about 30 miles to Solway Firth. Strong tidal river. Several good pools on river N of Annan. Some spring salmon, excellent sea trout in June and July, and excellent salmon in late autumn, Oct–Nov; a few brown trout in spring and summer.

Annan (Dumfriesshire). Warmanbie Hotel has stretch; salmon, sea trout and brown trout, free

to residents. Hotel also has access to many other waters, including on **Rivers Nith** and **Eden**, plus access to Sunday trout fishing. Rod and tackle hire, bait, tuition and ghillie can be arranged. Hotel also stocks a range of tackle for sale. For further information contact Warmanbie Hotel, Annan DG12 5LL, Tel: 01461 204015.

Ecclefechan (Dumfries & Galloway). Annan, 2m SW; salmon, herling (late July onwards), brown trout. Hoddom & Kinmount Estates, Estate Office, Hoddom, Lockerbie DG11 1BE, Tel: 01576 300244, have Hoddom Castle Water, over 2m stretch on Annan. Salmon; grilse late July onwards; sea trout, May-Aug. Dt £8–£14; limited to 15 rods per day. Fly only, except when river height is above white line on Hoddom Bridge when spinning is permitted. Hoddom & Kinmount Estates also have trout fishing on **Purdomstone Reservoir**; and coarse fishing on **Kelhead Quarry** and **Kinmount Lake**, which has first-rate pike fishing. Purdomstone Reservoir, brown trout; 2 boats; 2 rods per boat; dt £8 per boat. Kelhead Quarry; brown and rainbow trout, perch, roach, bream, carp, pike, tench, eels; dt £3.50–£4.50; suitable for disabled. Permits for Hoddom Estates waters may be booked from Water Bailiff, Estate Office, Hoddom, Lockerbie DG11 1BE, Tel: 0157 300417; Kelhead Quarry permits, from Water Bailiff, Kinmount Bungalows, Kinmount, Annan, Tel: 01461 700344.

Lockerbie (Dumfriesshire). R Annan 1½m W; salmon, sea trout, brown trout. Castle Milk Estate (Tel: 01576 510203) has two beats on R

Annan and **Castle Milk Water**; salmon and sea trout, brown trout; 1¾m, left bank; fly only. Limited dt £20 (early season) and £30 (late season). **Royal Four Towns Water**; salmon, sea trout, brown trout, herling, chub, grilse; 3¾m, both banks. Dt £10 (early season) and £12 (late season), also st, £35–£55. A tributary of Annan is **River Milk**, and there are 13 miles of fishing above and below Scroggs Bridge; sea trout and brown trout; fly only. Permits and bookable holiday cottages from Anthony Steel, Kirkwood, Lockerbie, Tel: 01576 510200. In the main river **Kirkwood** water: 1⅓m single bank with good salmon and sea trout fishing. Wt from £50–£170. **Jardine Hall** water: 2½m, some double bank, good sea trout, and late salmon. Wt from £50–£200. Contact Anthony Steel, *above*. **Halleaths Water**, west bank of Annan, near Lockerbie and Lochmaben; salmon and trout, fly only. Three tickets per week in the season, 25 Feb–15 Nov. Permits from McJerrow and Stevenson, Solicitors, 55 High St, Lockerbie DG11 2JJ. Upper Annandale AA has salmon and trout fishing in two beats: upper beat, between **Moffat** and **Johnstonebridge**, 4m double bank from just south of Moffat d/s to Cogries railway viaduct; and Applegarth beat, 4m double bank from Johnstonebridge and Lockerbie, and also 1m of **Kinnel Water**. Grayling and chub, which are also caught on this beat, may only be fished in salmon season. Permits £8 day, £25 week, conc, from Video Sports, 48 High St; Annandale Arms Hotel, Moffat; Moffat Petrol Station; or A Dickson, secretary of Upper Annandale AA (Tel: 01683 300592). **Black Esk Reservoir**: bank fishing; fly and spinner only. Salmon and sea trout fishing on **River White Esk**, 6m, both banks, with a number of named pools, 12m from Langholm. Salmon and sea trout run from late July.

Lochmaben (Dumfries & Galloway). Salmon, sea trout, brown trout, chub (good). Royal Four Towns Water, Hightae. Salmon season, Feb 25 to Nov 15; trout, March 15 to Oct 6. No Sunday fishing. Permits from Clerk, Mrs Kathleen Ratcliffe, Jay-Ar, Preston House Road, Hightae, Lockerbie DG11 1JR, Tel: 01387 810 220. From Sept–Nov advance booking advisable. Brown trout fishing on **Water of Ae** in Forest of Ae; fly, worm and spinning; Forest Enterprise, Ae Village, Dumfries DG1 1QB. Permits from Hart Manor Hotel, Eskdalemuir, Lockerbie 013873 73217. Coarse fishing on **Castle Loch**; permits from Warden, Brian McClimonds, Lochfield Cottage, Lochmaben (Tel: 01387 811767). **Hightae Mill Loch**, bream, carp, perch, tench,

rudd, chub and roach; boat fishing only. Permits from J Wildman, Annandale Cottage, Greenhill, Lockerbie. Hotels: Balcastle; Royal Four Towns, Hightae.

Wamphray (Dumfriesshire). Two beats of R Annan controlled by Upper Annandale AA. Permits for these, and 1 beat of Annandale FC, totalling 13m in all, from Red House Hotel, Wamphray, nr Moffat DG10 9NF, Tel: 01576 470470, who have special rates for anglers.

Moffat (Dumfries & Galloway). Upper Annandale AA has 4m double bank of Annan; with salmon, brown trout, and sea trout fishing. Permits obtainable. Refer to Lockerbie, above, for details.

AWE and LOCH AWE and LOCH ETIVE

A short river, but one of best-known salmon streams of west coast. Connects Loch Awe to sea by way of Loch Etive, which it enters at Bonawe. River fishes best from July onwards.

Taynuilt (Argyll). Salmon, sea trout, trout. Inverawe Fisheries, Taynuilt, Argyll PA35 1HU (Tel: 01866 822446) has ½m on River Awe, salmon and sea trout; and three lochs stocked daily with rainbow trout. Fly only. Wt and dt, with half-day and father/son concessions. Tuition, tackle for hire and refreshments on site. Salmon and trout fishing also from A R Nelson, Muckairn, Taynuilt, who has a stretch on R Awe. Loch Etive, brown, sea, rainbow trout and sea fish; no permit required. Hotel: Polfearn Hotel. Inverawe Holiday Cottages on estate.

LOCH AWE. Salmon, sea trout, wild browns (av. half pound), char, occasional large rainbows, perch and pike. British record brown trout caught in 1996, 25lb 6oz, and 20lb pike not uncommon. Protected and controlled by Loch Awe Improvement Association, and fished by permit only, which does not include salmon and sea trout. There is a road right round loch. Salmon are most often caught by trolling. Sea trout are rarely caught and only at north end. Trout can be caught anywhere and average just under ½lb; best months Mar, Apr, May, Jun and Sep. Char are caught on a very deep sunk line. Pike and perch can be taken on a spun lure but are rarely fished for. Boats may be hired at Loch Aweside Marine, Dalavich, or Loch Awe Boats, Ardbreckinish, from £30 with motor, to £10 without, half-day.

Lochawe (Argyll). The Loch Awe IA is open to all who buy season tickets £36, but also sells weekly (£12), 3 day (£6), and daily (£3) tickets. Assn also has trout and pike fishing on **River Avich** and **Loch Avich**. Concessions for OAPs and juniors. Permits from D Wilson, Ardbrecknish House, Dalmally Lochawe Stores, Lochawe, Dalmally, PA33 1AQ; and many other sales points including tackle shops throughout Scotland (a full list is issued by Assn).

Kilchrenan (Argyll). Taychreggan Hotel, on lochside, has pike, trout and salmon fishing on Loch Awe. Fish run to good size. 2 boats with outboard engines. Ghillie can be arranged. Fishing also on River Awe (salmon), and Loch Etive (sea trout). Good sea fishing. Hotel has own jetty and it is possible to arrive by seaplane from Glasgow. Permits and further information from Mrs Annie Paul, Taychreggan Hotel, Kilchrenan, By Taynuilt, Argyll PA35 1HQ (Tel: 01866 833211, Fax: 01866 244). .

Portsonachan (Argyll). Portsonachan Hotel on shore of Loch Awe has fishing in loch; trout, salmon, sea trout, perch pike. Boats for hotel guests. Salmon fishing and fishing on hill lochs also arranged. Sonachan House, also on shore of Loch Awe, issues permits for boat fishing on Loch Awe.

Dalavich (Argyll). Forestry Commission has fishing on Loch Awe (brown trout, rainbow trout, char, perch, pike), **Loch Avich** (brown trout) and **River Avich** (salmon and brown trout). Dt £2.50. Permits, boat hire and rod hire, from N D Clark, 11 Dalavich, By Taynuilt (Tel: 01866 844209).

Ford (Argyll). **Cam** and other hill lochs: brown trout, bank fishing, dt £3. Permits for hill lochs and also for Loch Awe (dt 2.50) from D Murray, Ford Hotel.

Tributaries of the Awe

ORCHY: Good salmon.

Dalmally (Argyll). River flows into Loch Awe here, excellent salmon fishing in May, June, Sept and Oct. GlenOrchy AC fishes lower Orchy. Permits for several beats on Orchy, and pike and trout permits for **Loch Awe** and **Loch Avich**, from Loch Awe stores, Loch Awe (Tel: 01838 200200), who can also supply fishing tackle for sale or hire. D Hadley, Ebor Cottage,

St Patricks Rd, Hucknall Notts NG15 6LU, has 7m single roadside bank, excellent fly fishing water. Wt from West Highland Estates, Oban (Tel: 01631 563617). Cottage to let, if required. Hotels: Glenorchy Lodge; Orchy Bank; Craig Villa. Self-catering and B & B accommodation in area.

Bridge of Orchy (Argyll). For permits contact Loch Awe Stores (see *Dalmally*); G Coyne, Achline Estate, Killin (Tel: 01567 820487); Inveroran Hotel, Black Mount, Bridge of Orchy (Tel: Tyndrum 220); and Alan Church, Croggan Crafts, Dalmally.

AYR

Rises in Glenbuck and flows into Firth of Clyde through town of Ayr opposite south end of Isle of Arran. Good brown trout river (av ½lb) with fair runs of salmon and sea trout.

Ayr (Ayrshire). Mostly preserved, but tickets can be had for ¾m Cragie stretch at Ayr (no Sunday fishing) from the Director of Strategic Services, South Ayrshire Council, Burns House, Burns Statue Square, Ayr KA7 1UT (Tel: 01292 612270), and from Gamesport (see below). Ayr AC has stretch on River Ayr at Ayr and near Annbank (salmon, sea trout, brown trout); and on **Loch Shankston** and **Loch Spallander** (rainbow and brown trout). Members only. Wading essential for good sport. Water restocked with brown trout. Membership from Gamesport (below). Troon AC has fishing on **Collenan Reservoir**, rainbow and brown trout. Dt £13 from Torbets (below), and the Spar shop, Barassie. Prestwick AC has fishing on **Raith Waters**, rainbow trout. Dt £7, 4 fish limit, conc for juv and OAPs, from Gamesport (below); Newall's Newsagent, Monkton; Wallace's Shoe Repairer, Prestwick; and from Torbet's Outdoor Leisure, Portland Street, Troon. Block bookings (outings etc.), R McFarlane, Tel: 01292 520150.

Belston Loch at **Sinclairston**, a small rainbow trout fishery, 6m from Ayr. Other fisheries: Springwater, Tel: 01292 560343, nr Dalrymple, stocked with steelheads, browns, rainbows, permits from fishery; Burns Fishery, Tarbolton; Coyle Water, stocked with steelheads and rainbows, permits at fishery; Prestwick Reservoir nr Monkton, stocked brown and rainbow, permits from Gamesport and Monkton newsagent; tickets for town and other waters on Rivers Ayr and **Doon** may be obtained, and for coarse fishing lochs. For further information contact Gamesport of Ayr, 60 Sandgate, Ayr, Hotel: Manor Park, Monkton.

Mauchline (Ayrshire). Salmon, sea trout and brown trout fishing on Rivers **Ayr**, **Cessock** and **Lugar**; and brown and rainbow trout fishing on **Loch Belston** at Sinclairston. Boats on Loch Belston. Permits from Linwood & Johnstone, Newsagent, The Cross.

Muirkirk (Ayrshire). Fish pass has been built at Catrine Dam, allowing fish to run to headwaters at Muirkirk. Muirkirk AA has approx 6m on River Ayr, both banks; salmon, sea trout, brown trout, grayling. Assn also has fishing on **Greenock Water**; fishing allowed till 30 Sept on Greenock W; on R Ayr salmon and sea trout 1 Apr–31 Oct, browns 15 Mar–6 Oct. Brown trout restocking program. Limited season tickets sold but membership full. Dt £8, Mon–Fri, limited to 6 per day. Wt £20. Apply to Mr Scott Davidson, President, 3 Lapraik Avenue, Muirkirk (Tel: 01290 661800). Concessions and 3 competitions per year for juveniles. Limited tackle from Moorheads. Hotel: Coach House Inn.

Tributaries of the Ayr

COYLE: Sea trout, trout, grayling, few salmon. **Drongan** (Ayrshire). Drongan Youth Group AC issues permits for **River Coyle** and **Snipe Loch**; brown and rainbow trout stocked weekly; fish up to 11lb are being caught. Permits from J Wilson, Hawthorne Cottage, Watson Terrace Drongan KA6 7AG, and Snipe Loch.

BEAULY

Beauly is approximately 9m long, and flows from the junction of Glass and Farrar into Beauly Firth and thence into Moray Firth. Salmon, sea trout good from beginning of season. Main grilse runs in July/August. Plentiful food supply in Beauly Firth, hence the presence of bottlenose dolphins, porpoises and seals.

Beauly (Inverness-shire). Salmon, sea trout, occasional brown trout. Beauly AA has water below Lovat Bridge, and river mouth to Coulmore Bay, north shore, and **Bunchrew Burn** on south shore (sea trout and occasional bass). Strictly fly only from Lovat bridge to Wester lovat. Permits £10, conc, for Assn water and for sea trout fishing on Beauly Firth from Morison's, Ironmonger, Westend, Beauly IV4 7BT. Members only, Thursdays and Saturdays. For **Loch Achilty** and **Loch Nam**

Bonnach, also enquire at Morison's. Sea trout fishing on Beauly Firth at Clachnaharry and North Kessock; permits from Grahams, 37 Castle St, Inverness, Tel: 0463 233178; Kessock PO, North Kessock, Tel: 01463 731470. Good sea trout from the beginning of the season. **Loch Ruthven**, trout fly fishing by boat, 12m from Inverness; **Tarvie Lochs**, rainbow trout, fly and boat only, 25m from Inverness; **Loch Ashie** and **Loch Duntelchaig**, fly and spinning, 10m from Inverness. Tickets for these, for 3m double bank of **R Ness**, and 9m on **R Nairn**, from J Graham, *above*. Hotels: Lovat, Priory, Caledonian, all Beauly.

Tributaries of the Beauly

FARRAR and GLASS:

Struy (Inverness-shire). Permits from Mr & Mrs F R Doyle, Kerrow House, Cannich, Strathglass, Inverness-shire IV4 7NA (Tel: 01456 415 243), for 3½m of brown trout fishing on River Glass (fly only). Special rates for guests of Kerrow House (B&B and self-catering). Fly fishing on **R Farrar** and **Glass**. Dt £15–£40 (salmon) and £10 (trout); from F Spencer-Nairn, Culligran House, Glen Strathfarrar, Struy, nr Beauly, Tel/Fax: 01463 761285. Priority given to guests of Culligran Cottages (self-catering), brochure issued. Hotels: Cnoc; Chisholm Stone House, Kerrow House.

Tomich (Inverness-shire). Tomich Hotel, Tomich, Strathglass, By Beauly IV4 7LY, has fishing in **Guisachan Hill Lochs**; brown and rainbow trout. Season: 1 May–6 Oct.

CANNICH: Tributary of the Glass.

Cannich (Inverness-shire). At confluence of Cannich and Glass. Glen Affric Hotel issues permits for brown trout fishing on **River Cannich**, **Loch Benevean**, **Loch Monar**, **Loch Beannacharan**, **Loch Mullardoch**, **Loch A-Bhana** and **Knockfin Forestry Hill Lochs**. Also salmon fishing on ½m of **River Glass**. Permits for Loch Benevean, Loch Mullardoch and Knockfin Hill Lochs only if not required by hotel guests. Pike and eel fishing can also be arranged after 15 Oct. Reservations direct to Glen Affric Hotel, Cannich, by Beauly (Tel: 01456 415 214). Fishing from boat. Fly only. No Sunday fishing. Caledonian Hotel, Beauly, offers a special trout fishing package; seven nights DBB, £350 per person subject to 2 persons sharing a boat; hotel also has dt from

£4 per hour on choice of local fisheries, and £12 dt on Beauly AA water.

BERVIE

Rises on Glen Farquhar Estate and flows 14m to North Sea near Inverbervie. Essentially an autumn river for finnock, sea trout and salmon although also good for brown trout.

Inverbervie (Kincardineshire). Finnock, sea trout, salmon (best Sept–Oct). Free tickets for foreshore for fortnightly periods (restricted; advance booking advised), bookable from Joseph Johnston & Sons, 3 America Street, Angus DD10 8DR (Tel: 01674 672666). For fishing upstream from Donald's Hole; dt £2 from Aberdeen Council, Area Officer, Church St, Inverbervie, Montrose DD10 0RU, or Leisure Centre, Kirkburn, Inverbervie.

BRORA

After being joined by tributaries Blackwater and Skinsdale, Brora flows through Loch Brora and into sea at Brora.

Brora (Sutherland). **Loch Brora**; salmon, sea trout and brown trout. Permits and boats on Loch Brora can be hired from Rob Wilson's Tackle Shop, Fountain Square (Tel: Brora 621373). Hotel: Royal Marine.

CARRON (Grampian)

Rises in Glenbervie and flows about 9m to the North Sea at Stonehaven. Trout.
Stonehaven (Kincardineshire). About 2½m brown trout fishing offered to visitors by Stonehaven and Dist AA. Permits also issued for **River Cowie** (about 1¼m), sea trout, salmon and brown trout. Best July, August and Sept. Permits from David's Sports Shop, 31 Market Sq. Good sea fishing. Hotels: Eldergrove, Arduthie House.

CLYDE

Rises near watershed of Tweed and Annan, and flows about 50m to the Atlantic by way of Glasgow. Once a famous salmon river, then spoiled by pollution. Now, river has improved, with salmon and sea trout returning annually. Controls are in force, to conserve stocks. Trout and grayling fishing, especially in higher reaches. The Clyde's most famous tributary, the Leven, which connects with Loch Lomond, has run of

salmon and sea trout. In north-west corner of Renfrewshire is Loch Thom, linked by water spill with Loch Compensation, which, when water is high, drains into River Kip in Shielhill Burn. United Clyde Angling Protective Association Ltd controls much of Clyde and tributaries upstream of Motherwell Bridge to Daer Reservoir, in three sections, the Upper, Middle and Lower Reaches, and restocks annually. Permits are prices as follows: annual £21, day £5, salmon £25 wt, OAP free, juv conc. These are obtainable from various tackle dealers and sports shops in Lanarkshire and Glasgow. Avon AC, Stonehouse, Lanarkshire, controls some leases on Avon. Accommodation can be arranged through Greater Glasgow and Clyde Valley Tourist Board.

Greenock (Strathclyde). On the estuary of Clyde. Greenock & Dist AC preserves **Loch Thom** (365 acres, trout – three to the pound), and has rights on **Yetts**, **No. 8 and No. 6** (Spring Dam), good trout. Permits from Brian Peterson, The Fishing Shop, *below*, or Jean Caskie, Garvocks Farm. Club membership restricted to persons resident in Greenock and district, but permits sold to visitors; Sunday fishing; no parties. Fly only. Bank fishing only. Tickets for trout fisheries in vicinity; Lawfield, Houston Rd, Kilmacolm PA13 4NY (Tel: 01505 874182), brown trout, rainbow and brook, permits and instruction at fishery; Fairlie Moor (10 acres), Dalry Moor Rd, Fairly (Tel: 01850 162543); Pine Wood, Kilmacolm (Tel: 01589 042393); and Haylie (3 acres), Largs (Tel: 01475 676005), Ardgowan Fly Fishery (37 acre loch, dt £9–£15, boats extra), Daff Fishery (65 acre loch, dt £10–£15, conc), and Kip River, (dt £13) from The Fishing Shop, 24 Union Street, Tel: 01475 888085. Good sea fishing for cod, skate, dogfish, conger, haddock and plaice. Hotel, Tontine, 6 Ardgowan Square.

Glasgow (Strathclyde). Glasgow has excellent trout, sea trout and salmon fishing within a radius of 60m. Lochs Lomond, Dochart, Awe, Tay, Ard, Leven, Lubnaig, Venachar, Lake of Menteith, etc, and Rivers Annan, Goil, Cur (head of Loch Eck), Clyde (trout and grayling only), Teith, Tweed, Allan, Dochart, Leven, Kinglass etc, all accessible from here. Coarse fishing on whole of **Forth and Clyde Canal**; pike, perch, roach, tench, eels, mirror carp, occasional brown trout. No close season. Permits from J B Angling, Kirkintilloch. For further details apply to British Waterways, 1 Applecross St, Glasgow G4 9SP, Tel: 0141 332 6936. Free coarse fishing in 5m radius of

Glasgow at **Auchinstarry Pond**, Kilsyth (tench, roach, perch and rudd); **Kilmadinny Loch**, Bearsden; **Bardowie Loch**, Balmore; **Mugdock Park Pond**, Milgavie; **Tench Pool**, Milgavie; **Carp Pond**, Seafar; and **Hogganfield Loch**, Glasgow. United Clyde Angling Protective Association issues annual tickets for stretches on Clyde and **R Douglas** near Motherwell, Lanark, Carstairs, Roberton and Thankerton; brown trout and grayling fishing. Permits from Hon Sec or tackle shops. Kilsyth FPS controls **Townhead Reservoir**. Tackle shops: Anglers Rendezvous, 74–78 Saltmarket; William Robertson & Co Ltd, 61 Miller St; Hooked in Scotland, Cambuslane.

Coatbridge (Lanarkshire). **Lochend Loch** is Monklands Dist water; pike, perch, brown and rainbow trout. Permits from waterside. Monklands District Coarse AC manages **Monklands Canal** west of Coatbridge; bream, 2lb–6lb, perch, gudgeon, common and mirror carp, dace, rudd and tench. St £12 and dt £1, conc. Day tickets on bank, fishing is allowed during close season, all anglers are welcome. Linlithgow Coarse AC has water on canal between Preston Rd Bridge and Woodcockdale Bridge; and Cobbinshaw AA also has water. Hotel: Georgian.

Airdrie (Lanarkshire). Airdrie AC has **Hillend Reservoir**; brown and rainbow trout 1lb–12lb stocked weekly, pike and perch. All legal methods. Bag limit 6 fish. Boat and bank fishing, good access for disabled. No ground bait. Permits at water £5, 4 fish limit, St £50. Clarkston Independent AC has **Lilly Loch** at Calderdruix; rainbow and brown trout. Season 15 Mar–6 Oct. Any legal method (fly only from boats). Dt £3 (£2 OAPs & juniors). Tickets from bailiffs on site. Hotel: Old Truff Inn, Caldercruix, By Airdrie.

Motherwell (Lanarkshire). United Clyde APA has water on **Clyde** and **Douglas**; brown trout and grayling. Permits from local tackle shops. Coarse fishing on **Strathclyde Country Park Loch** and adjacent R Clyde; carp, bream, roach, pike, perch and dace. No close season. No fly fishing. Lead free weights recommended. Also trout and grayling fishing; 15 Mar–29 Sept. Permits from Booking Office, Strathclyde Country Park, 366 Hamilton Rd, Motherwell. Tackle shop: Macleod's Tackle Shop, 176 High St, Newarthill, Motherwell.

Strathaven (Lanarkshire). Avon; trout and grayling. United Clyde Angling Protective Assn has water on Clyde; permits from tackle shops in Glasgow and Lanarkshire.

Lanark (Lanarkshire). Trout and grayling. United Clyde APA water on Clyde and **Douglas**; permits from local tackle shop J Ritchie, Bannatyne St. Coarse fishing on **Lanark Loch**; carp and tench. No close season. Hotel: Cartland Bridge.

Carstairs (Strathclyde). Trout and grayling. United Clyde APA water on Clyde and **Douglas**; permits from local tackle shops.

Thankerton (Strathclyde). Lamington AIA has 9m of water from Thankerton to Roberton; trout and grayling st £20, wt £15, dt £5; grayling st £5 and dt £2, conc. Permits from Hon Sec or Bryden Newsagent, Biggar. Concessions for OAP and junior. No Sunday fishing. Tickets from Post Offices, hotels, newsagents. United Clyde APA water below Thankerton.

Biggar (Lanarkshire). Lamington AIA fish from Roberton Burn mouth to Thankerton boat bridge, approx 9m, both banks, with brown trout and grayling. Good wading. Prices, see *above*. Hotels: Hartree Country House; Shieldhill. Tackle shop: Bryden, Newsagent, 153 High Street (Tel: 01899 220069).

Abington (Lanarkshire). Trout and grayling; UCAPA (United Clyde) water. Other assn water at **Crawford** and **Elvanfoot**. Hotel: Abington.

Tributaries of the Clyde

LEVEN and **LOCH LOMOND**: Salmon, trout, pike and perch.

Loch Lomond (Strathclyde). Loch is the largest area of inland water in Britain, being 22.8 miles long and up to 5 miles wide, and has over 40 islands on it. The powan, a freshwater herring, is unique to its waters, the loch holds the record for Britain's largest pike, and there are 17 other species present. Good trout, sea trout and salmon fishing (also perch and pike) can be had from various centres on loch. Under control of Loch Lomond Angling Improvement Assn, c/o R A Clements & Co, 29 St Vincent Place, Glasgow G1 2DT (Tel: 0141 221 0068). Fishing reserved for full members only on **Fruin**, **Blane** and some stretches of **Endrick**. Dt are issued for Leven and Loch Lomond at all local tackle shops, boat hirers and hotels. St and children's permits also obtainable for Leven. No Sunday fishing. Late April and May earliest for fly on Loch Lomond (sea trout and salmon). Tackle shops: McFarlane & Son, The Boatyard, Balmaha (boats for hire); and Balloch Tourist Information Centre, Balloch.

Rowardennan, By Drymen (Stirlingshire). Convenient for Loch Lomond; permits and boats. Hotel: Rowardennan.

Balloch (Dumbartonshire). Trout, good sea trout and salmon fishing on River Leven and Loch Lomond; large perch and pike in loch; fishing controlled by Loch Lomond AIA. Vale of Leven & Dist AC issues permits for brown trout fishing on **Loch Sloy**. Fly only, dt £4. Apply to Hon Sec, Fisherwood, Balloch. Hotel: Balloch, Tullichewan.

FRUIN: (tributary of Loch Lomond).

Helensburgh (Strathclyde). Salmon, sea trout and brown trout. Fly only. Permits issued by Loch Lomond AIA. Full members only.

Ardlui (Dumbartonshire). Trout, sea trout and salmon fishing in Loch Lomond. Hotel: Ardlui.

ENDRICK: (tributary of Loch Lomond).

Killearn (Stirling). Good trout, sea trout and salmon fishing. Loch Lomond AIA has water. No worm fishing; spinning restricted. No Sunday fishing. Accommodation arranged. Ghillie and boat hire. Full members only.

GRYFE (or GRYFFE): Brown trout, salmon, sea trout.

Bridge of Weir (Strathclyde). Bridge of Weir River AC has 3m of water. Trout: 15 Mar–6 Oct. Salmon: 15 Mar–31 Oct. St (locals only) from Hon Sec. Day tickets from M Duncan, Newsagent, Main St; Mon–Fri only.

Kilmacolm (Strathclyde). Strathgryfe AA has water on R Gryfe and tributaries **Green Water**, **Black Water** and **Burnbank Water**; approx. 25m in all, with brown trout and grayling. St £15 plus £10 entrance, with concessions. Permits from Hon Sec, or from Cross Cafe, Kilmacolm. No day tickets on a Sunday. Two fisheries with rainbow trout in Kilmacolm area: Lawfield and Pinewoods. Enquire M Duncan, Newsagents (see *Bridge of Weir*).

CALDER and **BLACK CART**:
Lochwinnoch (Strathclyde). St Winnoch AC has stretch of Calder (brown trout); and **Castle Semple Loch**, pike, perch, roach and eels. St £6 and dt £1–£3. Concessions for juniors. Permits from Hon Sec or A&G (Leisure) Ltd, 48 McDowall St, Johnstone. Also from Rangers Centre at loch.

AVON:
Strathhaven (Lanarks). Avon AC fishes approx 14m of excellent brown trout and grayling water, with additional salmon and sea trout, near Strathhaven Stonehouse and Larkhall. Restocked annually. Members only, membership £14 p.a., £18 salmon and sea trout, with concessions, from Sportsman Emporium, Hamilton; Gibson, Union St, Larkhall; or from bailiffs.

CONON
(including Blackwater)

Drains Loch Luichart and is joined by Orrin and Blackwater before entering the Moray Firth and North Sea by way of Cromarty Firth. Spring fishing has declined and main salmon runs now take place from July to September. Sport then among best in Highlands.

Dingwall (Ross-shire). Salmon, sea trout and brown trout. Dingwall & District AC has lower beat on R Conon. Fly only, for salmon, sea trout and brown trout. Thigh waders only. Season: Jan 26 to Sept 30, best months May, Aug and Sept. Dt £7–£10 from H C Furlong, Sports & Model Shop, High Street, Dingwall IV15 9RY. Permit also covers **Loch Chuilin** and **Loch Achanalt**. At **Brahan** there are 3 beats of brown trout fishing on **R Conon** and a stocked, brown trout pond. Coarse fishing on **Loch Ussie**, pike and eels. Permits from Seaforth Highland Estates, Brahan, by Dingwall (Tel: 01349 861150). Tackle shop: Maclean Sport, High St. Hotels: Conon at Conon Bridge; Craigdarroch and Coul House, both Contin.

Strathpeffer (Ross-shire). R Conon, above Loch Achonachie, salmon and brown trout; fly or spinning. **River Blackwater** above Rogie Falls, salmon, brown trout and pike. **Loch Achonachie**, brown trout, perch and occasional salmon; bank and boat fishing; use of a boat produces best results; fly or spinning. Coul House Hotel issues permits for beats on Rivers Conon, **Blackwater** and **Beauly** (salmon, sea trout, brown trout); and for **Lochs Tarvie**

(rainbow trout), **Achonachie** (brown trout) and **Meig** (brown trout). Apply to Coul House Hotel, Contin, by Strathpeffer IV14 9EY (Tel: 01997 421487). Hotel provides full angling service, including rod racks, rod and reel hire, small tackle shop, guest freezer, drying room and fish-smoking arranged.

Garve (Ross-shire). Garve Hotel (Tel: 01997 414205) has excellent fishing on **Loch Garve**, which holds large trout (fish up to 12lb taken) also pike to 30lb and perch; and brown trout fishing in 1½m of **River Blackwater** within hotel grounds. Free fishing for hotel patrons. **Loch an Eich Bhain (The Tarvie Loch)**, 25 acres, Ross-shire's first Troutmaster water; stocked with rainbow trout to 15lb and brown trout to 4lb; fly only. Fishing exclusively by boat. **Loch Ruith a Phuill**, 12 acres; wild brown trout, stocked rainbow to 6lb; coarse and fly fishing tackle allowed; third loch, 7 acres, stocked browns to 6lb, fly only, with boat. Permits from Tarvie Lochs Trout Fishery, Tarvie, by Strathpeffer, Tel: 01997 421250; Morison, Ironmonger, Beauly; Sports & Model Shop, Tulloch St, Dingwall; and J Graham & Co, 37/39 Castle St, Inverness. **Loch Glascarnoch**, brown trout, pike and perch; fly only. Contact Aultguish Inn, by Garve, Tel: 019975 254.

CREE and BLADNOCH

Cree drains Loch Moan and flows about 25m to sea at Wigtown Bay. Runs of salmon and sea trout in summer and early autumn. **Minnoch**, tributary of Cree, is also a salmon river, joining Cree about 6 miles from Newton Stewart. Bladnoch, a strong tidal river, flows into Cree Estuary at Wigtown. Salmon in season. Good pools.

Newton Stewart (Wigtownshire). Salmon, sea trout; best early in season. Newton Stewart AA has fishing on Cree, salmon and sea trout; **Bladnoch**, salmon; and **Bruntis Loch**, brown and rainbow trout, bank fishing only; **Kirriereoch Loch**, brown trout, bank fishing, fly only, **Clatteringshaws Loch**, browns, pike and perch, plus other waters. Assn spends between £10,000–£15,000 annually, restocking 4 stillwaters with trout. Permits £2–£10, salmon weekly, £75, from A J Dickinson, Galloway Guns & Tackle, 36A Arthur St, Newton Stewart DG8 6DE (Tel: 01671 403404) who supply all game, coarse and sea fishing tackle together with frozen and live bait.

Forestry Commission has fishing on **Palnure Burn**, salmon, sea trout, brown trout; **R Minnoch**, brown trout (Mar–Jun) and salmon (Mar–Oct); **Black Loch**, brown trout, stocked, fly only until 1 July; **Loch of Lowes**, brown trout, fly only; **Lilies Loch**, brown trout; **Lochs Spectacle** and **Garwachie**, pike, perch, tench, roach, rudd; **Loch Eldrig**, pike, perch, roach. Permits from Forest Enterprises, Newton Stewart Forest District, Creebridge, Newton Stewart DG8 6PJ (Tel: 01671 2420); and Galloway Wildlife Museum. Creebridge House Hotel, Newton Stewart DG8 6NP, Tel: 01671 402121, offers fishing on **R Bladnoch**, good spring run of grilse, Feb-Oct, 2m for up to 4 rods; **R Minnoch**, a tributary of Cree fed by Glentrool Loch, 4m for up to 12 rods, spawning pools; 2 beats offered, 22 pools in all. Hotel has excellent food and accommodation, can store rods in a lockable room and has freezer and drying facilities. Permits from £15–£25, only from A J Dickinson, *above*. **Upper Cree**, at Bargrennan, 2m salmon fishing: also assn water on stretch of Cree which runs through town to estuary mouth. Corsemalzie House Hotel, Port William, DG8 9RL *(see advt.)*, has salmon and trout fishing on **Bladnoch** and **Tarf**, 5m on each, dt £18, wt £80; trout fishing on **Malzie Burn**; and coarse fishing in nearby lochs. Ghillie for hire. Salmon, brown trout and pike fishing on Tarf; pike and perch fishing on **Whitefield Loch**; and trout and coarse fish on **Torwood Lochs**. Permits from David Canning, Torwood House Hotel, Glenluce, Newton Stewart. Trout fishing on **Black Loch**, and mixed coarse and pike fishing on **Lochs Heron** and **Ronald**; permit and boat hire from A Brown, Three Lochs Caravan Park, Nr Kirkcowan, Newton Stewart DG8 0EP (Tel: 0167183 304). Castlewigg Hotel, nr Whithorn, 19m S of Wigtown, can arrange salmon and trout fishing in local lochs and rivers; and sea angling from Port Patrick and Isle of Whithorn. Tel: 0198 85–213. Permits for salmon and trout fishing on River Bladnoch **Torhousekie** (6 rods) and **Low Malzie** (2 rods) fisheries, also 6 acre trout loch, from Bladnoch Inn, Wigtown DG8 9AB (Tel: 01988 402200). River beats have salmon and wild browns. Fishing holidays at inn, ghillie on site, £20 per day (10am to 4pm.) Local tackle shops have drying and freezing facilities. Cree and Bladnoch fishing holidays are arranged on private waters by J Haley, Mochrum Park, Kirkcowan, Tel: 01671 830471. Galloway Angling Centre, Managers House, Bladnoch Bridge Estate,

Wigtown DG8 9AB (Tel: 01988 403363) has permits for most waters in the area, covering coast, game and pike fishing, and large stock of various baits.

Barrhill (Ayrshire). Drumlamford Estate Fisheries comprising 1m of salmon and trout fishing on **River Cree**; three stocked trout lochs; and **Loch Dornal**, a coarse fish loch. Boats, permits.

CROSS WATER OF LUCE

Dependent on flood water for good salmon fishing, but very good for sea trout after dark. Best July onwards.

Stranraer (Wigtownshire). Excellent centre for river, loch and sea fishing. Stranraer & Dist AA has **Soulseat Loch**, rainbow and brown trout, fly and bait; **Dindinnie Reservoir**, brown and rainbow trout, fly only; **Knockquassan Reservoir**, brown and rainbow trout, fly only; and **Penwhirn Reservoir**, brown trout, fly only. All these waters are near Stranraer. Permits, £10, £50 weekly, from The Sports Shop, 86 George St DG9 7JS (Tel: 01776 702705). Torwood House Hotel issues permits for **Torwood Lochs,** trout, bream, tench, carp, roach, rudd, perch; and **Whitefield Loch**, pike and perch. Apply to R Goodship, Cock Inn, Auchenmalg, Glenluce (Tel: 01581 500224). Dunskey Estates, Port Patrick, Stranraer, has 2 lochs with stocked brown and rainbow trout. Contact Keeper, P Hoyer (Tel: 01776 810346). Sea fishing in **Loch Ryan**, Irish Sea and Luce Bay. Charter boats and bait obtainable locally. Hotel: Ruddicot.

DEE (Aberdeenshire)

Second most famous salmon river of Scotland; for fly fishing probably the best. Also holds sea trout and brown trout. Rises in Cairngorms and flows into North Sea at Aberdeen. Best months for salmon: February to mid–June. Best for finnock (small sea trout) mid–August to end of September.

Aberdeen. Salmon, sea trout, brown trout; sea fishing. Many owners let for whole or part of season, but some good stretches held by hotels. Some hotel waters free to guests during summer. Lower reaches give good finnock fishing. Sea fishing is good in vicinity of Aberdeen. Hotels: Bucksburn Moat House; Cults; Dee Motel.

Banchory (Kincardineshire). Salmon and sea trout. Banchory Lodge Hotel by river can arrange salmon and trout fishing on Dee for 5 rods, bait fishing to April 15, fly only after. Ghillies and tuition on site. Apply to Mr & Mrs Dugald Jaffray, Banchory Lodge Hotel, Banchory AB31 3HS (Tel: 0133 082 2625). Feughside Inn, Strachan, by Banchory, issues Aberdeen Dist AA permits for 1½m on **River Feugh**, salmon and sea trout, dt £30. Tor-na-Coille Country House Hotel also provides fishing. Other hotels: Invery House, Raemoir House.

Aboyne (Aberdeenshire). Dee, salmon and sea trout; and **Aboyne Loch**, rainbow trout, stocked. Fly only. No Sunday fishing on Dee. Permits from Glen Tanar Estate, Brooks House, Glen Tanar AB34 5EU (Tel: 013398 86451). Coarse fishing on Aboyne Loch; pike and perch; permits from the Office, Aboyne Loch Caravan Park AB34 5BR (Tel: 013398 86244). **Tillypronie Loch**, brown trout, fly only. Permits hourly or daily, Tel: 013398 81332. Hotels: Birse Lodge; Huntly Arms.

Ballater (Aberdeenshire). Balmoral, Mar, Glenmuick and Invercauld Estates preserve most of Upper River Dee salmon fishings. **River Gairn**, brown trout, fly only. St £9, wt £5, dt £1.50; from tackle shop. Ballater AA has fishing on 5 lochs with brown and rainbow trout, beats of Rivers **Muick** and **Gairn** by Ballater, with brown trout; Dee at **Maryculter** and **Deveron** at **Banff**, with salmon and sea trout. These waters are mostly for members only, but permits for **Loch Vrotichan**, with brown trout, fly only, are obtainable from Hon Sec and tackle shop: Countrywear, 15 Bridge St, Ballater (Tel: 013397 55453). Annual membership is currently £30, plus £30 joining fee. Many hotels and guest houses in vicinity.

Braemar (Aberdeenshire). Salmon fishing: Invercauld Estate lets Crathie, Lower Invercauld and Monaltrie beats, 20m in all, details from The Factor, Invercauld Estates Office, Braemar, By Ballater AB3 5TR (Tel: 013397 41224). Brown trout fishing on **Rivers Gairn** and **Clunie**. Permits from Invercauld Estates Office; Tourist Office, Braemar. **Lochs Bainnie** and **Nan Ean,** brown trout, fly only; permits from Invercauld Estates Office, Braemar AB35 5TR (Tel: 01339 761224); and the keeper, Mr K Peters, Wester Binzean, Glenshee, PH10 7QD (Tel: 01250 885206). Hotels: Invercauld Arms; Braemar Lodge.

DEE
(Kirkcudbrightshire),
(including Lochs Dee and Ken)

Flows through Loch Ken about 16m to Solway. Salmon, sea trout and brown trout. Netting reduced and river stocked with salmon fry. An area in which acidification problems have been reported. Some lochs affected.

Castle Douglas (Kirkcudbrightshire). Forestry Commission has fishing on **R Dee**, trout; and **Stroan Loch,** mainly pike but also perch, roach and trout. Dt £1, from dispenser at Raider's Road entrance. **Woodhall Loch**, best known as pike water but also roach, perch and large trout; good winter venue with big pike catches, including 20lb plus fish. Dt £1.50 from Mossdale Shop. Castle Douglas & Dist AA has 7m stretch on **River Urr**; salmon, sea trout and brown trout; re-stocked annually; good runs of sea trout and grilse starting in June. Dt £5 and £15 (Sept, Oct, Nov). Assn also has brown and rainbow trout fishing on **Loch Roan**; 4 boats. Dt £25 per boat for 2 rods. Permits from Tommy's Sports, 178 King Street, Tel: 01556 502851. **Loch Ken**, pike and perch; open all year for coarse fish. Permits from local hotels and shops. Wild brown trout fishing on **Lairdmannoch Loch** at Twynholm; boat fishing only. Permits from G M Thomson & Co Ltd, 27 King St D67 1AB; self-catering accommodation. Other tackle shop: McCowan & Son, 50/52 King St (branch also in Dalbeattie). Hotels: Douglas Arms; Imperial; Urr Valley Country House.

Crossmichael (Kirkcudbrightshire). Boats for **Loch Ken** from Crossmichael Marina, which has been recently upgraded and re-equipped; boats for hire all year round. Loch Ken, pike, perch, roach, brown trout, rainbow trout, sea trout, salmon, some bream, eels. Hotel: Culgruff House Hotel.

New Galloway (Kirkcudbrightshire). Dee private. Forest Enterprise controls fishing on 11 lochs, trout, coarse, or mixed, including **Loch Dee**, stocked brown trout; **Lillies Loch**, wild browns (ideal for beginners), and **Stroan Loch**, pike and perch, and stretches of Rivers **Palnure** and **Minnoch**, with salmon and sea trout. Weekly permits £25, with concessions, from Forest Enterprise, 21 King St, Castle Douglas DG7 1AA (Tel: 01556 503626); and Clatteringshaws Forest Wildlife Centre, New Galloway DG7 3SQ (Tel: 01644 420285). New Galloway AA controls stretch of **River Ken**, brown trout, salmon, pike, roach, perch; stretch of **Loch Ken**, brown trout, pike, perch, and salmon run through loch during season; **Blackwater of Dee** (N bank only), brown trout, salmon, pike; **Mossdale Loch**, native brown trout and stocked rainbow trout, fly only; and **Clatteringshaws Reservoir**, brown trout, pike, perch, roach. Fishing on Clatteringshaws Reservoir shared with Newton Stewart AA. Visitors permits, for all except Loch Ken and Mossdale Loch, £2 per rod per day or £10 per week; Loch Ken, dt £2 plus 50p surcharge if permit bought from bailiffs; Mossdale Loch, dt £12 per boat (1 rod) per day, from Mossdale shop. Permits from hotels in town; Ken Bridge Hotel; Mr Hopkins, Grocer, High St; Post Office, Mossdale; and Kenmure Hotel: Concession for jun. Ken Bridge Hotel has own stretch on R Ken (wt £10, dt £2). **Barscobe Loch**; brown trout, fly only; dt (incl boat) £5 from Lady Wontner, Barscobe, Balmaclellan, Castle Douglas.

Dalry (Kirkcudbrightshire). Dalry AA has fishing on **River Ken** from Dalry; good stocks of brown trout and occasional salmon; fly spinning and worm, bank fishing only. Assn also has water on **Carsfad Loch,** brown and rainbow trout, bank fishing only; **Earlstoun Loch**, brown trout, fly only, two boats. No Sunday fishing. Visitors tickets sold from 15 Mar–30 Sept, dt £4–£5, wt £16 from N W Newton (Grocers), 17 Main St, Castle Douglas DG7 3UP. Milton Park Hotel (Tel: 01644 430 286/655 Fax) has rainbow and brown trout fishing on **Lochs Moss, Roddick, Brack** and **Earlston**, wild brown and rainbow trout; boats for hire; also wild browns in R Ken. Tickets for all, from hotel. Lochinvar Hotel can arrange fishing in rivers, lochs and reservoirs (salmon, trout, pike and perch). Permits from Duchrae Farm for **Lochinvar Loch**; wild brown trout, no shore fishing, fly only. Hotel: De Croft.

DEVERON

Rises in Cabrach and flows some 45m into the Moray Firth at Banff. A salmon river, with brown trout fishing, some sea trout, June to September; finnock spring months.

Banff (Banffshire). Salmon, sea trout, brown trout. Fife Lodge Hotel, Banff Springs and County Hotel can sometimes arrange fishings. Early bookings advisable as best beats are heavily booked. Best months: salmon, March to Oct; sea trout June to Aug; brown trout, April, May and Sept. Sea trout improving. Sea trout fishing (July onwards) in **Boyne Burn**, 6m away. Tickets from Seafield Estate, Cullen (no charge, but limited).

Turriff (Aberdeenshire). Turriff AA has salmon, sea trout and brown trout fishing on Deveron. Wt £80 Jun–Aug, £100 Sept–Oct, Mon–Fri. Day tickets Feb–May only, £5; 6 rods per day limit. Permits from tackle shop. Fly only when level falls below 6in on gauge. Best months July, August and Sept; also a fishery on opposite bank, dt £5. Bognie, Mountblairy and Frendraught Group has salmon, grilse, sea trout and brown trout fishing on Bognie Pool, Upper and Lower Mountblairy, 4m (part double bank), salmon, grilse, sea trout, brown trout. 11 Feb to 31 Oct. Wt £70–£330 depending on time of year. Fishing is open to all, usually on a weekly basis along with holiday cottages. Day permits only up until May, from Mrs Joanne McRae, BMF Group, Estate Office, Frendraught House, Forgue, Huntly AB54 6EB (Tel: 01464 871331, Fax: 01464 871333). Enquiries to Bell Ingram, 7 Walker Street, Edinburgh for **Beldorney Castle Water**. £55 per rod per week. Tackle shop: Ian Masson, Fishing Tackle, 6 Castle St. Hotels: Union, White Heather. B & B suitable for anglers, from Jenny Rae, Silverwells, St Mary's Well, Turriff AB53 8BS (Tel: 01888 562469).

Huntly (Aberdeenshire). Salmon, sea trout, brown trout. Permits for **Deveron**, **Bogie** and **Isla**; st £70, mt £40, wt £30, dt £15 from Clerk, Huntly Fishings Committee, 27 Duke Street, Huntly AB54 8DP. Only 10 day tickets per day and none on Saturdays or Public Holidays. Castle Beat: ½m double bank fishing for two rods, access via Castle Hotel, 1 mile from Huntly; salmon, sea trout and brown trout, by arrangement either daily or weekly; contact Emma Plumpton, Loanend, Cartly, nr Huntly, AB54 4SB (Tel: 01466 720708). Forbes Arms Hotel at Rotheimay issue permits for Deveron; salmon, sea trout and brown trout; fly fishing and spinning.

DIGHTY

Drains some small lochs and falls into the Firth of Tay not far from Dundee. Banks built up on lower reaches. Now considered a negligible fishery.

Dundee (Angus). Trout with occasional sea trout; free. 10m east, **Monikie** and **Crombie Reservoirs** leased to Monikie AC, stocked browns and rainbows to 5lb. Visitors welcome, boats £25 for two, with concessions, 12 fish, via bailiff (Tel: 01382 370300). Access for disabled. **Lintrathen Reservoir** leased to Lintrathen AC. Good trout fishing; boats for hire; catch limit 15 fish (over 10in) per boat. Club bookings from Dr Parratt, 91 Strathern Road, Broughty Ferry, Dundee, Tel: 01382 477305. During season, reservations from boathouse (Tel: 01575 560327). Access and boats for disabled. Tackle from Broty Tackle, King St, Broughty Ferry, Dundee. Hotel: Station.

DON (Aberdeenshire)

Rises near Ben Avon and flows for nearly 80m to North Sea at Aberdeen. Long famed as a dry fly trout water, the river is also becoming known for its salmon, which run from April to October. Sea trout numbers are on the increase.

Kintore (Aberdeenshire). Salmon and trout fishing on both banks of River Don; 2½m on right bank and 3½m on left bank. Permits from Sloans of Inverurie, 125–129 High St, Inverurie AB51 3QJ (Tel: 01467 625181). No Sunday fishing.
Inverurie (Aberdeenshire). **River Don** (2½ miles) and **River Urie** (3½ miles) salmon, brown trout and occasional sea trout. No Sunday fishing on Don. Salmon best March, April, May and Sept–Oct. Permits from Sloans of Inverurie, 125–129 High St, Inverurie AB51 3QJ (Tel: 01467 625181).

Kemnay (Aberdeenshire). Salmon, sea trout, brown trout. Mrs F J Milton, Kemnay House, AB51 5LH (Tel: 01467 642220) issues very limited permits for one beat on Don at Kemnay; dt £25 and £8 (trout). Booking essential. Hotel: Parkhill Lodge. Tackle from Inverurie.

Alford (Aberdeenshire). 25m from Aberdeen. Salmon, brown trout and some sea trout. Forbes Arms Hotel, Bridge of Alford AB33 8QJ (Tel: 019755 62108) has 3¼m of Don for guests and also issues permits. Wt £45–£85, dt £8–£17. Preference given to guests. Some good trout burns (free) in vicinity.

Kildrummy (Aberdeenshire). Kildrummy Castle Hotel has good stretch of salmon and brown trout fishing. Trout best early, salmon late.

Glenkindie (Aberdeenshire). Glenkindie

Arms Hotel issue permits for salmon and trout fishing. No Sunday fishing; 4 rod limit.

Strathdon (Aberdeenshire). Colquhonnie Hotel, AB36 8UN, Tel: 019756 51210, has 9m of salmon and trout fishing. Permits for salmon fishing also from Glenkindie Arms Hotel; and Kildrummy Castle Hotel, Kildrummy.

DOON

Drains Loch Doon on the Firth of Clyde watershed and flows right through the old County of Ayr to the Firth of Clyde, near Ayr Town. Good salmon, sea trout and brown trout water.

Ayr (Ayrshire). On Rivers Doon and Ayr. Salmon and sea trout July onwards. Brig o' Doon Hotel, Alloway (Tel: 01292 442466) has water on Doon. Salmon and sea trout fishing on 3 beats at Skeldon Estate (1m from Dalrymple) with self-catering accommodation, from Mr Campbell, Skeldon Estate, Dalrymple KA6 6AT (Tel: 01292 560656). District Council issues permits for **Ayr**. Club membership and permits for various club waters issued by Gamesport of Ayr, 60 Sandgate, Ayr KA7 1BX (Tel: 01292 263822). Hotel: Parson's Lodge, 15 Main St, Patna.

Dalmellington (Ayrshire). Good salmon and sea trout (July onwards). **Loch Doon**, 6m; plenty of small brown trout and occasional salmon and char; fishing free; boats for hire. Craigengillan Estate KA6 7PZ (Tel: 01292 550237) has both banks of River Doon from Loch Doon to the Straiton Road Bridge, and coarse fishing from bank at Bogton Loch. Tickets from keeper. Brown trout and occasional salmon and sea trout. Apply Farm, Craigengillan (Tel: Dalmellington 550 366).

EDEN (Fife)

Rises in Ochil Hills not far from Loch Leven and falls into North Sea in St Andrews Bay. Provides some very fair trout fishing. Slow-flowing stream suitable for dry-fly fishing. Some sea trout below Cupar.

St Andrews (Fife). **Cameron Reservoir**, brown trout; stocked by St Andrews AC (trout av 1¼lb). Fly only. Sunday fishing. Boat and bank fishing. Boat hire (3 rods per boat) £30 per session. Bank permit £10 per session. Permits sold at reservoir. Newton Farm, Wormit, 8m from St Andrews, bank only, rainbows. Permits on site. Tackle shop: J Wilson & Son, 169–171 South St,

St Andrews KY16 9EE (Tel: 01334 72477).

Cupar (Fife). Clatto and Stratheden AA has brown trout fishing on **Clatto Reservoir**; morning and afternoon £8, evening £10, 4 fish limit; one boat, £4; from Waterman's Cottage at reservoir (Tel: 01334 652595).

Ladybank (Fife). Fine dry-fly fishing; trout. Some free, but mostly preserved. **Lindores Loch**, 3m from **Newburgh**, holds brown and rainbow trout; fly only; no bank fishing (Tel: 01337 810488). Permits from A G Mitchell, 28 Main St, Cupar, Fife KY15 5SQ.

ESK (North)

Formed by junction of Lee and Mark, near Loch Lee, and flows for nearly 30m to North Sea near Montrose. Good river for salmon and sea trout.

Montrose (Angus). Salmon, sea trout, finnock (whitling) and brown trout. Joseph Johnston & Sons Ltd, 3 America Street, Montrose DD10 8DR (Tel: 01674 672666) issue permits for salmon fishing on the Canterland beat, 5 rods, charges from £25 to £55, according to time of year. Spring and autumn best fishing. North Esk tickets from Post Office, Marykirk. Gallery fishing now owned by Garrochy Estate (Tel: 01356 650280). For Mill of Criggie Trout Fishery, St Cyrus, nr Montrose, rainbows and browns, open all year, contact Kevin and Helen Ramshore (Tel: 01674 850868). Limited disabled access, tuition, tackle, snacks on site. Montrose AC fishes Craigo beat of North Esk and Bridge of Dun beat of **South Esk**. Permits from £10–£18 on S Esk, £25–£45 on N Esk, from tackle shop: Cobsport, 7 Castle Place DD10 8AL (Tel: 01674 673095). Hotels: Carlton, George, Hillside, Marykirk.

Edzell (Angus). Salmon and sea trout. Dalhousie Estates, Brechin DD9 6SG, has boats to hire for trout fishing on **Loch Lee** in Glen Esk; no bank fishing, and fly only. Permits from Mrs Taylor, Kirktown of Invermark, Glenesk, by Brechin (Tel: 01356 670208); also salmon beats to let by the week on North Esk at Edzell, dt when no weekly lets; 2 beats at Millden, 4 and 3 rods, salmon and sea trout; mill dam at Edzell stocked with browns, fishable on day permit; details from Dalhousie Estates. Panmure Arms Hotel has 1m of fishing on **West Water** (trout, sea trout and occasional salmon); and can arrange fishing on North Esk and Loch Lee.

Hotels: Glenesk and Central. Self-catering cottages through Dalhousie Estates Office.

ESK (South)

Rises in Glen Clova and flows some 49m to North Sea near Montrose. Good salmon river with plentiful runs of sea trout. Best months for salmon are February, March and April. Good autumn river (mid-September onwards), sea trout May–July.

Brechin (Angus). Good centre for North and South Esk. Salmon and sea trout; fishing good, but mostly reserved. South Esk Estates Office, Brechin, let beats on 2½m, usually by the week or longer periods, but very limited. Sporting Scotland, Parklea, Park Rd, Brechin DD9 7AP (Tel: 01356 625436), offers 3 and 5 day fishing breaks in Grampian and Tayside, with accom, transport, ghillie, permits and equipment included in prices. Brechin AC has fishing on Matrix Beat of South Esk; **Loch Saugh** near Fettercairn, brown trout, fly only; and **River West Water**, brown trout, salmon and sea trout. Permits for **L Saugh** from Drumtochty Arms Hotel, Auchenblae; and Ramsay Arms Hotel, Fettercairn. Robertson's Newsagents, Swan St, Brechin, issue limited dt and wt for West Water.

Kirriemuir (Angus). Kirriemuir AC has approx 7m on South Esk. Salmon, sea trout, a few brown trout. Permits from Hon Sec (Tel: 01575 73456). Some fly only water, but much of it unrestricted. Concessions to jun. No Sunday fishing and no permits on Saturdays. Strathmore AIA has rights on lower **Isla** and **Dean,** both near **Blairgowrie**; st £8.50, dt £2, conc, from tackle shops in Dundee, Blairgowrie and Forfar.

EWE

This river has good runs of salmon (best May onwards) and sea trout (end June onwards) up to Loch Maree. Fishing again excellent, after problems caused by disease. Owned by Inveran Estate.

Aultbea (Ross-shire). Bank fishing for wild brown trout on **Aultbea Hill Lochs**. Permits from Bridgend Stores, Aultbea, Achnasheen, Ross-shire IV22 2JA (Tel: 01445 731204); Aultbea Lodges, Drumchork, Aultbea; Post Office, Laide. Bridgend Stores, as well as issuing permits, has a comprehensive range of tackle.

Hotels: Aultbea; Drumchork Lodge; Sand (Tel: 01445 731385).

Poolewe (Ross-shire). Salmon, sea trout, brown trout. The National Trust for Scotland, Inverewe Estate, Visitors' Centre (Tel: 01445 781299) offers trout fishing on several lochs: **Kernsary, Tournaig, Na Dailthean** and **A'bhaid**, Luachraigh, either by part ownership, or on behalf of owners. Dt £4.50, boat £3. No Sunday fishing. Reduction for members. Self-catering accom at Waterside of Poolewe IV22 2JX (Tel: 0870 7474 784).

LOCH MAREE (Ross & Cromarty). Spring salmon fishing from April until June. Sea trout from June until Oct. Also brown trout fishing.

Talladale (Ross-shire). Salmon, sea trout, brown trout. Loch Maree Hotel has fishing. Heavy demand for sea-trout season so early booking advised. Hotel owned by anglers' syndicate which provides excellent facilities. Boat fishing only. Apply to Loch Maree Hotel, Talladale, By Achnasheen, Wester Ross IV22 2HL. Gairloch Angling Club has brown trout fishing in many hill lochs, including **Bad na Scalaig, Tolliadh, Garbhaig**. Pike in Lochs Bad an Scalaig, Dubh and Fuar, salmon fishing in **R Kerry** (book at Creag Mor Hotel). Membership closed but permits £2–£12 from K Gunn, Strath Square, Gairloch.

Kinlochewe (Ross-shire). Salmon and sea trout fishing on loch. Boats for hire. Permits from Kinlochewe Hotel (Tel: 01445 760253) and Kinlochewe Holiday Chalets (Tel: 0144584 234). Brown trout, char and sea trout fishing on **Loch Bharranch**; and brown trout, pike and perch fishing on **Loch a'Chroisg**. Permits from Glendocherty Craft Shop.

Achnasheen (Ross-shire). Nr A832, **Loch a' Chroisg**, brown trout, pike, perch; permits from Ledgowan Lodge Hotel, Achnasheen, Ross-shire IV22 2EJ (Tel: 01445 720252).

FINDHORN

Rises in Monadhliath Mountains and flows over 60m to Moray Firth. Salmon, sea trout and brown trout. Good spate river with many rock pools, fishing begins mid- to late April. Best months: May/June and August/Sept. Grilse from summer to end of season. Recent native hardwood regeneration schemes along substantial lengths of the river have enhanced the quality of the spawning beds; and helped to limit erosion previously caused by livestock.

Drynachan (Nairnshire). Cawdor Estate has fly only salmon fishing on Findhorn, 4 beats with 2 rods per beat; and trout fishing on **Loch of Boath** (brown). Excellent accommodation is bookable on Estate at Drynachan Lodge. Contact the Factor, Cawdor Estate Office, Cawdor, Nairn IV12 5RE (Tel: 01667 404666, Fax: 01667 404787). Good trout fishing on nearby lochs; **Loch of Blairs**, **Loch Lochindorb**. Tickets for 7m stretch of **R Nairn** with sea trout and salmon, from tackle shop: Pat Fraser, 41 High St, Nairn. Permits for Lochindorb direct from keeper.

Forres (Moray). Broom of Moy beat, 1½m double bank, with salmon and sea trout. Fly only. Permits from The Tackle Shop, 188 High St, Elgin (Tel: 01343 543129). Permits for **Loch of Blairs**, from Ian Grant, Tackle Shop, High St, Forres.

Tomatin (Inverness-shire). 14 miles south of Inverness on A9 road, three beats of right bank, one on left, for two and three rods, with holding pools and many streams and runs; ghillie service; permits £45 per rod day, ghillie £35. Contact Mr A J Bell, Balemenoch, Hazelbank, Tomatin IV13 7YN (Tel: 01808 511439). 2m east of **Nairn** on A96 road, Boath House; rainbow trout fishing on lake, telephone bookings (01667 454896/455808). Dt £10–£18.

FLEET (Kirkcudbrightshire)

Formed by junction of Big and Little Water, empties into the Solway Firth at Gatehouse. Good sea trout and herling, and few grilse and salmon; best months July and August.

Gatehouse-of-Fleet (Dumfries and Galloway). Murray Arms Hotel, Gatehouse-of-Fleet DG7 2HY (Tel: 01557 814207) issue permits for Rusko and Cally Estate waters on River Fleet. Sea trout and herling with some grilse and salmon. No Sunday fishing. Gatehouse and Kirkcudbright AA has **Loch Whinyeon**, 120 acres, 3½m from town, brown trout, stocked and wild; fly only. Two boats; bank or boat fishing. Assn also controls **Loch Lochenbreck**, 40 acres, 3m from Lauriston, rainbow and brown trout. Fly only. Bank or boat fishing. Permits £10, boats £3, from Watson McKinnel, 15 St Cuthbert St, Kirkcudbright. Hotels: Angel; Selkirk Arms, Kirkcudbright.

FORTH (including Loch Leven and Water of Leith)

Formed from junction of Avendhu and Duchray not far from Aberfoyle, and thence flows about 80m to its firth at Alloa, opening into North Sea. Principal tributaries, Teith and Allan, flow above Stirling. A large salmon river, which at times, and especially on upper reaches, provides some good sport. Good run in lower reaches during February and March, as a rule. This river and Teith, Balvaig, Leny Water and Allan Water being extensively restocked with salmon and sea trout by Forth District Salmon Fishery Board. Trouting in upper reaches and tributaries, particularly in lochs, where salmon also taken.

Dunfermline (Fife). **Loch Fitty**, excellent brown and rainbow trout water, also steelheads. Bank and boat fishing, 30 boats, tackle shop and coffee shop to which visitors are welcome. Boats, including o/b, for 3 anglers, day (10am–5pm) £33; evening (5.30pm–dusk) £10 per angler with reductions during Apr, Aug, Sept; bank permits £15 per session; boats for single anglers, £16; "father and son/daughter", £18; OAP, (Tues and Thurs) £20–£23. Apply to Fife Angling Centre, The Lodge, Kingseat, by Dunfermline, Fife KY12 0TJ (01383 620666). Halfway House Hotel by Loch Fitty welcomes anglers and can arrange fishing for guests. Apply to Douglas Fleming, Halfway House Hotel, Main St Kingseat, by Dunfermline KY12 0TJ (Tel: 01383 731661). Further accom from Mrs E Fotheringhan, Bowleys Farmhouse (Tel: 01383 721506). Permits for **River Devon**, trout, £3 from D W Black, The Hobby and Model Shop, 10–12 New Row, Tel: 01383 722582. Other tackle shop: Aladdin's Cave, 259 High St, Leslie. Hotels: Abbey Park House, Auld Toll Tavern, King Malcolm Thistle. B & B, Loch Fitty Cottage, Tel: 01383 831081.

Stirling (Stirlingshire). Forth, **Allan** and **Teith** may be fished from here. Herling in Forth in spring and autumn. Salmon fishing from Lands of Hood to mouth of Teith (7½m) including Cruive Dykes is controlled by District Council. Good run in lower reaches, March and Aug–Sept. **North Third Trout Fishery**, Greathill, Cambusbarron, FK7 9QS (Tel: 01786 471967): rainbow and brown trout (record rainbow, 19lb 2oz; brown, 9lb 14oz); fly only; 23 boats and bank fishing, tuition by appointment. Permits and season tickets from fishery. Tackle shop: J

Henderson, Country Pursuits, Henderson St, Bridge of Allan (Tel: 01786 834495).

Aberfoyle (Perthshire). Brown trout. Aberfoyle APA has brown trout fishing on **Loch Ard**; fly only; stocked with young brown trout. Dt £3. Boats for hire; £15 per day. Apply to The Farm Shop, Kinlochard, by Aberfoyle (Tel: 01877 387284). Free fishing on Loch Ard for guests at Altskeith Hotel, Kinlochard by Aberfoyle Stirling FK8 3TL (Tel: 01877 387266). Brown trout fishing on **Loch Arklet, Loch Katrine** and **Glen Finglas**; permits now issued by Trossachs Fishings, Loch Vennacher, by Callander. Forest Enterprise controls fishing for brown trout, pike and perch on River Forth and **Loch Chon**, brown trout on **Loch Drunkie**, and **Lochan Reoidhte**, and salmon, sea trout and brown trout on **Loch Lubnaig**. Bank fishing only. Permits from £5.50 to £3 from Queen Elizabeth Forest Park Visitor Centre, Aberfoyle (Tel: 01877 382258) (open Easter to Oct). Access to Loch Drunkie via Forest Drive; no vehicle access after Oct. **Lake of Menteith** has brown and rainbow trout, largest b 5lb, r 12lb, 1,000 stocked weekly. Fly only, boat and facilities for disabled. Permits from Lake Menteith Fisheries Ltd, Port of Menteith, Stirling (Tel: 01877 385 664). Tackle shops: James Bayne, 76 Main St, Callander. Hotel: Inverard.

Tributaries of Forth

LEVEN: Flows from Loch Leven to Firth of Forth at Leven, Fife. Good sea trout runs from Jul–Oct. Any legal method (on shrimp or prawn). Tickets £5 day, £20 week, from Swan Pond Pet Shop, Leven, Gift shop, Station Rd, Windygates. Bank fishing for brown trout at **Upper Carriston Reservoir**, Star, **Markinch**; fly only, dt £9, 4 fish limit.

ALMOND: West of Edinburgh the river flows into the Firth of Forth at Cramond.

Cramond (West Lothian). Cramond AC has fishing leases on most of River Almond and tributaries. Salmon, sea trout and brown trout. Permits from Post Office, Cramond.

Livingston (West Lothian). River Almond AA has ½m of Almond with salmon and sea trout, and 2m with brown trout. Permits from Hon Sec; Livingston Sports, Almondvale Centre; Country Life, Balgreen Rd, Edinburgh. **Crosswood Reservoir**, closed in 1999. For

further information, contact East of Scotland Water, Fishing Desk, 55 Blackstone Terrace, Edinburgh EH10 6XH (Tel: 0131 4456462). **Morton Fishery**, brown and rainbow trout; fly only; bag limits 3–6 fish. Advanced bookings. Permits from Morton Fishery, Morton Reservoir, Mid Calder, West Lothian.

NORTH ESK and **SOUTH ESK**: These two rivers are fed by Lothian regional reservoirs and join near Dalkeith to form the River Esk. The Esk flows a short way down to enter the Firth of Forth at Musselburgh. Simpsons of Edinburgh offer salmon fishing on the North Esk Burn beat. Cost is between £40 per rod day, spring, and £810 per three rod week, autumn. Bookable cottage sleeps six. Contact Simpsons, 28/30 West Preston St, Edinburgh EH8 9PZ (Tel: 0131 667 3058, Fax: 0131 662 0642).

Musselburgh (East Lothian). Musselburgh and District AA has salmon, sea trout and brown trout fishing on Esk, from estuary, 2m upstream of Musselburgh; permits from Musselburgh Pet Centre, 81 High St; Mike's Tackle, 41 High St, Portobello. No Sunday fishing.

Penicuik (Midlothian). Esk Valley AIA has rainbow and brown trout fishing on North and South Esk; fly rod and reel only to be used. Permits from Hon Sec. **Glencorse** and **Gladhouse Reservoirs**. Brown and rainbow trout; fly only; boat only. Contact East of Scotland Water, Fishing Desk, 55 Blackstone Terrace, Edinburgh EH10 6XH (Tel: 0131 4456462). **Rosebery Reservoir**; 52 acres; brown and rainbow trout, pike, perch.

West Linton (Peeblesshire). Brown trout fishing on **West Water Reservoir**; 93 acres; fly only. 2 boats. No bank fishing. Permits from Slipperfield Estate, c/o Romano Inn, Romano Bridge, Peeblesshire (Tel: 01968 60781).

DEVON: Fair brown trout stream; sea trout and salmon lower down.

Alloa (Clackmannanshire). Devon AA has salmon, sea trout and brown trout fishing on 9 beats of Devon, from Glendevon to Devonside. Assn also has brown trout fishing on **Glenquey Reservoir**, near Muckhart; fly only on all waters to mid–April, no spinning; bank fishing only. Sunday fishing permitted on reservoir, prohibited on river. Season tickets for sea trout and salmon are only obtainable from Hon Sec (postal application only). Permits for brown trout fishing from Hobby & Model Shop, 10 New Row, Dunfermline; McCutcheons Newsagents, Bridge St, Dollar (Tel: 01259 742517); and Marco Palmieri, The Inn, Crook of Devon KY13 7UR; Muckhart PO; and Mrs Small, Riverside Caravan Park, Dollar, FK14 7LX (Tel: 01259 742896). 6m west of **Kinross**, Glensherrup Trout Fishery, Frandy Farm, Glendevon FK14 7AJ (Tel: 01259 781631) has fly only, rainbow and brown trout, stocked regularly, fish to 15lb 12 oz; boat and bank fishing, dt from £12.36.

Gartmorn Dam Fishery, stocked rainbow trout, plentiful browns also, fly and spinning, artificials only; bank and boat fishing, 9 boats and wheelyboat for disabled. Permits (from st £90 to boat dt £28.50, bank dt £6, conc,) from Gartmorn Dam Country Park, by Sauchie (Alloa 214319); and Clackmannan District Council, Leisure Services Dept (Tel: Alloa 213131). Fife Regional Council control **Upper** and **Lower Glendevon Reservoirs**, and **Castlehill Reservoir**; rainbow trout, some browns; fly only. No Sunday fishing on **Glendevon Reservoirs**. Permits from Fife Regional Council, Craig Mitchell House, Flemington Rd, Glenrothes; and from The Boathouse, Castlehill Reservoir, Muckhart. Fife Regional Council also lease out a number of reservoirs to local clubs; **Cameron Reservoir** to St Andrews AC; **Craigluscar Reservoirs** to Dunfermline Artisan AC, rainbow trout dt £11 for 5 fish, conc, from bailiff's hut; **Glenquey Reservoir** to Devon AA; **Lochmill Reservoir** to Newburgh AC; **Upper Carriston Reservoir** to Methilhaven & District AC (Tel: 01592 713008). **Stenhouse Reservoir**, 35 acres, run by John Low, Dunearn Farm, Burntisland Fife KY3 0AH (Tel: 01582 872267); fly fishing only, regularly stocked with brown trout; dt at loch, access for disabled. Hotels: Castle Campbell, Dollar; Castle Craig, Tillicoultry; Tormaukin, Glendevon.

Gleneagles (Perthshire). The Gleneagles Hotel, Auchterarder PH3 1NF, has access to Lower Scone and Almondmouth beats on **River Tay**; salmon, grilse and sea trout. Trout fishing on **Fordoun Loch**; and also on **Laich Loch**, in hotel grounds. Trout fishing costs £45, salmon £80–£600, including ghillie and tackle hire. Should venues be fully booked hotel will arrange alternative fishing on **River Tay** at **Upper Kinnaird**. Apply to The Club at Gleneagles, Gleneagles Hotel, Perthshire PH3 1NF (Tel: 01764 694331, Fax: 662134).

AVON: Flows 18m to estuary of Forth near Grangemouth. Lower estuary reaches polluted; good brown trout elsewhere (av ½lb with few around 4lb). River fishes best in late June, July and Aug.

Linlithgow (West Lothian). Linlithgow AC (Tel: 01506 847913) has 5m stretch of Avon north of Muiravonside Country Park, with trout, pike, perch, carp, roach. Permits obtainable. Avon Bridge AA offer excellent value season tickets on a lengthy stretch in Avonbridge area. Access to river regulated through R Avon Federation, which holds migratory fishing rights. Membership is available to members of the local fishing clubs. Muiravonside Country Park, The Loan, by Whitecross (Tel: 01506 845311): brown trout and coarse tickets, £3, conc. **Union Canal** from Edinburgh to Falkirk: pike, perch, roach, carp, eel, bream, mirror and leather carp, and tench; no close season. St £5.88 from British Waterways, Canal House, 1 Applecross Street, Glasgow G4 9SP, Tel: 0141 332 6936.

CARRON:
Larbert (West Lothian). Larbert & Stenhousemuir AC issue permits for **Loch Coulter**, near Carronbridge; brown and rainbow trout. Fly only. No Sunday fishing. Outlets: Scrimgeour Fishing Tackle, 28 Newmarket St, Falkirk (Tel: 01324 24581); Paton's Newsagent, Larbert.

Denny (Stirlings). East of Scotland Water controls **Carron Valley Reservoir**, together with 16 other trout fisheries in various localities. No bank fishing at Carron Valley, 16 boats, wild brown trout fishing, fly only. On the day booking: contact East of Scotland Water, Fishing Desk, 55 Blackstone Terrace, Edinburgh EH10 6XH (Tel: 0131 4456462). **Drumbowie Reservoir**, fly only brown trout permits from Bonnybridge AC (Tel: 01324 813136), £5, visitors accompanied by member, st £25.

TEITH: Noted salmon and brown trout fishery, with good sea trout in summer.

Callander (Perthshire). Stirling Council controls part of Teith, with excellent salmon, sea trout, and brown trout (average ¾lb). Fishing open to visitors; st £105, dt £25. Conc for residents, OAP & jun, from Baynes Fishing Tackle (below). **Loch Venachar** controlled by L Ven Assn; mainly brown trout, but some sea trout and salmon; trout average 1lb; fishing from bank permitted on parts of loch; mapped details from Baynes, with prices; boats for hire. Permits also for **River Leny**, 1m from town, salmon, fly and spinning; **River Balvaig**, 10m north, trout fishing, any method; **Loch Lubnaig**, 2m north, trout, perch, char, £4 dt, £2 juv; and Loch Venachar, from James Bayne (*below*). **Loch Drunkie** (brown trout) and **Lochan Reoidhte** (brown trout, fly only); permits £3–£5 from Queen Elizabeth Forest Park Visitors' Centre, Aberfoyle, and James Bayne, Fishing Tackle, 76 Main St FK17 8BD (01877 330218).

BALVAIG and **CALAIR** (Tributaries of Teith): salmon and brown trout.

Balquhidder (Perthshire). Salmon and brown trout fishing on **R Balvaig**, **Loch Voil** and **Loch Doine**; from Kings House Hotel, Balquhidder, Perthshire FK19 8NY (Tel: 01877 384646). Boat hire and ghillie can be arranged. Dt £3 for Loch Voil trout fishing also from Baynes Fishing Tackle (see *Callander*). Mrs Catriona Oldham, Muirlaggan, Balquhidder FK19 8PB (Tel: 01877 384219) has fishing dt £2.50, or st £15 on Loch Voil and Loch Doine, brown trout, boats for hire. 2 self-catering cottages on site, with free fishing on L Voil. Rod and tackle hire, and tuition from Craigruie Sporting Estate, Balquhidder, Perthshire FK19 8PQ (Tel: 01877 384262).

Strathyre (Perthshire). Salmon and brown trout fishing from Munro Hotel: Season 1 Feb–1 Oct. No boats.

LOCH LEVEN

Famous Kinross-shire loch which produces quick-growing trout. Loch is nowhere deep so feed is good, and practically whole area is fishing water. Under efficient management, this has become one of the most notable trout fishing lochs of Scotland.

Kinross (Kinross-shire). Loch Leven Fisheries is a predominantly brown trout loch which boasts the famous Loch Leven trout. These average over 1lb pound with many specimen of 3–4lb being taken. It is also stocked each year with high quality rainbow trout. Fly fishing by boat only. The pier is ¼m out of Kinross. Boats are bookable by letter or phone. For full information on charges and booking conditions, apply to The Pier, Kinross, Tayside KY13 8UF (Tel: 01577 863407). Tackle can be bought at the pier.

Heatheryford Fishery: top quality trout fishing on **Heatheryford**, and 10 acre spring fed water, with brown and rainbow trout; bank fishing only, access for disabled. Permits from office on site, Kinross KY13 0NQ (Tel: 01592 414312).

Ballingry (Fife). Rainbow and brown trout fishing on **Loch Ore**; 260 acre loch, with bank and boat fishing, regularly stocked, access for disabled. Permits from Lochore Meadows Country Park, Crosshill, Balligry, Fife KY5 8BA (Tel: 01592 414312).

Glenrothes (Fife). Permits may be had from East of Scotland Water, Graig Mitchell House, Flemington Rd, Glenrothes (Tel: 01592 614000) for reservoir trout fishing on **Holl**, **Castlehill**, and **Glenfarg Reservoirs**.

WATER OF LEITH

Local people who know river well get fair numbers of trout.

Edinburgh (Mid Lothian). Water of Leith, running through the city, is stocked annually with brown trout. Permits issued free of charge. Trout fishing at **Gladhouse**, **Glencorse**, **Clubbiedean**, **Crosswood**, and **West Water Reservoirs**. Contact East of Scotland Water, Fishing Desk, 55 Blackstone Terrace, Edinburgh EH10 6XH (Tel: 0131 4456462). Bank permits for **Harperrig** from ticket machine on site. **Rosebery Reservoir**, brown and rainbow trout, pike, perch; permits from Mrs Grant, Keeper's Cottage (Tel: 01875 830353). **Talla** and **Fruid Reservoirs**, brown trout; permits from Crook Inn, Tweedsmuir, Biggar, Lanarkshire ML12 6QN (Tel: 0189 880272). Permits for **Whiteadder Reservoir** and for **Hopes Reservoir** from Goblin Ha' Hotel, Gifford (Tel: 01620 810244). Coarse fishing on **Duddingston Loch**; carp and perch. Loch situated in a bird sanctuary, therefore a restricted area. Bank fishing by permit only, no charge. No lead weights. No close season. Permits from Holyrood Park Visitor Centre, Holyrood Lodge, Edinburgh EH8 8AZ (Tel: 0131 556 1761). **Union Canal** from Edinburgh to Falkirk; pike, perch, roach, carp and tench; no close season. Permits from British Waterways (see *Linlithgow*). Tackle shops: John Dickson & Son, 21 Frederick Street; Shooting Lines Ltd, 18 Hope Park Terrace and 23 Roseburn Terrace; F & D Simpson, 28/30 West Preston Street; Countrylife, 299 Balgreen Rd; Mike's Tackle Shop, 48 Portobello High St. **Balerno** (Edinburgh). Trout fishing on Water of Leith; permits from Balerno PO, 36 Main St; and Colinton PO. Brown and rainbow trout fishing on **Threipmuir** and **Harlaw Reservoirs**. Fly fishing only. Bank fishing only. Season tickets are balloted for; contact The Factor, Dalmeny Estate Office, Dalmeny Estate, South Queensferry, West Lothian EH3O 9TQ (Tel: 0131 331 4804). Day tickets from Flemings Grocery Shop, 42 Main Street, Balerno (Tel: 0131 449 3833). Concessions for OAP and jun. **Harperrig Reservoir**, 237 acres; brown trout. Fly only, bank fishing. Permits from machine at reservoir (coins required).

GIRVAN

Drains small loch called Girvan Eye and thence runs 25 miles to the Atlantic at Girvan. Good salmon and sea trout; fair brown trout. Salmon run March onwards; sea trout from June.

Girvan (Ayrshire). Salmon, sea trout, brown trout. Carrick AC issues permits, from Gilmour, Knockushan St, Girvan KA26 9AG (Tel: 01465 712122). **Penwhapple Reservoir**, near Barr, stocked with brown trout; Penwhapple AC water. Fly only. Dt £10 and evenings £8, boats £5, Sundays members only; apply Mrs Stewart, Lane Farm, Barr (½m beyond reservoir). Hotel: Ailsa Craig.

Kirkmichael (Ayrshire). Salmon and trout fishing on 3m stretch, limited rods; accommodation in Scottish baronial house in 50 acres of ground. Also lake fishing in small private loch, stocked with brown ad rainbow trout. Contact M L Hambly, Kirkmichael House, Maybole KA19 7PR (Tel: 01655 750212).

Straiton (Ayrshire). Salmon (late), sea trout, brown trout. Blairquhan Estate water, fly only. Permits from D Galbraith, The Kennels, Blairquhan Estate, Straiton. Forestry Commission controls fishing in Galloway Forest Park, with brown trout fishing · on **Lochs Bradan**, **Loch Dee**, **Black Loch**, and **Loch of the Lowes**; **Lilies Loch**, and **Dhu Loch**. Pike and perch fishing, with other coarse on **Linfern Loch**, **Spectacle**, **Garwachie**, **Eldrig**, and **Stroan**.

HALLADALE

Rises on north slope of Helmsdale watershed and empties into sea at Melvich Bay. Early salmon March onwards, 10–16lb. Grilse run from June, 5–7lb.

Melvich (Sutherland). Melvich Hotel, Melvich, By Thurso, Sutherland KW14 7YJ (Tel: 016413 206), 18m from Thurso, offers trout fishing on several lochs, one of which has a boat. Fly only. Dt £7.50 for bank fishing and £15 for boat fishing.

Forsinard (Sutherland. Forsinard Hotel has salmon fishing on River Halladale, 2½m stretch from Forsinain bridge to junction with River Dyke; and on **River Strathy**; both fly only. Hotel also has trout fishing on 6 lochs exclusively for guests and on 14 lochs open to non-residents. Apply to Forsinard Hotel, Forsinard KW13 6YT (Tel: 016417 221).

HELMSDALE RIVER

Formed by two headstreams near Kinbrace, this river flows 20m southeast through Strathullie to sea. Excellent salmon river, where there is now no netting.

Helmsdale (Sutherland). Salmon and sea trout. Salmon beat lettings from Roxton Bailey Robinson, Fishing Agents, 25 High St, Hungerford, Berks RG17 0NF (Tel: 01488 683222). Lower Helmsdale only: permits from Strathullie Crafts, Dunrobin St (Tel: 01431 821343). Information from J A Douglas Menzies, Mounteagle, Fearn, Ross-shire. Navidale House Hotel KW8 6JS, Tel: 01431 821 258, has limited salmon fishing on river from Jan–March, and arranges brown trout fishing on 6 lochs, fly only on all but one. Hotel has permits for Lower Helmsdale. Other hotels: Bridge: Belgrave Arms.

INVER (including Kirkaig and Loch Assynt)

Draining Loch Assynt, this river flows into a sea loch on the west coast of Sutherland known as Lochinver (village and loch having the same name), a little north of the old Ross-shire border. Holds salmon and sea trout but fishing is hard to come by.

Lochinver (Sutherland). Inver Lodge Hotel has salmon fishing on the River Inver, the upper beat of which is bookable. The hotel has further fishing on **River Kirkaig**, 3½m S of Lochinver and the upper Oykel, about 30m east of Lochinver. Hotel has first refusal of beats and brown trout lochs covering estate including **Loch Culag**, **Fionn Loch**, Loch Assynt, and numerous other hill lochs. Apply to Inver Lodge Hotel, Lochinver

IV27 4LU (Tel: 01571 844496). Assynt AC also has rights on Loch Assynt, and 10 boats are for hire, at £10 per day. The Assynt Crofters own the North Assynt Estate. Through the Trust, anglers may fish a large number of hill lochs, in a landscape of great natural beauty, including **Loch Poll**, the biggest, with boat obtainable from Old Drumbeg P O, **Loch Drumbeg**, (boats from Assynt Sporting Co (see below)), **Lochs Roe**, **Manse**, **Tuirk**, which can produce excellent sea trout runs, and many others. 10 boats are for hire, £10, and £5 permits may be bought at Stoer and Drumbeg Post Offices, and Lochinver Tourist Office. Inchnadamph Hotel (Tel: 01571 822202) has fishing on east end of **Loch Assynt**. Kylesku Hotel, Via Lairg IV27 4HW (Tel: 01971 502231) has fishing on a number of lochs in the Kylesku area. Assynt Sporting Co provide sporting holidays in this area, with guided wild brown trout fishing, tuition, boat and tackle hire, ghillie and accom. Contact Mr Millar, Schoolhouse, Drumbeg, nr Lochinvar, Sutherland IV27 4NW (Tel: 01571 833269).

Ledmore (Sutherland). The Alt Motel, 20m N of Ullapool, has brown trout and first rate Arctic char fishing on **Loch Borralan**. Boat £18 and bank £5 per day. Also, 12m of double bank salmon and sea trout fishing from Rosehall to Bonar Bridge on the Kyle of Sutherland at £18 per day; jetty for disabled. Bed and breakfast, and self-catering accommodation. Further information from Bruce and Alba Ward, The Alt Motel, The Altnacealgach, nr Ledmore Junction, By Lairg, Sutherland IV27 4HF (Tel: 01854 666220).

LOCH ASSYNT

Inchnadamph (Sutherland). Salmon fishing (fair) from June on upper end of Loch Assynt. Inchnadamph Hotel (Tel: 01571 822202) has fishing on loch, also celebrated **Gillaroo Loch** and **Loch Awe** (£6 per rod or £18 for boat which includes 2 rods, 8 boats for hire). Season: salmon from May 15 till Oct 15, trout, 15 Mar to 6 Oct.

IRVINE (including Annick)

Rises near Loudonhill and flows about 20m to Firth of Clyde at Irvine Town. Main tributaries are Cessnock Water, Kilmarnock Water and Annick. Fishing controlled largely by clubs. Salmon and sea trout July onwards; brown trout average ½lb; early season best.

Irvine (Ayrshire). Salmon, sea trout, trout; Irvine and Dist AA issues permits for 2m on Irvine and 3m Annick (no dt Saturdays). Irvine Water runs from estuary to Red Bridge, Dreghorn, on north bank and to Bogie Bridge on south bank. Annick Water is from confluence with Irvine to Perleton Bridge, both banks.

Dreghorn (Ayrshire). Salmon, sea trout, trout; Dreghorn AC issues st, wt and dt for 12m water on both banks of Irvine and Annick; obtainable from N Galloway, 13 Marble Ave, Dreghorn, or Alyson's Flowers, 10 Bank St, Irvine. July to Sept best for salmon and sea trout. Brown trout average ½lb.

Kilmarnock (Ayrshire). Salmon, sea trout, trout. Permits for stretches on Irvine at Hurlford and Crookedholm from P & R Torbet, 15 Strand St. Alexander Baird, 2 Avon Place, Kilmarnock KA1 3PW (Tel: 01563 530808) offers salmon and trout fishing with tuition and guiding on R Doon.

GARNOCK: Trout, sea trout, salmon. Joins Irvine at harbour mouth. Its tributary is **River Lugton**.

Kilwinning (Ayrshire). Garnock and Irvine join in tidal water and have common mouth. Salmon, sea trout, brown trout. Kilwinning Eglinton AC has 9m on Garnock and **River Lugton**. No Saturday or Sunday fishing. Permits from Craft Shop, 42 Main St.

Kilbirnie (Ayrshire). Kilbirnie AC has water on river Garnock **Kilbirnie Loch** (brown and rainbow trout) and two reservoirs. Yearly stocking of brown trout; monthly stocking of rainbow trout. Kilbirnie Loch best trout: brown 9lb 2oz. Kilbirnie Loch, any legal method. St £15; wt £7, dt £5. Club has excellent brown trout fishing on **Camphill Reservoir**; fly and boat only. Season holders £5 per boat per day and non-holders £12 per boat per day. Permits from Hon Sec; R T Cycles, Glengarnock, Beith KA14 3AA (Tel: 01505 682191); and Glengarnock PO. Tackle from R T Cycles. For other trout fisheries in vicinity, see Greenock.

ANNICK: Brown trout; small runs of salmon and sea trout Sept–Oct.

Irvine (Ayrshire). Dreghorn AC issues permits for 12m of water on Irvine and Annick. Permits from Ticket Sec, N Galloway, 13 Marble Ave, Dreghorn.

Kilmaurs (Ayrshire). Kilmaurs AC has fishing on Annick and **Glazert**; sea trout and brown trout, with salmon in autumn. Other fishing: North Craig Reservoir, Kilmaurs: Burnfoot Reservoir, Kilmaurs; Loch Gow, Eaglesham. Permits £6, conc, from Spar supermarket, Kilmaurs. St £25 (membership £20) from J Graham, 99 East Park Drive, Kilmaurs.

Stewarton (Ayrshire). Stewarton AC has water on Annick and tributaries, and **White Loch**; permits from Hon Sec and John Gordon, 6 Main Street KA3 5AE, Tel: 01560 482007.

THE ISLANDS

The term "The Islands" includes the Inner and Outer Hebrides, the Orkney and Shetland Islands and, for convenience, Kintyre.

ARRAN: In the rivers, brown trout are generally small, although fish up to 1lb have been recorded. In Aug, Sept and Oct there is often a good run of sea trout, especially in post-spate conditions, along with good salmon catches, particularly in **Sliddery**, **Kilmory**, **Sannox** and **Cloy**. **Benlister** and **Monamore** are also worth fishing under spate conditions. The Tourist Office at Brodick pier provides a free information sheet detailing all the main freshwater fishing opportunities on Arran, with charges. It also issues day and 6-day permits for various Arran AA waters. These include Kilmory (from above the bridge at Lagg Hotel), Cloy, Benlister, Monamore, Sannox, **Ashdale**, Sliddery Water and **Loch Garbad** (stocked with sizable brown trout). There is no Sunday fishing on rivers.

Machrie. Machrie Fishings consistently record excellent sea trout and salmon returns. A fine spate river which has numerous named pools extending from the sea pool for approx 3 miles. Fly water, but worming area for 2 rods. Season, 6 Jun–15 Oct, 6 rods maximum (2 per beat); enquiries should be made to Mrs Margo Wilson, 10 Leysmill, by Arbroath, Angus DD11 4RR Tel/Fax: 01241 828755, 9am–5pm), or to the Water Bailiff, Riverside Cottage, Machrie 840241. No Sunday fishing.

Dougarie. The **Iorsa River** has two beats, the upper beat includes **Loch Iorsa** (with boat). A spate sea trout river, with occasional salmon. The lower beat stretches from Gorge Pool to sea. Catches in 1998 were 11 salmon, 52 sea trout. Fishing is fly only and let by the week, from £125 (June) to £140 (July–Aug), and £160 Sept–Oct). Enquiries should be directed to The Estate Office, Dougarie, Isle of Arran KA27 8EB (Tel: 01770 840259).

Blackwaterfoot. **Blackwater** offers good sea trout catches and also salmon under suitable conditions; permits are obtainable from the post office, Blackwaterfoot. Port-na-Lochan Fishery, Kilpatrick (Tel: 01770 860444) has two small lochans of 3½ and 2 acres, with good quality rainbow trout fishing, one fly, one bait. 4 hours (2 fish limit), £10.50. Tickets and tackle at fishery, G & M Bannatyre, Lochside, Blackwaterfoot KA27 8EY.

Brodick. The **Rosaburn** is now let to a local syndicate. Brodick Boat Hire, The Beach, (Tel: 01770 302868): boats with tackle and baits supplied, for fishing in Brodick Bay area.

BENBECULA: Lies between N and S Uist. Numerous lochs, giving good sea and brown trout fishing.

Balivanich. South Uist AC has brown trout fishing on many lochs in South Uist and Benbecula. Bank and boat fishing. Permits from Colin Campbell Sports. Creagorry Hotel, Creagorry, Tel: 01870 602024, has fishing for guests on 15 lochs and 3 sea pools; boats on some waters; waders useful; trout to 1lb; all within five miles of hotel. June–Sept best for brown trout and August–Sept for sea trout. Sea trout up to 8lb in sea pools.

BUTE: 5m from Ayrshire coast; 16m long and 3–5m wide. Trout and coarse fish.

Rothesay. Loch Ascog, 1½m pike, perch and roach. **Loch Quien**, 5m first-class trout fly fishing (fish averaging 1lb). Fishes best early and late in season for brown trout. Applications to Mr Cain, The Tackle Shop, Deanhood Place (Tel: 01700 502346). **Loch Fad**, 175 acres, rainbow and brown trout fishing. Boat and bank fishing. 30 boats; booking advisable. Permits from bailiff's hut at Loch (Tel: 01700 504871). All information from Loch Fad Fisheries Ltd, Loch Fad, Isle of Bute PA20 9PA (Tel: 01700 504871). Hotel: Palmyra (Tel: 01700 502929), Ardbeg Lodge 505448, Port Royal, 505073. B & B: Commodore 502178, Tigh-na-Camus 502782, Vanetzia 502203. B & B on shore of L Fad regularly accommodates anglers: A Walters, Woodend House PA20 0PZ. Sea fishing: from rocky shore popular and good; by boat from Rothesay pier.

Tighnabruaich. Kyles of Bute AC has fishing on **Loch Asgog**, brown and rainbow trout, fly only; on **Upper** and **Lower Powder Dams**, brown and rainbow trout, fly and bait only; and on **Tighnabruaich Reservoir**, brown trout. Permits £5, conc, from Kames Post Office, Spar supermarket, and Glendaruel Hotel. Hotels: Kames, Royal, Kyles of Bute.

COLONSAY: Island of 28 square miles, reached by car ferry from Oban. Colonsay Fly Fishing Association was been formed in 1989 with the aim of protecting the native Colonsay brown trout loch fishing, which includes **Lochs West Fada**, **Mid Fada**, **East Fada**, **Ina Sgoltaire** and **Turamin**. The season is from mid-March to Sept 30, fishing is fly only, but children under 12 may spin. catch limit is 4 fish, sized 8in or more. Permits cost £10 per day, boats £2 per half day, from Mrs McNeill, Machrins Farm, who also arranges Assn boat hire. Further information from CFFA, Alex Howard, Colonsay Estate Argyll PA61 7YU (Tel: 01951 200211), or from Isle of Colonsay Hotel, Argyll PA61 7YP (Tel: 01951 200316). Hotel supplies permits to guests.

CUMBRAE: Small islands lying between Bute and Ayr coast. Largs is nearest mainland town, and there is a 10-minute ferry crossing from Calmac.

Millport. Cumbrae AC has fly only, brown and rainbow trout fishing on two reservoirs, **Top Dam** and **Bottom Dam**. Juveniles must be accompanied by an adult and be over 12 years. Permits, £10 dt and £30 wt from McFarlane's Newsagents, 2 Glasgow St, or Ritz Cafe, Stuart St, Millport. Sea fishing good from shore or boats. Tackle shops: Mapes, Guildford St, Millport; Hasties, 109 Main St, Largs. Hotel: Royal George.

HARRIS: Southern part of the island of Lewis and Harris, comprising the two distinct areas of North and South Harris. Accessible by car ferry from Ullapool, Isle of Skye, and North Uist. Daily flights from Inverness and Glasgow to Stornoway. Most of the trout, salmon and sea trout fishing in North Harris belongs to the North Harris Estate and is centred around Amhuinnsuidhe Castle, which is let along with the fishing on a weekly basis. There are six river systems with lochs, which all contain salmon and sea trout. Enquiries to the Estate Office, Lochmaddy, North Uist, HS6 4AA (Tel: 01876 500329, Fax 500428). For dt £70, incl boat, on

Saturdays and unlet weeks, contact Roddy Macleod, Head Keeper, Amhuinnsuidhe (Tel: 01859 560232).

South Harris, Good fishing for salmon and sea trout; brown trout lochs and lochans. Near Tarbert, salmon and brown trout fishing at Ceann an Ora Fishery, on **Lochs Sgeiregan Mor**, **A'Mhorghain** and **Na Ciste**. Fly and bank fishing only. Further information from The Anchorage, Ardhasaig, Isle of Harris HS3 3AJ (Tel: 01859 2009). Accommodation at Macleod Motel, HS3 3DG, Tel: 01859 502364, with waterfront location, and sea angling competitions arranged by Harris Sea AC. Borve Lodge, Scarista, 7m west of Tarbert, has fishing on sea trout lochs. Day tickets sometimes obtainable. Enquire Tony Scherr, Factor, Borve Lodge Estate Fisheries, Isle of Harris HS3 3HT (Tel: 01859 550202). Finsbay Fishing, 4 Ardslave, HS3 3EY (Tel: 01859 530318) has accommodation with over 100 lochs for salmon, land-locked salmon, sea trout and brown trout fly fishing, including **Lochs Humavat** and **Holmasaig**. For Finsbay, Flodabay and Stockinish Estates, contact A Mackinnon (Tel: 01859 530318): Interesting loch and stream fishing, bank and boat. For salmon and sea trout fishing on the Obbe Fishings at Leverburgh, contact David Rankin, Keeper, at Leverburgh (Tel: 01859 520466)

ISLAY: Most southern island of Inner Hebrides. Lies on west side of Sound of Islay, in Argyllshire. Greatest length is 25m and greatest breadth 19m. Sport with salmon, sea trout and trout. Hotel: Harris.

Bridgend. Salmon and sea trout fishing on **Rivers Sorn**, **Laggan** and **Grey River**; all within 2m of Bridgend; fly only. Brown trout fishing on **Lochs Gorm**, **Finlaggan**, **Skerrols** and **Ardnahoe**, with boats. Also trout fishing on numerous hill lochs without boats. Permits and self-catering accommodation from B Wiles, Headkeeper, Head Gamekeeper's House, Islay House Square, Bridgend, Isle of Islay, Argyll PA44 7NZ (Tel: 0149 681 293).

Port Askaig. Port Askaig Hotel has trout fishing nearby in **Lochs Lossit**, **Ballygrant** and **Allan**. Dt (boat) from Post Office. Sport on other lochs by arrangement. Salmon fishing in **River Laggan**. Best months: May, June and Sept.

Port Ellen. Machrie Hotel has salmon and sea trout fishing on **R Machrie**, and **Kinnabus**

Loch. Apply to Machrie Hotel, Port Ellen, Isle of Islay, Argyll PA42 7AN.

KINTYRE: This peninsula is part of Argyll and lies between Islay and Arran.

Campbeltown (Argyll). Kintyre AC has brown trout fishing on **Lochs Lussa, Ruan, Auchy Lochy, Crosshill**, and Southend River (small spate river, fishable Sept–Oct), fly only, brown trout in all lochs, av ½lb to 3½lb, steelhead to 10lb in Crosshill; permits from McGrory *below*. Carradale AC has fishing on **Tangy Loch**, 60 acres, trout to 2lb. Access road to waters edge. Permits from tackle shop. Sea fishing in harbour and **Firth of Clyde**. Permits from A P McGrory, Electrical Hardware, 16–20 Main Street (Tel: 01586 552132). Hotel: White Hart.

Carradale (Argyll). Excellent salmon and seatrout fishing may be had on **Carradale River**, a small spate river. Carradale Estate lease the water to Carradale AC. Bait and spinner under certain conditions, otherwise fly only. Club also has brown trout fishing on **Tangy Loch**, members only, and on river, permits offered, apply to J Semple, The Garage; Mr William Shaw, Westhill, Carradale (River Keeper); A P McGrory, Fishing Tackle, Main St, Campbeltown. Hotel: Argyll Arms.

Crinan (Argyll). Near west end of Crinan Canal, brown trout lochs controlled by Lochgilphead Dist AC. Canal (trout).

Lochgilphead (Mid Argyll). At east end of Crinan Canal, Forest Enterprise, White Gates, Lochgilphead PA31 8RS, has leased fishing on **Loch Coille Bhar, Cam Loch, Loch An Add, Daill Loch, Seafield Loch, Lochs Glashan, Blackmill** and **Bealach Ghearran** to Lochgilphead AC; brown trout, fly only. Club also leases bottom mile of Duntrune Castle water on R Add. On remaining 5m of Duntrune Castle water, six holiday cottages, from Kilmichael Bridge to tidal pools, fly only, mid-June–mid-Sept: normally, 2 or 3 day permits for non-residents, £15, £75 weekly. Also dt £3.50–£6 trout, £10 salmon, conc, from Fyne Tackle, 22 Argyll St, Lochgilphead PA31 8NE (Tel; 01546 606878). Holiday bookings from Robin Malcolm, Duntrune Castle, Kilmartin, by Lochgilphead, Argyll PA31 8QQ (Tel: 01546 510283). Permits from Andrew Malcolm (Tel: 01546 510283).

LEWIS: Some salmon and sea trout; almost unlimited amount of wild brown trout fishing on a large number of lochs and streams, much of which is free.

Stornoway. Permits for salmon and sea trout fishing in **River Creed** and **Lochs Clachan** and **An Ois**, approx 5m from town, cost £10–£12, £20–£22 with boat. For more details enquire of the Factor, Stornoway Trust Estate Office, Leverhulme House, Percival Square, Stornoway (Tel: 01851 702002). Stornoway AA is local association, with boats on **Lochs Breulagh** and **Thota Bridein**. Permits from Sportsworld, 1–3 Francis St (Tel: 01851 705464). Soval AA has brown trout fishing on several lochs within easy distance of Stornoway. Wt £5 if staying in Soval area and £10 if not, dt £2, from Hon Sec; and N Mackenzie, Treasurer, Tabhaigh, Keose, Lochs (Tel: 01851 830 242). **Loch Keose**, a beautiful 90 acre loch with plentiful wild brown trout. Permits and information brochure from Murdo Morrison, Handa Guest House, 18 Keose Glebe, Lochs, Isle of Lewis HS2 9JX (Tel: 01851 83334). Hotels: Caberfeidh, Caledonian. Tackle and waterproof clothing from Lewis Crofters Ltd, Island Rd, Tel: 01851 702350.

Garynahine. The Grimersta Estate Ltd owns fishing on **Grimersta River** and system of lochs. Mostly for guests and members of Stornoway AA, but occasional permits are obtainable, through Estate Office, Grimersta Lodge, Isle of Lewis HS2 9EJ (Tel: 01851 621358). The Garynahine Estate control all the fishing on the River Blackwater and its freshwater lochs. Salmon run from mid-June–mid- October, sea trout from early April. Accom at Garynahine Lodge for parties of up to 10. Contact C Buxton, Garynahine (Tel: 01233 811355).

Uig. Salmon, sea trout and brown trout fishing on Scaliscro Estate including **Langavat**. Bank and boat fishing. Permits, boat and tackle hire, and ghillies; apply to Estate Office, Scaliscro Lodge, Uig, Isle of Lewis HS2 9EL (Tel: 01851 672325). Uig and Hamanavay Estate, 10 Ardroil, Uig HS2 9EW (Tel: 01851 672421) offers extensive fly only salmon and sea trout fishing, with self-catering accom, on the **Hamanavay**, **Red River** and **Croistean** systems, also Lochs Cragach and Fuaroil. Estate also has brown trout fishing on over 100 lochs. Contact Estate Manager.

Kintarvie. The Aline Estate, on the march of Lewis and North Harris, has one salmon fishery, **Loch Tiorsdam**, plus 12 brown trout lochs and numerous lochans. Boat and bank fishing for both salmon and trout on **Loch Langavat** and trout lochs. Wild browns to 10lb have been caught in recent years, salmon are mostly grilse, Arctic char taken every year in Loch Langavat. Cottage and lodge to let. Boat and ghillie. Contact The Aline Estate, Lochs HS2 9JL (Tel: 01859 502006). Further fishing contacts on Lewis are: Barvas Estate, D Macdonald, Keeper, Tel: 01851 840267; Soval Estate, J Macleod, Keeper, Tel: 01851 830223; Mike Reed, 23 Gravir, South Lochs, Lewis HS2 9QX, Tel/Fax: 01851 880233.

MULL:

Tobermory. Salmon and sea trout fishing on **Rivers Aros** and **Bellart**. No Sunday fishing. Salmon, sea trout and brown trout fishing on **Loch Squabain**; boat fishing only. Fishing on **Torr Loch**, sea trout, wild browns; no Sunday fishing; 2 boats; banks clear. Bank fishing on **Loch Frisa**. Permits for all these, prices £3–£12 daily, £8–£36 weekly, depending on water and season, from Tackle & Books, 10 Main St (Tel: 01688 302336). Tobermory AA has fishing on **Mishnish Lochs**, well stocked, native brown trout only, 3 boats for hire on daily basis; and **Aros Loch**, open all year for rainbow. Dt £10 and wt £30. Boat hire (Tel: 01688 302020): £5 for 4 hrs and £12 all day. Permits from A Brown & Son, General Merchants, 21 Main Street PA75 6NX (Tel: 01688 302020). Fishing on **Loch Frisa**, good brown trout, some salmon and sea trout; and **River Lussa**. Apply to Forest Enterprise, Mull Office, Aros (Tel: 01680 300346). For fishing near **Salen** on **River Ba** contact (Killeiechronan Estates (01680 3004030); and on River Ba and **Loch Ba** (Tel: 01680 300356). List of hotels from Tourist Office, Tel: 01688 302182.

Bunessan. Argyll Arms Hotel has good salmon, sea trout and brown trout fishing on **Loch Assapol**, with boats. Fly and spinner only. No Sunday fishing.

RAASAY:

The Isle of Raasay is near Skye. Free trout fishing in lochs and streams; waders should be taken.

RUM:

The fishing on the Isle of Rum is all owned and managed by Scottish Natural Heritage, The White House, Rum National Nature Reserve, Isle of Rum PH43 4RR, Tel: 01687 462357.

Permits to fish are required, and SNH reserves the right to restrict fishing over certain areas in the interests of successful ornithological conservation, most particularly, red throated divers. But there are always fishing opportunities in various lochs on the island, along areas at the mouth of the **Kinloch River**, mainly browns and sea trout.

NORTH UIST: Island in Outer Hebrides, 17m long and 3–13m broad. More water than land with over 400 named lochs and lochans, and many more unnamed, some probably unfished. Plenty of lochs by roadside for elderly or infirm anglers.

Lochmaddy. Fishing on North Uist is controlled by the North Uist estate, Lochmaddy HS6 5AA (Tel: 01876 500 329, Fax: 01876 500 428). This covers all the salmon and sea trout systems on North Uist, and comprises 16 brown trout lochs, most of which are provided with a boat, and 11 salmon and sea trout lochs, 6 of which have a boat. Visitors' charges range between £38 per day, two rods, salmon and sea trout, to £6 per day, brown trout. Salmon and sea trout fishing is available to guests staying at the Lochmaddy Hotel (Tel: 01876 500331) (see *advt*) or the Langass Lodge Hotel, Locheporti, HS6 5HA (Tel: 01876 580285); residents have the first option. Non-residents day tickets cost £35 per rod per day, when obtainable; ghillies on premises. Brown trout fishing costs visitors £20, weekly, or £6 daily, bank only, plus £15 per day boat hire. All permits from the Lochmaddy Hotel. North Uist AC, c/o Langass Lodge (*above*), offers brown trout permits for the Newton Estate waters, comprising numerous lochs with boats on 3 of them, st £35, wt £20 and dt £5, from J Matheson, Clachan stores, Clachan, and J Handyside, Stag Lodge, Lochmaddy (Tel: 01876 500364). North Uist AC also offers permits on Balranald Estate, from W Quarm, Bayhead Shop (Tel: 01876 510257). Other North Uist accommodation: Lochportain House, Lochmaddy HS6 5AS, Tel: 0131 447 9911, self catering; Sealladh Traigh, Claddach Kirkibost, Tel: 01876 580248.

SOUTH UIST:

Bornish. South Uist AC has trout fishing on many lochs in South Uist and **Benbecula**. Bank and boat fishing; boats on 12 lochs: Secretary, W P Felton, Tel: 01870, 610325. Permits from Mrs Kennedy, Bornish Stores. For South Uist Estates fishing, Captain J Kennedy, Tel: 01878 700332 (Hotel).

Lochboisdale. Lochboisdale Hotel issues permits for brown trout fishing on many lochs; sea trout and salmon fishing may also be open. Boats on several lochs. Fly only. Contact John Kennedy, Lochboisdale Hotel (Tel: 01878 700332) (see advt.).

ORKNEY

While sea fishing for skate, ling, halibut (British record), haddock, cod, etc, is general in waters about Orkney, good fun may be had in the evenings with saithe comparatively close to the shores.

Trout fishing is prolific, there are a multitude of lochs which hold excellent stocks of wild brown trout, and sea trout also are plentiful. **Loch of Harray** is the most famous and will produce fish from the first day of the season to the last, with May, June and July the best months. **Boardhouse Loch** in Birsay is ideal for the visiting angler as there are no skerries and the fish average ¾lb. The best months to fish at Boardhouse are May, June, and early July. **Loch of Swanney**, again in Birsay, is another favourite with visiting local anglers, with the best months being May and June. The **Loch of Stenness** is a challenge, connected to the sea, it is partly tidal. Native brown trout and sea trout thrive in this environment, growing big and strong on the abundant marine life. The **Loch of Skaill** in Sandwick should also be mentioned as it holds specimen trout, with fish averaging 2lbs. The lochs on the islands of Sanday and Westray also contain a number of very large trout.

The Orkney Trout Fishing Association is a non-profit making voluntary body, dedicated to the preservation and enhancement of game fishing throughout the islands of Orkney. The Association operates a trout hatchery. Restocking has yielded excellent results, notably in the **Loch of Swanney**. Membership is £20, visitors season £15, OAP, jun and disabled season £10. Membership entitles anglers to use Assn facilities, which include access to fishing on Loch of Skaill. Subscriptions are accepted at **Orkney Tourist Board Office, Kirkwall**; Barony Hotel, Boarhouse Loch, Birsay KW17 2LS (Tel: 01856 721327), who offer flies, transport and other services to anglers; J I Harcus, Bridge St, Kirkwall; Merkister Hotel (see below); The Longship, Broad St, Kirkwall; W S Sinclair, Tackle Shop, Stromness; E Kemp, Bridge St,

Kirkwall. Further information from OTFA Hon Sec, Capt. James E Purvis, Pier House, 3 Maitland Place, Finstown, Orkney KW17 2EQ. A Trout Fishing Guide to Orkney by Stan Headley is on sale at most newsagents and booksellers in Orkney.

There is good quality accommodation throughout Orkney and there are taxi services to fishing waters. The Merkister Hotel, Harray KW17 2LF (Tel: 01856 771366) is close to Loch of Harray (now the best of the Orkney Lochs) and offers excellent loch fishing: boats, incl for disabled, outboards, ghillies. The Standing Stones Hotel, Stenness, is fully licensed, and can provide boats, outboards, ghillies. The hotel is situated on the shores of Loch of Stenness and is also convenient for the Loch of Harray, while Smithfield Hotel (Tel: 01856 771 215) and The Barony (Tel: 01856 721 327) are convenient for the Lochs of Boardhouse, Hundland and Swanney.

SHETLAND

Shetland was formerly renowned for its sea trout fishing, but for a variety of reasons this fishing has now drastically declined and anglers are recommended to concentrate on the excellent wild brown trout fishing in over 300 lochs containing trout up to 5lb in weight.

Taking the Shetland Islands as a group, the majority of the fishing is controlled by the Shetland Anglers' Association, who charge a fee of £20 per season, £5 per day for unlimited fishing, juniors free. Boats are bookable on five of the best lochs at a daily cost of £5. Details of all fishing and permits are obtainable from Rod and Line Tackle shop, Harbour Street, Lerwick, and also from the Association secretary, Alec Miller, 55 Burgh Road, Lerwick, Shetland ZE1 0HJ, Tel: 01595 695903 (day), 01595 696025 (evening), Fax: 01595 696568. The Association publishes a comprehensive local guide covering over 200 trout lochs. There are now several hotels specialising in catering for anglers, and among the best are Hildasay Guest House, Scalloway; Herrislea Hotel, Tingwall; Westings Hotel, Whiteness; Baltasound Hotel, Baltasound, Unst.

SKYE

Trout and salmon fishing generally preserved. Sea trout especially good in places. Excellent sea fishing.

Dunvegan. Numerous streams in area can be very good for sea trout in May and June. Hotels: Atholl House; Misty Isle.

Sleat. Brown trout and Arctic char fishing on a number of small rivers and lochs in the South of Skye. Permits £5–£7 from Hotel Eilean Iarmain, An t-Eilean, Sgiathanach (Tel: 01471 833332). Tackle shop: Dunvegan Boats and Fishing Tackle, Main Rd, Dunvegan; The Gun & Tackle Room, Unit 4, Dunvegan.

Portree. The **Storr Lochs** called **Fada** and **Leathan** are 4m away, and have good brown trout (average 1lb, occasionally 5lb). Bank fishing; 10 boats. Mid-May to mid-June and early Sept best. Permits for these and other hill lochs from Jansport (below). The Portee AA controls all river fishing in the area, except south bank of **R Lealt**. Lealt is most productive of these; also **Kilmuluag**, **Kilmartin**, and **Brogaig** rivers, small spate streams with the odd sea trout and salmon, suitable for fly, small spinner and worm. Dt £10 from Janesport (below). Enquiries to Hon Sec, Portree AA. Also sea fishing, for pollack and saithe in harbour. Tackle shop: Jansport, Somerled Sq. Hotel: Cuillin Hills.

Skeabost. Skeabost House Hotel, Skeabost Bridge, Isle of Skye IV51 9NP (Tel: 0147 532202) has salmon and sea trout fishing (8m double bank) on **River Snizort**, reputed to be the best salmon river on Skye, and trout fishing; dt £15, and free fishing for three-day residents.

Sligachan. Sligachan Hotel (Tel: 01478 650204) currently issues permits at £10 for salmon and sea trout fishing in 2m **Sligachan River** and brown trout fishing in **Loch na-Caiplaich** free for guests; salmon few, sea trout quite plentiful; best months, mid-July to end Sept. Brown trout fishing by arrangement in Storr Lochs (15m); boats for hire; season, May to end Sept. No permit is required for brown trout fishing in **Loch Marsco**.

Broadford. Sea trout and salmon in the **Broadford River**. 1½m south bank, fishing permits £5 from Broadford Hotel (Tel: 01471 822204). **Loch Sguabaidh** and **Lochan Stratha Mhor**, brown trout, sea trout, occasional salmon, permits £5 from Keith Miller (Tel: 01471 866260).

Staffin. Salmon, sea trout, brown trout. Portree AA hold the fishing rights. Tickets from D Burd, College of Agriculture, Portree.

Struan. Ullinish Lodge Hotel, IV56 8FD (Tel: 01470 572214) has salmon, sea trout and brown trout fishing in three lochs (Connan, Duagrich and Ravag) and on **Rivers Ose** and **Snizort**. £10 for loch fishing, special rates for residents of hotel. Residents only on Loch Ravag. **Glen Brittle**: Permits £10 for salmon and trout in River Brittle (in spate); from Glenbrittle Campsite Shop (Tel: 01478 640404).

Uig. Uig Hotel, IV51 9YE (Tel: 01470 542205, Fax: 542308) can arrange fishing on north bank **River Hinnisdale** and **Storr Lochs**; also on various hill lochs on which Portree AA has rights. River Hinnisdale is run by angling club. Permits £12 daily, for salmon and trout fishing on **Rivers Rha**, **Connan** and north bank R Hinnisdale from Ferry Inn, Uig (Tel: 01470 542242).

LOCHY
(Nevis and Coe)

Drains Loch Lochy and, after joining the Spean at Mucomir, flows about 8m to salt water in Loch Linnhe close to Fort William. Very good salmon and sea trout river but affected by hydro works at Falls of Mucomir. Best months: July, August and Sept. Whole river is on weekly lets only. Further information from River Lochy Association, c/o A M V Mann, Keeper's Cottage, West Hatch, Tisbury, Salisbury Wilts SP3 6PE.

Tributaries of the Lochy

SPEAN: Flows from Loch Laggan. A rocky river with good holding pools. Good fishing for salmon and sea trout from May to October. For lettings and permits enquire at Rod & Gun Shop, 18 High Street, Fort William.

Spean Bridge (Inverness-shire). Beats open on dt for left bank only, also for **Lochs Arkaig** and **Lochy**. Enquire at Spean Bridge Hotel.

ROY (tributary of Spean): Salmon. A spate river; fishes best July onwards.

Roy Bridge (Inverness-shire). Lower half let to Roy Bridge AC; contact Ian Matheson (Tel: 01397 712370). Upper half owned by Roy Fisheries: only available to lodge guests from Aug–Nov; permits from CKD Finlayson Hughes, Lynedoch House, Barossa Pl, Perth PH1 5EP (Tel: 01738 451600) and keeper, Braeroy Estate. Roy Bridge AC has fishing on **Loch na Turk**; stocked rainbow trout; apply to Hon Sec.

NEVIS: A short river flowing around south

side of Ben Nevis and entering Loch Linnhe at Fort William, not far from mouth of Lochy. Very good salmon and sea trout fishing.

Fort William (Inverness-shire). River Nevis; salmon, grilse, sea trout. Fort William AA has about 6m; dt from tackle shop after 9am on day required. No spinning; best June onwards. Good brown trout fishing on **Loch Lundavra** 6m from town. Dt £15, boat and £3, bank; from Mrs A MacCallum, Lundavra Farm, Fort William PH33 6SZ (Tel: 01397 702582). For **Loch Arkaig** and **Loch Lochy**, sea trout and brown trout; bank fishing only. Permits from West Highland Estates Office, 33 High St. Tackle shop: Rod & Gun Shop, 18 High St (licences and permits for town beat on River Lochy). Hotels: Imperial, Grand, Alexandra, West End, Milton.

COE: River flows through Glen Coe to enter **Loch Leven** and from there into **Loch Linnhe**. Salmon, sea trout and brown trout.

Glencoe (Argyll). The National Trust for Scotland have stopped issuing tickets on their stretches of R Coe till stocks recover. Contact Ballachulish Tourist I.C. (Tel: 01855 811296) for further information. Brown and rainbow trout fishing on **Loch Achtriochtan**. Rainbow trout fishing on **Glencoe Lochan**, nr Glencoe Village; managed by Forest Enterprise. Permits from Scorrybreac Guest House PA39 3HT (Tel: 01855 811354), adjacent to the lochan, or from Forest Enterprise Camp, outside village. Boat for disabled on water. Nearest tackle shop, Rod & Gun, in Fort William.

LOSSIE

Drains Loch Trevie and flows about 25m to the Moray Firth at Lossiemouth. A good trout stream; salmon runs improving, July onwards. Provides good sport with sea trout from June onwards, especially near estuary.

Lossiemouth (Moray). Salmon, sea trout. Elgin and Dist AA, has water; estuary and sea; salmon, sea trout and finnock. Permits and information on other fishings from tackle shops in Elgin and Lossiemouth. Hotels: Stotfield, Huntly House.

Elgin (Moray). Elgin AA has water on Lossie at Elgin (salmon, sea trout and brown trout) and **Loch Park** fishings (brown trout). For membership apply to Membership Secretary, A F Garrow, 8 School Walk, New Elgin, Elgin, Moray (Tel: 01343 546168), enclosing £1 to cover administrative costs. Trout fishing can be had on the Town Council's Millbuies Estate: **Glenlatterach Reservoir**, brown trout, boats on site; **Loch of Blairs**, stocked rainbows, boat fishing only, and **Millbuies Loch**, mainly rainbow trout, also boat fishing only. Boat dt £11.80, one angler in boat, £8.80 each for two; bank fishing on Glenlatterach £4.80. Conc. Permits for Millbuies and Glenlatterach from The Warden, Millbuies Lochs, Longmorn, Elgin (Tel: 0134386 234); for Blairs: Fishing Tackle Shop, 79d High St, Forres (Tel: 01309 72936). Information from Moray District Council, Environmental and Development Services Dept, High St, Elgin IV30 1BX (Tel: 01343 543451). Hotels: Braelossie; Mansefield House; Mansion House.

LUNAN

Rises near Forfar and flows about 13m to North Sea between Arbroath and Montrose. Some good trout. Sea trout and finnock in autumn. A protection order now in force requiring all anglers to be in possession of proper permits, obtainable through Arbroath Angling Club.

Arbroath (Angus). Lunan and its tributary, the **Vinney**, about 8m of water, leased to Arbroath AC by riparian owners; restocked each year, holds good head of brown trout, also sea trout and occasional salmon. Bag limit 6 fish. River mouth, sea trout and salmon. Upstream, st £15 and dt £3; river mouth, dt £3. Concession for OAPs and juniors. Permits from Arbroath Cycle & Tackle Centre, 274 High Street, Arbroath DD11 1JE (Tel: 01241 73467). Good sea fishing. Local sea angling trips daily.

Forfar (Angus). Canmore AC (members of Strathmore Angling Improvement Association) have trout fishing on **River Dean**, fly only; **Cruick**; R **Kerbet**, fly only; Club also hold rights for **Den of Ogil Reservoir**, boat and bank fishing for brown trout; **R Isla**; and **Forfar Loch**. All Canmore AC permits from C Kerr (below). Rescobie Loch Development Assn runs **Rescobie Loch**, 200 acres, 3m E of Forfar; a Troutmaster loch with boat and bank fishing to rainbows and browns; full dt £10, 4 fish limit; boat 2/3 rod £25 per day, single angler £14; from Rescobie Boathouse, Clocksbriggs, Montrose Rd by Forfar (Tel: 01307 830367). Tackle Shop: C Kerr, 1 West High St, Forfar.

NAIRN

Rises in Monadhliath Hills and flows about 36m to Moray Firth at Nairn. Salmon, sea trout, finnock and brown trout.

Nairn (Nairn). Tickets for the lower reaches (estuary to Cantray Bridge, approx 6½m) can be had from Nairn AA; salmon and sea trout. Best months: July to September for salmon. Visitors permits £41 weekly, £13.50 day, conc, from Pat Fraser, Radio, TV and Sports Shop, 41 High Street (Tel: 01667 453038) or J Ormison, Inverness (Tel: 01463 225182). Clava Lodge Holiday Homes, Culloden Moor, By Inverness IV12 2EJ (Tel: 01463 790228) also issues permits for a stretch on Nairn. **Lochs Lochindorb, Allan,** and **Loch-an-Tutach** privately owned; brown trout; dt and boat. Other tackle shop: Sportscene, Harbour St. Other hotels: Meallmore Lodge, Daviot (private stretch of river); Newton (river and loch fishing by arrangement).

NAVER (including Borgie and Hope)

Drains Loch Naver and flows about 24m to north coast at Naver Bay. The Borgie, which also debouches into Naver Bay, drains Loch Slaim and has course of about 7m. Both are good salmon and sea trout rivers; all preserved, but beats can be arranged, usually for weekly periods.

Altnaharra (Sutherland). Altnaharra Hotel, By Larg, Sutherland IV27 4UE (Tel/Fax: 0154 411 222), which specializes in catering for fishermen, provides salmon fishing in **Loch Naver** and **River Mudale**; sea trout fishing in **Loch Hope** and brown trout fishing in a number of lochs; all lochs have boats and are close to the road. Some are open to non-residents. Dt £18 to £30. Excellent sea trout water; also holds salmon. No bank fishing; fly only. Hotel has fully stocked tackle shop; and provides outboard motors, tuition and accommodation.

Tongue (Sutherland). Three limited day tickets for quality salmon fishing on River Naver from The Store, Bettyhill. Salmon and sea trout fishing on **Loch Hope**; approx £100 per week. Early booking advisable. Contact Ian MacDonald, Keeper (Tel: 0184756 272). Tongue Dist AA (HQ at Ben Loyal Hotel) has brown trout fishing on 8 lochs; fly only. Boats on **Lochs Loyal, Cormach, Craggie, Bealach na Sgeulachd, and Lochan Hakel**. Ghillie by arrangement. St £20, wt £12 and dt £3; from hotel: Drying room and freezer space at hotel: Kyle of Tongue estuary also assn water; excellent sea trout when shoals are running; fly or spinner. Permits from local hotels, post office and general store. For **R Borgie** private beats, Mar–Sept, fly only, contact Peter MacGregor, Borgie Lodge Hotel, Skerray by Tongue KW14 7TH (Tel: 01641 521231). Salmon fishing £380–£450 + VAT, brown trout dt £5. Hotel has brown trout fishing on 20 lochs, with salmon in three, boats on three at £10 hire, spinning and worm permitted on some. Hotel runs fishing packages with ghillie and all other facilities, and is HQ of Borgie Angling Club. **River Naver** permits from The Store, Bettyhill.

NESS

Drains Loch Ness and flows to Moray Firth at Inverness. Notable salmon and sea trout river. Best July to October.

Inverness (Inverness-shire). Salmon, sea trout, brown trout. Inverness AC has stretch from estuary upstream for about 3¾m, both banks. No Sunday fishing. Permits £15 per day or £75 weekly, conc, from tackle shops, or Tourist Board, High St. **Loch Ruthven,** brown trout; fly only; boat only; permits from J Graham & Co; and R Humfrey, Balvoulin, Aberarder. Sunday fishing permitted. **Loch Choire,** brown trout; fly only; permits from R Humfrey, Balvoulin, Aberarder. Sea trout fishing on North Kessock sea shore; permits from North Kessock PO; and J Graham & Co. Tourist Office: Castle Wynd, IV2 3BJ (Tel: 01463 234353) issues permits and local fishing information. Tackle shops: J Graham & Co, 37–39 Castle St (Tel: 01463 233178); Ormiston & Co., 20 Market Brae Steps (Tel: 01463 222757). Hotels: Glen Mhor; Loch Ness House; Haughdale.

LOCH NESS: Sea trout at Dochfour and Aldourie; salmon, especially out from Fort Augustus and where **Rivers Moriston** and **Foyers** enter the loch. Brown trout all round the margins. Boats and boatmen from hotels at Fort Augustus, Drumnadrochit, Foyers, Lewiston and Whitbridge.

Dochgarroch (Inverness-shire). Dochfour

Estate has brown trout fishing on **Loch Ness** and **Loch Dochfour**; north bank only. No Sunday fishing. Permits from Dochfour Estate Office, Dochgarroch, Inverness IV3 8GY (Tel:01463 86218, Fax: 01463 861366).

Drumnadrochit (Inverness). Salmon and brown trout. **Loch Meiklie**, brown trout, fly only; permits from Mrs Taylor, Kilmartin House, Glenurquhart.

Foyers (Inverness). Foyers Hotel has salmon and brown trout fishing on Loch Ness. Boats and ghillie service. Several other lochs may also be fished, including **Lochs Bran**, **Garth**, **Farraline** and **Killin**. Neil Ellis, Foyers House B & B, IV1 2XU, hires fishing boats on Loch Ness, for all types of fishing.

Invermoriston (Inverness). **River Moriston** enters Loch Ness here. An early river, best February to June. Permits for river and trout fishing on hill lochs from Glenmoriston Lodge Estate Office, IV63 7YA (Tel: 01320 351300, Fax 301); and salmon fishing by boat on **Loch Ness**; from Headkeeper, Levishie House, Glenmoriston (Tel: 01320 51219).

Fort Augustus (Inverness). Salmon and brown trout. Salmon season opens Jan 15. Trout season, March 15. Brown trout fishing on **Loch Quoich**; permits and boats from Lovat Arms Hotel. Other Hotels: Caledonian, Brae, Inchnacardoch.

Tributaries of Loch Ness

FOYERS: Free brown trout fishing.

Foyers (Inverness-shire). **Loch Mhor**, 18m from Inverness, is 4m long by ½m broad, and contains trout averaging ½lb. Outlet from loch enters Loch Ness via River Foyers. Accommodation ½m from loch at the Old Manse Guest House, Gorthleck and 2½m from loch at Whitebridge Hotel, Whitebridge, Inverness IV1 2UN (Tel: 01456 486226). Tackle for purchase or hire, and boats (£12 per day); from Whitebridge Hotel: **Loch Ruthven** can be fished, also **Loch Bran** and **River Fechlin**.

Whitebridge (Inverness). Whitebridge Hotel has boats for use of guests on **Loch Knockie** and **Loch Bran**; brown trout; fly only. Arrangements also made for guests wishing to troll on Loch Ness. River and burns dried out in course of hydro-electric development. Other

hotel: Knockie Lodge.

MORISTON: Salmon, brown trout.

Glenmoriston (Inverness-shire). Glenmoriston Lodge Estate has fishing rights on Loch Ness, salmon and brown trout; R Moriston, salmon and brown trout; and **Glenmoriston hill lochs**, brown trout. (See *Invermoriston*.) **Loch Cluanie**, brown trout. No Sunday fishing.

OICH and **GARRY**: Garry rises in loch SW of Loch Quoich and runs into that loch at western end, thence to Lochs Poulary, Inchlaggan and Garry. Good salmon and trout river. Outlet to Loch Garry dammed by North of Scotland Hydro-Electric Board. At Loch Poulary are fish traps; at Invergarry, a hatchery.

Invergarry (Inverness). Glen Garry FC controls fishing on the whole of Upper Garry (both banks), **Lochs Quoich**, **Poulary**, **Inchlaggan** and **Garry**. Loch Quoich holds brown trout record and Loch Garry holds Arctic char record; both lochs hold char. Salmon only good July onwards, closing mid-Oct. Boats on all lochs and some of pools of Upper Garry. Permits from Tomdoun Hotel (Tel: 018092 218) and Garry Gualach, Glengarry (Tel: 018092 230). Garry Gualach also issues permits for Loch Inchlaggan; fly only. Peter H Thomas, Ardochy Lodge, Glengarry PH35 4HR, has boat fishing for trout and Arctic char. P Williamson, Ladyscroft, Invergarry PH35 4HP lets excellent early spring fishing on both banks of R Garry and sole salmon fishing on Loch Oich. Agent is Invergarry Hotel (Tel: 01809 501206). Day or weekly bookings, for up to 6 rods. Tomdoun Hotel issues permits for **Lochs Quoich**, **Poulary**, **Inchlaggan**, **Garry** and **Loyne**, and Upper River Garry; trout, salmon, char and pike (no salmon in Quoich and Loyne, and no pike in Quoich). Upper Garry reserved for hotel guests. Boat fishing only on Quoich. Bank fishing only on Loyne. Boats from hotel for all waters except Loyne. Apply to G F Heath, Tomdoun Hotel, Invergarry, Inverness-shire PH35 4HS (Tel: 018092 218/244). Bed and breakfast accommodation plus a self-catering chalet from Mrs P A Buswell, who can arrange fishing holidays and operates a small mini bus to collect and transport clients who have no transport. Apply to Mrs P A Buswell, Nursery Cottages, Invergarry, Inverness-shire PH35 4HL (Tel: 01809 501 297).

NITH

Rises on south side of Ayr watershed and flows south and east to Solway, which it enters by an estuary with Dumfries at its head. Is the largest and best-known river in the Dumfries and Galloway region and has established a reputation for the quality of its salmon and sea trout which continue to improve. Carries a good head of small trout.

New Abbey (Kirkcudbrightshire). New Abbey AA has 2m on a small tributary of Nith; occasional salmon, good sea trout and herling, and stocked with brown trout and rainbow trout. Visitor's st £12 and dt £3. Concession for jun. Permits from Hon Sec; The Shop, The Square; and Criffel Inn, The Square. Hotels: Abbey Arms, Criffel Inn.

Dumfries (Dumfries & Galloway). Dumfries Common Good Fishing, 3m on Nith, 1½m on **Cairn** (tributary); salmon, sea trout, brown trout and grayling; best, March–May and Sept–Nov. Visitors st £210, wt £110, dt £30. Reductions for residents, OAP, juveniles, from Dumfries and Galloway Regional Council, Housing Services, 52–60 Queensberry Street, Dumfries DG1 1BF (Tel: 01387 260739), and from Tourist Board, 64 Whitesands. Dumfries and Galloway AA has 3m on Nith and 16m on Cairn; salmon, sea trout and brown trout. Fly fishing anytime; spinning and bait fishing restricted to water level. Daily and weekly tickets; no daily tickets on Saturday. Concessions for juniors. Permits from D McMillan, Fishing Tackle Specialists. **Glenkiln Reservoir** (trout) controlled by Dumfries and Galloway Regional Council, Director of Water and Sewage, Marchmount House, Marchmount, Dumfries DG1 1PW. St £20, wt £10, dt (bank) £2.75. Boats on site. Bank fishing free to OAP and disabled residents.

Jericho Loch (Dumfries & Galloway. Rainbow and brown trout; fly only; bank fishing only. Permits from Mousewald Caravan Park, Mousewald, By Dumfries; Thistle Stores, Locharbriggs, Dumfries. Tackle shops: D McMillan, 6 Friar's Vennel (Tel: 01387 52075); Malcolm Pattie, 109 Queensberry Street.

Thornhill (Dumfriesshire). Mid Nithsdale AA has 3½m on Nith and tributary **Scaur**; salmon, sea trout and brown trout. No permits on Saturdays. Assn also has brown and rainbow trout fishing on **Kettleton Loch** 4m NE of

Thornhill, 40 acres. Advanced booking for autumn fishing. Permits from Hon Sec. Drumlanrig Castle Fishing on the Queensberry Estate offers salmon and sea trout fishing on River Nith, 7m, both banks, 4 beats; **Morton Castle Loch** and **Starburn Loch**, rainbow and brown trout; and **Morton Pond**, coarse fish. Accommodation at Auchenknight Cottage on estate. Apply to The Factor, The Buccleuch Estates Ltd, Drumlanrig Mains, Thornhill, Dumfriesshire DG3 4AG (Tel: 018486 283). Barjarg Estate has stretch on Nith; salmon, grilse, sea trout, brown trout and grayling. Daily or weekly permits until end August; normally weekly from Sept to end Nov. Self-catering accommodation. Apply to Andrew Hunter-Arundel, Newhall, Auldgirth, Dumfriesshire DG2 0TN (Tel: 01848 331342). **Loch Ettrick** near Closeburn DG3 5HL, 32 acre loch, well stocked with rainbow and brown trout. Hotels: Buccleuch, George, Elmarglen. Tackle shop: The Fishing Tackle Shop, 35 Drumlanrig St, Thornhill.

Sanquhar (Dumfries & Galloway). Upper Nithsdale AC has approx 11m of Nith; and stretches on tributaries **Kello**, **Crawick**, **Euchan** and **Mennock**. Salmon, sea trout, brown trout and grayling. No Sunday fishing, Saturdays must be booked in advance. Reduced membership charge for resident juveniles; and Forsyth Shield presented each year in Jan to resident boy for heaviest fish caught. Permits from K McLean Esq, Solicitor, 61 High Street, Sanquhar (Tel: 01659 50241). Day tickets for grayling fishing, Jan and Feb, from K McLean, Solicitor, 61 High St. Hotels: Nithsdale, Glendyne, Blackaddie House.

New Cumnock (Ayrshire). New Cumnock AA has brown trout fishing on River Nith, **Afton Water** and **Afton Reservoir**; and on parts of **Rivers Deugh** and **Ken**, and **Carsphairn Lane Burn**. Club also has grayling fishing on River Nith and rainbow trout fishing on **Creoch Loch**. Creoch Loch open all year. Permits from Phillips Auto Electrics, and from Kelly's Grocery. Hotels: Lochside House, Crown.

OYKEL (including **Carron**, **Cassley**, **Shin** and **Loch Ailsh**):

Rises at Benmore Assynt, flows through Loch Ailsh and thence 14m to enter the Kyle of Sutherland at Rosehall. Excellent salmon and sea trout fishing. The Lower Oykel has produced an average catch of over 780 salmon in recent years.

Oykel Bridge (Sutherland). Lower reaches fish very well for salmon early on and good grilse and sea trout run usually begins in the latter half of June. Loch Ailsh. Good sea and brown trout fishing with occasional salmon. Best months **Lower Oykel**, March to September. **Upper Oykel** and **Loch Ailsh**, mid-June to September. Inver Lodge Hotel has salmon and trout fishing on Oykel. Contact Inver Lodge Hotel, Lochinver IV27 4LU.

CASSLEY: Some 10m long, river is divided at Rosehall into upper and lower Cassley by Achness Falls. Below falls fishing starts early. Upper Cassley fishes well from May to Sept. Sea trout July and Aug.

Rosehall (Sutherland). Rods let by week (av £200) on both banks. Sole agents: Bell Ingram, Estate Office, Bonar Bridge, Sutherland IV24 3AE. Hotel: Achness House.

SHIN (**Loch Shin** and **Kyle of Sutherland**): Loch Shin is largest fresh water loch in Sutherland, 16m long. Brown trout in loch av ½lb, but very large fish taken early in season. Outlet from Loch Shin controlled by hydro-electric works. River flows about 7m and empties into Kyle of Sutherland at Invershin. Salmon fishing privately let.

Lairg (Sutherland). Lairg AC has trout fishing in Loch Shin and hill lochs, including **Loch Beannach** (brown trout, 5m from Lairg, 1m walk). Loch Shin, brown trout including ferox up to 12lb. Loch Craggie, members only. Competitions held on Loch Shin throughout the season – details from club hut at loch side. St £10 from Hon Sec; wt £16 for L Shin, and dt £5 from local tackle shop. Concessions for juveniles. Boats for hire on hill lochs of Doulay, Craggie and Tigh na Craig, from D Walker, Park House, Lairg (Tel: 01549 402208). Bookings from Hon Sec (Tel: 01549 402010). Best mid-May to end of July. No Sunday fishing. Overscaig Hotel, on shore of **Loch Shin**, has boats there, and also on **Lochs A' Ghriama** and **Merkland**. Many hill lochs within walking distance. There are usually facilities for sea trout and salmon fishing on **Lochs Stack** and **More**. Hotel ghillies, advice and instruction. Large brown trout caught on hotel waters in recent years. Fishing free to residents. Boats with ob motors. For further information contact Overscaig Lochside Hotel, Loch Shin, By Lairg IV27 4NY (Tel: 01549 431203). Tackle shop: Sutherland Sporting Co. Main St.

DORNOCH FIRTH:
Dornoch (Sutherland). At entrance to Firth. Permits from Dornoch AA for sea trout at **Little Ferry**; wt £6, dt £2 and brown trout on **Lochs Lannsaidh**, **Buidhe**, **Laoigh**, **Lagain**, **Laro** and **Cracail Mor**, boat, £12 per day and bank on Buidhe, Laoigh and Lagain £5. Assn has recently acquired salmon, sea trout and brown trout fishing on **Loch Brora**; boat only, £15 per day. Fly only on lochs. Spinning allowed on Little Ferry. No Sunday fishing. Permits from W A MacDonald, Hardware Store, Castle St. Hotels: Burghfield House; Castle.

KYLE OF DURNESS

Durness (Sutherland). Simpsons of Edinburgh offer fishing on the first six beats of **River Dionard**, from the sea pools. Sport best after heavy rain. This fishing also includes four trout lochs, and costs £30 per day salmon, £12 trout. Ghillie hire, £12. Fishing with accommodation, £670 per week double, £345 single. Contact Simpsons, 28/30 West Preston St, Edinburgh EH8 9PZ (Tel: 0131 667 3058, Fax: 0131 662 0642). Cape Wrath Hotel at Keoldale has good salmon and sea trout fishing on Rivers Dionard **Grudie** and **Dall**, and the Kyle of Durness. Best for salmon and sea trout mid-June to mid Sept. Big brown trout in **Lochs Calladale**, **Crosspool, Lanlish**, and **Borralaidh** – well-conditioned fish of 8lb in weight have been taken – and there are several lochs, three with boats. Lochs and rivers stocked with salmon, sea trout, brown trout fry. Hotel open throughout year. Enquiries to Cape Wrath Hotel, Keoldale, by Lairg, Sutherland.

SCOURIE
(Lochs Stack and More)

Scourie (Sutherland). Excellent centre for sea trout, brown trout and salmon fishing. About 300 trout lochs. Scourie Hotel has extensive fishing rights on over 250; four with salmon and sea trout. Boats on many. Ghillies may also be hired. Dt varies between £4 and £50, depending on season. Days on **Loch Stack** and **Loch More** open to guests during July, Aug and Sept. Salmon, sea trout (good), brown trout. For further information apply to Patrick and Judy Price, Scourie Hotel, Scourie, By Lairg IV27 4SX (Tel: 01971 502396). Scourie & Dist AC has rights on 33 lochs to N of village and 2 lochs S; trout around ½lb mark, but some larger fish. Wt £12 and dt £4 (boat £4 extra) from R McKay, 12 Park Terrace (Tel: 01971 502425).

SHIEL
(Argyll/Inverness-shire)
(including Moidart
and Loch Shiel)

Short salmon river, only about 3m long, draining Loch Shiel. Moidart is a good spate river with excellent holding pools. Loch Shiel is fed by four major rivers, **Slatach**, **Finnan**, **Callop** and **Alladale**, which all tend to be spate rivers. Fishing in the loch has been poor of late.

Acharacle (Argyll). River preserved. **Loch Shiel**, 17m long, holds salmon and sea trout, and a few brown trout. No bank fishing. Boats and permits for Loch Shiel from D Macaulay, Dalilea Farm (Tel: 0196 431 253); Fergie MacDonald, Clanranald Hotel; and Loch Shiel Hotel. Also apply to Fergie MacDonald, Clanranald Hotel, for salmon and sea trout fishing on **Rivers Carnoch**, **Strontian** and **Moidart**; boats. The Ardnamurchan Peninsular has fly fishing in **Lochs Mudle** and **Mhadaidh**; wild brown trout, sea trout and the occasional salmon. Permits obtainable from Estate Office, Mingary House, Kilchoan, Acharacle PH36 4LH (Tel: 01972 10208), from all local shops, T.I.C. (Tel: 01972 510222), and hotels and visitors centres. All other 12 hill lochs and salmon and sea trout fishing on the Achateny water and at Choire Mhuilin reserved for estate guests. Tackle, boat hire and self-catering accommodation at Ardnamurchan Estate. Fly fishing tuition £7 per hour, tackle and boat hire, and sea fishing from Nick Peake, Sithean Mor, Achnaha, nr Kilchoan, By Acharacle, Argyll PH36 4LW (Tel: 01972 510212). Boats and information from Kilchoan Tourist Office (Tel: 01972 510333). Hotels: Sonachan (Tel: 01972 510211); Kilchoan House (Tel: 01972 510200).

Glenfinnan (Inverness-shire). **Loch Shiel**: fishing now sub-standard and not recommended.

SPEY

One of the largest rivers in Scotland, from its source Loch Spey, it flows 97 miles to Moray Firth, emptying between Banff and Elgin. The total catchment area is 1,154 sq miles. The Spey is an alpine river, with melting snow supplementing flow well into spring. The waters are low in nutrients, and have remained fairly free from pollution. The main river is also relatively free from obstructions. Historically, one of the great salmon rivers, net fishing ceased at the end of the 1993 season, and there is now no commercial netting for salmon within the Spey district.

Fochabers (Morayshire). Extensive salmon fishings are let by the Factor, Estate Office, Gordon Castle IV32 7PQ (Tel: 01343 820244). These include Upper Brae Water, the Brae Water, Gordon Castle Water, and the two Gordon Castle Lower Water beats, in total approx 9m of double bank salmon, sea trout and finnock fishings. Accom for parties of up to 12 on Estate. Fochabers AA have four visitors day permits (subject to availability). These are booked at the Coat and Swagger Shop, Baxters of Speyside (Tel: 01343 820393). Gordon Arms Hotel, High St IV32 7DH (Tel: 01343 820508/9) and Mill House Hotel, Tynet, By Buckie, Banffshire AB56 5HJ (Tel: 01542 850233) caters for fishermen and fishing parties.

Craigellachie (Banffshire). Salmon, sea trout, trout. Craigellachie Hotel, Craigellachie, Speyside, Banffshire AB38 9SR (Tel: 013940 881204) arranges salmon fishing on Spey and brown trout fishing on local lochs for residents. **Aberlour** (Banffshire). Salmon, sea trout. Aberlour Association water. Six tickets per day on first-come-first-served basis. Hotels Dowans and Aberlour have 3 bookable tickets for residents. Dt £20 and wt £100. No day tickets issued on Saturdays. Permits from J A J Munro, Fishing Tackle, 93–95 High St, Aberlour, Banffshire AB38 9PB (Tel: 01340 871428). Season 11 Feb–30 Sept. Best season usually March till June but can be very good in July and August too. J A J Munro is a specialist supplier of hand-tied salmon flies, also re-felts wader soles with traditional felt with studded heels.

Grantown-on-Spey (Moray). Salmon and sea trout. Strathspey Angling Improvement Association has 7m on **Spey**, and 12m on **Dulnain**; salmon, sea trout and brown trout. Permits offered to visitors resident in Grantown, Cromdale, Duthill, Carrbridge, Dulnain Bridge and Nethy Bridge areas. Permits from tackle shop. Strathspey Estate, Old Spey Bridge Rd, Grantown-on-Spey PH26 3NQ (Tel: 01479 872529) has 5 beats on Spey, incl three Castle Grant beats. Contact Estate Office of further information. Trout fishing on **Avielochan**, bank fishing only; **Loch Dallas**, fly only; **Loch Mor**, fly only; and **Loch Vaa**, boat fishing only. Permits from tackle shop.

Arthur Oglesby runs occasional game angling courses at the Seafield Lodge Hotel; for dates and information apply to Alasdair Buchanan, The Seafield Lodge Hotel PH26 3JN (Tel: 01479 872152). Tackle shop: Mortimer's, High St.

Boat of Garten (Inverness-shire). Salmon, sea trout, brown trout. Abernethy AC, incorporating Aviemore Improvement Assn, issues tickets for Abernethy Waters, 6 mile stretch of Spey, both banks, 15 named pools. Certain stretches restricted to fly only when river below certain level, otherwise spinning and worming allowed; no prawn or shrimp allowed at any time. Brown trout fishing – fly only at all times. Permit only for those staying locally, wt £110, dt £33; from A J Allen, Allen's, Tackle Shop, Deshar Rd, Boat of Garten PH24 3BN (Tel: 01479 831372), and Speyside Sports, Aviemore.

Aviemore (Inverness-shire). The principal Spey Valley tourist centre. Kinara Estate has salmon and trout fishing on Spey and loch fishing (bank or boat) for trout and pike; apply to Major Campbell, Kinara Lodge, Aviemore (Tel: 01479 811292). The Aviemore Waters consist of 3½m of double bank salmon fishing, at reasonable price: dt £28, wt £85, conc for juv, permits from Speyside Sports, (*below*). **Avielochan**, 10 acre brown trout water, dt £15, evening £10, boat £5, from Mrs G A McDonald, Lochside, Avielochan (Tel: 01479 810847), or Speyside Sports (*below*). Trout and pike fishing on Rothiemurchus Estate, including rainbow and brown trout lochs, and beats on R Spey with salmon and sea trout; apply to Rothiemurchus Trout Fishery, Aviemore PH22 1QH (Tel: 01479 810703). Ghillie service and instruction on site, disabled access on bank. Trout fishing on **Loch Morlich** at Glenmore. Permits from Warden's Office, Glenmore Forest Camping and Caravan Park, Glenmore, by Aviemore. Permits 3½m single bank of Spey, £22 day, £65 weekly, conc, from Allens, Boat of Garten *above*. Tackle shop: Speyside Sports, 2 Station Square PH22 1PD (Tel: 01479 810656).

Kingussie (Inverness-shire). Alvie Estate has fishing on Spey, salmon and trout; **Loch Alvie**, brown trout and pike; and **Loch Insh**, salmon, sea trout, brown trout, pike and Arctic char. Fly fishing or spinning. Apply to Alvie Estate Office, Kincraig, by Kingussie PH21 1NE (Tel: 01540 651255); and Dalraddy Caravan Park, Aviemore PH22 1QB (Tel: 01479 810330). Loch Insh Watersports & Skiing Centre, Insh Hall, Kincraig PH21 1NU (Tel: 01540 651272) also has fish-

ing on loch, and stocked trout lochan; boats for hire, and tuition on site, facilities for disabled. Badenoch AA has fishing on River Spey from Spey Dam down to Kingussie, Loch Ericht at Dalwhinnie, and Loch Laggan on the Fort William Road. All brown trout fishing, stocked monthly, very few salmon. Spey Dam has 2 boats, fly only, the other waters allow worm and spinning. Permits £7 for all waters, boat £7, from Hamish Cromarty Fishing Tackle, Kingussie; Sandy Bennet, Water Bailiff (Tel: 01540 661645); and local hotels. Ossian Hotel has private fishing; salmon and brown trout. Permits from Ossian Hotel, Kincraig, By Kingussie PH21 1NA (Tel: 01540 651 242). Tuition from Jock Dallas, Castwell, Fishing Instruction School, Kingussie. Tackle shop: Spey Tackle, 25 High St, PH21 1HZ (Tel: 01540 661565).

Newtonmore (Inverness-shire). Badenoch AA has trout fishing on Upper Spey, **Loch Laggan, Loch Quoich** and **Spey Dam**. Boat and permits: Mains Hotel.

Tributaries of the Spey

AVON: Main tributary of Spey.

Ballindalloch (Banffshire). Ballindalloch Estate owns 5m stretch on Avon from junction with Spey; salmon and sea trout. Weekly and daily permits. Permits from The Estate Office, Ballindalloch, Banffshire AB37 9AX (Tel: 01807 500 205).

Tomintoul (Banffshire). Sea trout, grilse and salmon. Gordon Arms Hotel guests can fish 2m of Avon and 1m of Livet. Price varies depending on duration of stay. Fishing only open to residents of hotel.

STINCHAR

One of west coast streams, rising on western slope of Doon watershed and flowing about 30m to Atlantic at Ballantrae. Has a late run of salmon, and fishes best from mid-August till late October. Yearly catch is normally over 1,200 salmon. Also good sea trout and brown trout.

Colmonell (Ayrshire). River rises and falls rapidly after rain. Salmon and sea trout. Boar's Head Hotel, 4 Main St, KA26 0RY (Tel: 01465 881371) can arrange fishings on river. Permits for Kirkholm Farm from W Marshall, Tel: 01465 831297. For Knockdolian (best beat): Estate Office, Colmonell, Ballantrae (Tel: 01465 881

237), or A Boag, 881254. For Kirkhall Water: Mrs Shankland, 881220. Badrochet Estate: Bob Anderson, 881202. Hallow Chapel fishing: David Telfer, 881249. Almont: D Love, 841637. Dalreogh Estate: David Overend, 881214. These are the main beats on the river, of which majority are fly only, prices range between £15 and £60 per day, depending on season. Queen's Hotel, 21 Main St KA26 0RY (Tel: 01465 881213) can supply information to visiting anglers.

TAY

A great salmon river. Tay proper runs out of Loch Tay, but its feeder, the Dochart, at head of loch, takes its head water from slopes of Ben Lui. After a course of some 120m it empties into North Sea at Dundee, by a long firth. River fished mainly from boats, but certain beats provide spinning and fly fishing from banks. Notable in particular for run of spring fish, though autumn fishing often gives good results. All netting has now been removed in the Tay estuary, and salmon and sea trout have run unhindered for several years. At least half a dozen of its tributaries are salmon rivers of slightly less repute than main stream. An excellent run of sea trout, big brown trout (less often fished for), grayling, and coarse fish (scarcely fished at all). Loch Tay itself has been improving over recent years as a salmon fishery, the largest taken being a little over 40lb. For fishing hotels on loch, see *Killin*.

Perth (Perthshire). Scone Estate offers salmon fishing on two beats of Tay. Daily lets in spring, and weekly, sometimes daily in July and August. Stormont AC has salmon fishing on Tay, 3 beats; and on **R Almond**, 2 beats. Members only (c. 550). Permits for 3 beats of brown trout and coarse fishing on Tay and Almond, from tackle shops. Perth & Dist AA has various leases for brown trout and salmon fishing on Tay. Assn also has fishing on **Black Loch**, rainbow trout; **Loch Horn**, rainbow and brown trout; and **Balthatock Loch**, brown trout. All game fishing members only. Brown trout on Tay permits from P D Malloch. Permits for Perth Town Water; salmon, trout, grilse and also coarse fish; from Perth and Kinross Council, Leisure & Cultural Services, 5 High St, Perth PH1 5JS (Tel: 01738 475211); and Tourist Information Centre, 45 High St, Perth PH1 5TJ (Saturday only). Advisable to book in advance; only 20 permits per day and only 2 permits in advance by any one person. Tackle shops: P D Malloch, 259 Old High St; and Perthshire Field Sports, 13

Charlotte St. Hotels: Royal George; Tayside, Stanley.

Stanley (Perthshire). Stanley & Dist AC has brown trout and grayling fishing at Luncarty, Upper Redgorton, Stanley Taymount, Burnmouth and Meikleour. A limited number of permits are offered at £2 per day, from Stanley PO (Mon–Fri). Tayside Hotel PH1 4NL (Tel; 01738 828249, Fax: 827216) offers permits for salmon and sea trout during the summer lettings (May to July) on Linn Pool, Burnmouth, Catholes, Pitlichrie, Benchil, and Luncarty. Special rates to residents. Hotel has tackle for sale, and special anglers' facilities. Ballathie House Hotel (Tel: 01250 883268) lets rods on the Ballathie beat and elsewhere, when available, to residents.

Dunkeld (Perthshire). Dunkeld & Birnam AA and Perth & Dist AA have trout fishing on **Tay**. Wt £10; dt £2 and £1, respectively. Permits are also issued for grayling, mostly in the trout close season. Coarse fishing on **Loch Clunie**; dt £2. Concessions for OAP & jun. Permits from Kettles of Dunkeld, Atholl St, Dunkeld PH8 0AR (Tel: 013502 727 556). Dunkeld & Birnam AA also has brown trout fishing on **River Braan**; and **Loch Freuchie** at Amulree, trout and pike, bank fishing only. Permits for R Braan from Kettles and for L Freuchie from Amulree PO. Stakis Dunkeld House Hotel has salmon and trout fishing on Tay; 2 boats 3 rods; 8 bank rods; experienced ghillies; no salmon fishing on Sundays. **Butterstone Loch**, put and take rainbow and brown trout; fly only. 17 boats on water. Permits (day and evening) from Butterstone Loch Fishings, Butterstone, by Dunkeld PH8 0HH (Tel: 01350 724238).

Dalguise (Perthshire). Perth and Dist AA fishes Dalguise and Newtyle beats, permits £1 from Kettles, Atholl St, Dunkeld; also Kinnaird-Balnaguard fishing, north bank, from Ballinluig Post Office (Tel: 01796 482220). Permits, with boat and ghillie from Finlayson Hughes, 29 Barossa Place, Perth (Tel: 01738 630926/625134). £22–£50 per rod per day, depending on season.

Grandtully (Perthshire). Permits for Tay from Grandtully Hotel (Tel: 01887 840207); salmon, brown trout and grayling; fly, bait or spinning. Boat and ghillie on site. Booking advisable. For Tay at Edradynate and Upper Grandtully, permits from Robert Cairns (Tel: 01887 840228). Boat, ghillie and tuition offered.

Aberfeldy (Perthshire). Salmon and brown

trout fishing on Tay. Grayling tickets no longer issued, owing to out-of-season trout fishing. Weem Hotel, Weem, By Aberfeldy, Perthshire PH15 2LD (Tel: 01887 820 381) has trout and salmon fishing open to guests on River Tay, salmon, trout sea trout; Loch Tay, salmon, and trout; and various hill lochs, including coarse fish and wild brown trout. Permits also issued to non-residents. Special fishing breaks with accommodation either serviced or self-catering. Full ghillie service, tuition and tackle hire on request. Brown trout permit from R Kennedy, Borlick Farm (Tel: 01887 820463).

Kenmore (Perthshire). Tay leaves **Loch Tay** at Kenmore. Salmon and trout fishing on river and loch for guests at The Kenmore Hotel, Kenmore PH15 2NU (Tel: 01887 830 205); boats. Permits for non-residents from hotel or Post Office.

Killin (Perthshire). Killin & Breadalbane AC has fishing on **Loch Tay, River Dochart**, **River Lochay**, and **Lochan an Laraig**; salmon, brown trout, rainbow trout, perch, pike and char. Stocking policy includes annual stocking with mature brown trout. Salmon of up to 30lb are caught; rainbows of 5–6lb. An excellent venue for visiting anglers who are made very welcome. Rods for hire. Permits £5 for these waters, with concessions, from J R News, Newsagent & Tackle Shop, Main St.

Crianlarich (Perthshire). Trout fishing on **Loch Dochart** (good early in the season), **Loch Iubhair** and **River Fillan**, a tributary of Tay. In summer, salmon find their way into loch and up Fillan and tributaries. Best months: May, June, July and Sept. Dt £5. Day tickets for River Fillan from Ben More Lodge Hotel, Crianlarich FK20 8QS (Tel: 01838 300 210). Permits £5 for Lochs Dochart and Iubhair from Portnellan Lodge Estate FK20 8QS (Tel: 01838 300284). Boats, engines, and ghillies for hire.

Tributaries of the Tay

EARN: Salmon, sea trout, brown trout (av ½lb) and excellent grayling. Loch Earn fishing closed in winter.

Bridge of Earn (Perthshire). Rainbow trout fishing on **Sandyknowes Fishery**, 8 acres; fly only; bank fishing only. Bag limit 4 trout. Permits from E C Christie, The Fishery Office, Sandyknowes, Bridge of Earn (Tel: 01738 813033).

Auchterarder (Perthshire). Salmon, sea trout, brown trout and grayling. James Haggart, Haugh of Aberuthven, Auchterarder (Tel: 01738 730206) has fishing for the same at **Lower Aberuthven**: salmon on application, grayling ticket £4. All legal baits allowed. Tickets for **Orchill Loch** trout fishery, from A Bond, see below. Dupplin Estate, **Dupplin**, Perth PH2 0PY, Tel: 01738 622757, has £3 permit on offer for brown trout and grayling, issued Mon–Fri from estate office.

Crieff (Perthshire). Crieff AC has Drummond Castle, Braidhaugh and Upper Strowan beats, totalling 4½m, mostly double bank; brown, sea trout, salmon, dt £5 b trout, £5–£20 migratory fish, depending on month. Season 1 Feb–15 Oct; no Saturdays in Oct; also Drummond Loch, brown trout, dt £25 per boat for two. Laird Management Ltd has Lochlane and Laggan fishings, with sea trout and salmon, dt £12–£40, 1 Feb–31 Oct. Permits for Crieff AC waters from A Boyd (below), or from Crieff Tourist Office, 33 High St PH7 3HU (Tel: 01764 652578, Fax: 655422); for Laird Management waters from Tourist Office or from John Young, Whitecot, Camp Rd, Comrie PH6 2HA (Tel: 01764 670361). Brown trout fishing on **Loch Turret**; fly only; boats for hire. Permits from A Boyd (below). Drummond Trout Farm and Fishery, **Comrie** PH6 2LD (Tel: 01764 670500), 1m off A85, has three lochans stocked daily with trout, open all year, from 10am, dt £1.50, conc half price, easy disabled access. Braincroft Loch: brown trout permit from £5, at Braincroft Farm, By Crieff (Tel: 01764 670140). Cowden Loch: brown and rainbow trout permit at Lochyview Farm, Mill of Fortune, Comrie 01764 670677. A £5 grayling permit is obtainable for R Earn, from 15 Nov–15 Jan, from tackle shop: A Boyd, Newsagents and Tackle, 39 King St, Crieff PH7 3AX (Tel: 01764 653871).

St Fillans (Perthshire). Trout and charr fishing for visitors in **Loch Earn**. Whole of loch controlled by St Fillans & Lochearn AA. Stocked with brown trout, between 12oz and 2½lb. For permits, see Lochearnhead.

Lochearnhead (Perthshire). Loch Earn, natural brown trout, stocked browns, occasional rainbows and char. St Fillans & Lochearn AA water. Visitors day permits £6, boats £15–£29, from Drummond Estate Boat Hire, Ardveich Bay, Lochearnhead (Tel: 01567 830400). Permits also from Village Shop, Lochearnhead (Tel: 01567 830214); Village Shop, St Fillans (Tel: 01764

685309); and hotels. Nearest tackle shops in Crief, Killin, Callander. Hotels: Mansewood House; Lochearnhead: Clachan Cottage.

ISLA: Trout (av ½lb and up to 3lb) and grayling. Pike also in lower reaches.

Dundee (Angus). Permits for brown trout and grayling fishing from Strathmore AIA; and local tackle shops. Assn also issues permits for **Dean Water**, tributary of Isla; brown trout. Cameron Loch, **St Andrews**, brown trout; Lintrathen Loch, **Kirriemuir**, brown trout; Mill of Criggie, **Montrose**; Newton Farm, **Newport on Tay**; Rescobie Loch, **Forfar**; all brown and rainbow; details and permits from tackle shop: John R Gow Ltd, 12 Union St, Dundee DD1 4BH (Tel: 10382 225427).

ALYTH (tributary of Isla):

Alyth (Perthshire). Several streams in neighbourhood. Isla contains trout and grayling in lower reaches. Above Reekie Linn trout very numerous but small. Alyth Hotel can arrange salmon and trout fishing on River Tay and a number of its tributaries; also trout fishing on a selection of lochs. Both day fishermen and coach parties are catered for. Apply to The Alyth Hotel, Alyth, Perthshire PH11 8AF, Tel: 01828 632447.

ERICHT (tributary of Isla):

Blairgowrie (Perthshire). Salmon and brown trout. Blairgowrie, Rattray and Dist AC has fishing on part of Ericht. St £100; dt £15 and £2, trout; from local tackle shops and Tourist Information Centre. Salmon fishing for non-club members on Mon, Wed and Fri. Advance booking only on 4m stretch, £35–£40 per day, from Roger McCosh (Tel: 01250 875518). For information on this, contact Bridge of Cally Hotel. Various fishings on tributaries **R Ardle**, **R Blackwater**, **R Shee**; full information from Tourist Board, West Mill St, Perth PH1 5QP (Tel: 01738 627958); permits from tackle shops. **River Isla**: Jim Wilson (Tel: 01828 627205), Kate Fleming or James Crockart *below*; in Glen Isla, inquire from Mr Maynard (Tel: 01575 582278). For salmon and trout fishing on Isla and **Dean**, contact Strathmore AIA (Tel: 01382 668062). Permits from local tackle shops. Plentiful loch fishing in area, including **Lochs Marlee**, bank fishing only; **Tullochcurran** and **Shandra** (wild browns); enquire at tackle shops or Perth Tourist Office (*above*); **Butterstone Loch**, boat fishing for brown and rainbow, per-

mit from Bailiff, Lochend Cottage, Butterstone, By Dunkeld (Tel: 01350 724238); **Monksmyre Loch**, brown and rainbow, permit from Jim Wilson (Tel: 01828 627205); **Loch Nan Ean** and **Loch Bainnie**, brown trout, fly only, boat on Bainnie, permits from Invercauld Estate Office, Braemas; and others. Tackle shops: Kate Fleming, Shooting and Fishing, 26 Allan St, Blairgowrie PH10 6AD (Tel: 01250 873990); James Crockart & Son, 28 Allan St, Blairgowrie PH10 6AD, Tel: 01250 872056, who supply ghillie and instructor on R Isla. Other hotels: Bridge of Cally.

Blacklunans (Perthshire). Dalrulzion Hotel, Glenshee PH10 7LJ (Tel: 01250 882222) has salmon and trout fishing on **River Blackwater** from hotel grounds. Free to guests. Day permits offered to non-residents. Other fishings in vicinity.

BRAAN: runs from Loch Freuchie.

Dunkeld (Perthshire). Forestry Commission, National Trust and riparian owners have leased water on R Braan to Dunkeld and Birnam AA. Brown trout. Permits for Hermitage beat and beats 1 and 2 from Kettles of Dunkeld, Atholl St. Permits for beat 3 and for assn **Loch Freuchie** fishing (perch, pike, brown trout) from Amulree Tea Room, Amulree (Tel: 01350 725200). Amulree Hotel, Amulree, by Dunkeld, has private trout fishing on R Braan for hotel residents; fly only. Hotel has boat hire, also.

TUMMEL: Salmon, trout and grayling.

Pitlochry (Perthshire). Pitlochry AC has salmon fishing on R Tummel from marker post below Pitlochry Dam to bottom of Milton of Fonab Caravan Site; south bank only. Spinning, worm or fly only. Dt £6–£30; 3 anglers per day. Advance booking recommended, particularly for Apr–Jun. Recent average annual catch, 89 salmon and grilse. Contact Ross Gardiner, Pitlochry Angling Club (Tel: 01796 472157, evenings). Club also has fishing on **Lochs Bhac** and **Kinardochy**, brown trout. Bank and boat fishing on Bhac; boat only on Kinardochy. Fly only. Permits from Mitchells of Pitlochry (Tel: 01796 472613); or Pitlochry Tourist Office. East Haugh House Hotel Pitlochry PH16 5JS has various salmon beats on R Tummel and R Tay, dt from £25 per rod. Permits for trout fishing on R Tummel also from Tourist Office, Atholl Rd; Milton of Fonab Caravan Site; Ballinluig PO; and Ballinluig Service Station. **Loch Faskally**; created in 1950s by damming of R Tummel.

Salmon and sea trout ascent fish pass at dam, and may be caught from end of Mar–Oct 15; brown trout, pike, perch; any legal lure. Permits, boats and bait from D McLaren, Pitlochry Boating Station, Loch Faskally, Pitlochry PH16 5JX (Tel: 472919/472759). Tackle Shop: Pitlochry Fishing Tackle.

GARRY: Tributary of Tummel, good river for about 6m.

Killiecrankie (Perthshire). Pitlochry AC has salmon fishing on east bank. Dt £20, 4 anglers. For advance booking and information contact Hon Sec (Tel: 01796 472157, evenings). Bookings at short notice from Mitchells of Pitlochry.

Blair Atholl (Perthshire). Trout fly fishing on R Garry and **Tilt** (approx 4m), and salmon fishing on **R Tilt** (3m), combined dt £3, wt £12, conc; large trout and pike in **Errochty Dam**, dt £3; rainbow trout on Blair Walker Pond, dt £12. Permits from The Highland Shop, Blair Atholl, Perthshire PH18 5SG (Tel: 01796 481303).

Dalwhinnie (Inverness-shire). **Loch Ericht**, 22 mile long brown trout loch, and rivers; weekly permit £24, day permit £6, from Loch Ericht Hotel, Dalwhinnie, Inverness-shire PH14 1AF (Tel: 01528 522257). Open all year, boats for hire.

LOCH RANNOCH: Trout, some large but averaging 9oz; best May to October, also ferox trout, char, pike. Trout fishing in River Tummel, below loch.

Kinloch Rannoch (Perthshire). Loch Rannoch Conservation Assn has fishing on Loch Rannoch; brown trout, pike and char. Permits from Hon Sec, and local shops and hotels. **Dunalastair Loch** is a short distance east of Kinloch Rannoch, with brown trout; 5 boats, no bank fishing, fly only. Permits from Lassintulloch Fisheries (Tel: 01882 632330); or Dunalastair Hotel (Tel: 01882 632323). Moor of Rannoch Hotel, Rannoch Station PH17 2QA, Tel: 01882 633238, has trout fishing on **L Laidon**, **R Gaur** and **Dubh Lochan**, which is stocked with brown trout. Permits £3 per rod, £25 per day with boat and outboard. Rannoch & District AC has fishing on **Loch Eigheach**, 1m from Rannoch Station; brown trout and perch. Fly fishing only. Bank fishing only. June best month. St £15, wt £8, dt £3, from J Brown, The Square, Kinloch Rannoch. Permits for Loch Rannoch

and **R Tummel**, dt £4, wt £14, st £25, conc, OAP free, from Kinloch Rannoch hotels; Post Office; Country Store, Bridge End, Kinloch Rannoch PH16 5PX, who also sell limited tackle. Hotels: Loch Rannoch; Dunalastair; Bunrannoch.

LYON (near Loch Tay): Good salmon and trout river in the magnificently forested Glen Lyon, reputedly the longest glen in Scotland. River runs from two dammed lochs at glen head.

Aberfeldy (Perthshire). Salmon and brown trout fishing on **Lyon**; max 4 rods; no bait fishing. Permits from Coshieville Hotel, by Aberfeldy PH15 2NE (Tel: 01887 830319). Rods and ghillies for hire.

Fortingall (Perthshire). Fortingall Hotel has 3m on Lyon; dt £20 (salmon) and £5 (trout). Also **River Tay** and **Loch Tay** by arrangement from £20 per day. Special rates for guests. Apply to Alan Schofield, Fortingall Hotel, By Aberfeldy, Perth-shire PH15 2NQ (Tel: 01887 830 367).

Glen Lyon (Perthshire). Brown trout and salmon permits from Post Office House, Bridge of Balgie (Tel: 01887 886221). North Chesthill Beat: Gregor Cameron, Keeper's Cottage, Chesthill Estate (Tel: 01887 877207), £10–£15 per day, fly and spinning. Mrs Norma McDougall, Roromore Farm PH15 2PW (Tel: 01887 877213) has 1.3m south bank of R Lyon, with three pools. Main salmon run in autumn, average 10.4lb. Salmon dt £15, trout £3. Brown trout permits from the following: Mr Walker, Slatich (Tel: 01887 877221, £2.50 per day, fly only, except in spate; Mr Sinclair, Keepers Cottage, Cashlie (Tel: 01887 886237), £3–£5 per day, fly only, except in spate; River Lyon, £12.50–£15 salmon dt, £2.50 brown and rainbow trout dt, fly only, on application from Mr Drysdale, Keepers Cottage, Innerwick (01887 886218). **Loch an Daimh**: brown trout permit for north bank only, £3 from W Mason, Croc-na-keys (Tel: 01887 886224).

DOCHART (feeds Loch Tay):

Killin (Perthshire). At confluence of Dochart and Lochay, near head of Loch Tay. Salmon fishing best in July, Aug and Sept. Trout numerous and run to a fair size. Water is very deep and sluggish from Luib to Bovain, but above and as far as Loch Dochart there are some capital streams and pools. Auchlyne & Suie Estate

Water; trout and salmon. Permits issued by G D Coyne, Keeper's Cottage, Auchlyne, Killin FK21 8RG; Luib Hotel; and Glendochart Caravan Park. Trout fishing best April–May, good run of autumn salmon. Ardeonaig Hotel, South Lochtayside, Perthshire FK21 8SU, has own harbour with 4 boats on **Loch Tay**; salmon, trout and char. Salmon fishing for residents only, trout fishing tickets from Killin newsagents. Loch Tay Highland Lodges, Milton Morenish, by Killin FK21 8TY (Tel: 01567 820 323, Fax: 581), have salmon and trout fishing on Loch Tay; 18 boats with outboard motors for hire, trolling is the usual method. Hotel is ideally placed for fishing middle and western beats of the loch.

THURSO

A noted salmon river and one of the earliest in Scotland. The spring run has been improving recently, after a period of decline. Water level may be regulated by a weir at Loch More on the upper reaches. The river is entirely preserved.

Thurso (Caithness). Thurso AA has Beat 1 (from River Mouth up to the Geise Burn, including tidal water), which produces 10% of total river catch; members only, but possibility of permit if no members fishing; brown trout permit on Assn waters from Harpers (*below*). Salmon fishing (fly only) can be arranged through Thurso Fisheries Ltd, Thurso East, Thurso KW14 8HW (Tel: 01847 893134). Bookings usually by week, fortnight or month, but day lets arranged. Weekly charges, including accommodation, range from £515 to £900, according to date. Fishing improves progressively from opening on Jan 11 to close on Oct 5. First-class loch, burn and river fishing for trout. Salmon permits (on the day) from Cycle Shop, 35 High St. Brown trout loch fishing in vicinity: **Loch Calder**, **Lochs Watten**, **St John's** and **Stemster**; **Loch Hielan**; **Brubster Lochs**, **Dunnet Head Lochs**; permits for all these from tackle shop: Harper's Fly Fishing, 57 High St KW14 8AZ, Tel/Fax: 01847 3179.

Lesley Crawford, Caithness & Sutherland Angling Services, Askival, Reay, Caithness KW14 7RE, has fly fishing for wild brown trout on various lochs in Caithness. Contact L Crawford, or Harpers Tackle (*above*). Hotels: Park; Pentland: St Clair; Royal.

Halkirk (Caithness). The Ulbster Arms Hotel has fishing on **Loch Calder** and many other hill lochs; excellent accommodation and fishing, £410–£900 per week. Salmon fishing on **Thurso River**. Information from The Manager, Ulbster Arms Hotel, Halkirk, Caithness KW14 6XY (Tel: 01847 831 206/641).

Dunnet (Caithness). House of the Northern Gate, Dunnet Estate. 7 estate lochs for good brown trout. Contact Michael Draper (Tel: 01847 851622), or Internet: dunnet.estate.jab.net. St John's Loch AA has fishing on **St John's Loch**; bank and boat fishing. Permits from Northern Sands Hotel.

TWEED

Rises in corner formed by watersheds of Clyde and Annan, and flows over 100m to North Sea at Berwick-upon-Tweed, forming, for some of its course, the boundary between England and Scotland. The Tweed is probably the most popular of large Scottish rivers, partly owing to its proximity to England. It contains over 300 named casts and its salmon harvest is considerable. It has the longest season (1st February to 30 November), but at its best in autumn, especially from mid- to late October, when the run is noted for the size and number of salmon caught. There is a good spring run, and sometimes even the most famous beats such as the Junction at Kelso are open for permit fishing, for around £25 per day. Summer fish may be difficult to catch at low water. Ghillies are employed by most beats. The Tweed produces a strain of sea trout, formerly called bull trout, which are remarkable both for size and distance they are known to travel in sea. The best sea trout fishing is on tributaries, the Till and Whiteadder, both of which fish well in summer. The season on the Tweed is the same as for salmon, and the permits are combined.

Over recent years there has been a decline in wild brown trout fishing in the Tweed and Lyne. To combat this, the rivers have been stocked with brown trout. These are marked with a blue spot on the underbelly, and there is a bag limit of 4 stocked fish in force. Further, a policy of catch and release for indigenous trout is in operation. There has been improved brown trout fishing since 1995. There exists a code of conduct with regard mainly to fly fishing for salmon and sea trout, and full copies may be obtained from River Tweed Commissioners or from most tackle shops and letting agents.

"Tweedline" is a service for fishermen provided

by the Tweed Foundation, a charitable trust established by the River Tweed Commissioners to promote the development of salmon and trout stocks in the Tweed river system. It provides information on the following: Fishing reports and prospects (Tel: 09068 666410); River levels (updated daily) (Tel: 09068 666411); Last minute rod vacancies (Tel: 09068 666412). J H Leeming, Letting Agents, Stichill House, Kelso, Roxburghshire TD5 7TB, Tel 01573 470280, Fax: 01573 470259, provide a 24hr information service (01573 470322) and Internet: www.leeming.co.uk. There is a *Borders Angling Guide* produced by the local tourist board, which gives comprehensive information on the whole river, cost £1.50 from any Borders T I Centre. For further information write to Tweed Foundation, Drygrange, Steading, Melrose TD6 9DL (Tel: 01896 848 271, Fax:277). SEPA operate a local 24-hour pollution emergency response on 01896 754797. Anglers are requested to report incidents with urgency.

Berwick-upon-Tweed (Northumberland). Salmon, sea trout, trout, grayling, coarse fish. Tidal Tweed gives free fishing for roach and grayling. Salmon fishing on Tweed offered by J H Leeming, Letting Agents, Stichill House, Kelso, Roxburghshire TD5 7TB; 11 beats between Tweedhill, near Berwick, and Peebles; from £30 to £100, one or two rods per day; early booking advisable. Berwick and Dist AA has salmon and brown trout fishing on 8m of **River Whiteadder**, which joins Tweed 1m from Berwick. St £40, wt £20, dt £7.50, conc, for trout, from Game Fair, Marygate (Tel: 01289 305119); and Hoolets Nest, Paxton. **Till** enters Tweed 2½m above Norham, 9m from Berwick. **Coldingham Loch**, near Great North Road, Ayton. Brown and rainbow trout, 4 boats, bank fishing for 4 rods. Permits from Dr E J Wise, West Loch House, Coldingham, Berwickshire (Tel: 018907 71270), who has chalets and cottages to let. Booking essential. Coldingham is noted for the quality and size of the trout caught there. Tackle shops: Game Fair, 12 Marygate; and Jobsons, Marygate. Hotels: Castle; Kings Arms; Chirnside Hall, Chirnside; Hay Farmhouse, Cornhill-on-Tweed; Coach House, Crookham, Cornhill-on-Tweed. The owner of Wallace Guest House is prepared to arrange early starts and late returns for fishermen and has private parking; apply to J Hoggan, Wallace Guest House, Wallace Green, Berwick upon Tweed (Tel: 01289 306539).

Horncliffe (Northumberland). Tidal. Salmon,

trout, grayling, roach, dace and eel. No permits required for trout and coarse fishing. Salmon fishing on Tweedhill Beat; 3m single bank; 6 rods; 2 ghillies; 2 huts. Obtainable from J H Leeming, Letting Agent, Kelso.

Norham (Northumberland). Salmon, trout. Salmon fishing on Ladykirk and Pedwell Beats from J H Leeming, Letting Agent, Kelso. Ladykirk, 3½m single bank, 4 huts, 5 boats and up to 1–5 ghillies, 6–10 rods; over 3 years average catch 195; also good sea trout water. Pedwell, 1½m single bank for 2 rods with boat and ghillie; Mon, Tues, Fri, Sat only. Prices range from £30, to £120, 2 rods for 2 days. Ladykirk & Norham AA has fishing from Norham boathouse to Horndean Burn, both banks, brown trout, grayling, eels. Reputed to be one of the best waters along border. St £30, dt £5, concessions OAP, junior free if accompanied. Permits from Mace Shop; Masons Arms Hotel TD15 2LB; and Victoria Hotel.

Coldstream (Berwickshire). Salmon, sea trout. Salmon fishing on West Learmouth obtainable from J H Leeming, Letting Agent, Kelso. Mrs Jane Douglas-Home has rods to let at The Lees, TD12 4LF (Tel/Fax 01890 882706), £40–£60 per day. The Lees is a prime quality spring and autumn beat including the well known Temple Pool; 2m, 4 rods, 2–3 ghillies, 2 huts, 4 boats. West Learmouth is a good spring and autumn beat for 2 rods opposite The Lees; 2/3m of single bank with boat and ghillie. Prices vary considerably, from £25, to £540, 2 rods for 6 days. Tillmouth Park Hotel, Cornhill-on-Tweed TD12 4UU, has facilities for anglers. Sale & Partners (see *Fishery Agents)(see advt.)* offer fishing by weekly or daily booking on beats 2 to 7 of Tillmouth Water, **Cornhill-on-Tweed**. Prices range from £300 to £2,000 per week, and from £50 to £90 per day, depending on season. October is the most productive month. All prices include boat, ghillie, and use of fishing huts, plus VAT, Tweed levies and taxes. Head Ghillie: Tel/Fax: 01289 382443. Hotels: Collingwood Arms, Purves Hall.

Kelso (Roxburghshire). Salmon and sea trout preserved, trout and grayling. Salmon and sea trout fishing can be obtained daily during summer months on some of the best beats of the Tweed. For further information contact James H Leeming, Stichill House, Stichill, By Kelso (Tel: 01573 470280, Fax: 259). Kelso AA has about 8m of Tweed and **Teviot**, and short stretch on **River Eden**; brown trout and grayling. No

Sunday fishing; size limit 10in; restrictions on spinning; trout season, April 1 to Sept 30. Trout fishing good. St £20, wt £10, dt £5. Concessions for OAPs and juniors. Permits from local tackle shops. Brown and rainbow trout fishing on **Wooden Loch** at Eckford. 4 boats on site. No bank fishing. Advance booking necessary. Apply to Forrest of Kelso. Tackle shops: Forrest & Son, 40 The Square, Tel: 01573 224687; Intersport, 43 The Square; Tweedside Tackle, 36/38 Bridge St TD5 7JD (Tel: 01573 225306). Hotels: Cross Keys; Ednam House; Sunlaws House, Heiton, By Kelso.

St Boswells (Roxburghshire). St Boswells & Newtown District AA rent miscellaneous stretches on River Tweed between Ravenswood and Mertown; brown trout; rod limits on 4 stretches. Christine Grant, Newsagent, Newtown St Boswells. Assn also has rainbow trout fishing on **Eildon Hall Pond**, nr Newtown St Boswells. Permits from Brian Shackleton, Langlands Garage, Newtown St Boswells. Dryburgh Abbey Hotel (Tel: 01835 822261) is close to river, with excellent facilities for anglers.

Melrose (Roxburghshire). Salmon fishing on Bemersyde Beat, prime beat superbly set in beautiful wooded gorge; 1m with 6 rods, 1–2 ghillies, 4 boats. Prices range between £25 and £190, 6 days, 2 rods. Apply to J H Leeming, Letting Agent, Kelso. Melrose and Dist AA has 2m of Tweed around Melrose open to visitors for wild trout and grayling fishing. No Sunday fishing; no spinning or use of natural minnow or maggot permitted. St £12, dt £4 from Croal Bryson Garage, or Sec. Season 1 Apr–6 Oct trout, 1 Aug–1 Mar grayling. Barbless hooks and strict limit. 50% of permit sales donated to Tweed Foundation. Hotel: Burts.

Earlston (Berwickshire). A good centre for Leader and Tweed trout fishing. Earlston AA controls about 5m of **Leader** adjacent to Earlston, with the exception of two small private stretches. St £5 (OAP & jun £1), dt £1, from local hotels and shops. No Sunday fishing and Saturday fishing for st holders only. Two day permits at £1 each on River Tweed at Gledswood estate for st holders. Other portions of Tweed are reserved. No salmon or sea-trout fishing is open on trouting portions of Tweed. Hotel: Red Lion, Black Bull, White Swan.

Galashiels (Selkirkshire). Salmon fishing on

Fairnlee Beat, good varied autumn beat in lovely scenery; 3m of single bank, 20 small pools; 9 rods; ghillie, huts and full facilities. Prices, from £40 to £100, 1 rod for 6 days, depending on month. Contact J H Leeming, Letting Agent, Kelso. Gala AA has trout fishing on 13m of Tweed, part **Gala Water**, and part **River Ettrick**, st £20, wt 15, dt £10, schoolboys £2 (no Sunday tickets; no spinning). Tickets from J & A Turnbull, Tackle Shop, 30 Bank St; and hotels. April to Sept provides best daytime sport; Mid-June to Aug best evenings. Sunderland Hall (Tel: 01750 21298) has 2 rods let, £46–£394 per rod week, up to 30 Aug. The School of Casting, Salmon and Trout Fishing, offer weekly salmon and trout fly fishing courses throughout the season. Further information from Michael Waller or Margaret Cockburn, The School of Casting, Salmon and Trout Fishing, Station House, Clovenfords, Galashiels, Selkirkshire TD1 3LU (Tel/Fax: 01896 850293). Hotels: Kingsknowes, Woodlands.

Selkirk (Selkirkshire). Salmon fishing preserved. Good centre for Tweed, **Yarrow** and **Ettrick**, covering 80m of trout fishing. Selkirk and Dist AA has water on Ettrick and Yarrow; restocks annually from own hatchery; size limit 10in. Permits from Hon Sec; also from Honey Cottage Caravan Site, Ettrick Valley TD7 5HU (Tel: 01750 62246); Gordon Arms; Bridge End PO; Rodgersons, 6 High St. Trout average 4 to the pound and go up to 3lb. No spinning allowed. Rodgersons also have boat fishing permits £15 at Lindean Reservoir, for rainbow trout. Enquiries to D Mitchell, 28 Scotts Place, Selkirk TD7 4DR (Tel: 01750 20748). Hotels: Glen, Heatherlie House, Woodburn, Priory. Nearest tackle shops: Anglers Choice, 23 Market Sq, Melrose TD6 9PL. J A Turnbull, 30 Bank St, Galashiels.

Walkerburn (Peeblesshire). Salmon, trout. Tweed Valley Hotel, EH43 6AA, has salmon fishing on hotel's private beat. Peak season spring and autumn. Hotel also has river and loch, trout and grayling fishing on private and Peeblesshire Trout FA water; open all season. Hotel offers fishing courses at £97.50 one week adult. Tackle hire on site. Season: salmon, 1 Feb–30 Nov; trout, 1 Apr–30 Sep. Reservations direct to hotel (Tel: 01896 870636, Fax: 870639). George Hotel (Tel: 01896 870336) has permits from £40.

Innerleithen (Borders). Salmon, trout. Salmon fishing on Traquair Beat, good late autumn beat in grounds of Scotland's oldest inhabited historic house; 3m with easy casting and access for 10 rods; ghillie. £40 to £55, 1 rod. Contact J H Leeming, Letting Agent, Kelso. Peeblesshire Trout FA has trout and grayling fishing on Tweed; tickets sold by Traquair Arms Hotel.

Peebles (Borders). Salmon fishing on approx 1½ miles of River Tweed. Season Feb 21 to Nov 30. Fly fishing only. Tickets (limited in number) issued by Peeblesshire Salmon FA. St £130, apply by Jan 31, to Blackwood & Smith WS, 39 High St, Peebles EH45 8AH. Dt £25 and £35–15 Oct to 30 Nov. Permits only from Tweeddale Tackle Centre, 1 Bridgegate, Peebles EH45 8RZ (Tel/Fax: 01721 720979). Salmon and trout fishing on Town Water and Crown Water. Permits: £44 per 3 day, 16 Sept–30 Nov; £11 per week, 21 Feb–14 Sept. Apply to Tweeddale District Council, Rosetta Road, Peebles. Peeblesshire Trout FA has approx 23m on Tweed and 5m on **Lyne**; trout and grayling. Season April 1 to Sept 30. No spinning or float fishing. Fly only April and Sept and all season on upper reaches. Catch and release policy is described under main river heading; waders desirable. Good trout April/May on wet fly then dry best. St £36, wt £24, dt £8. Permits from Hon Sec (Tel: 01721 720131); Tweeddale Tackle Centre; Peebles Hotel Hydro; and Rosetta Caravan Park. Tweeddale Tackle Centre, 1 Bridgegate (Tel: 01721 720979), besides issuing permits on the waters above, will arrange fishing on private beats for salmon, sea trout and trout; and also arrange casting tuition by qualified specialists in all fly fishing techniques. Kingsmuir Hotel, Springhill Rd, Peebles EH45 9EP (Tel: 01721 720151) can arrange salmon and trout fishing on Rivers Tweed, Lyne and tributaries. Gytes Leisure Centre, Walkershaugh (Tel: 01721 723688) has permits for Town water from old railway bridge to Vennel, and Crown water from Hay Lodge, Vennel, to Manor Bridge. Peebles Angling School, 10 Dean Park (Tel: 01721 720331) offers instruction in salmon and trout fishing, and fishing parties on private water.

Tweedsmuir (Peeblesshire). Crook Inn, by Biggar ML12 6QN (Tel: 01899 880272) issues permits for Peeblesshire Trout FA water on Tweed; and on **Talla Reservoir** (300 acres) and **Fruid Reservoir** (293 acres); wild brown trout. Talla: fly only. Fruid: fly fishing, spinning and worm fishing. 2 boats and bank fishing on each reservoir. Permits also from Reservoir Superintendent, Victoria Lodge, Tweedsmuir (Tel: 018997 209). Hotels: Kingsmuir; Park.

Tributaries of the Tweed

WHITEADDER: Runs from junction with Tweed via Cantys Bridge and Allanton Bridge to source. A good trout stream which is well stocked with both natural fish. Upper waters, from Blanerne Bridge to source, including tributaries, are mainly controlled by Whiteadder AA.

Allanton (Berwickshire). Blackadder joins river here. Waters from ½m above Allanton Bridge (including lower Blackadder) down to tide are mainly controlled by Berwick & Dist AA. Salmon and sea trout fishing tickets on six recognised beats cost £40 season, £20 week, and £7.50 day, and are obtainable from Allanton Inn (Tel: 01890 8182600); R Welsh & Sons, Duns (Tel: 01361 883466); Game Fair, Berwick-upon-Tweed (Tel: 01289 305119). Allanton Inn caters for anglers; also excellent B & B at High Letham Farmhouse nr Berwick (Tel: 01289 306585), run by experienced angler.

Chirnside (Berwickshire). Trout. Chirnside is good centre for Whiteadder. From here to source, except for stretches at Ninewells, Abbey St Bathans Estate, Chirnside Paper Mills and Cumledge Bridge, river is controlled by Whiteadder AA, including all tributaries entering above Chirnside, except **Monynut** above Bankend; **Fasney** above Fasney Bridge; and certain stretches of the **Dye**. Tickets from bailiffs, hotels and public houses. **River Eye**, runs parallel to Whiteadder a few miles to N, entering sea at Eyemouth. Eye Water AC has water on River Eye at town, Ayton and East Reston, 3½m, and **Ale Water**; river stocked annually with brown trout. Tickets from McMurchies, High Street, Eyemouth. Hotels: Ship, Whale, Home Arms, Dolphin, Glenerne.

Duns (Berwickshire). Trout. The following streams are within easy reach: **Blackadder**, **Whiteadder**, **Fasney**, **Bothwell**, **Dye**, **Blacksmill**, **Monynut** and **Watch**. These, except Blackadder, are, with main stream, largely controlled by Whiteadder AA. Tackle shop: R Welsh, 28 Castle Street TD11 3DP (Tel: 01361 883466) sells tickets for local associations. Hotels: White Swan, Barnikin, Plough, Black Bull, Whip & Saddle.

Longformacus (Borders). 7m from Duns. On Dye, Watch and Blacksmill burns. Permits from

R Welsh, see *Duns*. Trout fishing from boat and bank on **Watch Reservoir**; 119 acres, fly only, stocked with rainbows from 1¾lbs, also "blues" and browns. Permits and refreshments from Bill Renton, The Fishing Lodge, Tel: 01361 890331/0860 868144.

Cranshaws (Borders). East of Scotland Water manage **Whiteadder Reservoir**; 193 acres, brown trout. Fly only. Bag limit 10 trout, bank fishing only at present. Permits from Mr Whitson, Waterkeeper's House, Hungry Snout, Whiteadder Reservoir (Tel: 01361 890362, (Office: 257).

BLACKADDER (tributary of Whiteadder): Very good for brown trout early in season.

Greenlaw (Borders). About 12m held by Greenlaw AC. Season from 1 April to 6 Oct, very good for brown trout, early in season, stocked every year. St £8 and dt £4, conc for OAP and juniors from Butcher's Shop, Blackadder Mini Market, 20 West High St TD10 6XA; Post Office; and hotels. Hotel: Blackadder,Cross Keys.

TILL and **BREAMISH**: Trout, sea trout, salmon, good grayling, some pike and perch.

Milfield (Northumberland). Local beats on River Till all have good seasonal runs of salmon and sea trout with resident stocks of brown trout and grayling. No Sunday fishing. Ford Public Water, 3m stretch; daily, weekly and seasonal tickets sold by Post Office, Milfield; and Post Office, Ford. Ford and Etal Estates, Estate Office, Ford, Berwick-on-Tweed, Tel: 01890 820224, has fishing as follows. Top Beat, 1m u/s of Redscar Bridge, single bank: Flodden Beat, 2m d/s to Tilesheds; Middle Beat, 1½m from Tilesheds d/s to Ford Bridge; let by day or week, max 3 rods. Upper and Lower Tindal Beats, 3m total, single bank, 33 pools for 8 rods; let by day or week. Bookings from Brian R Thompson, River Keeper, Redscar Cottage, Milfield, Wooler, Northumberland NE71 6JQ (Tel: 01668 216223). Prices range from £20 dt to £150 wt per rod.

Wooler (Northumberland). Upper Till private fishing, also **Glen**. Wooler and Doddington AA preserves 2m of the Till and 1m of **Wooler Water**; limited dt £6 issued to visitors staying locally, but not for Sundays; fixed-spool reels prohibited; no maggot fishing; fly only, Feb–April inclusive and from Sept 14 to Nov 30.

Tickets from Hon Sec. Some miles from Wooler, at Bewick Bridge, Breamish becomes Till. Wading in Till dangerous. **Bowmont**, also preserved. **Kale Waters**: Trout (small), grayling, with good sea trout in wet season.

Chatton (Northumberland). Trout, grayling; and some fine roach: preserved by Chatton AA for 6½m. Limited number of associated members' tickets, waiting list 5 years; st apply by Jan 1 to Hon Sec; dt from hotel.

EDEN: Wild brown trout

Ednam (Borders). No salmon fishing open to general public. Kelso AA has trout fishing for short stretch. Permits from Kelso tackle shops, dt £5, st £10.

Gordon (Berwickshire). Permits for brown trout fishing from Gordon FC, Hon Sec J H Fairgrieve, Burnbrae, Gordon, and from newsagents in village. £3.50 st, juvenile £1. No spinning. No Sunday fishing. Tackle, Tweedside Tackle, Kelso.

TEVIOT: First class for trout and grayling.

Roxburgh (Roxburghshire). Kelso AA controls some miles of brown trout fishing on Teviot and Tweed. Visitors tickets, day £5, season £20, conc; grayling day £4, week £8, from Kelso tackle shops (see *Kelso*).

Eckford (Borders). Eckford AA issues dt for Teviot; salmon and trout. The Buccleuch Estate has Eckford Beat. Contact Andrew Graham (Ghillie), Eckford Estate Cottage, Eckford, Kelso (Tel: 01835 850774). Morebattle & Dist AA has brown trout fishing on Kale Water, **Bowmont Water** and **Oxnam Water**. Permits from Hon Sec; the Garage; and Templehall Hotel.

Hawick (Roxburghshire). Hawick AC has fishing on River Teviot and tributaries **Slitrig**, **Borthwick** and **Ale**; salmon, sea trout, brown trout and grayling. Club also has fishing on **Lochs Alemoor**, pike, perch and brown trout; **Hellmoor**, brown trout, perch and pike; **Acremoor**, brown trout and perch; **Williestruther**, rainbow trout and brown trout; **Acreknowe**, rainbow trout and brown trout; **Synton Mossend**, rainbow trout and brown trout. Day permits £5–£10 from Hon Sec; The Pet Store, 1 Union Street; Hawick Tourist Office, and Sanford's Country Sports, 6/8 Canongate, Jedburgh. Hotels: Elm House.

Jedburgh (Roxburghshire). Jedforest AA has 3 stretches on Teviot, salmon, sea trout, browns and grayling; and **Hass Loch**, rainbow trout. Trout st £30, dt £5, salmon wt £130–£60, dt £35–£15. Conc for OAP & jun. Visitors permits for salmon from Hon Sec; for Hass Loch from Kenmore cafe or First & Last Shop, Jedburgh; for trout from Sanford's Country Sports Shop, 6/8 Canongate, Jedburgh TD8 6AJ (Tel: 01835 863019), and W Shaw, Canongate. Sandfords also sell Hawick AC tickets. Jedforest Hotel has stretch of Jed Water, which runs by hotel (brown trout). Royal Hotel can arrange fishing in Jed Water and Teviot.

LEADER: Trout (4 to lb).

Lauder (Borders). Lauderdale AA controls 6m of Leader and 20m of tributaries upwards from Whitslaid Bridge to Carfraemill with the exception of waters in Thirlestane Castle policies and Kelphope Burn above Carfraemill. St £4, wt £3, dt £2, conc, from Hon Sec, shops, hotels and Post Office. Earlston AA has water. Hotels: Tower, Oxton; Carfraemill (4m from Lauder); Lauderdale; Black Bull.

Oxton (Borders). Lauderdale AA has Leader Water from Carfraemill and tributaries.

GALA WATER: Popular trout water; fish average about 5 to lb.

Stow (Borders). Salmon and trout fishing on Gala Water. No permit required for local trout fishing. Royal Hotel stands on banks of Gala; apply to The Royal Hotel, Townfoot, Stow, nr Galashiels TD1 2SG (Tel: 01578 730 226).

ETTRICK and **YARROW**: Salmon.

Bowhill (Selkirkshire). The Buccleuch Estates Ltd has 12m double bank on Rivers Ettrick and Yarrow; salmon and trout, Tweed rules apply. Dt £20–£40, according to season, fishing best in autumn. Estate also has brown and rainbow trout fishing on **Bowhill Upper Loch**; fly only; dt £40 per boat, 2 rods, 4 fish per rod limit. Permits for loch and salmon fishing from Estate Office, Bowhill, Selkirk TD7 5ES (Tel: 01750 20753). All trout fishing in Ettrick and Yarrow by ticket; water being restocked with brown trout by Selkirk AA. Permits from Hon Sec; also from Honey Cottage Caravan Site, Ettrick Valley, Selkirk TD7 5HU (Tel: 01750 62246); Gordon Arms, Selkirk; Bridge End PO; Rodgersons, High St, Selkirk.

Ettrick Bridge (Selkirkshire). Ettrickshaws Hotel, Selkirk (Tel: 01750 522229) has 2½m single bank salmon and trout fishing, concessions for hotel guests; also private loch fishing for trout.

St Mary's Loch (Selkirkshire). East of Scotland Water manage **Megget Reservoir**; 640 acres; stocked brown trout, also Arctic char. Fly only. 6 boats and bank fishing. Bag limit: 6 trout. Permits from Tibbie Shiels Inn, St Mary's Loch TD7 5NE (Tel: 01750 42231). St Mary's Loch AC has fishing on **St Mary's Loch** (500 acres) and **Loch o' the Lowes** (100 acres); brown trout, pike and perch. Season 1 Apr–30 Sept, fly only until 1 May. Boat and bank fishing; fly and spinning; no private boats allowed. Outboard motors are really essential on St Mary's Loch, but they must be supplied by the angler as none are for hire. Permits £5 fly, £8 spinning, junior £2.50, boats £10 extra from Mr Brown, Keeper, Henderland East Cottage, Cappercleuch (Tel: 01750 42243); Tibbie Shiels Inn; The Glen Cafe, Cappercleuch; Gordon Arms Hotel, Yarrow; Tweeddale Tackle Centre, Eastgate, Peebles.

TYNE (Lothian)

Rises on north slopes of Lammermuir Hills and flows about 25m to North Sea a little south of Whitberry Ness, known best as brown trout stream.

Haddington (East Lothian). Brown and sea trout, and salmon. East Lothian AA controls most of water in county. St £10–£12 from Main & Son, 87 High Street, and East Linton Post Office, High St; also river watchers. No Sunday fishing; no spinning. Concessions OAP & jun. **Markle Fisheries** near Dunbar; 3 lochs total 10 acres, stocked daily with rainbow trout, also brown, blue, golden, tiger; fly only; one loch stocked with large carp, tench etc. Open all year, partial access for disabled. Permits from Lodge, Markle Fishery, East Linton, East Lothian EH40 3EB. North Berwick AC has no club water but organises 15 outings per year on various waters, for example, Loch Leven, Loch Fitty and North Third Fishery. **Hopes Reservoir**, near Gifford; 35 acre; brown trout. Fly only. Bag limit 6 trout. 2 boats. No bank fishing. Permits from East of Scotland Water, Alderston House, Haddington (Tel: 0162 082 6422). Tackle from Mike's, 46 High St, Portobello, Edinburgh.

UGIE

A small river entering the sea at Peterhead. Salmon, good sea trout, some brown trout. Salmon and sea trout best from July to October; good run of finnock in February and March.

Peterhead (Aberdeenshire). Permits for approx 13m of fishing leased by Ugie AA. St £125–£150, wt £50–£60, limited dt for tourists only, from Robertson Sports, 1 Kirk Street, Peterhead (Tel: 01779 472584); and Dick's Sports, 54 Broad Street, Fraserburgh (Tel: 01346 514120). Concessions OAP & jun. Braeside Fishery, Stirling Hill, Boddam AB42 3PB (Tel: 01779 473903) has fly fishing for rainbow, brown and brook trout, on 2.5 acre loch, stocked. Open all year.

Rathen Reel Affair Trout Fishery, Rathen by Fraserburgh, AB43 8UL (Tel: 01346 513329): lochs of 7 acres and 5 acres with fly fishing for rainbow, brown, tiger, steelhead and blue rainbow trout, ave 3½lb; dt £8.50–£19.50, access for wheelchairs. **Crimonmogate Trout Fishery**, Lonmay, Fraserburgh AB43 4UE (Tel: 0374 224492/01779 471432): fly fishing on two trout lakes. Crimonmogate Lake, 6 acres, wild brown trout and stocked with rainbow. Dt £18, limit 4 fish. **Loch Logie**, newly formed, 5 acres, stocked rainbow trout and wild brown trout. Open all year. Full day £18, limit 4 fish. Half day, £12, 2 fish. Tuition for beginners and tackle hire on site. Permits issued on bank. Hotels: Albert, Waterside Inn.

Tributaries of the Ugie

STRICHEN (or North Ugie):
Strichen (Aberdeenshire). Free trout fishing (subject to permission of riparian owners). Salmon fishing strictly preserved.

URR

Drains Loch Urr and flows to Solway. Late run of salmon; also sea trout, herling and brown trout.

Dalbeattie (Kirkcudbrightshire). Dalbeattie AA has Craignair beat, with salmon, sea trout, and brown trout, best Sept–Nov; fly, worm, spinning. Assn also has trout fishing on **Buittle Reservoir**; fly only; stocked monthly with rainbows. Various permits offered, incl dt for river

£17–£22, reservoir £12, conc, from M McCowan & Son, 43 High Street. (Branch also in Castle Douglas). Castle Douglas AA has about 5m of Urr; brown trout, sea trout and salmon. Assn also has fishing on **Loch Roan**, 60 acres, no bank fishing, 8 fish limit. Permits from Tommy's Sports Goods, 178 King St, Castle Douglas. Carp fishing on **Barend Loch**; permits from Barend Holiday Village, Sandyhills, By Dalbeattie (Tel: 01387 780663).

WEST COAST STREAMS AND LOCHS

Some complex fisheries and one or two smaller – though not necessarily less sporting – streams are grouped here for convenience. Other west coast waters will be found in the main alphabetical list.

AILORT

A short but good sea trout river which drains Loch Eilt and enters sea through saltwater Loch Ailort. One of the few rivers where run of genuine spring sea trout takes place.

Lochailort (Inverness-shire). Salmon and sea trout fishing on **Loch Eilt** and River Ailort; loch is renowned for some of largest sea trout caught in Britain. Fly only. Permits from Lochailort Inn. **Loch Morar**, a few miles north; good brown trout and occasional salmon and sea trout. Fly, spinning and trolling allowed. Boats from A G MacLeod, Morar Hotel, Morar, Mallaig, when not taken by guests. Also from Loch Superintendent, Tel: 01687 462388. Permits £4, weekly £20, boats £25 per day, or £2.50–£5 per hour.

LOCH BROOM (including Rivers Broom, Dundonnell, Garvie, Oscaig, Polly and Ullapool) **Achiltibuie** (Ross-shire). Sea trout, brown trout and sea fishing. Summer Isles Hotel has much fishing for guests on rivers and lochs in the vicinity. Sea trout and brown trout: **Lochs Oscaig** and **Lurgain**. Boat on Oscaig £24.50; no boats on Lurgain. Brown trout lochs, dt £5. Own boats for sea fishing. Apply to Robert Mark Irvine, Summer Isles Hotel, Achiltibuie, By Ullapool, Ross-shire IV26 2YG (Tel: 0185 622282). Inverpolly Estate, Ullapool IV26 2YB (Tel: 01854 622452) has salmon, sea trout and brown trout fishing, with accommodation, on the following: **River Garvie** (very good little sea trout river which runs from Loch Osgaig); **River Osgaig** (running from Loch Badagyle to Loch Osgaig, fishes best in late season); **River**

Polly, mainly below road bridge (numerous lies and pools), **Polly Lochs**, **Loch Sionascaig** and **Loch Badagyle**; **Black Loch**, **Green Loch**, **Loch Lurgainn** and others. Mostly fly only, Sunday fishing allowed. Loch permits with boat, £12–£15 (o.b. £10); bank, £5. Accommodation with fishing, £500–£550 weekly.

Ullapool (Ross-shire). **Ullapool River,** sea trout, brown trout and salmon; dt £15 (upper beat) and £6 (lower beat). **Loch Achall**, salmon, sea and brown trout; dt £12 (boat) and £6 (bank). Permits from Loch Broom Hardware (*below*). Salmon and sea trout fishing on **River Kaniard** at Strathkanaird; prices according to time in season. Also brown trout fishing in hill lochs. Full details from Langwell Estate (Tel: 01854 666268). Ullapool AC has brown trout fishing on Strathkanaird hill lochs: **Lochs Dubh** (brown trout), **Beinn Dearg** (brown and rainbow trout) and **na Moille** (brown trout and char). Membership for residents in area. 2 rainbow limit, no brown trout limit. All lochs fly only except Loch na Moille where under 15s may spin or bait fish. Open annual pike fishing competition on third Sunday in October. Day tickets £6. Permits from Mountain Man Supplies, West Argyle St IV26 2TY (Tel: 01854 613383) who have large range of fly rods, reels and flies; and Lochbroom Hardware, Shore Street (Tel: 01854 612356). Hotel: Argyle; Arch Inn.

Leckmelm (Ross-shire). Brown trout fishing on Leckmelm Estate lochs; excellent fish up to 4lb. Permits from Leckmelm Holiday Cottages, Loch Broom IV23 2RN (01854 612471).

Inverbroom (Ross-shire). **River Broom** is a spate river sometimes suitable for fly-spinning. Inverlael Lodge has approx 1½m, single bank, including 10 pools. The bottom pool is tidal. Inverlael Lodge also has fishing on **River Lael** and on some hill lochs. Apply to Inverlael Lodge, Loch Broom, by Ullapool (Tel: 01854 612471).

Dundonnell (Ross-shire). **Dundonnell River**; salmon and sea trout.

LOCH DUICH
(including Shiel and Croe)

Glenshiel, by Kyle of Lochalsh (Ross-shire). Salmon and sea trout. Fishing on **River Croe**, a spatewriter with late runs. National Trust for Scotland, Morvich Farm House, Inverinate, By Kyle IV40 8HQ, issues £12 permits on alternate

days by arrangement with neighbouring estate. Reductions for members. Sea fishing on Loch Duich. Hotels: Kintail Lodge; Loch Duich; Cluanie Inn, Loch Clunie.

EACHAIG
(including Loch Eck)

Drains Loch Eck and flows about 5m into Atlantic by way of Holy Loch and Firth of Clyde. Salmon and sea trout.

Kilmun (Argyll). On Holy Loch and Firth of Clyde. Eachaig enters sea here. Salmon, sea trout in Loch Eck (5m), where Whistlefield Inn, Loch Eck, has boats for guests: fly best at head of loch where **River Cur** enters. Other hotel: Coylet, Eachaie.

Dunoon (Argyll). Salmon and sea trout; limited weekly lets on River Eachaig from R C G Teasdale, Fishing Agent, Quarry Cottage, Rashfield, nr Dunoon, Argyll PA23 8QT (Tel: 01369 840510). Coylet Hotel, Loch Eck (Tel: 01369 840426) and Whistlefield Inn have salmon (mainly trolling), sea trout and brown trout fishing on **Loch Eck** for guests (preferential terms for residents); st £50, wt £25 and dt £5; boats for hire at hotels. Loch Eck is about 7m long. No good for salmon until early June; best in August, Sept. Apply to Whistlefield Inn, Loch Eck, By Dunoon PA23 8SG (Tel: 01369 860440). Dunoon & Dist AC has **Rivers Cur**, **Finnart** and **Massan**, salmon and sea trout, any legal lure; **Lochs Tarsan** and **Loskin**, brown trout, fly only; and **Dunoon Reservoir**, rainbow trout, fly only. Permits £7, £10, £11, conc, from Purdies of Argyll, 112 Argyll Street (Tel: 01369 703232). Permits for River Finnart; sea trout, and occasional salmon; £6, half day £4, conc, from S Share, Keeper's Cottage, Ardentinny, Argyll PA23 8TS. Good sea fishing in estuary for mullet and flatfish, etc. Glendaruel Hotel at **Glendaruel** (Tel: 01369 820274) has salmon, sea trout and trout fishing on **River Ruel** (best Aug to Oct). Permits £15, free to residents. Dunoon hotels: Lochside; Graigieburn.

LOCH FYNE
(including Rivers Douglas, Fyne, Kinglas, Shira and Garron, and Dubh Loch)

Large sea loch on west coast of Argyll, which provides good sea fishing. In rivers, stocks of wild salmon and sea trout have declined seriously, and Argyll Estates no longer offer fishings.

GAIRLOCH

A sea loch on the west coast of Ross.

Gairloch (Ross-shire). Gairloch AC manages several trout lochs, including Lochs **Bad na Scalaig Tollie**, **Garbhaig**. Permits for these from Mr K Gunn, Strath, Gairloch. Gairloch Hotel has sea angling, and trout fishing in hotel's own hill lochs. **Lochs na h-Oidhche, na Curra**, **Maree** and other fishing in remote mountain scenery; from Post Office, Pier Rd, Gairloch (Tel: 01445 712175); fishing from mid-June. Salmon and sea trout fishing in **River Kerry**, a spate river; easily accessible; season May–Oct; best Aug–Oct. Permits from Creag Mor Hotel. Shieldaig Lodge Hotel, by Gairloch IV21 2AW (Tel: 01445 741250) has salmon and trout fishing on **Badachro River** and trout fishing on a dozen hill lochs, boats on most. Priority to guests. Casting instruction for salmon and trout, rod repairs and special fly tying service from D W Roxborough, The Old Police Station, Gairloch (Tel: 01445 712057). Tackle, ghillie service and boat hire from Chandlers, Pier Rd (Tel: 01445 72458).

GLENELG

Rises in Glen More and flows about 10m to the sea at **Glenelg**. Preserved by Scallasaig Lodge. No fishing at present, owing to dramatic decline of stock.

LOCH LONG
(including Rivers Finnart and Goil)

A sea loch opening into the Firth of Clyde. Good sea trout, some salmon in streams. Finnart good in spates.

Ardentinny (Argyll). River Finnart enters Loch Long at Ardentinny. Dunoon and District AC lease both banks of **River Finnart** from Forestry Commission on condition that river is kept open to the public at a low cost. Grilse and sea trout, season July to mid-October. Small brown trout in plenty; healthy wild stock. Catch and return policy advised for late coloured spawning fish. Spate and high rivers due to wet Argyll climate makes all parts of river fishable – not many permits. Fishing peaceful and enjoyable. Permits for River Finnart and advice on

local fishing from S Share, River Warden, Keeper's Cottage, Ardentinny, Argyll PA23 8TS (01369 810228), also Purdies 112 Argyll St, Dunoon.

Arrochar (Dumbartonshire). Cobbler Hotel (Tel: 013012 238) overlooks Loch Long, where good sea fishing obtainable. Hotel has trout fishing in **Loch Lomond** (1½m).

Carrick (Argyll). Carrick Castle Hotel has salmon, sea trout and brown trout on River and **Loch Goil**, free to guests. Boat on loch.

Lochgoilhead (Argyll). River Goil Angling Club has 15 years lease on **River Goil** salmon and sea trout fishings, and has bought the salmon netting stations on **Loch Goil** with the intention of closing them for good. Club also stocks the river. Membership fee £100 pa plus £25 joining fee. Visitors dt £15. Loch Goil (sea fishing) – mackerel, dabs and cod. Strictly limited permits, boat hire and accommodation from J Lamont, Shore House Inn (Tel: 01301 703340). A tackle shop in village and at Carrick Castle.

FIRTH OF LORN
(including Loch Nell)

Forming the strait between Mull and the mainland on the west coast. Lochs Linnhe and Etive open into it. Good sea trout and a few salmon.

Oban (Argyll). Oban & Lorn AC has trout fishing on **Oude Reservoir** and on 26 fly-only lochs in the Lorn district; all brown trout, two with char. Oude Reservoir, stocked brown trout; club boat often located on this loch; bank fishing can be difficult because of fluctuating water level. **Loch Nell**, salmon, sea trout, brown trout and char; salmon best in summer; sea trout all through season. Other brown trout fishing include **Lochs Nant** and **Avich**, the largest of these waters. No bait fishing and fishing with more than one rod is illegal. Except for Loch Nell and Oude Reservoir, where spinning, bubble and fly are permitted, all lochs are fly only. There is a junior section which has separate outings and competitions; and juniors are given instruction, etc. Permits from tackle shops in Oban; and Cuilfail Hotel, Kilmelford (see Kilmelford). Forest Enterprise, Lorne Forest D.O., Millpark Rd PA34 4NH (Tel: 01631 566155) has brown trout fishing on **Glen Dubh Reservoir**. Permits J Lyon, Appin View, Barcaldine, Argyll. Brown trout fishing on **Loch**

Gleann a'Bhearraidh at Lerags. Permits from Forest Enterprise, Oban; and The Barn Bar, Lerags, by Oban. Accommodation one mile from loch: Cologin Chalets, Lerags, by Oban PA34 4SE, Tel: 01631 564501. **MacKays Loch**, well stocked with rainbows, plus natural browns, fishing from bank or boat, 10 minutes from town centre. Permits for this, and other hill lochs from Anglers Corner. Tackle shops: Anglers Corner, 114 George St, Oban PA34 5NT (Tel: 01631 566374); David Graham's, 11–15 Combie St, Oban PA34 4HN (Tel: 01631 566374). Hotel: Ayres; Columba; Manor House.

Kilninver (Argyll). On **Euchar** estuary (10m south of Oban on A816). Tickets for 1m of good salmon, sea trout and brown trout fishing on Euchan may be had from Mrs Mary McCorkindale, Glenann, Kilninver, By Oban (Tel: 01852 316282). Boat + 2 rods on **Loch Scammadale** £15 per day. Bank and river fishing dt £3. As the Euchar is a spate river, bookings are not accepted more than a week in advance. Price concession for full week booking. Permits for Euchar also from Andrew P Sandilands, Lagganmore, Kilninver; salmon, sea trout and brown trout; fly only; 3 rods per day only; no Sunday fishing.

Knipoch, by Oban (Argyll). **Dubh Loch** (Loch Leven and brown trout) and **Loch Seil**, (sea trout and brown trout); dt £10 with boat. **River Euchar**, salmon and sea trout; dt £10. **Loch Tralaig**, near Kilmelford; trout; bank fishing only. Permits from Mrs J Mellor, Barndromin Farm (Tel: 01852 316 273/297).

LOCH MELFORT

A sea loch opening into the Firth of Lorn south of Oban. Sea trout, mackerel, flounders, etc.

Kilmelford (Argyll) 15m from Oban. Cuilfail Hotel, Kilmelford, Argyll PA34 4UZ (Tel: 01852 200274 ext 264), can arrange fishing on **Lochs nan Drimnean** (10 min walk, trout; March–May, Aug–Sept best; fly only; 10in limit); **a'Phearsain** (15 min walk; trout, char; fly only; April–June, Aug–Sept best); **Avich** (5m by road; trout; May–Oct best); **na Sreinge** (8m by road and 35 min walk; trout; May–Oct best), and **Scammadale** (8m by road; sea trout, salmon; end June–Sept). Melfort (10 min walk; sea trout, mackerel, flounders, skate, etc; June-Aug best), and 5 hill lochs (hour's walk and climb; trout; June–Oct). Wt £25, dt £5. Membership from Oban & Lorn AC. Season: March 15 to Oct 15.

MORVERN

Lochaline (Argyll). Salmon and sea trout fishing on both **River Aline** and **Loch Arienas**. Native brown trout in over 16 hill lochs. River fishing £33 per day for 2 rods; loch fishing dt £5. Boats on site. Contact Ardtornish Estate Co Ltd, Morven, By Oban, Argyll PA34 5UZ (Tel: 01967 421 288). Fishing tackle from Estate information centre and shop; and self-catering accommodation in estate cottages and flats.

LOCH TORRIDON

River Torridon, small salmon and sea trout river, flows into Upper Loch Torridon. Outer Loch Torridon offers excellent sea angling for a wide variety of species.

Torridon. **Rivers Torridon**, and **Thrail**, **Lochs an Iascaigh** and **Damph**, and hill lochs. Loch Torridon Country House Hotel, Torridon, By Achnasheen, Wester Ross, IV22 2EY (Tel: 01445 791242), can advise on these, and also arrange fishing on Loch Maree, subject to availability. Salmon and sea trout fishing on **River Balgy**, which drains Loch Damph into southern shore of Upper Loch Torridon. Tigh an Eilean Hotel, Shieldaig IV54 8XN (Tel: 01520 755251) can advise on R Balgy and on other local fishing including sea angling, and has good local contacts at the Shieldaig Angling Club, and Torridon House Estate.

WEST LOTHIAN
(lochs and reservoirs)

Allandale Tarn Fisheries, Gavieside, **West Calder** EH55 8PT (Tel: 01506 873073): brown, rainbow, blue, gold, and tiger trout; minimum 1½lb to 16lb plus; dt (4 fish limit), £15, 5 fish limit, barbless hooks only; good facilities for disabled.

Beecraigs Loch, Beecraigs Country Park, **Linlithgow** (Tel: 01506 844516). Rainbow, brown trout, fly fishing, 6 boats on site. Limit, 12 fish per boat (2 rods). No bank fishing, conservation area. All facilities, including tackle hire and visitors centre. Advance booking essential.

Bowden Springs Trout Fishery, Carribber, **Linlithgow** EH49 6QE (Tel: 01506 847269), 2 lochs 5 and 2 acres, stocked daily with large rainbows, dt £10, 3 fish limit, open 7 days a week.

Crosswood Reservoir, West Calder (Tel: 01506 414004), fly fishing for brown, rainbow, American brook trout. Limit 6 fish. 3 boats on site. Tickets from reservoir.

Linlithgow Loch, Linlithgow. Rainbow and occasional brown trout, Mar–Oct, 20 boats incl one for disabled, and bank fishing. Limit, 6 fish per rod. Permits from Forth Federation of Anglers, PO Box 7, Linlithgow, West Lothian EH49 7LH (Tel: 01831 288921) or at lochside.

Morton Fishery, Morton Reservoir, **Mid Calder** (Tel: 01506 880087), fly only brown and rainbow trout, 8 boats on site, and bank fishing, limit 3–6 per rod. All facilities, tickets from Fishery.

Parkley Fishery, Edinburgh Rd, **Linlithgow** (Tel: 01506 842027), fly and bait fishing for rainbow trout. 5 fish limit, £15.

WICK

Salmon, sea trout and brown trout fishing on Wick. Spate river with good holding pools. River controlled by Wick AA. Famous Loch Watten (trout) is 7m from Wick.

Wick (Caithness). Wick AA has fishing on River Wick; salmon, sea trout and brown trout. River well stocked from Assn's own hatchery. Fly and worm fishing. Tackle specialist Hugo Ross, 56 High St, Wick KW1 4BP (Tel: 01955 604200) has boat and bank fishing permits on **Lochs Watten**, **St Johns**, **Toftingall**, **Calder**, **Stemster** and **Dunnett**: wild brown trout. Fly only on Watten and St Johns; all legal methods on Calder. Bank fishing is open on most other Caithness lochs, including those on the Thrumster Estate.

Lybster (Caithness). Lybster is 12m S of Wick at mouth of Reisgill Burn. Portland Arms Hotel, Lybster KW3 6BS can usually arrange salmon fishing on **Berriedale River**, also by arrangement on **River Thurso**. Trout fishing on several hill lochs by arrangement, also on **Lochs Watten** and **Calder**. Hotel has a boat on **Loch Sarclet**.

YTHAN

Rises in "Wells of Ythan" and runs some 35m to North Sea at Newburgh. Late salmon river, of no great account for brown trout, but noted for sea trout and finnock, which run up from June through to September, with some fish in October. Ythan has very large estuary for so small a river and is markedly tidal for the lower five miles or so of its course.

Newburgh (Aberdeenshire). Sea trout and finnock and salmon. Fishing on the large estuary controlled by Ythan Fisheries. Sea trout average 2–2½lb run up to 12lb; finnock May onwards with large ones in September. Fly fishing and spinning only; spoons. Ythan Terrors, devons and Sutherland Specials fished on a 7–8ft spinning rod with 8–12lb line as most usual tackle. Worm, maggot, bubble float and other bait not allowed. Lead core lines, sinking lines not allowed. Floating line with sinking tip allowed. Much fishing from bank, but boats for hire. Best months June to September. Limited fishing open from 1 June to 30 Sept. Prices on application to Mrs A J Forbes, Fishing Manager, Ythan Fisheries, 3 Lea Cottages, 130 Main Street, Newburgh, Ellon, Aberdeenshire AB41 6BN (Tel: 01358 789 297), who also stocks tackle.

Ellon (Aberdeenshire). Buchan Hotel (Tel: Ellon 720208) issues permits for Ellon Water on River Ythan.

Methlick (Aberdeenshire). Some spring fish, but main run Sept to Oct. Good early run of finnock; a second, smaller run in the autumn. Sea trout; June–Oct. Fishing on Haddo Estate water; now leased to Haddo House AA. Dt £6–£15. Permits from S French & Son, Methlick. Hotel: Ythanview.

Fyvie (Aberdeenshire). Brown trout, sea trout and salmon. Sept and Oct best months for salmon. Fyvie AA has approx 3m on upper River Ythan, single bank. St £25, before 30 Aug only, and dt £5 Feb-Aug, £10 Sept-Oct; obtainable from Vale Hotel or Spar Grocer.

Scottish Sea Fishing Stations

It is only in recent years that the full sea angling potential of the Scottish coast, indented by innumerable rocky bays and sea lochs, has come to be appreciated. Working in conjunction, tourist organisations and local sea angling clubs smooth the path for the visiting angler. He is well supplied in matters of boats and bait, natural stocks of the latter remaining relatively undepleted in many areas. The Scottish Federation of Sea Anglers can supply information about more than 50 annual sea fishing festivals, championships and competitions, at venues all around the Scottish mainland and islands.

Note: *The local name for coalfish is "saithe" and for pollack "lythe".*

Kirkcudbright (Dumfries & Galloway). Centre for excellent shore fishing. Rocky points give good fishing for dogfish, with occasional conger, bull huss and thornback. Clear water gives pollack, garfish, mullet. The Dee estuary produces bags of plaice, dabs and flounders. Boats may be launched at harbour, Ross Bay and Brighouse. Baits: lug and ragworm may be dug locally, mackerel and herring are obtainable in town. Tackle from Watson Mckinnel.

Stranraer (Dumfries & Galloway). Loch Ryan, the W coast of Wigtownshire and Luce Bay offer first-class sea fishing, boat and shore. Loch Ryan: codling, whiting, plaice, flounders, dabs, skate, conger, tope and dogfish. Other species found in Luce Bay and off Irish Sea coast include pollack, coalfish, bass, wrasse, mackerel, plaice, dabs, whiting, dogfish, conger. Tackle shop supplies blast frozen ammo sea baits, and live baits. Boats: Mike Watson, Main St (Tel: 01776 85 3225). Local club: Lochryan Sea AA, J Keith, Motehill, Glenluce DG6 0PE (Tel: 01581 300371). Tackle shop: Sports Shop, 86 George St, Stranraer DG9 7JS (Tel: 01776 702705) has information and tickets for Stranraer AA trout waters.

Girvan (Ayrshire). Pier fishing. Mostly plaice, codling, rays, flounder, pollack and ling, wrasse, mackerel, dogfish, conger, all from boat. pollack, wrasse, dogfish, codling, flounders from shore. Horse Rock is popular local fishing mark, approachable at half tide, nr Stranraer Rd. Lugworm and ragworm may be dug locally. Boat hire: Mark McCrindle, 7 Harbour St KA26 9AJ (Tel: 01465 713219); Tony Wass, 22 Templand Rd, Dalry (Tel: 01294 833724). Hotel: Mansefield.

Ayr (Ayrshire). On the estuaries of the Rivers Ayr and Doon. Beach fishing for flounders from Newton Shore, where baits may be dug; flounders and eels in harbour, mullet in tidal stretches of Ayr. Good mackerel and herring fishing from May to October. Good boat fishing for cod, spotted dogs, and other species. Tackle shop: Gamesport, 60 Sandgate.

Saltcoats and **Ardrossan** (Ayrshire). Shore fishing in the South Bay, and around the harbours, for pollack, wrasse, dogfish, eels, cod, saithe, flat fish and herring. Ragworm and lugworm may be obtained locally, at Fairlie Pier and Saltcoats Harbour. 3m north, Ardneil Bay, codling. Club: Ardrossan and District SAC.

Brodick and **Lamlash** (Isle of Arran). Cod, plaice, mackerel, conger, wrasse, pollack, gurnard and flatfish. Brodick has good fishing from Markland Point to Clauchlands Point. Boats from Brodick Boat Hire, The Beach, Brodick (Tel: 01770 302868/840255). Lamlash is the main centre for sea fishing on Arran, with boats for hire for mackerel fishing at Lamlash Pier (Tel: 01770 600 998/349). Johnston's Marine Store, Old Pier, Lamlash (Tel: 01770 600333) has tackle and comprehensive chandlery stock, with information on wrecks, etc.

Campbeltown (Argyll). Good sport with cod, haddock, flatfish, etc, in Kildalloig Bay and from The Winkie, causeway between Davaar Island and mainland. Plenty of loch and river trout fishing in vicinity. Details from the Tourist Information Office Mackinnon House, The Pier PA28 6EF (Tel: 01586 552056); or Kintyre Angling Club, Shore St. Tackle shop: A P MacGrory & Co, Main Street; Country Sports, Main St, both with permits for Kintyre AC waters.

Oban (Argyll). Best fishing off south and west sides of Kerrera Island. Best shore marks,

Salmore Point, North Connel at road bridge. Good mackerel fishing in Oban Bay. Species found from shore and boat: tope, conger, whiting, codling, cod, pollack, coalfish, skate, thornback ray, spurdog, dogfish, mackerel, ling, wrasse and gurnard. Boats from R Campbell, 14 Kenmore Cottages, Bonawe (Tel: 01631 75213). Charter boat 'Gannet', licensed for 10, all tackle provided. Contact Adrian A Lauder, 3 Kiel Croft, Benderloch, by Oban PA37 1QS (Tel: 01631 720262). Tackle shop: Anglers' Corner, 114 George Street PA34 5NT (Tel: 01631 566374) has information on all local fishing.

Portree (Isle of Skye). Sheltered harbour, with fishing marks in and around it. Free anchorage. Cod, haddock, whiting, coalfish, pollack and mackerel. For bait, unlimited mussels and cockles in tidal areas. Camastianavaig is a sheltered bay 4m south east of Portree, where heavy bags of skate, cod, whiting, haddock, spurdog, gurnard, pollack may be caught with trace or paternoster. Boat for hire: Greshornish House Hotel (Tel: 0147082 266).

Kyle of Lochalsh (Ross-shire). Pollack and mackerel frequent; occasional cod, ling, conger, skate. Wreck fishing around Isle of Skye waters. Mussels, clams and cockles are local baits. Tackle shop: Maclennan & Co, Marine Stores (Tel: 01599 4208). Boat fishing trips from Vango Marine Leisure, Blairdhu House, Kyle Farm Rd, Kyleakin, Isle of Skye (Tel: 01599 534760). Tackle supplied, disabled facilities aboard.

Shieldaig (Ross-shire). Skate, cod, conger, saithe, ling, huss, dabs, sole and mackerel. Fishing in sea lochs of Shieldaig, Torridon and Upper Torridon; sheltered water nearly always. Outside lochs conditions can be dangerous.

Gairloch (Ross-shire). Cod, haddock, mackerel, whiting, pollack, saithe, ling, thornback and flatfish in Loch Gairloch. Disabled anglers have free access to Gairloch Pier. Boats for sea angling, including skippered cruises from West Highland Marine Ltd, Chandlers, Pier Rd, Gairloch IV21 2AH (Tel: 014458 712458, Fax: 712511). Charter boats from Kerry sea Angling, Caberfeidh, Auchtercairn, Gairloch IV21 2BP (Tel: 01445 712369); full and half-day trips, tackle provided, common skate fishing and mixed. B & B and self-catering accommodation Gairloch Tourist Information Centre, Achtercairn, Gairloch IV21 2DN (Tel: 01445 712130).

Ullapool and **Summer Isles** (Ross-shire).

Skate, also haddock, whiting, codling, pollack, coalfish, mackerel, gurnard, flatfish, thornback ray, conger, dogfish, turbot and wrasse. Inshore sport from dinghies and in charter boats around the Summer Isles. Good shore fishing at Morefield, Rhu and Achiltibuie. Charter boats from I McLeod, Achiltibuie. Boats and fishing tackle for hire, from Ardmair Point Caravan Site and Boat Centre (Tel: 01854 612054). Tackle shop: Lochbroom Hardware, Shore Street, Ullapool.

Lochinver (Sutherland). Cod, halibut, skate, tope, saithe, codling, lythe, mackerel. A large fleet of fishing boats operates from harbour. Tackle from Lochinver Chandlery, Culag Sq (Tel: 015714 228/398). Hotel: Lochinver.

Stornoway (Isle of Lewis). Cod, conger, pollack, ling, dabs, bluemouth, flounder, dogfish, wrasse, whiting, saithe, skate, etc. Fast-growing centre with local club, Stornoway Sea AC, South Beach Quay, whose secretary will gladly help visiting anglers. Club organises Western Isles Sea Angling Championships in August. Accommodation and information from Maryann Macnar, Western Isles Tourist Board, 26 Cromwell St, Stornoway Isle of Lewis HS1 2DD (Tel: 01851 703088, Fax: 705244).

Kirkwall (Orkney). Sheltered waters in Scapa Flow hold variety of fish (record skate; halibut over 150lb, ling of 36lb). Also plaice, pollack, coalfish, haddock, mackerel, wrasse, from shore or boat. Boats mainly booked by divers, hence hard to obtain. Orkney Tourist Information, Broad Street, Kirkwall KW15 1NX. Tackle shops: E Kemp, 31–33 Bridge St; W.S. Sinclair, 27 John St, Stromness. Hotels: Stromness; Royal Hotel, Stromness.

Lerwick (Shetland). Superb skate fishing: Nearly 200 skate over 100lb taken. Also excellent mixed fishing for ling, cod, tusk, haddock, pollack, etc, and chance of halibut. Area holds British records for tusk, homelyn ray, grey gurnard and Norway haddock. Also Scottish hake record. Tackle shops: J A Manson, 88 Commercial St; Cee & Jays, 5 Commercial Rd. Hotels: Lerwick, Shetland; and Busta House, Brae.

Thurso (Caithness). Conger from harbour walls, and rock fishing. Cod, ling, haddock, conger, pollack, coalfish, dogfish, spurdog, plaice, wrasse, mackerel, dabs, whiting, rays, halibut, porbeagle shark. Thurso Bay and Dunnet head are sheltered areas. Baits: mussel and lugworm at lower water. Most boats are based at **Scrabster**. Tackle shop: Harpers, 57 High St KW14 8AZ (Tel: 01847 63179).

Wick (Caithness). Mainly rock fishing for conger, pollack, saithe, cod, haddock, mackerel and flatfish. Porbeagle shark off Caithness, and excellent halibut fishing. Good points are: Longberry, Broadhaven, Sandigoe and Helman Head. Excellent cod fishing off Noss Head. Best months: June to Sept. Hotels: Nethercliffe; Mackay's; Norseman; Queen's. For further information contact Wick Tourist Information Centre: Whitechapel Rd (Tel: 01955 60 2596, Fax: 4940).

Portmahomack (Ross-shire). Good opportunities for cod, ling, pollack, etc. The best of the season runs from April to October, probably peaking in August and September. Good reef and limited wreck fishing. Charter vessel for parties of up to 12; boats charged at £30 per hour or £160 per day including roads and bait. Accommodation can be arranged. Contact John R MacKenzie, Carn Bhren, Portmahomack, by Tain IV20 1YS (Tel: 01862 871257). Tackle shop: R McLeod, Tackle Shop, Lamington St (wide and comprehensive stock including bait). Hotels: Caledonian; Castle: and Oystercatcher.

Lossiemouth (Moray). Notable centre for sea-trout fishing off east and west beaches; spinning into breakers provides splendid sport. Also mackerel, saithe, flatfish from beach, pier and boats. Tackle shops: Angling Centre, Moss St, Elgin; The Tackle Shop, High St, Elgin.

Aberdeen (Aberdeenshire). Excellent rock fishing for codling, saithe, mackerel, whiting, haddock and flatfish. Few boats. Hotels: Caledonian, Imperial, Royal.

Stonehaven (Kincardineshire). Rock fishing for haddock, flounder and mackerel very good. Cod, haddock, ling, etc, from boats; available from A Troup (Tel: 01569 62892), W Lawson (Tel: 01569 63565) and J Lobban (Tel: 01569 65323). Bait may be ordered from the above. Tackle shops: Davids, Market Square. Hotel: Arduthie House.

Nairn (Nairn). Sea angling on Moray Firth. Most fishing is done from two piers at the entrance to the harbour which is tidal, or on the beach at low water. Tackle shop: Pat Fraser, Radio, TV and Sports shop, 41 High St (Tel: 01667 453038); issues permits for 7m stretch of R Nairn, with sea trout and salmon, and stillwaters. Hotels: Altonburn; and Greenlawns Guest House.

Dundee (Angus). Fishing from rocks, pier and boats at Broughty Ferry, Easthaven and Carnoustie for mackerel, cod, saithe, lythe and flatfish. Fishing from boats at Arbroath; for bookings apply to Doug Masson, 12 Union St DD1 4BH (Tel: 01382 225427). Tackle shop: John R Gow Ltd, 12 Union Street, who issue permits for Strathmore AA waters.

Dunbar (Lothian). Excellent rock, pier and boat fishing. Saithe, cod (up to 10lb), codling, dabs, plaice, flounders, eels and, at times, small whiting, gurnard and mackerel can be caught.

Fishing Clubs & Associations in Scotland

Included in the list of fishing clubs and associations in Scotland are those organisations which are in England, but which have water on the Tweed and its tributaries or on the Border Esk. Further information can usually be had from the secretaries and a courtesy which is appreciated is the inclusion of a stamped addressed envelope with postal inquiries. Please advise the publishers (address at the front of the book) of any changed details for the next edition.

National Bodies

Association of Salmon Fishery Boards
5A Lennox Street
Edinburgh
EH4 1QB
Tel: 0131 343 2433
Fax: 0131 332 2556

Committee for the Promotion of Angling for Disabled People
Scottish Sports Association for Disabled People
Fife Sports Institute
Viewfield Road
Glenrothes
Fife KY6 2RB
Tel: 01592 415700
Fax: 01592 415721

Federation of Highland Angling Clubs
K Macdonald
30 Swanston Avenue
Scorguie
Inverness IV3 8QW
Tel: 01463 240095
Over 30 clubs and associations registered

Fisheries Research Services, Freshwater Fisheries Laboratory
Faskally
Pitlochry
Perthshire PH16 5LB
Tel: 01796 472060
Fax: 01796 473523
Internet: www.marlab.ac.uk

Forestry Enterprise
Information Office
231 Corstorphine Road
Edinburgh EH12 7AT
Tel: 0131 334 0303

Fax: 0131 334 3047
Internet: www.forestry.gov.uk

Handicapped Anglers' Trust
Taigh na lasgair
Russell Close
Little Chalfont
Bucks HP6 6RE
Tel/Fax: 01494 764333

Institute of Aquaculture
University of Stirling
Stirling FK9 4LA
Tel: 01786 473171
Fax: 01786 472133

International Fly Fishing Association
Ian Campbell, Secretary and Treasurer
Cruachan
16 Marindin Park
Glenfarg
Perth & Kinross
PH2 9NQ
Tel/Fax: 01577 830 582

Scottish Anglers' National Association
Caledonia House
South Gyle
Edinburgh EH12 9DQ
Tel: 0131 339 8808
Fax: 0131 317 7202
Internet: www.sana.org.uk

The Scottish Executive Rural Affairs Department
Pentland House
47 Robb's Loan
Edinburgh EH14 1TY
Tel: 0131 244 6231
Fax: 0131 244 6313
Internet: www.scotland.gov.uk

Scottish Federation of Sea Anglers
Caledonia House
South Gyle

Edinburgh EH12 9DQ
Tel: 0131 317 7192

The Scottish Office Agriculture and Fisheries Department
Marine Laboratory
PO Box 101
Victoria Road
Aberdeen AB9 8DB
Tel: 01224 876544.
Fax: 01224 295511

Scottish Record Fish Committee (Saltwater)
G T Morris
8 Burt Avenue
Kinghorn, Fife
Tel: 01592 890055
Aims as for British Record Fish Committee
sportscotland
(formerly Scottish Sports Council)
Caledonia House
South Gyle
Edinburgh EH12 9DQ
Tel: 0131 317 7200
Fax: 0131 317 7202

Scottish Tourist Board
23 Ravelston Terrace
Edinburgh EH4 3TP
Tel: 0131-332 2433
Internet:
www.holiday.scotland.net
Gives information on fishing holidays in Scotland

CLUBS

Aberfeldy Angling Club
G MacDougall
60 Moness Crescent
Aberfeldy
Perthshire PH15

Aberfoyle Fishing Club
J McGuire
Dunbiggan
Blairholle
Port of Menteith
Perthshire

Achnasheen Angling Club
c/o Ledgowan Lodge Hotel
Achnasheen
Ross-shire IV22 2EJ

**Airdrie and District
Angling Club**
J Potter
c/o 12 Sharp Avenue
Coatbridge
Lanarkshire ML5 5RP

Assynt Angling Club
A Munro
Ardglas Guest House
Lochinver, Sutherland

Avon Angling Club
P Brooks
3 The Neuk
Stonehouse
Lanarkshire ML9 3HP

**Badenoch Angling
Association**
Alexander Bennett
113 High St
Kingussie
Inverness-shire PH21 1JD

**Ballater Angling
Association**
Dr T Fallowfield
Ben Avon
Kindrochit Drive
Braemar
Aberdeenshire AB35 5YW

Beauly Angling Club
D K Sellers
Mingulay
Easter Moniak
Kirkhill
Inverness-shire IV5 7PP

**Berwick and District
Angling Association**
D Cowan
129 Etal Road
Tweedmouth
Berwick TD15 2DU

**Blairgowrie, Rattray and
District Angling
Association**
Walter Matthew
9 Mitchell Square
Blairgowrie
Perthshire PH10 6HR

Brechin Angling Club
W Balfour
Tanera
9 Cookston Crescent
Brechin, Angus DD9 6BP

Carradale Angling Club
Donald Paterson
21 Tormhor
Carradale
Argyll PA28 6SD

**Castle Douglas and
District Angling
Association**
Stanley Kaye
2 Cairnsmore Road
Castle Douglas, Galloway
DG7 1BN

**Central Scotland Anglers'
Association**
Kevin Burns
53 Fernieside Crescent
Edinburgh
EH17 7HS

**Chatton Angling
Association**
J Douglas
10 Church Hill
Chatton, Alnwick
Northumberland

**Cobbinshaw Angling
Association**
J Glynn
6 Rosshill Terrace
Dalmeny Station
Kirkcaldy
EH30 9JS

**Coldstream and District
Angling Association**
H F Bell
12 Priory Hill
Coldstream
Berwickshire

Cramond Angling Club
Craig Campbell
2 Canmore Street
South Queensferry
West Lothian
EH30 9ND

Crieff Angling Club
Patrick McEwan
11A Sauchie Road
Crieff
Perthshire PH7 4EF

Cumbrae Angling Club
P J Lonsdale
Isle of Cumbrae
Scotland KA28 0HA

**Dalbeattie Angling
Association**
J Moran
12 Church Crescent
Dalbeattie
Kirkcudbrightshire DG5 4BA

Dalry Angling Association
N Harvey
Lochside Cottage
Balmaclellan
Castle Douglas
Kirkcudbrightshire DG7 3QA

**Devon Angling
Association**
R Breingan
33 Redwell Place
Alloa
Clackmannanshire FK10 2BT

Dreghorn Angling Club
R Irvine
54 Dunlop Crescent
Dreghorne
Ayrshire KA11 4HN

**Dunfermline Artisan
Angling Club**
W B Stewart
13 Foresters Lea Crescent
Dunfermline
Fife KY12 7TE

**Dunkeld and Birnam
Angling Association**
A Steele
21 Willowbank
Birnam
Dunkeld
Perthshire PH8

**Dunoon and District
Angling Club**
A H Young
Ashgrove
28 Royal Crescent
Dunoon, Argyll PA23 7AH

**Earlston Angling
Association**
D G Stafford
36 Queensway
Earlston, Berwickshire

**East Lothian Angling
Association**
John Crombie
10 St Lawrence
Haddington
East Lothian EH41 3RL

**Eckford Angling
Association**
The Buccleuch Estates Ltd
Bowhill, Selkirk

**Esk and Liddle Fisheries
Association**
G L Lewis
Buccleuch Estates Ltd
Ewesbank, Langholme
Dumfriesshire
DG13 0ND
**Esk Valley Angling
Improvement Association**
Kevin Burns
53 Fernieside Crescent
Edinburgh
Evanton Angling Club
P F Cumberlege
Balavoulin
Evanton
IV16 9XW
Eye Water Angling Club
William S Gillie
2 Tod's Court
Eyemouth
Berwickshire TD14 5HW
**Federation of Highland
Angling Clubs**
W Brown
Coruisk
Strathpeffer
Ross-shire IV14 9BD
Fyvie Angling Association
J D Pirie
Prenton
South Road
Oldmeldrum, Inverurie
Aberdeenshire AB51 0AB
Gairloch Angling Club
Mrs L MacKenzie
4 Strath
Gairloch
Ross-shire IV21 2BX
**Galashiels Angling
Association**
S Grzybowski
3 St Andrews Street
Galashiels, Selkirkshire
TD1 1EA
Gartmore Fishing Club
W D Hodge
Buchanan Cottage
Gartmore
Perthshire
3 St Andrews Street
Galashiels, Selkirkshire
TD1 1EA
**Gatehouse and
Kirkcudbright Angling
Association**
C M Jeffrey

Pulcree Cottage
Gatehouse of Fleet
Castle Douglas
DG7 2BS
GlenOrchy Angling Club
I MacIntyre
4 Scott Terrace
Dalmally
Argyll PA33 1BX
Goil Angling Club
Ian K Given
"Bonnyrigg"
25 Churchill Drive
Bishopton
Renfrewshire PA7 5HB
Gordon Fishing Club
J Fairgrieve
Burnbrae, Eden Road
Gordon
Berwickshire TD3 6UU
**Greater Glasgow and
Clyde Valley Tourist
Board**
11 George Square
Glasgow G2 1DY
Tel: 0141 204 4480/4772 Fax
**Greenlaw Angling
Association**
Mr T Waldie
26 East High Street
Greenlaw, Berwickshire
TD10 6UF
**Haddo House Angling
Association**
J French
Kirkton
Methlick
Ellon, Aberdeenshire
Hawick Angling Club
E J Stewart
24 Borthaugh Road
Hawick
Roxburghshire TD9 0BZ
Inverness Angling Club
K Macdonald
30 Swanston Avenue
Inverness IV3 8QW
**Jedforest Angling
Association**
G Page
34E Castlegate
Jedburgh
Roxburghshire TD8 6EX
Keithick Angling Club
John Carrick
c/o Athole Arms
Coupar Angus

Kelso Angling Association
Euan M Robson
Elmbank
33 Tweedside Park, Kelso
Roxburghshire TD5 7RF
**Killin and Breadalbane
Angling Club**
Dave Murray
"Clan Alpine"
Main Street
Strathyre
Perthshire FK18 8NA
Kilmaurs Angling Club
Colin Ritchie
48 Hillmoss
Kilmaurs, Ayrshire
Kilsyth Fish Protection
P Clark
9 Jeffery Place
Kilsyth G65 9NQ
**Kinlochewe Angling
Association**
c/o S Condon
Glendocherty Craft Shop
Kinlochewe
Ross-shire IV22 2PA
Kintyre Angling Club
N J McNaughton
75 Ralston Street
Campbeltown,
Argyll PA28 6LG
**Kyles of Bute Angling
Club**
Allen Richardson
Allt Beag
Tighnabruaich, Argyll
PA21 2BE
**Ladykirk and Norham
Angling Association**
R G Wharton
8 St Cuthberts Square
Norham
Berwick-upon-Tweed
Northumberland TD15 2LE
(Tel: 01289 382467)
Lairg Angling Club
J M Ross
St Murie
Church Hill Road
Lairg, Sutherland IV27 4BL
**Lamington and District
Angling Improvement
Association**
B Dexter
Red Lees
18 Boghall Park
Biggar, Lanarkshire ML12 6EY

Lauderdale Angling Association
Donald M Milligan
The Torrs
Portling
By Dalbeattie
Kirkcudbrightshire
DG5 4PZ

Linlithgow Coarse Angling Club
See Scottish Federation of
Coarse Angling
T C Macnair
MacArthur Stewart
Boswell House
Argyll Square
Oban, Argyll PA34 4BD

Lochgilphead and District Angling Club
D MacDougall
23 High Bank Park
Lochgilphead
Argyll PA31 8NL

Loch Lomond Angling Improvement Association
R A Clement & Co,
Chartered Accountants
29 St Vincent Place
Glasgow G1 2DT

Loch Rannoch Conservation Association
E M Beattie
2 Schiehallion Place
Kinloch Rannoch
Perthshire

Lochryan Sea Angling Association
J Keith
Motehill
Glenluce DG6 0PE
Tel: 01581 300371

Melrose and District Angling Association
T McLeish
Planetree Cottage
Newstead
Melrose
Roxburghshire TD6 9DD

Monikie Angling Club
I Smith
6 Collier Street
Carnoustie
Angus DD7 7AJ

Monklands District Coarse Angling Club
John McShane
5 Crinian Crescent

Townhead
Coatbridge
Lanarkshire ML5 2LG

Montrose Angling Club
c/o Community Office
George Street
Montrose
Angus

Morebattle Angling Club
D Y Gray
17 Mainsfield Avenue
Morebattle
Kelso
Roxburghshire

Muirkirk Angling Association
J Timmins
38 Hareshaw Crescent
Muirkirk
Ayrshire KA18 3P

Musselburgh and District Angling Association
George Brooks
29 Eskside West
Musselburgh
East Lothian EH21 6PP

Nairn Angling Association
K Macdonald (Treasurer)
Mu Dheireadh
Claymore Gardens
Nairn
Inverness IV12 4JB

New Cumnock Angling Association
T Basford
1 Pathhead
New Cumnock KA18 4DS

New Galloway Angling Association
Allan Cairnie
4 Carsons Knowe
New Galloway
Castle Douglas
Kirkcudbrightshire DG7 3RY

Newton Berwick Angling Club
Bertie Marr
1 St Coans Place
Newtown Stewart
Wigtownshire

North Berwick Angling Club
Norman M Morrison
Kidlaw Farm
Gifford
East Lothian EH39 4JW

North Uist Angling Club
P Harding
Claddach, Kyles
North Uist HS6 5EW

Oban and Lorne Angling Club
c/o Anglers Corner
114 George St
Oban
Argyll PA34 5NT

Orkney Trout Fishing Association
Captain James E Purvis
3 Maitland Place
Finstown
Orkney Isles KW17 2EQ

Peeblesshire Salmon Fishing Association
Messrs Blackwood & Smith,
W.S.
39 High Street
Peebles, Peeblesshire
EH45 8AH

Peeblesshire Trout Fishing Association
David G Fyfe
Blackwood and Smith, W.S.
39 High Street
Peebles, Peeblesshire
EH45 8AH

Portree Angling Association
Neil Cameron
Hillcroft, Treaslane
By Portree
Isle of Skye
IV51 9NX

Rannoch and District Angling Association
John Brown
The Square
Kinloch Rannoch
Perthshire
PH16 5PN

River Almond Angling Association
H Meikle
23 Glen Terrace
Deans, Livingston
West Lothian
LH54 8BU

River Goil Angling Club
See Goil AC
Peter F Malcolm
54 St Nicholas Street
St Andrews
Fife KY16 8BQ

St Fillans and Loch Earn Angling Association
President
T J Turner
22 Turleum Road
Crieff
Perthshire

St Mary's Loch Angling Club
Neil Macintyre
8 Rosetta Road
Peebles
Borders EH45 8JU

Scottish Federation of Coarse Angling
S Clerkin
2 Dotham Farm Cottages
Kirkcaldy
KY2 6QP

Selkirk and District Angling Association
D Heatlie
8 Knowepark
Selkirk

Shetland Anglers' Association
Alec Miller
55 Burgh Road
Lerwick
Shetland Isles ZE1 0HJ

Soval Angling Association
W France
45 Leurbost
Lochs
Stornoway
Isle of Lewis HS2 9NS

Stanley and District Angling Club
S Grant

7 Murray Place
Stanley
Perth PH1 4LX

Stornoway Angling Association
Malcolm Crate
Northern Cottage
Shuilishader
Point, Isle of Lewis

Stranraer and District Angling Association
D Pride
Almar View
Ochtrelure
Stranraer DG9 8HU
or
c/o The Sports Shop
86 George Street,
Stranraer DG9 7JS

Strathgryfe Angling Association
Kingsley Wood & Co,
Solicitors
Burnside Chambers
The Cross, Kilmacolm
Renfrewshire PA13 4ET

Strathmore Angling Improvement Association
Mrs M C Milne
1 West Park Gardens
Dundee DD2 1NY

Thurso Angling Association
N Murray
20 St Magnus Road
Thurso
Caithness
or
T Stitt, President

Horndean
Glengolly
By Thurso KW14 7XP

Tobermory Angling Club
W G Anderson
Carna, 7 West Street,
Tobermory
Isle of Mull PA75 6QJ

Turriff Angling Association
R Masson
6 Castle Street
Turriff,
Aberdeenshire AB53 7BJ

Ullapool Angling Club
D Taggart
37 Morefield Place
Ullapool
Ross-shire

United Clyde Angling Protective Association
Joseph Quigley
39 Hillfoot Avenue
Cambusnethan, Wishaw
Lanarkshire ML2 8TR

Upper Annandale Angling Association
A Dickson
Braehead, Woodfoot
Beattock
Dumfriesshire DG10 9PL

Whiteadder Angling Association
Cdr R Baker
Millburn House
Duns
Berwickshire TD11 3TN

Fishing in Northern Ireland

Boards of Conservators, Close Seasons, etc.

For game fisher and coarse fisher alike, Northern Ireland is still largely undiscovered country. There is a wealth of lakes, large and small; miles of quiet unpolluted river, plentifully stocked with large, healthy fish, anything but well-educated to anglers and their methods. By the standards of most other parts of Britain, all of it is underfished. In recent years, coarse fishermen have begun to find out what Northern Ireland has to offer, and there is much, too, for the game fisherman. The visitor as yet unfamiliar with the province is recommended to concentrate on the waters owned and managed by the Department of Agriculture, possibly the largest single fishery proprietor in Northern Ireland. They include some of the very best.

The Dept of Agriculture (Fisheries Division, Annexe 5, Castle Grounds, Stormont, Belfast BT4 3PW (Tel: 028 9052 3434, Fax: 028 9052 3121) is the ultimate authority for fisheries in Northern Ireland. In addition to the Department, and working in co-operation with it, there are two Conservancy Authorities, The Foyle Fisheries Commission; and The Fisheries Conservancy Board for Northern Ireland. They operate in separate areas.

The Department publishes an Angling Guide to the waters under its control, available from Fisheries Division at the above address, and from many tackle shops.

The Foyle Fisheries Commission (8 Victoria Road, Londonderry BT47 2AB, Tel: 028 7134 2100, Fax: 028 7134 2720) act as conservator and issues rod licences in the Foyle area: i.e. the North-Western parts of the province drained by the Foyle/Mourne/Camowen river systems and the rivers Faughan and Roe. The Commission is also responsible for a number of river systems in Co Donegal, R.O.I., including the Finn, Culdaff and Deele. The Foyle Fisheries Commission is controlled jointly by the Governments of Northern Ireland and The Republic of Ireland, including in the total area the former Moville District in the Republic and the former Londonderry District in N.I.

The Fisheries Conservancy Board for Northern Ireland (1 Mahon Road, Portadown, Co Armagh BT62 3EE, Telephone: 028 3833 4666, Fax: 028 3833 8912, E-mail address: tfearon@fcbni.force9.co.uk). This board issues licences for the remainder of the province.

The Northern Ireland Tourist Board (St Anne's Court, 59 North Street, Belfast BT1 1NB (Tel: 028 9024 6609, Fax: 028 9031 2424) is also involved in angling, concerning itself with development and promotion, and issues literature on travel and accommodation.

Under the provisions of The Fisheries Act (N.I.) 1966, **The Fisheries Conservancy Board** and **The Foyle Fisheries Commission** co-operate with the **Dept of Agriculture** in the development and improvement of fisheries. As a result, there has been in recent years a dramatic improvement in the quantity and quality of angling, game and coarse, available to visitors. The Department's Rivers Agency is also actively engaged in the improvement of fisheries in watercourses under its control. Works include the construction of fishery weirs, groynes and deflectors; restoration of gravel, landscaping of altered watercourses and comprehensive schemes of tree-planting.

Rod Licences. The Fisheries Conservancy Board for Northern Ireland, whose jurisdiction extends to all fisheries in Northern Ireland except the Foyle Fisheries Commission area, requires a rod licence for **ALL** freshwater fishing for each rod and line. A Game Rod Licence covers coarse fishing only *on waters designated as coarse fisheries*. The following licences are available.

Game fishing:
Season game fishing rod licence, £20.50.
8-day game fishing rod licence, £10.
1-day game fishing rod licence, £4.
Additional amount payable by the holder of a Foyle Fisheries Commission season game fishing rod licence to use a single game rod, £16.50.
8-day joint licence/DANI permit, £24.50.
1-day joint licence/DANI permit, £12.50.

Coarse Fishing (FCB):
Season coarse fishing rod licence, £8.

8-day coarse fishing rod licence, £4.
3-day joint coarse fishing rod licence/DANI coarse fishing permit, £7.50.
8-day joint coarse fishing licence/DANI coarse fishing permit, £12.50.

Foyle Fisheries Commission, whose jurisdiction extends to all waters in the Foyle catchment in both the South and the North including the feeders into the Foyle estuary, requires a **Game Fishing** rod licence for salmon, sea

trout, brown and rainbow trout. These are available in the following categories:
Season game fishing rod licence, £21.
14-day game fishing rod licence, £15.50.
1-day game fishing rod licence, £4.50.

Under 18 years of age juvenile game fishing rod licence, £10.
Licence endorsements for holders of FCB licences or licences issued in the Republic of Ireland are now £17.

Fishing Stations in Northern Ireland

As in other sections, principal catchment areas are dealt with in alphabetical order, and details of close seasons, licences, etc, will be found on the preceding page. Anglers wanting further details of accommodation, etc, should write to the Northern Ireland Tourist Board, St Anne's Court, 59 North Street, Belfast, BT1 2NB, or 24 Haymarket, London SW1Y 4DG (Tel: 020 7766 9920).

BANN (Lower)
(For close seasons, licences, see under Boards)

A mainly sluggish river running approx 30m from where it leaves Lough Neagh to where it enters the sea below Coleraine. River is canalised at upper end. Good coarse fish and salmonoid population; sea trout fishing in the tideway. Non-canal stretches, both coarse and game, are controlled by Bann System Ltd, and permits are obtainable. Ten-year average salmon catch, 1,300 on Camroe Beat.

Coleraine (Co Londonderry). River tidal below Cutts. Good game and coarse fishing above tidal stretches. Bann System Ltd, The Cutts, 54 Castleroe Rd, Coleraine BT51 3RL (Tel: 028 703 44796) offers beats but these must be booked by the end of January. For **River Bush**, contact Sir Patrick Macnaghten, Dundarave, Bushmills (Tel: 028 2073 1215). Coleraine AA allow dt fishing on R Ree, and Ballyinreese Reservoir, obtainable from E Kee, 3 Kings Rd, Coleraine. Agivey AA has 12m stretch on R Agivey plus stretch on **Wee Agivey**, nr **Garvagh**. Salmon and brown trout. Permits (£12, £5) from Mrs J McCann, 162 Agivey Rd, Aghadowey; or Albert Atkins (*below*). Fishing has access for disabled. **Ballyrashane Trout Lake**, Creamery Rd: fly only, stocked r trout, dt £10, 4 fish limit, season 1 May to mid-Oct, Contact Council Offices, 41 Portstewart Rd,

Coleraine, Tel: 028 7035 2181. For Ballylagan Fishing and Conservation Club water, dt £10, contact Smyth's. Tackle shops: Smyth's Country Sports, 1 Park St BT52 1BD; Albert Atkins, 71 Coleraine Rd, Garvagh, BT51 5HR (Tel: 028 2955 7691). Hotels: Lodge, Bohill Auto Inn, Brown Trout, Aghadowey.

Kilrea (Co Derry). Pike and perch in local canals and loughs. Trout day tickets on Kilrea & Dist AC waters, from Sean Donaghy, Electric Goods, Kilrea. Salmon and trout tickets for Lower Bann at Portna from J E Templeton, 34 Coleraine Rd, Gavagh, BT1 5HP (Tel: 57009), or from Albert Atkins (*above*). Hotel: Portneal Lodge.

Portglenone (Co Antrim). **Clady River** joins Bann below town. Brown trout, late salmon and dollaghan. Dt £5 (1 Mar–30 Sept), £10 (Oct), from Clady & Dist AC, who control whole river and tributaries. Obtainable from Weirs, Clady Rd, or M Cushanan, Main St, both Portglenone. Kingfisher Angling Centre, 24A Hiltonstown Rd, Portglenone, BT44 8EG (Tel: 028 2582 1630) has self-catering accommodation and fishing on Upper and Lower Bann, with salmon and trout, and mixed coarse fishing. St £13.80 from Bann Guns & Tackle. Other tackle shop: McGall's, Main St.

Toomebridge (Co Antrim). Here, the Lower Bann leaves L Neagh. Dept of Ag controls

Lower Bann Navigational Canal at **Toome**, **Portna** and **Movanagher**. Tickets from tackle shops. Bann Systems Ltd, Dundarave, Bushmills BT57 8ST issues permits for Portna fishing on Lower Bann, all legal methods except maggot. **Lough Neagh**, with an area of 153 sq miles, is the largest inland water in the British Isles. It supports an immense commercial eel fishery, but apart from that, its potential is as yet largely untapped. The bottom-feeding habits of Lough Neagh trout and the exposed conditions on this enormous stretch of water have so far discouraged anglers from trying to exploit it. A principal problem is the absence of sheltered bays.

BANN (UPPER)

Flows west and north from its source in the Mourne Mountains to enter Lough Neagh near the middle of its southern shore at a point north of Portadown.

Portadown (Co Armagh). Pike, perch, roach, bream and trout. Dept of Ag has 10m stretch from Portadown to Lough Neagh; a designated coarse fishery which is one of the best in Europe. Licences from Fisheries Conservancy Board, (Tel: 028 3833 4666); permits from The Field and Stream, Moy. Hotels: Carngrove; Seagoe.

Banbridge (Co Down). Late salmon, brown trout and coarse fish. Water from Hilltown Bridge to **Katesbridge**, and at Drumlouga, controlled by Rathfriland AC; membership £20 plus £20 joining. Contact J Dougan (Tel: 028 406 389343). Banbridge AC fishes from Katesbridge to **Lenaderg**, browns and late salmon, and has 76 acre **Corbet Lough**, rainbow trout, 4m from town. Dt £8 lake, £4 river, conc, from tackle shops. Gilford AC fishes from Lenaderg to Moyallen, plus **Kernan Lake**. **Lough Brickland**, 62 acres, Dept of Ag, fly only, b and r trout. **Altnadue Lake**, stocked with rainbows, dt £5 from tackle shops. Coarse fishing: **Newry Canal** (roach, bream, rudd, perch, pike); **Lough Shark**; Lakes **Drummillar**, **Drumaran**, **Drumnavaddy**; **Skillycolban** (Mill Dam, perch, pike, eels); Lakes **Ballyroney**, **Hunshigo**, **Ballyward**, **Ballymagreehan**, pike, perch, F C B coarse licence required. Tackle, licences and permits from Coburns Ltd, 32 Scarva St, Banbridge, Tel: 028 4066 2207. Rathfriland tackle shop: W R Trimble, Downpatrick St. Hotels: Belmont, Banville, Downshire. Wright Lines, Tel: 028 4066 2126, offers 2-day Angling Breaks for £43.

Mrs J Fleming, Heathmar, 37 Corbet Rd, Banbridge (Tel: 028 4062 2348) has accommodation close to Corbet Lough, above.

Hilltown (Co Down). Dept of Ag have 4 good trout lakes, totalling more than 350 acres in the area: **Spelga**, **Castlewellan**, **Hillsborough**, **Lough Brickland**. Castlewellan and Annsborough AC fish **Ballylough**, **Annsborough**, a few miles north east. Brown and rainbow trout, fly only. Day tickets from Chestnut Inn (see below). Shimna AC has **Altnadue Lough**, stocked with rainbows. Dt £5 from The Four Seasons, Newcastle. Tackle shops: J Coburn, 32 Scarva Street Banbridge; W McCammon, Main St, Castlewellan; W R Timble, 25 Downpatrick St, Rathfriland. Hotels: Downshire Arms and Belmont, Banbridge. Chestnut Inn, Lower Square, Castlewellan, offers trout fishing weekends and mid-week breaks on Ballylough.

BLACKWATER
(For close seasons, licences, see under Boards)

The largest of the rivers flowing into L Neagh, rising in S Tyrone to enter the lough at its SW corner. Coarse fish and trout.

Blackwatertown (Co Armagh). Dept of Ag has 1½m, mainly coarse fishing but short stretch of good game fishing. Permits from K Cahoon (below). Ulster Coarse Fishing Federation has water from Bond's Bridge to end of Argory Estate, a mixed fishery with excellent match weights. Individuals may fish free on F C B licence. Several trout lakes near **Dungannon**: Dungannon Park, 12 acres (Tel: 028 8772 7327); **Aughadarragh** (Tel: 028 8554 8320), r trout; **Altmore Fishery**, 5 acres, (Tel: 028 8775 9977); **Ballysaggart Lough**: bream, eels, perch, pike, roach, rudd, tench. No permit needed. Other local fishings include **Lough More**, Clogher, wild browns, **Annaginny Lake**, Newmills, rainbow trout (Tel: 028 8774 7808); **Carnteel Lough**, pike, perch and roach; Carrick and Greeve Loughs, **Brantry**, pike, perch, bream. Information from Director, Leisure Services, Council Offices, Circular Rd, Dungannon BT71 6DT (Tel: 028 8772 0300). Tackle shops: K Cahoon, Irish St, Dungannon, (Tel: 028 8772 2754); Tight-Lines, Killyman Rd, Dungannon (Tel: 028 8772 2001). Inn on the Park, Moy Rd (Tel: 028 8772 5151) offers various types of fishing holiday.

Moy (Co Tyrone). Moy AC has coarse fishing on Blackwater at Moy, tickets from tackle shop

The Field and Stream, Killyman St, Moy. Hotels: Charlemont House; Tomneys Licensed Inn (Tel: 028 8778 4895).

Benburb (Co Tyrone). Trout for 2½m downstream. Armagh & Dist AC leases or owns stretch on river, and 7 lakes. Dept of Ag has **Brantry Lough** (brown trout); and **Loughs Creeve** (pike to 35lb) and **Enagh** (pike, perch, bream). Permits from Outdoor World, 67 Chapel St, Cookstown. Dept of Ag also has coarse fishing on **Clay Lake**, nr **Keady** (Co Armagh); 120 acres, pike rudd and perch, open all year. Hotel, Salmon Leap View offers private fishing on riverbank, at £10 B & B, plus £1.50 fishing.

Clogher, **Augher** and **Aughnacloy**. (Co Tyrone). Local stretch of river has undergone fishery rehabilitation following a major drainage scheme of the Blackwater River. Permits from Aughnacloy AC, Clogher & Dist AC, Augher Dist & Upper Blackwater AC and landowners. Permission from landowners for tributaries. **Callan**, **Oona** and **Torrent**. Dept of Ag has rainbow trout fishing on **White Lough**. 4 fish per day, min. size 10in. Fly only from boats, otherwise, spinning and worming permitted. Permits from R Morrow, 48 Rehaghey Road, Aughnacloy. Accommodation: Mrs K Hillen, 48 Moore St, Aughnacloy.

Armagh (Co Armagh). Beside **River Callan**, centre for Blackwater and its tributaries, with many fishing lakes in district. Six of these are controlled by Armagh AC, who offer day tickets on three, with brown and rainbow trout. Fly only on **Shaws Lake** and **Seagahan Reservoir**, all legal methods on **Aughnagorgan Lake**. Loughgall Country Lake, 11/14 Main St, Loughgall BT61 8HZ (Tel: 028 3889 2906): coarse fishery, open in April 2000, with pike, perch, roach, rudd, eels, tench; stand for disabled; st £30, wt £12, dt £4, conc for juv. Carnwood Lodge Hotel, 61 Castleblaney Rd, Keady (Tel: 028 3753 8935) is close to **Keady Trout Lakes**, and caters for anglers.

SMALLER RIVERS EMPTYING INTO LOUGH NEAGH

MAINE (Co Antrim): Flows 25m from source in Glarryford Bogs to enter lough south of Randalstown, Co Antrim. With tributaries **Kellswater**, **Braid**, **Clough** and **Glen-**

wherry provides good fishing for salmon, trout and dollaghan. Gracehill, Galgorm and Dist AC has 3m water at **Ballymena**, brown trout with salmon from July; 6 fish limit, no spinning until Aug 1, no maggot fishing; stretch for disabled. Dt £3 Mar–Aug, £5 Sept Oct, with conc, from Galgorm Spar; Maine Fishing Equipment, 158 Finaghy Rd, Cullybackey, Ballymena (Tel: 028 2588 1444); Slaght P O. Randalstown AC controls Maine from **Randalstown** Road Bridge to Andraid Ford. Trout, with salmon and dollaghan in season. Dt £3 from C Spence, 32 New Street, Randalstown. Membership £20 pa juv £5. Kells and Connor AC has dt £3 or £1 for fishing on Kells and Glenwherry. B and r trout and late salmon run. Apply to Duncan's Filling Station, Kells. Dept of Ag has brown trout fishing on **Dungonnell** and **Killylane Reservoirs**, 70 and 50 acres. Limit 4 fish. Maine AC issues 12 day tickets (£3) on 4 miles of river from above **Cullybackey** to Dunminning Bridge; brown trout and salmon. From Simpsons, 52 Main St, Cullybackey, Ballymena. Tackle shops: Spence Bros, New St; Groggans, 34 Broughshane St, Ballymena. Hotels: Adair Arms; Leighinmore House and Tullyglass House, Ballymena.

SIXMILEWATER: Flows 15m from Ballyclare to enter lough at Antrim, at its NE corner. A heavily fished but highly productive trout water, salmon and dollaghan Sept–Oct. Antrim & Dist AC issues £8, £5 and £3 permits for water between **Doagh** and **Antrim**; brown trout, salmon from August; from Templepatrick Supermarket. Mrs Marigold Allen, The Beeches Country House, 10 Dunadry Rd, Muckamore (Tel: 028 9443 3161) has accommodation convenient for Sixmilewater between Antrim and Doagh. Dunadry Hotel and Country Club, 2 Islandreagh Drive, Dunadry BT41 2HA (Tel: 028 9443 4343) has fishing for guests on Sixmilewater, which passes through hotel grounds. Ballynure AC issues dt £5 Mar–Jul, £8 Aug–Oct, for water between Doagh and **Ballynure**, from Ballyclare Filling Station, Main St, Ballyclare, BT39 9AB; Doagh Petrol Station, Main St, Doagh. **Potterswalls Reservoir**, off Steeple Rd, nr Antrim, has rainbow trout fishing for members and visitors. Dept of Ag has trout fishing on **Woodburn Reservoirs**, nr **Carrickfergus**. Upper South, 65 acres, Middle South 64 acres, Lower South 22 acres, North 18 acres. Upper and Lower South, fly only. Lough Mourne, 127 acres, Copeland (Marshallstown) 24 acres. North Woodburn,

Rainbow, others, rainbow and brown. Limit 4 fish. Fishing at trout farm nr **Ballycarry**: Mr J Caldwell, 73 Bridgend Rd, Ballycarry, Tel: 028 9337 2209. Tackle shop: Country Sports & Tackle, 9 Rough Lane, off Steeple Rd, Antrim. Hotel: Deer Park, Antrim. Ballyclare accommodation: Five Corners B & B.

CRUMLIN and **GLENAVY** (Co Antrim): small rivers which flow west through these villages to enter lough. Trout fishing near their mouths. Centre: Crumlin. Tackle shop: Fur, Feather and Fin, 3a West Terrace, Mill Rd, Tel: 028 9445 3648. Accommodation: Hillvale Farm, 11 Largy Road.

BALLINDERRY: Flows east for approx 30m, through **Cookstown**, to enter lough about midway along west shore. Good fishing for brown trout and dollaghan for 20m up from the mouth. Permission from Cookstown AC and landowners. Kildress AC has fishing 3m from Cookstown, on A505 Omagh road, with trout, dollaghan and salmon, main species. Members only, membership from Secretary (Tel: 028867 64345), £10 per season, or £15, after 31 May. Competition supervised for juveniles. Moy AC has stretch at Coagh. Tickets from The Field and Stream, Moy. **Lough Fea** is fished by the Mid Ulster AC. Tackle shop: Outdoor World, 67 Chapel St, Cookstown (Tel: 028 8676 3682). Hotels: Glenavon House, Drum Rd, Greenvale, Drum Rd; both Cookstown, Co Tyrone.

MOYOLA (Co Londonderry): Flows east and south from its source in S Derry to enter lough at NW corner. Brown trout in lower reaches and a good run of salmon from July. Fishing rights held by Moyola and Dist AC, dt from G Ewings Confectionery, 41 Main St, Castle Dawson, or tackle shop H Hueston, 55 Main St, Castledawson, Magherafelt BT45 8AA (Tel: 028 7946 8282). Accommodation: Laurel Villa Guest House, 60 Church St, Magherafelt BT45 6AW (Tel: 028 7963 2238).

BUSH
(For close seasons, licences, see under Boards)

The Bush flows 30m west and north through Bushmills, Co Antrim, to enter the sea near Portballintrae. The fishing rights of the entire catchment (except the stretch from the sea to Bushmills) have been acquired by the Dept of Agriculture primarily as an experimental river for studies into the biology and management of salmon. Within the terms of this programme,

salmon angling is maintained at the highest possible level. Trout in the Bush and its tributaries are small but plentiful: there is a modest run of spring salmon and a grilse run for which the river is best known which begins in June or July, according to flow. It is important to report catches of fin-clipped fish. Bush season has been extended to 20 October.

For angling management, the river is divided into the following sections: the *Town Stretch* about 200 yds downstream of the Project Centre at Bushmills; the *Leap Stretch* upstream (approx 600 yds of water); the *New Stretch* (500 yds); and the *Unrestricted Stretch*, the remaining 24m of fishing water. Special daily permits, which may be booked in advance, are required for the Town, Leap and New stretches, as shown under "Licences, permits and close seasons". Weekend or bank holiday angling must be booked and paid for by 1400 hours on the preceding Friday or normal working day. Half day tickets are sold for the Town and Leap stretches from 1 June to 20 Oct. Tributary: **River Dervock**, flowing through the village of that name, offers 2m of good trout fishing. *(For details of permit charges, see under Boards).*

Bushmills (Co Antrim). Salmon, sea trout and brown trout. Dundarave Estates Ltd, Dundarave, Bushmills BT57 8ST, have excellent salmon fishing stretch from Bushmills to the sea. Dt £25 and £50. Fishing lodge also on site. Dept of Ag has short stretches (Town, New, and Leap) near Bushmills; stands for disabled on bank. Dt from The Hatchery, and should be booked in advance. Contact Fisheries Division, 21 Church St, Bushmills (Tel: 028 2073 1435). Permits from R Bell, 40 Ann St, Ballycastle (Tel: 028 2076 2520). Other Bushmills tackle dealer: Bushside Tackle, 108 Main St (Tel: 028 2073 2700). Hotels: Bushmills Inn; Antrim Arms, Ballycastle.

Ballymoney (Co Antrim). **Bush River** may be fished for brown trout, as can the Ballymoney Burn. Good coarse fishing on **Movanagher Canal** and **R Bann**. Brown and rainbow trout fishing on **Altnahinch Reservoir**, at head of R Bush. Dept of Ag water, 44 acres, bag limit 4 fish, bank fishing only. Permits from Pollocks Filling Station, Rodeing Foot, also E J Cassell, 43/45 Main St, both Ballymoney. Newtowncrommelin tackle shop: Taga Sport Ltd, D Anderson, 6 Old Cushendun Rd BT43 6RS (Tel: 028 2575 8572); Various permits for game and coarse fishing.

LOUGH ERNE
(Upper and Lower)
(For close seasons, licences, under Boards)

Upper and Lower Lough Erne, with the R Erne and tributaries feeding the loughs, comprise 15,300 hectares of mixed game and coarse fishing owned and annually restocked by the Dept of Agriculture and offering some of the best sport in Europe. The flow is in a NW direction, through the beautiful and largely unspoilt Fermanagh countryside, via Belleek, to where the R Erne reaches the sea at Ballyshannon. Infinitely varied fishing in the lakes, with innumerable secluded bays, inlets and small islands. Rich, unpolluted waters teeming with fish-life, the Erne system is truly an angler's paradise. Centres: Belleek; Kesh; Enniskillen; Bellanaleck; Lisnaskea; Newtownbutler; Derrygonnelly (Timavar).

RIVER ERNE. River heavily populated with large bream and roach, pike of record-breaking proportions. Good salmon runs in late summer and autumn. **Belleek**, Co Fermanagh, is a good centre for fishing river and Lower Lough. Dept of Ag has 3¾ miles with brown trout and salmon. Limit, 6 fish; also b and r trout on **Lough Keenaghan**, 38 acres. **Scolban Lough** (171 acres) has pike to 20lb as main quarry, also perch, and is stocked with rainbow trout to 2lb by Dept of Ag. **LOWER LOUGH ERNE**. The trout fishing areas, in which the fish may run very large, are in the north and west of the lake. Recommended areas are from Roscor Bridge up to the Heron Island, and across to the **Garvary River**. South and east of a dividing line, the lake may be fished on coarse fishing licence and permit only.

TRIBUTARIES FEEDING LOWER LOUGH: **Ballinamallard** River flows south through the village of Ballinamallard, to enter the lake near St Angelo Airport. Dept of Ag controls 1 mile nr Ballinamallard; brown trout. **Colebrook** and **Tempo** enter lake from the east. 2 miles of Colebrook is Dept of Ag Designated Coarse fishery, nr Lisnaskea: roach, bream, perch, rudd, eels, the occasional pike, trout and salmon. Ballinamallard and Colebrook rivers are currently being stocked with juvenile salmon as part of a cross-border salmon enhancement initiative for the Erne system. Tackle shop: J A Knaggs, Main St, Ballinamallard.

UPPER LOUGH ERNE: Principally coarse fish: pike, eel, perch, rudd, bream, roach, occasional salmon and sea trout. Centres:

Lisnaskea; **Newtown Butler**; **Enniskillen**. The National Trust at Crom Estate has fishing on Inisherk and Derryvore Islands, with excellent bream and roach. Dt £3 in advance from Sharon Sey, Gate Lodge, Crom Estate, Newtownbutler, Fermanagh (Tel: 028 5773 8825). Stocked pike lake dt £20, very limited. Boats for hire, contact Visitors Centre (Tel: 028 5773 8118). Accommodation at National Trust Holiday Cottages (Tel: 028 4488 1204); Carrybridge Hotel & Marina, 171 Inishmore Rd, Lisbellaw (Tel: 028 6638 7148) is situated on Upper Lough Erne, and has boats on site. **Mill Lough**, **Bellanaleck**: 100 acres Dept of Ag r and b trout fishery 4 miles from Enniskillen, 4 fish limit. At Castle Coole, **Lough Coole**, National Trust Fishery. B and r trout to 5lbs. ½ dt (boat) £3. **Killyfole Lough**, 56 acres, nr Lisnaskea, has a variety of coarse fish, incl perch and pike. Permits from F Dowler, Main St, Lisnaskea. Tackle shops: J E Richardson, East Bridge Street, Enniskillen (tickets for local fishing); Erne Tackle, Main Street, Lisnaskea; J & K Mullen, Sligo Road, Enniskillen, Co Fermanagh. Hotels: Killyhevlin Hotel, Dublin Rd (Tel: 028 6632 3481), has chalets on banks of Erne, with fishing stages; other hotels, Manor House; Railway; both Enniskillen; and Ortine, Lisnaskea. Riverside Farm, Gortadrehid, Enniskillen (Tel: 028 6632 2725) has accommodation with boats and bait supplied. Derryad Cottages, Lisnaskea (Tel: 020 8567 4487): fishing holidays with motor boats supplied. Other accommodation at Lough Erne Cottages, Bolusty, c/o J E Richardson, see above. Boats and engines on site.

TRIBUTARIES FEEDING UPPER LOUGH ERNE: **Swanlinbar River** flows north from Co Cavan to enter the lough midway on the S side. Coarse fish in lower reaches, trout in upper. Permission from landowners. The **Sillees River** flows from above Derrygonnelly to enter the lough between Enniskillen and Lisgoole Abbey. Excellent coarse fishing, some trout. **Arney River** flows from Lower Lough Macnean to Upper Lough Erne (large trout and exceptional pike fishing) to enter Upper L Erne near **Bellanaleck**. Good mixed fishing all the way to **Lough Macnean**. Upper and Lower L Macnean both have coarse fishing on them, notably pike. Permits from tackle shops in Bellanaleck and Enniskillen. Also 10 Dept trout lakes of various sizes in the area (5 acres to 100 acres), including the famous **Navar Forest Lakes**, and **Mill Lough** at Bellanaleck which holds trout to 5lb. Dept of Ag permits for Mill Lough, Navar Forest Lakes, and

Keenaghan Lough, from Belleek Angling Centre, Main St, Belleek BT93 3FX (Tel: 028 686 58181), and tackle shops in Enniskillen.

FOYLE
(For close seasons, licences, see under Boards)

The Foyle system is half in Northern Ireland, half in the Republic. It is formed by the **Derg** (draining Lough Derg) and the **Strule**, constituting the **Mourne**, which unites with the **Finn** at Strabane to become the Foyle proper, which enters the sea at Londonderry. That part of the system in Northern Ireland, including the **Faughan** and **Roe**, is the largest salmon and trout fishery in the country. It drains the north and west slopes of the Sperrin Mountains and most of Co Tyrone.

Londonderry. River tidal here, with fishing for salmon in tidal pools from July. Also a run of sea trout. Permits from Foyle Commission. Tackle shops: Rod and Line, 1 Clarendon St, Tel: 028 7126 2877; P McCrystal, Spencer Rd; Fitzpatrick Sports, Spencer Rd; Hills (Derry Ltd), Spencer Rd, all Waterside, Londonderry; Tom's Tackle, Ardlough Rd, Drumahoe BT47. Hotels: White Horse Inn, Everglades, Broomhill House.

Strabane (Co Tyrone). Here **Mourne** and **Strule** unite to form Foyle. Salmon and sea trout. Permits from Foyle Commission. Dept of Ag has 5 lakes in the area. Fir Trees Hotel, Melmount Rd, Tel: 028 7138 2382, offers weekend fishing breaks, £99.

Tributaries of the Foyle

MOURNE: Salmon, sea trout, brown trout; excellent fishing in the 10m between Strabane and Newtownstewart, but largely private. Two weekly tickets obtainable, from Abercorn Estates, Newtownstewart (Tel: 028 8166 1683).

Sion Mills (Co Tyrone). Excellent 4m stretch from Strabane to Victoria Bridge managed by Sion Mills AC, salmon, brown, white and rainbow trout; no bag limits, fly, spinning worm allowed; access for disabled; permits from Angling Information, 151 Melmount Rd; Tourist Office, Main St, Sion Mills (Tel: 028 8165 8027), and from tackle shop: N M Tackle, 9 Alexandra Place, BT82 9HR (Tel: 028 8165 8501). N M Tackle has own private fishing with dt offered, also day and week permits for various other waters, and advice and information on fishing, local clubs, and accommodation.

Newtownstewart (Co Tyrone). The **Owenkillow** and **Glenelly** enter here, offering 30m of ideal game fishing waters noted for their sea trout and salmon. Owenkillen is spate river, only worth fishing in Jun/Oct. For **Gortin** fishing on Owenkillow and Owenrea, contact G Treanor (Tel: 028 8164 8543). Blakiston-Houston Estate has fishing on 6m stretch of **Owenkillen** and 3m stretch of **Owenrea**; salmon and sea trout; limited fly only dt, £10, from Gabriel Treanor, 56 Main St, Gortin (Tel: 028 8164 8534/8824), or K Fleming, 51 Gorticashel Rd, Gortin. Omagh AA holds most of fishing rights on Mourne, Strule and Owenkillow around this area (some 28 miles) and offers dt £12. These, also Gaff AC dt (£5) on **Glenelly River**, and £6–£10 dt on Owenkillen from tackle shop: Campbell's Mourne Valley Tackle, 50 Main St, Newtonstewart, Tel: 028 8166 1543/1167. Campbell's also offer accommodation with private fishing on Rivers **Mourne**: Salmon, brown trout, sea trout. Baronscourt Cottages, Tel: 028 8166 1013, has pike fishing for guests. Weekend break, £54, mid-week, £46.50. B & B and self-catering: Anglers Rest, Mr & Mrs D Campbell, 12 Killymore Rd, Newtownstewart

STRULE: Very good trout fishing from Omagh to Newtownstewart, sea trout and salmon.

Omagh (Co Tyrone). Dept of Ag controls the coarse fishing on a stretch of R Strule by arrangement with Omagh AA. Roach and eels. Assn also controls stretches of **Camowen**, **Owenkillen** and **Drumragh Rivers**. More good fishing upstream of Omagh, to Camowen, but fish smaller. Salmon in season. **Owenragh**, **Quiggery/Fintona** and **Drumragh** enter near **Omagh**. Dept stillwaters, **Loughs Bradan** and **Lee**, 60 and 37 acres, 5 miles from **Castlederg**; Brown trout fishing, 4 fish limit, per day, min. size 10in. Permits for Omagh AA water £12, weekday, £6 weekends, from tackle shops: Chism Fishing Tackle, 25 Old Market Place, Omagh (Tel: 028 8224 4932); David Campell, 50 Main St, Newtownstewart, (Tel: 028 8166 1543). Omagh hotels: Royal Arms, Silverbirch.

FAIRYWATER: Flows E from Drumquin (trout) to enter **Strule** below Omagh. Remarkably good roach fishing in lower reaches. No permit required. **Burn Dennett River**, **Dunamanagh**: Small brown trout, occasional salmon and sea trout in season. Fly, spinning and worm. Permit from Burn Dennet AA.

DERG: flows E from Donegal for 50m to enter Mourne N of **Newtownstewart**. Spate river. Good trout water for 15m to above Castlederg, Co Tyrone, with salmon, brown trout, and occasion sea trout. Castlederg AC has 5m, both banks. Permits £15, £20 weekly from H Irwin, 5 John St, Castlederg, Tel: 028 8167 1050 (day). Tackle shop: Campbell's Mourne Valley Tackle, 50 Main St, Newtownstewart (Tel: 028 8166 1543). Hotel: Derg Arms, 43 Main St Castlederg (Tel: 028 8167 1644).

FAUGHAN AND ROE
(For close seasons, licences, see under Boards)

The Faughan flows N for 20m to enter the Foyle area E of Londonderry city; the Roe flows the same distance in the same general direction to enter the Foyle Estuary N of Limavady, Co Londonderry. Salmon, sea trout and brown trout in Faughan; principally sea trout in Roe, but also salmon from July.

FAUGHAN: River Faughan Anglers Ltd lease the fishing rights of tributaries and main river, a 30 mile stretch of water divided into two sections, approx 2m tidal and 28m freshwater, situated between Londonderry and Park. Both sections are productive of sea trout and salmon. Access for disabled anglers, left-hand bank below Campsie Bridge. Waiting list for season permits; daily £15, with concessions, and licences, from Club Office, 26A Carlisle Rd, Londonderry, or from Foyle Fisheries Office, 8 Victoria Rd, Londonderry BT47.

ROE:
Limavady (Co Londonderry). Good fishing for 15m from Limavady to Dungiven. Dept of Ag has 1¼m at **O'Cahan's Rock**, S of Limavady, with salmon and sea trout. Roe AA offers 26 day tickets for most of a 34 mile stretch, both banks, from source to river mouth, from Limavady tackle shops, £5; no dt during Oct. Sea trout av 1lb, salmon 8lb. Dungiven AC controls 6m between Ross' Mill and Bovevagh Bridge, salmon, sea trout, best Sept/Oct. Dt £5 from P McGuigan, 24 Station Rd, Dungiven, and Bovevagh P O. Tackle shops: R Douglas & Son, Rod & Gun, 6 Irish Green St, Limavady; S J Mitchell, 29 Main St, Limavady, who displays map of all local fishings, issues permits and is a reliable source of local information. Hotels: Gorteen House, Limavady; Alexander Arms; many guest houses.

GLENS OF ANTRIM RIVERS
(For close seasons, licences, see under Boards)

CUSHENDALL: Enters sea at Cushendall. Good runs of sea trout Jul–Oct. Occasional late salmon, small native brown trout. Fly, spinning, worm permitted, no bait digging allowed.

GLENARIFF: Small sea trout river which enters sea at Waterfoot. Good runs of sea trout Jul–Oct, occasional late salmon, small native brown trout. Fly, spinning, worm permitted, but no bait digging allowed.

GLENDUN: Enters sea at **Cushendun**. Fair run of late salmon, primarily Sept–Oct, and sea trout Jul–Oct. Fly, spinning, worm permitted, but no bait digging allowed. All three rivers controlled by Glens AC. Dt £10 in Oct, otherwise £5; available at O'Neills Country Sports, Unit 1, 25 Mill St, Cushendall, Co Antrim BT44 0RR (Tel: 028 217 72009). Many guest houses in locality.

MARGY/CAREY/GLENSHESK: a system of small rivers entering the sea at **Ballycastle**. Sea trout, brown trout and salmon. Dept of Ag waters. Tickets from R Bell, 38/40 Ann St, Ballycastle, Tel: 028 2076 2520. Hotels: Antrim Arms, Ballycastle; Thornlea, Cushendun. Tackle shop: R Bell, 40 Ann St, Ballycastle, Tel: 028 2076 2520.

LAGAN
(For close seasons, licences, see under Boards)

A productive river which flows into the **Belfast Lough**. Trout fishing upstream from Magheralin, Co Down, for 12m.

Belfast (Co Antrim). Dept of Ag has 2¼m of coarse fishing on R Lagan. Permits from: Tight Lines, 198/200 Albertbridge Rd, Tel: 028 9045 7357; J Braddell, 11 North St; H D Wolsey, 60 Upper Newtownards Rd. Dundonald AC fishes **Lough Creevy**, Ballylone Rd, nr Saintfield: rainbow trout, pike. Limited dt £10 from Legge Bros, 56 Belmont Rd, Belfast 4.

Lisburn (Co Antrim). Iveagh AC has stretch of 7 miles from Thornyford Bridge, Dromore, to Spencer's Bridge, Flatford. 10 free dt for holders of Dept. of Ag annual game season permit. Tickets from Premier Angling, 17 Queen St, Lurgan. Lisburn & Dist AC fish on 7 miles of **Lagan** between Lisburn and Moira, containing a fair head of b trout, roach, bream;

also a stretch of a small tributary, the **Ravarnette**, with b trout to 3lb not uncommon, also roach and bream. This fishing is open to general public with no charge. Club membership is £12 pa Dept of Ag has brown and/or rainbow trout lakes, totalling more than 700 acres, in the Lagan Valley area. Near to Belfast, these waters are fished more heavily than most in N Ireland. They include: **Stoneyford** and **Leathems-town Reservoirs**, 160 and 28 acres, b and r trout, fly, spinning and worm, 4 fish limit, no boat angling; **Ballykeel Loughherne**, 53 acres, b and r trout, fly only. Abundant coarse fishing on canals and loughs **Henney**, **Begney**, **Aghery**, **Beg**, **Neagh**. All with pike, perch, etc. Tackle shop: Lisburn Sports, 9 Smithfield Square. Hotels: Beechlawn; Forte Crest, both Dunmurry.

Lurgan (Co Armagh). Dept of Ag water: **Craigavon City Park Lakes**, 168 acres, South Lake, r trout, fly, spinning, worming, 4 fish limit. North Lake, coarse fishery with pike and roach. Permits from F C Computers & Tackle, 28 High St; Premier Angling, 17 Queen St.

Dromore (Co Down). Dromore AC has 2 miles of river below, and 5 miles above Dromore: good trout water, for wet and dry fly. Season starts 1 March. Dt £3.50, juv £1, from J McCracken's Confectionery, Gallows St, Dromore. 5 miles away at **Hillsborough**, 40 acres r trout fishery, Dept of Ag water, season 1 Feb–31 Dec. Accommodation at Win Staff B & B, Banbridge Rd; Mrs Rhoda Marks, B & B, Milebush Rd, both Dromore.

LOUGH MELVIN
(For close seasons, licences, see under Boards)

A 5,000 acre natural lake, approximately one fifth of which lies in Northern Ireland (Co Fermanagh). A good spring run of salmon starts in February and a grilse run in June, but the lake is famous chiefly for the variety of its native brown trout. In addition to fish of orthodox appearance, there are dark "sonaghan" caught over the deeper water, and the yellow-bellied "gillaroo", found in the shallows near the shore. Regarded as the Dept of Agriculture's best game fishery. No coarse fishing. **Garrison**, Co Fermanagh is the centre for fishing the lough and **Lough Macnean**, Upper and Lower, also in the vicinity. (Pike, large trout, general coarse fishing.) Small trout in **L Lattone** may be caught from the roadside between Belcoo and Garrison.

NEWRY RIVER
(For close seasons, licences, see under Boards)

A small system flowing into the head of **Carlingford Lough** at **Newry**, Co Down. 3m of fair brown trout water above Cambane Industrial Estate. Newry & Dist AC issues dt £4 for **Clanrye River**, **Greenan Lake**, stocked with brown and rainbow trout and **McCourt's Lake**, **Poyntzpass**, brown trout, fly only. Apply to Mrs E McAlinden, 12 Lisgullion Park, Armagh Rd, Newry. 3m from town, Cooper's Lake, fly fishing for brown trout. Two Dept of Agriculture trout lakes in area: **Lough Brickland** and **Glassdrumman**. Warrenpoint, Rostrevor and Dist AC has fly fishing at Mill Dam, Warrenpoint; Sec (Tel: 028 4177 3525). Tackle shop: J C Smyth, 7/9 Kildare Street, Newry; Bennett's Bar, Warrenpoint.

NEWRY SHIP CANAL

The first ship canal in British Isles, ceased operation in 1976. The fishable section which runs from Newry to sea locks on Omeath road, 3½m approx, has produced match weights of over 50lb. Summer algae improves roach and bream catches, while large pike are to be caught in winter. Most winter fishing is in Albert Basin. There is free fishing for licence-holders.

QUOILE
(For close seasons, licences, see under Boards)

Flows into top of **Strangford Lough** at **Downpatrick**, Co Down. Coarse fish and some trout in lower reaches; fair trout waters between Annacloy Bridge and Kilmore. Dept of Ag has fishing rights on **Quoile Basin** (100 acres) and 7m of Quoile River from Downpatrick to Kilmore; pike, perch, rudd, eels and brown trout; south bank fishing only. No fishing on nature reserve d/s of Steamboat Quay. No wading. Other Dept of Ag fisheries, **Portavoe Reservoir**, nr Donaghadee and Bangor, 31 acres b and r trout, fly only, 20 rods per day, 4 fish limit; **Lough Money**, 53 acre coarse fishery with pike, perch, eels, nr **Downpatrick**. Bridgewater Trout Fishery, 1 Logan, 91 Windmill Rd, Donaghadee (Tel: 028 9188 3348): rainbow trout, B & B on site. Downpatrick & Dist AA hold fishing rights to **Loughinisland Lake** and **Magheraleggan Lake**; guests only when accompanied by a member. A new fishery for disabled anglers has been opened at **Marybrook Mill**, nr Ballynahinch. Rainbow trout and coarse fish. Tel: 028 4483 0173. **Lough Cowey**, 2 miles north of **Portaferry**, natural 70 acres lough with rainbow and brown trout mostly 2lb plus, fly fishing. Dt and boats on site; contact Manager, The Fishery, Lough Cowey Rd, Portaferry (Tel: 028 4272 8946). Tackle shops: H W Kelly & Son, Market Street, Downpatrick; Dairy Fishery, 179 Belfast Rd, Ballynahinch. Hotel: Portaferry (Tel: 028 4272 8231) offers fishing breaks on Lough Cowey.

SHIMNA
(For close seasons, licences, see under Boards)

Small attractive river with deep rocky pools flowing from E slope of Mournes to enter sea at **Newcastle**, Co Down. Sea trout and salmon from July. Dept of Agriculture fishery in forest areas. Bag limit 2 fish. No Sunday fishing. Permits from Forest Office at Tolleymore Forest Park and the Forest Ranger. The rest of the river is controlled by Shimna AC. Wt £25 and dt £7, from Four Season, see below. Fishing is by all legal methods. Dept stillwaters: **Spelga**

Reservoir, 148 acres, b trout; **Castlewellan Lake**, 4 miles from Newcastle, 103 acres, b and r trout, 4 fish limit. Fly, spinning and worming. Tackle shop: The Four Seasons, 47 Main Street, Newcastle. Hotels: Slieve Donard, Enniskeen.

WHITEWATER
(For close seasons, licences, see under Boards)

Small attractive water flowing into sea W of **Kilkeel**, Co Down; 3m of fishing, mainly for sea trout, with some brown trout and a few salmon. Kilkeel AC offers 6-day tickets, £10 per rod day, for Kilkeel and Whitewater Rivers, from Sub Post Office, The Square, Kilkeel (Tel: 028 4176 2225), or Kilmorey Arms (below). Spelea Reservoir is Dept of Ag brown trout fishery, bank only, permits only from Graham Sports. Tackle shops: Graham Sports, 47 Greencastle St, BT34 4BH (Tel: 028 4176 2777); McConnell & Hanna, 19 Newcastle St, both Kilkeel. Hotel: Kilmorey Arms, 41/43 Greencastle St, Kilkeel (Tel: 028 4176 2220).

Sea Fishing Stations in Northern Ireland

The popularity of sea fishing in N Ireland has grown immensely in recent years, leading to the discovery of new and exciting possibilities. 300 miles of unpolluted coastline offers fishing for a variety of species from rock and beach alike. Sheltered inlets, of which Strangford and Belfast Loughs are the largest and best known, offer protection to the boat angler when the open sea may be unfishable due to adverse weather. Twenty-four species of sea fish are caught regularly, including blue shark, skate, tope, cod, bass and flatfish.

Magilligan (Co Antrim). From point, surf fishing for dogfish, flounder, occasional bass. From strand, where lug and ragworm can be dug, beach fishing for flounder. Other venues are: Benone Strand, Downhill Strand, **Castlerock** beach and breakwater, **Barmouth** pier (spinning for mackerel) and beach; flatfish, coalfish, whiting, occasional mullet and bass.

Portrush (Co Antrim) and **Portstewart** (Co Derry). Near mouths of Lough Foyle and River Bann. Rock, pier and beach fishing for pollack, mackerel, wrasse, dogfish, coalfish, flounder, plaice, conger and bass. Conger fishing in Portrush harbour. Rock fishing from Ramore Head east and west, Blue Pool rocks, and **Dunseverick**. Skerries, 2m off Portrush produce good catches of turbot, plaice, dogfish, dab. Causeway bank off **Giants Causeway**

good rock fishing for wrasse, coalfish, pollack, plaice, turbot. Boats for hire: "Wandering Star", Geoff Farrow, 6 Sunset Park, Portstewart BT55 7EH (Tel: 028 7083 6622); experienced skipper for day and evening deep sea angling trips. Club: Portstewart SAC. Tackle shop: Joe Mullan, Sea Angling Specialist, 74 Main Street, Portrush. Hotels: Northern Counties; Magherabuoy House, Eglington, Kiln-an-Oge; all Portrush (and many more).

Ballycastle (Co Antrim). Rock fishing for wrasse, pollack, coalfish, mackerel from Ballintoy. At Ballycastle strand, codling, plaice, small coalfish and whiting. Best in autumn, on evening tides. Spinning or float fishing for cod and pollack. Night fishing at ferry pier is recommended, using float tackle with ragworm, obtainable in town. **Rathlin Island**, just off the coast opposite Ballycastle, has wreck fishing for conger in Church Bay; and cod, coalfish, dogfish, plaice, pollack, turbot, haddock, ling, herring, conger eel, spurdog and skate off Bull point. Boats from C McCaughan, 45 Ann St (Tel: 028 2076 2074) and others. Tackle shop: R Bell, 40 Ann St. Hotel: Antrim Arms. Hilsea B & B, 28 North St Ballycastle BT54 6BW (Tel: 02657 62385) has accommodation with sea fishing trips arranged.

Larne (Co Antrim). No fishing from harbour, but bottom fishing at nearby beach for coalfish, cod, dogfish, wrasse. Lugworm can be dug at Larne, **Glynn** and **Magheramorne** strands or bought at McCluskey's. Local venues are: Glenarm, popular night fishing mark for codling, flatfish; **Murlough Bay**, spinning from rocks for coalfish, mackerel, pollack; Garron point, codling, wrasse, pollack, coalfish, dogfish. Club: Larne & Dist SAC. Tackle shops: Larne Angling Centre, 128 Main St BT40 1RG; S McCluskey, 47 Coastguard Rd. Hotels which cater for anglers: Magheramorne House, Curran Court, Halfway House, Kilwaughter House.

Whitehead and **Carrickfergus** (Co Antrim). Opposite Bangor at entrance to Belfast Lough (Belfast 16m). Pollack, mackerel, coalfish, cod, whiting, from rocks, beach and boats. Wrecks off Blackhead for cod, pollack, coalfish. Local venues are Whitehead Promenade, Carrickfergus Harbour and East pier, Ballycarry Causeway, nr **Islandmagee**. Below Blackhead lighthouse, conger, wrasse, cod, mackerel. Boat trips from Marina, Rogers Quay (Tel: 028 9336 6666), as well as Sailing Club, The Harbour (Tel: 028 9335 1402). Clubs: Woodburn AC and Greenisland AC. Hotels: Dobbins Inn; Coast Road, both Carrickfergus.

Bangor (Co Down). Bangor is on Belfast Lough, 12m from capital. Cod, plaice, turbot, whiting. Lugworm can be dug on beaches at Bangor, ragworm at Kinnegar. Smelt Mill Bay and Orlock point are good summer venues for wrasse, codling, coalfish, dogfish, mackerel. Bangor and **Donaghadee** piers for mackerel, coalfish, flatfish. Boats from Tom Martin (Tel: 028 9145 4672), £15 per angler, charter £150. Tackle shop: Trap & Tackle, 6 Seacliff Rd (Tel: 2047 458515).

Donaghadee (Co Down). Fishing from pier or rocks for pollack, codling and mackerel. Rigg sandbar (3m off Donaghadee) for cod, whiting, gurnard, coalfish, flatfish, mackerel, rays, dogfish, plaice, pollack. Back of Sandbar for big huss. Boats from Q Nelson, 146 Killaughey Rd (Tel: 028 9188 3403) specialising in wreck and reef drift fishing. Twice daily June–Sept, and weekends Sept–Nov, around the Copeland Islands. All tackle provided for beginners. Club: Donaghadee SAC. Tackle shop: Kennedy's, 1 The Parade.

Strangford Lough (Co Down). Good boat fishing in estuaries and inlets around the lough. Big skate (Aug–Oct), spurdog, huss, thornback. Skate and tope are protected species in lough, and must be returned to the water alive. Codling, turbot, whiting, haddock, mackerel, spurdog and wrasse at deep-water entrance to lough. Best fishing in slack water. Lugworm is plentiful at Island Hill nr Comber and shore at Kircubbin. Wreck fishing for big ling and conger outside lough. Boat in **Portaferry**: 'Cuan Shore', D Rogers, 200A Shore Rd (Tel: 028 4272 8297); tackle shop on board. Tackle and bait from Country Sports, 48a Regent St, Newtownards.

Kilkeel (Co Down). Harbour fishing for coalfish and mackerel; West strand for flatfish, dogfish. Black Rock, **Ballymartin**, produces mackerel, dogfish, thornback and codling; **Carlingford Lough**, flatfish, dogfish, thornback, a few bass. Good points are Cranfield and Greencastle, mackerel, dogfish, bass, a few conger, and Bloody Bridge, 1½m outside Newcastle towards Kilkeel, rock cod, mackerel, pollack; Cranfield Point, 3m SW of Kilkeel, fishing for bass, sea trout, pollock and codling. Lugworm can be dug in **Newcastle** harbour and **Greencastle**, rag and lug at **Warrenpoint** beach. Whitewater River has two piers for disabled. Boats are available at Newcastle, phone Newcastle Centre (Tel: 028 4472 2222), or Harbourmaster (Tel: 028 4472 2106/2804). Boats for hire from Carlingford Lough Sea Angling Centre, O Finnegan, 25 Chestnut Grove, Newry BT34 1JT (Tel: 028 3026 4906), for wreck and deep sea fishing, species caught incl cod, pollack, tope, conger, ling; also at Warrenpoint (Tel: 72682 or 73776). Tackle shops: Graham Sports, 47 Greencastle St BT34 4BH); McConnell & Hanna, 19 Newcastle St; Four Seasons, 47 Main St, Newcastle (Tel: 028 4472 5078). Hotel: Kilmorey Arms, 41/43 Greencastle St (Tel: 028 4176 2220) is HQ of Kilkeel AC, who have trout and salmon fishing in Kilkeel and Whitewater Rivers.

Fishing Clubs & Associations in N. Ireland

The following is an alphabetical list of fishing clubs and associations who fish in Northern Ireland. Particulars of the waters held by many will be found by reference to the Index, in the section headed 'Fishing Stations in Northern Ireland', and information about the others, which may not have their own water, could be had from the secretaries. A courtesy they appreciate is the inclusion of a stamped addressed envelope with postal inquiries. Please advise the publishers (address at the front of the book) of any changed details for the next edition.

National Bodies

Fisheries Conservancy Board for Northern Ireland
1 Mahon Road
Portadown,
Craigavon
Co Armagh BT62 3EE
Tel: 028 3833 4666
Fax: 028 3833 8912
E-mail:
tfearon@fcbni.force9.co.uk
Fisheries Office
Riversdale
Ballinamallard
Co Fermanagh
Handicapped Anglers' Trust
Taigh na Iasgair
Russell Close
Little Chalfont
Bucks HP6 6RE
Tel/Fax: 01494 764333
Ulster Coarse Fishing Federation
Robert Buick, Chairman
7 Knockvale Grove
Belfast BT5 6HL

Clubs

Agivey Anglers' Association
Ian Pollock
Ballinamean Avenue
Garvagh
Co Londonderry
Antrim and District Angling Association
B McNeill
41 Derry Road

Newtown Abbey
BT36 7UF
Ards Fly Fishing Club
James Crothers
c/o Lough Cowey Fishery
Lough Cowey Road
Co Down
Ards & District Sea Angling Club
J Purdy
Ivy Cottage
22 Glenmount Park
Rosehill
Newtownards BT23 4QL
Armagh Angling Club
c/o Armagh Colour Copy
Shop
Dobbin Centre
Armagh
Armagh and District Angling Club
Contact
Amagh District Council
The Palace Demesne
Armagh BT60 4EL
Ballylagan Fishing and Conservation Club
c/o Smyths Country Sports
1 Park Street
Coleraine
Co Londonderry BT52 1BD
Ballymoney and District Angling Club
J McKay
15 Pharis Road
Ballymoney
Ballynure Angling Club
John Arneill
17 Collinview Drive
Ballyclare
BT39 9PQ
Banbridge Angling Club
J Curran

2 Ballydown Road
Banbridge
Co Down BT32 4JB
Belfast Anglers' Association
John A Collinson
7 Hawthorne Drive
Belfast BT4 2HG
Blue Circle Angling Club
N Hutchinson
c/o Blue Circle
Sandholes Road
Cookstown
British Legion Angling Club
C McFetridge
c/o British Legion
Burn Road
Cookstown
Co Tyrone
Burn Dennet Angling Association
W O'Neill
Carrickatane Road
Dunamanagh
Co Tyrone
Castlecaldwell Anglers
c/o Leggs Post Office
Fermanagh
Castlederg Anglers' Club
R R Harron
36 Ferguson Crescent
Castlederg
Co Tyrone BT81 7AG
or
c/o H Irwin, Grocer
5 John Street
Castlederg, Co Tyrone
Castlewellan and Annsborough Angling Club
S P Harrison
Garden Cottage

Forest Park
Castlewellan
**Clady and District
Angling Club**
H Doherty
95 Clady Road
Portglenone
Co Antrim BT44 8LB
Clogher Angling Club
Seamus McGirr
2 Richmond Drive
Clogher
Co Tyrone BT76 0AD
Coleraine Angling Club
B Liddell
53 Seapark
Castlerock BT51 4TH
Derg Angling Club
c/o Campbells
50 Main Street
Newtownstewart
Co Tyrone
**Donaghadee Sea Angling
Club**
Billy Greer
29 Ravenscroft Avenue
Belfast BT5 5BA
Dromore Angling Club
R Russell
49 Ravenscroft Avenue
Belfast
Dundonald Angling Club
Peter Grahame
13 Cherryhill Drive
Dundonald
Belfast BT16 0JG
**Dundonald Sea Angling
Club**
Sam Burns
24 Tara Crescent
Newtownards BT23 3DF
Dungiven Anglers' Club
Now amalgamated with Roe
AA
Enler Fishing Club
Comber
Co Down
**River Faughan Anglers'
Ltd**
L F Thompson
Office:
26A Carlisle Road
Londonderry BT48 6JW
Gaff Angling Club
c/o Campbell's Mourne Valley
Tackle
50 Main Street

Newtownstewart
Co Tyrone
**Galgorm and District
Angling Club**
N Anderson
56 Ballykennedy Road
Gracehill
**Garrison & District
Angling Club**
Garrison
Fermanagh
Gilford Angling Club
M Magee
Station Road
Scarva Craigavon
**Glenravel & Clough
Angling Club**
D Anderson
6 Old Cushendun Road
Newtowncrommelin
Co Antrim
Glens Angling Club
Secretary
5 Middle Park Crescent
Cushendall
Co Antrim
**Gracehill, Galgorm and
District Angling Club**
M Weir, Chairman
23 Beechwood Avenue
Ballymena
Co Antrim
BT42 1ND
Greenisland Angling Club
W Hinton
18 Glenkeen Drive
Greenisland
Carrickfergus
**Holywood Fly Fishing
Club**
C F Kyle
2 Seymour Park
Crawfordsburn Road
Bangor
**Kells and Connor Angling
Club**
N Wilson
35 Templemoyle
Kells, Ballymena
Co Antrim
Kildress Angling Club
Bobby Cox
10 Millburn St
Cookstown
Co Tyrone
BT80 8EG
or Headquarters

Upper Kildress Road
Cookstown
Kilkeel Angling Club
c/o Kilmorey Arms
41 Greencastle Street
Kilkeel
**Kilrea and District
Angling Club**
David Laughlin
Bann Road
Kilrea
Co Londonderry
Kingsbridge Angling Club
c/o The Dunleath Bar
Church Street
Cookstown
**Kings Road Game
Angling Club**
c/o 8 Kim Park
Dundonald BT5 7GA
**Larne and District Sea
Angling Club**
S Givran
16 McGee Park
Larne BT40 1PP
**Lisburn and District
Anglers' Club**
H H Crombie
16 Plantation Avenue
Lisburn, Co Antrim
BT27 5BL
Maine Angling Club
Bill McCartney
7 Demesne Manor
Holywood
Co Down BT18 9NW
**Mid-Antrim Angling
Club**
R Topping
24 Cameron Park
Ballymena
Co Antrim
**Mid-Ulster Angling
Club**
D Boner
57 Molesworth Road
Cookstown
Co Tyrone
Moy Angling Club
D Tomney
10 The Square
Moy, Dungannon
Co Tyrone
**Moyola and District
Angling Club**
T Maguire
3 Graigmore Road

Maghera
Co Londonderry
Newry and District
Angling Club
D Kidd
8 Cloneden
Dallan Road
Warrenpoint
Co Down
Omagh Angling
Association
c/o D Campbell
Fishing Tackle Shop
50 Main Street
Newtownstewart
Co Tyrone
Portstewart Sea Angling
Club
A McCallion
23 Hillview Park
Cleraine
Co Londonderry
BT51 3EH
Randalstown Angling

Club
R Magee
67 Muckamore Garden Village
Antrim
BT41 1NB
Rathfriland and District
Angling Association
John Dougan
33 Newry Road
Rathfriland, Co Down
Roe Anglers
c/o R Douglas and Son
6 Irish Green Street
Limavady
Co Londonderry
Shimna Angling Club
P Mornin
84 Bryansford Road
Newcastle, Co Down
BJ33 0LE
Sion Mills Angling
Club
Angling Information Centre
151 Melmount Road

Sion Mills
Co Tyrone
Strangford Lough Sea
Angling Club
19 Joe Tumelty Drive
Portaferry
County Down BT22 1RP
Tullylagan Angling Club
Jim Warnock
133 Dungannon Road
Cookstown
Co Tyrone
Warrenpoint, Rostrevor
and District Angling Club
P Murphy
1 Carrickview Burren
Warrenpoint
Co Down BT34 3FB
Woodburn Angling Club
W Moore
544 Upper Road
Woodburn
Carrickfergus

Fishing in Ireland

The Irish Republic is world famous for the quality of its fisheries. Salmon, sea trout, brown trout, pike and other coarse fish, are to be found there at their best. The seas around Ireland contain very good quantities of many varieties of fish which provide excellent sport for visiting and native sea anglers. Where to fish in Ireland is virtually everywhere. Fisheries are administered by a Central Fisheries Board and by seven Regional Fisheries Boards coordinated by the Central Board. The function of each Regional Board is to conserve, protect, develop and promote every aspect of the inland fisheries (salmon, trout, coarse fish, eels), including sea angling, within the Board's fisheries region.

Rod/Line Licences

Salmon/Sea Trout – Season (All districts) £25
Salmon/Sea Trout (Single district only) £12
Salmon/Sea Trout Juvenile £8
Salmon/Sea Trout 21-Day £10
Salmon/Sea Trout 1 Day £3
Foyle Area Extension £17

Central/Regional Fisheries Board Permits on trout fisheries
Ordinary (Season) From £5 to £20
Pensioner/Juvenile (Season) From £2 to £10, (Day) from £0.50 to £5

South Western Board Permits
Annual £20. Three week £10. Day £3

Shannon Board Permits
Adult Annual £20. Day £5
Pensioner Annual £20. Day £5
Juvenile Annual £20. Day £1

Share Certificates
There are eight fisheries development societies in the country, and their purpose is to raise funds for the development of coarse and trout fishing. At present the Northern and Upper Shannon regions are the only ones where a share certificate is obligatory. Elsewhere their purchase is voluntary. Annual share certificates cost £12; 21 days: £5; 3 days: £3. They may be obtained from tackle shops.

The modified close seasons now in force for salmon, sea trout and brown trout differ not only as between regions, but also within regions, in a formulation too complex for repro-duction here in detail. The general pattern is that seasons for migratory fish tend to open early and close early, while that for brown trout opens early in many places (Feb 15) and does not close until a date in October. There are, however, important exceptions and anglers proposing to visit the Republic, especially early or late in the year, should make careful enquiries with the appropriate Regional Board before making firm plans, whether the intention be to fish for salmon, migratory or brown trout.

There is no annual close season for angling for coarse fish or for sea fish.

Overall responsibility for the country's fisheries rests with the Department of the Marine, Leeson Lane, Dublin 2, Tel: 01 678 5444, Fax: 01 661 8241.

The Central Fisheries Board consists of the chairmen of the seven Regional Boards and from four to six members nominated by the Minister for the Marine. The functions of the Central Board are prescribed in the Fisheries Act 1980 and include such things as co-ordination and, where necessary, direction of the regional boards in the performance of their functions, which are: management, conservation, protection, development and promotion of inland fisheries and sea angling resources, and the protection of molluscs. Pollution, poaching and environmental incidents should be reported immediately to the appropriate regional board (addresses below). The head office of the **Central Fisheries Board** is at **Mobhi Boreen, Glasnevin, Dublin 9**, Tel: 379206/7/8, Fax: 01 360060.

The Central Fisheries Board owns and operates an important commercial and rod salmon fishery on the River Corrib at Galway, Co Galway (inquiries to the Manager, The Fishery, Nun's Island, Galway, Co Galway, Tel: 091 562388), and the famous Erriff Fishery in Co Galway. Enquiries for fishing and accommodation here – at Aasleagh Lodge or Cottage – to the Manager, R Erriff Fishery, Aasleagh Lodge, Leenane, Co Galway (Tel: 095 42252).

The Electricity Supply Board also holds extensive fishing rights: principal salmon waters are the River Mulcair and the Shannon at Parteen, above Limerick, and at Castleconnell, Co Limerick. The Board preserves and develops the fisheries under its control. Inquiries to

Electricity Supply Board, Fisheries Division, Ardnacrusha, Co Clare (Tel: 061 345588).

Inquiries about accommodation and general tourist angling information (e.g. leaflets, brochures about local angling resources and amenities throughout the country) should be addressed to **Bord Failte, Baggot Street Bridge, Dublin 2, Tel: 01 602 4000, Fax: 602 4100** or **The Irish Tourist Board, 150 New Bond Street, London W17 0AQ, Tel: 020 7493 3201**.

The Regional Boards

The Eastern Regional Fisheries Board. Covers all lakes and river systems entering the sea including coastal waters between Carlingford Lough, Co Louth and Kiln Bay, Co Wexford. Inquiries to: Regional Manager, Balnagowan House, Mobhi Boreen, Glasnevin, Dublin 9 (Tel: 01 8379209, Fax: 8360060).

The Southern Regional Fisheries Board. Covers all lakes and river systems entering the sea, including coastal waters, between Kiln Bay, Co Wexford and Ballycotton Pier, Co Cork. Inquiries to the Board's Regional Fisheries Manager, Anglesea St, Clonmel, Co Tipperary (Tel: 052 23624, Fax: 052 23971).

The South Western Regional Fisheries Board. Covers all lakes and river systems entering the sea, including coastal waters, between Ballycotton Pier, Co Cork and Kerry Head, Co Kerry. Inquiries to the Board's Regional Fisheries Manager, Nevilles Terrace, Massey Town, Macroom, Co Cork (Tel: 026 41221/2, Fax 026 41223, e-mail: swrfb@swrfb.ie).

The Shannon Regional Fisheries Board. Covers the inland fisheries of the Shannon catchment, the River Feale catchment in North Kerry and the rivers of Co Clare flowing westwards to the Atlantic. The coastal boundary stretches from Kerry Head, Co Kerry to Hag's Head, Co Clare. Inquiries to the Board's Regional Fisheries Manager, Thomond Weir, Limerick (Tel: 061 455171, Fax: 061 326533, Internet: www.shannon-fishery-board.ie, e-mail: info@shannon-fishery-board-ie).

The Western Regional Fisheries Board. Covers all lakes and rivers entering the sea, including coastal waters, between Hag's Head, Co Clare and Pigeon Point, near Westport, Co Mayo. Inquiries to The Board's Regional Fisheries Manager, The Weir Lodge, Earl's Island, Galway City (Tel: 091 563118/9, Fax: 091 566335).

The North Western Regional Fisheries Board. Covers all lakes and rivers entering the sea, including coastal waters, between Pigeon Point, just north of Westport, Co Mayo, and Mullaghmore Head, Co Sligo. Inquiries to the Board's Regional Fisheries Manager, Ardnaree House, Abbey St, Ballina, Co Mayo (Tel: 096 22788, Fax: 096 70543, e-mail: nwrfb@iol.ie).

The Northern Regional Fisheries Board. Covers all lakes and rivers entering the sea, including coastal waters, between Carrickgarve, Co Sligo and Malin Head, Co Donegal. Inquiries to the Board's Regional Fisheries Manager, Station Road, Ballyshannon, Co Donegal (Tel: 072 51435/ 52053, Fax: 072 51816).

Fishing Stations in Ireland

Details of close seasons, licences, etc, for Irish rivers and loughs listed alphabetically here will be found in pages on the previous pages. Anglers wanting further details of accommodation should write to **Bord Failte (Irish Tourist Board), Baggot Street Bridge, Dublin, 2. Tel: 0602 4000 (4100 Fax).** *Anglers in the* **Western Fisheries Region** *should note the fact that the killing of sea trout is now illegal.* **All sea trout must be returned alive to the water.**

BALLYSODARE and LOUGH ARROW
For close seasons, licences, etc, see The Regional Fisheries Board)

River Ballysodare formed by junction of three rivers, **Unshin** or **Arrow**, **Owenmore** (not to be confused with Owenmore River, Co Mayo), and **Owenbeg**, near Collooney, flows into Ballysodare Bay. Near mouth of river, at Ballysodare Falls, is earliest salmon ladder erected in Ireland (1852). Salmon, trout, very few sea trout. R Arrow, which runs out of Lough Arrow, contains small stock of brown trout for which fishing is free. The Owenmore has good coarse fishing, especially bream, at Ballymote. Lough Arrow is a rich limestone water of 3,123 acres on the border of Sligo and Roscommon, situated 14 miles from Sligo town and 4 miles from Boyle. It is about 5m long and varies in width from ½m to 1½m. The lough is almost entirely spring-fed and has a place of honour among Ireland's best known mayfly lakes. Nowhere else is the hatch of fly so prolific or the rise so exciting. The brown trout rise to mayfly from late May to mid-June and sport is varied at this time by dapping, wet-fly and dry-fly fishing with green drake and the spent gnat. This is followed soon after (mid-July to mid-Aug) by a late evening rise to big sedge called the Murrough and Green Peter which may give the lucky angler as much fun as mayfly. The lough is regularly stocked with trout. Boats and ghillies may be hired at all seasons and at many centres on lake shore. **Loughs Bo** and **na Súil** are in close proximity, and ideal bank fishing for trout. Coarse fishing may be found nearby at **Lough Haugh, Temple House Lake, Ballanascarrow (Ballymote)**, and the **Owenmore River**. Coarse and trout fishing at **Cavetown Lake**; stand for disabled; Cavetown and Croghan AC, Kit O'Beirne (Tel: 079 68037). Salmon may be fished at Ballysadare (10 miles from Lough Arrow). Miss

Eileen McDonagh, Pub, Lough Bo, Geevagh Via Boyle, (Tel: 071 65325) supplies permits for brown trout fishing in Lough Bo, and rainbow trout in Lough na Súil; boats and access for disabled; st £25, dt £5. Boats: R and J Acheson, Andresna House, Lough Arrow, Boyle (Tel: 079 66181); Annaghloy Boat Hire (Tel: 079 666666), and F Dodd (see *Castlebaldwin*); D Grey (Tel: 071 65491); Eileen Carty, Ballinafad (Tel: 079 66001). A boat for disabled is being funded for year 2000, and piers for disabled at Lough Bo. For information about Lough Arrow, contact Arrow Community Enterprises Ltd, Castlebaldwin Via Boyle (Tel: 071 65738), a company existing to promote economic and social development of region; Lough Arrow Fish Preservation Society, F Dodd (Tel: 071 65065); or J Hargadon, Annaghloy Boat Hire (Tel: 079 66666). For L Arrow and Dist AC (Tel: 071 65304). Tackle from Brian Flaherty, Boyle; Barton Smith, Sligo. Accommodation in Lough Arrow area includes Andresna House (*above*); Cromleagh Lodge, Ballindoon (Tel: 079 65155); Rockview Hotel, Riverstown (Tel: 079 66073/66077); Tower Hill B & B, Castlebaldwin (Tel: 079 66021). Tackle from Louis Carty, Ballinafad (Tel: 079 66001).

Collooney (Co Sligo). Best season, May to July. Fishing dependent on sufficient rain. Permission to fish for sea and brown trout sometimes obtainable. Good dry fly. River contains sizeable pike. **Lough Bo** fished from here (See *above*).

Castlebaldwin via **Boyle** (Co Sligo). Trout fishing on L Arrow, free. Season 1 Apr–30 Sept. Bank fishing not recommended. Boats can be hired on lake shore from Dodd Boats, Ballindoon, Riverstown (Tel: 071 65065), and Annaghloy Boat Hire (Tel: 079 66666). L Arrow FPS fishes in Loughs **Arrow** and **Augh** (pike, perch, b trout in L Arrow). NWRFB permits required for L Bo and L na Leibe, but not L

Arrow; season £12, £5 conc, daily £3–£1. **Lough Bo** in hills provides good shore fishing for brown trout. Fly only. Season 1 April–30 Sept. **Lake na Leibe** has rainbow trout stocked by Central Fisheries Board. Season 1 April–30 Sept. Fishing from shore or boat. Good stock of brown trout in **Lough Feenagh**; boats for hire. River fishing on **R Unshin** and **R Feorrish** (above Ballyfarnon); trout. Coarse fishing on **Templehouse Lake** and **Cloonacleigha Lake**; good pike fishing; boats for hire. Coarse and trout fishing on **Lough Key**, 3m east of Arrow. Contact Sec, L Arrow FPS, F Dodd (Tel: 071 65065); or J Hargadon, Annaghloy Boat Hire (Tel: 079 66666). For L Arrow and Dist AC (Tel: 071 65304). Hotels: Cromleach Lodge, Rock View.

Boyle (Co Roscommon). L Arrow, trout, free; contact Fishery Inspector (Tel: 079 66033) for information. **River Boyle**, a tributary of R Shannon, connects **Loughs Gara** and **Key**, both with very large pike. Upstream of town are quality bream, rudd, perch, roach, eels, hybrid and brown trout. Downstream, pike are to be found. A short distance southwest at **Ballaghaderreen** is the **Lung River** connected to **Breedoge Lough**, and several other waters, among them **Loughs Cloonagh**, **Urlaur**, and **Cloonacolly**. This area holds some of the best coarse fishing in Ireland, with many species incl pike to 30lb. Contact J Cogan, Ballaghaderreen AC (Tel: 0907 60077). **Lough Nasool**, 13m north, contains rainbow trout, dt from Eileen McDonagh, Lough Bo, Geevagh Via Boyle (Tel: 071 65325). Tackle shops: Abbey Marine and Field Sports, Carrick Rd (Tel: 079 62959) provides ghillies; Christy Wynne, Main St, supplies live and ground bait; Boyle Tourist Office (Tel: 0796 2145); Martin Mitchell, Abbey House, (*below*), bait stockist; Michael Rogers, Ballymote. Accommodation for anglers: Mrs Mitchell, Abbey House (Tel: 079 62385), situated beside R Boyle, with much fine game and coarse fishing within easy reach; Arrow Angling Accommodation (Tel: 079 66181/66050); Mrs Eileen Kelly, Forest Park House, Rathdevine, Boyle (Tel: 079 62227); Arrow Lakeside Accommodation; Rockview Hotel, Ballindoon via Boyle (Tel: 079 66073). Arrow Lodge, Kilmactranny, via Boyle (Tel: 079 66298): period lakeside accom, with private mooring and boat hire; ghillie service; salmon fishing arranged at Ballysodare, coarse fishing close by.

BANDON

(For close seasons, licences, etc, see The South Western Regional Fisheries Board)

45 miles in length, rises in Sheshy Mountains, flows 45 miles, and drains 235 square miles. Salmon fishing extends all the way from **Inishannon** u/s to **Togher Castle**, depending on conditions. An estimated 1,300 salmon are caught each season; about 300 of these are spring fish. Grilse run at end of June. Big run of sea trout from early July to end of Aug, and good stocks of browns, mostly small, but fish up to 2lb taken. Fishing can be excellent on 4m stretch from Bandon to Inishannon. Ghillies are for hire. Season 15 Feb–30 Sept.

Bandon (Co Cork). About 8m double bank controlled by Bandon AA. Dt £15, wt £75. Bag limit 6 fish, size limit 10in. Visitors welcome, tickets from M J O'Regan, 21 Oliver Plunkett St, Bandon (Tel: 023 41674).

Ballineen (Co Cork). The 4m stretch of river to about 1m above Ballineen Bridge is controlled by Ballineen and Enniskeane AA; salmon and trout. St and dt from Tom Fehilly, Bridge Street, Ballineen. Kicoleman Fishery, Enniskeane (Tel: 023 47249) offers lodge accommodation and private fishing on Bandon with 10 named salmon pools, and excellent stocks of wild brown trout. Season Feb 15–Sept 30, spate fishing, mainly fly only. Av salmon catch 103 per annum. Manch House Fishery, Manch, Ballineen (Tel: 023 47256) has 2m double bank fishing for salmon and wild brown trout, many holding pools, fly only. Rods limited, dt £30 where available.

Dunmanway (Co Cork). Above Manch Bridge is Dunmanway Salmon and Trout AA water. Tickets from P MacCarthy, Yew Tree Bar, Dunmanway. River fishable for about 8m. Many small trout loughs in region, incl **Cullenagh** (4½m west), **Coolkeelure** (2¼m north west), **Ballynacarriga**, **Atarriff**, **Chapel Lake**; free fishing, small browns; for **Curraghalickey Lake**, contact P MacCarthy, *see above*.

CAHA RIVER. Joins Bandon 3m north of Dunmanway. Holds good stock of trout to 14 oz, for 3m up from confluence. Free fishing, best in early season, because of weed. Free fishing on **Neaskin Lough,** 3¼m north of Dunmanway. Difficult access, but plenty of 6oz browns.

Clonakilty (Co Cork). **River Argideen**, rises northwest of Clonakilty, flowing into Courtmacsherry Harbour, rated among best sea trout rivers in SW Ireland, occasional salmon. Lower fishery owned or managed by Argideen AA. Maximum 6 rods per day, bag limit 10 trout, size limit 9in. Permits from Fishery Office, Inchy Bridge. Tackle shop: Jeffersports, South Main St, Bandon.

BARROW
(including Nore)
(For close seasons, licences, etc, see The Southern Regional Fisheries Board)

A limestone river which has been underrated in its potential, and not heavily fished. The second longest in Ireland, it rises well in the centre of the country on the eastern slopes of the Shannon watershed and flows over 120m south to the sea at Waterford Harbour, entering by a long estuary. An excellent head of wild brown trout, salmon run from Apr, best angling during grilse run in Sept. Bream, pike, rudd and hybrids provide good coarse angling, and annual May run of twaite shad is popular with visiting and local anglers.

Waterford (Co Waterford). Reservoirs managed by SRFB, **Knockaderry** and **Ballyshunnock**: both 70 acres at normal level, with wild brown and stocked rainbow, 6 fish limit. Boats on Knockaderry, no bank fishing, fly only, book in advance (Tel: 051 84107). All legal methods on Ballyshunnock, bank only, no maggot. Dt from Carrolls Cross Inn (Tel: 051 94328). **Mahon River** (15m) holds sea trout and salmon, and mackerel, bass and pollack abound along the coast.

Graighuenamanagh (Co Carlow). Good coarse fishing, with pike and large bream. Local venues are Tinnehinch Lower Weir and Bahanna. Contact J Butler, Tinnahinch, Graighuenamagh.

Carlow (Co Carlow). Bream, rudd, pike. Trout fishing on Rivers Barrow, Milford to Maganey, 8m, **Lerr**, 4m, **Greese**, 3m approx, and **Burren**, 8m, controlled by Barrow AC and restocked yearly. Members only, membership £6 from tackle shop, or secretary. Other club: Carlow and Graiguecullen Anglers. Free fishing from Milford Weir to canal mouth d/s of Milford Bridge. Tackle shop: Murph's, Tullow St, Carlow. Hotel: Dolmen, Kilkenny Rd.

Athy (Co Kildare). Trout, bream, rudd, pike.

Several tributaries within easy reach. **R Greese**, from Dunlavin to Barbers Bridge, Kilkea, approx 8m, fishable on permit from Greese Anglers. Bream to 8lb are regularly caught in Barrow, as well as pike above 30lb, perch, rudd and game fish. **Grand Canal** holds good head of tench, pike, perch, rudd and bream. There is some good free dry-fly water on left bank d/s of Athy, known as the Barrow Track. Kilberry & Cloney AC fish 5m **Boherbaun River** from Milltown Bridge to Forth of Dunrally Bridge, Vicarstown, eastside, (natural browns, 1–4lb); **Stradbally River**, 6m away, with trout; permits from Griffin Hawe (*below*). Vicarstown & Dist AC club waters extend on west side of R Barrow from Laois/Kildare border northwards to the Glasha River. Athy & Dis AC fishes Barrow to Maganey Lock. In Sept 1992 club released 20,000 brown trout into Barrow as part of a general improvement programme. There are no fishing rights on Barrow, but a club card allows access from landowners. Membership £5 pa and accom list from tackle shop: Griffin Hawe, 22 Duke St, Tel: 0507 31221 (Fax: 38885). Self-catering accom: Mrs C Crean, Vicarstown Inn (Tel: 0502 25159); Mr Jim Crean, Milltown Cottage, Tel: 0502 25189, Fax: 0502 25652; many B & B in locality.

Portarlington (Co Laois). River at town is easily accessible, and holds some salmon from March. Portarlington AC has approx 6 miles of good dry fly trout fishing on **Upper Barrow**. Best mid-May to mid-Sept. Mountmellick AC has 7m, good trout, a few salmon. Bracknagh AC has approx 5 miles of the **Figile River**, a tributary of the Barrow. Mainly coarse, a few trout around Millgrove Bridge. St £5 for all these waters are readily obtainable from Portarlington AC treasurer Mr Pat Maher; Inchacooley, Monasterevin; or Mick Finlay, publican, Bracklone St. Another tributary, the **Cushina River**, north of **Monasterevin** is fished by Cushina AC: tickets from P Dunne, Clonsast, Rathangan. For general information about local fishing, and tickets, contact Mick Finlay (*above*); Kieran Cullen, Gun and Tackle, Monasterevin (Tel: 045 25902/25329); or Donegan, Tackle, Main St Portarlington. Fishing accommodation near aqueduct, where Grand Canal crosses R Barrow: Owen Cullen, Coole, Monasterevin.

GRAND CANAL (Co Kildare). Much free fishing. Canal runs through **Prosperous** and **Robertston** and **Sallins**, where there is first-class fishing for bream, best early morning. Also rudd, tench, hybrids and some pike. Prosperous Coarse AC fishes on a length of some 20m. At **Edenderry**, Co Offaly, canal has large bream, tench, carp, rudd, roach, perch, eels. Edenberry Coarse AC controls 18m first-class coarse angling, with bream, tench, roach, rudd, carp; membership £10, £2 conc. Contact Pauric Kelly, Edenderry Angling Supplies, 48 Murphy St, Edenderry, Tel: 0405 32071 (home).

GRAND CANAL, BARROW BRANCH (Co Kildare and Co Laois). Fishing for bream, roach, tench, hybrids, rudd and pike, 5 minutes' walk from **Rathangan**. Information from M J Conway, Caravan and Camping Park, Rathangan (Tel: 045 524331). At **Monasterevin** canal has pike, perch and bream. Contact Pat Cullen, Tackle Shop. At **Vicarstown**, Co Laois, fishing for bream, tench, pike and rudd. For permits, accom and information contact Jim Crean, Vicarstown Inn, Vicarstown (Tel: 0502 25189). Naas tackle shop: Countryman Angling Ltd. Bait stockists: Griffin Hawe, Athy; Countryman Angling, Haas; Jim Cream.

SUIR

(For close seasons, licences, etc, see The Southern Regional Fisheries Board)

Considered to be one of Europe's finest dry fly trout rivers, with average trout size of ¾lb, and fish up to 3lb often caught. Predominantly a trout river, there is also a good salmon run. It is fairly shallow with deep glides, and drains large areas of limestone. Runs into the same estuary as Nore and Barrow, reaching sea at Waterford. Fishes best from mid-May to the end of September. Daytime fishing is more productive in May, and evenings during the summer months. Record salmon for Ireland, 57lb, was caught in Suir, in 1874. Salmon fishing opens on 1 March, and in good years large springers up to 25lb are caught. Grilse run usually begins in late May and continues to end of Sept. Late August and Sept often bring bigger fish, over 10lb. There are large stocks of wild brown trout in river, but they are not easily caught, and best fished in faster glides, from May to mid-June. Season 1 Mar–30 Sept. A wide network of tributaries, excellent fishing in their own right, includes the Rivers Nire, Tar, and Anner (see below).

Carrick-on-Suir (Co Tipperary). Start of tidal water. **Duffcastle** to Carrick-on-Suir is last freshwater section, well stocked with trout. Carrick-on-Suir AA has north bank from Miloko to Duffcastle, also **Coolnamuck Fisheries**, 3 miles south bank, fishing for salmon, trout, twait shad. Tickets and ghillies though J O'Keeffe, *see below*. Free trout fishing on tributary **Lingaun River**, which runs from north into tidal water east of Carrick-on-Suir; landowners consent reqd. Up river there is good trout fishing and occasional sea trout; free for 400m on left bank d/s of **Kilsheelin**. 1½m south bank permits from Mrs Maura Long, Glencastle, Kilnasheelin (Tel: 052 33287); salmon and trout, £15, £5. About 4m to south mountain loughs, largest of which are **Coumshingaun** and **Crotty's**, provide very good fishing as also does **Clodiagh River**, which springs from loughs and is close to road for part of way. Good salmon and trout fishing from Carrick to Cashel. Most of river preserved for salmon, but some owners give permission to fish for trout. Tackle shop: O'Keeffe, OK Sports, New St (Tel: 051 40626). Hotel: Orchard House.

Clonmel (Co Tipperary). Moderate to good stocks of trout to 30cm. Free fishing between the bridges in town. Clonmel and Dist AC controls water from **Knocklofty Bridge** d/s one mile on south bank, also from Clonmel New Bridge to **Anner River**. Permits from J Carroll (Tel: 052 21123/21966). Private fishing u/s of Knocklofty Bridge reserved for residents of Knocklofty House Hotel. Fishing on Marlfield Fisheries through Jean Loup Trautner, Marlfield Lodge, Clonmel (Tel: 052 252340). Clonmel & Dist Salmon and Trout Anglers control fishing rights on both banks from Deerpark to Kilmanahan Castle. Permits from John Kavanagh (*below*). At **Kilsheenan** left bank d/s is free fishing for 400m. 2m private salmon and trout fishing is obtainable from Mrs Maura Long, Glencastle, Kilsheelin (Tel: 052 33787). Local tributaries of main river are **Nire** (mountain stream with trout av ½lb, to 6lb), **Tar** (lowland stream with exceptional fly life, densely populated with trout av ½lb), **Duag**, **Anner** (fast moving stream with good stocks of trout av ¾lb, very good fishing in early season by u/s nymph method). Andrew and Eileen Ryan, Clonanav Fly Fishing Centre, Ballymacarbry, Clonmel (Tel: 052 36141, Fax: 36294) offer accommodation and instruction, and arrange dry fly fishing on Nire, Tar, Duag, Anner, Suir, and Blackwater Rivers; Nire and Glenahiry Lakes; Knockaderry and Ballyshunnock Reservoirs. Tickets sold for these waters, guide service and tackle shop. Nire Valley AC has 6m of **Nire**, st £5 from Mrs Wall, Hanoras Cottage, Ballymacarbry. Mountain loughs can also be reached from this centre. Tackle shop: Kavanagh's Sports Shop, Westgate,

Clonmel. Hotels: Clonmel Arms; Hotel Minella.

Ardfinnan (Co Tipperary). Good numbers of trout to 30cm. Ardfinnan AC has much trout fishing in locality, d/s of Rochestown to Corabella. Permits from John Maher, Green View, Ardfinnan. Limited rods at Cloghardeen Fishery, Cloghardeen Farm.

Cahir (Co Tipperary). Cahir and Dist AA controls Suir from Ballycarron Convent 4m below Golden Village, d/s to meetings, and from Swiss Cottage Bridge d/s 4m to Garnavilla ford; all fishing fly only, mostly brown trout, some salmon, limited dt £8, wt £45, from The Heritage, Mr Pat O'Donovan, 1 The Square, Cahir. Tackle from Kavanagh Sports, Clonmel; flies from Alice Conba, fly dresser (Tel: 062 52755). Hotels: Castle Court, Cahir House (Tel: 052 41729); Kilcoran Lodge (Tel: 052 41288); 8m salmon and trout water; Theresa Russell, Bansha Castle, Bansha (Tel: 062 54187).

Cashel (Co Tipperary). Brown trout and salmon. Cashel, Tipperary and Golden AA issues visitors' permits for 8m both banks **Suir** from Camas Bridge south to **Ballycarron Bridge**, fly only, wild brown trout to 2lb, dt £5, wt £15 from Mrs Ryan, Tackle Shop, Friar St, Cashel. Dundrum Dist AA fly fishes on **Marl Lake, Dundrum**. Permits from Dundrum House Hotel. Cashel Palace Hotel, Main St, owns rights on good stretch of Suir and Aherlow Rivers, about 8m south of town, with brown trout fly fishing; ghillie service, permits on request from hotel. Best fishing from early spring to mid-summer. Other hotels: Ardmayle House, Baileys, Cashel, Ryans, and many excellent guest houses and B&Bs.

Thurles (Co Tipperary). Good centre for upper river trout fishing. Thurles, Holycross and Ballycamas AA has water from **Holycross** to Kileen Flats both banks, fly only. Dt £5 from Hayes Hotel. Club also fishes **R Clodiagh** and **R Drish**. Good stocks of trout to 40cms. U/s from Drish Bridge weeded in summer; d/s fishable throughout season, usually. Accommodation and permits: J & T Grene, Farm Guesthouse, Cappamurra House, Dundrum, Tel: 062 71127.

Templemore (Co Tipperary). Templemore AA water; visitors' dt for Suir (trout only, av ½lb).

BLACKWATER RIVER (Co Kilkenny): This tributary joins the Suir about 2 miles upstream of Waterford City. It is tidal as far as the weir below **Kilmacow**, and holds good stocks of small trout between Kimacow and **Mullinavat**. Some fishing with landowners' consent. Enquire at local tackle shops.

PORTLAW CLODIAGH (Co Waterford): Tributary, which joins **Suir** east of Portlaw. Moderate trout stocks. Fishing rights on entire river owned by the Marquis of Waterford, but fishing is open u/s of **Lowrys Bridge** and d/s of **Portlaw**.

ARA/AHERLOW (Co Tipperary): Tributary joins Suir north of Cahir, flowing from a westerly direction. Significant numbers of trout to 28 cm. Ara AC has trout fishing from **Tipperary Town** to **Kilmyler Bridge**, where R Ara meets R Aherlow; fly, spinning or worming, wt £5, from J Evans, Main St, Tipperary.

NORE

(For close seasons, licences, etc, see The Southern Regional Fisheries Board)

River rises in Co Tipperary, flows east through Borris-in-Ossory and then south through Kilkenny to join River Barrow near New Ross, about 8 miles south of Inistioge. 87 miles long with a total catchment of 977 square miles, Nore is a limestone river with abundant fly life. Increased salmon run in recent years. Because the salmon fishing is good, the trout fishing is somewhat neglected, although trout are plentiful in the river. Mills and weirs are a feature of this river, and long deep stretches provide excellent dry fly fishing even in low water.

Thomastown (Co Kilkenny), Thomastown AA has excellent salmon and trout stretch of Nore and issues temporary cards to visitors. Trout fishing is fly or worm only. Inistioge AC controls 3m both banks at **Inistioge**, from Ballygalon Weir to Red House Stream. Salmon, sea trout, brown trout and eels. Visitors are welcome, salmon dt £5, 1 Feb–30 Sept. Brown trout dt £5, 1 Mar–30 Sept; st £15, from Castle Inn, Inistioge (Tel: 056 58483). Tanguy de Toulgoet, Moyne Estate, Durrow, Co Laois, organises dry fly fishing trips at Kilkenny, Durrow, Rathdowney, Kells and Callan, with instruction, and his own flies. Dry fly catch and release, permits through local clubs. Tel/Fax: 0502 36578.

Kilkenny (Co Kilkenny). Kilkenny AA has some excellent salmon and trout fishing on

Nore, left bank from **Dinin R** to **Greenville** weir, and from **Maddockstown** to 1m u/s of **Bennetsbridge**; also **Dinin R**, Dinin Bridge to Nore. Assn issues permits to visitors, from P Campion, Tackle Shop, Kilkenny. Durrow & Dist AC fishes from **Watercastle Bridge** to **Owveg** confluence, and **Erkina R** from **Durrow Castle** to R Nore; all with 3m of Durrow. Dt £5 from Susan Lawlor, Foodmarket, The Square, Durrow (Tel: 0502 36437). Durrow AC Sec (Tel: 0502 36437). Rathdowney AC fishes approx 4m of **Erkina R** from local meat factory to **Boston Bridge**, early season best for open fishing, May–Sept for fly. Brown trout from 8oz to 2lb, dt £2 from M White, Moorville, Rathdowney. **Kings River**; good brown trout. Free fishing at Ballinakill Lake: good tench, perch, rudd, pike. New coarse fishery at Grandtown Lake: Mat Doyle, Grandtown, Ballacolla, Portlaoise. Tackle shops: M McGrath, 3 Lower Patrick Street, Kilkenny; Kilkenny Sports Scene, 1 Irishtown, Kilkenny. Hotels: Castel Arms, The Durrow Inn, both Durrow. B & B, James Joyce, The Square, Durrow.

Abbeyleix (Co Laois). Trout and salmon. Abbeyleix & Dist AC fishes from **Shanahoe Bridge** to **Waterloo Bridge**, dt £8, conc, from Liam Dunne, Bridge-Well Hardware, Abbeyleix. Accommodation: Harding Guest House.

Mountrath (Co Laois). Nore; brown trout, pike, perch, roach, eels. Mountrath & Dist AC stocks and fishes Nore main channel from Nore/**Delour** confluence to New Bridge at **Donore**, and **Whitehorse River**, which runs through town. Good salmon fishing for 2m between Mountrath and Castletown. Tourist permit £4, 21 days; £3 wt; £1 dt from Hon Sec Tom Watkins (Tel: 0502 32540). Tackle and salmon permits from Mrs Kelly, Main St. Accommodation: Mrs Geraldine Guilfoyle, Redcastle (Tel: 0502 32277); Mrs Fiona Wallis, Coote Terrace (Tel: 0502 32756).

KINGS RIVER (Co Kilkenny). Tributary which joins Nore above Thomastown. Water quality bad at present, stocks low.

BLACKWATER
(For close seasons, licences, etc, see The Southern Regional Fisheries Board)

Perhaps most famous salmon river in the Republic, and the most prolific for 1998 season, with a remarkable total of 8,063 fish caught, sur-

passed in North Atlantic area only by Kola Peninsula, Russia. Rises west of Killarney Mountains and flows eastward about 70m until it reaches town of Cappoquin, where it becomes tidal and turns sharply south, entering sea by estuary 15m long at Youghal Bay. 20m tidal, from Lismore to Youghal. Salmon (best stretches mainly between Mallow and Lismore), sea trout, brown trout, but large quantities of dace, roach, perch and pike in some parts. Best fishing strictly preserved. Big runs of spring salmon from Feb to April; grilse June to Sept; and often good run of autumn salmon during Aug and Sept. Sea trout in Blackwater and Bride, June onwards.

Youghal (Co Cork). Youghal Sea AC has fishing on main river and tributaries. All arrangements through secretary. At **Castlemartyr** on Cork/Youghal road is **Lough Aderry**, rainbow trout fishery, 6 fish limit, fly, worm and spinning.

Cappoquin (Co Waterford). The freshwater here is backed up by the tide and fishing is best when the water is either rising or falling. Salmon and trout, good coarse fishing for roach and dace throughout year but best autumn and spring. Cappoquin Salmon & Trout AC have 4 miles of water on both sides of town. Day tickets £12–£15, wt £60–£70, depending on season, from tackle shop. Good stocked tench fishing at **Dromana Lake**, south of Cappoquin. Trout fishing on **Rivers Owenshed** and **Finisk** and on R Blackwater downstream of **Lismore Bridge**. Lismore Trout ACA fishes 1½m south bank from Lismore town d/s, and 1m north bank; also Abhan-na-Shad, Blackwater tributary, good in spate from July; fly only, browns and sea trout. Dt £5, wt £10, from John O'Gormans Newsagent, or Maddens Pub, both Lismore. Tackle shop: Tight Lines Tackle & Gift Shop, Main St, Cappoquin. Hotels: Richmond House (Tel: 058 54258); Ballyrafter House, Lismore, Tel: 058 54002. Anglers' accommodation: "The Toby Jug"; Flynn's River View Guesthouse, Tel: 058 54073; Mrs Power, Pine Tree House, Ballyanchor, Lismore (Tel: 058 53282).

Upper Ballyduff (Co Waterford). Ballyduff Trout FAA has approx 3m east of bridge and 3m west, both banks. Restricted to local club members only. Blackwater Lodge Hotel, Upper Ballyduff (Tel: 058 60235, Fax: 60162) (see advt) controls 15m private salmon fishing, day tickets for both residents and non-residents; self-catering accommodation, complete service for angler incl tackle, smokery and ghillies, and website with up-to-date river report. Tackle shop: Bolger's, Ballyduff.

Conna (Co Cork). Beats owned by Mrs Green, Ballyvolane House (see below), and Mrs McCarthy, Elgin Cottage, Ballyduff, Co Waterford (Tel: 058 60255).

Fermoy (Co Cork). Salmon, brown trout, dace, roach, perch, gudgeon and pike. Four coarse fishing beats are open by courtesy of Fermoy Salmon AA, best being Barnane Walk, Jones Field and Hospital bank. Permits from Toomey's, see below. Salmon fishing on R Blackwater at **Careysville Fishery**, 1¾m stretch, both banks with well defined pools. One of the most prolific salmon fisheries in the country. Grilse run in June. Fishing peaks on the lower beats in June and on the rest of river in July. Max 2 to 4 rods per day depending on month. Ghillie price included in fishing charges. Permits from Careysville House (Tel: 025 31094) or Lismore Estates Office (Tel: 058 54424). Salmon fishing arranged at Blackwater Fly Fishing, Doug and Joy Lock, Ghillie Cottage, Kilbarry Stud, Fermoy (Tel: 025 32720). Stretches near town which hold roach and dace; waters accessible and banks well kept. For information on coarse fishing contact John Mulvihill (Competition Secretary and Live Bait) 3 Casement Row, Fermoy, Tel: 025 32425, or Brian Toomey, Sports Shop & Fishing Tackle, 18 McCurtain St, Fermoy, Tel: 025 31101. U/s of Fermoy are 8 private salmon beats owned by Merrie Green, Ballyvolane House, Castlelyons (Tel: 025 36 349, Fax: 781), at Ballyduff, Fermoy, Killavullen and Ballyhooly Castle Fishery. Fishing Feb–Apr, May–Sept, spring run Apr/May. Accommodation, tackle, and ghillies. Chest waders recommended. Local facilities for smoking or freezing salmon. **Araglin** holds brown trout; good dry fly. **Funshion** (**Funcheon**) runs in near Careysville on north bank; trout, dace, rudd. Contact Peter Collins, Tel: 022 25205. Hotel: Grand. B & B information from Slatterly Travel, 10 Pearse Sq, Fermoy, Tel: 025 31811.

Mallow (Co Cork). Salmon fishing from 1 Feb to end of Sept; trout 15 Feb to end of Sept. Coarse fishing for dace, roach, pike. Mallow Trout Anglers have 4m both banks, salmon, trout, dace and roach. Dt for this and for other private beats from tackle shop; coarse fishing free. Information from the Bridge House Bar.

Tackle shop: Pat Hayes, the Spa, Mallow. Hotels; Hibernian; Central.

BRIDE: This tributary of the Blackwater holds salmon and sea trout as well as brown trout, also dace.

Tallow (Co Waterford). River is 500 yds from town. Tallow & Dist AC have 4½m fishing from Mogeely Bridge to Bride Valley Fruit Farm. Brown trout, sea trout; salmon and peal from June onwards. Fly only between Mogeely and Tallow Bridges, otherwise, maggot, worm, etc. There is also coarse fishing for big dace and roach. Visiting anglers welcome. St (£10) and dt (£5) from Treasurer, Paul Hampton (Tel: 058 56358), or tackle shops: John Forde; Dan Delaney, both Main St. Ghillie service: Lonnie Corcoran, Ballyduff. Hotels: Bride View Bar; Devonshire Arms.

AWBEG: Tributary which runs into the Blackwater midway between Mallow and Fermoy. A very good trout stream, especially for dry fly.

BOYNE
(For close seasons, licences, etc, see The Eastern Regional Fisheries Board)

Rises near Edenderry and flows for about 70m, entering the sea near Drogheda north of Dublin. One of Ireland's premier game fisheries, in main channel and tributaries. Good salmon fishing between Navan and Drogheda. Excellent run of sea trout as far up river as Slane Bridge. Superb stocks of brown trout in Boyne and tributaries. Virtually no free fishing, but permits are sold on many club waters. Contact Joint Council of Boyne Anglers, Mrs T Healy, Little Grange, Drogheda, Tel: 041 24829. Fishable tributaries include **Rivers Trimblestown** (small browns), **Kells Blackwater** (trout, u/s of Headford Bridge), **Borora** (7m good trout fishing from Corlat d/s to Carlanstown), **Martry** (small stream, trout to 1lb), **Stoneyford** (excellent trout water, Rathkenna Bridge to Shanco Bridge), **Deel** (a few salmon at Riverdale, trout), **Little Boyne** (spring trout fishery, club based at Edenberry), **Nanny** (sea trout up to Julianstown, browns to Balrath Bridge).

Drogheda (Co Louth). Drogheda and District AC has prime salmon and sea trout fishing below Oldbridge and u/s at Donore, and **Nanny**; and also **Reservoirs Killineer** and **Barnattin** which are stocked with brown and rainbow, and Rosehall, a mixed coarse fishery. Permits £10–£6, conc, from Mr Ace, Tackle Shop, 8 Laurence St. Lower parts of Boyne and Mattock preserved. Brown trout in two reservoirs; St from Drogheda Corporation. Hotels: Central, White Horse, Boyne Valley, Rosnaree, Cooper Hill House (Julianstown).

Navan (Co Meath). Salmon and sea trout. Navan and Dist AA has approx 8½m of fishing on R Boyne and on R Blackwater. Details from Secretary (Tel: 046 22103, or mobile: 086 8197228). Membership from M Fox, 12 Flower Hill, Navan. Dt from Boyne Fisheries Manager, 1 Bedford Place, Navan. Hotels: New Grange, Ardboyne, both near river. Many B & B.

Slane (Co Meath). Slane, Rossin & Dist AC have salmon and sea trout fishing at Oldbridge, also excellent salmon and brown trout below Slane. Dt £10, juv £5, from Sec, Ray Foster, Tel: 01 8315406, or Mr Ace, Tackle Shop, see *Drogheda*. Hotel: Conyngham Arms.

Trim (Co Meath). Good trout in main river and tributaries. Trim, Athboy and Dist AA preserves and restocks **Athboy River** and some stretches on Boyne itself; st £16; dt £5. Concessions to jun and OAP, from sec. Deel and Boyne AA has trout and salmon water on tributary **Deel**. Longwood Anglers also have salmon and trout fishing on Boyne. Hotel: Wellington Court; Brogans Guest Accommodation.

Kells (Co Meath). Good trout fishing on **River Blackwater**, a tributary of R Boyne, dry fly. Mayfly fishing good. 15m preserved and restocked by Kells AA; permits from Tom Murray, *below*. Trout up to 7lb may be had in the river, also large pike and salmon, 1½m of free fishing from source. Hotel: Headford Arms. Tackle shop: Tom Murray, Flying Sportsman, Carrick St (Tel: 046 40205).

Virginia (Co Cavan). On headwaters of R Blackwater. Lough Ramor gives good trout fishing and excellent fishing for bream, roach, perch and pike; boats for hire, two tributaries. Ten lakes and four rivers within 5m; trout and coarse fish. Virginia Coarse AC has fishing on **Lough Ramor**, with large bream, pike above 25lb, 200lb catches of coarse fish per day recorded. Membership £10 per annum, conc. Other fisheries: **Lisgrea Lake** (all species); and **Rampart River** (roach, perch and bream). **Mullagh Lake** is a popular pike fish-

ery. For further information contact Pat McCabe, Rahardrum (Tel: 049 47649); Nattie Dogherty, Salmon Lodge, Main St; and Edward Tobin, Mullagh Rd. Accommodation: Mrs McHugho, White House, Tel: 049 47515; P & M Geraghty, Knocknagarton, Tel: 049 47638, both Virginia. To north east, **Bailieboro** is an ideal centre for good coarse fishing, with innumerable lakes within easy reach containing bream, roach, rudd, perch, dace, plentiful pike to 30lb; all free, incl **Castle**, (with stands for disabled), **Parker's**, **Gallincurra**, **Galboly**, **Drumkeery**, **Skeagh**, **Town**, **Gallin**, all with pike, perch, roach, bream, tench, rudd, and others, and under-fished. Bailieboro AC local club, membership £10 per season; Sec (Tel: 042 65382, daytime). Bailieboro tackle shop: Raymond Lloyd, Main St (Tel: 042 65032). Bailieboro hotels include Bailie and Brennans, Main St; Hilltop Lodge, Curcish Lane.

BUNDROWES RIVER AND LOUGH MELVIN
(For close seasons, licences, etc, see The Northern Regional Fisheries Board)

About 4m south of Erne, the Bundrowes River carries water of Lough Melvin to sea in Donegal Bay. The entire 6 mile river is open to anglers except for private stretch from Lareen Bay to the Four Masters Bridge. For accommodation and information, contact T Gallagher (*see below under Kinlough entry*). The lough is 8m by 2m, approx 5,000 acres; part of it is free and part under private ownership. It is renowned for its three different species of trout, these being sonnaghan, gilaroo and ferox. Good run of big spring salmon in Feb and March; smaller fish arrive in April and May; grilse in late May and run right through to June. Best time for fly fishing for salmon late April to end June. Trolling baits, where permitted, takes place from early Feb.

Bundoran (Co Donegal). Salmon, trout. Bundrowes R, 1½m, and west end L Melvin, 3m. Salmon season 1 Jan–30 Sept (Bundrowes); 1 Feb–30 Sept (Melvin). **Bunduff River**, 3½m from Bundoran, flows 8m to enter Donegal Bay near Castlegal; salmon, brown trout. Best salmon, June to Aug. Brown trout in upper reaches. Bunduff Angling Syndicate has water; dt £12 from Mrs Kathleen McGloin, The Shop, Bunduff Bridge, Co Leitrim. Also Kinlough Anglers, c/o John Fahy, Kinlough. Tackle shops: Mrs McGloin (*above*); Pat Barrett, Main St; Rogans, Bridgend, Ballyshannon, Co Donegal

(Tel: 072 51335). Hotels: Allingham, Foxes Lair. Gillaroo Lodge, West End, Bundoran, has permits and licences, boats and ghillie service, and all other angling facilities.

Kinlough (Co Leitrim). Salmon, grilse, trout. Season for spring salmon, Jan to Apr; grilse, sea trout, May to Sept. Boats and tickets for **Bundrowes** fishing at Drowes and Lareen Fisheries from Thomas Gallagher, Lareen Angling Centre, Kinlough (Tel: 072 41055); Thomas Kelly (Tel: 072 41497). Tackle shop: The Fishery Office, Lareen Park.

Rossinver (Co Leitrim). Salmon, grilse, son-aghan and gillaroo trout. Rossinver Bay strictly fly only, rule extended to Eden and Dooard, from 15 May. All legal methods elsewhere. Ghillies in vicinity. Salmon and trout dt £10 until 15 Jul, £5 thereafter; boat, engine and 2 rods £30, from Peter Bradley, Rossinver Fishery, Eden Quay (Tel: 072 54201). Part of Lough Melvin is in Northern Ireland and is served by village of Garrison (Co Fermanagh). Tickets and boats for Garrison AC fishing from Sean Maguire, tackle shop, Garrison.

CLARE

Flows into **Lough Corrib**, near Galway, and is one of best spawning streams for salmon entering the Galway or Corrib River. Best season: spring salmon, April and May; grilse, June and July; brown trout, April to September. Holds large trout, similar to Corrib fish, and suitable for dry fly. Fishing in main river and tributaries is controlled by riparian owners and angling clubs. WRFB Angling Officer (Tel: 091 563118) has detailed information.

Galway (Co Galway). For lower reaches. Sea and lake fishing. Several clubs have fishing rights, and issue permits. Contact WRFB. At **Carraroe**, 26m west of Galway, Carraroe Ac controls a number of brown and sea trout loughs, incl Lough Atoureen, Lough an Gleanna, Lough an Bric Mor, and Lough Cora Doite. Sea trout mainly from July onwards. Boats on request.

Tuam (Co Galway). For upper waters. Tuam and Dist AA controls Clare River from Gardenfield, several miles u/s of Tuam, to Clonmore Bridge, also left bank d/s at Turloughmartin, for 930 yds past Grange junction. **Castlegrove Lake**; pike, perch, bream, rudd.

Tributaries of the Clare

ABBERT: Enters from east, 7m south of Tuam. Good trout fishing, with excellent fly hatches. Brown trout of 3lb regularly taken, and salmon in flood conditions. The best angling is at Ballyglunin junction with Clare.

GRANGE: Joins Clare from east, 4m south of Tuam. Brown trout and salmon in lower reaches. U/s of Castlemoyle for a distance of 3m is a very good area for large brown trout. Salmon when in spate.

SINKING: Enters from east, 8m north of Tuam. Salmon may be taken in lower reaches, following flood conditions anytime after the end of May, but primarily a brown trout fishery, the best areas being from Dunmore as far as Cloonmore. Good fly hatches. **DALGAN**: Runs into Sinking. Stocks of brown trout, salmon may be caught from the end of May, depending on water conditions.

CLARE
(streams and loughs)

A number of salmon and sea trout rivers and streams run from Co Clare to the Shannon estuary or to the west coast. Most of them offer free fishing, with landowners' permission. Trout and coarse fishing lakes abound in the East Clare "lakeland" and in the south west. The rivers are listed here in their geographical order, westwards from Limerick.

BUNRATTY. Enters Shannon at Bunratty Castle, and holds a small stock of ½lb brown trout; modest grilse and sea trout run, best in June/July, from tide to D'Esterres Bridge, 3m. Free fishing. At source, **Doon Lough** nr **Broadford**, is a fine coarse fishery with large bream and other species; boats on hire locally. Several other coarse fishing loughs in region: **Rosroe** and **Fin**, nr Kilmurry: pike over 20lb, from boat; **Cullaun**, 400 acres, 2m from **Kilkishen**, specimen pike and large bream, best from boat; just south, **Stones Lough**: big tench. As well as these, there are other less accessible lakes for the angler to explore. Further north east is another notable group of coarse fishing loughs: **Kilgory**, nr **O'Callaghan's Mills**, with large bream; 4m West of Tulla are **Bridget Lough** and others, with pike, perch, rudd, bream, tench, roach, hybrids; by **Scarriff**, **O'Grady** (**Canny's Lough**), shallow water, difficult access, but good bream fishing, with pike, tench and big rudd; and **Keel Lough,** inaccessible and unfished, with large tench, bream and rudd. On the **Scarriff River**, shoals of good bream and pike, easily accessible. On **R Graney** is **Lough Graney, Caher**, at 1,000 acres the biggest lake in the county with abundant perch, bream, pike, rudd and eel, boat essential, on hire at Caher and Flagmount. **Tulla** is central to much lake fishing: north are **Loughs Clondanagh** and **Clondoorney**, easily accessible with rudd, with pike and perch. At **Kilkishen** are **Loughs Cullaunyheeda, Avoher, Doon, Rathluby, Clonlea**, and others, with similar species. Accommodation at **Broadford**: Lake View House, Doon Lake, Broadford, Co Clare (Tel: 061 473125); on shore of lake, anglers catered for, boats for hire, much excellent coarse fishing in easy reach.

RINE (QUIN RIVER). Runs from the lakes of East Clare to the estuary of the **Fergus**. Fishing similar to Bunratty; about 5m fishing from Latoon Bridge u/s to Quin. Permission to fish **Dromoland Castle** water from Rec. Manager, Tel: 061 71144. Castle also has 20 acre lough in grounds, stocked trout fishery. Rest of fishing free. A few miles SE of Rine are **Loughs Caherkine, Fin, Ballycar, Rosroe, Teereen, Castle** (at **Kilmurry**) and others, with pike, perch, bream and rudd.

FERGUS. This medium-sized, limestone river with several loughs along its course, rises in Burren region of North Clare and flows southward to join Shannon at Newmarket-on-Fergus. Holds good stocks of brown trout, av ¾lb, with fish to 3½lb. Good dry fly water, both banks fish well for trout, best in Feb–May and Sept. Pike fishing also good. Approx 200 spring salmon and grilse each year, salmon Feb–March, grilse June–Sept, from Ennis u/s. Much free fishing in **Corofin** locality. **Loughs Dromore** and **Ballyline**. 6m east of Ballyline; limestone waters with trout to 5lb. Best March–May and Sept. Free fishing, boat hire, contact M Cleary, Lakefield Lodge, Corofin, Tel: 065 37675. **Ballyteige Lough**: 50 acre limestone fishery, trout to 7lb. Best in March/Apr, at dusk in June/July. Boat necessary; contact M Cleary. **Inchiquin Lough**, 280 acres: excellent stock of wild browns, av 1¼lb. Fishes well in early season, and Sept. Boats from Burkes Shop, Main St, Corofin (Tel: 065 6837677). **Lough Cullaun** (Monanagh Lake): limited stock of big trout; also a good pike fishery. Trolling popular method. **Muckanagh Lough (Tullymacken**

Lough): 60 acre shallow lake with good trout and pike. Boat necessary. Boats through M Cleary for both these loughs. **Lough Atedaun**, 1m from Corofin, has excellent fishing for large pike, tench and rudd. Best fished from boat. **Lough Ballycullinan**, 1½m from Corofin, has good stocks of large pike, perch, bream, tench and hybrids. Boat essential. Contact Burke's, Corofin, Tel: 065 37677. **Ballyeighter Lough**: a rich limestone water which holds pike, rudd and large tench. On this water in 1994, Mr Nick Parry of Tubber broke Irish record with 7lb 15¼oz tench, then broke his own record with one 8lb 2oz (June 1995).

CLOON. This small river enters north east corner of Clonderalaw Bay. It gets a sea trout run in June/July, and is fishable for 2m d/s of new bridge on secondary road. Free fishing. Nearby trout loughs are **Knockerra**, 50 acres, **Gortglass**, 80 acres, and **Cloonsneaghta**, 30 acres. Boat hire on Gortglass (M Cleary, Tel: 065 37674), free fishing on all.

DOONBEG. A better known salmon and sea trout river, rising in Lissycasy, flowing west to the sea at Doonbeg. Small spring salmon run, fair grilse and sea trout from June. Overgrown in places; best fishing on middle and upper reaches. Free with permission. For **Knockerra Lough**, see Kilrush, under Shannon.

CREEGH. Small spate river, running to west coast north of the Doonbeg, on which 150 to 200 grilse are taken each season. Small brown trout, and sea trout under the right conditions. Free fishing. Near Kilmihil is **Knockalough**, with good stock of small browns. Boat is helpful; dapping with daddy-long-legs in Aug/Sept. Free fishing.

ANNAGEERAGH. Runs into **Lough Donnell**. Sea trout fishing at dusk for about 1m u/s of lough in June/July. Sea trout fishing and a few grilse in rest of river. **Doo Lough**, 220 acres, a little north west of Glenmore, holds good stock of small browns.

KILDEEMEA. A small spate river which enters sea 2m south west of **Miltown Malbay**. Excellent sea trout, to 3lb. Best June/July, fishable over ½m stretch on south bank from Ballaclugga Bridge u/s. Fly and spinner, fly best at night. Free fishing.

CULLENAGH (INAGH). This river is a good coarse fishery for 8m from Inagh towards sea.

Open banks for pike and rudd fishing, easily accessible. Near village, **Inagh Loughs** contain good numbers of small brown trout. Free fishing. 2m west of Inagh, **Lough Caum**, 45 acres, pike fishery, boat fishing only. Contact M Fitzgerald, Fishing Tackle, Strand St, Castlegregory (Tel: 066 39133), or Landers Leisure Lines, Courthouse Lane, Tralee (Tel: 066 71178).

DEALAGH. Joins sea from north east at Liscannor. Spate river with sea trout and grilse in June/July. Sea trout best at night, between first and fourth bridges u/s from tidal water. Free, with permission. **Lickeen Lough**, 200 acres, 2m south of **Kilfenora**, contains small wild browns and stocked rainbows to 2lb. Boat for hire. Contact John Vaughan, sec of Lickeen Trout AA, Tel: 065 71069.

AILLE. Small spate river running from **Lisdoonvarna** to **Doolin**. Stock of 14in browns, moderate grilse and sea trout. Best between Roadford and Lisdoonvarna; access difficult, banks overgrown. Free fishing.

CORK SOUTH WEST
(rivers and loughs)

ARGIDEEN. Runs from west, above Clonakilty, and enters sea at **Timoleague**. A sea trout river, most of which is jointly managed by Argideen AA and SWRFB. Best methods are single worm by day, or fly at night. Tickets from Bob Allen (Tel: 023 39278), or SWRFB (Tel: 026 41222). Fishing with accommodation is obtainable from Tim Severin, Argideen River Lodges, Inchy Bridge, Timoleague, Tel: 023 46127 (Fax: 46233). To west of river, **Lough Atariff**, permission from P McCarthy, Dunmanway Salmon & Trout AC, Yew Tree Bar, Dunmanway; and **Curraghalicky Lake**, free fishing. Both with good stock of small wild brown trout. At **Midleton**, 16m east of Cork City, **Lough Aderra**, a popular stocked trout fishery of 30 acres, fairly shallow water, with large stocks of rudd and eels; 6 boats on water, fly, spinning and worm permitted. Contact SWRFB (Tel: 026 41222), or TH Sports, 37 Main St, Midleton, Cork (Tel: 021 631800).

ILEN. A medium-sized spate river about 21 miles long, scenically pretty, rising on watershed of Bantry district and flowing into sea through long estuary, from Skibbereen. Spring salmon from late March. Main salmon runs in Apr–Jun. Average size 10lb. Good grilse run from mid-June. Sea trout begin in February, August is the most prolific month, fish run from ½lb to over 4lb. Fly, spinning and worming are practised. Prawn and shrimp not permitted.

Skibbereen (Co Cork). R Ilen AC has about 8m fishing on river, with salmon, grilse and sea trout. Visitors welcome, access for disabled 1m from town. Dt £15, wt £60, from Fallons (below), and Houlihans Newsagent, North St. 3m east, stocked rainbow and wild brown trout fishing on **Shepperton Lakes**, 35 and 15 acres, with boats; st and dt from E Connolly, Shepperton, Skibbereen (Tel: 028 33328). West nr Schull is **Schull Reservoir**, 5 acres, small native browns and stocked rainbows. Both these are SWRFB fisheries. 2m north of **Leap**, **Ballin Lough**: wild stock supplemented with brown trout fingerlings and limited number of 2 year-olds, by Ballin Lough AC. Boats and tickets at lough, season 1 Apr–30 Sept. Information from Sec, Jim Maxwell, Tel: 028 33266, or HQ, Bee Hive Bar, Connonagh, Leap. 3m south west of Dunmanway is **Garranes Lake**, 25 acres, Stocked rainbows and wild browns. Jointly run by SWRFB and Dunmanway & Drinagh AA. Dt and boats from G Carolan, Filling Station, Garranes, Drimoleague. 3m south of Leap, **Lough Cluhir**, free fishing on small lough for tench, pike and roach. Tackle shop: Fallon's Sports Shop, 20 North Street, Skibbereen. Full range of accommodation, from T.I. Office, North St (Tel: 028 21766).

Bantry (Co Cork). Bantry Trout AC fishes **Lough Bofinne**, 3m east of Bantry, 25 acres, first-class rainbow and brown trout fishery, stocked weekly by Fisheries Board. Tickets (st £20, dt £3) from Sports Shop or from Mrs P Spillane, Supermarket, Chapel St (Tel: 027 51247). Tackle shops: Vickery's Store; McCarthy's Sports Shop, Main St, Bantry. Hotels; Vickerys, New St (Tel: 027 50006); Bantry Bay Hotel, The Square (Tel: 027 50062).

MEALAGH. 1m north of Bantry, salmon and sea trout. Free except for bottom pool below falls.

OUVANE and **COOMHOLA**. Small spate rivers which run into north east Bantry Bay. Salmon and sea trout, the latter declined in Ouvane, better in Coomhola R. Ouvane has four good pools in first mile, and three more below Carriganass Falls. Coomhola has a good supply of brown trout. Coomhola Anglers, O'Brien's Shop, Coomhola Bridge, Bantry, offer permits to fish some 20 pools.

GLENGARRIFF. This small river flows into Bantry Bay at north east end through one of Ireland's most beautiful national parks, and has good salmon fishing when in spate, sea trout and browns. Rights are held by Glengarriff AA, who offer dt £5 for river or loughs (see below), conc, from Bernard Harrington, Maple Leaf Bar, Glengarriff. Limited tackle from Shamrock Stores and Maureen's, Glengarriff. Hotels incl Eccles, Caseys.

BEARA PENINSULA. (Co Cork). **Adrigole River** runs into Bantry Bay on north side: 6m long spate river with grilse and sea trout, controlled by Kenmare AA. Contact J O'Hare, 21 Main St, Kenmare, Tel: 064 41499. Beara AA has tickets for local lough fishing. **Upper** and **Lower Loughs Avaul** contain wild brown trout, and are stocked with rainbows, fish to 17lb being caught. Tickets £5, conc, from Glengarriff AA, c/o M Harrington, Mace Supermarket, Castletownbere; or B Harrington, Maple Leaf Bar, Glengarriff. High in the Caha Mountains, south west of Glengarriff, free fishing on **Loughs Eekenohoo-likeaghaun** and **Derreenadovodia**, and **Barley Lake**, 100 acres: small wild brown trout. Other small loughs in area with similar stock: **Glenkeel, Moredoolig, Begboolig, Shanoge** (larger fish, many over 1lb). Best in April/May and Sept. South of **Ardgroom** is **Glenbeg Lough,** leased by Berehaven AA. Big stock of small browns; tickets from Harrington, see *above* Hotel: Ford Rí, Castletownbere (Tel: 027 70379) has local fishing information.

CORRIB SYSTEM
(For close seasons, licences, etc, see The Western Regional Fisheries Board)

River Corrib drains Lough Corrib and runs 5½m to Galway Bay passing virtually through the city of Galway. Salmon, trout. Salmon fishing very good. For particulars as to present conditions and rods apply Central Fishery Board, Nuns Island, Galway. Best fishing for springers early in season; grilse, May–June. Rods let by the day or by week.

Galway (Co Galway). Salmon fishing at Galway Fishery, situated in City of Galway, less than 1m from sea. Applications to The Manager, Galway Fishery, Nun's Island, Galway, Tel: 091 562388. Dt £30 to £16, depending on season. The flow of the river is controlled by a regulating weir and the short stretch downstream of the weir is the salmon angling water.

Kilcolgan River (10m E) part tidal, salmon and sea trout. WRFB controls 645 yards of north bank in town land of Stradbally East. Dt £3, from WRFB, Tel: 091 63118. Tackle shops: Freeney's, 19 High St.

LOUGH CORRIB

This, the largest lough in the Republic is 65 square miles of water, and dotted with islands, around which are shallows that make for good fishing. Specially noted for large brown trout, each season a number of specimen fish are taken, and the record stands at 26lb. The lough is so immense that anglers unfamiliar with it will do best using the services of a local ghillie. Trout fishing opens on Feb 15, and commences with the duck and olive season, but lough best known for dapping with mayfly (beginning sometimes as early as first week in May), and daddy-long-legs (mid-July to end of season). Some dry-fly fishing on summer evenings. Salmon taken mainly by trolling, and in June on wet fly in many of the bays. Also big pike and other coarse fish in Corrib, so that angling of some kind is possible all year. Fishing free, but salmon licence required. Many hotels issue licences. Boats and boatmen at Portacarron, Oughterard, Baurisheen, Derrymoyle, Glan Shore, Cong, Greenfields, Doorus, Carrick, Salthouse, and Inishmacatreer. A detailed list and angling map of Lough Corrib may be purchased from WRFB, Weir Lodge, Earl's Island, Galway City.

Oughterard (Co Galway). Best fishing is from April to early June. **Owenriff River** flows through Oughterard; good in high water late summer. Local club is Oughterard Anglers and Boatmens Assn; actively involved in stream and river development, information from Tucks (*below*). There is additional good fishing for bream and roach on **Moycullen Lakes**, Moycullen, on Galway/Oughterard Rd. Currarevagh House Hotel (Tel: 09182 313) provides boats, ghillies, outboard motors with fuel and tackle if necessary for a charge of £40 per day, also has boat on top lake of **Screebe** sea trout fishery. Hotels: Oughterard House (free fishing on Corrib; private water within 12m; salmon and sea trout); Lake Hotel (Tel: 91 552275). Also new motel: Connemara Gateway (reservations: Tel: 01 567 3444) and Ross Lake Hotel, Rosscahill (boats and boatmen). Tackle shops: Tucks, Main Street; M Keogh. Galway tackle shop: Freeney's, 19 High St.

Clonbur (Co Galway). Good centre for **Loughs Corrib** and **Mask**. Clonbur AC fishes these waters, **Loughs Coolin**, **Nafooey** (pike over 36lb) and others, and is affiliated with Corrib Federation. Tackle shop: Ann Kynes, Clonbur (Tel: 092 46197); O'Connors, Cong. Accommodation: Fair Hill Guest House, Clonbur (Tel: 092 46197) caters for anglers, and arranges fishing trips with local boatmen; Noreen Kyne (Tel: 092 46169); Ann Lambe, Ballykine House (Tel: 092 46150). Self-catering with boats, J O'Donnell, Tel: 092 46157.

Headford (Co Galway). Convenient for the east side of Lough Corrib. **Black River** (limestone stream) provides excellent if somewhat difficult dry fly water. Affected by drainage work. Best near village of **Shrule**. A £3 dt is sold by WRFB, Weir Lodge, Galway, Tel: 0915 63118. Tackle shop: Kevin Duffy. Accommodation at Angler's Rest Hotel and guest houses.

Greenfields, nr Headford (Co Galway). Trout, salmon and coarse fish. Situated on shore of **L Corrib**. Boatmen in vicinity. Rooms-en-suite, tackle, boats, apply to Ower House Guesthouse, Greenfields, Headford, Co Galway (Tel: 093 35446, Fax: 35382). Local boatman: Michael Walshe, The Parks, Ower P O, Co Galway (Tel: 093 35380).

Cong (Co Mayo). On shores of L Corrib, good centre for **Lough Mask** also; Cong Canal, coarse fishing; and R Mear, with salmon and trout, pike and perch. Boats from Michael Ryan, River Lodge (Tel: 092 46057); boats and accommodation from Mike and Rose Holian, Bayview Angling Centre, Derry Quay, Cross P O, nr Cong (Tel: 092 46385), open during winter for pike fishing. Tackle shops: O'Connors, Cong; T Cheevers, Northgate Street, Athenry.

Tributaries of Lough Corrib.

BLACK RIVER: Fifteen miles in length, it enters lough just north of Greenfields. Access is easy from Shrule, Co Mayo. A rich limestone river with a good stock of brown trout. Best in early season, before weed accumulates.

CREGG RIVER: Rises half mile upstream of old Cregg Millhouse, and flows four miles to Lower Lough Corrib. Upper stretch is nursery for stocking into Corrib, and fishing is not encouraged. Salmon and brown trout angling is permitted on lower stretches.

CLARE RIVER: for this river entering L Corrib at the easternmost end, and its own tributary system, see Clare.

LOUGH MASK

Limestone lake of 22,000 acres connected by underground channel with Lough Corrib, holding large ferox trout, pike, eels, perch and a few char. Angling is free. Trout to 15lb are taken by trolling and on dap (5–6lb not uncommon). Mayfly best from mid-May to mid-June; daddy-long-legs and grasshopper, late June to Sept; wet fly, Mar-April and July-Sept. Dry fly fishing can be successful May–Sept. **Ballinrobe**, **Cong**, **Clonbur** and **Tourmakeady** are good centres. At Cong is Cong AA; (st £5), at Ballinrobe is Ballinrobe and Dist AA (st £5), open to visitor-membership. Tackle shops: Fred O'Connor, Cong; Dermot O'Connor, Main Street, Ballinrobe. Boats for hire at Cushlough Pier, Bay of Islands Park, Rosshill Park, Caher-Tourmakeady Pier. Good anglers' accommodation at Ard Aoidhinn Angling Centre, Cappaduff, Tourmakeady (Tel: 92 44009) (HQ of Tourmakeady AA), tickets for salmon fisheries, good boat access for disabled; Mask Lodge and Mask Villa on lake shore, both run by David and Helen Hall, Lakeshore Holiday Homes, Caher, Ballinrobe (Tel: 092 41389): boats, engines and ghillies provided; Red Door Restaurant, Ballinrobe (Tel: 092 41263). River fishing on **Finney** and canal joining Mask and Corrib. At Tourmakeady are some good spate rivers, and mountain lake fishing can be had in **Dirk Lakes**; brown trout.

LOUGH CARRA. Connected to Lough Mask, 4,003 acres, limestone, relatively shallow with brown trout which are considered to be freer rising than those in Lough Mask, and on average heavier. All are derived entirely from natural population of wild fish. Shore fishing, difficult, boat essential. Boats and anglers' accommodation from Roberts Angling Service and Guest House, Lough Bawn, Kilkeeran, Partry (Tel: 092 43046); Mrs J Flannery, Keel Bridge, Partry, Tel: 092 41706; Mr R O'Grady, Chapel St, Ballinrobe, Tel: 092 41142. Local clubs: Ballinrobe and Dist Anglers, c/o Ballinrobe P O; Partry Anglers, c/o Post Office, Partry. East of L Carra, **Claremorris** and **Irishtown** are notable centres for little-known coarse lakes, containing large numbers of perch, pike, bream and roach.

Lough Nafooey. Connected to Lough Mask, and contains trout, pike and perch.

Tributaries of Lough Mask

ROBE RIVER, has brown trout fishing, free, best u/s of Robeen Bridge as far as Clooncormack, from Hollymount u/s to Hollybrook, and from Crossboyne through Castlemagarrett Estate as far as the Claremorris/Tuam road. Also d/s from Ballinrobe.

KEEL RIVER. Enters west of Ballinrobe, holds a fair stock of brown trout, and is an ideal dry fly water.

NORTH DONEGAL
(streams)
(For close seasons, licences, etc, see The Northern Regional Fisheries Board)

Donegal is mostly salmon and sea trout country. Its waters are generally acid; rocky or stony streams and small lakes in which the brown trout run small – though there are one or two fisheries where they may be taken up to 2lb and more.

LENNON. Rises in Glendowan Mountains and flows through **Garton Lough** and **Lough Fern** before entering **Lough Swilly** at Ramelton. Historically is one of the best salmon rivers in Donegal. It is best known as a spring river and its most famous pool, The Ramelton Pool, is privately owned. The rest of the river is a "free fishery" and only a state licence is required. Season I Jan–30 Sept. June to Sept for grilse. Trout fishing equally good on upper and lower reaches; best April to July. Loughs Garton and Fern have stocks of small brown trout, and fishing is free.

Ramelton (Co Donegal). Salmon fishing on lower portion of river at Ramelton owned and fished privately by Ramelton Fishery Ltd. **Lough Fern** is best fished from a boat and produces mostly grilse. Other brown trout loughs in vicinity, Akibbon, Sessigagh, Glen and Keel. Information on these and all other local waters from Anglers Haven Hotel, Kilmacrennan, Co Donegal (Tel: 074 39015).

SWILLY. Flows into Lough Swilly. Much free salmon and trout fishing of good quality in region. Recently, the river has undergone major development with work being carried out by the Northern Regional Fisheries Board and the Letterkenny and District AA.

Letterkenny (Co Donegal). Letterkenny AA has salmon, sea trout and brown trout fishing on Rivers **Swilly, Lennon, Owencarrow**, and more than 25 lakes; trout av ½lb. Salmon run into Lakes **Glen, Gartan** and **Lough Fern**. Boats on Glen Lake: J Doherty, Tel: 38057; on Lough Keel: W Gallagher, Tel: 39233. Membership and permits from A McGrath, Port Rd. Hotel: Mount Errigal.

Churchill (Co Donegal). **Lough Beagh** situated in the heart of the **Glenveagh National Park**; 4m long by ½m wide; salmon, sea trout and brown trout. Best known for quality of sea trout fishing in August and Sept. Boat fishing only; 2 boats for hire. Anglers are requested to respect the bird life on this lake, as there are some rare and interesting species residing. Season 15 July–30 Sept. Dt £20, from The Superintendent, Glenveagh National Park, Churchill, Letterkenny (Tel: 074 37090/37262).

CRANA. Enters **Lough Swilly** at Buncrana. Primarily a spate river which gets a good run of grilse and sea trout. Access to fishing is excellent.

Buncrana (Co Donegal). Salmon and sea trout. Buncrana AA issues permits. For first week £25 and for each subsequent week £10. Licences from Bertie O'Neill's Fishing Tackle Shop, Bridgend, Tel: 077 68157. Other waters: **Mill River**; brown trout to ½lb numerous; free. **Inch Lake** (6m): good sea trout; free. **Dunree River** (6m) free; brown trout, occasional salmon and sea trout. **Clonmany River** (5m); salmon sea trout and brown trout fishing; fair sport in good water; best June onwards. Hotel: Lake of Shadows.

CULDAFF. A small spate river on the Malin Peninsula, with brown trout, sea trout from mid-June onwards, and salmon in August and September. Nearest towns, Malin and Carndonagh. Season, I April–20 Oct. Fly spinning and worm, no float fishing. Permits from Faulkners, Main St, Culdaff.

DEELE. East Donegal rather than North, a tributary of the Foyle which enters downstream of Strabane. Fished by Deele AC from 3m u/s of Convoy to 4m d/s, for brown trout, sea trout, and grilse from July on. Season I Apr–20 Oct, fly, spinning, worm, no floats. Dt £5, st £30 from Billy Vance, Milltown, Convoy, Co Donegal (Tel: 074 47290); Tony Gibson, Ballyboe, Convoy (Tel: 074 47462); Liam Hoey, Convoy (Tel: 074 47613).

WEST AND CENTRAL DONEGAL (streams)
(For close seasons, licences, etc. see The Northern Regional Fisheries Board)

EANY and **ESKE**. Eany fishery consists of Rivers Eany, Eany More, and Eany Beg, giving about 10 miles of fishing. Eany itself is a spate river which flows for 10m SW from Blue Stack Mountains and enters sea in Inver Bay close to Inver village. Good run of salmon and sea trout and has resident population of small brown trout. **Eske River** drains **Lough Eske** (900 acres) then runs SW for about 5m to join sea at Donegal Bay. The system gets a good run of salmon and a fair run of sea trout; and has a resident stock of brown trout and char. Salmon 1 March–30 Sept. Trout 1 March–30 Sept. Most fishing is on the lake from boats and the river has a number of good pools. In recent years the system has been getting a declining run of fish but this may be temporary.

Donegal (Co Donegal). Donegal Town & Dist AC controls fishing on Eany. Eske Anglers control fishing on Eske River and Lough Eske. Dt £10 from C Doherty, Tackle Shop, Main St (Tel: 073 21119).

Frosses (Co Donegal). Fishing controlled by NRFB. Fishery has been upgraded with improved access. Excellent run of salmon and sea trout, best fishing June to Sept. Permits £10, and licences from Eany Angling Centre, Gragrim, Frosses (Tel: 073 36559).

GLEN. Flows S for 8m from Slievetooe to enter sea at Teelin Bay beside the town of Carrick. A spate river but has a number of good holding pools. Salmon, sea trout, brown trout. Fishes best in summer after a flood. Slieve League AA has fishing, Donal Ward, Ardcrin, Carrick (Tel: 073 39004). Also Sliabh Liág AA.

Carrick (Co Donegal). Salmon and trout. Private fishing. Tackle shop: Hugh Cunningham.

LACKARGH (Co Donegal). At Creeslough in extreme north of county, river system has spring salmon run mid-March to mid-May. Creeslough & Dist Anglers. Contact NRFB.

FINN. Governed by Foyle Fisheries Commission. Flows from Lough Finn nr **Fintown** in an easterly direction until it joins Mourne above **Strabane** and **Lifford**, to form River Foyle. Spring salmon best in March–May,

between Lifford Bridge and Salmon Leap at Cloghan, depending on flow. Grilse, main run in May–July, best in middle section between **Liscooley** and **Letterbrick**, and at **Commeen** on **R Reelan**; sea trout, good runs in May–July, best in middle and upper sections. Brown trout and coarse, lower reaches. Foyle Fisheries Commission water, near **Clady**, is best for spring salmon. Finn AC and Glebe AC fish sections from Liscooley Bridge to near Edenmore. Ballybofey and Stranorlar AA fish water from Edenmore to Dooish townland, limited rods. Tickets £10 from Ken Rule, Killygordon, and Ballybofey T I. Cloghan Lodge Fisheries, **Cloghan** (Tel: 074 33003), has over 30m both banks of R Finn, from Dooish to Lough Finn, plus tributaries **Reelan**, **Cummirk, Elatagh**. Excellent fly fishing, spinning and worm also permitted, with spring salmon and grilse, autumn salmon, average take per year increasing (a record of 3,300 in 1998). Good sea trout run in May–July. Limited tickets, st from £250, dt from £10; ghillie service, B & B, by advance booking. Lower part of this fishing is held jointly with Glenmore Estate. 20 loughs are also fishable, incl Finn, Nambraddan, Shivnagh, Muck. Glenmore Estate, T McCreery, Altnapaste, **Ballybofey** (Tel: 074 32075) has good fly fishing with day tickets, on 10m of Rivers Reelan, Letterkillew and Finn, and one bank of Cummirk River; spate system, with more than 40 named pools; salmon with good grilse run, and sea trout. Killygordon Fishery, "The Curragh", Killygordon (Tel: 074 42931) has dt for salmon, sea trout and brown trout fishing on R Finn, nr Ballybofey. At **Lifford**, Mrs Nell Bradley, Swallows Rest Guest House (Tel: 074 49400) owns rights on 1m single bank of R Finn, fly fishing; good service offered to visiting anglers.

OWENEA AND OWENTOCKER. Short rivers running into head of Loughrosmore Bay near Ardara. Owenea is primarily a spate river, taking 1 or 2 days to run after a good flood, with a run of spring fish, grilse, sea trout, and a resident stock of small brown trout. It has 9 beats on 8m of river, with good pools spread throughout river, much good fly water, and when in condition is one of the best in the country for salmon. Season 1 Mar–30 Sept.

Ardara and **Glenties** (Co Donegal). Fishing controlled by Northern Regional Fishery Board, Glenties, Co Donegal (Tel: 075 51141). Fishery has been upgraded and there are additional facilities for anglers, incl access for disabled along one section. Excellent run of salmon and sea trout from March to Sept. Dt £10; wt £100. Permits, licences and bookings from Owenea Angling Centre, Glenties. Salmon and sea trout fishing on River Brackey. Many mountain lakes free to fish. Hotels: Nesbitt Arms, Ardara; Highlands Hotel, Glenties.

GWEEBARRA. Drains **Lough Barra** and flows south-west about 7m to Doochary Bridge, where it becomes tidal and flows hence through long estuary between high hills a further 6m to the Atlantic.

Doochary (Co Donegal). Bridge here marks end of tidal water; several trout lakes in vicinity. Salmon, sea trout. Best season: Spring salmon, Feb–May; grilse and sea trout, end of June to Sept. Fishing belongs to riparian owners, leave obtainable. Salmon and sea trout run into Lough Barra in large numbers and into tributaries.

THE ROSSES. The Rosses Fishery is made up of five salmon and sea trout rivers, including **River Dungloe**, and 130 lakes, some of which contain salmon and sea trout, all of which contain brown trout.

Dungloe (Co Donegal). Salmon and sea trout. Rosses Fishery controlled by Rosses AA. **Loughs Meeala**, **Dungloe**, **Craghy**, stocked with browns and rainbows. Season 2 Feb–12 Oct. Fly only on all lakes. Prices are: dt £6, boat £5 per angler; with ghillie, £25. Juv free. River prices vary for season on **Crolly River** and **Clady River**. Permits and boat hire from Charles Bonner, Tackle Shop, Bridge End (Tel: 075 21163); Bill McGarvey, Main St, Dungloe. Hotels: Sweeney's; Ostan na Rosann. Wide range of accommodation.

EAST COASTAL STREAMS
(For close seasons, licences, etc, see The Eastern Regional Fisheries Board)

AUGHRIM RIVER. Approx 5m long, flows south-east to meet Avoca River at Woodenbridge; limestone catchment, good trout water. River and tributaries controlled by Aughrim and Dist Trout AC. Permits £2 per day, £5 per week, from Michael and Bridget Morris, Newsagents, Main St, Aughrim, Co Wicklow (Tel: 0402 36234), or Woodenbridge Hotel, Vale of Avoca, Arklow (Tel: 0402 35146).

AVONMORE RIVER. Runs through Rathdrum, Co Wicklow, from **Loughs Tay** and **Dan**, approx 8m north. It joins **River Avonbeg**, runs into the **Avoca** and reaches sea at Arklow. Big stocks of small brown trout. Rathdrum AC controls lower reaches. Tickets £3, from Tourist Office, Main St, Rathdrum (Tel: 0404 46262); McNabbs Newsagents, Lower Main St, Rathdrum (Tel: 0404 46103). Stirabout Lane Guest House, Rathdrum, caters for anglers with ghillie service, fly-tying room, etc.

BROADMEADOW RIVER. Dublin District; trout. Drainage scheme has affected sport. Broadmeadow AC fishes river and **Tonelgee Reservoir**. Contact K Rundle, Tel: 01 438178.

DARGLE RIVER. Short river which reaches sea at Bray. Principally sea trout, plenty of 2–4lb fish between May and Sept, salmon Apr–May, Aug–Sept, also brown trout. Dargle AC has fishing rights on lower reaches; permits from Viking Tackle, 79 Castle St, Bray (Tel: 01 286 9215). Tinnehinch Fishery: private water on Dargle, fly only. £20 permits for visitors, from H Duff, Tinnehinch House, Enniskerry (Tel: 01 286 8652).

DELVIN RIVER. In Drogheda District. Fair brown trout stream entering sea at Gormanstown holds few sea trout. Gormanstown and Dist AA has water. River being stocked and developed with cooperation of landowners and members. Balbriggan is convenient centre. Hotel: Grand.

RIVER DERRY. Rises near Knockanna, flows south through Tinahely, Shillelagh and Clonegal to meet R Slaney near Kildavin; occasional salmon, small brown trout. Fishing controlled by Derry and Dist AC.

DODDER. Dublin District; brown trout (av 9oz, but fish to 2lb caught), with some sea trout fishing in tidal portion. Dodder AC controls all fishing; contact R O'Hanlon, 82 Braemor Rd, Dublin 14, Tel: 01 982112. Fishing on Dublin Corporation's **Bohernabreena** and **Roundwood Reservoirs** (10m from Dublin); by st £10, wt £4, dt £1.50 from Dublin Corporation, Block 1, Floor 3, Civic Offices, Fishamble St, Dublin 8. No boats. Conc for OAP. Members of these clubs are entitled to reduced rates: Dublin Trout AA; Wicklow AA; Dodder AC.

GLENCREE RIVER. In Dublin District. Enniskerry is a centre; small brown trout. Mostly free.

NANNY RIVER. In Drogheda District. River enters sea at Laytown, Co Meath. Fair brown trout fishing; some sea trout in lower reaches. Drogheda and Dist AC has water and issues permits. Club also fishes R Boyne, and three stillwaters. *See Drogheda.*

TOLKA RIVER. In Dublin District. A once excellent trout stream which has suffered from pollution. Best fishing is from Finglas Bridge to Abbotstown Bridge. For fishing information contact secretary, Tolka AC, Tel: 01 361730.

VARTRY. Small river which drains **Roundwood (Vartry) Reservoir** and flows into sea near Wicklow, with sea trout from late August, and small brown trout. Vartry AC controls lower reaches of river, also **Ashtown Reservoir**; stocked rainbow trout fishery nr **Wicklow Town**. Dt for river from Sec (Tel: 0404 69683); for reservoir, £6 from Bridge Tavern, Wicklow (Tel: 0404 67718). Vartry Reservoir is fly only, brown trout water, run by Dublin Corporation; permits £1.50, from Vartry Lodge near water, or D C Vartry Waterworks (Tel: 01 281 8368). Hotels: Hunter's, Tinakilly House.

ERNE
(For close seasons, licences, etc, see The Northern Regional Fisheries Board)

A hydro-electric scheme has turned the River Erne into two large dams. Excellent sea trout fishing in estuary, for 2 miles from the Mall Quay in Ballyshannon to the Bar at the mouth, with easy access, especially on north shore, season 1 Mar–30 Sept. Coarse fishing excellent; bream, rudd and perch abundant and roach multiplying following their introduction in recent years, also large numbers of pike.

Ballyshannon (Co Donegal). Boats for sea trout fishing, on hire at Mall Quay. **Assaroe Lake** is a reservoir resulting from the Erne Hydro-Electric Generating Scheme, located above Kathleen Falls Power Station. Fishing is available at four points on north side, controlled by ESB, and a permit to cover salmon, brown trout and coarse may be purchased from ESB Fisheries Office, Ardnacrusha, nr Limerick; ESB Generating Station or ESB Shop, both Ballyshannon; Mr T Kelly, Edenville, Kinlough, Co Leitrim; st £15, dt £5, conc; boats from Jim McWeeney, *see below.* Other ESB waters are Gweedore Fishery: Rivers **Clady** and **Crolly**, st £25, wt £15, dt £5, conc, from ESB Office (*above*); C Bonner, The Bridge, Dungloe, Co

Donegal. Tackle shops; Jim McWeeney, Arena, Rossnowlagh Road, Ballyshannon (Tel: 072 51165); Rogan's, Bridge End, Ballyshannon (Tel: 072 51335), Erne sea trout fishing permits sold; McGrath's Fishing Tackle, Belleek.

Belturbet (Co Cavan). Good centre for **Rivers Erne**, **Annalee**, and **Woodford**, and some 37 lakes, with most coarse fish and some trout. **Putighan** and **Derryhoo Lakes** are popular venues, tench to 5lb in L Bunn, to 3lb in L Carn. New developments at Loughs Grilly, Killybandrick, Bunn, Drumlaney, Greenville, Round. Bait, boats and tackle from J McMahon, Bridge St, Tel: 049 22400. Anglers accommodation includes Kilduff House, 2m from Belturbet, and Fort View House, Cloverhill, Belturbet (Tel: 049 4338185) provides guide, bait, drying room, and all other facilities.

Cavan (Co Cavan). All lakes and rivers in the area hold coarse fish except **Annagh Lake** (100 acres) which holds brown and rainbow trout; fly only, no bank fishing, 6 fish limit. Trout season 1 March–30 Sept. **Lough Oughter**, a maze of lakes fed by **R Erne** and **R Annalee**, holds a wealth of coarse fish; bream, rudd, roach, pike, perch, tench. Further details from The Secretary, Cavan Tourist Assn. Tackle shop: Magnet Sports Store, Town Hall. Accommodation catering for anglers: Mrs Myles, Halcyon, Cavan Town; Lakevilla, Blenacup, and Forest Chalets, both Killykeen.

Lough Gowna (Co Cavan). Coarse fishing on Lough Gowna, the source of R Erne. Information from Lough Gowna Tourist Assn. Anglers' accommodation can be found at Hastes Hotel Bar and Restaurant, Main St; Greenville House, both Carrigallen; Lakeview House, Lough Gowna; Frances and Sean Barry, Farrangarve House, Arva, Co Cavan (Tel: 049 4335357).

Cootehill (Co Cavan). A notable fishing centre, with more than 30 coarse fishing lakes within 15 mile radius, and **Rivers Dromore** and **Annalee**: trout, bream, rudd, tench, pike, hybrids, roach, perch. Fishing free in Dromore and Annalee, permit required for **Bunoe** and **Laragh Rivers**. **Moyduff Lake** is brown trout fishery, controlled by NRFB. Permit at lake. Local clubs are Cootehill AC, Laragh AC, Moyduff AC and Bunnoe AC: contact through Cootehill Tourist Development Assn, Riverside House, Cootehill (Tel/Fax: 049 5150). Boats from same address. Tackle shop: C J Bait and Tackle, Bridge St. Anglers' accommodation:

Riverside House; Cabragh Farmhouse; Hillview House, Cootehill.

Clones (Co Monaghan). Coarse fishing. **River Finn**, a sluggish tributary of Upper Lough Erne, excellent bream fishing. There are 60 lakes within 5m of town: pike, perch, rudd, bream, roach, eel, and other species. A few miles north of **Monaghan** is **Emy Lake Fishery**, Emyvale, 136 acres trout fishing, fly only, 6 fish limit. Also at Monaghan, Peters Lake, roach, rudd, tench pike; run by Rossmore CAC. Tackle shop: Dick Kiernan, Venture Sports, Glasslough St, Monaghan. Hotels: Creighton, Lennard Arms.

WOODFORD RIVER.
Ballinamore (Co Leitrim). Well developed centre for angling, close to river, which produces large catches of bream av 2½lb, roach, perch, pike and other coarse fish. River runs into **L Garadice**, one of 25 fishing lakes in this area, all free fishing; voluntary subscription appreciated, contact Angling and Tourist Development Assn, Ballinmore. Riversdale Farm Guesthouse (Tel: 078 44122) caters for anglers, also McAllister's Hotel; Kennedy, Glenview (Tel: 078 44157); Ivan and Dorothy Price, Ardrum Lodge (Tel: 078 44278), all Ballinamore. Tackle from G Owens, High St (agent for Irish Angling Services).

FANE
(For close seasons, licences, etc, see The Eastern
Regional Fisheries Board)

Rises in **Lough Muckno** at Castleblaney and flows SE to enter sea at Blackrock, 4m S of Dundalk. Good supply of salmon in lower reaches, and well up river, depending on water levels; small run of grilse in June, autumn run of salmon. Upper reaches have wild brown trout, good fly fishing water, plenty of fish are caught as large as 3–5lb.

Dundalk (Co Louth). Waters from Knockbridge to border (except 1m at Balentra), plus all **Castletown** and **Ballymascanlon** Rivers and tributaries controlled by Dundalk & Dist Trout AA, Sec (Tel: 0801693 888378). Assn stocks each year with browns, and there is a good run of sea trout and salmon (Aug–Oct best). Membership £12, dt £3, conc, from tackle shops and tourist office. 7m both banks from Knockbridge to sea, Dundalk Salmon AA; catch returns '98 season, 400+ salmon, 400+ sea trout; dt £6, until 31 Aug, £10 Sept, £15 Oct, from Island Tackle, and Devenney's Stationery,

Crowe St. Tackle shops: Island Tackle, 58 Park St; Mac's Sports, 3 Demense, Dundalk. Hotels: Ballymascanlon (3m north); Derryhale; Imperial.

Inniskeen (Co Monaghan). Waters in Inniskeen area controlled by Inniskeen AC. Trout, fly only. Salmon, fly, spinning, lure or shrimp. Membership from A Campbell, Monvallet, Louth, Co Louth. Dt £5 from Ruddys Filling Station, Dundalk.

Castleblayney (Co Monaghan). Good centre for Rivers Fane, **Clarebane**, **Frankfort** and **Mullaghduff**, brown trout. Several coarse fishing loughs in area; **Lough Muckno**, 325 hectares, with pike, perch, roach, bream, and other species; good fishing from several islands in lough. Permission and access controlled by Lough Muckno Leisure Park. **Lough Egish** (5m), pike, perch and eel. **Dick's Lake**, large roach; **Smith's Lake**, good tench fishing, also bream, roach, perch; **Loughs Na Glack** and **Monalty**, big bream. Castleblayney Trout AA has trout fishing on **Milltown Lough** (3m); stocked annually with 3,000 brown trout; dt from Hon Sec. Tackle shop: The Mascot, Main St. Hotel: Glencarn. B & B at Hill View, Kathy Wilson, Bree, Castleblaney (Tel: 042 9746217), 1m from Lough Muckno.

Ballybay (Co Monaghan). Excellent coarse fishing centre for **Dromore River** and loughs, of which there are a large number; some, it is claimed, have never been fished. Boats and ghillies are to be found on the more important local fisheries, including **Bairds Shore**, **Corries**, **Convent**, **Derryvalley**, **Mullanary**, **Corkeeran** and **White Lakes**. There is much free coarse fishing for visiting anglers, and typical weights per day exceed 40lb, mainly bream and roach. Local pike fishing is also very good. Town holds annual coarse angling festival. Local Assn: Corkeeran and Dromore Trout and Coarse AA. Dt £5. Tackle from Martin O'Kane; Mick Harte, both Main St. Accommodation: Riverdale Hotel (Tel: 042 41188) caters for anglers: boat hire and ghillie service, bait and tackle, special rates for angling packages.

GLYDE: Rises near Kingscourt in Co Cavan and flows E for 35m to join River Dee before entering the sea at Annagassan. Flows through some prime coarse fisheries in upper reaches, notably **Rahans** and **Ballyhoe Lakes**. Small run of spring salmon and fair run of grilse in late summer depending on water levels. Good stock of brown trout. Excellent Mayfly hatch. Due to drainage works some years ago, there are some steep banks on which care should be taken. A good centre for anglers is **Carrickmacross**, with several fine coarse lakes near to hand with bream, roach, tench, rudd, hybrids, perch, pike, etc, incl **Lisaniske, Capragh** and **Monalty Lakes, Lough Na Glack**, and fishing accommodation: Mrs Haworth, Rose-Linn Lodge, Carrickmacross, Tel: 042 61035; Mrs Campbell, Glencoe, Tel: 042 67316; Mrs Tinnelly, Corglass, Tel: 042 67492, both Kingscourt.

Castlebellingham (Co Louth). Salmon, sea trout, brown trout. Season 1 Feb–30 Sept. Dee & Glyde AC protect and fish river. Hotel: Bellingham Castle.

DEE: Rises above **Whitewood Lake**, near Kilmainham Wood. Flow E for 38m, joining **River Glyde** at **Annagassan**. Fair runs of spring salmon, some grilse and good runs of sea trout to 5lb (May). Lower reaches below **Ardee** and **Drumcar** yield most salmon and sea trout. Brown trout water above Ardee. Due to drainage works some years ago, many banks are steep and dangerous. Weeds can be a problem during dry summers, ruining fishing in many sections. Season 1 Feb–30 Sept.

Dunleer (Co Louth). Salmon, sea trout. Drumcar Fishery has water. St £10 and dt £3, from The Reception, St Mary's, Drumcar House. Permits 9am–5pm only. Sea trout fishing allowed after dark.

Ardee (Co Louth). Dee & Glyde AC has water on Rivers Dee and Glyde. St £7 and dt £2, from Moonan's Tackle Shop. Other tackle shop: Ardee Sports Co, John St. Hotel: The Gables.

Drumconrath (Co Meath). Drumconrath AC issues permits. Dt and information from Fergus Muldoon, Bar and Lounge, Main St (Tel: 041 54119). **Ballyhoe Lakes**, tench fishing, plus bream, roach, perch, pike; coarse fishing in **Lough Mentrim** (specimen bream and tench), **Lake Balrath**, Corstown. Fishing accommodation at Inis Fail, Tel: 041 54161, and Ballyhoe, Tel: 041 54400/54104.

Nobber (Co Meath). Nobber AC has stretch from **Whitewood Lake** to Yellow-Ford Bridge. Mainly brown trout, occasional salmon

in late autumn, usually during flood water. Weeds can be a problem during low water.

MULLAGHDUFF: Tributary which enters Lough Muckno. A good trout stream, wet fly fishing best from April onwards, dry fly late in season.

FRANKFORT: Short river which connects Milltown Lough with Lough Muckno, stocked by local assoc. Trout to 3lb. Best in May–July.

FEALE

(For close seasons, licences, etc, see The Shannon Regional Fisheries Board)

Rises in North Cork on the southern slopes of Wullaghereick Mountain, then flows west through Abbeyfeale, Listowel, and enters Shannon Estuary south of Ballybunion. Its total length is an estimated 46 miles, and there are 11 main tributaries: the **Gale**, Oolagh, **Allaghaun, Cahir, Brick, Smearlagh, Tullylease, Owveg, Glashacooncore, Clyddagh** and **Breanagh**. A spate river, with salmon, sea trout and brown trout. Season is from 1 Mar–30 Sept. Sometimes salmon run poor owing to low water. The Feale system is controlled almost entirely by five associations. (See below.)

Abbeyfeale (Co Limerick). Best centre for Feale. Waders essential. Abbeyfeale AA has 6m of single and double bank d/s of town, with salmon and sea trout; st £40, plus £25 joining fee and dt £15 from Ryan's, New Street, Abbeyfeale. Brosna AA has 6m upstream; trout permit from S Quinlan, Kilmanahan, Abbeyfeale. Hotel: Leen's. Tackle shops: P Ryan, New Street; Lane (manufacture of the famous "Lane" artificial minnow), New Street.

Listowel (Co Kerry). North Kerry AA has 7m single and double bank on R Feale and on **River Smearlagh**; salmon and sea trout, all legal methods allowed; wt and dt, from Hon Sec or tackle shops. Killocruin/Finuge Club controls 3m d/s of town, best stretch for spring salmon and grilse. Tralee AA has 5m u/s, both banks; dt issued. Fly fishing for salmon quite good from mid-Aug. Brosna/Mountcollins Club has 8m on upper reaches of Feale, with good sea trout fishing from mid-Aug to end of Sept. Salmon licences and permits from Mr Jim Horgan, Woodford, Listowel. Tackle shops: Halpins; Landers Leisure Lines, Courthouse Lane, Tralee. Hotels: Stack's, Listowel Arms.

GALWAY AND MAYO
(rivers and smaller loughs)
(For close seasons, licences, etc, see The Western Regional Fisheries Board)

BALLYNAHINCH

An extensive system of lakes, tributaries and connecting rivers draining into Bertaghboy Bay. One of the most important salmon and sea trout fisheries in the west of Ireland.

Recess. Salmon and sea trout. The famous Ballynahinch Castle Hotel Fishery consists of **Ballynahinch River** (2½m) and **Ballynahinch Lake**; situated at bottom of 25m long system of river and lakes. Salmon best June to Sept. Sea trout best July to Oct. Fly fishing dt £30–£60. Max 28 rods. Ghillies £35 per day. Permits for non-residents from The Manager, Ballynahinch Castle Hotel (Tel: 095 31006). Near **Roundstone**, The Anglers Return Fishery comprises several joined lakes draining into the Owenmore (Ballynahinch) River, as well as a chain of brown trout lakes. **Tombeola Lough**, south, has good browns, av 1lb. Permits and fishing help from Lynn Hill, Anglers Return, Toombeola Roundstone (Tel: 095 31091). No charge for residents. Lough Inagh Lodge Hotel, Recess, is central to the **Lough Inagh Fishery**, seven beats including two outstanding loughs, **Inagh** and **Derryclare**, and associated rivers; situated at top of Ballynahinch system in heart of Connemara. Dt, boats and ghillies. Permits from Maire O'Connor, Lough Inagh Lodge (Tel: 095 34706); Della MacAuley, Inagh Valley Inn (Tel: 095 34608). Tackle for sale or hire at fishery office. **Athry Fishery** comprises five loughs on Upper Ballynahinch, including **Lough Athry**. Lower loughs get run of sea trout and occasional salmon, and upper loughs sea trout only. Season mid-July to 12 Oct. Dt £25 (boat and 2 or 3 rods). Max 9 rods. Ghillies £25 per day. For fishing on **Bealnacarra River** and **Glendollagh Lake**, apply to W Hollinger and B Gilmore, Recess House. Tackle shops: Ballynahinch Castle Hotel; Percy Stanley, Clifden, Co Galway.

Maam Cross (Co Galway). Salmon and sea trout. Top Waters Ballynahinch Fishery comprises six lakes and part of **Owentooey** and **Recess Rivers**. **Lough Oorid**, at top of system, is 2m W of Maam Cross with **Loughs Shannakeela**, **Derryneen** and **Cappahoosh** forming a chain westward. Season mid-June to 30 Sept. Wt (boat) £150, dt (boat) £25

and (bank) £20. Permits and accommodation from Mr L Lyons and Mrs Iris Lyons-Joyce, Tullaboy House (Tel: 091 552 305/462).

CARROWNISKEY: rises in Sheefry Hills and flows 6m to sea beyond Louisburgh. Spate river, overgrown by trees in parts, making fishing difficult. Lower reaches characterised by long flat stretches. There are runs of salmon and sea trout from June onwards. Roonagh Lough, into which river runs, offers fishing for both, either by fly or dapping. St and wt £50, dt £12 from Charles Gaffney's Pub, Louisberg, Tel: 098 66150.

Louisburgh (Co Mayo). Permits for Carrowinsky fishing from Charles Gaffney's Pub (*above*). Salmon and trout in **Altair Lake**. Good shore fishing for bass, pollack, etc; boats at Roonagh and Old Head.

BUNOWEN: spate river with some deep pools, providing excellent lies for salmon and sea trout. Sea trout and salmon, best from mid-June. Season: 1 Apr to 30 Sept. Tagged salmon were introduced into river in 1992, any tagged fish caught should be reported to an officer of WRFB. Permits £50 season and week, £12 day, for river and **Lough Namucka** from Charles Gaffney's Pub, as above. **Mother Lough**, in vicinity of **Westport**; stocked annually by WRFB with 2,000 brown trout, ave 1lb; fly only, dt £15, 4 fish limit; permits from M McDonnell, Liscarney, Westport (Tel: 098 21638). Tackle shop: Hewetsons, Bridge St, Westport, Co Mayo (Tel: 098 26018). Hotels: Old Head, Durkans. For sea fishing Bay View Hotel, Clare Island, recommended; boats for hire.

CASHLA: drains a complex system of lakes then flows into Cashla Bay at Costelloe. Good run of salmon up to 22lb, but it is as a sea trout fishery that it really excels.

Costelloe (Co Galway). Sea trout, salmon. Costelloe and Fermoyle Fishery: Lower fishery includes R Cashla and **Lough Glenicmurrin**, and holds excellent sea trout and good salmon; Upper fishery Loughs **Fermoyle Clogher**, **Carrick** and **Rusheen**, and holds excellent sea trout. Dt £20–£45, £60–£70 with ghillie service. Permits and tackle from Tim Moore, Bridge Cottage, Costelloe (Tel: 091 572196, Fax: 572366); accommodation may be booked through fishery. Tackle shops: Freeney's, 19 High St; Hugh Duffy, Mainguard St, all Galway, Co Galway; Costelloe and Fermoyle Fishery Office.

DAWROS: drains Kylemore Lakes then flows 5m before entering Ballinakill Harbour. Run of spring salmon, grilse, sea trout. Best July to Sept (sea trout); Aug (salmon).

Kylemore (Co Galway). Salmon, grilse, sea trout. Mrs Nancy Naughton, Kylemore House Hotel (Tel: 095 41143) issues permits. Tackle shops: Percy Stanley, Clifden, Co Galway; Hamilton's, Leenane, Co Galway.

DOOHULLA: drains a number of lakes, then runs one mile to Ballyconneely Bay. Holds some summer salmon and sea trout. Best sea trout July to Sept. Best salmon June to Aug.

Ballyconneely (Co Galway). Between Roundstone and Ballyconneely lies the Doohulla Fishery, consisting of The Pool at Callow Bridge, **Doohulla River**, and **Loughs Maumeen**, **Emlaghkeeragh**, **Carrick** and others. Salmon, sea trout, browns. Dt £10 (The Pool) and £5. Hire of boats £10. Permits from N D Tinne, Emlaghmore (Tel: 095 23529). Clifden tackle shop: Stanley.

ERRIFF AND BUNDORRAGHA: good salmon and sea trout rivers lying short distance north of Ballynahinch country and flowing into Killary Harbour near Leenane.

Erriff Fishery, **Leenane** (Co Galway). At the east side of Killary Harbour, fishery consists of River Erriff (8m) and **Tawnyard Lough**. Noted for salmon and some sea trout. Fishery acquired by Central Fisheries Board in 1982. Dt £10 from April, £35 June–July, £30 Aug–Sept. River season 1 Apr–30 Sept. Tawnyard Lough, boat for 2 rods, £50, from 1 July. Accommodation at Aasleagh Lodge. Enquiries to Erriff Fishery Office, Aasleagh Lodge, Leenane, Co Galway (Tel: 095 42252, Fax: 42361).

Delphi Fishery, **Leenane** (Co Galway). On the north side of Killary Harbour, fishery has the following waters: **Bundorragha River** (1m), 4 rods, salmon from 1 Feb–30 Sept, some sea trout from July onwards; **Finlough**, two boats, and **Doolough**, three boats, salmon from March onwards, sea trout from July. **Glencullin** and **Cunnel Loughs**, some trout from July. Fly only, dt with boat £40 to £60. Ghillies, £40. Apply to Fishery Manager, Peter Mantle, Delphi Lodge, Leenane, Co Galway (Tel: 095 42222, Fax: 42296, E-mail: delfish@iol.ie). Accommodation at Delphi Lodge and 4 fishing cottages. Tackle shops: The

Fishery Office, Delphi Lodge; Hamilton's Bar, Leenane.

Knock (Co Mayo). Situated in east of county, a notable centre for coarse fishing. Local loughs include **Cloontariff**, pike and perch, **Carrownamallagh**, excellent pike, **Clooncurry**, pike and perch, **Curragh**, bream and pike, **Derrykin**, pike, **Lakehill Pond**, specimen tench, **Nanonagh**, mixed coarse. Boats are available on all lakes. Hotel and B & B accommodation is plentiful locally.

NEWPORT: drains Lough Beltra and runs into Clew Bay, at Newport. River over 7m long and usually fished from banks. Good for salmon and very good sea trout. There are about 20 pools, some for both day and night fishing. Fly only. River known for length of season, 20 March–30 Sept.

Newport (Co Mayo). Salmon and sea trout. Newport House Hotel has fishing on **Newport River**, **Lough Beltra**, **East** (fine run of spring fish) and 4m on **River Skerdagh**, a tributary. Fly only, all sea trout to be returned alive. Dt £26, £85 for 2 rods with boat and ghillie, from The Fishery Manager, Newport House (Tel: 098 41222). Newport AC, whose members are free to fish Newport River by concession of Newport House, issue permits for salmon and sea trout fishing (June to Sept) on **Owengarve**, a small spate river near **Mulrany**. Fly only, all sea trout must be returned alive. Dt £10. Various small trout loughs around Newport. Hotel also issues tickets to non-members, when available. A few miles from Newport, boat fishing for salmon and sea trout at **Burrishoole Fishery** which consists of **Loughs Feeagh** and **Furnace** with short tidal stretch of river. Fishery owned and administered by Salmon Research Agency of Ireland; fishing season effectively mid-June to end September. Boats with or without boatmen, package holidays arranged by request incorporating local accommodation of varying grades. Full details from SRAI, Newport, Co Mayo, Tel: 98 41107. Agency also controls **Ballinlough Fishery**, 54 acres, 2m north west of Westport: stocked rainbow and brown trout, £30 per boat per day (2 rods), limit 6 fish. Permits from Mrs Gill, Ballinlough, (Tel: 098 26128). Tackle shop: Hewetson Bros, Bridge St, Westport, Co Mayo (Tel: 098 26018).

OWENDUFF: Good for salmon from end of

Mar. Grilse and sea trout, mid-June to end of Sept. Provides excellent all-round fishing when water right.

Ballycroy (Co Mayo). Salmon, sea trout. Middle reaches owned by Craigie Bros, Owenduff, Celbridge, Co Kildare (Tel: 01 6272671); occasional weekly lettings with accommodation, for up to 16 guests and 6 rods. Lower down, at Shranamanragh Lodge a small beat is owned by Mr Colm O'Brian of New Park, Bray Rd, Foxrock, Dublin 18, Tel: 01 2895337. Good accommodation, let with fishing by the week. Good for salmon (April/May), grilse and sea trout (July onwards).

OWENGARVE: Spate river. Salmon, grilse and sea trout, early June to early Oct.

Mulrany (Co Mayo). Most of river controlled by Newport AC, which has mutual agreement with Dr J Healey, Rosturk Castle, Rosturk, Westport, Co Mayo, whereby whole river can be fished. Daily (£2), weekly and monthly rods from club Hon Sec or from Rosturk Castle.

ACHILL ISLAND: Off Mayo coast, has become famous in recent years for its sea fishing (see Sea Fishing section). Excellent sea trout. There are three main trout lakes: Loch Gall, recently stocked with rainbows; Loch na Breach, with good stock of natural browns; Keel Lake, with a sea outlet, and a good run of sea trout; controlled by Achill Sporting Club, permits from Secretary Roger Gallagher, Valley House, Dugort, Achill; disabled access. Tackle from P Sweeney, Achill Sound. Hotel: Slievemore, Dugort. Accommodation list from Achill Tourism, Achill Island, Tel: 098 47353.

OWENGOWLA and **INVERMORE**: two short rivers, each draining a complex of lakes. Owengowla flows into Bertraghboy Bay and Invermore flows into Kilkieran Bay. Both are excellent sea trout fisheries.

Cashel (Co Galway). Sea trout. **Gowla Fishery** consists of **R Owengowla**, with holding pools, and about 14 loughs, permits from Fishery Office. **Invermore Fishery** has 10 sea trout lakes and an additional brown trout lake; sea trout, and some salmon at fishery. Upper lakes are remote, but accessible by path. Lower lakes fish from mid-June; upper lakes governed by summer rainfall. There are 10 boats on the fishery, and accommodation. Dt (boat) £25 from Mrs Margaret McDonagh,

Glen View B & B (Tel: 095 31054). Ghillies at both fisheries.

OWENMORE: 20m long and principally spate river from Bellacorick Bridge, rises near Ballycastle and flows into Blacksod Bay. Principal tributary is **Oweninny** (Crossmolina AA). River divided among number of owners. Good for spring salmon from April 1, given really high water; good grilse and sea trout from mid-June to end of Sept, if water is right. To the south of river are a number of small loughs with brown trout. Some of these have free fishing, including **Loughs Brack**, **Nambrock**, and **Nalagan**. They are remote, but worth exploring.

Bangor Erris (Co Mayo). Upper and middle reaches owned by syndicate, not for letting. Part of fishery let to Bangor Erris AC. Permits from Seamus Henry, see below. Enquiries respecting **Carrowmore Lough**, salmon, sea trout and brown trout, plus 4m of **Owenmore** and **Glenamoy** Rivers, to Seamus Henry, West End Bar, Bangor Erris, Ballina, Tel: 097 83487. Bellacorick Fisheries have salmon and trout fishing on **Srahnakilly** and **Oweninny** Rivers. Permits from Musical Bridge Inn, **Bellacorick**, Tel: 096 53094.

SCREEBE: drains a group of lakes, including Lakes **Ardery**, **Shindilla**, **Loughanfree**, **Ahalia** and **Screebe**, then flows into Camus Bay at Screebe. Gets good run of grilse and some summer salmon.

Screebe (Co Galway). Salmon and brown trout. Screebe Estate Fishery is professionally managed and includes Screebe River and numerous lakes. It also has its own hatchery. Fly fishing only. Permits from The Manager, Screebe Estates, Camus (Tel: 091 74110). Hotel: Currarevagh House Hotel, Oughterard, Co Galway (Tel: 091 552312/3), situated beside L Corrib on NW shore, good centre for local fishing, caters for anglers. Tackle shops: Tommy Tuck (Oughterard AA); M Keogh, both Oughterard, Co Galway.

MAYO NORTH
(streams)

Several small sea trout rivers run to the coast in north west of county. **Bunnahowen** is a short river near Belmullet, with free fishing for brown trout (to 1lb), and sea trout. **Glenamoy** and **Muingnabo** both empty into a sea lough at **Broad Haven Bay**, and have salmon and sea trout. Fishing on the Muingnabo River is free. Near **Ballycastle** are **Glencullin** and **Ballinglen Rivers**, both with sea trout, late run on Glencullin, a few salmon in Ballinglen. Free fishing on both. The **Cloonaghmore River** runs into **Killala Bay**, west of the Moy. It has both salmon and sea trout. Free fishing with permission of local assn. **Leafony** is a small spate river which runs into east side of Killala Bay, and has free fishing for salmon and sea trout (late run, Aug–Sept). **Easkey River** runs north from **L Easkey** (brown trout, free), and has salmon and sea trout. Some of this river is preserved, elsewhere free fishing. **Drumcliffe** and **Grange Rivers** run into sea loughs north of Sligo. Grange has brown trout, free fishing; Drumcliffe (connected to Glencar Lough) is assn water, with salmon fishing. Contact Mr Harold Sibbery, The Waterfall, Glencar, Co Leitrim.

GARAVOGUE AND LOUGH GILL

(For close seasons, licences, etc, see The North-Western Regional Fisheries Board)

Garavogue River connects Lough Gill with the sea, which it enters in Sligo Bay to south of Donegal Bay and Erne. Salmon, trout, coarse fish. Lough Gill is a fine coarse fishery, with pike to 30lb and excellent stock of bream at Hazelwood, Dooney, Aughamore and Annagh Bay.

Sligo (Co Sligo). Salmon, trout. **Lough Gill**, a large lake 5m long. Good run of spring salmon; best Feb to March. Northern and eastern shores controlled by Sligo AA. Dt £10, from Barton Smith, Tackle Dealer, Hyde Bridge. Fishing on the rest of the lake is free. Boats £10 per day, from Blue Lagoon, Public House (Tel: 071 42530/45407), also tackle hire and ghillie service. **Drumcliffe River** and **Glencar Lake**, 6 to 9 miles north of Sligo, controlled by Sligo AA and Manorhamilton Anglers. Small brown trout. Good spring salmon run from mid-Feb. Some very large sea trout caught. **Ballisodare River**, 5m south, excellent run of summer salmon. **Lough Colga**, 4m; brown trout; free. Permits from Barton Smith, Tackle Shop, Hyde Bridge (Tel: 071 42356).

Dromahair (Co Leitrim). **River Bonet** feeds Lough Gill; salmon, trout. Best for salmon in summer. Dromahair AA fishes locally. Permits from McGoldricks Mace Foodmarket. T McGowan, Stanford Old Inn (Tel: 071 64140), has private fishing for guests, and patrons of bar and restaurant. Manorhamilton AA also pre-serve some water on river and **Glencar Lake**. St £12, dt £5, from A Flynn, Post Office. Manorhamilton (Tel: 072 55001). Also abundance of coarse fishing in river and **Loughs Belhavel**, **Glenade** and **Corrigeencor**; all free, with pike and perch. Tackle from Spar, Main St.

CO KERRY
(rivers and loughs)
(For close seasons, licences, etc, see The South Western Regional Fisheries Board)

KENMARE BAY. Several small salmon rivers empty into this bay, which provides excellent sea fishing (large skate, tope, etc). Best season, May to August.

Kenmare (Co Kerry). Salmon, sea trout, small wild brown trout. Kenmare Salmon Angling Ltd owns 1¼m of **Roughty** at Ardtully Castle, 5 miles from Kenmare-Cork Road. Spring salmon, March to June; good grilse runs, June to Aug; fly, spinning, prawning and worming permitted; spring salmon average 9lb, grilse 4lb. Permits (dt £12, wt £35) for visitors staying locally, from John O'Hare, 21 Main St, Kenmare, Tel: 064 41499. No Sunday fishing for visitors. **Sheen River** runs in on south shore and is preserved by owner. It produces approx 1,000 salmon and grilse every season. Contact the Manager, Sheen Falls Lodge, Kenmare, Tel: 064 41600. **Finnihy River** is overgrown and requires determination, but has grilse run: free fishing. **Lough Barfinnihy** 35 acres, is 6½m from Kenmare, off Killarney Rd. Good brown and stocked rainbows. **Lough Inchiquin**: char, sea trout, salmon, browns. One boat on site. Permits for these and for **Uragh Lough** from J O'Hare, see above. **Cloonee Loughs**, on the south shore, have excellent game fishing. Permits, £13 per day, and boats from May O'Shea, Lake House, Cloonee (Tel: 064 84205). For fishermen with taste for mountain climbing there are at least 40 lakes holding brown trout on plateau of **Caha Mountains**, all easily fished from Kenmare. See also South West Cork. **Kerry Blackwater** 10m long, drains Lough Brin, spring salmon run, sea trout and browns. Fishing part over 4m long, with about 30 pools. Good fly fishing up near Lough Brin itself. Dt £20–£25 may be obtained from Fishery Manager, SWRFB, Macroom, also from hut on river bank, limit 2 salmon. **Lough Brin**, 65 acres, 10m northwest; trout to 1lb, and sea trout from August, dt £5, boat with outboard £20. Controlled by SWRFB. **Sneem River**, farther west, is controlled by Sneem River Assn;

permits £7–£12 per day, from Tourist Office, South Sq, Sneem (Tel: 064 45270). Limit 2 salmon per day, 4 sea trout. Fishing with accom at fishing lodge: H Cowper, Sneem (Tel: 054 36230). Run of grilse and sea trout July/August. For trout fishing on SWRFB **Lough Fadda**, contact Monica O'Shea, Tahilla, Sneem (Tel: 064 82901). Hotels: Sheen Falls Lodge (Tel: 064 41600) permits; Park Hotel; Kenmare Bay; Riversdale; Dunkeron Lodge.

WATERVILLE RIVERS. Waterville River or **Currane**, short river joining **Lough Currane**. Popular with visitors. Salmon, sea trout, brown trout. All migratory fish running to Lough Currane go through this river, which also has spring run of large sea trout. Lough Currane: famous for its large sea trout and spring salmon fishing, grilse from June; fishing predominately by boat, free to licence-holders. All sea trout under 12in to be returned alive. Season 17 Jan–30 Sept. Boat hire, Waterville AA, c/o Lobster Bar, Waterville (Tel: 066 74183), and others.

Cummeragh River, spate river with five upper loughs, **Derriana**, **Niamona**, **Cloonaghlin**, **Na Huisce** and **Coppal**, feeding main river which flows into Lough Currane. All these loughs contain salmon, sea trout and browns, and river has good catches of salmon in summer and autumn. Tickets for all these may be obtained from Tadhg O'Sullivans Fishing Tackle, Waterville, Co Kerry (Tel: 066 74433/75384). Local hills contain numerous small loughs rarely fished.

Inny River, a fair sized spate river some 15m in length, with good run of salmon and sea trout from June onwards. Salmon fishing on these rivers is from 17 Jan–30 Sept. Spring fish average 11lb, fish over 15lb caught, record 32lb. An unusual feature is that fish may be caught by a small fly on a floating line from opening day, although many are taken on rapallas, toby spoons and other baits. The system is noted for its large sea trout, with over 70% of Irish specimen (6lb plus) fish taken. Season 14 Feb–30 Sept. The bigger fish are caught in Lough Currane and Derriana. Tickets from Tadgh O'Sullivan (*above*). **Waterville House, Tel: 0667 4244, lets occasional rods on R Waterville** and R Inny, for 4 hour periods. Spinning allowed in spring, thereafter, fly only. Several other owners have fishing to let on Inny, incl Butler Arms Hotel, Waterville, Tel: 0667 4156; J

O'Connell, Foildrenagh, Mastergeehy, Killarney (Tel: 066 9474523), lake and river with salmon, sea trout, brown trout, tickets from Butler Arms Hotel; J O'Shea, Killenleigh, Mastergeehy; M J O'Sullivan, Tel: 0667 4255. Tackle shops: Tadgh O'Sullivan (*above*); Coomaciste Crafts; Sean O'Shea. Other hotels: Silver Sands, White House.

CARHAN and FERTA: small spate rivers which enter Valentia Harbour. Small run of grilse and sea trout. Carhan is overgrown and worm is the best method. **Kells Lough** is between **Glenbeigh** and **Caherciveen**. Plentiful stock of small browns.

CARAGH: river runs through **Caragh Lake** to sea at Dingle Bay. Salmon, sea trout, trout. Salmon best from May, sea trout late, good fishing at night. Bass and mullet in estuary. Permits for lower river from Mrs Maureen O'Grady, Ferndale Heights, Glenbeigh (Tel: 066 68228). 7 beats on upper river from Glencar Hotel, Glencar (Tel: 066 976 0102/0167 Fax); weekly only Mar–mid-Jul, dt and wt mid-Jul–30 Sept; access for disabled. tackle shop at hotel. Immediately to the east of Caragh Lake is a large group of small loughs, incl **L Nakirka**, 20 acres, with good stocks of small wild browns and stocked larger fish. For permit contact SWRFB, 1 Neville Terrace, Macroome, Co Cork (Tel: 026 41222), or Kate O'Connor, Oulagh, Caragh Lake, Killorglin (Tel: 066 69279).

Glenbeigh (Co Kerry). For lower water; wt £26 and dt £6, from Towers Hotel. Hotel also issues permits for 6m of **Laune** (single bank only), 8½m of **Feale**, 3m of **Flesk**, **Behy** and **Loughs Caragh** and **Currane**. To south west of Glenbeigh is a group of small trout loughs drained by **R Behy**, incl **Coomnacronia** and **Coomaglaslaw**: free fishing on all of them.

Glencar (Co Kerry) Glencar House Hotel has 7 beats, one rod per beat, reserved for guests only; salmon; best months, Feb to end of June; grilse June onwards; sea trout. Average salmon catch over 10 years, 310 per annum. The hotel also has fishing on **Loughs Cloon**, **Acoose** and **Reagh**. Many smaller rivers and lakes holding brown trout. Ghillies and boats in vicinity. Tackle and licences at hotel, Tel: 066 60102, Fax: 60167).

MACGILLYCUDDY'S REEKS (Co Kerry). In the Gap of Dunloe, a line of three small lakes drain into **Laune** at Beaufort Bridge: **Black Lake**, **Cushvalley** and **Auger**. Free fishing for plentiful small brown trout that fight extremely well. Very small fly recommended. At head of Black Valley are **Cummeenduff Loughs** and **Lough Reagh**, which are approached via Gap of Dunloe. Free fishing with spring salmon and good grilse run. Boats from J O'Donoghue, Black, Valley, Killarney.

DINGLE PENINSULA (Co Kerry). Several small rivers and loughs are fishable in this area; **Rivers Milltown**, free fishing with some sea trout; and **Owenascaul**, or **Annascaul** on south side, rights owned by Patricia Scully, Bunanear, Annascaul, permission required to fish; **Owencashla**, **Glennahoo**, **Scarid**, **Owenmore** on north side: some migratory fish in spate, worth fishing. Mostly free. Owencashla overgrown. Loughs incl **Annascaul**, with sea trout in Aug/Sept; **Gill**, west of **Castlegregory**: free, for small browns; **Adoon**, with sea trout from August, free; and many others worth exploring. **Lough Caum** at Castlegregory is SWRFB trout fishery with small native browns and stocked rainbows. Boats for hire on water.

LAUNE AND MAINE
(including Killarney Lakes)
(For close seasons, licences, etc, see The South-Western Regional Fisheries Board)

LAUNE: Drains Killarney Lakes and flows 8m to Castlemain Harbour on Dingle Bay. Salmon, sea trout, brown trout. Late summer best time for trout. Laune Salmon and Trout AA has 18 fisheries on river; £10 permits for beat 3 of State Fishery from O'Sullivan's Foodstore, Beaufort Bridge, and Angler's Lodge, Lahard Beaufort (Tel: 064 44559). Access for disabled. Permits for Beats 1 and 2 of State Fishery from SWRFB. Dungeel Farmhouse, on river nr Killorglin, has B & B catering for anglers. Tackle shops in Killorglin, Killarney and Tralee.

Beaufort (Co Kerry). For upper reaches. Permits and light tackle from O'Sullivan's, Beaufort Bridge, Killarney, Tel: 064 44397. Self-catering house on banks. Accom at Angler's Lodge, Beaufort.

MAINE: Maine and tributaries **Little Maine** and **Brown Flesk** hold salmon, sea trout and brown trout. Salmon fishing is at times very good. Brown Flesk has at least 35 holding pools; over 200 salmon per season, sea and brown trout fishing often good. River is late. Best at

medium to low water; good grilse from end of June, sea trout in July. Little Maine has 7 or 8 salmon pools and good fishing for small browns. Sea trout best at night. Part of this system is free fishing; check with SWRFB.

KILLARNEY LAKES: Consist of three lakes: **Upper Lake**, **Muckross Lake**, **Lough Leane**, last being much the largest at 4,500 acres, connected with sea by **R Laune**. Good free trout fishing, excellent stocks of wild browns av 8oz. Numerous boatmen for hire, £50 per day, two fishing; boats for disabled. Boats: Henry Clifden, Ross Castle, Killarney (Tel: 064 322252. **R Flesk** feeds **Lough Leane**. Medium-sized spate river, with good grilse run: Saratoga House Hotel, Muckross Rd, Killarney, offers free fishing to guests. Many small mountain lakes; free trout fishing. **Barfinnihy Lake**, 10m away on Sneem Road, is well stocked with brown trout, fishing by permit only, contact O'Neills (see *Killarney*) or J O'Hare (see *Kenmare*).

Killarney (Co Kerry). Salmon fishing best in May/June. Sea trout fishing poor, brown trout excellent, best June, and Sept to mid-Oct. Fishing on R Flesk is open for £10 per week from Lough Leane AA. **Lough Leane** (4,500 acres), largest of Killarney lakes; famous for beauty of scenery; estimated that local fishermen get hundreds of salmon and grilse by trolling baits every season. Free fishing; max rods 40–50. Boats from Harry Clifton, Ross Castle (Tel: 064 32252); Abbey Boating & Fishing Tours, Tel: 064 34351. Tackle shops: O'Neill's, 6 Plunkett St (Tel: 064 31970, Fax: 35689), supplies tickets for rivers and lakes, ghillies and boats; The Handy Stores, Main St; Harry Clifton. Many hotels and guest houses, incl Saratoga House B & B, run by M J O'Neill (*above*).

LEE
(For close seasons, licences, etc, see The South-Western Regional Fisheries Board)

Draining **Gougane Barra Lake** and flowing 53m in an easterly direction to Cork Harbour, Lee was formerly notable early salmon river, but fishing partly spoilt by hydro-electric schemes; salmon sport restricted to lower 9m, d/s of Inniscarra Dam. At least 300 salmon and 800 grilse are caught in a typical season. Trout are more plentiful below Inniscarra Dam. There is also good coarse fishing in system, for bream, tench, perch, eels. Salmon season, Feb–30 Sept. SWRFB Fisheries: **Inniscarra Lake**, River Lee:

530 ha, and over 25 miles of bank side, possibly Ireland's best bream fishing. Bags in excess of 100lb are common; also to be found are bream-rudd hybrids. **Inniscarra Salmon Fishery** is a ¾m double bank salmon fishery, below hydro-electric station. Fishable from March, peaks in April–May, mid-June for grilse, brown trout 15 Feb–12 Oct. State salmon permits £12, additional payment for fishing, £15, from Amenity Officer, ESB Fisheries, Carrigadrohid, Co Cork (Tel: 026 4122/48132).

Cork (Co Cork). Salmon fishing on lower R Lee at Inniscarra Dam and below Millbro; season Feb 1 to Sept 30. Fishing is privately owned or leased and controlled mainly by Lee Salmon A and Cork Salmon A (dt £10, from Hon Sec). Salmon fishing licence is required, obtainable from tackle shops. Trout fishing on **R Shournagh, Martin, Bride, Sullane** and **Dripsey**; small streams with brown trout; fishing mostly free. For information contact Cork Trout AA, Blarney AA and tackle shops. Lough in Cork City, 10 acres, has large carp (Irish record 22lb) and eels, 2lb to 6lb. Tackle shops: T W Murray & Co, 87 Patrick St; The Tackle Shop, 6 Lavitts Quay. Hotels: Jurys, Metropole, Imperial.

Macroom (Co Cork). Stocked brown trout fishing on **Inniscarra Reservoir**; contact SW Fisheries Board, Macroom, Tel: 026 41222. **Carrigohid Reservoir** is good pike fishery, with perch shoals. Other venues for pike are lower **Sullane River, Middle Lee, Lough Allua**. Middle Lee, Rivers Sullane, Laney and Foherish, and **Gougane Barra** lake are good fisheries for small trout. Local club: Macroom Trout AC, c/o Mary Anne's Bar, Masseytown, Macroom. Hotels: Castle, Victoria.

LIFFEY
(For close seasons, licences, etc, see The Eastern Regional Fisheries Board)

Winding river with two reservoirs along its course, rises some 13m SW of Dublin but flows over 80m before entering sea at Islandbridge, Dublin. Subject to hydro-electric floods, it has brown trout and some sea trout in lower reaches. Very poor salmon run in 1999. Mayfly hatch end of May. Best trout fishing from Lucan upstream. Best salmon between Straffan and Islandbridge.

Dublin (Co Dublin). Most water controlled by clubs. Dublin & Dist Salmon AA: Liffey at Islandbridge, Lucan, and below Leixlip Bridge;

Dublin Trout AA: about 6m on Upper and Lower Liffey at Ballyward Bridge, Clane, Straffan/Celbridge, **Leixlip, Blessington** and **Upper** and **Lower Bohernabreena Reservoirs**; mainly trout fishing, some salmon in Liffey, and pike, also. Dt £5–£2, depending on water. Clane Trout and Salmon AA: approx 4m of excellent brown trout water, best from early May. Dt £5 from Patrick Cleere and Son (below); fly, bait fishing discouraged, no coarse; North Kildare Trout & Salmon AA: Millicent Bridge to Kilcullen Bridge; Kilcullen Trout and Salmon AA, Kilcullen u/s to Harristown; Ballymore Eustace Salmon and Trout AA, Ballymore Eustace to Harristown; Kilbride AC: Ballyfoyle to Ballysmutton; Lucan AC fishes Lucan stretch. Chapelizod AC has water from Old Mill Race River to Laurence Brook Weir; game and coarse fishing, no dt, membership £20 pa, conc. Broadmeadow AC fishes **Broadmeadow R** and **Tonelgee Reservoir**. Tickets from tackle shops. Dt £2 for Dublin Trout AA waters from Dan O'Brien, New Rd, Blackhall, Clane, Co Kildare and Sy Gallagher, Reeves, Straffan, Co Kildare. Dublin Corporation controls fishing on **Roundwood Reservoir** (20m) and on **Bohernabreena Reservoir** (8m); the former leased to Co Wicklow AA; fly only; bank fishing; st and dt. **Grand Canal**, which runs alongside Liffey for some distance, holds brown trout, bream, rudd, perch and pike. Coarse fishing also in **Royal Canal**, similar species. Tackle shops: P Cleere & Son, 5 Bedford Row, Temple Bar, Tel: 01 677 7406); Rory's, 17a Temple Bar, Dublin 2 (Tel: Dublin 6772351), who sells permits for Dublin Salmon A, Dodder A, North Kildare A, Tolka A.

Naas (Co Kildare). Ballymore Eustace Trout & Salmon AA has fishing on Liffey from **Ballymore Eustace** to **Harristown**, and also **Golden Falls Lake**. St and dt are from Michael Murphy, Publican, The Square, Ballymore Eustace. Kilcullen & Dist Trout and Salmon AA fishes Liffey at Kilcullen, u/s to Harristown. Prosperous Coarse AC fishes 20m of **Grand Canal**, see Grand Canal. Tackle shops: Cahills Sports; J Prescott, Pachelli Rd, both Naas; bait from Prescott. Hotel: Ardenode, Ballymore Eustace. Several guest houses.

MOY
(For close seasons, licences, etc, see The North Western Regional Fisheries Board)

Flowing 63m from its source in the Ox Mountains to enter Killala Bay at Ballina, its tributaries drain an area of some 800 square miles. One of Ireland's premier salmon rivers, particularly famous for its grilse and summer salmon. Stretches to suit all forms of angling from fly fishing to spinning to worm fishing. Spring run starts in early Feb; main grilse run starts in May and peaks in June/July. Estuary contains good stocks of sea trout, boats obtainable. Detailed information on all fisheries from NWRFB, Ardnaree House, Abbey Street, Ballina (Tel: 096 22788).

Ballina (Co Mayo). Famous salmon water, with catches of over 5,000 in a season. Fishing on 8 beats owned by **Moy Fishery**. Apply to Moy Fishery Office, NWRFB (*above*). Moy Fishery can also arrange boats and engines for **Lough Conn** fishing. Ballina Salmon AA issues permits for a 3m stretch, with estimated 1,000–3,000 salmon per season; apply to NWRFB, or Billy Egan, Barret St, Ballina. 4m south of Ballina, Mount Falcon Castle Hotel has in total 3m of Moy; ghillie service and casting instructors provided. Apply to Fishery Manager, Mount Falcon Castle (Tel: 096 21172). Attymass Fishery, 2 beats of 1½m, bait and spinning water, permits from P Garret, (094 58151). Armstrong Fishery has adjoining left bank stretch of about 1m. Contact George Armstrong at Fishery (Tel: 094 56580). For Gannons Fishery, 1½m single bank, contact Gannons, Post Office, Foxford (Tel: 094 56101). Ballina Angling Centre arranges boat fishing trips in Moy Estuary, also on Lough Conn. Tackle shops: M Swartz, Ballina Angling Centre, Dillon Terrace; Ridge Pool Tackle Shop; Boozy O'Brien's Pub, Ballina; John Walkin, Tone St; Edward Doherty, Tackle and Bar, Bridge St. Hotels: Belleek Castle, The Bartra House, Downhill Motel.

Foxford (Co Mayo). Foxford Fishery, double bank, from 400m north of Foxford Bridge, d/s for 1m. Limited rods, book in advance; from Chris Downey, 9 Moy View, Foxford (Tel: 094 56824). New Bakers Fishery, about 400m d/s from Eel weir, Foxford; 2 good salmon pools. Foxford Salmon Anglers, 1m double bank, permits from Tiernan Bros (*below*). Cloongee Fishery, both banks above and below Lough Cullin: dt £20 from Sean O Ruain, Cloongee (Tel: 094 56534), guides available; East Mayo AA, 8m both banks above Foxford, fly only, ghillie service; dt £20: contact Hazel Wills, Ballylahan Bridge (Tel: 094 56054); Permits for most of these fisheries from Tiernan Bros (*below*). Free fishing on **Loughs Conn** and

Cullin, 2m from town, and on a short stretch of R Moy downstream of Foxford Bridge. Healys Hotel, **Pontoon** (Tel: 094 56443) has boats at southern end of Lough Conn and at Lough Cullin. Jon Binley, Flysport Ltd, Cashel (Tel: 094 56310) provides ghillie and driver service to anglers on R Moy and tribs, Loughs Conn, Cullen, and Carra Beltra. Tackle shops: Tiernan Bros, Upper Main St (Tel: 094 56731); Angling Advice Centre (Tel: 094 56731), both Foxford; J J Connor, Spencer St, Castlebar, Co Mayo.

Crossmolina (Co Mayo). Salmon, grilse, trout. Free fishing on **Lough Conn**. Boats and ghillies from J Murphy, Mossbrook, Ballina (Tel: 096 51079); P Kelly, Cloghans, Ballina. Cloonamoyne Fishery, Enniscoe, Castlehill, Ballina, Tel/Fax: 096 31851, provides a complete angling service covering brown trout fishing on Loughs Conn and Cullin, and salmon fishing on Loughs Carrownore, Beltra, Furnace and Feeagh; also river fishing for salmon, sea trout, browns, and pike; accom arranged. Tackle shop: Munnelly, Centre Supermarket (Tel: 096 31215). Accommodation: Kilmurray House, Castlehill (Tel: 096 31227).

Swinford (Co Mayo). Spring salmon best from mid-March, grilse June onwards. Swinford AA issues permits, apply to Mrs Wills, Ballylahon Bridge (Tel: 094 56221); Seamus Boland, Bridge St. **Lough Talt** is good brown trout lake, free.

Tributaries of the Moy

BUNREE: Joins just below Ballina. End of season salmon fishing, sea trout, brown trout. Free fishing.

GWEESTION: Glore River and **Trimoge River** join to become **Gweestion**, flowing from southeasterly direction. Both have a large stock of small brown trout, with free fishing.

MULLAGHANOE and **OWENGARVE**: These two rivers flow from the **Charlestown** area westwards. They contain a good stock of browns to 1½lb. Fishing free, excellent on Owengarve d/s of Curry Village.

EINAGH: Joins main river from **Lough Talt** near **Aclare**. Brown trout to 3lb, but average at 10oz. Sea trout run; free fishing in river and lough (browns, av ½lb).

LOUGH CONN SYSTEM: Lough Conn, 12,000 acres, together with **L Cullin**, has free fishing for salmon, main run from end of March through April, grilse run from May through July. Salmon adhere to known localities, and are taken by trolling spoon or Devon minnow, a few on wet fly. Trout fishing starts around March 17. The vast majority of trout caught on Lough Conn are taken on wet flies during seasonal hatches. L Conn has one of the longest mayfly hatches in the country, from about 20 May until almost the end of June. Trout fishing slows in July, but improves in August. Specimen fish are sometimes taken. Several rivers run into **Loughs Conn** and **Cullin** which offer free fishing for game and coarse fish. From north west, **Deel River**: salmon in spring and summer, brown trout u/s of Deel Bridge. From the south, **Clydagh** and **Manulla Rivers**, and the outflow from **Castlebar Lakes** all join a few miles above lough. On Clydagh free salmon fishing; on Manulla free trout fishing between **Moyhenna** and **Ballyvary** bridges. Some free fishing for wild browns on location in **Islandeady Bilberry Lough**. **Upper** and **Lower Lough Lannagh** and **Lough Mallard**, nr **Castlebar**, have been developed as free trout fisheries. There is a wide range of accommodation approximate to the Lough Conn fisheries. Contact NWRFB, Ardnaree House, Abbey St, Ballina, Tel: 096 22788, for further information on L Conn fishing.

SHANNON
(For close seasons, licences, etc, see The Shannon Regional Fisheries Board)

Largest river in these islands, 160m long with catchment area covering greater part of central Ireland. Enters Atlantic on west coast through long estuary. A typical limestone river, rich in weed and fish food, of slow current for most part, and though some of its sources rise in peat, acidity is counteracted by limestone reaches. Many of the adverse effects of hydro-electric scheme now overcome by re-stocking and other forms of fishery management. With exception of the famous Castleconnell stretch, Shannon mostly sluggish. Salmon run from March to May, grilse from end of May to September. Primary sea trout waters are **Rivers Feale** and **Doonbeg**. Permits from local tackle shops. Trout fishing is a feature of Shannon and tributaries, **Mulcair, Newport, Nenagh, Brosna, Little Brosna, Fergus**, and **Maigue**. There is a mayfly rise, when excellent sport can be enjoyed, free of charge, in **Loughs Derg** and **Ree** at Athlone. Trolling is the usual method, otherwise; trout grow large. Salmon fishing rights on Shannon and

tributaries are reserved by the ESB, and a permit is required, which is sold as st, wt, or dt, from ESB Fisheries Office, Ardnacrusha (Tel: 061 345589). Brown trout fishing is in part free, and in part leased to the Central Fisheries Board or fishing clubs. River has well-deserved reputation for its coarse fishing. Excellent fisheries for rudd, perch, shoals of bream and roach, at Plassey, O'Brien's Bridge, u/s of Portumna, Banagher, Shannonbridge. The three main pike fisheries of the system are R Shannon itself, Lough Derg, and R Fergus. There is a limit on the killing of pike: one per angler per day, max size, 3kgs. Coarse fishing may also be had in Derg and Ree. **Lough Allen**, northernmost lake of Shannon, specially good for pike. Eel fishing is growing more popular in Shannon region, which has sluggish stretches ideal for the species, large catches coming from Shannon, **R Fergus, L Derg** and **East Clare Lakes**; Mouth of Suck at Shannonbridge and mouth of Brosna are good spots to try. A licence is required to fish for brown trout and coarse fish upstream of Banagher Bridge, £5 for 21 days, and a licence costing £25 is required to fish for sea trout and salmon in whole of region. For angling guide and detailed pamphlets on angling in Shannon region, contact Shannon Development, Shannon Town Centre, Co Clare (Tel: 061 361555, Fax: 361903), E-mail: info@shannon-Dev.ie; or Shannon Regional Fisheries Board, Thomond Weir, Limerick (Tel: 061 455171). A *Three Counties Angling Guide* is also available, covering fishing in upper Shannon catchment, from Mr Michael Flaherty, Lack, Whitehall, Co Longford (Tel: 053 4326439).

Kilrush (Co Clare). West Clare AA has fishing in this corner of Co Clare, on Lakes **Knockerra** (50 acres), **Knockalough, Doolough, Kilkee Reservoir**, all fly and worm only. Trout permits £5 from Jack Horgan, Cree PO and Doonbeg Tourist Office. Tackle, information and advice from Michael O'Sullivan & Son, 49/50 Moore St (Tel: 065 51071). Hotels: Strand, Kilrush Creek Lodge, both Kilkee. salmon and sea trout fishing locally on **Cree, Annageeragh** and **Doonbeg Rivers**.

Limerick (Co Limerick). On tidal Shannon. Clancy's Strand is the lowest bottom fishery on Shannon, mainly trout fishing, which can be very good, on fly, worm, dead minnow or spinner. ESB permit required. On outskirts of city is the Long Shore Fishery: wide, deep tidal water with spring salmon run; it can be fished from both banks. Good spring salmon fishing at **Plassey**

(2m); 500 yds salmon fishing which peaks in May, and trout. ESB permit reqd. Limerick tackle shops: McMahon, Roches Street; Limerick Sports Stores, 10 William Street; J Donerty, 3 John St; Steve's Tackle, Michael St.

Castleconnell (Co Limerick). Principal centre for salmon angling on Shannon and within 3m of **Mulcair River**. Traditional big fish water; catches improved recently. Good run of spring salmon, grilse from May, and Sept fishing is usually good. Fishing on 8 Castleconnell beats controlled by Regional Manager, Hydro Generation Region, Ardnacrusha, nr Limerick, who will book beats and provide information. Permits £10 to £25, from Head Warden, M Murtagh, O'Briens Bridge, Tel: 061 377289, or from Kingfisher Angling Centre (below). Advance booking advisable, from ESB, Tel: 061 345588. Best beats to book are nos 8, 4, 5, 1, 7, 6, 3, 2. Best spring beats are 8, 5, 7, 4, 1, 3, 2. Best months for spring salmon, April to mid-May, grilse mid-May to end June. Fly, spinning and worm. Trout fishing free. The best coarse fishing in Limerick area is located just below Castleconnell salmon fishery. This is free fishing. Tackle shop: Kingfisher Angling Centre (Tel: 061 377407) supplies boats, ghillies, hires tackle, supplies permits and licences, and runs Kingfisher AC. Also agent for stocked fishery, with trout 2lb–12lb. Accommodation at Edelweiss, Stradbally, Tel: 061 377397; J Moloney, Riverside, O'Brien's Bridge, Tel: 061 377303.

Killaloe (Co Clare). At outlet from Lough Derg, good centre for trout and coarse fishing on lake. Trout angling can be very good in May and autumn; fish average 3–4lb. Boats for hire. **Doon Lough**, 8m west, is a fine coarse fishery, with a good stock of bream to 3lb, also boat fishing for large pike. Boats for hire. Good bream fishing at caravan park on west shore. Tackle shop: McKeogh's, Ballina. Hotel: Lakeside.

Scariff Bay (Co Clare). From Aughinish Point into bay there is good fishing for specimen pike, also stocks of bream, tench, perch and rudd. Boat essential. Further west shore centres for coarse fishing are **Mountshannon/ Whitegate**: Church Bay contains large tench, pike, bream and rudd; **Williamstown Harbour**: big tench from boat, quay fishing for pike, perch and bream; **Rossmore** pier: good place for same species, and a nice spot for camping. Boats and ghillies are for hire.

Dromineer (Co Tipperary). Best centre for middle sections of **Lough Derg**. Large trout taken spinning or trolling; also good centre for dry fly and dapping; trout up to 10lb caught. Mayfly starts about first week in May. Coarse fishing very good at **Youghal Bay**, Dromineer, **Kilgarvan** and **Terryglass** from quays, harbour walls and shore; Carrigahorig Bay has shoals of big bream and large pike: boat essential; fishing free. Eight fishing clubs on lake are represented by Lough Derg AA. **River Nenagh** flows into R Shannon at Dromineer; a major trout fishery with small number of salmon; in wider stretches trout can reach 2lb, about ½lb in narrows. No coarse fish except between Ballyartella Weir and mouth of river (1m); 22m of fishable water. Fly fishing best Mar–May, wet and dry fly. Minimum size removable, 10in. Nenagh and tributary **Ollatrim** (trout fishery only, no maggot fishing) are controlled by Ormond AA; st £5 from tackle shop: Whelan's, Summerhill, Nenagh, Co Tipperary. Hotels: Abbey Court; Hibernian Inn. At **Nenagh**, Ashley Park House, Ardcroney, (067 38223), has Lough Ourna, private lake in grounds of Ashley Park, stocked with brown trout. Dt £15, fish may be taken under prior agreement.

Portumna (Co Galway). At northern inlet end of **Lough Derg**. Some dapping bays within reach. Good centre for coarse fishing, proposed location for world angling championships of 2002. In Shannon, bream, roach, pike, perch, eels, tench and rudd. Best pike months are March to May, and Oct. Perch in summer months. Local club membership £5 from tackle shop. Tackle shop: Bait stockist, accom and information, Adrian Cummins, Ballycrissane, Portumna (Tel: 0905 75205). Hotels: Westpark, Portland House. Many guest houses.

Lough Rea (Co Galway). 19m NW of Portumna; fairly large limestone lake with trout, pike and perch. Fishing on lough and river open to members of Loughrea AA, which has improved and restocked water; trout average 2lb, pike run to over 30lb; for dt and boats contact Sweeney Travel, Loughrea (Tel: 091 841552). Loughrea tackle shop: Beatty's, Church St; also Sweeney's. Hotel: O'Deas, Bride St.

Banagher (Co Offaly). Brown trout, coarse fishing good: bream, rudd, hybrids, pike, perch, eels. River is wide at **Meelick**, with islands, pools and weirs. There is some east bank fishing for salmon, mainly from boat. Access to west bank is from **Kilnaborris**: bank fishing possible, in fast water. Occasional spring salmon, mainly grilse. **Brosna** and **Brosna River** and small tributary **Camcor River**, nr **Birr**, controlled by Central Fisheries Board; brown trout; a licence to fish required. Coarse fishing on **Grand Canal**. **Ferbane** is a good centre, with bream, rudd, pike. Shannon Regional Fisheries Board stock **Pallas Lake** (18m E) with rainbow and brown trout. Season 1 May–12 Oct. Bank fishing. Fly only. 6 fish limit. Permits from Jim Griffin, Tackle Shop, Rahan, Co Offaly; Al Conroy, Tackle Shop, Kilbride St (Tel: 0506 21283), and Joe Finlay, 15 William St, both Tullamore, Co Offaly. Other tackle shops: Donegans, Lyons, Kellerhers, all Banagher. Hotels: Brosna Lodge, Shannon.

Shannonbridge (Co Offaly). Junction of Shannon and **Suck** is a fine centre for coarse fishing; long stretches of bank ideal for bream, hybrids, tench and rudd. Hot water from the power station attracts tench. Eel and roach fishing also is good here. Dennis Maher, Abbey Lodge, Abbey St, Portumna, Co Galway, has fishing rights on 2m stretch of R Suck, at Shannon confluence, coarse fishing, permits offered. Five bog lakes have been opened 10–14m distance, stocked individually with trout, tench, small carp, roach. Assn: Shannonbridge AA. Tackle and baits from Dermot Killeen, Bar & Grocery, Main St (Tel: 0905 74112). For information contact Information Centre, Shannonbridge (Tel: 0905 74344).

Athlone (Co Westmeath). Athlone AA has water within 20m radius; restocked with trout. Some salmon. Shannon and Lough Ree abound with trout (good rise to mayfly, late May to late June), pike, roach and bream; bank or boat. Tench plentiful on **Lough Ree**. **Lough Garnafailagh**, which has produced remarkable catches of tench and bream, may be fished from here. At Barrymore Point, Lough Ree, is good fishing for rudd and bream. Anglers accommodation: Mrs Duggan, Villa St John, Roscommon Rd, Tel: 0902 92490; Mrs Denby, Shelmalier, Tel: 0902 72245.

Lanesborough (Co Longford). Bream, rudd, rudd-bream hybrids, perch, pike, eels. Coarse fishing on **R Shannon**, **Suck, Lough Ree** and **Feorish River**. Good stock of big fish early in season on hot water stretch of Shannon below power station; from July these move out into lake. Baits from Holmes Tackle Shop; M

Healey, Lakeside Stores. Tackle from Holmes Tackle Shop. Accommodation for anglers: Abbey Hotel, Roscommon, Tel: 0903 26240.

Strokestown (Co Roscommon). Free fishing in locality, some on £5 dt. Convenient centre for Shannon and **Lough Lea**, a chain of small lakes with rudd, perch, bream, pike and tench. **Cloonfree Lake**, one mile from town, is another good coarse fishery, especially for rudd. **Kilglass Lake**, a five-mile long chain, is 4 miles out on Dumsa Rd: plentiful bream and rudd. **Annamore Lake**, record rudd caught in 1995. **Lough na Blaith** has new fishing development with 70 fishing stands erected; rudd, bream, tench, roach. Local club, Strokestown AC. Approved accommodation: Mrs Cox, Church View House, Strokestown (Tel: 078 33047), central for much local free fishing.

Rooskey (Co Leitrim). Centre for coarse fishing on Rivers Shannon, **Rinn** or **Rynn**, and many small lakes in the area. Bream, tench, rudd, perch, pike, roach. Some brown trout in Shannon. Good catches in **Drumdad Lake** near **Mohill**. Mohill is also a good centre for **Loughs MacHugh**, **Erril**, **Lakes Cloonboniagh** and **Creenagh**: fine waters for tench and bream, with pike. Tackle shops: Roosky Quay Enterprises; Lakeland Bait, Knocknacrory. Accommodation catering for anglers: Lakeland House; Mrs Davis, Avondale, Tel: 078 38095; Mrs Duffy, Killianiker, Tel: 078 38016.

Carrick-on-Shannon (Co Leitrim). Centre for **Shannon**, **Boyle, Loughs Key, Allen, Corry, Drumharlow** and many others. Trout and coarse fish. Boyle carries heavy head of roach. Good venues are: **Hartley Bridge, Drumsna, Carrick, Albert Lock**. Heavy catches are consistent. Tackle shops: The Creel, Main St; Tranquillity Tackle, Kilclare. Many guest houses and hotels offer special anglers accommodation, including Weir House, with 200m Shannon and 41 lakes within 6 miles; **Lough Bran**, with boats for hire; Aisleigh House; Ard-na-Greine House.

Drumshanbo (Co Leitrim). R Shannon rises in Cuilcagh Mountains a short distance N of here. Free coarse fishing on R Shannon, **Lough Allen** and 12 small lakes, incl. **Acres, Derrynahoo, Carrickport** and **Scur**. Trout fishing on Shannon, esp. below **Bellantra Bridge**, in fast water. Lough Allen

Conservation Assn has stocked L Allen with over 100,000 trout in past five years. Lough also has a good stock of coarse fish, including specimen pike over 30lb and some big trout. However, as lough acts as a reservoir for the power station near Limerick and has sluice gates at lower end, the waters fluctuate considerably and at low water there are many hazardous rocks; and also there can be sudden strong winds. Local club is Lough Allen AC, visitors welcome, membership £10. Two trout streams run into L Allen, on which fishing is regarded as free. The **Yellow River** enters from east, a spate river, with brown trout in lower reaches. The **Owennayle** is a mountain stream entering from north. Trout average ½lb. Tackle shop: McGaurty's, The Square. Anglers' accommodation: Paddy Mac's, High St, Tel: 078 41128; Woodside Guesthouse, Tel: 078 41106; Mrs Costello, Forest View, Tel: 078 41243; McGuires Rent a Cottage, Tel: 078 41033.

Principal Tributaries of the Shannon

DEEL: Enters estuary near Askeaton some miles below Limerick. Fishing stations; **Rathkeale** (Limerick), and **Askeaton** (Limerick), (best Feb–May), white trout (on summer floods), a few salmon and good brown trout (best mid-Mar to Sept). Parts of river preserved by Mrs R Hunt, Inchirourke, Askeaton, and Altaville Estate. Hotels at Rathkeale; Central, Madigan's. Deel AA issues st £5 for 15m at Rathkeale. Nearest tackle shop at Limerick.

MAIGUE: Enters estuary between mouth of Deel and Limerick. Brown trout, and a few salmon.

Adare (Co Limerick). Adare Manor Hotel, Tel: 061 396566, has 2m stretch for guests. Ghillie on site. Dunraven Arms Hotel has 1¼m fishing free to guests. Contact hotel for details of Bleech Lake, 5m, good trout and pike fishing. Rathkeale, 7m, trout, with ghillies and boats. Some free tidal water below town.

Croom (Co Limerick). Maigue AA has brown trout fishing. Season 1 March–30 Sept. Fly only. Bag limit 6 fish. Trout ¾lb–3lb. St £25, mt £17, wt £10, dt £5, from Hon Sec. Preserved water below town, free above to Bruree and beyond. Tributaries Camogue, Loobagh and Morningstar mostly free and very good for trout.

Kilmallock (Co Limerick). Kilmallock & Dist AC has brown trout fishing near town on **R Loobagh**, from Riversfield Bridge to Garrouse Bridge, fly only. River is recovering from drainage scheme, and fish average small. Tickets from club members.

MULCAIR: Enters Shannon 4 miles east of Limerick, and is joined by **Slievenohera River**, which is a confluence of the Newport and Annagh Rivers. Mulcair River is spate system, mainly grilse from March, small brown trout d/s of Annacotty Bridge. The Slievenohera system gets spate runs of grilse from late June. St, wt and dt from Regional Manager, Hydro Generation Region, Ardnacrusha, nr Limerick.

KILMASTULLA: Enters Shannon above O'Briens Bridge from east, near Montpelier. River holds some good trout at Shalee, and a moderate stock to 1lb immediately u/s of Kilmastulla Bridge. E.S.B. permit reqd.

FERGUS: Limestone stream with gin-clear water, trout fishing good; few salmon in spring. Fishing free. See also Co Clare Streams and Loughs.

Ennis (Co Clare). Good centre for fishing principal waters of Co Clare, including several coarse fish lakes and rivers (tench, pike, perch, rudd). Good brown trout fishing in Fergus and lakes it drains. **Knockerra Lake** has rainbow trout to 8lb. Tackle shop in Ennis: M F Tierney, Fishing & Cycle Centre, 17 Abbey St, Tel: 065 29433. Accommodation: Auburn Lodge; Old Ground; Queen's; West Country Inn; G & J Finn, Druimin, Tel: 065 24183.

Corofin (Co Clare). Numerous lakes very good for trout, others for perch, rudd and tench, and all for pike. Accommodation at number of family guest houses. Lakes Inchiquin, Atedaun and Ballycullinan and R Fergus close by; boats.

Tulla (Co Clare). Area is noted for its excellent bream fishing; also roach, tench and pike; fishing free in about 20 lakes within 10m radius (Ennis 10m).

BROSNA: Enters Shannon from the north east, at junction with Grand Canal, north of Banagher. A brown trout fishery, controlled by Inland Fisheries Trust, Dublin 9.

SUCK: Flows through 30-mile valley linking West Roscommon and East Galway, joins Shannon at Shannonbridge, between Banagheer and Athlone. Wild brown trout and excellent coarse fishing for tench, pike, bream and rudd. Tench to 6lb at Shannonbridge Power Station, where "hot water stretch" attracts fish. Specimen rudd in L Ree. Good fishing in Coreen Ford area, nr Ballinasloe.

Ballinasloe (Co Galway). River Suck deep and slow, providing excellent coarse fishing with large shoals of bream to 8lb, bags of 100lb common, also rudd to 2lb. Other local waters include **Lough O'Flyn**, **Ballinlough**, 600 acres trout fishery, controlled by CFB. **Bunowen** and **Shiven** hold excellent stock of trout, especially good early in season. **Lough Acalla**, nr Kilconnell; rainbow trout, season 1 May to 30 Sept, st and dt purchased locally. Shannon Regional Fisheries Board permits from Salmon's Department Store, Ballinasloe. Hayden's Leisure Hotel, Ballinasloe (Tel: 0905 42347) offers anglers' accommodation with salmon and coarse fishing in Rivers Shannon and Suck.

Ballygar (Co Galway). For middle R Suck and also tributaries, **Rivers Bunowen** and **Shiven**. Excellent coarse fishing. St £5 from Tom Kenny, Public House, The Square. Tackle from Hanley's Tackle Shop.

Roscommon (Co Roscommon). Coarse fishing on R Suck and **Lough Ree**. River is good for trout in mayfly season. Irish record rudd (3lb 1oz) caught in nearby **Kilglass Lake**. Roscommon Gun and Rod Club has Hind River; trout; dry-fly water. Hotels: Grelly's, Royal, O'Gara's, Abbey.

Castlerea (Co Roscommon). For upper R Suck reaches which hold trout in some areas. **Lough O'Flynn** now has excellent trout fishing, thanks to CFB improvement work. SRFB permit required, season £20, conc, day £5. Permits and boats from Padraig Campbell, O'Flynn Bar, Ballinlaugh. Trout and coarse fish in **Lough Glinn** and **Errit Lakes**. Hotels: Don Arms, Tully's.

INNY: A slow-flowing river densely populated with roach, pike, and large bream. Trout between Abbeyshrule and Shrule Bridge. Inny AA controls much fishing.

Mullingar (Co Westmeath). Many coarse loughs in area, including **Kinale** (roach, pike), **Slevins**, bream, trench, pike, perch (with new platform for disabled), **Patrick** (tench), **Sheever** (bream, tench, pike, perch), **Ballinafid** (specimen bream, carp), **Doolin** (carp, tench, bream), **Derravaragh** (pike, roach and trout); trout loughs are **Lene**, north of Collinstown, fly and trolling, good fly hatches on water; **Bane**, northeast of Mullingar, access through ghillies only, very large brown trout; **Glore**, 4km from Castlepollard, excellent stocks of wild browns, average over 2lb, good fly hatches; famous limestone loughs, **Sheelin** ((4,654 acres, see below), **Ennell** (3,200 acres) and **Owel** (2,500 acres); and also **Mount Dalton Lake**, a small fishery stocked with brown trout. Season 1 March–12 Oct Ennell and Owel; on Ennell, wet fly fishing productive in March, fly hatches from May; on Owel, large hatches of fly from mid-Apr, and sedges from end of Jul to mid-Aug; on both lakes, dapping grasshopper and daddy long-legs in Aug. Mt Dalton season 1 Mar–12 Oct. Size limit 30cm. Bag limit 6 fish. Fly only on Mt Dalton Lake. St £20 and dt £5, from Shannon Regional Fisheries Board, Tudenham, Mullingar (Tel: 044 48769); David O'Malley, see below. **Royal Canal** nr Mullingar contains tench, roach, rudd, tench, pike. West of Mullingar to Ballinea Bridge is one of Ireland's prime tench fisheries. Local assns: L Owel Trout PA, membership £7 pa; L Ennell Trout PA; Mullingar Coarse AC. Boats on L Ennell from J Gavigan (Tel: 044 26167); Myles Hope (Tel: 044 40807), or Jim Roache (Tel: 044 40314); L Owel: John Doolan, Levington, Mullingar (Tel: 044 42085), £22 per day with engine, also Shannon Board fishing permits; Mount Dalton: Mrs C Gibson Brabazon, Mt Dalton, Rathconrath, Mullingar (Tel: 044 55102); L Sheelin: Stephen Reilly, Finea, tel: 043 81124; L Patrick, Oliver Daly (Tel: 044 71220). Tackle shops: David O'Malley, 33 Dominick St (Tel: 044 48300); Sams Tackle, Castle St (Tel: 044 40431), both Mullingar. Hotels: Bloomfield House, Greville Arms. Lakeside accommodation: Mrs A Ginnell, Lough Owel Lodge, Tel: 044 48714; Mrs A Smyth, Whitehall Farm House, Tel: 044 61140.

Castlepollard (Co Westmeath). Trout and coarse fish. **Lough Derravaragh** (2,700 acres), a limestone lake once famous for trout but in recent years trout stocks have decreased to be replaced by a large population of roach. **Lough Glore** (86 acres) holds excellent stock of wild brown trout; boat fishing only. **White Lake** (80 acres) is stocked annually with rainbow trout and some brown trout. Lakes controlled by Shannon Regional Fisheries Board. Season 1 March–12 Oct (Derravaragh and Glore); 1 May–12 Oct (White Lake). Bag limit 6 fish. St £9.50, dt £2; from Thomas Murphy, Fishing Tackle & Hardware, The Square (Tel: 044 61137). Boats from Mrs Nancy McKenna, Fore (Tel: 044 611781) for White Lake; Fergus Dunne, Oldcastle Rd, for L Glore.

Kilnaleck (Co Cavan). Brown trout fishing on **Lough Sheelin** (4,654 acres); rich limestone lough which produces and maintains a large stock of big brown trout. Fishing controlled by SRFB. Season 1 March–12 Oct. Mayfly from about mid-May to early June. hatches from Derry Point to Curry Rocks, Merry Point, Sandbar, Plunkett's Point to Crane Island. Bag limit 6 fish. Coarse fishing is prohibited. No live bait fishing. Suitable flies and dt from Kilnahard Pier, Mountnugent, L Sheelin; dt also direct from Shannon Regional Fisheries Board, Mullaghboy, Ballyheelan (Tel: 049 36144). Local assn: Lough Sheelin Trout PA. Tackle, boats and Lough Sheelin information from Robert Chambers Guest House, Mullaghaboy, Ballyheelan, Kilnaleck (Tel: 049 36682). Tackle and in-depth fishing information from Tom Murray, The Flying Sportsman, Carrick St, Kells, Co Meath (Tel: 046 40205). Hotels: Sheelin Shamrock; Crover House, both Mountnugent. Boats from both hotels. B & B Accom at Sheelin House, Kilnahard: Josephine Leggette; boat and engine hire.

Two tributaries of the Inny are fishable, on a fisheries board permit: the **Tang River** joins Inny downstream of Ballymahon, and the **Rath River**, upstream. Both have a stock of small brown trout, and are best fished early in the season, before they run low. Permits from David O'Malley, Tackle Shop, 33 Dominick St, both Mullingar.

SLANEY

(For close seasons, licences, etc, see The Eastern Regional Fisheries Board)

Rises in corner between Barrow and Liffey watersheds and flows south 73m to Wexford Harbour. During most of course has rocky beds, rapids alternating with deep pools. Good spring salmon river, especially in Tullow-Bunclody reaches (Mar, April, May best; no autumn run), but of little account for brown trout save in upper reaches and in some tributaries. Good sea trout lower down and in tributaries Urrin and Boro. Best sea trout fishing in lower reaches, late June to August. Most salmon fishing private, but certain parts let from season to season and no permission needed to fish for salmon or sea trout from Enniscorthy Bridge to Ferrycarrig (Feb 26 to Sept 15). Fly fishing only, from 1 Apr to 31 Aug.

Wexford (Co Wexford). Garman AC has made efforts to restock; good white trout fishing in June, July and Aug. **Sow River** near Castlebridge good for brown trout and sea trout; permits from angling club. Fishing for brown trout on **Wexford Reservoir**. Sea fishing (incl sea trout, bass and mullet) in estuary. Tackle shop: Bridges of Selskar, North Main Street. Hotels: Talbot, White's, County.

Enniscorthy (Co Wexford). Sea trout good; brown trout poor; free fishing downstream of bridge. Tackle shops: Paddy Lennon, 26 Main Street; Nolan, 3 Wafer Street, and C L Cullen, 14 Templeshannon. Hotels: Portsmouth Arms, Slaney Valley.

Bunclody (Co Wexford). Salmon and sea trout, browns and rainbows, coarse fishing for eels. Much fishing in area on Slaney, Clody and Derry, either free or for nominal fee. Bunclody Trout AC has fishing for visitors. Tackle shop (licences): John Nolan's Sports Shop, Ryland Rd. Accommodation: P Kinsella, Meadowside, Tel: 054 77459.

Tullow (Co Carlow). Tullow Trout and Salmon AA have water on Slaney. Permits £20 salmon, £5–£7 trout, from O'Neill's Garage, Carlow Rd (Tel: 0503 51288). Trout and salmon fishing is free on Slaney from Rathvilly to Baltinglass, and also on **River Derreen** with permission from landowners. Hotel: Slaney.

Sea Fishing Stations in Ireland

As elsewhere, the sea fishing in the Irish Republic has been growing in popularity. The inshore potential of these waters is now widely appreciated. Bass are much sought after along the south and west coasts, and pollack are abundant off the rocks. Deep-sea boats land specimen skate, conger, halibut, turbot and so on. Fishing facilities are improving all the time. There are, however, reports on the east coast of reduced sport for anglers, owing to over-fishing by trawlers. Space will not permit more than a few centres to be listed, but club secretaries and local tackle shops will be pleased to give further information and to help visitors.

Dundalk (Co Louth). Bay is shallow for the most part, but contains spurdog, ray and flatfish for boat anglers off north shore. Quay fishing from **Gyles Quay** at high water for flatfish and dogfish; the quay on **Castletown River** south bank, mullet in summer. 8m south at **Glyde** and **Dee** junction, spinning from southern breakwater for bass, mackerel, occasional sea trout. Good fishing rocks north of **Drogheda** at **Clogher Head**: pollack, coalfish, codling and mackerel. Club is North Louth Sea AC. Town also has two game angling clubs. Tackle shops: Macs Sports, Demesne Shopping Centre; Island Fishing Tackle, Park St (permits and licences); Military Connection, 8 Laurence St, Drogheda. Hotels: Ballymascanion, Imperial and others. Boats operate from **Carlingford**: Peadar Elmore, North Commons, Carlingford (Tel: 042 73239, Fax: 73733)

Dublin and **Dun Laoghaire** (Co Dublin). To north, **Howth Harbour** is popular venue: from piers, whiting, pollack, coalfish and codling; from rocks, mackerel, flatfish and others. Good boat fishing for large spurdog. Howth club holds annual festival. Estuary at **Sutton** is a good place to dig lugworm and clam. Ragworm can also be found. In Dublin Bay good points are: Dollymount Strand (some large bass, flounder, eels, codling, good in autumn at evening); sea wall running south (pollack, codling, whiting, bass and flounder); Liffey between Ringstead Basin and Pidgeon House Power Station (mullet and bass in large numbers); spinning below Poolbeg Lighthouse (bass, mackerel); Sandymount Strand, a large beach with gullies and pools, with bass, mullet, big flounder. This beach can be dangerous at flood tide. Ferryport at **Dun Laoghaire** provides pier fishing from head of West Pier, and bandstand at East Pier: dabs and conger in summer, whiting, codling, pouting, coalfish in autumn/winter. Sandymouth

Strand, north towards Dublin, produces flatfish and bass. South, from Bullock Harbour to Greystones Harbour there are seven popular fishing venues, with pollack, coalfish, codling, whiting, flatfish, conger, and mackerel. Dublin has over 30 sea angling clubs affiliated to the Leinster Council of the IFSA; information from Central Fisheries Board. Boat hire at Dun Laoghaire: "Lander II", Charles Robinson, Sea Angling Charter, Stella Maris, Church Hill, Wicklow (Tel: 0404 68751); booking agent (Tel: 01 284 2462); £30 per angler, incl tackle and bait, daily charter £360. Main species caught, big tope, spurdog, ray, thornback, ling, red and grey gurnard, and others. Dublin Tackle shops: Rory's, 17a Temple Bar, Dublin 2 (Tel: 677 2351); Watts Bros, 188 Upper Ormond Quay, Dublin (Tel: 677 8574), and several others; Dun Laoghaire Angling, 129 Lower George's St, Dun Laoghaire (284 2462).

Arklow (Co Wicklow). Local boats offer deep sea angling over inshore banks for dogfish, ray, codling, whiting, bull huss, plaice, flounder, and tope. Codling and dabs may be fished for from Roadstone Pier. Beach fishing on Clones Strand: codling, bass, flounder. There are more than two dozen good shore venues between Arklow and **Wexford**. Club: Arklow Sea Anglers. Tackle from Bolands, Pat Kelly, both Main St. Hotel: Arklow Bay.

Rosslare (Co Wexford). Good pier fishing for conger, occasional bass and flatfish. Access is difficult because of shipping. Fishing from shore at St Helens for bass, flatfish, mackerel and other species. Rock and surf fishing for bass and tope between Rosslare and **Kilmore Bay**. **Ballyteigue Lough** is a fine venue for flounders, and beach fishing is very good at **Cullenstown**, for bass and flounders. Ballytrent beach is good for flatfish by night.

Boats can reach Splaugh Rock, a massive reef, and Tuskar Rock: mainly cod fishing. Charter boat operating from Wexford Town: Peter Jackson, 3 Mary St, Wexford.

Kilmore Quay (Co Wexford). Record Irish pouting taken in 1983, and large coalfish taken recently. Fishing at high tide from pier produces flounder and occasional bass. Mullet may sometimes be taken by ground baiting. **St Patrick's Bridge**, reef of rocks to east of harbour, is boat mark for good bass fishing. Excellent pollack, bass and tope around **Saltee Islands**. Surf fishing for bass and tope at **Ballyteigne Bay**. Mullet and flatfish abound. Lugworm from harbour. **Burrow** shore is popular beach for competitions, best at night. Wexford Boat Charter: 143 The Faythe, Wexford (Tel: 053 45888). Base, Kilmore Quay Marina. Club: Kilmore Quay SAC. Tackle shops in Rosslare, Wexford and Kilmore Quay.

Fethard Bay (Co Wexford). Bottom fishing for flounder, bass, plaice, best at night. Hook Head has spinning at high tide for pollack, coalfish, mackerel, bottom fishing for conger and other species. Along shore at Cummins Quay, **Ballyhack**, conger fishing.

Dunmore (Co Waterford. Shore fishing in estuary; shark, reef and wreck fishing; base for charter boats. Contact J A O'Connor, Dunmore East Angling Charters, Pelorus, Fairy Bush, Dunmore East (Tel: 051 383397). Daily charter £150–£250, 12 persons. Club: Dunmore East Sea Anglers, Chairman, J A O'Connor, (above). Tackle shop: Shootin' N Fishin', Ballybricken.

Dungarvan Bay (Co Waterford). From **Ballinacourty** pier, bass, flatfish and dogfish, half flood to early ebb. Abbeyside and Barnawee; spinning for bass, bottom fishing for flounder. Fishing at Dungarvan for bass and flatfish. A number of large bass, 6lb to 9½lb are caught, but mackerel have been scarce. Pier at **Helvick** provides good sport with congers; distance casting catches ray. Mullet taken in Helvick Harbour. Fewer blue shark than there were. Conger, mackerel, pollack, wrasse (specimen taken) off Helvick Head. Crab and lugworm on foreshore. Boats for hire. Local clubs are Abbeyside Shore AC and Dungarvan Sea AC, which holds 6 or 7 boat competitions, from end of May to beginning of Sept. Recent 2-day event yielded 1,037 fish, from 18 boats, conger, ling, dogfish, pollack, pouting, coalfish, garfish, whiting, cod, scad, gurnard, cuckoo and ballan wrasse, and thornback ray. Membership £10 per annum, contact secretary (Tel: 058 41298). Tackle shop: Baumanns Jewellers and Fishing Tackle, Mary St. Hotels: Lawlers, Park, Gold Coast.

Ardmore and **Youghal** (Co Cork). Several venues around Ardmore and Ram Head, incl surf fishing from Ballyquin Strand for bass and flatfish (flounder to 3½lb), Ardmore beach and pier, bass, flatfish; Goat Island and Whiting Bay, similar species. Fishing from Mangans Cove through Youghal, to Knockadoon Head and pier offers more than a dozen venues. Species caught include flounder, plaice (to 5lb), codling, ray, turbot, bass, dogfish, conger (to 41lb), ling (to 38lb), cod (to 28lb 12oz), pollack, coalfish, gurnard, whiting, wrasse, blue shark (135lb) and most deep sea species. Clubs: Ardmore Sea Anglers; Youghal Sea AC also has freshwater fishing on Blackwater and tributaries. Hotels: Hilltop, Devonshire Arms, Avonmore Roseville and Green Lawn Guest Houses.

Ballycotton (Co Cork). One of the best-known of Irish sea fishing centres; large catches of prime fish and excellent facilities. Many specimen caught, including blue shark, conger, ling, pollack, coalfish, bass, hake, spur and spotted dog. Big cod in winter months. Fishing from pier at Ballycotton and **Knockadoon**, rocks from Knockadoon Head, Ballinwilling Reef and other marks, or boat; surf fishing at **Ballymona**; bass, flounder and codling. Good mullet in harbour. Lugworm may be dug at Ballycrennan and Ardnahinch. Boat hire: Ballycotton Angling Centre (Tel: 021 646773), (£100 per boat min, 10.30 to 17.30); South Coast Angling centre (Tel: 021 646002). Monthly competitions May to Oct. Local clubs: Ballycotton Deep Sea AC, c/o Sheila Egan, Main St; Aghada SAC, E Cull, Woodlands, Garryduff, Midleton. Tackle shops: T H Sports, Main St, Midleton; Guileen Tackle Shop, Ballycotton (Tel: 021 661515). Hotels: Bayview (Tel: 021 646746), Garryvoe (Tel: 021 646718); Mrs B Murray (Tel: 021 646713); Mrs M Tattan (Tel: 021 646177). Many hotels around Midleton.

Cobh (Co Cork). Good area for fishing Cork harbour; conger, ling, dogfish, cod, pollack, rays, also base for shark fishing. Cobh Sea AC (c/o Geary, below) runs an international sea angling festival each year in first week of September. Species caught include skate, bass, pollack, coalfish, tope, 1 s dogfish. Conger 44lb 12oz has been weighed in. For deep sea fishing there are charter boats from Geary Angling Services, Sycamore House, Ballynoe, Cobh (Tel: 021 812167), or Donnacha Geary (Tel: 021 813417). Tackle shop: Geary, contact for Cobh Sea AC, membership £15 per annum, juv £5. Hotel: Commodore. Guest house: Bellavista House (Tel: 021 812450).

Cork (Co Cork). Fishing both inside and outside harbour offers the following species: dogfish, codling, conger, pollack, turbot, plaice, ray, wrasse. 144lb blue shark caught in harbour, and record angler fish. Various charter boats operate from Cork harbour and **Crosshaven**, for shark, wreck and bottom fishing, incl: Cobh Angling Centre (Tel: 0211 813417); Carrigaline Deep Sea Angling Charters (Tel: 021 372896); Barry Twomey, Crosshaven (Tel: 021 831843, Fax 831679). Daily charges, £130. Tackle for hire. Club: Cork Sea Anglers. Tackle shop: The Tackle Shop, Lavitts Quay.

Kinsale (Co Cork). Fine natural harbour. Old Head Sea AC holds closed competitions. Best-known centre on the south coast for deep-sea fishing, especially for shark, ling, conger, dogfish, ray, pollack, coalfish, red bream and wrasse. Well-equipped boats and experienced skippers; all operators offer rod and tackle hire. Kinsale Sea AC run many competitions during season. For boat hire and full information contact Castlepark Marina, Kinsale (Tel: 021 774959/958 Fax). "Loyal Mediator" is 24 foot ex-Navy training ship operating from Milford Haven, on 5-day trips off Irish coast, wreck fishing in vicinity of Kinsale and elsewhere. Contact Jim Cowling, Lincoln Villa, Ferryside SA17 5ST. Hotels: Trident, Actons, Perryville House, Atlantic, Garretstown.

Rosscarbery (Co Cork). Noted for surf fishing for flatfish, mackerel, occasional bass; three fine beaches. Bass and mullet also taken in small harbour, and from mouth of estuary. Mackerel spinning from pier. Lugworm and ragworm in estuary, sand eel from beach. Club: Rosscarbery SAC.

Baltimore (Co Cork). Shark (very good, July–Oct), skate, conger, tope, ling, cod, pollack and mackerel from boats; pollack, bass and mackerel from shore. Best June–Oct. Deep sea boat charter: T Brown, Baltimore Harbour Cottages (Tel: 028 20319); M Walsh, Marine Services (Tel: 028 20145/20352), £200, £35 per angler; Baltimore Angling Centre (Tel: 028 20438), £180, £30 per angler; Nick Dent (Tel: 028 21709). Tackle shop: Kieran Cotter Ltd, Baltimore.

Mizen Peninsula (Co Cork). Fishing in harbours, rocks, coves, for pollack, mackerel, coalfish, flatfish, etc. Schull Pier offers bottom fishing for flounder, float fishing for mullet. Barley Cove at point of Peninsula is recommended. Wreck fishing within easy reach. Schull boat operator: Ciarán O'Carroll, Mizen Charters, Derryconnell House, Derryconnell (Tel/Fax: 028 37370); good shark fishing and large skate; reef and drift fishing for large pollack, ling, coalfish, spurdog, bull huss. Tackle from Barnett's, Main St, Schull. Hotel: East End. B&B, Mary Murphy, Schull.

Bantry (Co Cork). Town is convenient centre for Bantry Bay deep sea fishing. Large conger are caught, rays, ling, whiting, bull huss, l s dogfish, pollack. Shore fishing best on south side of bay. Dunmannus Bay boat: Luke Brasens (Tel: 027 67201). Boat hire costs £20 per angler. Club: Bantry Sea Anglers, membership £20. Tackle and boat hire from McCarthy's Sports, Main St; J J Crowley's, The Square. Hotels: West Lodge (Tel: 027 50360); Vickery's (Tel: 027 50194); Bantry Bay (Tel: 027 50289).

Castletownbere (Co Cork). Fine harbour for sheltered fishing in Berehaven and offshore at marks in Bantry Bay. Shark, pollack, ling, conger, tope, ray, skate, pouting, bass, bream, wrasse, spurdog, gurnard, flounder, plaice, grey mullet, whiting and mackerel. Boats are always available. Shore fishing at harbour pier, Muccaragh, Seal Harbour and Zetland Pier. Tackle shop and tourist agent: C Moriarty, The Square. Hotel: Cametrignane House. **Kenmare**: charter boats operated from Kenmare Pier by Seafari, 1 Reenkilla, Lauragh, Killarney (Tel: 064 83171). £200 daily, £25 per angler. **Sneem**: Two deep sea boats operate from here, for cod, ling, skate, blue shark, etc; Gulf Stream Fishing (Tel: 064 45159); Jack and Mick O'Shea (Tel: 064 45332).

Waterville (Co Kerry). Centre for Ballinskelligs Bay, which has various points for rock and surf fishing. Bass readily taken. Angling club: Waterville AC. Boats may be chartered for shark and other species: Skellig Aquatics, Caherdaniel (Tel: 066 9475277); M Fenton, Castlecove Angling, Castlecove (Tel: 066 75305), with equipment for disabled; Bealtra Boats, Bunavalla, Caherdaniel (Tel: 066 75129); or contact tackle shop: Tadhg O'Sullivan, Main St, Waterville (Tel: 066 94744433). Much excellent game and coarse fishing in vicinity. Boats for disabled anglers from O'Sullivan, or Lakelands Guesthouse, Lake Rd.

Cahirciveen (Co Kerry) and **Valentia Island**. Rock fishing for mackerel, pollack, wrasse, dogfish, pouting, conger, and others, over 20 species. Deep sea angling for ling, cod, conger, pollack, skate, blue shark, bull huss, and other species. Charter boats operate. Catches include conger (up to 50lb), ling (to 35lb), cod (to 30lb), pollack (to 15lb); also cuckoo wrasse, gurnard, haddock, and others, record fish caught here, in various species. Cahirciveen chosen for European Boat Championships, 2001. International Deep Sea Festival at Cahirciveen in Aug. Club: Cahirciveen Sea & Shore AC (Tel: 066 947 2087 day, 2976 evening), membership £25 per annum. At Valencia, Brendan and Kathleen Casey operate charter boat (Tel: 066 72437), shark and bottom fishing, £25 per angler, £140–£200 charter. Boats and tackle from Hugh Maguire, Anchor Bar and Tackle Shop (Tel: 066 9472049). Wide range of hotels and B & B, contact Tourist Office, The Old Barracks (Tel: 066 9472777).

Dingle Peninsula (Co Kerry). Rock fishing for pollack, wrasse, conger. Inshore fishing for ray; offshore for pollack, coalfish, bream, conger, ling, tope, cod, whiting, huss, spurdog, gurnard, pouting and shark. Club: Dingle SAC. Charter boats operate from Dingle: N O'Connor, Dingle Marina (Tel: 066 59947), £25 per angler, charter £200. Tackle shop: Walter Sheeny's, Dingle.

Shannon Estuary. Locations for shore fishing on the south side are: **Beal Point** and **Littor Strand**, bottom fishing for dogfish, flatfish, and bull huss; several marks around **Carrig Island** and **Saleen Quay**, where good bottom fishing is to be had from rocks and quay: ballan wrasse, dogfish, bull huss, some tope. **Tarbert** and **Glin** piers are best at high tide for flatfish, conger at night; **Foynes'** piers produce conger, thornback ray, codling, whiting and flounder. Best baits, crab, lugworm, mackerel. North side of estuary has pier fishing available at **Kildysart** (flounder, crab bait essential), and **Innishmurray** (bull huss, thornback, conger, freshwater eels), Kilrush (see below), and **Carrigaholt** (bottom fishing for dab and flounder, spinning for pollack and wrasse). Beach fishing at **Shanahea** and **Killimer** for bass, flounder, flatfish, Spanish Point for bass, and rock fishing at **Aylvaroo Point** for similar species, plus codling and whiting in winter. Plenty of opportunities for bait digging. Charter boats for estuary from Kilrush. Car ferry runs from Killimer to Tarbert hourly, summer: 7 to 21.30 (Sundays: 9 to 21.30), winter: 7 to 19.30 (Sundays: 10 to 19.30).

Kilrush (Co Clare). Important sea fishing centre. Pier fishing from **Cappagh** pier, conger, whiting, flounder, dogfish on flood tide, large catches of mackerel in warm weather. Beach fishing at White Strand and Doughmore, Sandhills and Seafield Beaches. Mackerel and pollack fishing from Dunlickey cliffs and Bridges of Ross. Species commonly caught in Lower Shannon include large tope, pollock, conger, thornback ray, bull huss, dogfish, bass. Several towns on the coast of Co Clare have charter boats available for shark, wreck and bottom fishing, 35ft average, tackle for hire. Kilrush Deep Sea Angling, Cappa Rd, Kilrush (Tel: 065 9051327) has boat charter. Kilrush Creek Marina (Tel: 065 9052072, Fax: 9051692), has every facility for hiring and mooring boats, incl hoist and repair services, and accom, shops, bars, restaurants. "Liscannor Star", M McLaughlin, Doonbeg, Co Clare, operates from Kilrush, tope, blue shark, and other species caught. Gerald Griffin (Tel: 065 9051327) runs angling boat trips, on Shannon. Tackle and information from Michael O'Sullivan & Son, 49/50 Moore St (Tel: 065 9051071); Martin Clancy, Henry St (Tel: 065 9051107), all sea and freshwater tackle, and all emergency repairs. B & B: The Central (Tel: 065 9051332).

Kilkee (Co Clare). Short distance from Kilrush, on north of peninsula. Fishing for mackerel, eel, pollack, ray, and cod. Rocks near golfcourse are good mark, also Pollack Holes, at low tide.

Liscannor (Co Clare). Boats: O'Callaghan Angling, Roslevan, Tulla Rd, Ennis (Tel: 065 906821374). Fishing trips around Aran Islands, tackle and baits supplied.

Galway Bay (Co Galway). **R Spiddal** enters on north side, with skate, tope, ray, huss, dogfish, monkfish, cod, ling, conger, flatfish. Boats from Galway Bay Sea Safaris, K McGowan, Spiddal (Tel: 091 553286); Aran Islands Sea Angling, Enda Conneely, Innishere (Tel: 099 75073).

Clifden (Co Galway). First-class boat and shore angling in sheltered conditions. Blue shark, tope, coalfish, pollack, skate, ray, ling, cod, turbot, brill and plaice. Good marks include: Slyne Head; Barrister wreck off **Inishark**; Inishbofin; Inishturk and Fosteries Shoals. Other good bays are Mannin, Ballinakill, Killary, Roundstone,

Cleggan and Bunowen. Tackle shops: E Sullivan, Main Street, and P Stanley, Market Street. Deep sea charter boats: J Britain (Tel: 095 21073) £25 per angler daily; J Ryan (Tel: 095 21069), £35, £350 charter, tackle on board; Bluewater Fishing, Sharamore House, Streamstown Bay. Charter boats from **Letterfrack**: John Mongan (Tel: 095 43473), 31ft, 12 persons, £15 per day. Club: Clifden Sea AC. Hotels: Clifden Bay, Alcock & Brown, Abbeyglen, Clifden House, Atlantic Coast and Celtic. Boats for hire at Bunowen and Roundstone.

Westport (Co Mayo). Good boat and shore fishing in shallow water. Local clubs run sea angling competitions in the area each year. Fish caught include: the record monkfish (69lb), skate (up to 167½lb), tope and conger (to 40lb and more), cod, codling, pollack, flounders, plaice, gurnard, coalfish, bass, wrasse, turbot, dogfish, white skate (146lb), blue shark, and porbeagle shark, bull huss. Good marks include Tower in Inner Bay, off Lighthouse, Pigeon Point, Cloghormack Buoy. Sheltered sport in **Clew Bay**. 36 ft boat available from Austin Gill (Tel: 098 64865), £150-£200 charter, 10 persons; F Clarke, The Mews, Rosberg (Tel: 098 25481), £30 per angler, £200 charter; R Roynon (Tel: 098 26514), £17 per angler, £140 charter; Westport Sea Angling Boats, 36ft, 10 persons (Tel: 098 25481), £200. Clubs: Westport Sea AC, Secretary (Tel: 098 27297); runs 3 day annual boat festival and 1 day shore event in June; and Westport AC, which has trout fishing on Ballinlough, by Westport-Newport Rd: dt £10, incl boat. Tackle shop: Hewetson's, Bridge St. Hotels: Helm, Clew Bay, Grand Central.

Achill Island (Co Mayo). Excellent boat fishing; up to 40 species, incl pollack, conger, ling, ray, cod, etc; fish run large. Noted area for blue shark and porbeagle. Holds records for heaviest fish caught in Irish waters for both men and women: 365lb (man), 362lb (woman), plus blue shark record, 206lb. Pollack and wrasse fishing off rock produces specimens in 15lb class. Good marks are Carrick Mor, Gubalennaun, Alennaun Beag, Dooega and Dugort. Flatfish from **Tullaghan Bay** on north side of island. Good shore fishing at Keel Strand and Keem Bay; mackerel and pollack fishing from **Cloughmore Pier**. Sea trout late June to early Aug (plentiful and good size); mackerel; plaice etc. Charter boats from **Purteen Harbour**: Tony Burke (Tel: 098 47257), £120, one angler £25. Local club: Achill Sea AC.

Tackle shops: Sweeney and Son, Achill Sound (Tel: 098 45211); O'Malleys, Keel PO (Tel: 98 43125, 43444 Fax). Hotels: Island House, Dookinella, Keel (Tel: 098 43180); Bervie Guest House, Keel (Tel: 098 43114); Atlantic Breeze, Poolagh (Tel: 098 43189), and many others. For Achill Deep Sea Angling Holidays, contact Mary Burke, Cashel, Achill (Tel/Fax: 098 47257).

Newport (Co Mayo). Central for Clew Bay, which has more than 20 popular shore fishing venues. Flounder fishing at outskirts of estuary. Good shore fishing at Mallaranny and Corraun. At Newport Quay, bottom fishing for flounder; Rossmoney, casting over mud for dogfish, bull huss and conger; Rossanrubble, bottom fishing for ray, dogfish and bull huss; also Ross and Rossnakilly, dogfish, bull huss, small pollack, flounder. Other species found in Clew Bay include mackerel, gurnard, whiting, common skate. Bait may be dug at Carrowmore Strand and Mallaranny (sand eel), Murrick, Rossbeg, Rossturk, Rossmurrevagh, Corraun (lugworm). Charter boat for shark and bottom fishing from Mary Gavin Hughes, Clynish View, Derradda, Newport (Tel: 098 41562), Ireland's only lady charter skipper; £100 daily, disabled provided for; Pat O'Malley, Comploon, Newport (Tel: 098 41265), operating from Newport Quay, for bottom and reef fishing. Club: Newport Sea Anglers. Tackle from Hewetson's, Bridge St, Westport. Hotels: Black Oak Inn, Newport House.

Belmullet (Co Mayo). Rapidly rising in popularity as sea-fishing centre. Sheltered water. 39 species and many specimen caught to date, incl present Irish record red gurnard and halibut; turbot, bream and pollack especially good. Belmullet Sea AC, Secretary, Michael Nallen (*below*) has been active in improving sea fishing in the area, and holds competitions in June, July, Aug. Local venues include Annagh Head: spinning for pollack, coalfish and mackerel from rocky outcrops, float fishing for wrasse, bottom fishing for dogfish and occasional conger; Cross: bottom fishing for flounder, dogfish and small turbot. Lugworm may be dug at various nearby localities, including the shore lying west of town. Deep-sea charter boats for shark, reef and bottom fishing from Belmullet: Padraic Sheeran (097 81105), £15 per angler, £80–£100 charter; **Blacksod Bay**: Vincent Sweeney (Tel: 097 85774), charter £100 per day min, £25 per angler; Martin Geraghty (Tel: 097 85741), charter £100; Michael Lavelle (Tel: 097 85669), charter £80. Tackle shop: Nallen, American St,

Belmullet (Tel: 097 82093). Hotel: Western Strands; numerous guesthouses.

Ballina (Co Mayo). Estuary of R Moy opens into Killala Bay. Lugworm may be found in sandy patches, sand eel, crab and clam are alternative baits. From Kilcummin Head at the west, to Lenadoon Point at the east, there are eight recognised shore fishing areas. These include Palmerstown Channel (Cloonoghmore Estuary), spinning for sea trout and bottom fishing for flounder; Ross Beacon, the same, Innishcrone Strand (beach fishing for flounder, dab, dogfish) and Pier (conger, dogfish, occasional ray, wrasse.

Donegal Bay (Co Donegal). There are more than 20 good shore fishing points around bay, from **Darbys Hole** in south through **Erne Estuary** (flounder), **Donegal Quays** (float fishing for mullet with ground bait), spinning from St John's Point, **Killybegs Harbour** (mackerel, etc from East Pier), beach fishing at Nun's Cove for flatfish, mackerel from **Muckross Pier** and Head; **Teelin**, pier, rock and shore fishing, with more than 20 species to be caught, incl red gurnard, whiting, conger, mackerel, haddock, cod, ling, flatfish; and White Strand, flatfish from beach plus mackerel. Shark fishing for blue shark Jul–Sept. Deep sea charter boats operating from **Bundoran**: "Ellen Louise", bookable at Bundoran Sea Leisure Centre, Sea Rd (Tel: 072 41526); **Killybegs**: E O'Callaghan (Tel: 073 31288); 36ft charter boat for shark or bottom fishing, 6 rods shark, 10 rods bottom. £20, £160 charter; Brian McGilloway (Tel: 073 31144, mobile 087 2200982), 34ft, 8–10 persons, £20–£25 per person, £100 charter. Local clubs are Donegal Bay SAC; Killybegs SAC.

Kilcar (Co Donegal). Boat and shore angling, from rocks, reefs, estuary and sandy beaches, for pollack, coalfish, cod, ling, conger, bull huss, spurdog, whiting, tope, shark, skate, flatfish, etc. Club: Kilcar Sea AC, Chairman (Tel: 073 38337); holds annual competition in August; membership £10 per annum. Charter boats operate. Tackle shop: Jimmy's, Main St (Tel: 073 38492) for tackle, boat hire, and information. At **Teelin**, Smith Campbell, Teelin Bay Charters, Carrick (Tel: 073 39117); 32ft, 8 persons, £20, charter £100–£120. Species caught include pollock, ling, conger to 30lb, cod to 15lb, mackerel, coalfish, wrasse, flatfish and others.

Burtonport (Co Donegal). By Aran Island,

and the Rosses, famous trout fishery. Good base for shark and bottom fishing, with up to 30 species caught. Boats for hire from Burtonport Sea Angling, Roshine Tel: 075 42077). Equipment also for hire.

Downings (Co Donegal). On Melrose Peninsula, in Sheep Haven Bay; site of Home International Competition in 1999, and selected by Shark Club of Ireland for first shark competition. Beach, rock, estuary fishing for sea trout and other species; charter boats operate. Information from Downings SAC Secretary (Tel: 074 39029), HQ, Beach Hotel (Tel: 074 55303).

Rosapenna (Co Donegal). Boat fishing for tope. For deep-sea bookings apply Mrs C O'Donnell, The Fleets Inn, Downings. Boat charter: Pat Robinson, Dunfanaghy (Tel: 074 36290), 38ft, shark, wreck, bottom fishing, £200.

Lough Swilly (Co Donegal). Sea trout in estuaries, good sea fishing to be had, with rays, flatfish, tope, May–July; cod, haddock, pollack, ling, conger, wrasse on offshore wrecks; blue shark in Aug/Sept. Lough Swilly SAA is local assn, at Rathmullen, runs a major annual top angling festival, first week in June. Charter boat, The Cricket, 38ft, operates at **Dunfanaghy**, 12 persons, £200. Pat Robinson (Tel: 074 36290). At **Rathmullan** pier, "Enterprise I" 12 persons, £140 min; tackle on board, disabled access; Colm Gallagher, Skipper (Tel: 087 2880190), or Agent, Angela Crerand (Tel: 074 58315/58131). **Malin** (Co Donegal). Charter boats operate from Bunagee and Culduff, specialising in wreck fishing; species caught are whiting, haddock, cod, conger, ling, gurnard, pollock, tope, turbot, plaice. Contact Inishowen Boating, J McLaughlin, Carrowmore, Malin (Tel: 077 70605). Tackle shop: nearest at Letterkenny, 14m from Rathmullan. Hotels: Malin; McGrory Guest House; Mrs Ann Lynch, Culdaff and others.

Moville (Donegal). Estuary of River Foyle; haddock, pollack, cod, tope, whiting, red gurnard, wrasse, flatfish and dogfish. Foyle Sea AC arranges Lough Foyle Festival of Sea Angling, an annual 8-day festival in August. Club owns boat and can arrange wreck fishing. Membership £10 per annum. Secretary (Tel: 077 82627). Plenty of boats (20ft–30ft) and bait. Tackle from Pat Harkin, Malin Rd. Hotels: Foyle, Redcastle, Greencastle, McNamara's, Moville.

Clubs & Associations in Ireland

The following is an alphabetical list of angling clubs and associations in Ireland. Particulars of the waters held by many will be found, by reference to the Index, in the section headed Fishing Stations in Ireland, and the information about the others, which may not have their own water, could be had from the secretaries, whose addresses are given. An addressed envelope should be enclosed with inquiries. Please advise the publishers (address at the front of the book) of any changed details for the next edition.

National Bodies

Bord Fáilte (Irish Tourist Board)
Baggot Street Bridge
Dublin 2
Tel: Dublin 765871
Central Fisheries Board
Balnagowan House
Mobhi Boreen, Glasnevin,
Dublin 9
Tel: 379206/7/8
Fax: 01 360060
Department of the Marine and Natural Resources
Leeson Lane
Dublin 2
Tel: 353 1619 9200
E-mail:
contact@marine.irlgov.ie
Irish Federation of Sea Anglers
Hon. Sec.
67 Windsor Drive
Monkstown
Co Dublin
Tel: 01 806873/806901
Irish Sea Angling, Accommodation and Charters
c/o Secretary
Loughcarrig House
Midleton
Co Cork
Tel: 021 631952
Charter boats and accommodation for sea anglers
Irish Specimen Fish Committee
Mohbi Boreen

Glasnevin, Dublin 9
Tel: Dublin 837 9206
North-West Angling Services Ireland
Rathedmond
Sligo
E-mail: henryken@hotmail.com
Ghillie service, boats, permits, etc
Sligo, Leitrim, Mayo, Roscommon.

Clubs

Abbeyfeale Anglers' Association
Pat O'Callaghan
Ballybehy
Abbeyfeale,
Co Limerick
Abbeyleix Anglers
M O'Brien
Ballyruan
Portlaoise
Co Laois
Abbeyside Sea Anglers
M Cowming
Clonea Road
Abbeyside
Dungarvan
Co Waterford
Achill Sea Anglers
Tony Burke
Cashel, Achill
Co Mayo
Ardfinnan Anglers
John Maher
Green View
Ardfinnan
Clonmel, Co Tipperary
Ardmore Sea Anglers
Mary Moloney
Fountain House

Ardmore
Youghal, Co Cork
Arklow Sea Anglers
E Doyle
55 Fr Redmond Park
Arklow
Co Wicklow
Athy Anglers
J Shaughnessy
c/o Athy Library
Athy
Co Kildare
Bailieborough Angling Club
Tom Gorman
4 Tanderragee
Bailieborough
Co Cavan
Ballybofey and Stranorlar Angling Association
D McCollum
Edenmore
Ballybofey, Lifford
Co Donegal
Ballyduff Trout Fly Angling Association
Eamon Bolger
Post Office
Ballyduff, Co Waterford
Ballyhooly Trout Anglers
Jim Ahern
Ashgrove
Ballyhooly
Co Cork
Bandon Angling Association
Michael O'Regan
21 Oliver Plunkett Street
Bandon
Co Cork
Bannow Bay Anglers
J Whitty

Wellington Bridge
Co Wexford
Bantry Sea Anglers
Con O'Leary
Baurgorm
Bantry
Co Cork
Barrow Anglers
E A Moore
Chaplestown
Carlow
Co Carlow
**Belmullet Sea Angling
Club**
Michael J Nallen
American Street
Belmullet
Co Mayo
**Boyle and District
Angling Club**
Eamonn Conroy
Marian Road
Boyle, Co Roscommon
**Cahir Anglers'
Association**
Kevin Rowe
Clonmore
Cahir
Co Tipperary
**Cahirciveen Sea and
Shore Angling Club**
Sean O'Shea
Carhan Lower
Cahirciveen
Co Kerry
**Cappoquin Salmon and
Trout Angling Club**
Jeremy Nicholson
Littlebridge Inches
Cappoquin, Co Waterford
**Carraroe Angling
Club**
Sean Finnerty
Carraroe
Co Galway
**Carrick-on-Suir Angling
Club**
N Power
Tinhalla
Carrick-on-Suir
Co Tipperary
**Cashel, Tipperary and
Golden Angling Club**
James Doyle
2 Moor Lane
Cashel
Co Tipperary

**Castlelyons Trout
Anglers**
P O'Dwyer
Glenarousk
Castlelyons
Co Cork
Cavan Anglers
Brendan Coulter
Blaiwith, Ceighan
Co Cavan
Chapelizod Anglers' Club
Paul Deveroux
23 Liffey Terrace
Chapelizod
Dublin 20
**Clane Angling
Association**
A McDonald
Downstown Lodge Stud
Maynooth, Co Kildare
**Clodiagh Anglers'
Association**
Timmy Delaney
Rathmoyle
Borrisoleigh
Co Tipperary
Clonbur Angling Club
Edward Lynch
Clonbur
Co Galway
**Clonmel Salmon and
Trout Anglers**
John Kavanagh
West Gate Clonmel
Co Tipperary
Clonmel Anglers
John Carroll
3 Dr Croke Place
Clonmel
Co Tipperary
Cobh Sea Angling Club
Mrs Mary Geary
Sycamore House
Ballynoe
Cobh, Co Cork
**Corkeeran and Dromore
Trout and Coarse
Anglers' Association**
Talbot Duffy
4 Lake View
Ballybay
Co Monaghan
Cork Salmon Anglers
J Buckley
Raheen House
Carrigrohane
Co Cork

Cork Sea Anglers
M Curran
22 Dundanion Road
Beaumont Park
Cork
**Cork Trout Anglers'
Association**
J A O Connell
87 Patrick Street
Cork
**Corofin Anglers'
Association**
Michael Cullina
Gortcleva
Claregalway
Co Galway
**Culdaff Angling
Association**
c/o Faulkner's
Main Street
Culdaff
Co Donegal
Dargle Anglers Club
A Grehan
45 The Drive
Boden Park
Rathfarnham
Dublin 16
Deele Angling Club
Billy Vance
Convoy, Lifford
Co Donegal
**Derry and District
Angling Club**
Steppen Kavanagh
Carnew, Co Wicklow
**Downings Bay Sea
Angling Club**
Joe Nash
Aughharooney Lodge
Ramelton
Co Donegal
**Drogheda and District
Anglers' Club**
c/o John Murphy
39 Anneville Crescent
Drogheda, Co Louth
Duff Angling Syndicate
John Fahey
Kinlough
Co Leitrim
**Dundalk and District
Trout Anglers'
Association**
J Clarke
3 Mill Road
Forkhill

Co Armagh
BT35 9SJ
**Dundalk Salmon Anglers'
Association**
Hubert Smith
Green Road
Dromiskin
Co Louth
**Dundrum and District
Anglers**
Sean Breen
Garryduff West
Dundrum
Co Tipperary
**Dungarvan Sea Angling
Club**
Ann Fuller
Friars Walk
Abbeyside
Dungarvan
Co Waterford
**Dunmore East Sea
Anglers**
J Dunphy
68 Grange Heights
Waterford
**Durrow Angling
Club**
Michael Walsh
18 Erkindale Drive
Durrow
Portlaois
**Edenderry Coarse
Angling Club**
Pauric Kelly
48 Murphy Street
Edenberry
Offaly
**Fermoy Salmon
Anglers**
E Glendon
21 Connaught Place
Wellington Road
Fermoy
Co Cork
**Fermoy and District
Trout Anglers'
Association**
M Fanning
41 Saint Mary's Terrace
Fermoy
Co Cork
Finn Angling Club
Francis Curran
1 Derry Road
Strabane
Co Tyrone

**Foxford Salmon Anglers'
Association**
Michael Tiernan
Riverside
Foxford, Co Mayo
Foyle Sea Angling Club
Kevin McGhee
Quay Street
Moville
Co Donegal
Freshford Anglers
Mr Pearce
Doherty
Freshford
Co Kilkenny
Glebe Angling Club
William Cochrane
87 Mourne Park
Newtownstewart
Co Tyrone
**Glengariff Anglers'
Association**
Jim Fegan
Old Snave Church
Ballylickey
Bantry, Co Cork
Greese Anglers
P Leigh
Woodhill, Narraghmore
Ballitore
Co Kildare
Headford Anglers' Club
Michael Walshe
Ower Post Office
Galway
River Ilen Anglers' Club
A Taylor
Cois Abhann
Coolnagarrane
Skibbereen
Co Cork
Inistioge Anglers' Club
Bill Doherty
High Street
Inistioge, Co Kilkenny
**Kenmare Trout
Anglers**
John O'Hara
21 Main Street
Kenmare
Co Kerry
**Kilcar Sea Angling
Club**
E Roberts
Umiskin
Kilcar
Co Donegal

Killarney Sea Anglers
R O'Riordan
Inchycullane
Kilcummin
Killarney
Co Kerry
Killeshandra Angling Club
Jim Murphy
Coragh
Killeshandra
Co Cavan
**Kilkenny Anglers'
Association**
Edward Stack
c/o Garda Station
Kilkenny
Permits from
Sports Shop
Kilkenny, Co Kilkenny
**Killybegs Sea Angling
Club**
Mary Roullier
Evergreens
Killybegs
Co Donegal
Kilmore Sea Angling Club
B McLoughlin
Spencertown
Murrintown
Co Wexford
**Kiltane Sea Angling
Club**
Seamus Geraghty
Shraigh West
Bunnahowan, Ballina
Co Mayo
**Kinsale Sea Angling
Club**
Evelyn Morrissey
Butcher's Row
Kinsale
Co Cork
**Laune Salmon and Trout
Anglers' Association**
T O'Riordan
50 Oak Park Demesne
Tralee, Co Kerry
Lee Salmon Anglers
Brendon O'Flaherty
5 Brampton Court
Bishopstown
Co Cork
**Letterkenny and District
Anglers' Association**
Gerry McNulty
Hawthorne Heights
Letterkenny, Co Donegal

**Lismore Salmon
Anglers**
B Hogan
Main Street
Lismore
Co Waterford

**Lismore Trout Anglers
and Conservation
Association**
B McCarthy
Main Street, Lismore
Co Waterford
or
J Celisse
Parks Road
Lismore
Co Waterford

**Lough Arrow and District
Angling Club**
Muriel Frazer
Ballindoon
Riverstown
Co Sligo

**Lough Arrow Fish
Preservation Association**
J Hargadon
Annaghloy via Boyle
Co Sligo

**Lough Ennel Trout
Preservation
Association**
M Murphy
9 Old Ballinderry
Mullingar, Co Westmeath

**Lough Owel Trout
Preservation Association**
S McKeown
Irishtown
Mullingar, Co Westmeath

**Lough Sheelin Trout
Protection Association**
M Callaghan
Dublin Road
Ballyjamesduff
Co Cavan

**Monasterevin Anglers'
Club**
P Moran
Rathangan Road
Monasterevin
Co Laois

**Mountmellick
Anglers**
B Lynch
5 Wolfe Tone Road
Mountmellick
Co Laois

**Mountrath and District
Anglers Club**
Tom Watkins
6 Fintan Terrace
Mountrath
Co Laois

**Mullingar Coarse
Anglers' Club**
Brian Conlon
Outdoor Pursuits
35 Dominic Street
Mullingar
Co Westmeath

**Navan and District
Angling Association**
Betty Tracey
168 Woodlands
Navan
Co Meath

**Newport Sea
Anglers**
Fionuala O'Malley
Comploom
Newport
Co Mayo

**North Kerry Anglers'
Association**
Jim Horgan
Woodford
Listowel, Co Kerry

**Old Head Sea
Anglers**
Vincent McDwyer
Aghadoe
Carrigmore
Carrigaline
Co Cork

**Ormond Angling
Association**
Joe O'Donoghue
Cameron
Gortlandroe
Nenagh
Co Tipperary

**Portarlington Angling
Club**
Patsy Farrell
White Hart Lane
Kilmalogue
Portarlington
Co Laois

**Rathdowney Anglers'
Association**
M White
Mooreville
Rathdowney
Co Laois

**Rathdrum Trout Angling
Club**
Peter Driver
Glasnarget
Rathdrum
Co Wicklow

**Rinnashark Sea
Anglers**
L Ryan
6 Lynwood
Ashley Court
Waterford

Rossin and Slane Anglers
Ray Foster
181 Foxfield Grove
Raheny

**Rosses Anglers'
Association**
John Ward
Dungloe, Co Donegal
353 73 31114

St Colmans Angling Club
Corofin
Co Galway

Schull Sea Angling Club
Kieren Higgins
47 Mountain View
Naas
Co Kildare

**Shannonbridge Anglers'
Association**
c/o Dermot Killeen
Shannonbridge
Co Offaly

**Slane, Rossin and District
Anglers' Club**
c/o "Mr Ace"
8 Laurence Road
Drogheda, Co Louth
or Secretary
Ray Foster
01 8315406

**Sliabh Liág Anglers'
Association**
Frank O'Donnell
Carrick Lower, Carrick
Co Donegal

**Tallow and District
Anglers' Club**
Treasurer, Paul Hampton
Tel: 058 56358

**Tar Trout Anglers'
Association**
Tony O'Brien
27 Fr. Sheedy Terrace
Clogheen
Co Tipperary

Thomastown Anglers
P Heafey
Castel Avenue
Thomastown
Co Kilkenny
Thurles/Hollycross/
Ballycamas Anglers
Jimmy Purcell
Rathcannon
Holycross
Thurles
Co Tipperary
Tramore Anglers
J Cashin
33 Rockinham
Ferrybank
Waterford
Co Waterford
Tuam and District
Anglers
Sonny Martyn
Esso Station
Galway Road
Tuam
Co Galway
Tullamore Coarse Fishing

Club
Pat Gorman
Tullamore
Co Offaly
Tullow Trout and Salmon
Anglers
Richard Burgess
The Lodge
Tullow
Co Carlow
Vartry Angling Club
P McDevitt
22 St Manntan's Park
Wicklow Town
Village Anglers
Arthur Campbell
Monvallet
Louth, Dundalk
Co Louth
Virginia Angling Club
Raymond Lloyd
Main Street
Bailieborough
Co Cavan
Virginia Coarse Angling
Club

Pat McCabe
Rahardrum
Virginia
Co Cavan
Waterford Sea Anglers
J O'Brien
20 Beechwood Avenue
Lower Grange
Waterford
Co Waterford
West Clare Anglers'
Association
Gerard Kelly
Cooraclare
Co Clare
Westport Sea Angling
Club
Julie Connolly
Monamore
Lodge Road, Westport
Co Mayo
Youghal Sea Anglers
M Goggin
I Ardrath
Youghal
Co Cork

Index